BLACK POPULAR MUSIC IN AMERICA

ARNOLD SHAW

Author, *Honkers and Shouters*

BLACK POPULAR MUSIC IN AMERICA

FROM THE SPIRITUALS, MINSTRELS, AND RAGTIME TO SOUL, DISCO, AND HIP-HOP

ARNOLD SHAW

SCHIRMER BOOKS
A Division of Macmillan, Inc.
NEW YORK

Collier Macmillan Publishers
LONDON

Schirmer Books
A Division of Macmillan, Inc.
866 Third Avenue, New York, NY 10022

Collier Macmillan Canada, Inc.

Library of Congress Catalog Card Number: 85-24191

Printed in the United States of America

printing number
1 2 3 4 5 6 7 8 9 10

Library of Congress Cataloging in Publication Data

Shaw, Arnold.
Black popular music.

Includes index.
1. Afro-Americans—Music—History and criticism.
2. Music, Popular (Songs, etc.)—United States—History and criticism. I. Title.
ML3556.S5 1985 781.7'296073 85-24191
ISBN 0-02-872310-4

CONTENTS

INTRODUCTION

This history of black popular music is the product of a long journey, one that began almost forty years ago. At that time, *The New York Times* published my first article on popular music. It dealt with a black novelty song, "Open the Door, Richard," which became a resounding pop hit in 1947, recorded initially by a West Coast black artist, tenor-man Jack McVea, on a small Rhythm and Blues (R & B) label, then by Dusty Fletcher, on whose vaudeville routine it was based, and covered by Count Basie and Louis Jordan. I was then working as a minor executive at a major New York popular-music publishing company, more hospitable than most Broadway publishers to black songwriters.

In 1961, by which time I had become a major executive at another popular-music publishing company, I was invited by musicologist Paul Henry Lang to contribute a survey of 100 years of popular music to a centennial volume being edited by him and published by G. Schirmer, Inc., on the occasion of its hundredth anniversary *(One Hundred Years of Music in America)*.

In the opening segment of that survey, "Popular Music from Minstrel Songs to Rock 'N' Roll," I noted that different ethnic sounds and "feeling tones" infiltrated our music at various times: "the sadness of the Jews, the tender nostalgia of the Irish, the Italian love of soaring melody, the Latin American leaning towards contrapuntal rhythms." But, I concluded: "The influence of no group has been as pervasive and decisive, or as frequently denied and depreciated, as that of the American Negro."[1]

In the more than two decades since I made that observation, the denial and depreciation have been corrected. "The Negro was the primary source," composer/songwriter/arranger Alec Wilder observes, "of the emergence of a new native music in America."[2] Wilder is just one of many musicologists, historians, and critics who have made due recognition of the black contribution to our popular music. And it is the magnitude of that debt that is a burden of the present work.

But I am really concerned with a more complex problem: the

precise nature of that debt, how the white commercialization of the black original has affected the black style as well as the white, and the overall result of that interrrelationship. Studies of our popular music make it clear, as I did in that essay, that black songwriters, singers, and musicians have been the source of styles that gave their names to periods like the Jazz Age, Ragtime Years, Swing Era, Age of Rock, etc. Unwittingly, what these studies have done is to develop the concept of our popular music as a broad mainstream (white) into which a black tributary overflows to change and refresh it.

Another aspect of the development that has not been properly annotated is the dialectical character of the change. As black music accomplishes a transformation of white, it, too, changes. Moreover, the white transformation is sometimes performed by blacks.

In recognizing that white musicians, singers, and songwriters have profited greatly—I have used the word *rip-off* in some of my writing—and that blacks have suffered economically and in other ways, we have tended to disregard the *musical* contribution made by whites. Whether we approve or like what white musicians have done in adapting, polishing, refining, and commercializing a black style, it is those changes that have created an audience for the "original"; no longer, of course, the original. But without the refinements, the black style and its originators might have remained a satellite.

The Motown development of the 1960s exemplifies what I have been suggesting. It came after white Rock 'n' Roll (R 'n' R) had emerged from black Rhythm and Blues. Pop Gospel, as the Motown Sound has been typed, represented the synthesis by blacks in the triad of thesis (R & B), antithesis (R 'n' R) and synthesis (Motown Sound). Again, Swing music originated with black bands. But after the white bands adapted it, they in turn affected the intonation of the black bands. Soul music is a fusion of Gospel and R & B. In recent years, Soul has been fused with R 'n' R and synthesizers to produce Funk.

Clearly, I am not trying to force the triadic concept. But what is true is that the white adaptation of the black original constitutes a synthesis, the word I employ in describing the transformation. I have chosen that word by way of trying to say that popular American music is neither white nor black, but a fusion, and the result of an interplay. That interplay has been at work since at least the middle of the nineteenth century. Our popular American music is a *blend* whose designation should properly be *Afro-American*. Regardless of the social situation and the relations between black and white musicians, our popular music has always been integrated.

Afro-American is the word that Henry Pleasants employs in referring to the pop tradition in his perceptive study *The Great Ameri-*

can Popular Singers. Viewing our music as an expatriate, with the bifocal vision of one versed in classical as well as popular music, London music critic of the *International Herald Tribune* and London editor of *Stereo Review,* he writes: "Musical society today is dichotomous, one part of it identified with a European idiom we think of as Serious or Classical, the other with an Afro-American idiom we think of as Popular. The singers I shall be writing about have worked, and many are still working, in the Afro-American idiom."[3]

The journey about which I spoke at the outset of this introduction included rather extensive contact with black music and black popular singers between 1950 and 1966, when I served as the "hitfinder" of three major Broadway publishers—Vice-President and General Professional Manager was the formal title. Of the hit songs developed under my auspices during these years, there were, among others, "What A Diff'rence A Day Makes" (Dinah Washington); "Wonderful, Wonderful" (Johnny Mathis); "Hotel Happiness" (Brook Benton); "Brokenhearted Melody" (Sarah Vaughan); "Night Lights" (an instrumental I composed, recorded by Oliver Nelson); "Sh-Boom" (The Chords); "Watermelon Man" and "Brown Baby" (Oscar Brown); "Matilda" (Harry Belafonte); "I Cry Alone" (Dionne Warwick); and "If You Go Away," also known as "Ne Me Quitte Pas" (Damita Jo). I also produced recordings by a number of black artists, the most successful of which was "Lollipop," by Ronald and Ruby, a mixed duo.

Betweentimes, I dealt with various aspects of black music in a number of books: *Belafonte, An Unauthorized Biography; The World of Soul: Black America's Contribution to the Pop Music Scene; The Street That Never Slept,* also called *52nd St.: The Street of Jazz; Honkers and Shouters: The Golden Years of Rhythm & Blues;* and *Dictionary of American Pop/Rock.* But when I began teaching the course "Black Popular Music" seven years ago, I found that neither these nor any other single book covered the entire development of the field. Efforts to use histories of popular music proved futile, because their focus was on the white mainstream, and black music was simply treated as an influence. Inevitably this resulted in limited attention to black music and, by unintended inference, to a minimization of its significance and scope. Treated as an influence, the black styles were denied recognition for what they were in themselves.

In my opinion, the concepts of *interaction* and of our popular music as a *blend,* basic to this volume, emerge most vividly when that music is viewed from the black end of the spectrum.

American popular music did not have a voice of its own until the middle of the nineteenth century, when Stephen Foster poured forth the golden melodies of his creative genius. Until then, our popular music was largely imported from the countries whose immigrants settled and developed the American continent. During those years, a native style was being developed; but it was the folk expression of the slaves—and it remained theirs in the segregated and divided world of the seventeenth and eighteenth centuries. In the nineteenth century, as America became a more mobile society, the sounds of black music began filtering into the white world, at first through the aegis of the minstrel show.

Five dates stand out as critical in the process of acculturation:

1. February 6, 1843: the first performance of the Virginia Minstrels
2. October 6, 1871: the Fisk University Jubilee Singers set forth on their first historic concert tour
3. 1899: publication of "Maple Leaf Rag," by Scott Joplin
4. 1917–1918: appearance of Original Dixieland Jazz Band in New York City and of King Oliver's Creole Jazz Band in Chicago
5. November 1920: release of Mamie Smith's recording of "Crazy Blues"

These dates signal the initial entry of five black styles into popular white culture: (1) Minstrelsy, (2) Spirituals, (3) Ragtime, (4) Jazz, and (5) the Blues. It was the fusion of these sounds that produced the native style that characterized and identified our popular music from the Jazz Age until roughly the Supreme Court decision of 1954, desegregating schools.

Known variously as the Tin-Pan Alley years, the Big Ballad era, and the age of the Big Baritones, they were the years when Jazz, the Blues, the musical theater, Hollywood films, and Tin-Pan Alley produced a rich storehouse of songs that remain the popular standards of American music—and to which a certain number of Rock and Country artists (Linda Ronstadt, Carly Simon, Toni Tenille, Barry Manilow, and Willie Nelson, among others) are currently returning. But even in their peak years, black music groups such as the Ravens ("Ol' Man River"), Supremes *(Sing Rodgers and Hart)*, Temptations ("Try to Remember" and "The Impossible Dream"), Drifters ("White Christmas"), and others were singing and recording the standards of Jerome Kern, *The Fantasticks*, Irving Berlin, and others. Most recently, in his solo debut album, David Lee Roth, lead singer of the Heavy Metal group Van Halen, recorded "Just a Gigolo," an Austro-American hit of the 1930s.

Since the mid-1950s, the infusion of black music and, especially, black artists into the music scene has continued pace. In 1964, *Billboard* magazine discontinued its Rhythm and Blues chart on the ground that it was virtually identical with the Pop chart of the Top 100. Twenty years later, in a year-end survey of 1984, Robert Palmer wrote in *The New York Times:* "The most popular black artists—the Jacksons, Prince, Tina Turner—achieve their own ingenious fusions of black gospel and soul roots with the flash of white guitar rock. White pop artists almost unconsciously capitulated to the sway of black dance rhythms." Moreover, in the January 1985 American Music Awards, when Lionel Richie was named top Male Vocalist and top Male Video Vocalist, and his song "Hello" won out as the top Video Single, he gained these awards not just in the Black category but in the Pop classification as well—the six awards thereby underscoring the persistent conjunctive, biracial character of our popular music. In short, the blending and the interplay on a black base continue to determine the sound of that music.

While this is a study of black popular music, it is in a sense a history of the development of American popular music, save that the view is from the other side of the tracks.

Arnold Shaw
Las Vegas, Nevada, July 1985

BLACK POPULAR MUSIC IN AMERICA

ARNOLD SHAW

Author, *Honkers and Shouters*

CHAPTER ONE

"THAT GREAT GETTIN'- UP MORNING"

On October 6, 1871, a windy fall day in Nashville, Tennessee, a group of nine young black singers left Fisk University by train in what appeared to be a vain effort to prevent the closing of the institution. Cincinnati, Ohio, was to be the first stop on a concert tour whose foolhardy purpose was to raise $20,000. No one could have anticipated that the tour would become a historic event not only in the annals of Fisk University but in the development of American popular music.

Except for one of the contraltos, the nine student singers — five women and four men — were all emancipated slaves.[1] Fisk had been founded by the American Missionary Association, a wing of the Congregational Church, in 1865 as one of seven institutions to educate ex-slaves. Taking its name from Union Army General Clinton Fisk, head of the Missionary Association, and housed in an abandoned army hospital barracks, Fisk opened its doors in 1866. In financial straits from the beginning, it was on the verge of bankruptcy in 1870, when George L. White, the treasurer of the university, who was also the director of its choir, proposed a concert tour to raise funds.

The son of a Cadiz, New York blacksmith and a veteran who had fought at Chancellorsville and Gettysburg, White had been a schoolteacher in Ohio. Working with the Freedman's Bureau in Nashville, he had taught a Sunday-school class of black children in the year that

Fisk began functioning. Using songs in his work, he made an initial acquaintance with the slave songs, developing a feeling for them that burgeoned when he added the chore of choir director to his work at Fisk. Within a short time, White's collegiate choir was giving small, off-campus concerts not only in Nashville, but in neighboring towns. The program consisted largely of operatic arias, patriotic anthems, temperance songs, and popular ballads of the day. There was a reluctance on the part of the ex-slaves to sing songs that had been part of a past best forgotten.

White's proposal that the choir undertake a fund-raising tour met with no enthusiasm at the tottering university. Neither the administration nor the trustees would offer any support, feeling that the undertaking was rash and doomed to failure. The omens were not good. Blackface minstrelsy was enjoying a great vogue at the time. The program of White's choir did not include any of the elements that made the minstrel shows so popular—dances, comedy, banjo solos, ensemble instrumental numbers, etc. The choir was just a group of students who were, from a theatrical standpoint, amateurs. Moreover, the slave songs or Spirituals were largely unknown to a world whose hotels, restaurants, and other facilities would not be very receptive to a black group in the bitterly racist days of Reconstruction. But George L. White was "a man with a cause and a purpose," in the words of W. E. B. Du Bois,[2] and something of a visionary, as time proved.

When the University offered no budget at all, a determined White pawned possessions to raise whatever sums he could. After an initial concert at the Vine Street Congregational Church in Cincinnati, the choir spent the rest of October concertizing in various Ohio cities. Plagued by bad weather, a shortage of funds, and racial animosity, they literally lived for much of the time in railroad stations. The concert at Chillicothe, Ohio, was noteworthy: Despite its financial straits, the choir donated the $50 raised by a collection to the victims of the Great Chicago Fire, which destroyed miles of the city on October 8–9 and left 100,000 homeless. During concerts in Columbus, Ohio, on October 28–29, the choir, at the behest of White, adopted a name by which it became known to the world, the Jubilee Singers.[3]

It was not until late in December that the turnaround came in the group's fortunes. Henry Ward Beecher, minister of the Plymouth Church in Brooklyn, New York, and a noted abolitionist, had heard the choir sing at the Council of Congregational Churches in Oberlin, Ohio, and urgently invited it to appear at his church. The performance so stirred the audience that Beecher turned out his pockets and emptied all his money into the collection plate, urging his parishioners to do likewise. The proceeds of the concert totaled $1,300.

Now bookings and receipts took a welcome upturn. A series of March 1872 concerts in several Connecticut cities earned them $3,900. A single concert at Boston's Tremont Temple netted $1,235. The group made appearances in New York over a six-week period. Despite increasing acceptance, its members were denied accommodations at the American Hotel in Jersey City. But a few days later, during concerts in Washington, D.C., they were received warmly not only by Howard University students but by President Ulysses S. Grant himself. By early May, when they were heading home, a concert at Louisville, Kentucky, elicited the prophetic comment that "they were likely to sing themselves into history."[4] On their arrival in Nashville, they presented to the university the sum of $20,000, which they had set as their goal.[5]

Perhaps the most exciting appearance made by the group occurred in June 1872, when it sang in Boston by invitation at the mammoth World Peace Jubilee, produced by the eminent military bandmaster Patrick S. Gilmore. "The great audience was carried away with a whirlwind of delight," J. B. T. March wrote in his book on the Jubilee Singers. "The men threw their hats in the air and the Coliseum rang with cheers and shouts of 'The Jubilees! The Jubilees forever!' "[6] To Eileen Southern, discussing it in her book *The Music of Black Americans*, this was "the event that catapulted the singers to fame . . . (that made) the reputation of the Fisk Jubilee Singers.[7]

In the spring of 1873, the singers gave concerts in England, the first of many that eventually brought them before audiences all over Europe. In England, they were entertained by Prime Minister and Mrs. Gladstone, and sang for Queen Victoria, who was so moved by their performance of "Go Down, Moses" and "Steal Away to Jesus" that she presented them with a beautiful tapestry carpet. It still hangs today in Jubilee Hall. Even before their arrival in Great Britain, English friends of Mark Twain were apprised of the treat that awaited them. "I do not know when anything has so moved me," Twain wrote of the Spirituals, and he went on to contrast the minstrel songs of the day's blackface entertainers with the true plantation music of the Jubilees. By the time they toured England, the programs of the Jubilees had changed from the potpourri of sentimental, temperance, and patriotic songs, sacred anthems and Irish ballads,[8] to an exposition of Spirituals and other slave songs.

Before the original group of Jubilee Singers disbanded in 1878—the Jubilees are a continuing tradition, as October 6 is a sacred holiday at Fisk[9]—it sang before audiences in Holland, Switzerland, Ireland, and Scotland, as well as for Frederick the Great of Prussia, the Czar of Russia, and crowned heads of Europe. By commencement 1875, the original $20,000 contribution of the group had grown so that a new building, Jubilee Hall, was dedicated in its honor. Three years later, the contribution of the Jubilee Singers was estimated at $150,000.

"To me, Jubilee Hall seemed ever made of the Sorrow Songs themselves," W. E. B. Du Bois has written. "The Negro folk-song—the rhythmic cry of the slave—stands today . . . as the most beautiful expression of human experience born this side of the seas . . . The Fisk Jubilee Singers sang the slave songs so deeply into the world's heart that it can never wholly forget them."[10]

Although the Fisk singers were the first to make the world aware of the beauty, poetry, and power of Spirituals, their role was quickly abetted by another college choir whose path crossed theirs at Steinway Hall in Brooklyn on March 27, 1873. Hardly as well known as the Jubilees, the Hampton Institute group choir was organized in February 1873, specifically to sing Spirituals. Composed of 16 students, the choir took another cue from the Jubilees and undertook by touring to raise $75,000 for a chapel, dining room, and girls' dormitory; it was named Virginia Hall on its dedication. Capitalizing on the interest aroused by the Jubilees, the Hampton choir was warmly received at initial concerts in Washington, D.C.—where it, too, was greeted by President Grant—in Philadelphia, and in New York. The concerts in New York elicited high praise from the *New York Weekly Review*, which commented: "It has remained for the obscure and uncultured Negro race in this country to prove that there is an original style of music peculiar to America."[11]

In Cambridge, Massachusetts the singers were made welcome by the eminent poet and professor Henry Wadsworth Longfellow, at whose home they sang, afterward paying their respects to the memory of the civil rights activist Senator Charles Sumner, at whose grave they delivered the Spirituals "O Dust and Ashes" and "My Lord, What a Morning."[12]

The Hampton singers, who did not achieve the renown of the Fisk choir, experienced little difficulty in raising the funds required to erect Virginia Hall. Two years later, they added $25,000 to build a boys' dormitory. As with the Jubilees, their journeys were not without racial incidents. As at Fisk, the choir and the singing of Spirituals became a continuing tradition, with notable musician/composers serving as choirmasters.[13]

Spirituals have been variously, and sometimes poetically, described as songs "forged of sorrow in the heat of religious fervor," songs that "transform the spear of frustration into a shaft of light," and songs "of a folk, created by a folk, giving emotional voice to the emotional life of a folk."[14] Having served as an emotional source of solace, diversion, strength, hope, and determination during slavery days, Spirituals performed a more utilitarian function in the post–Civil War period. Of the greatest significance is that the more perceptive listeners early discerned in them the beginnings of a uniquely American style.

The process of transforming Spirituals from folk songs transmitted orally, into published songs began in the Civil War decade, not very long before the debut tour of the Fisk singers. "Roll, Jordan, Roll" is recognized as the first of the Spirituals to be published with music. The year was 1862; the city, Philadelphia, and the collector, Lucy McKim. During the succeeding five years, two more Spirituals came into print: "Done Wid Driber's Dribin" and "No More Peck of Corn for Me," also called "Many Thousands Go," both of which made reference to Emancipation.[15] In 1867, the first collection of spirituals was published, *Slave Songs of the United States,* edited by William Francis Allen, Charles Richard Ware, and Lucy McKim Garrison.[16]

How old were the Spirituals when these collectors gave them printed form? When did the Spirituals take shape, and how? Doubtless, the earliest of the songs developed by the slaves, dating back to the late seventeenth century, were the work songs.[17] Apart from continuing the African tradition of wedding music and movement, the slaves were encouraged to sing while working, since it increased productivity. As they toiled in the cotton, rice, and tobacco fields from "can see 'til can't," hoeing, chopping, planting and harvesting, rowing or paddling boats on the rivers, loading lumber on vessels under the watchful eye of the "driver"—after Emancipation, the "Cap'n"—songs took shape in the antiphonal relationship between a singing leader and the responding work gang. River-rowing songs, rollicking sea shanties, stevedore roustabout chants—all figured in the work routines of the slaves.

Then there were the field hollers, or arhoolies, cries, calls, or shouts, solo exclamations of individual slaves, half-sung, half-yelled, half-yodeled fragments of song, sometimes rising into falsetto. These were, in Harold Courlander's words, "to communicate messages of all kinds . . . (or) to make one's presence known . . . (or) simply a form of self-expression, a vocalization of some emotion."[18]

Both the work songs and the field hollers were of direct African derivation not only in the call-and-response patterns of the former, but in the guttural vocal textures and the sliding tonalities of both the former and the latter. The Spirituals, developing later, after generations of slaves had become intimate with Christianity and European music, were Afro-American, the result of a process of acculturation.

The musical cultures of the whites and the blacks developed independently of each other, at least until after the Revolution. By the middle of the eighteenth century, advertisements for runaway slaves or slaves for sale in various colonial newspapers occasionally indicated that the individual in question was a fiddler, played the fife, the flute, or even the French Horn.[19] But during the first 100 years of the American experience, contact of the slaves with the music of the white world—instruments, concerts, or even Anglo-Scottish folk songs—was so limited as to allow for little influence, black to white or white to black.

The musical culture of the white world was, of course, derivative, European-oriented. Beginning with the *Bay Psalm Book* (1640), the first book published in the colonies, the psalms and hymns were derived from British sources, as were the folk songs of Appalachia. Thomas Jefferson, who played the violin, and George Washington, who played the flute, were interested not in folk music but in chamber music and opera, Italian, French, German, or English ballad-opera. By 1799, New York had a Philharmonic Society, and Boston, soon after, a Handel and Haydn Society. The post-Revolution development to enrich American life flowered in the early nineteenth century with the spread of the Singing Schools movement and the evolution of Shape-Note pedagogy. Soon concert halls rang with the music of the great German classicists—Beethoven, Mozart, Mendelssohn, and so on—the romantic Europeans—such as Berlioz, Liszt, and Chopin—and some indigenous composers, of whom only Louis Moreau Gottschalk (1829–1869) turned to the New World (New Orleans, Caribbean, black music) for inspiration.[20]

From these developments, the slaves were largely removed. It was only with the rise of populist religious movements, the Great Awakening in the eighteenth century and, especially, the Camp Meetings of the early nineteenth century, that the slaves became much involved with white hymnody. In this interaction, the psalms, hymns, and spirituals of Dr. Isaac Watts, published earlier in 1707 and 1719, played a vital role, arousing enthusiastic slave reactions.

Witness to such reactions, the Reverend Samuel Davies reported in letters (1750–1752) to John Wesley, founder of Methodism: Of books he made available to Negroes in Virginia, "none were more acceptable than the Psalms and Hymns (of Dr. Watts), which enable them to gratify their peculiar taste for hymnody." When he awoke at two or three in the morning, having left some of the slaves in his kitchen singing Dr. Watts's hymns, "a torrent of sacred psalms poured into my chamber. In this exercise, some of them spent the whole night."[21] In exercises like these, some see the genesis of Spirituals, dating them back to the late eighteenth century.

The nub of the dating problem, as Dena J. Epstein has observed, is the conversion to Christianity, "an essential prerequisite for the development of the Afro-American Spiritual, which was not completed by 1800."[22] Acceptance of this concept would put the genesis into the early nineteenth century, as Eileen Southern contends. But William Tallmadge, together with others, balks at this later date: "The delay in the consummation of conversion," he argues, "in no way prevented the slave from creating and singing Spirituals."[23] The point is not to confuse conversion with church membership, which slaves were prevented from achieving, because of slave-owner opposition, until the nineteenth century.

Eileen Southern proposes the beginning of the nineteenth century as the most likely period for the origin of the Spirituals. "They originated," she asserts, "in the independent churches of the North where black congregations, freed from the supervision of white clergymen, could conduct their religious services as they wished." Mother Bethel, formed in Philadelphia in July 1794 by black Methodists who seceded from white churches, appeals to Southern as a fertile breeding ground. The Reverend Richard Allen, who led the secessionist movement against discrimination within the church, published two collections of hymnals in 1801, in which he included hymns beloved by blacks, regardless of Baptist, Methodist, Congregational, or even Camp Meeting origin. According to Dr. Southern, these could have "inspired the invention of well-known Spirituals." She rejects as myth the idea that Spirituals "were born on plantations of the South, invented by slaves as they labored in the cotton fields under the blazing sun."[24]

A related area of investigation, subject to more precise analysis than the dating of Spirituals, is the matter of white or black origins. Beginning in 1893 with *Primitive Music,* by Richard Wallaschek, and capped by George Pullen Jackson in his *White Spirituals in the Southern Uplands* (1933), a number of scholars have maintained that the African source of Spirituals is a myth; that both the black and white spirituals originated from a common source in the Camp Meetings and white southern rural churches, and/or that Spirituals are "mere imitations of European compositions . . . military signals, well-known marches, German student-songs, etc."[25]

In 1914 Henry Krehbiel, longtime musical reviewer of the *New York Tribune,* made a detailed analysis of 527 Spirituals, setting forth the specifics of African influences.[26] In 1981 William Tallmadge presented a study of the 116 Spirituals adduced by Jackson to establish Camp Meeting hymns as the source of Spirituals. Tallmadge demonstrated that "the identifying characteristic of the camp-meeting song, *the structure,* was a black contribution."[27] More specifically, "the verse-refrain-chorus structure of the camp-meeting hymns was derived from the oral practice of black singers."[28] Tallmadge concluded categorically: "George Pullen Jackson's claim of a white source for the tunes of the Negro spirituals is denied."[29]

In 1983 Dena J. Epstein, long a student of the subject, sought to resolve the conflict. Noting that performance was the crucial factor in any study of folk music, she suggested that those who found a white basis for Spirituals relied on notation, which did not and could not delineate characteristic aspects of African vocal style; furthermore, that an investigation of performance procedures established the direction of influence from black to white. However, she indicated that she would readily accept "the idea of exchange or mutual influence" and that "a process of syncretism must have taken place —the fusion of cultures."[30]

"The motivation of those scholars who have tried to deny the Negro credit for the creation of this art," John and Alan Lomax have stated, "is as ignoble as it is foolish." They add: "No amount of scholarly analysis and discussion can ever make a Negro spiritual *sound* like a white spiritual" [Emphasis added].[31] Surely, that is the crux of the matter: what Spirituals are in themselves as song and poetry. Sources and influences do not alter their significance, impact, or character any more than Beethoven's use of German folk lieder in his *Pastoral* Symphony impugns or depreciates its appeal, artfulness, and beauty.

No one who traces their melodies to tunes of white origin could demonstrate that Spirituals sounded like their supposed sources. The fact is that Spirituals are palpably different from English and European hymnody in structure, rhythm, feeling, and sung melodies—differences that are in part the product of African traditions and in part the result of an interaction between the American environment and slave psychology, which yielded something uniquely Afro-American.

No real insight into Spirituals is possible without an understanding of the *ring-shout,* a form of black expressiveness originating in Africa, which fuses dance and song, and, at a peak, results in a state of ecstasy described by the word *possession.* The word *shout* seems to come from the Arabic word *saut,* encountered on the west coast of Africa and signifying "to walk or run around the Kaaba."[32] In *The Book of American Negro Spirituals,* James Weldon Johnson describes the ring-shout as follows.

A space is cleared by moving the benches, men and women arrange themselves, generally alternately, in a ring, their bodies quite close. The music starts and the ring begins to move. Around it goes, at first slowly, then with quickening force. Around and around it moves on shuffling feet that do not leave the floor, one foot beating with the heel in a decided accent in a strictly 2/4 time. The music is supplemented by the clapping of hands. As the ring goes around, it begins to take on signs of frenzy. The music, starting perhaps with a Spiritual, becomes a wild, monotonous chant. The same musical phrase is repeated over and over, 1, 2, 3, 4, 5 hours. The words become a repetition of an incoherent cry. The very monotony of sound and motion produces an ecstatic state. Women, screaming, fall to the ground, prone and quivering. Men, exhausted drop out of the shout. But the ring closes up and moves around and around.[33]

Here is the form from which sprouted the unique patterns and singing style that mark the Spiritual. The essence is collective participation and the interplay of music and movement, song and dance. Out of this interplay come such basic elements of the Spiritual as coarse vocal textures, propulsive rhythms, heightened emotional level, antiphony of call-and-response, polyphony of two or more melodies sung simultaneously or overlapping, spontaneous improvisation, pyramiding repetition.

Now, what are the African-derived characteristics of the Spiritual?

1. The interplay between the lead singer and a group—call-and-response in African music—produced a structure in which a refrain may appear after every four lines, two lines, or even a single line:

Then spoke the Lord, bold Moses said.
Let me people go.
If not, I'll strike the firstborn dead.
Let my people go.

Unlike English-Scottish folk music, a refrain will appear in the verses (see the preceding) as well as in the chorus, which follows:

Go down, Moses,
Way down in Egypt land,
Tell old Pharaoh
To let my people go.

2. The rhythms are more complex, involving syncopation and polyrhythms as the group echoes and-or answers the lead singer, sometimes overlapping his delivery. The rhythms are intensified

through handclapping, finger-snapping, foot-tapping, and exclamations in a music that is always conjoined with movement.

3. Instead of the eight-note scale of English and European music, Spirituals frequently use the five-note, pentatonic scale of African music. One hundred-eleven of the 527 Spirituals analyzed by Krehbiel were pentatonic.[34]

4. Religious in outlook and imagery, Spirituals are less concerned with sin, evil, right and wrong, or other moral problems, a preoccupation of white Spirituals, than with the day-to-day trials and troubles of the slave. Like the Blues later, these Spirituals are existential, concerned with what is, not with what might or should be, except for the yearning for freedom, freedom from the pains, anguish, deprivations, and cruelties of slavery.

No more peck of corn for me.
No more, no more.
No more driver's lash for me,
No more, no more.

5. Abstractions such as death assume a concrete form in Spirituals, and the act of dying is viewed in terms of everyday experience. Death is "a man goin' 'roun' takin' names" or someone who "comes tippin' in the room." Consider the earthly realism of "when my blood runs chilly and cool" then there will be a "little black train comin'" and "if I got my ticket, I'm goin' to ride."

6. There is no wall or distance between God, Jesus and humans. Because the African gods were not Sunday gods, but involved in day-to-day situations, Spirituals dealt with God and Jesus on a level of intimacy, verging on the blasphemous in white hymns:

Some of these days
I'm goin' tell my Jesus 'howdy.'

When I get to Heaven,
I'm goin' take my stand,
Goin' wrestle wid my Lord
Like a nachul man.

7. Because religion was not a philosophy or a theological system to the slave but an emotional experience, feeling took priority over meaning. Extensive repetition and melisma were used to achieve a heightened emotional level:

Sometimes I feel like a motherless child.
Sometimes I feel like a motherless child.
Sometimes I feel like a motherless child
A long way from home, a long way from home,
O Lawd, a long way from home.

In black Spirituals, there was an outpouring of feeling for which there was no parallel or equal in song—not in English-Scottish balladry, not in Dr. Isaac Watts's very popular hymns, and not in white Spirituals. What gives the Negro Spirituals their continuing appeal is not only that they deal with fundamental aspects of living and dying, but that they approach these with an overpowering intensity:

You got to walk that lonesome valley
You got to go there by yourself
Ain't nobody here can go there for you.
You will see de coffins bustin',
You will see po' sinners creepin',
Den you'll hear de hell-hounds barkin',
With the rumblin' of the thunder,
Then you see the moon a-bleedin',
See the stars a-fallin'
See the elements a-meltin'
And time will be no longer.

The thousands of extant Spirituals have been classified in various ways for purposes of study.[35] There are *Sorrow Songs,* generally sung in slow tempi, plaints weighted down with the burdens, troubles, and deprivations of slave existence, such as "Sometimes I Feel Like a Motherless Child," "Keep Me from Sinking Down," "Poor Me," "Nobody Knows De Trouble I See," and "All My Troubles Soon Be Over." In *The Souls of Black Folk,* W. E. B. Du Bois (1868–1963) titles his chapter on Negro folk songs, "Of the Sorrow Songs."[36]

But there are also songs of jubilation, or *Jubilees.* The largest group of spirituals are songs dealing with the veneration of Jesus and God, the celebration of biblical heroic figures such as Moses, Samson, and David, the rejection of the Devil, the anticipation of Judgment Day, and the hope of Heaven. Many titles are self-revelatory: "Lord, I Want to Be a Christian," "He is the King of Kings," "See the Sign of Judgment," "Satan Am a Liar," "You'd Better Run (to the City of Refuge)," "Want to go to Heaven When I Die," etc. Among these are uptempo songs, sung in a spirit of exhilaration and excitement, such Jubilees as "Go Tell It on the Mountain," "Goin' to Shout All Over God's Heaven," "Little David (Play on Yo' Harp)," "Gimme Dat Ole Time Religion," "In That Great, Gettin' Up Mornin'," etc.

A third group, ostensibly deriving its name from African cult meetings secretly attended by slaves, is known as *Cult Songs.* In these, news was conveyed in a code, as it were, understood by the slaves as directions for meetings or even escape routes, but perceived by the masters simply as religious statements. Perhaps the best known of these is "Follow the Drinking Gourd," in which the gourd was a metaphoric allusion to the Big Dipper, an allusion to escape to the North and freedom. Other Cult Songs include "Hush, Somebody's Calling My Name," "You Gonna Reap," "I'm Packing Up," "There's a Meeting Here Tonight," etc.[37]

Apart from source and chronology, scholars differ as to how militant they believe Spirituals to be. Some contend that the slave's embrace of Christianity led to a benign acceptance of their miserable lot. Instead of striving to change conditions or rebelling against bondage, they looked to Heaven for release, Heaven being a place where they would wear long white robes, golden waistbands, starry crowns, and golden slippers.[38]

But a growing number of scholars believe that Spirituals were motivated by "the longing for freedom"[39] and that the religious tenor of the songs disguised their true motivation and shielded the slaves from slave-owner reprisals and punishments. Ex-slave Frederick Douglass (1817–1895) wrote: "A keen observer might have detected in our repeated singing of 'O Canaan, Sweet Canaan, I'm bound for the land of Canaan' something more than a hope of reaching Heaven. We meant to reach the North, and North was our Canaan . . . On our lips, it simply meant a speedy pilgrimage to a free state . . . and deliverance from all the evils of slavery."[40]

Taking a cue from Douglass, it becomes clear that religious references in some or many of the Spirituals invite a social as well as a spiritual interpretation. When slaves sang of "stealing away 'home,'" flying to "Mt. Zion," crossing over Jordan to the "Promised Land," etc., is one to believe that mention of these places did not embrace a yearning for freedom as well as Heaven, that the deliverance sought was not just from this weary life but from slavery itself?

In *Army Life in a Black Regiment,* published in 1870, Colonel Thomas Wentworth Higginson (1823–1911) printed the words of some of the Spirituals he heard his black troops sing. Writing of "We'll Soon be Free," Higginson reported that at the outbreak of the war, Negroes were put in jail in Georgetown, South Carolina, for singing this Spiritual. When he questioned a drummer boy about the song, the youngster focused on the line "When de Lord calls us home" and explained: "Dey tink de Lord, mean for say de Yankees."[41]

In addition to Spirituals with the freedom motif concealed in religious imagery, there are those that are explicit freedom songs. Higginson prints the words of "Many Thousands Go," with its pointed rejection of "No more peck o' corn for me," "No more driver's lash for me," "No more pint o' salt for me"—the peck of corn and the pint of salt were slavery rations—which, the colonel states, were "sung in secrecy to avoid detection."[42] Rebellion or escape are indicated or implied in such titles as "Oh, Freedom," "Singin' Wid a Sword in My Hand," "Dere's a Han' Writing on de Wall," "Rise, Shine, For Thy Light Is A-Comin' (My Lord Has Set His People Free)," and many others.

That the slaves saw an analogy to their situation in the Old Testament narratives of the sufferings and struggles of the Jews under Egyptian slavery is manifest in quite a number of Spirituals; for instance, "Joshua Fit the Battle of Jericho," "Didn't My Lord Deliver Daniel (And Why Not Every Man)," "Little David (Play on Yo' Harp)," "Tryin' to Cross the Red Sea," "Samson Tore the Building Down," and, of course, "Go Down, Moses . . . Tell Old Pharaoh . . . Let My People Go." It surely is significant that the Jews celebrated in these songs were fighters and leaders of rebellion who triumphed over their slave captors.

I believe that the time has come for us to recognize that Spirituals as a whole are *songs of liberation*—spiritual liberation in most, physical liberation in the rest. It does not matter whether the yearning for freedom is covertly or directly stated. All are informed with the heavy feelings of a people in bondage. The yearning for freedom is a positive state of mind, necessary psychologically to maintain a people existing under intolerable conditions and a possible prelude to the escapes and uprisings that did take place.[43] It is this hope of liberation, whether in Heaven or on earth, that gives Spirituals their special quality emotionally, ideologically, and musically.

As with the Blues, there has been resistance at various times, especially among middle-class blacks, to performances of Spirituals. The opposition stemmed from a desire not to be reminded of an ugly and wretched past. With the passage of time and the growth of Black Nationalism, the unique character of spirituals as an art form and of their beauty as song, earlier underestimated or disregarded, have largely eliminated the opposition to performances. For some time, in fact, Spirituals have figured in the programs of most black concert artists.

The process of rediscovery had its beginnings, as with the Blues, during the era of sparkling black creativity known as the Harlem Renaissance. In 1925 Paul Robeson (1898–1976), the great actor/singer who made his singing debut in New York City, devoted his entire program to Spirituals; it was the first time that such a repertoire had been presented on the formal concert stage. In 1925, too, Hall Johnson (1888–1970) organized his famous Hall Johnson Choir, which gave its first concert of slave songs the following year.

As early as 1904, the noted Afro-English composer Samuel Coleridge-Taylor (1875–1912), having heard the Spirituals performed by the Fisk Jubilee Singers in London in 1899, completed a collection of piano arrangements under the title *Twenty-Four Negro Melodies.*[44] By 1917 Henry T. Burleigh (1866–1949) published his famous arrangement of "Deep River," the first of a series *(Jubilee Songs of the United States of America)* in which he arranged Spirituals for solo voice with piano accompaniment in the style of art songs. In 1925–1926 John Rosamond Johnson (1873–1954) and his brother, James Weldon Johnson (1871–1938), edited the two historic volumes of *The Book of American Negro Spirituals.*[45]

In organizing his choir, Hall Johnson later explained that its purpose was not to entertain but "to show how the American Negro slave . . . created, propagated and illuminated an art-form, which was, and still is, *unique* in the world of music."[46] In addition to giving concerts over a period of almost 35 years, the choir appeared in several Hollywood films and in a number of Broadway shows, including *Run, Little Chillun* and Marc Connelly's *The Green Pastures* (1930). In 1938 RCA Victor recorded a dozen Spirituals as sung by the choir, which gave its last public concert in June 1960.

Some years later, when he was greatly concerned that the sound of the choir should be preserved on record, Hall Johnson asserted, not without artistic and historic justification: "No soloist nor small vocal ensemble can hope to produce the necessary effects. The authentic Negro Spiritual is a *choral* form, requiring many voices to color the lush harmonies and to bring out the brilliant, syncopated counterpoint so characteristic of the genuine Spiritual."[47]

The unique character of the Spiritual as an *American* art form was first recognized, not by an American, but by a European composer, Anton Dvořák. When he arrived in this country in 1892 to become Director of the National Conservatory of Music, in New York City, "art music in America was dominated by a genteel tradition that looked to postromantic Germany for inspiration."[48] American composers were still traveling abroad, as they had been all through the nineteenth century, to study composition, and to return to write symphonies, oratorios, and other works in a European-derived idiom, dissociated from American life and the American spirit.[49] It is, perhaps, not surprising that musicologists of that day were then asking, as Frederic L. Ritter did in an 1883 history of American music: "How are we to account for the utter absence of national people's music and poetry in America?" And another musicologist, Louis C. Elson, said bluntly: "It must be admitted that in the field of folk music, America is rather barren."[50]

It was barren—as art music was, too, of an indigenous idiom—if one failed to investigate and become acquainted with the music being created by black people on the plantations, in the churches, and, after the Civil War, as itinerant Blues singers. Dvořák was fortunate in that he quickly became acquainted with Spirituals through some of his black students. Harry T. Burleigh has told of how "it was my privilege to sing repeatedly some of the old plantation songs for him at his home and one in particular, *Swing Low, Sweet Chariot,* greatly pleased him."[51]

When Dvořák's Symphony No. 5, titled *From the New World,* Op. 95, received its premiere at a November 1893 concert of the New York Philharmonic Society, the influence of Spirituals was unmistakable, as it was also in his succeeding String Quartet in F, *The America.* Op. 96, and the Quintet in E Flat, Op. 97. In a statement before the premiere, Dvořák frankly acknowledged the Negro source of his inspiration: "These beautiful and varied themes," he said, "are the product of the soil. They are American. They are the folk songs of America and your composers must turn to them. In the Negro melodies of America, I discover all that is needed for a great and noble school of music."[52]

To this, Edward MacDowell (1861 – 1908), speaking for the genteel tradition and subservience to music from abroad, replied: "What the Negro melodies have to do with Americanism in art still remains a mystery . . . Masquerading in the so-called nationalism of Negro clothes cut in Bohemia will not help us."[53]

Dvořák was not to be dissuaded from his conviction. In the New York *Herald* in May 1894, he declared once again: "Negro melody furnishes the only sure basis for an American school of music."[54] He was prescient, anticipating the future development of American popular music and, when one thinks of George Gershwin (1898–1937), art music as well. As an Afro-American fusion, the Spiritual was the beginning of the process by which American popular music freed itself from domination by foreign traditions and rooted itself in American soil and the American experience.[55]

CHAPTER TWO

"GENTLEMEN, BE SEATED!"

Sometime in 1898, Al Jolson (1886–1950), later one of the celebrated singers of the first half of the twentieth century, attended a vaudeville show at the Bijou Theater in Washington, D.C. Onstage was the popular blackface minstrel Eddie Leonard (1875–1941), later the writer of "Ida" and "(Roll Dem) Roley Boley Eyes," when Jolson, seated in an inexpensive balcony seat, rose—spontaneously or calculatedly—and joined in the singing of one of the day's hits. It was not unusual in those years for publishers to have their songs plugged in exactly that way.[1] Leonard was so impressed by young Jolson's singing that he hired him as an adjunct to his act.

Several years later, Jolson worked in blackface as a member of Lew Dockstader's Minstrels. Although the minstrel show was essentially a nineteenth-century entertainment, theatergoers as late as 1908 saw a minstrel show at the New York Theater that included Eddie Leonard as well as George "Honey Boy" Evans and Julian Eltinge, two other burnt-cork minstrels. George M. Cohan (1878–1942), the eminent songwriter/actor, and his partner, Sam Harris, were trying to revive a dying tradition. Despite the limited business in a twenty-four-performance run, the Cohan and Harris Minstrels returned to the New York Theater again in August 1909 with a full-fledged production that included all the traditional elements of the minstrel show—interlocutor, end-men gags, jingling tambourines, clacking bones, clog dancers, cakewalkers, an olio and walkaround, etc. It was the last time that such a production appeared on Broadway. The era of the minstrel show was ended.[2]

By 1909 the world had been enjoying the blackface minstrel show for over sixty years. Its importance, despite its pejorative black caricature, cannot be overestimated, since it was not only America's first export in the world of entertainment—Spirituals came later—but it was the incubator of Ragtime, vaudeville, the revue, burlesque, and musical comedy, the major forms of American entertainment before the advent of radio.[3]

In *Black Manhattan* (1930), James Weldon Johnson (1871–1938) assessed the contribution of the minstrel show as follows:

> Minstrelsy was, on the whole, a caricature of Negro life, and it fixed a stage tradition which has not yet been broken. It fixed the tradition of the Negro as only an irresponsible, happy-go-lucky, wide grinning, loud laughing, shuffling, banjo-playing, singing, dancing sort of being. Nevertheless, the companies did provide stage training and theatrical experience for a large number of coloured men . . . which, at the time, could not have been acquired from any other source."[4]

The "companies," in Johnson's text, were companies of black minstrels, who also worked in blackface and emerged after the Civil War, attaining a popularity that challenged the vogue of white, burnt-cork minstrels.

The minstrel show was born in 1843. In that year, on the evening of February 6, four performers pooled their talents to present a musical entertainment at the Bowery Amphitheater on the Lower East Side of Manhattan. Appearing under the designation the "Virginia Minstrels," the four white men performed in blackface as part of a circus show. In the announcement of their presentation, the New York *Herald* described them as "a novel, grotesque, original and surprisingly melodious Ethiopian band" and their music as a combination of the sounds of "the banjo, violin, bone castanets and tambourine." Remaining for one week in their performance of a "Negro Concert" as part of the circus program, they not only sang, but participated in two circus scenes.[5]

No one could have anticipated or predicted that these appearances of the quartet would launch a uniquely American form of entertainment—a form whose popularity would sweep the nation in the 1840s and 1850s, that would dominate the popular theater into the twentieth century, and through which America's first major popular songwriters and performers would emerge. It was the minstrel show that introduced the songs of Daniel Decatur Emmett, Stephen Collins Foster, Gussie Davis, James A. Bland, and the talent of William Christopher Handy. Among a notable array of black and white performers who worked in blackface, the world became acquainted with the artistry of Dan Bryant, E. P. Christy, Eddie Leonard, George "Honey Boy" Evans, McIntyre and Heath, George Primrose, and the great Bert Williams.

Working in blackface was not an innovation of the Virginia Minstrels. The tradition has been traced back to British music-hall performers in the late eighteenth century. In the early nineteenth century, a number of Americans performed impersonations of Negroes on the stage, among whom George Washington Dixon (1808–1861) and Thomas Dartmouth "Daddy" Rice (1808–1860) stand out. As early as 1827 Dixon presented stage portrayals of blacks in Albany, and two years later performed at the very Bowery Theater where the Virginia Minstrels first appeared, introducing "Coal Black Rose," a favorite song of the minstrels. Dixon claimed authorship of another minstrel song favorite, "Long Tail Blues," which described a Negro dandy on a Sunday stroll in a high-fashion swallow-tail coat. (Two standard characters of the minstrels were Zip Coon, the city dandy, and Jim Crow, the plantation slave, as in many skits of Williams and Walker.)[6]

"Daddy" Rice, known as the "father of American minstrelsy," is credited with introducing the first international song hit of American popular music. "Jim Crow" was a song he developed as the result of seeing a deformed black stable-hand perform a strange, quirky dance routine as he worked and sang

Turn about an' wheel about an' do jes so
An' ebery time I turn about, I jump Jim Crow.[7]

Appearing in blackface and old rags, and imitating the dance, "Daddy" Rice scored a sensation when he introduced the routine for the first time, once again at the Bowery Theater, in November 1832. "Jim Crow" made him famous not only in the United States, where his performances were greeted with enthusiasm in city after city, but in England, where he made a standout tour in 1836.

The fact is that all four members of the Virginia Minstrels had also made appearances in blackface before the show they gave on February 6, 1843. Daniel Decatur Emmett (1815–1904), the songwriter of the group and the best known, worked briefly as a printer and then as a musician in the years before the quartet was formed. Self-taught on the fiddle, he later learned to play drums, fife, and, while in the orchestra of the Cincinnati Circus, the banjo. It was "a new interest in Negro impersonation," Hans Nathan tells us, "that led to his debut as a banjo player and singer in the circus ring, undoubtedly in blackface."[8] In this capacity, he worked with Francis Marion Brower (1823–1874), another member of the Virginia Minstrels, who was a highly regarded bones player and "one of the foremost blackface dancers of the day."[9] Performing separately and together in various circuses, the two settled in New York City by late 1842. Here, their appearance in a new variety theater attracted newspaper notices, hailing Emmett as "the great Southern banjo melodist" and Brower as "the perfect representation of the Southern Negro character."[10]

The other two members of the Virginia Minstrels, William M. Whitlock (b. 1813) and Richard Ward Pelham (b. 1815), were both New Yorkers and experienced blackface performers. Whitlock, whose banjo-playing skill attracted the great P. T. Barnum as his manager, was said to have acquired "his accurate knowledge of the peculiarities of plantation and cornfield Negroes"[11] by close observation of Southern life while on tour. As a dancer, "defying all de niggers in de world to charm de people," according to a contemporary playbill,[12] Whitlock was surpassed by Pelham, who frequently performed with his younger brother in "Negro Peculiarities, Dances and Extravaganzas."[13]

What made the February 6 presentation of the four unique was not the burnt cork they used to blacken their faces but the format, their performing together as an ensemble and, through their clothes, makeup, and dialect, creating an identifiable (plantation) setting; in short, their creating a framework that made their individual contributions into a *show*.

The presentation at the Bowery Amphitheater was followed by appearances at the Cornucopia, a "sporting saloon" on Park Row, and the Olympic Circus at the Park Theatre, where they added new bits in the form of "lectures" and conundrums. It was not until March 7 and 8, at the Masonic Temple in Boston, that their "Ethiopian Concert" occupied a full evening for the first time and that the format of "minstrel music and scenes by a minstrel band,"[14] garbed as Negro plantation slaves, approached what later became known as a minstrel show. The instruments they played, especially the banjo, bones, and tambourine, became *the* instruments of the minstrel show, as the semicircle, with the bones player at one end, the tambourine man at the other, and the emcee or interlocutor in the middle became standard.

Edwin P. Christy, who tried unsuccessfully to dispute the priority of the Dan Emmett troupe as the originators of the minstrel show, is generally credited with stylizing it. Born in Philadelphia in 1815, Christy was involved with Afro-American culture early in his career and performed as a blackface musician and comic singer before forming his minstrel troupe. Working with a group of slaves in New Orleans in his early twenties, he had ample opportunity to view and savor the famed Congo Square singing and dancing of the slaves. Settling in Buffalo in the late 1930s, where he later organized his first minstrel company, he entertained in blackface and amplified his knowledge and store of Negro lore through contact with a black church singer whom he acknowledged as One-Legged Hanson.[15]

Christy's Original Band of Virginia Minstrels was what he called the troupe of four performers he founded in about 1843. After touring through the West, he made his first New York appearance at Palmo's Opera House, on April 27, 1846. He apparently timed this debut to coincide with the departure on a British tour of the Ethiopian Serenaders, who had entertained at the White House just a year after the rise of the Virginia Minstrels. In 1847 Christy leased Mechanics' Hall on Broadway for what lengthened into a ten-year stand. During those years, the Christy Minstrels became as popular a New York entertainment as Barnum's Museum, surpassing all minstrel troupes, including the Ethiopian Serenaders, who returned for a New York appearance at Palmo's in 1847. Comparing the two shows, a critic indicated he had little desire to return to Palmo's but said of Christy's troupe: "We listen and laugh and desire to go again and again."[16]

It was during the long run of the troupe at Mechanics' Hall that the format and routines of the Minstrel Show crystallized into a pattern thereafter followed by other troupes. The blackface minstrels, with the exaggerated, elliptical mouths outlined in white, and wearing white gloves, marched onstage to a spirited, up-tempo overture. Christy as the interlocutor sounded the words that marked the traditional minstrel opening—"Gentlemen, Be Seated!"—and proceeded to exchange gags, generally plays on words, with the end men, Mr. Tambo, on his right, and Mr. Bones, on his left. The humorous banter would be interspersed with a song or two.

The second part of the show, known after a time as the *olio*—presumably from the Spanish *olla,* for "salmagundi," or "potpourri"—involved a succession of specialty numbers: disregarding chronology, George "Honey Boy" Evans singing "In the Good Old Summertime"; a banjo solo on "Ballin' the Jack"; a soft-shoe tap dance to Eddie Leonard's "Ida (Sweet as Apple Cider)"; Bert Williams delivering in his talk/comic style "Play That Barbershop Chord" or his self-deprecating "Nobody"; a silver-voiced tenor singing almost in falsetto a sentimental ballad, "Can't You Hear Me Calling Caroline," followed shortly by the basso profundo of the company, descending to the lowest notes he could reach in "When the Bell in the Lighthouse Rings (Ding, Dong)."

In the final segment, there might be a "stump speech," a humorous address by one of the end men on a topical subject in black dialect and full of malapropisms; or a farcical parody, a Negro version of *Macbeth* such as Henry Woods's Minstrels presented in 1852; or a slapstick scene, involving shenanigans such as pie-throwing. The entire company participated in a rousing finale, known after a time as a *walk-around,*[17] in which singers and dancers did a bit to handclapping, tambourine-shaking, and bones-clacking by the company, arranged in a colorful circle.

Bryant's Minstrels are most often remembered because of Daniel Decatur Emmett's association with the troupe, and especially because Emmett's great song, "Dixie," was written for and introduced by it. But Dan Bryant deserves recognition as one of a group of Irishmen who contributed to the vogue of minstrelsy—George Christy, Matt Campbell, and Billy Emerson were others—and as the organizer and producer of one of the best early minstrel troupes, along with Christy.

A company of 12, Bryant's Minstrels was formed by Dan Bryant in 1857, after he had worked with various other troupes. Associated with him in his new venture were his brothers Jerry, who played tambourine and bones, and Neil, who was an outstanding performer on accordion and flutina. Dan was himself proficient on banjo, bones, and tambourine, and was a superior dancer and comic, talents he shared with Jerry. Both were expert in handling Negro dialect. Opening on February 25, 1857, at Mechanics' Hall, a showplace at 472 Broadway previously occupied and popularized by the Christy Minstrels, Bryant's troupe remained in residence for almost 10 years, eliciting continued praise and drawing crowds even during the financial crisis of 1858.

That Emmett had much to do with the success of the Bryant troupe seems unquestionable. Joining in October–November of 1858, he remained with the company until 1866, the year of its demise, except for one brief season at the outbreak of the Civil War when he mistakenly thought their business would slacken off. During those years, Emmett sang, acted in comical skits (some of which he probably wrote), played several instruments, and, most important of all, wrote songs and the music for the rousing walk-arounds.

The high point of Emmett's association with Bryant and, perhaps, in retrospect, the high point of Bryant minstrelsy came with the presentation of "Dixie" on April 4, 1859. According to interviews he gave, Emmett wrote the piece on a rainy Sunday in response to Bryant's request for a walk-around for a Monday rehearsal. The inclement weather supposedly accounted for the basic idea, when Emmett or his wife remarked, "I wish I was in Dixie." The word *Dixie* had become an emblem for the South in the years before the

Civil War, though its origin is a matter of uncertainty. A contraction of "Mason and *Dix*on line"? A derivation from the French word for 10 *(dix),* employed in New Orleans and given currency through a 10-dollar bill issued by a Louisiana bank and referred to as a "dixie"?[18]

On its introduction, according to Emmett, "Dixie" was received with such enthusiasm that "before the end of the week, everybody in New York was whistling it." By April 10, 1861, the New York *Clipper* called the song "one of the most popular compositions ever produced . . . It has been sung, whistled and played in every quarter of the globe."[19] By then, the song had begun to settle in as a favorite of the Confederacy, the first Southern performance having been given by the Rumsey and Newcomb Minstrels in December of 1860. Less than a year later, in March 1861, it was interpolated in a Zouaves production of *Pocahontas* at the Variétés Theater in New Orleans. So exciting was the presentation by the full Zouaves company that the audience demanded numerous encores. Soon soldiers of the Confederacy were singing "Dixie" with improvised martial lyrics. Before they made their assault at Gettysburg, General Pickett reportedly ordered the playing of the song to raise the morale of his troops.

Although the Civil War established "Dixie" as a ballad of the Confederacy, at the war's end it had acquired the same duple status as "Lilli Marlene" did in World War II. A German sentimental ballad about a prostitute and a favorite of German soldiers, "Lilli Marlene" was picked up by British troops, and in English translation became a wartime favorite and, still later, an American hit. After Lee's surrender at Appomattox, President Lincoln suggested that "Dixie" was part of the North's spoils of war and requested that the band outside the White House play it. Opposed to Southern separatism but not necessarily pro-Negro, Emmett said earlier: "If I had known to what use they (Confederate bands) were going to put my song, I will be damned if I'd have written it."[20]

Emmett derived more renown than returns from the song, for he sold it outright to Firth, Pond & Co. for a total payment of $300 in February 1861. "I Wish I Was in Dixie's Land," the title under which the first authorized edition appeared, was reprinted in songsters and newspapers, while minstrel companies coopted the melody for walk-arounds, adapting and parodying its words. After performances in the South, a New Orleans company published a pirated edition, on which Emmett was not even credited with authorship.[21] All of these developments serve to emphasize the popularity of the song, which, in Hans Nathan's words, "became one of the greatest song successes of the nineteenth century, not only in America but abroad as well."[22]

As the Virginia and Bryant's Minstrels gave the world one of

America's major songwriters in Daniel Decatur Emmett, Christy's Minstrels has the distinction of having introduced the songs of Stephen Foster, the foremost creator of plantation songs and one of America's supreme songwriters.

Foster has also been described as "the first American songwriter to support himself with his compositions."[23] It was more of an attempt than an achievement. In 1849, when he was 23 years old, Foster, having worked as a bookkeeper in his brother's commercial house in Cincinnati for several years, made a decision to leave the business world. Inspired by his contact with the publishing firm of Firth and Pond, he returned to his hometown, Pittsburgh, and set up an office as a full-time songwriter. By then he had already written "Oh! Susanna" and "Uncle Ned." With performances by the popular Nelson Kneass and his Ethiopian Troupe, the Original Christy Minstrels, and the celebrated Southern Sable Harmonists, and publication in New York, as sung by the Christy Minstrels, and in Cincinnati, "Oh! Susanna" had become a nationwide favorite. It ranked in popularity with the famous "Zip Coon" song, as sung by G. W. Dixon. Firth and Pond had, in fact, published an arrangement of "Oh! Susanna" by the brilliant pianist Henri Herz even before Foster was in touch with them.

The contract that Foster signed with Firth and Pond in 1849 provided for a two-cent royalty per copy sold, this at a time when most songwriters had to be satisfied with a flat fee. (Foster had himself sold "Oh! Susanna" for a $100 fee plus some free copies of the sheet music, to W. C. Peters, who eventually earned $10,000 and more on the song.) Nevertheless, it was an intrepid move on Foster's part, since then-successful songwriters such as John Hill Hewitt (1801–1890), composer of the popular "The Minstrel's Return'd from the War," and Henry Russell (1812–1900), the writer of "Woodman! Spare that Tree!" could not exist simply on song royalties and had to supplement with teaching, journalism, and music publishing (Hewitt) and recitals and concerts (Russell).

Subsequent contracts with Firth and Pond, beginning in 1853, when his royalty was raised to 10% and an advance, were as favorable as any songwriter could then expect. Yet from 1853 until his death, in 1864, Foster's financial history was one involving constant borrowing from his brother, Morrison; drawing money from publishers against anticipated royalties; selling the rights to future earnings on various songs for flat sums; and in his final years, when his exclusive contract with Firth, Pond & Co. expired, scribbling potboilers and selling them outright. In other words, while Foster devoted his life to songwriting and worked as a full-time professional songwriter (except for a brief period in about 1851), he was not able to support himself and his small family (one child) through his songs, popular best-sellers and widely performed though they were. When he died in a ward in Bellevue Hospital in New York City, having suffered an alcoholic fall in the Bowery fleabag hotel where he lived (separated from his wife and child), they found a purse in his frayed suit, which contained 3 pennies, 35 cents in scrip, and a slip of paper containing the words for a possible future song, "Dear Friends and Gentle Hearts." (The words were adapted for a popular song of 1949, titled "Dear Hearts and Gentle People," written by Bob Hilliard and Sammy Fain, and recorded by Dinah Shore and Bing Crosby).

"Vacillating skunk" was Christy's scrawled comment on the back of a letter written to him by Foster on May 25, 1852. Admitting that he had solicited Christy's permission to place his name as writer and composer on "Old Folks at Home," Foster was asking to have his own name reinstated on the "Ethiopian Melody," as it was described on the sheet music in 1851. Christy never consented to the change, and his name remained on the song ("Written and Composed by E. P. Christy") until the copyright's first term expired, at the end of 28 years, in 1879.

In his deferential letter, Foster explained that he originally wanted his name omitted, "owing to the prejudice against (Ethiopian songs) by some, which might injure my reputation as a writer of another style of music." But having found that, by his efforts, he had "done a great deal to build up a taste for Ethiopian songs among refined people . . ." he wanted his name reinstated; moreover, he had decided "to pursue the Ethiopian business without fear or shame and lend all my energies to making the business live, at the same time that I will wish to establish my name as the best Ethiopian songwriter . . ."[24]

That he succeeded in being "the best" is unquestioned. But it was not without manifesting the ambivalence that so irritated Christy, who was paying Foster then and later a $10 fee for prepublication performances of his Ethiopian numbers. Foster's relationship to blackface minstrelsy actually began when he was still a boy. We know from his brother Morrison that as a nine-year-old—in 1835, eight years before the Virginia Minstrels emerged—Stephen was part of a thespian company, performing in a nearby carriage house, and that he starred as the singer of the Ethiopian songs then popular—"Zip Coon," "Long-Tailed Blue," "Coal Black Rose," and "Jim Crow."[25] Ten years later, as part of the Knights of the Square Table, a group that met at his Pittsburgh home to harmonize for fun, Foster produced his first two Ethiopian songs: "Lou'siana Belle," published in 1847 by W. C. Peter of Cincinnati, and "Old Uncle Ned."

It was for this group that Foster also wrote "Oh! Susanna," the first of his songs to be associated with the Christy Minstrels.

The bulk of the "plantation melodies," as Foster's minstrel songs in slave dialect are designated, were written before 1853, with his peak creativity between 1851 and 1853, when he produced "Old Folks at Home" (1851), "Massa's in de Cold Ground" (1852), "My Old Kentucky Home, Good Night" (1853) and "Old Dog Tray" (1853), 4 of his most popular numbers. By 1850 Foster had actually published 12 minstrel songs, which, though they are not now as well known as the four, were staples of the minstrel-show repertory. But even these surpassed standard minstrel repertory, were written by Foster in four-part harmony, and contained choruses, which are not to be found even in his so-called "English" songs. In contrasting the "Ethiopian" melodies with the "English" songs, Charles Hamm observes that Foster "transformed the genre (Ethiopian) and made it expressive of sentiments far removed from those of the 'nigger songs.'"[26]

Despite this achievement and the recognition that came to him as a result of this genre, Foster was apparently more concerned about the acceptance of his "English" songs. He called songs of the "Jeanie with the Light Brown Hair" type "poetic," the "Oh! Susanna" genre "comic," and the "Old Folks at Home" style "pathetic"; that is, expressing pathos. In an evocative study of these three types and their changing meanings for different artists, critics, and times, William H. Austin concludes that Foster's interest in the two Ethiopian types fluctuated, but "his interest in the 'Jeanie' type was constant."[27]

Nevertheless, as we know, Foster's position in the annals of popular song is based on the Ethiopian songs. Of the "poetic" or "English" type—that is, the sentimental ballads—only two have achieved widespread acceptance: "Beautiful Dreamer" and "Jeanie with the Light Brown Hair." The posthumous fame of "Beautiful Dreamer" was almost predictable, since it was "the last song ever written by Stephen C. Foster, composed but a few days before his death."[28] But "Jeanie," written in 1854 presumably because of Foster's separation from his wife, Jane, did not become a hit until 1941. It was then in the public domain, so that Foster's estate received no royalties from the extensive performances of the ballad that year.[29]

If the tremendous popularity of the minstrel show needed confirmation, the rise and growth of companies of black minstrels, which occurred after the Civil War, provided invincible proof.

W. C. Handy (1873–1958), author of "St. Louis Blues," worked as bandmaster and cornet soloist with Mahara's Minstrels, starting in 1894 for "twelve or fourteen years."[30] In his autobiography, he tells of a tragic incident involving a member of the company. Louis Wright was a proud minstrel, who defiantly cursed a crowd of whites when he and his lady friend were snowballed in Missouri. An angry crowd stormed the theater where the troupe was appearing, threatening to lynch Wright, who dispersed them by firing a gun. Later that night, when the minstrels' railroad car was surrounded and Wright again refused to give himself up, the entire company was arrested. Beatings failed to force identification of Wright. However, one of the mob recognized him, and he was taken into custody. During the night, the sheriff released Wright to the mob. He was lynched, his tongue cut out, and his mutilated body shipped to his mother in Chicago.[31]

"Black minstrels experienced the widest possible range of discrimination from trivial to deadly," Robert C. Toll states in his illuminating study, *Blacking Up*. "Being denied their basic needs and regularly insulted and threatened with things like the 'Nigger Read and Run' signs . . . were everyday experiences."[32] Nevertheless, when a New York promoter advertised for 40 black minstrels, an estimated 2,000 Negroes appeared at his office and 1,012 left their names.[33]

Black minstrel shows were inordinately popular with black people, not "upper-crust" Negroes, throughout the nineteenth century. Being a minstrel gave an entertainer stature, class, and importance; a measure of financial stability; and, most of all, mobility, an opportunity to travel not only in this country but, at times, throughout the world. The minstrel show afforded black songwriters, singers, musicians, comics, dancers, and impersonators the first large-scale opportunity to enter American show business.

Although companies of black minstrels made ephemeral appearances as early as 1855, it was not until the organization of Brooker and Clayton's Georgia Minstrels in 1865 that a permanent, first-class black troupe came into existence. So impressive was this troupe, and it drew such enormous crowds throughout the North, that other companies sought to capitalize on the "Georgia Minstrels" designation, which was used so frequently that it became a synonym for Colored Minstrels. Seeking to distinguish their performers from blackface whites, Brooker and Clayton publicized them as men who "were slaves in Macon" and who "spent their former lives in bondage." Critics responded favorably to the claim of authenticity, showering praise on "the genuine plantation darkies" as "great delineators of genuine darky life in the South."[34]

Charles Hicks, who started his own company in 1866 after organizing and managing the Brooker and Clayton troupe, likewise advertised his black minstrels as Slave Troupes and Georgia Slave Brothers. Respected by his white contemporaries as an aggressive promoter, Hicks worked tirelessly but not entirely successfully to own a company. In 1870, after organizing several short-lived troupes, he took his first black troupe to Germany and England. On his return, he managed Callender's Georgia Minstrels as well as Sprague and Blodgette's Georgia Minstrels, after struggling with two unsuccessful companies of his own—African Minstrels and Georgia Minstrels. In 1877 he managed to lure a company of black minstrels from white owners, J. H. Haverly and Tom Maguire, and took them for a three-year tour of Australia.

In 1881–1882 he again persuaded a troupe to leave its management—this time it was Callender—only to buckle under the formidable power of the Frohmans, Gustave and Charles, who came to Callender's resuce. By 1885, when Billy Kersands (1842–1915), the most celebrated black comic minstrel, organized a company of his own, Hicks again surfaced as manager. Again Hicks left to form his own troupe, this time in a short-lived partnership with A. D. Sawyer, another ambitious black entrepreneur. After the breakup, Hicks again took a troupe to Australia and New Zealand. A versatile performer, accomplished as singer, end man, and interlocutor, and a dynamic manager—but successful "only in marginal areas that whites did not covet and control"[35]—Hicks died in Surabaya, Java, while touring with a black minstrel company in 1902.

By the early 1870s, whites owned the most successful black minstrel companies, and even though the success of these troupes depended on black stars, "Negroes had to struggle to retain ownership of any companies at all."[36] In the careers of black minstrels, three white entrepreneurs played large roles.

In 1872 Charles Callender, a white tavern-keeper, purchased the Sam Hague integrated minstrel troupe on its return from England. Employing Charles Hicks as business manager and featuring comedians Billy Kersands, Pete Devonear, and Bob Height, a comic who was later compared to Bert Williams, Callender attracted such crowds and favorable reviews that his name quickly joined "Georgia" as identification of outstanding black troupes. Despite competition from 27 other black companies, business boomed for Callender, whose troupe was the only black minstrel troupe mentioned in a list of leading American minstrel companies in 1877. But in June of the following year, Callender sold his Georgia Minstrels to J. H. Haverly, another white giant in the minstrel field, blackface as well as black. Haverly not only advertised as extensively as Callender but augmented the personnel to as many as 100 and focused the presentations on so-called realistic, but actually romanticized, portrayals of plantation life. Like Callender earlier, Haverly's Colored Minstrels played to turnaway crowds, attaining a peak in the summer of 1881, when they followed his blackface Mastodons to England for a sensational year's tour.

While Haverly's company was abroad, ex-advance men Gustave and Charles Frohman, later producers on Broadway, purchased Callender's new troupe, added Haverly's Colored Minstrels when Haverly overextended himself, and, retaining Callender's name, established Callender's Consolidated Colored Minstrels—"The Pick of the Earth's Colored Talent." Pursuing an eye-catching pattern of luxurious productions and flamboyant advertising, the Consolidated Minstrels gained such acceptance that by late 1882, three separate companies were touring the country.

"White-owned-and-structured shows had the greatest exposure," Robert C. Toll concludes, "made the most money and focussed audience expectations on stereotyped images of Negroes. Most of all, they illustrated that when blacks became marketable as entertainers, it was white men who reaped the profits."[37]

So marketable were black minstrels in the years between 1880 and 1884 that an advertisement for minstrels in the *Clipper* read: "Non-colored performers need not apply."[38] And W. C. Handy observed: "All the best black talent—the composers, the singers, the musicians, the speakers, the stage performers—the Minstrel Show got them all."[39]

The highest-paid black minstrel was Billy Kersands, whose renown was the result of a gigantic mouth, which could hold a cup and a saucer as he danced. Billy was such an attraction, according to Tom Fletcher, that in St. Louis, "prejudice was half forgotten as the owners arranged for colored customers to occupy a full half of the theater from the ground floor or orchestra section right up to the gallery with whites filling the other side."[40]

The second highest paid was Wallace King, the Sweet Singing Tenor of the noted Callender troupe of 1882. Among banjo virtuosos, there were the Bohees, James and George, and Horace Weston. Then there was Sam Lucas, "The Grand Old Man of the Negro Stage," as James Weldon Johnson dubbed him in *Black Manhattan*.

Sam Lucas (1840–1916) worked as a barber and constantly fell back on minstrelsy jobs as singer, composer and character actor while he sought serious dramatic roles. Costarring with the famous Hyer Sisters in such musical dramas as *Out of Bondage* and *The Underground Railroad* between minstrel appearances, he became the first black man to play the lead in *Uncle Tom's Cabin* (1878). In 1890 he performed in Sam T. Jack's *Creole Show*, an early, primitive example of black musical comedy, and, toward the end of the decade, in *A Trip to Coontown,* regarded as the first Negro musical to make a complete break with minstrelsy. As the climax to his career, he became the first black to star in a film *(Uncle Tom's Cabin).* Unfortunately, in one of the scenes, he had to jump into a partially frozen river to save Little Eva. He developed pneumonia as a result of the exposure and died in January 1916.

The list of minstrel performers of distinction is long. Into the twentieth century, the minstrel show served as a launching pad not only for white singers like Al Jolson and comics including Eddie Cantor, but for black artists, including several of the classic Blues singers. Gertrude "Ma" Rainey (1886–1939) traveled for a period with her own troupes as well as the Rabbit Foot Minstrels, whose personnel included a young Bessie Smith (1894–1937), later celebrated as Empress of the Blues.

One of the more significant phases of minstrelsy was its role in developing the creative talents of the first popular black songwriters: Ernest Hogan, Gussie L. Davis, James A. Bland, Bert Williams (who will be discussed in the next chapter), and W. C. Handy, among others.

Ernest Hogan (1859–1909) born Reuben Crowder, in Kentucky, served as end man with the great Bert Williams in minstrel shows; did a cakewalk in *Summer Nights* (1897) at the Casino Roof in New York City; produced the first show with syncopated music in 1905, starring the so-called Memphis Students—they were neither students nor from Memphis; and is best known for the biggest "coon song" hit, "All Coons Look Alike to Me" (1896), which he regretted writing all his life and which will be discussed later in this book.

Gussie Lord Davis (1863–1899), who is not as well-known as the other writer/performers under consideration, was described in the newspapers, circulars and sheet music of his day as "Cincinnati's Only Colored Author and Comedian," "the most popular author and composer the race has produced," and "the race's most prolific writer." He was unquestionably the most-published black songwriter of the years between 1880 and 1899, the year of his death in Whitestone, New York. He has more recently been described as "the first black songwriter to succeed in Tin-Pan Alley,"[41] which is acceptable if the reference to Tin Pan Alley is not taken literally, since that cognomen did not come into existence until 20 or more years after Davis's death. ("Tin Pan Alley," as a description of a closely knit microcosm of publishers and songwriters, was first applied to an area in New York City by songwriter/journalist Monroe H. Rosenfeld in about 1911. A concentration of music firms was then to be found on a block between Fifth Avenue and Broadway on 28th Street.) But it is a matter of record that Davis was successful in having 200 or more of his songs published by 24 different New York publishers, and by publishers in Cincinnati, Boston, Chicago, and St. Louis.

"Maple on the Hill," Davis's first song, was published in Cincinnati in 1880. Seeking to enhance his musical education, he applied for admission to the Nelson Musical College, in his native city. Rejected because he was black, he took a job as a janitor for $15 a month in order to receive private instruction. In 1887 he moved to New York with the support of white George Propheter, who had published several of his songs in Cincinnati, and who now published "Goodbye, Old Home, Goodbye" and "The Court House in the Sky."

Davis was a versatile professional writer, whose ability to create songs to fit the needs of various black minstrels for comic, sacred, or sentimental material, made him a favorite. During the "coon song" craze, he wrote quite a number, including "That Strange Coon," "The Coon That I Suspected" (1895), "I'm the Father of a Little Black Coon" (1897), "Nigger, You Won't Go" (1898), "Only a Nigger Baby" (1898), and "There'd Never Been No Trouble If They Kidnapped a Coon" (1899). For "Send Back the Picture and the Ring," entered in a contest sponsored by the *New York World* among the 10 most popular songwriters of the day, he won a prize of $500 in 1895. He also wrote larger works, including the musical *A Hot Old Time in Dixie,* which was on tour at his death. His biggest hit, the sentimental ballad "In the Baggage Coach Ahead," came in 1896. Introduced by Billy Johnson (1858–1916), a prominent minstrel and later a producer of Black Patti's Troubadours, and popularized by the white "female baritone" Imogene Comer, it reportedly sold over a million copies.

In an interview published in 1888 in the *New York Evening Sun,* Davis asserted that "the day of Negro and jubilee songs" was over, and that he was, accordingly, making a specialty of "waltz songs." The "coon song" was then in the making, along with cakewalk dance numbers, so that Davis was really reacting to a market developing among "refined people." Distinguishing between the reaction of men and women to a song, he stated: "A woman buys it and sings it at home. She cannot sing a minstrel or Negro song in the parlor, and refined people would not allow it in the house . . . Love and mother songs are the taking songs."[42] Davis became such a master of this genre of sentimental, lachrymose ballad—so dear to the hearts of readers of *Godey's Lady Book*—that historian Maxwell F. Marcuse properly observed: "Gussie Davis reached for the tender spots that lurk deep within all of us . . . In an era of 'sing-'em-and-weep' melodies, Davis did more than his share to open the tear ducts of America . . . [Year after year he filled] another bucket of tears to add to the lachrymal ocean pouring out of Tin-Pan Alley."[43]

The admiration minstrels felt for Davis found expression in a poem that appeared posthumously in the *Freeman*. Spelling out "Gussie L. Davis" vertically with the initial letter of each line, famous black minstrel Sam Lucas wrote a lament for the issue of October 20, 1900.

James A. Bland (1856–1911) vied in output and, perhaps, exceeded the 600 songs written by Gussie L. Davis. He has been called "the most prolific, famous and influential black minstrelsy songwriter," "first major professional song composer," and "the most distinguished creator of sentimental Southern songs after Foster."[44] As with Davis, sentimental ballads were, indeed, Bland's forte. But he plucked the heartstrings with songs, not about mother, children, romantic love, and death, but about plantation life. By contrast with Davis, Bland was a top notch performer, who was advertised as The World's Greatest Minstrel Man and The Idol of the Music Halls.[45]

Born in Flushing, New York, and educated in Washington and at Howard University, he began a distinguished career as a minstrel when he was 19. It was a performance of the Primrose Minstrels, we are told, that so excited him that he decided to leave Howard University after only two years.[46] Having early mastered the banjo, he gigged around Washington until in 1875. He became the manager of and starred in the Original Black Diamonds in Boston. There followed stints with the Bohee Brothers Minstrels, Sprague's Georgia Minstrels (when he reportedly outshone both Sam Lucas and Billy Kersands) and Haverly's Colored Minstrels, with whom he went to England. There he remained for eight years, playing solo performances to turnaway crowds in England and on the Continent, being billed as the Prince of Negro Songwriters and giving Command Performances before Queen Victoria and the Prince of Wales.

On his return to the United States in 1890, he joined the W. C. Cleveland Colored Minstrel Carnival, passing up an offer from the celebrated Kersands' Minstrels. In the 1890s, as variety and vaudeville began to supersede the minstrel show as an audience draw, his career went into a down-spin. Although he sang with Black Patti's Troubadours, a vaudeville company, in 1898, his efforts to reestablish himself failed. At the time that he rejected the Kersands' Minstrels offer, he seems to have purchased "the largest diamond ever worn probably by a colored person, its weight being 4½ carats."[47] But when he died, in May 1911, he was a pauper, and was buried in an unmarked grave in Merion, Pennsylvania. It was not until 1939 that the grave was located and not until 1946 that a tombstone was erected, with funds supplied by ASCAP.

By then, the State of Virginia had adopted as its official state song his "Carry Me Back to Old Virginny," published in 1878. "Oh, Dem Golden Slippers," published in 1879 and a sensation in his

London solo debut in 1882, has remained the theme of the Mummers' annual New Year's Day Parade in Philadelphia since the 1920s. His other best-known songs include "In the Morning by the Bright Light," described as an End Song in an 1879 publication;[48] "De Golden Wedding" (1880); "Hand Me Down My Walking Cane" (1880); and "In the Evening by the Moonlight," introduced by Sprague's Georgia Minstrels.

Unlike Gussie Davis, whose sentimental songs dealt with conventional subjects, Bland's best-known songs presented sentimental pictures of plantation life, which, perhaps, accounted for their popularity among the minstrel companies playing in the North. "His nostalgic old darkies expressed great love for their masters and mistresses," Robert Toll has observed, "his plantation songs were free from antislavery protests and from praise of freedom; his religious songs contained many stereotyped images of flashy dressers and of overindulgent parties; and his Northern Negroes strutted, sang, danced, and had flapping ears, huge feet and gaping mouths."[49] In short, Bland was a black Stephen Foster, as Foster was a white Bland.

William Christopher Handy, who called himself Father of the Blues, which is also the title of his autobiography, and whose career as a songwriter, instrumentalist, arranger, collector, editor, and publisher extended into the mid-1950s, was involved with minstrelsy during the first 15 years of his musical life. At the age of 15, in 1888, he joined a singing quartet that was part of a hometown minstrel show in Florence, Alabama. "I looked pretty funny," Handy wrote in his autobiography,

> stepping along with the 'walking gents' in my father's Prince Albert. We had seen the famous Georgia Minstrels in Florence, and we knew how to make the pivot turns. We were all acquainted with Billy Kersands, the man who could make a mule laugh and we remembered his trick of proving on the stage that his enormous mouth would accommodate a cup and a saucer. We had seen Sam Lucas and Tom McIntosh walking at the head of the parade in high silk hats and long-tailed coats."[50]

Even though the troupe was stranded in Jasper, Tennessee, after a few appearances and the manager skipped town, Handy's feeling for minstrelsy was not deflated. After working as a bandsman in Henderson, Kentucky, he seized the opportunity to join W. A. Mahara's Minstrels as cornetist, terming the day of his induction, August 4, 1896, as "the big moment that was presently to shape my course in life." He joined, even though "a large sector of upper-crust Negroes, including the family and friends of Elizabeth Price" (his future wife) viewed minstrels as "a disreputable lot."[51] His reason was that the best black talent of his generation became minstrels.

Soon he was onstage in the olio, a recognized cornet soloist; and, the following year, became the leader of a band consisting of 30 pieces in the parade and 42 in the night performances. It was a glorious life of "a bright uniform, golden epaulettes, a gleaming silk topper," excited, applauding audiences, and even a trip to Cuba[52]—which later accounted for his use of the *habanera* rhythm in his famous "St. Louis Blues." But it was also one fraught with dangers: white men who lynched a member of the troupe; cowboys who roped them during the morning parade; an Orange, Texas, mob that would riddle the group's Pullman car with bullets as it traveled through town; threats of lynching and having the Pullman burned when members of the troupe came down with smallpox.

Nevertheless, after a hiatus of two years when he served as musical director at A and M College, Handy readily returned to Mahara's Minstrels. Thinking back to those days, Handy remembered them as "well spent," a time that took him from Cuba to California, from Canada to Mexico; that threw him into contact with "a wistful but aspiring generation of dusky singers and musicians," and that "taught me a way of life that I consider the only one for me."[53]

When Eddie Leonard appeared in vaudeville, in about 1912, he was billed as The Last of the Great Minstrels. Others who were among "the last" would include Lew Dockstader, in whose troupe Leonard performed; George "Honey Boy" Evans; and, especially, black Bert Williams, whose remarkable talent carried him high into the Broadway theater as well as vaudeville, and whose work will be considered later.

According to music publisher Edward B. Marks, Eddie Leonard got his start in minstrelsy when he brought the young white hoofer to the manager of Primrose and West Minstrels.[54] Leonard was hired when he agreed to play the cymbals as well as dance. Early in that association (1903), Leonard wrote "Ida (Sweet as Apple Cider)," the song whose performance saved him when he was about to be fired. Years later, a young Eddie Cantor (1892–1964), who became known as Mr. Banjo Eyes and married a girl whose name was Ida, scored with his imitations of Eddie Leonard's rendition of the song. So did a young Al Jolson, working in blackface with Lew Dockstader's Minstrels. By the time he wrote and introduced "(Roll Dem) Roly Boly Eyes" in 1912, Leonard was working in vaudeville, and widely acknowledged for his dancing of the soft-shoe tap. He ultimately appeared on Broadway in a 1919 musical titled *Roly Boly Eyes,* in which he sang "Ida" as well as the title song.

Like Eddie Leonard, George "Honey Boy" Evans, another of the famous blackface minstrels, is remembered for two songs he wrote. "I'll Be True to My Honey Boy," written in 1894, gave Evans the cognomen by which he is known. "In the Good Old Summertime" (1902), one of the great gang-songs of all time, was introduced in the musical *The Defender,* with Evans standing in the wings, harmonizing with Blanche Ring, the star. Evans and Shields, who collaborated on "Summertime," also wrote "Come, Take a Trip on my Air-Ship," an early tribute to aviation. Despite his success as a minstrel and songwriter, Evans, like James Bland, died poor.

Lew Dockstader was a blackface performer as well as a minstrel-company owner. A writer of parodies and comic songs, he helped popularize "Everybody Works but Father," which he did not write, in about 1905. One of the last "stump speakers," he became known for his "political" speeches, in which he skilfully always inserted topical local references, and for his hilarious imitation of President Theodore Roosevelt. He was much concerned with keeping minstrelsy alive as a distinct form after variety and musicals had superseded it in popular favor.

"Minstrelsy in silk stockings," he complained, referring to the opulent innovations of competitors, "set in square cuts and big wigs is about as palatable as an amusement as a salad of pine shavings and sawdust with a little salmon, lobster or chicken. . . . What is really good is killed by the surroundings. . . . They have refined all the fun out of it."[55]

What competitors were doing was presenting variety and musicals within the framework of minstrelsy. When the famous troupe of Primrose and West broke apart, George Primrose, an outstanding blackface comedian, joined with Lew Dockstader. Although it was only for one lively summer at Hammerstein's Victoria, they were able to attract Eddie Leonard as a performer. Dockstader continued with his own troupe almost into the second decade of the twentieth century, launching among other careers that of Al Jolson in 1909.[56]

Minstrelsy flourished as a popular form of entertainment into the last decade of the nineteenth century. One of the blackface minstrel companies that was quite popular in this era but participated in changes that anticipated the emergency of vaudeville was Primrose and West. George Primrose, born Delaney in Canada, was so masterful a dancer that (to recall the incident) a young James Bland, viewing a performance, was inspired to turn away from the law, his family's choice of profession, to minstrelsy. Primrose and his partner, William West, were both working with Haverly's Minstrels when a dispute over salary led to their departure and the formation of their own company in 1877. As Primrose and West, they were so successful that in time they became known as the Millionaires of Minstrelsy.

The association of the company with an unusual number of very popular songs contributed to their renown. In 1884, tenor Banks Winter introduced his own "White Wings," a sentimental ballad that soon was "sung, whistled, warbled, hummed, ground out by hurdy-gurdies, banged on pianos and every other conceivable instrument," according to Douglas Gilbert,[57] and that became a request number for the rest of his career. In 1894, James Thornton's popular tear-jerker, "She May Have Seen Better Days," was effectively introduced by minstrel R. H. Widom.

The more significant development of 1894, and a novel departure from minstrel procedures, was the first use of illustrated slides to present and dramatize a new song for the public. West opposed the innovation. But publisher Edward B. Marks, who also wrote the lyrics of "The Little Lost Child," was so persuasive in discussions with George Primrose that the song was presented with a series of slides illustrating the sentimental story at the Grand Opera House, on 23rd St. and Eighth Avenue, in New York, with tenor Alan May singing the song. As "The Little Lost Child" went on to sell a million copies, other music publishers were soon using slide presentations with their new songs.

The year 1902 found Primrose and West riding high with two new hits. "Silver Threads among the Gold," introduced first in 1873, was revived by another silver-voiced tenor, Richard J. Jose, born in England but claimed by California as a native son. A minstrel with the Charlie Reed troupe and, later, Lew Dockstader, he also contributed to the popularity of "With All Her Faults I Love Her Still" (1888) and "I Love You in the Same Old Way (Darling Sue)" (1896); but neither of these achieved the popularity of "Silver Threads," which eventually sold over three million copies. The second Primrose and West hit of 1902 was "Oh, Didn't He Ramble," written by Bob Cole and Rosamond Johnson under the pseudonym Will Handy, introduced by George Primrose, and, in time, a favorite of black bands on the way home from a funeral.

When Lew Dockstader lamented the sacrifice of fun to refinement in the minstrel show, it was in reference to developments pioneered by Primrose and West. Impressed by the success of a British minstrel company (Sam Hague's) in which performers appeared in full evening dress and only the end men were in blackface, Primrose and West experimented with white minstrelsy and a cast dressed in Shakespearean costumes. By then, the company was known as Thatcher, Primrose and West, and it shortly presented a *Black Mikado,* which ran for two years, 1884–1886.

A photograph included in a program of the period—presumably the late 1880s—bears the inscription, "A New Departure: Modern Minstrelsy in Kingly Splendor."[58] Arranged in a large semicircle are 23 performers, attired in elegant colonial vests and britches, with no less than 5 Mr. Boneses on the left end and 5 Mr. Tambos on the right end. Except for these 10 performers in blackface, the rest are white. Seated behind this semicircle, in a raised semicircular box, there is an orchestra of strings, woodwinds, and brass, adding up to 21 musicians. By this time, apparently, other latter-day minstrel troupes were making limited use of blackface, low comedy, and plantation settings and material, and concentrating on lavish productions. Of these, as of the Thatcher, Primrose and West presentations, it could be said, as the *Clipper* wrote of the Sam Hague Minstrels: it was "more like a high class ballad or operatic concert than a minstrel show."[59]

It has been customary to regard vaudeville as a descendant of the olio segment of the minstrel show. The attribution of paternity is understandable—if questionable—since the olio, not unlike vaudeville, consisted of a series of specialty acts. Of course, there was a difference in that the performers in the olio were part of a troupe, not disparate acts, each traveling and performing separately. But the fact is that the minstrel show itself underwent a transformation in which its basic character changed. By the late 1880s, it was a minstrel show largely in name and, except for some vestigial elements, was really a variety or vaudeville show.

A sign of the change was J. H. Haverly's United Mastodon Minstrels, whose expanded personnel was blazoned in posters, playbills, and newspapers as consisting of "FORTY—40—COUNT 'EM—40—FORTY!" The enlarged cast was itself an indication of an elaborate production, flamboyant curtains, colorful sets, expensive costumes, and exotic themes. When Haverly bought the San Francisco Minstrels in the winter of 1883–1884, eliminating the last resident minstrel company in New York, a city that had once boasted dozens of minstrel troupes,[60] the disappearance of minstrelsy as it had flourished for 40 years was a reality.

Haverly has been described as the greatest minstrel entrepreneur and as a promoter and empire-builder of P. T. Barnum proportions. By 1881 he was the owner of an empire that embraced two large white minstrel companies and the biggest black troupe, four touring comedy theater groups, and six theaters, three in New York and one each in Brooklyn, Chicago, and San Francisco.

The modifications he made in the traditional minstrel show were the product, not of personal quirks, but of several socioeconomic factors. Decisive was the expansion of the American economy in the post–Civil War era, with the growth of population, transportation, and cities. Like other phases of the economy, minstrelsy was drawn into the Gilded Age trends toward large-scale enterprise and the elimination and absorption of small companies. Moreover, the rise and growth of black minstrelsy, admired for its ethnic authenticity in depicting plantation life in comparison with the burnt-cork brigade, compelled the white minstrel companies to move in the direction of visually exciting settings and dazzling specialty acts. Reacting also to the competition of other types of entertainment, such as drama, opera, and variety, and feeling that the minstrel show had not grown with the economy, Haverly was motivated to establish a minstrel troupe that "for extraordinary excellence, merit and magnitude will astonish and satisfy the most exacting seeker in the world."[61]

Inevitably, outsized extravaganzas and grandiose spectacles became the order of the day. As the first-part finale of an 1880 program, Haverly offered "a magnificent scene representing a Turkish Barbaric Palace in Silver and Gold."[62] In the mid-1880s, Haverly presented a Colossal Japanese Show, including jugglers, tumblers, necromancers, all ostensibly brought from the Court Theatre of his Imperial Majesty, the Mikado of Japan.

The cost of mounting these lavish productions forced the minstrels of the late nineteenth century to become traveling companies. Resident troupes could not achieve the long runs required to amortize costs, while one-nighters in the larger cities provided a substantial source of revenue. The smaller resident companies could not meet the competition, and went out of business or were bought out by the empire-builders, as Haverly had done in New York City with the San Francisco Minstrels, who had presented a traditional minstrel show, beginning in May 1865, for 19 years.

What Haverly was doing with his blackface Mastodons was in part the result of what he was doing with his Colored Minstrels. The latter presented "The Darky as He Is at Home, Darky Life in the Cornfields, Canebreak, Barnyard and on the Levee and Flatboat."[63] For the traditional semicircle opening of his blackface minstrels, Haverly substituted picturesque nonplantation settings. From the earliest black troupe, there had been an emphasis on "genuine plantation darkies from the South," so that critics and audiences began to feel "there is nothing like the natural thing. . . . A Negro can play Negro peculiarities much more satisfactorily than the white 'artist,' who with burnt cork is *at best a base imitator*."[64] Negroes depicted plantation life, said the New York *Clipper*," with greater fidelity than any 'poor white trash' with corked faces can do."[65]

In actuality, the black minstrels were really recapitulating the sham, romantic illusion of plantation life that the blackface minstrels had foisted on the public. But the belief in the authenticity of black portrayals worked to the disadvantage of the blackface troupes. As the black companies offered their versions of plantation life, the white blackface troupes were moved to seek out new locales and new subjects; in short, they were driven in the direction of variety.

In histories of American popular music, Ernest Hogan has achieved an unwanted notoriety as the guilt-ridden black author of the song "All Coons Look Alike to Me," the content of which belies the pejorative and prejudiced implication of the title. (The song will be considered at length in the section on "coon songs," in the next chapter). Overlooked in the Hogan accounts is the notable career he enjoyed as an actor/singer/composer/producer for almost two decades before his death.

Born Ernest Reuber Crowder in Bowling Green, Kentucky, he worked as a minstrel end man in Richard and Pringle's Georgia Minstrels. The song that became a runaway hit on its publication in 1896 and that caused him so much travail also sent his career into high gear. He was starred in *Clorindy, or the Origin of the Cakewalk* (1898), the path-breaking operetta by poet/author Paul Laurence Dunbar (1872–1906) and composer/producer Will Marion Cook (1869–1944), which was presented at the Casino Roof Garden in New York. In this, he sang a number of "coon" songs that became popular: "Who Dat Say Chicken in Dis Crowd," "Darktown Is Out Tonight," and "Hottest Coon in Dixie."

On leaving *Clorindy,* he succeeded Cole and Johnson as star of the famous Black Patti Troubadours, receiving equal billing with Black Patti herself and being featured opposite her as the "Unbleached American." Later, when he played Hammerstein's Victoria Theater, it was as a headliner, at a high figure. Nevertheless, he returned to minstrelsy in the 1899–1900 season, touring with Curtis's Afro-American Minstrels and being received vociferously in Australia and Hawaii. With his partner of the Australian and Hawaiian comedic triumphs, Billy McLain (1866–1949), he persuaded Gus Hill to finance the organization of the Original Smart Set Company, in which he successfully created the character of George Washington Bullion. After starring in *Uncle Eph's Christmas,* a musical with a book again by Paul Laurence Dunbar and music by Will Marion Cook, his career reached a new height with the lead role in *Rufus Rastus,* a Hurtig and Seamon production of 1905–1906, for which he wrote the songs and that yielded the hit, "Oh, Say, Wouldn't That Be a Dream."

By 1907 he was working on *The Oyster Man,* which he hoped

would be his crowning production. He staged the work, collaborated on the music, and, assisted by Miller and Lyles, two performing creators fresh out of Chicago's famous Pekin Stock Company, wrote the book. Starring with the noted comic John Rucker (1866–19—), he won accolades from the critics. By the time the show opened, he was ill from overwork, and left it briefly early in 1908. Returning shortly, he collapsed on the stage of the Globe Theater in Boston. Gravely concerned, producers Hurtig and Seamon sent him for a rest to the mountains. He never returned, dying in 1909, at the age of 50.

Ernest Hogan's creative journey, from minstrel end man to the star of pioneer black musicals, departing from the minstrel framework and ingredients, embodies changes that were occurring in black entertainment. While minstrelsy itself was being transformed,[66] from it sprouted new theatrical styles like variety and vaudeville, as well as new musical styles, including Ragtime, "coon" songs, and the cakewalk.

CHAPTER THREE

"MY RAGTIME BABY"

The Coon Song and the Cakewalk

When the great comedy team of Williams and Walker came to New York City in 1895, "coon" songs were the rage. One of the first shows in which they appeared, *Senegambian Carnival,* with music by Will Marion Cook and book and lyrics by Paul Laurence Dunbar, was competitive with Bob Cole's *A Trip to Coontown.* Trading on the current popularity of such songs, George Walker introduced his hit, "The Hottest Coon in Dixie," in the *Senegambian Carnival.* When the duo starred in *The Policy Players* circa 1900, they were billed as the "Two Real Coons." Coon songs were a development of the 1890s, concomitant with the popularity of the cakewalk songs and dance and the rise of Ragtime.

Unquestionably, the best known of the coon songs was Ernest Hogan's "All Coons Look Alike to Me," which appeared in the same year (1896) as Barney Fagan's "My Gal Is a High-Born Lady," Ben R. Harney's "Mister Johnson, Turn Me Loose," and Paul Dresser's "I'se Your Nigger if You Wants Me, Liza Jane." The Hogan song did not embody the prejudicial stereotype implied by its title. It was a ballad of a broken love affair in which a woman, now possessed of a new lover who spends money on her, airily dismisses her old love with the comment, "All coons look alike to me."[1] Despite its nonracial content, the song, according to Sigmund Spaeth, "was heartily resented by Hogan's own race, but white listeners loved it, and it remains one of the justly famous examples of true ragtime. . . . Hogan was a great comedian close to the standard of Bert Williams, but his all too popular 'coon song' gave him a permanent feeling of guilt, and he died regretting its composition."[2]

"The refrain [of 'All Coons Look Alike to Me'] became a fighting phrase all over New York," music publisher Edward B. Marks recalled. "Whistled by a white man, it was construed as a personal insult. Rosamond Johnson relates that he saw two men thrown off a ferry boat in a row over the tune. Hogan became an object of censure among all the Civil Service intelligentsia, and he died haunted by the awful crime he had unwittingly committed against the race."[3]

Coon Songs refers not merely to a type of song but to a style of singing as well. One of the earliest dynamic proponents of "coon shouting," as this style came to be known, was white May Irwin, of the well-known Irwin Sisters. With her sister Flora, May was the singer of Ragtime specialty songs at Pastor's Music Hall in New York. In her booming delivery of "Mamie, Come Kiss Your Honey Boy," a song she wrote for the musical *A Country Sport* (1893), and of "The Bully" in *Widow Jones* (1895), May anticipated robust and raucous singers such as Sophie Tucker (1887–1966), who billed herself as "the Last of the Red Hot Mamas," and, later, Willie Mae "Big Mama" Thornton (1926–1984), of "Hound Dog" fame.

The originator of "coon shouting," if one can be so designated, is a little-known black singer who is remembered simply as Mama Lou and who sang in a celebrated St. Louis brothel run by Babe Connors. Mama Lou is believed to be the writer of "Ta-ra-ra Boom-der-a" and "The Bully," songs credited to others. In each instance, someone who heard Mama Lou supposedly brought the song to the attention of a performer and revised it (probably eliminating the more risqué material), with the result that Charles F. Trevathan, a sportswriter, has his name on the published version of "The Bully" (1896) and Henry J. Sayers, a press agent, received credit on "Ta-ra-ra Boom-der-a" (1891). The latter song became a perennial for Lottie Gilson, a torch singer of the 1890s, who introduced it at Koster and Bial's in New York after scoring a sensation with it in London; Lottie later popularized the unforgettable "Sidewalks of New York."

Although few coon songs originated in brothels, they contrasted sharply with the sentimental, maudlin waltzes — "She's More to Be Pitied Than Censured," "Take Back Your Gold," etc.—that were then so popular among refined ladies. Coon songs were an infusion into the pop music scene of high spirits, revelry, and rhythmic drive, much as Rhythm and Blues was later in the 1950s. As a musical form and style, coon songs differed little from syncopated Ragtime songs such as Hughie Cannon's "Bill Bailey, Won't You Please Come Home?" or Ben Harney's three classic hits: "Cakewalk in the Sky," "Mister Johnson, Turn Me Loose," and "You've Been a Good Old Wagon, But You Done Broke Down," the latter two popularized into standards by May Irwin's boisterous performances in vaudeville. The symbiotic relationship between coon and Ragtime songs is suggested by the early career of Sophie Tucker, who was billed as a "coon shouter" when she appeared in blackface at Pastor's Music Hall, and, having dispensed with burnt cork, was then billed as the Mary Garden of Ragtime. Coon songs were, in fact, ragtime songs, but with a special, if unfortunate, racial orientation.

The word *coon,* from raccoon, evolved as a pejorative term during the post-Civil War era of Reconstruction, when prejudiced and "threatened" whites sought through intimidation and violence to keep the newly emancipated "niggers," or "coons" in their place. It is, perhaps, not surprising that the 1880s witnessed the inception of the deprecating coon song cycle with Jacob T. Sawyer's "Coonville Guards" (1881) and "The Coon Dinner" (1882), followed by Paul Allen's "New Coon in Town" (1883). Of "The Whistling Coon" (1888), by Sam Devere, historian Sigmund Spaeth wrote: "It represents a growing repertoire of pseudo-Negro material of the less respectful type."[4] The 1890s witnessed a flood of such songs, which, wedded to jouncy, syncopated rhythms, caught the ears of a wide public, black as well as white.

In 1897 a song that started as an instrumental two-step was developed by its writer, Kerry Mills, into a protest against coon songs and became a cakewalk classic as the result of its use by a well-known vaudeville song-and-dance team. "At a Georgia Camp Meeting" was the work of Kerry Mills (1869–1948), who was head of the violin department at the University of Michigan, and who later wrote the hit "Meet Me in St. Louis, Louis." He entered the world of popular music in 1895 with a syncopated cakewalk for piano, "Rastus on Parade," which he pubished under the imprint of F. A. Mills—his name was Frederick Allen Mills. Troubled by the deprecatory impact of coon songs, he added lyrics in 1899 to another two-step, using a southern religious revival gathering as the basis of "At a Georgia Camp Meeting." When the dance team of Genaro and Bailey, whom he interested in the song, performed it in vaudeville, they did a high-stepping cakewalk in the interlude.

The cakewalk was originally a plantation phenomenon, in which slave couples, dressed in their Sunday finery, vied for a cake. It was awarded to the couple who did the most elegant and demonstrative strut. At some point, minstrelsy converted the marching strut into a dance. Even Harrigan and Hart, of the famous *Mulligan Guard* burlesques, presented a version of the cakewalk in one of their productions, routined to a song titled, "Walking for Dat Cake" (1877). A feature of shows presented by Williams and Walker, it brought renown to George Walker, who became an outstanding cakewalker. Moving from the stage to the street, the dance became so popular that in 1892, the first annual Cakewalk Jubilee was held in Madison Square Garden, a three-night contest that drew dancers from cities and towns around the country. The cakewalk is still visible today in the high-stepping strut of drum majorettes leading marching bands during football halves, who march with their bodies bent backward to a 45-degree angle, as they twirl and juggle a baton.

The extent of the coon song craze is suggested by the number of black songwriters who contributed to it. In the repertoire of Williams and Walker, there were, in addition to "The Hottest Coon in Dixie" (1899), "The Ghost of a Coon" (1900) and "She's Gettin' Mo' Like the White Folks Every Day," all written by them. Bob Cole produced and wrote the pioneering show, *A Trip to Coontown* (1898), and the shows written by poet Paul Laurence Dunbar and Will Marion Cook included their share of coon songs. Although coon songs did not always contain objectionable material, there were songs that were explicitly deprecatory; for instance, "Every Race Has a Flag but the Coon" (1900) and "Coon, Coon, Coon (I Wish My Color Would Fade)" (1900).

It was to be expected of course, that Tin Pan Alley songwriters would join the parade. Harry Von Tilzer (1902–1946) wrote "Mammy's Kinky-Headed Coon" (1899) and "The Coldest Coon in Town" as an answer to "The Hottest Coon in Dixie." Paul Dresser (1857–1906), a master of the sob ballad, produced "You're Just a Little Nigger, Still You're Mine" as an answer to his own "I'se Your Nigger If You Want Me, Liza Jane." In 1905 Fred Fisher, another Tin Pan Alley bigwig, indulged in a bit of speculation: "If the Man in the Moon Were a Coon." Earlier in 1895, a youthful George M. Cohan (1878–1942) produced "Hot Tamale Alley," which was introduced by coon-shouter May Irwin. In 1911 Jerome Kern wrote the score for *La Belle Paree,* the musical with which the Shuberts opened their new Broadway theater, the Winter Garden. Kern's score included "Paris Is a Paradise for Coons," sung by a newcomer named Al Jolson.

Despite its reprehensible overtones and its role in continuing a deprecatory stereotype developed by the minstrel show, the coon song was musically a positive influence in popular music. By contrast with the dominant wave of schmaltzy, European-sounding waltzes—the sheet music of "After the Ball (Is Over)" sold two million copies—coon songs had verve, drive, buoyancy, humor, and syncopation. Like Ragtime songs, of which they were a phase, they contributed excitement and fresh, vibrant sound to popular music,[5] anticipating the development of Jazz.

The Ragtime Pioneers

On January 23, 1900, Ragtime pianists from all over the nation came to Tammany Hall in New York City to participate in a competition for the Ragtime Championship of the World. The keyboard players who made the semifinals were required to demonstrate their superiority by ragging for two minutes Ernest Hogan's very popular song, "All Coons Look Alike to Me."

Three years earlier, in 1897, Tony Pastor's Music Hall, on New York's Fourteenth Street, presented a backroom saloon-pianist/singer whom it billed as the Inventor of Ragtime. By then, Benjamin Robertson Harney (1871–1938) had made a reputation for himself as a coon-shouter, an exciting Rag pianist, and the writer of coon song-hits. In the year of his appearance at Pastor's, his *Rag Time Instructor* was published—a method book in which he demonstrated how pianists could take a folk ballad, a sacred song, or what-you-will, and rag it. For a long time, it was believed that Harney was white; but through Eubie Blake, it has been established that he was black.[6]

Between Harney's rousing performances at Pastor's and the World Championship competition, the first Ragtime best seller made its appearance out of a small Missouri town near St. Louis. "Maple Leaf Rag," named after the club where composer Scott Joplin (1868–1917) played, was published by John Stilwell Stark of Sedalia, Missouri in 1899, and caught the public's fancy to such a degree that it sold over a million copies. All three developments made the country cognizant of a new, bouncy sound in popular music. But by 1900, the sound had traveled across the Atlantic with the brass band of John Philip Sousa (1854–1932), which won a prize at the Paris Exposition of 1900 for its playing of Fred Stone's piece, "My Ragtime Baby" (1898).

The Stone opus is sometimes cited as the first piece specifically to use the word *Ragtime*. However, the word *rag* had already appeared in the title of a piano piece by a Chicago bandmaster, W. H. Krell whose *Mississippi Rag* was copyrighted in 1897, a matter of months before Harney's *Rag Time Instructor* (which contained "new selections in Rag Time by Theo. H. Northrup") and before *Harlem Rag*, by Thomas Turpin, a café owner, known as the Father of St.

Louis Ragtime. The Krell work was divided into four segments, with titles that suggest possible sources of Ragtime: "Cakewalk; Plantation Song; Trio; Buck-and-Wing Dance."

Scott Joplin did not view the 39 rags he ultimately completed as dance music but as art music, American art music comparable to the piano pieces of such composers as Chopin and Mozart. Nevertheless, black dance music was basic in the evolutionary development of Ragtime, especially the cakewalk. By 1892 William A. Pond & Co. published a banjo solo for piano titled, "Kullud Koons' Kake Walk," by D. Emerson. This was, perhaps, the first in an onrushing flow of cakewalk pieces that yielded such favorites as Sadie Koninsky's "Eli Green's Cakewalk" (1896), Kerry Mills's very popular "At a Georgia Camp Meeting" (1897), Abe Holzman's "Smokey Mokes" (1899) and J. Bodewalt Lampe's "Creole Belles" (1909), among others. Through the 1890s and into the twentieth century, the cakewalk grew in popularity, so that *Musical Courier* denounced the high-society folk of Newport, Rhode Island, for doing "the sex dance," as it termed it.[7]

The cakewalk craze peaked just as John Philip Sousa, heir to the mantle of brass-bandmaster Patrick Gilmore (1829–1892), was embarking on his notable career as the foremost American composer and conductor of marching-band music. Responsive to popular taste and fresh sounds, Sousa quickly added cakewalk music, with its syncopated rhythms, to the band's repertoire, imitating also the ragging of marches practiced spontaneously by black marching bands. Thus, the marching band and the march became factors, along with the cakewalk, in the rise of Ragtime. (Rags incorporated the march form, including a trio, and a steady tempo without acceleration was regarded as the correct way to play classic Ragtime.) Cakewalk pieces were marked: "A characteristic march which can be used effectively as a two-step, polka or cakewalk,"[8] and the two-step was danced to Sousa's "Washington Post March."

Before dancers took to the cakewalk, it was a specialty feature, together with the double quadrille, double shuffle, and "patting Juba" dances, of black minstrel troupes. Other features of the minstrel show that contributed to the development of Ragtime included banjo solos, buck-and-wing dancing, the spirited walk-arounds, and the coon songs. All of these made a spontaneous use of syncopated rhythms and offbeat accents that were absorbed by Ragtime.[9] For that matter, the black folk of southern cities, including St. Louis, Memphis, and many Mississippi River towns, danced and sang with an abandon that impressed Lafcadio Hearn as a "drunkenness of music" and "an intoxication of the dance" and that infused Ragtime.[10]

Basic to a musical explosion like Ragtime is its relationship to the temper of the time. As America approached the twentieth century, people were filled with a heady ebullience, a jangling optimism, a sense, in President Theodore Roosevelt's words, of the country's "manifest destiny" in the world. Ragtime reflected, as it gave expression to, the buoyant spirit of the years between the Spanish–American War (1898) and World War I. But this was a mark of the dance-derived pieces and of the jouncy Ragtime songs written by the white commercializers, not of the classic style developed by Scott Joplin and his followers.

Joplin's role in seeking to create a classic form of Ragtime is evident from the publication of his first popular rag, "Maple Leaf Rag," which he marked *Tempo di marcia,* to the aspirations of his last dismal years. Coming from a musical family in Texarkana, Texas—his mother played banjo, his father, the violin, and his brother, guitar—he made an early acquaintance with the great European composers, through a local German teacher, who gave him lessons on the square grand piano acquired by his family. During eight years spent in St. Louis, starting in his seventeenth year, in 1885, he gained an insight into the unbuttoned dance music and "jig-piano" played by blacks in waterfront clubs, on the levees, and on the Mississippi paddle steamers. After a while, he himself played piano in dives on Chestnut and Market streets. Before he settled in Sedalia, Missouri, he visited the World's Columbian Exposition in Chicago in 1893, where he heard such rural Ragtime piano players as Johnny Seymour, "Plunk" Henry, and Otis Saunders.

What brought Joplin to Sedalia? Possibly an interest in advancing his knowledge of music theory, since Sedalia was one of the few cities with a college for Negroes. There were two music publishers in town, John Stark and W. Perry. In the 1890s it also possessed one of the largest and most talked-about red-light districts in Missouri, with clubs offering employment opportunities to musicians. One of the most popular was the Maple Leaf Club, where Joplin played. It was owned by the black Williams brothers, who, together with Otis Saunders and John Stark, who was white, motivated Joplin eventually to set down on paper the off-the-cuff pieces he improvised during an evening's performance.

Playing piano at night at the Maple Leaf, Joplin attended George Smith College for Negroes, where he studied composition and theory. His first published compositions, two songs and three piano pieces (1895), were conventional, sentimental, and staid works in the "respectable" mode of the day. It was not until four years later that "Original Rags," followed by "Maple Leaf Rag," made their appearance, the former published by Carl Hoffman of Kansas City, who turned down the latter, which brought Joplin into a continuing 10-year relationship with John Stilwell Stark, then of Sedalia, later of St. Louis and New York.

"Original Rags" was in the genre of Rag medleys, which appeared at that time as Ragtime developed from its freewheeling folk status into a classic form. Composers "ragged" known songs and themes', as for example, in Ben Jerome's "A Bunch of Rags" (1889), which incorporated nine tunes, all of them coon songs: "Hesitate, Mr. Nigger, Hesitate," "I Wonder What Is That Coon's Game?" "No Coon Can Come Too Black for Me," etc. Joplin's "Original Rags" bore the notation, "Picked by Scott Joplin" and "Arranged by Chas. N. Daniels," and sounded like a Czerny exercise in Ragtime.

Neither Stark nor Joplin could have anticipated the reception of "Maple Leaf Rag." In form, it consisted of four segments or themes typical of marches (AA BB CC DD) in 2/4 march time, including a trio. It employed the behind-the-beat notes, anticipations, and offbeat accents adding up to the syncopation typical of Ragtime—and which Joplin had heard during his years in St. Louis. The first bar began with a sixteenth rest, which threw the accent on the afterbeat; contained an alteration of the oompah bass (oom-pah-pah-oom), which again threw the accent on the afterbeat; and employed a figure that put a note behind the fourth note in the bass. Offbeat accents appeared in bar 5, when octaves in the treble alternated with octaves in the bass. In bars 7 and 8, the marching beat was broken through the use of a running set of sixteenth notes. Throughout, broken chords typical of banjo playing were used. These devices for "ragging the march" had long been practiced by black bands and honky-tonk piano players. Apart from the fact that "Maple Leaf" seemed to come at just the right moment in time, its popularity was doubtless due to its melodious quality. It became a raging best seller, a classic model for the Rag composers that followed, and, employing a non-European language, helped usher in a new era in American popular music and music publishing.

Joplin went on to see 39 of his rags in print, 7 of which were written with students, imitators or competitors, none of whom matched his productivity. In a number of his compositions, such as the Ragtime waltz, "Bethena," "Heliotrope Bouquet," "Gladiolus Rag," and "Euphonious Sounds," he displayed a lyricism that went far beyond the jaunty syncopation of Ragtime. Throughout his career, his concern with melodic flow, and not just hop–skip rhythms, was evidenced in his insistence that his pieces should be played at a moderate tempo; in fact, virtually all of them contained the admonition, "Not Fast," and in his *School of Ragtime,* he wrote: "Never play ragtime fast at any time."

That he was interested in larger forms of composition was evident even in the year of "Maple Leaf Rag." That year he produced a folk ballet, *The Ragtime Dance,* which was performed at Sedalia's Woods Opera House.[11] By 1903 he had written the book and music of *A Guest of Honor,* a Ragtime opera, which received one concert performance in St. Louis by the Scott Joplin Drama Company. It was copyrighted by John Stark but never published by him, and the manuscript has not been found. Two years later, Joplin completed another Ragtime, or folk, opera, *Treemonisha,* whose production and publication preoccupied and embittered him until his death in 1917. Having broken with Stark, doubtless in part because of the publisher's lack of interest in *Treemonisha,* he himself published *The School of Ragtime* for piano (1908).

At Joplin's death, *Treemonisha* remained unproduced, save for one concert performance, which he himself staged in 1915 in a small Harlem hall, without scenery or costumes, and with himself supplying the thin accompaniment on piano. By then, he had been trying for almost 10 years to interest producers and publishers in the work, which he himself had fully orchestrated. John Stark, his friend and the publisher of his Rags until 1909, having rejected it, Joplin published the 230-page manuscript himself in 1911. It was in 1972, 67 years after its completion, that *Treemonisha* received its premiere, by an all-black cast, at the Memorial Arts Center in Atlanta, a performance that was repeated in August of 1972 at Wolf Trap Park for the Performing Arts in Virginia.

By then, a Joplin renaissance had begun to take shape, launched by a number of developments in 1971. That year, the New York Public Library published the *Collected Works of Scott Joplin* in two facsimile volumes, edited by concert pianist Vera Brodsky. In the summer of 1971, readers of *Billboard* magazine were perhaps surprised to find an LP of Joplin's *Piano Rags,* Volume I, on the chart of Best-Selling *Classical* Records. These were recorded by Joshua Rifkin, a pianist with degrees in composition and musicology from Juilliard and Princeton, and a member of the Brandeis University music faculty. In short, the Joplin renaissance began, not in Tin Pan Alley or with pop record artists, but as Joplin would have preferred it, with classically oriented artists.[12] There followed *An Evening with Scott Joplin* at Lincoln Center whose participants included Joshua Rifkin, William Bolcom, another classicist, and jazz pianist Mary Lou Williams (1910–1981).[13]

In 1974 the renaissance was in full bloom. Superstars Paul Newman and Robert Redford were appearing on the screen in an award-winning film, *The Sting,* in which Joplin's Rag, "The Entertainer" was used as the theme. By then, Rifkin had recorded Volume II of Joplin's Rags; William Bolcom had recorded *Heliotrope Bouquet,* with rags by Thomas Turpin and Joseph Lamb as well as Joplin; and the indefatigable collector/performer/promoter of Ragtime, Max Morath, had recorded *The Best of Scott Joplin*. Within a matter of months, the record scene was flooded with Rags by Joplin and other classic Ragtime composers, as played by every conceivable artist on every conceivable instrument.[14] An ironic situation also occurred in 1974: Joplin's music was nominated for two Oscars by the Motion Picture Academy of Arts & Sciences, but the awards were given, not to Joplin, but to Marvin Hamlisch, who had arranged and adapted the Joplin music for *The Sting*. During his life, Joplin had also been treated to the irony of seeing Irving Berlin billed as the King of Ragtime and Ben Harney as the Creator of Ragtime.[15]

In 1975 *Treemonisha* was on Broadway in a production by the Houston Grand Opera Company, which had earlier given several noteworthy performances, including one at the John Fitzgerald Kennedy Center for the Performing Arts in Washington, D.C. In 1978 Carmen Balthrop, who had starred in the Houston presentation, also played the leading role in a production by the Los Angeles Opera Company, which commissioned new orchestrations by composer Gunther Schuller, President of the New England Conservatory. Inevitably, in 1977, filmgoers were treated to a biopic based on Joplin's life, *King of Ragtime,* which fared like most Hollywood film biographies and was seen on TV the following year. Full-page advertisements run by Eastman Kodak in 1983 would have pleased the King: over a facsimile reproduction of Scott Joplin's handwritten signature, a headline read: "In ragtime, the Joplin signature says it's the genuine article. In photoprocessing, it's. . . ."

It is not inappropriate to view classic Ragtime as a Missouri frontier development and largely as a Sedalia development. (Sedalia came to be called the Cradle of Ragtime.) Two of Joplin's students in his Sedalia days were Scott Hayden and Arthur Marshall, with whose parents Joplin lived for much of his stay in that town. Just about the time when he moved to St. Louis, following John Stark's locating in the riverside city, Joplin married Belle Hayden, a sister-in-law of Scott's, who also married at that time. The newly married Joplins and Haydens lived in the same residence, and in 1903 moved to a 13-room house, which served as a boardinghouse as well. Later, in 1905, when Joplin's marriage broke up, the house was sold to Arthur Marshall, who operated it as a boardinghouse until he moved to Chicago. When Joplin went to Chicago in 1906, he first lived with Marshall, and, finding no work, returned to St. Louis, where he lived with Ragtime composer Tom Turpin. In short, Joplin was on intimate terms, as the local king of Ragtime, with three of the well-known writers of Rags.

However, the big three of Ragtime would seem to include, in addition to Joplin, Joseph Lamb (1887–1960) of Montclair, New Jersey, and James Sylvester Scott (1886–1938), another Missourian who may have studied with Joplin. Lamb, a white man who knew and admired Joplin's work before he met him, became a friend afterward and had his first Rag published in 1908 through Joplin. Scott, who was born in Neosho, Missouri, worked in a music store in Carthage, Missouri, when he wrote and had "Fascination" (1903) and other early pieces in the march-two step-cakewalk style published by Dumar's Music Store. Settling in Kansas City in 1914, Scott remained there for the rest of his life, active as a music teacher, arranger, organist, and theater musician. Of the 30 rags he wrote, starting with "Frog Legs Rag" in 1906, he is remembered for "Kansas City Rag" (1907); "Great Scott Rag," and "Sunburst Rag," both from 1909; "Grace and Beauty," "Hilarity Rag," and "Ophelia Rag," all from 1910; and "China Rag," written in 1914. All were published by John Stark, who also published Scott's final piece, "Broadway Rag," in 1912. Highly regarded by his contemporaries for his piano virtuosity, Scott wrote Rags, including "Honeymoon" and "Prosperity" (1916), in his mature years that make great technical demands on the performer.

Like Scott, Joseph Lamb was self-taught. Although he came from the East, he was versed in Joplin's works; John Stark published his Rags, as he did Joplin's and Scott's. With the passing of the Ragtime vogue during World War I, Lamb became an importer and disappeared from the music scene. In those years, it was assumed that he was a black Midwesterner of the Joplin–Scott circle. When he was rediscovered before his death in 1960, he manifested the same skill in playing and composing that had first given him access to Joplin. After the publication in 1908 of "Sensation Rag," as arranged by Joplin, there was a flow of Lamb rags until 1919. Bearing the tempo marking of "Slow March," they included "Ethiopian" and "Excelsior" Rags (1909); "Cleopatra," "Contentment," "Reindeer," and "Ragtime Nightingale" (1915); and "Bohemia Rag" (1919).

Other Ragtime Performer-Composers

The Ragtime narrative would be incomplete without mention of at least four other contributors.[16] Joe Jordan and Tom Turpin were both from St. Louis, while "Jelly Roll" Morton was originally from New Orleans and Eubie Blake was an Easterner, from Baltimore.

When Joplin first arrived in St. Louis in 1885, he got a job playing in the Silver Dollar, a saloon owned by the father of Tom Turpin (later the owner of the Booker T. Washington Theatre) and a gathering place for local and itinerant Ragtimers. Thomas Millin Turpin (1873–1922) owned many spots in the city's sporting-life district, including the Rosebud Café, where he frequently played the piano himself and acted as host to other Ragtime performers. Until it became known that Ben Harney was black, Turpin was acknowledged as the composer of the first published Rag by a Negro, "Harlem Rag," which appeared in December 1897.[17] Turpin's oft-anthologized Rags include "Bowery Buck" (1899), "A Ragtime Nightmare" (1900), "St. Louis Rag" (1903), and "Buffalo Rag" (1904).

In 1904, at the time of the St. Louis Fair (Louisiana Purchase Exposition), the Turpins sponsored a Ragtime competition, which drew black pianists from all over the country. First place went to a New Orleans eighty-eighter, Alfred Wilson, and second place, to Charles Warfield of St. Louis. After 1905, many of the St. Louis crowd moved to other cities, Kansas, New York, and especially Chicago, so that the Windy City superseded St. Louis as the center of Ragtime.

Joe Jordan (1882–1971), who was born in Cincinnati and raised in St. Louis, was among the Missourians who moved to Chicago. The year was 1903, he was just 21, and he had completed studies at the Lincoln Institute of Jefferson City, Missouri. During his St. Louis sojourn, he wrote a number of Rags, including "Double Fudge" (1902) and "Nappy Lee (1903); and after settling in Chicago, "Pekin Rag, Intermezzo" (1904) and "JJJ Rag" (1905). Jordan went on to a long, distinguished career as a composer and conductor, writing music for a dozen black choruses, being actively involved with productions of the Pekin Stock Company of Chicago, and collaborating with such notables as J. Rosamond Johnson and the famous producer/actor/writer J. Homer Tutt.[18] To the *Ziegfeld Follies* of 1910, Jordan contributed "Lovey Joe," sung by comedienne Fanny Brice (1891–1951) in her Broadway debut.

Ferdinand Joseph Morton née La Menthe (1885–1941), one of the most colorful figures of the time, whose braggadocio included the boast, "I invented Jazz,"[19] is generally classified as a jazzman. Growing up in New Orleans, he later recalled that the "spasm bands"—street musicians, some of whom played homemade instruments—"did a lot of adlibbing in ragtime style."[20] At 17 Jelly Roll was playing piano in a Storyville brothel, something that caused his grandmother to throw him out of the house as "a bum and a scalawag." She did not want him around his two sisters. He became a wanderer, and during the Fair of 1904, spent some time in St. Louis and then in Chicago. He also toured the South with a minstrel show in about 1909–1910. In a saloon in St. Louis where pianists hung out—it could have been the Rosebud—he had to prove his prowess by reading pieces set before him.

"They brought me all of Scott Joplin's tunes," he later said. "I knew 'em all by heart anyhow at the time; so I played 'em all"—pretending that he was reading them for the first time.[21] (It was inevitable that he should have known Joplin's work, since he was working in the New Orleans sporting-house district at the height of the Ragtime craze.) Making his piano solo recordings of his own compositions in 1923—"Kansas City Stomp," "Milenburg Joys," "Wolverine Blues," and "The Pearls," later recorded by him with his famous Hot Peppers, he used Ragtime figuration extensively. But his originals include such Rags as "Frog-i-More Rag," "The Naked Dance," "Superior Rag," "The Perfect Rag," "King Porter Stomp," and, of course, "Tiger Rag," which was based on a French quadrille and which, despite his claims, it is doubtful that he wrote. Jazz trumpeter Louis Armstrong credits Scott Joplin's Rags with great influence on pioneer jazzmen and asserts that "Snake Rag," written by King Oliver (1885–1938), really "owed much to Scott Joplin and his piano rags."[22]

The prime exponent of Ragtime in the East, James Hubert Blake (1883–1983), better known as Eubie Blake, was born of ex-slaves and became a legend in his own time. He wrote his first rag, "Charleston Rag," in the year of the appearance of the "Maple Leaf Rag" (1899), and became a leading figure in the rediscovery of Ragtime in the 1970s, at the age of 86. He learned Ragtime as a kid by listening outside the swinging doors of Baltimore bars to such colorful itinerant Ragtimers as Shout Blake (no relation), Big-Head Wilt, and Yellow Nelson. Although he was chastised by an extremely religious mother, "Get that ragtime out of my house!" he was playing at Aggie Sheldon's sporting house at the age of 15, when he was still in knickers. Possessed of an unusually large hand, so that he could span 12 notes—a tenth is a challenge for most pianists—he spent his twenties as a piano soloist, entertaining during the winter at the Goldfield Hotel in Baltimore and in the summertime at a number of clubs in Atlantic City.

It was toward the end of this period, in 1914, that he wrote "Fizz Water" and "The Chevy Chase," published by Joseph W. Stern & Co., to whom he was introduced by Ragtime and jazz pianist/songwriter/club owner Charles Luckeyeth Roberts (1890–1968). In an interview with Eileen Southern, Eubie said: "I don't like Ragtime—that is, for me to listen to. . . . But I had to play it to make a living . . ."[23]

In 1915, when he was playing with Joe Porter's Serenaders, he began a collaboration with Noble Sissle (1889–1975) of Indianapolis, who had joined the band as a vocalist. One of their earliest songs, "It's All Your Fault," was introduced by Sophie Tucker. Together the two worked as a piano-vocal team with James Reese Europe's Society Orchestra in New York; performed in vaudeville on the Keith-Orpheum circuit as the Dixie Duo, one of the first black acts to work without burnt cork and to play the Taj Mahal of vaudeville, the Palace Theater on Broadway (July 1919); and climaxed a highly successful collaboration with the writing of the legendary black musical *Shuffle Along* in 1921. The partnership ended in 1927, when Sissle went to Europe to lead a band, after which Blake teamed with lyricist Andy Razaf (1895–1976) on several shows. Out of this partnership came "Memories of You" from *Blackbirds of 1930*, Eubie's favorite song.

By the late 1940s, when he was in his sixties, Blake went into voluntary retirement and began a course of study in the Schillinger System of Musical Composition at New York University. But in 1951 he cut a new record album, *Wizard of Ragtime Piano*, which brought a remarkable renewal of his career as a Ragtime pianist. Even before the film *The Sting* energized the Scott Joplin revival in the mid-1970s, record producer John Hammond arranged for Blake to record a historic retrospective album, *The Eighty-Six Years of Eubie Blake*. Though he was nearing 90 years of age, Eubie embarked on an increasingly active program of TV interviews, performances, and appearances at major festivals. At a Carnegie Hall concert in the summer of 1972, he introduced "Classical Rag" and three other new Rags he had just written.

In 1978 *Eubie*, a revue composed of Blake's songs and compositions, opened on Broadway and ran for 439 performances, during some of which the 96-year-old pianist made surprise appearances. For his ninety-seventh birthday, in 1980, he appeared in *Memories of Eubie*, an hour-long TV special, tracing his history from the birth of Ragtime through vaudeville to the world of popular music and the American musical theater. In October 1981 he received the Medal of Freedom in a White House ceremony—the highest civilian award. One week before his ninety-ninth birthday, he appeared at a Eubie Blake Celebration Concert at the Eastman Theater in Rochester, playing "Memories of You," the song he also performed during an impromptu appearance at a free concert of his music by the U.S. Army Band at Damrosch Park in Lincoln Center on June 19, 1982.

A bout with pneumonia kept him from attending two celebrations of his hundredth birthday on February 7, 1983. One was at St.

Peter's Lutheran Church in midtown Manhattan, a church known for its concern with jazz musicians. The other, hosted by Robert Kimball, music critic of *The New Post* and coauthor (with William Bolcom) of *Reminiscing with Sissle and Blake* (1972), drew 1,600 people to Broadway's Shubert Theater. Eubie died seven days later.

The White Synthesis

Apart from the influence of Ragtime on the development of Jazz and popular music, its impact was so pervasive that noted European composers tried their hand at writing Ragtime or using raggy rhythms in their work. Among these, we find "Piano Rag Music" (1919), by the great Igor Stravinsky; "Shimmy, Ragtime," by Paul Hindemith; "Three Rag Caprices," by Darius Milhaud; "The American Girl's Dance" from the ballet *Parade,* (1916) by Erik Satie; and the most attractive and beguiling of these, "Golliwog's Cakewalk" from *Children's Corner* (1906), by Claude Debussy.

Among American classical composers, John Alden Carpenter used Ragtime in his Concerto for Piano and Orchestra (1917) and in a ballet, *Krazy Kat* (1922). Charles Ives, l'enfant terrible of the concert world, peppered an unconventional first Piano Sonata (1902) with Ragtime effects, and used Ragtime in a song, "Charlie Rutledge."

By the time that Ragtime was rattling the rafters of the coutry's music halls, variety theaters, and fashionable restaurants, the publication of popular music had become a flourishing commercial enterprise. In New York City, Union Square, near fourteenth Street and Fourth Avenue, was not only the entertainment capital of the country, with a complex of theaters, ballrooms, brothels, and music halls, but the Tin Pan Alley of popular music.[24] Music publishers, songwriters, and variety artists whose stock in trade was the sentimental ballads of the day, were quick to sense the appeal of the new black sound and began producing, publishing, and exploiting a flow of Rag-influenced and Rag-oriented songs. Some of these had little to do with Ragtime as a style, and merely used the word or a related word in the title for commercial advantage.

Of the more successful songs in the genre, apart from the coon songs by white writers, there was vaudevillian Joe Howard's "Hello Ma Baby" (1899); Harry von Tilzer's "Alexander" and "Goodbye Eliza Jane"; Theodore F. Morse's "Way Down in My Heart," and Hughie Cannon's evergreen "Bill Bailey, Won't You Please Come Home?"[25]

Three of the most creative figures in popular music began their careers during the Ragtime era, and their early work was rooted in Ragtime style. Of these, Irving Berlin (b. 1888) made the most extensive use of the style, starting in 1909 with "Ragtime Violin" and "That Mesmerizing Mendelssohn Tune," in which he developed a raggy version of the famous "Spring Song." The next year yielded "Dat Draggy Rag"; "Yiddle on Your Fiddle (Play some Ragtime)," later sung by Fanny Brice in *The Great Ziegfeld* (1936); "Stop That Rag," introduced by Nora Bayes (1880–1928); "Sweet Marie—Make a Rag-a-Time Dance with Me"; and "That Beautiful Rag," introduced and performed by Berlin himself, sporting a collegiate sweater and tennis racket in *Up and Down Broadway*. From Berlin's piano in 1911 came "Dying Rag," the popular "Everybody's Doin' It," "Whistling Rag," and one of the most performed and recorded songs emerging from that era, "Alexander's Ragtime Band."

Introduced by Berlin himself at a Friar's Frolic, "Alexander's Ragtime Band" attracted performances by female coon-shouter Emma Carus and; by Al Jolson, who was then embarking on his fabulous career as a singer with Lew Dockstader's Minstrels. Despite the limited syncopation in the number, it did more, perhaps, than any other song to excite an awareness of Ragtime.

The following year, 1912, saw a new flood of Berlin song rags: "Ragtime Mocking Bird," "Ragtime Soldier Man," "That Mysterious Rag," "Ragtime Jockey Man" (featured in *The Passing Show* of 1912) and "Ragtime Sextette," a parody arrangement of a well-known air from Donizetti's opera *Lucia di Lammermoor*. In 1913 while on shipboard during a crossing of the Atlantic for a successful music-hall tour of England, Berlin wrote "The International Rag." It was popularized by Sophie Tucker and revived, in the motion-picture musical *Call Me Madam*, by Ethel Merman in 1950. Playing in London at the Hippodrome Theatre, he was billed as The King of Ragtime, a title not conferred on the real king, Scott Joplin, until the 1970s.[26]

The craze for dancing, which swept the nation beginning in 1910, began to peter out as the world became more and more enmeshed in the travail of World War I. By the time that America entered the fray in 1917, the year of Joplin's death, Ragtime and the cakewalk had outlived their popularity. But in the years before then, Ragtime was frequently heard on Broadway. Irving Berlin's first complete show score, *Watch Your Step*, of 1914, was in Ragtime, and included "Play a Simple Melody," which employed a syncopated counter-melody. (He used the same device in *Call Me Madam*, starring Ethel Merman, in 1950 in the hit song, "You're Just in Love"). In *Watch Your Step*, the dancing Castles, Vernon and Irene, sang and danced his "Syncopated Walk," which was also used in the finale. Berlin's succeeding show score, for *Stop! Look! Listen!* of 1915, was also in Ragtime, opening with rhymed dialogue set to Ragtime and including the syncopated "I Love A Piano," played on six pianos, and closing with "Everything in America Is Ragtime." Other Berlin songs that traded on the reigning vogue of ragtime include "Just Give Me Ragtime Please," of 1916, a year in which Berlin shared the score of *The Century Girl* with the reigning king of operetta, Victor Herbert (1859–1924), to whose classic waltz, "Kiss Me Again," he wrote a Ragtime counter-melody, performed in the show; "Ragtime Razor Brigade," included in the Army revue *Yip, Yip, Yaphank*, produced at New York's Century Theater in August 1918, which yielded the well-known, "Oh! How I Hate to Get Up in the Morning," sung by Berlin himself in uniform; and "Everybody Step," which was featured in Berlin's first annual Music Box Revue (1921) and possessed more syncopation than some of the numbers with *Ragtime* in the title.

In 1917, George M. Cohan, who wrote half of the songs for the *Cohan Revue* of 1918, while Berlin wrote the rest, presented "Those Irving Berlin Melodies," in which he paid tribute to his colleague's popularity and appeal as a Ragtime songwriter by interpolating "The International Rag," "Everybody's Doing it Now," and "Alexander's Ragtime Band."

As Hoagy Carmichael (1899–1981) was growing up in Bloomington, Indiana, "popular music was mostly ragtime," he wrote in his autobiography, and his mother, who played piano, could not wait to get the latest Ragtime piece from a publisher in Chicago.[27] "Ragtime on the piano," his mother said, "were Hoagland's lullabies." Later, when he was going to high school and had himself learned to play piano, he performed in the Greek restaurants, joints, and sporting houses on North Illinois Street, seeking a "good audience for my ragtime jazz."

In the spring of 1923, when he was attending Indiana University, he booked the Wolverines with the great Bix Beiderbecke (1903–1931) on trumpet for several dances. By then he had become familiar with a series of piano novelties, written by white men such as Felix Arndt (1889–1918) and Zez Confrey (1895–1971), who adapted Ragtime in such pieces as "Nola" and "Kitten on the Keys." With Gennett Records located on the premises of the Starr Piano Company in Richmond, Indiana, the Wolverines made their first recordings on the label—and one of their first disks was "Riverboat Shuffle," written by Carmichael, which led to a contract from Mills Music Co. in New York.

"Washboard Blues" was followed by the development of a melody that later became one of the most popular standards in all of pop music, "Star Dust." In its original form, as recorded on Gennett by Emile Seidel's Orchestra, with Hoagy at the piano, the ballad was a Ragtime piece with "a verse, piano interlude and a passage for clarinet." Carmichael was still fooling around with the cornet, which he admittedly never learned to play too well, when he recorded another early Rag-inflected piece, "Walkin' the Dog." Out of the talent nurtured by Midwest Dixieland and rooted in Ragtime, later came "Rockin' Chair," the theme first of Mildred Bailey (1907–1951) and then Louis Armstrong (1900–1971); "Georgia on My Mind," now the State Song, largely as a result of Ray Charles's devotion to the song; and a large music stand of perennials, including "Lazy Bones." At his wedding reception in 1936 in New York City, where George Gershwin entertained at the piano, Hoagy's mother played her favorite piece, Scott Joplin's "Maple Leaf Rag."

Gershwin (1898–1937), the third of the popular-music giants who emerged from the Ragtime era, made a more sophisticated use of the style than either Berlin or Carmichael, transmuting it into a personal form of expression. Among his earliest attempts at composing, undertaken while he worked at the Jerome H. Remick Music Publishing Co. as a song-plugger and staff pianist, was a selection titled, "Ragging the Traümerei." While it went unpublished, his "Rialto Ripples," a Rag written with Will Donaldson, appeared in print in 1917. The following year—by then he had been hired as a staff composer by Max Dreyfus, the man who nurtured and published virtually all of the top show composers of the 1920s, 1930s, and 1940s—he and his brother, Ira, wrote their first professional song together, "The Real American Folk Song (Is a Rag—a Mental Jag)." In 1919 came the first hit song of Gershwin's notable career, "Swanee," interpolated and transformed into a best seller by Al Jolson in *Sinbad,* and as typical in its sound and its offbeat rhythms as any song of the era.

During the next five years, Gershwin wrote the music for five successive editions of *George White's Scandals.* That his genius was already stirring him to break out of the boundaries of the popular song and the show song into larger forms became evident in 1922. For that edition of the *Scandals,* he and B. G. DeSylva (1895–1950) wrote a 20-minute work titled *Blue Monday.* One of the less than friendly critics described it "as a sort of ragtime opera that drags the 'Mammy' motif to unbearable lengths."[28] Although the work was dropped from the show after a single performance on opening night, it led to the writing of *Rhapsody in Blue.* Paul Whiteman (1890–1967), featured in the *Scandals* with his orchestra, was so impressed by *Blue Monday* that he commissioned the writing of the *Rhapsody* when he planned his celebrated February 12, 1924, concert at Aeolian Hall, at which the world-famous work was introduced, with Gershwin himself at the piano.

Of all the show composers, Gershwin made the greatest use—a constant one—of a displaced accent at the opening of songs. Not only in rhythm tunes but in ballad after ballad— "Embraceable You," "Somebody to Watch Over Me," "That Certain Feeling," among others—the first melody note is elided and appears on the afterbeat. As much as a repetition of the same note, which one finds throughout the Gershwin oeuvre, the displaced accent (not just at the beginning of a piece) and catchy syncopation crop up in songs including "Fascinating Rhythm," "Clap Yo' Hands," "Liza," and "I Got Rhythm," as well as in larger works such as the *Rhapsody*, *American in Paris*, and *Concerto in F*. Fine melodist that he was and adept at the coloration achieved through fresh harmonies, Gershwin wrote in an age when the feverish pace and the jazzy rhythms of the Roaring Twenties found ebullient expression in his Rag-rooted music.

Piano Novelties

Ragtime not only became the basic style of American popular music into the early 1920s, but it spawned two piano styles. Stride Piano was developed by a group of black Harlem eighty-eighters, while Piano Novelties were part of the white synthesis.

Gershwin's collaboration on the raggy "Rialto Ripples" was the result in part of his hearing piano rolls made by Felix Arndt and a number of piano novelties composed by Arndt. The best known of these was and is "Nola," published in 1916 and introduced and popularized by pianist Vincent Lopez (1895–1975), who used it as a theme throughout a long career in vaudeville and as a bandleader in several New York City hotel grills. A bravura piano piece, involving a series of eight-and-sixteenth notes cum "breaks," played at a brisk or fast tempo, "Nola" was inspired by singer/pianist Nola Locke, whom Arndt married after giving her the piece as an engagement present. By then, Arndt had written a number of piano novelties—"Marionette," "Soup to Nuts," "Toots," among others—which he recorded on RCA Victor. He also cut hundreds of piano rolls of popular tunes, something that moved Gershwin to begin making piano rolls himself in 1916.

Piano Novelties employed the regular four-to-the bar bass of Ragtime but imposed on it a memorable flow of melody, not infrequently interrupted by syncopated breaks. Such pieces as "Twelfth

Street Rag" (1914), by Euday L. Bowman; "Ragging the Scale" (1915), by Edward B. Claypoole; and "Bugle Call Rag" (1916), a piano solo by Eubie Blake and Carey Morgan; were hardly distinguishable from typical Ragtime selections. But after a time, especially after the publication of "Nola," the genre was distinguished by its sophisticated harmonies, its departure from banjo and chordal figuration, its concern with catchy melodies, and its pseudo-Jazz sound.

One of the more prolific composers of the genre was Zez Confrey, who was born in Peru, Illinois, and received his musical training at Chicago Musical College. After serving in the Navy in World War I, he worked as a pianist and recorded several of his own novelty rags, including "Twaify's Piano," Twaify being a favorite night spot in La Salle, Illinois. The high point of his career came in 1924, when he performed at the famous Lincoln Day concert at which Paul Whiteman introduced *Rhapsody in Blue.* He played his "Nickel in the Slot" and scored a hit with "Kitten on the Keys," published in 1921 and a Vincent Lopez favorite. In time, Confrey's piano novelties mounted to 90 publications, the best-remembered of which, in addition to "Kitten on the Keys," are "Dizzy Fingers" (1922) and "Stumbling." The latter, which Confrey developed pentatonically on the black keys of the piano, included a lyric by him, which made it a hit song in 1923.

One reason for the vogue of Piano Novelties was the prestigious position occupied by the piano in American middle-class homes, and even among working people who could afford one, during the pre-Depression years of the twentieth century. The player piano, or pianola, was a source of home entertainment for those who could not play but could pedal, in the years before radio and the phonograph, still in its infancy. Until the advent of talking pictures in 1927, even motion pictures were accompanied by piano players.

Through the 1920s, pianists were challenged by Novelty Piano pieces such as "Flapperette" (1926), by Jesse Greer; "Manhattan Serenade" (1928), by Louis Alter, who served as an accompanist for Nora Bayes, Irene Bordoni, and Helen Morgan; and "Doll Dance" (1927), by Nacio Herb Brown, better known for such film ballads as "Pagan Love Song" and "Singin' in the Rain." Although it is not strictly a piano novelty, "In a Mist," a piece in a French Impressionist vein, was produced by Jazz trumpeter Bix Beiderbecke in 1928. Two years earlier, in 1926, Gershwin introduced his *Three Preludes* for piano at a concert in the Hotel Roosevelt in New York. These pieces do not have the pop sound of the Piano Novelty, but the first, in B-flat major, and the third, in E-flat major, employ Ragtime–Jazz rhythms and the showy, uptempo runs associated with piano novelties.

Stride Piano

The development of Stride Piano, a step upward from Ragtime toward Blues and Jazz, overlapped the vogue of the Piano Novelty. But unlike the latter, it was the creation of black Harlem ticklers, who entertained at "rent parties," where they frequently indulged in "cutting contests."

Of James P. Johnson (1891–1955), sometimes known as the father of the style, Duke Ellington said: "Everybody was trying to sound like *Carolina Shout* Jimmy had made on a piano roll. I got it down by slowing down the roll. . . ."[29] Classically trained, Johnson had begun playing professionally in 1912 in Coney Island; performed for a number of years in Harlem night spots, including Leroy's and Baron Wilkins; and began recording in 1921, the year that he cut "Carolina Shout"—though the piano roll to which Ellington referred might have been made earlier. The arc-like movement of the left hand, which became a Stride staple, involved striking a low-register tenth chord on the downbeat, looping to a middle-register triad on the second beat, hitting a low single note or octave on the dominant of the chord on the third beat, and arcing again to a middle-register chord on the fourth beat. It was a two-fisted style, whose proponents sneered at the Jazz pianists after the Bop revolution for their lack of a left hand.

As a theater composer, Johnson accounted for *Runnin' Wild* (1923), in which Elizabeth Welch introduced the song and dance "Charleston," which became an international fad. In 1924, a Charleston marathon held at the Roseland ballroom in New York City dragged on for almost 24 hours. The following year, *George White's Scandals* included a production number in which Tom Patricola and a chorus of 60 girls did the Charleston.

Later in 1926, Johnson wrote, "If I Could Be with You One Hour Tonight," featured by Ruth Etting (1898–1978) and the song that became a best-selling record and the theme of McKinney's Cotton Pickers. Composer of "Weeping Blues" and "Worried and Lonesome Blues," which he recorded for Columbia, Johnson proved himself a superb blues accompanist on a series of recordings with Bessie Smith, especially her "Backwater Blues" and "Preachin' the Blues."

Concerned after a time with compositions in larger forms, he composed *Symphony Harlem* (1932), having previously premiered *Yamecraw* at Carnegie Hall in 1928. He continued performing and recording through the 1940s and 1950s, despite strokes that left him bereft of speech in 1946 but made an invalid of him from 1951 until his death in 1955. He was a composer whose reach exceeded his grasp. Despite his formidable talent, he never attained the recognition that should have been his, except as the preeminent master of the Stride style.

One of the eighty-eighters who influenced James P. was Luckeyeth "Lucky" Roberts, who also assayed extended forms in his later years, wrote for the musical theater, played Barron Wilkins in Harlem, and likewise suffered incapacitating strokes. A partnership with Alex Rogers (1876–1930), who wrote much material for the team of Williams and Walker, yielded a flow of songs for the top singers of the day (Nora Bayes, Sophie Tucker, Al Jolson, Marie Cahill) and for innumerable black musicals. Together they wrote the material for the radio show *Two Black Crows,* starring Moran and Mack. As a performer, Roberts played not only many Harlem clubs but in vaudeville, served as a sought-after society bandleader during the thirties and forties, and was featured on Rudi Blesh's radio program, *This Is Jazz.* For over 14 years, beginning in 1940, Lucky Roberts owned a successful club in Harlem, the Rendezvous.

He became widely known as the result of Glenn Miller's introduction and performances of a piano piece he composed at the age of 17. The syncopated "Ripples of the Nile" (1912) was the basis, with a lyric by Kim Gannon, of "Moonlight Cocktail," which rose as high as number four on the celebrated *Your Hit Parade* shows of April–May 1942, and which became known as one of the most popular ballads of the World War II years.

Like J. P. Johnson, Roberts composed a number of extended concert works, including *Whistlin' Pete, Miniature Syncopated Rhapsody,* which he presented in concerts at Town and Carnegie halls in the early 1940s. In 1946 he performed together with Johnson on an album, *Harlem Rent Piano,* which included his "Ripples of the Rialto." Although a number of his instrumentals became Ragtime standards— "Junk Man Rag," "Nothin'," and "Pork and Beans," among others — he was recognized as an outstanding Stride pianist, whose playing also influenced white society and cocktail pianists.

Thomas "Fats" Waller (1904–1943) played "Carolina Shout" and won a talent contest at New York's Roosevelt Theater in 1918. It was the forecast of a relationship that included James P.'s tutoring young Waller and, later, working with him on the musical score of the all-black revue *Keep Shufflin'* (1928). Waller was both prodigious and profligate in his appetite for food and liquor, in a recording schedule that yielded several hundred sides, in bookings in key New York and Chicago clubs, in film appearances, in performances on the radio (Cincinnati's WLW and CBS in New York), and in an output of songs that produced more hits than any of his competitors. Waller crowded more activity into a brief life than was good for him or his talent, and that inevitably brought a sudden, possibly preventable, terminus at the age of 39. He died unexpectedly and unknowingly of pneumonia on a train bringing him from an exhausting routine of partying and performing in Los Angeles to New York. The Santa Fe Chief was pulling into Kansas City Union station when his inert body was discovered in his compartment.

Beyond his skill as a Stride pianist comparable to his mentor, Waller possessed a number of assets that made him an in-demand performer and a best-selling record-maker. He was not only a stellar showman, delivering in a jauntily tipped derby, but a superior comic, whose sly throwaway comments added a humorous dimension to his playing and singing. Those "asides" can be heard even on some of his recordings. In addition, he was an extremely gifted songwriter, with an almost unquenchable flow of appealing melody.

All of these qualities were deftly delineated in *Ain't Misbehavin'*, a Broadway musical that opened to rave notices in May 1978, won a flock of awards, and ran for 196 performances. In *Ain't Misbehavin'*, audiences savored such Waller perennials as the title song, "I've Got a Feeling I'm Falling," "Black and Blue," and "Honeysuckle Rose" —all four from his 1929 collaboration with Andy Razaf on the Connie's Inn stage show, *Hot Chocolates*— "Squeeze Me" (1925); "Keepin' Out of Mischief Now" (1932); "Yacht Club Swing" (1938); "The Joint Is Jumpin'," (1937) and the lilting "Jitterbug Waltz" (1942). The revue also offered songs by others that the Waller magic had turned into hits, starting with " 'T Ain't Nobody's Bizness If I Do," the first song he recorded, in 1922.[30] A high point of the show was the opening segment, in which a spotlight focused on an upright piano with an empty stool, and the audience heard Fats himself playing his Stride standard, "Handful of Keys" (1933).

One of the big draws on New York's 52nd St. in its heyday in the 1930s, Waller played to SRO audiences at the Yacht Club and the Famous Door. One evening, as he began his stint, he spotted pianist Art Tatum in the audience. "I play piano," he announced, "but God is in the house tonight!"

Pianist/singer Hazel Scott (1920–197—) told of how, one evening, she went to Café Society Downtown with former bandleader Artie Shaw (b. 1910) and the great concert pianist Vladimir Horowitz to hear Tatum. "Horowitz was bowled over," she reported. "After listening to Art play *Tiger Rag*, Horowitz exclaimed, 'It can't be true. I can't believe my eyes and ears!' Two nights later, Horowitz took the great conductor Arturo Toscanini, his father-in-law, to hear Tatum, and Toscanini was bowled over, too!"[31]

In short, Art Tatum (1910–1956) overwhelmed musicians not only in the Pop–Jazz world but in the concert-classical cosmos as well. Long before his death of uremia at 46, everybody was saying: "No one can imitatum! No one can overratum!"

Tatum's roots in Stride piano, of which he became the most eloquent and elegant exponent, are clear from a comment he made at one point: "Fats, man—that's where I come from." To the swinging rhythm of Stride, he added the horn-like inventiveness of Earl "Fatha" Hines (1903–1983), producing a style that staggered the imagination with its melodic, rhythmic, and harmonic freshness. No one could match the velocity or intricacy of his runs and arpeggios —Oscar Peterson (b. 1925) has tried—his lightning Stride bass, or the harmonic beauty and opulence of his chord changes.

Born in Toledo, Ohio, with cataracts on both eyes that left him virtually blind—he had some sight in one eye—Tatum became staff pianist at Station WSPF at 17. In short order, his 15-minute program was being heard on a national network. He began recording in 1933, his first sides ("Sophisticated Lady" and "Tiger Rag") revealing a pianist with a powerful striding left hand and a fleeting right hand whose decorative excursions dazzled by their harmonic inventiveness. In constant demand by clubs all over the United States and England, not to mention his vaulting popularity on Swing Street, as New York's 52nd St. was then and is still known, he did not record nearly as regularly as Fats Waller. Tatum never became a popular celebrity, as Waller did. But the Tatum piano magic is preserved through marathon recording sessions he had between December 1953 and January 1955, in which he cut over 100 selections for Jazz producer Norman Granz. Issued in 10 Verve albums under the apropos title, *Genius of Art Tatum,* they stand as mind-boggling examples of orchestral, Pop-Jazz piano playing at its best.

Tatum gloried, as did his followers, in his amazing ability for almost endless invention—his artistry in reshaping and varying a tune, rhythmically, harmonically, and melodically, for an unlimited number of choruses. This prodigious talent found its most challenging and exhilarating expression in "after hour" performances. These sessions were frowned upon by the Musicians Union (since they were unpaid exercises) as well as the police, whose entry into a club operating after curfew could bring a revocation of its liquor license. Nevertheless, there were clubs both in Harlem and on 52nd St. that appeared to be closed but where such musicians as Erroll Garner (1921–1977), Johnny Guarnieri (b. 1917) Tatum, and others played for fans who never left before daylight. While the Verve recordings provide an index to the Tatum inventiveness, they do not—they cannot for obvious limitations of time—approach what listeners (including this writer) experienced in hearing Tatum live.

Combining the foot-tapping rhythmic pulse of Stride with the decorative showiness of the Piano Novelty, Tatum produced music whose essence was spontaneity, unpredictability, and sophisticated improvisation—in short, Jazz.

CHAPTER FOUR

"SHUFFLE ALONG"

In the early years of the century, audiences at vaudeville theaters on the Keith–Proctor circuit were treated to a comic performance, which began with a spotlight being focused center stage on a white glove in which fingers were jiggling nervously against the closed curtain. After a moment, a hand was extended, then an arm in a blue jacket, followed by a drooping shoulder, and, finally, with some hesitation, a six-foot man in blackface slid through the opening in the curtain and ambled awkwardly to the footlights. Dressed in bedraggled black pants and a short jacket cut from a frock coat, he was a picture of dejection. As applause of recognition and admiration died down, the disconsolate figure in blackface began to half-sing, half-recite:

When all day long, things go amiss,
And I go home to find some bliss,
Who hands me a glowing kiss?

He paused, shrugged his shoulders, and answered: "Nobody!"

When summer comes all hot and clear,
And friends, they see me drawing near,
Who says, "Come in and have a beer?"

He shook his head unhappily and replied: "Nobody!" Then he sang with an air of resignation:

I ain't never done nothin' to nobody
I ain't never got nothin' from nobody, no time.
Until I get somethin' from somebody, some time,
I'll never do nothin' for nobody, no time.[1]

The black performer who enchanted audiences with "Nobody" for 17 years, starting in 1905, was Egbert Austin Williams, known as Bert Williams (1874–1922), of whom the noted comic W. C. Fields said: "Bert is the funniest man I ever saw and the saddest man I ever knew."[2] Widely acknowledged as "the greatest comedian of the Negro race," he was so popular that another gifted black comic, Charles "Charlie" Hart (1873–1917), later of the famous team of Avery and Hart, did imitations of him.

Bert William's journey from a blackface minstrel of the 1890s to a star of the *Ziegfeld Follies* on Broadway is emblematic of changes in American entertainment from the demise of the minstrel show to the growth of variety or vaudeville and the development of musical comedy; also of some changes in the artistic, if not social, status of the black performer.

Bert Williams

Egbert Austin Williams was born in the British West Indies (New Providence, Nassau) on November 12, 1874, a circumstance that later made him feel outside not only of white society but of the American Negro world as well. He met George Walker (1873–1911), who was born in Lawrence, Kansas, in San Francisco when, appearing as an end man in Martin and Selig's Mastodon Minstrels, he went looking for another end man. After working a five-month tour with the Mastodon troupe, they spent two years at Halahan Homan's Midway in San Francisco; performed in Chicago, Pittsburgh, and briefly in two New York shows; and, finally, made a reputation for themselves when they appeared at Koster and Bial's Music Hall, a leading vaudeville house, in 1897.

Coon songs were then the rage, and white and black stars in blackface, a big box-office attraction. The act that brought them fame began to take shape in Detroit, at Moore's Wonderland, in 1896, when they appeared in blackface for the first time. George Walker later explained that there were strong barriers to

> natural black performers . . . on account of racial and color prejudice . . . . [The problem was] how to get before the public and prove

> that ability we might possess. . . . As there seemed to be a great demand for blackface on the stage . . . we finally decided that as white men with black faces were billing themselves as "coons," Williams & Walker would do well to bill themselves as The Two Real Coons, and so we did. Our bills attracted the attention of managers and gradually we made our way in.[3]

Nevertheless, Walker conceded, as Bert Williams felt throughout his career: "Nothing seemed more absurd than to see a colored man making himself ridiculous (imitating the blackface white comedian) in order to portray himself."[4]

When they opened in New York, their billing was "The Two Real Coons." Walker, in flashy street clothes, played straight man to Bert Williams, who, dressed in mismatched, bedraggled clothes, brought the laughter. Consciously or unconsciously, the characters they adopted, encapsulated the two main contrasting black figures that emerged from the minstrel show—Jim Dandy and Zip Coon. At Koster and Bial's, they were applauded also for their dancing of the cakewalk, the popularization of which they continued when *Clorindy, or the Origin of the Cakewalk* was incorporated in their *Senegambian Carnival* in 1899. Despite flat feet, Walker was an outstanding cakewalker.

From their triumph at Koster and Bial's, they went on tour on the high-class vaudeville circuits, alternating between vaudeville and a series of farces they produced and starred in, including *A Lucky Coon* (1899), described as "a hodge-podge of nearly everything in the coon line from buck-dance and ragtime melodies to selections from grand opera";[5] *The Policy Players* (1899); *Sons of Ham* (1900–1902); and *In Dahomey* (1903).

In Dahomey was a high point in the career of Williams and Walker, for it was the first full-length musical, written and played by blacks, to be performed at a major Broadway theater, the New York Theater, at 59th St. and Broadway. What that meant to them as performers was stated by Williams in an interview: "The way we've aimed for Broadway and just missed in the past several years would make you cry." Observing that they would land either in a Third Avenue theater or a West 34th St. music hall, Williams said: "I used to be tempted to beg for a $15 job in a chorus just for one week so as to be able to say I'd been on Broadway once."[6]

In the favorable reviews that appeared, Williams was described in New York's influential *Theater Arts* magazine as "a vastly funnier man than any white comedian now on the American stage."[7] Playing 53 performances on Broadway, *In Dahomey* played for seven months a year later, in London. To cap their and the show's triumph, they were requested to give Command Performances at Buckingham Palace to help celebrate the birthday of the young Prince of Wales.[8] After the June 23 royal appearance, it was SRO at the Shaftesbury Theatre, with their dancing initiating a cakewalk craze among the social set in France as well as England. Among those who applauded Bert Williams, the distinguished playwright George Bernard Shaw was so impressed that he thought of him for a part in his *Caesar and Cleopatra.* On its return to the United States, *In Dahomey* played the Grand Opera House in New York (August 1904) and then went on a 40-week tour of the country.

The comic character that Williams played as part of Williams and Walker initially found expression in a song they wrote in 1897, "I Don't Like No Cheap Man." It was Bert's theme song after he introduced it with Hydes's Comedians. By 1903 Williams had a new song that more sensitively epitomized his role. Of "I'm a Jonah Man," written by Alex Rogers (circa 1880–1930) and interpolated at every performance of *In Dahomey,* Williams said: "I'm the man who, even if it rained soup, would be found with a fork in his hand and no spoon in sight."[9]

(Verse)
My brother once walked down the street
And fell in a coal hole
He sued the man that owned the place
And got ten thousand cold.

I figured this was easy
So I jumped in the same coal hole
Broke both my legs
And the judge give me one year for stealing coal.

(Chorus)
I'm a Jonah, I'm a Jonah man.
My family for many years
Would look at me and then shed tears.
Why am I dis Jonah
I sho' can't understand
But I'm a good, substantial, full-fledged
Real, first-class Jonah man.

But the song that best expressed the luckless, pathetic character he generally played was, of course, "Nobody," whose words were written by Alex Rogers to music by Bert Williams. Introduced by him in 1905 in vaudeville, it became the song that audiences demanded whenever and wherever he appeared. It was one of the showstoppers when he made his debut in the *Ziegfeld Follies* of 1910. "For seven whole years I had to sing it," he later said. "Month after month

I tried to drop it and sing something new, but I could not get anything to replace it and the audience seemed to want nothing else." In subsequent years, Perry Como and Bob Hope, among other artists, made recordings of the song. But the classic rendition was Bert Williams's.

Until illness forced George Walker to retire in 1909, Williams and Walker continued their very successful association. *In Abyssinia,* the most luxurious of their productions—large cast, elegant scenery, and even live camels—opened in 1906 at the Majestic Theater, on Columbus Circle and 58th St. It was succeeded by *Bandana Land,* which introduced the famous pantomime poker game, thereafter a Bert Williams trademark.[11] By the time that *Bandana Land* was playing Louisville, Ada Overton Walker (1870–1914), dressed in male attire, was singing her husband's numbers, including his well-known "Bon Bon Buddy" theme song. On his death in 1911, Walker was eulogized in the New York *Age* in a tribute that read in part:

> It was his desire to give us productions as elaborate as the white shows and to play the best theaters. For years he struggled valiantly . . . against managers who did not believe the time was ripe for the presentation of first-class colored shows . . . George Walker's character of the "dandy darky" brought out hundreds of imitators . . . The man was a dominating force in the theatrical world more because of the service he rendered colored members of the profession than for the type he originated . . .[12]

Appearing for the first time without his partner, briefly in *Bandana Land,* Bert Williams played lead in one other all-black show, *Mr. Lode of Koal* (1909). In demand as a solo comic/singer, he now began playing the best houses in the Keith-Orpheum vaudeville circuit. Although he was the headliner on each bill, his name did not appear at the top of the bill but always in second place, though the type was the largest and the blackest.

In May 1910, newspapers carried the announcement that Williams was to appear in the *Ziegfeld Follies of 1910,* a first for a black performer. In an article he later wrote for the *American Magazine,* Williams revealed that "when Mr. Ziegfeld first proposed to engage me, there was a tremendous storm in a teacup. Everybody threatened to leave; they proposed to set up a boycott if he persisted; they said all sorts of things against my personal character. But Mr. Ziegfeld stuck to his guns and was quite undisturbed by everything that was said."[13]

When the *Follies* opened in Chicago, Constance Skinner of the *Chicago Evening American* commented: "The principal congratulatory item is Mr. Bert Williams. Bert Williams is not one of the *Follies,* he is the wisdom and wit before F. Ziegfeld ever committed a folly."[14]

In the *Follies of 1911,* Williams's contribution was extended, and he performed in two sketches, one with white comic Leon Erroll. "It remained for that dusky vaudeville genius, Bert Williams," *The New York World* observed, "to make the big hit of the night. He had already been funny in *Everywife* but he was sidesplitting when he appeared as a 'red cap' to pilot an English tourist (Leon Erroll) over the almost inaccessible fastness of New York Central Station. . . ."[15] The New York *Morning Telegraph* said in part: "The big comedy hit of the night arrived late with Bert Williams. . . . Williams capped the climax of a glorious night for himself by telling the true story of a poker game in pantomime. . . . Whether serious, grotesque, or just simply funny, this dark-skinned man demonstrated again he is one of the most finished actors on the American stage. . . ."[16] Among the songs that Williams sang was "Woodman, Woodman, Spare That Tree," written especially for him by Vincent Bryan and the great Irving Berlin, whose song hits of 1911 included the immortal "Alexander's Ragtime Band."

The big hit again of the *Follies of 1912,* Williams engaged for the first time in dialogue with women of the cast, and at the finale of both the first and second acts, appeared onstage with all the principals. (Williams's first contract with Ziegfeld stipulated that "at no time would he be on stage with any of the female members of the company.") Except for the *Follies of 1914,* Williams continued to appear in each annual edition through the *Follies of 1919,* more than holding his own with such top comics as W. C. Fields, Ed Wynn, Will Rogers, and Eddie Cantor. He did not appear in the 1914 edition because he signed with the Keith circuit for a weekly stipend of $2,000—more than he was paid by Ziegfeld—which also included headline honors at the Valhalla of vaudeville, the Palace Theater on Broadway.

In the article that Williams wrote for *American Magazine* in December 1917, he addressed himself candidly to the problem of racism: "People sometimes ask me," he wrote,

> if I would not give anything to be white. I answer, in the words of the song, most emphatically "No." How do I know what I might be if I were a white man? I might be a sandhog, burrowing away and losing my health for $8 a day. I might be a streetcar conductor at $12 or $15 a week. There is many a white man less fortunate and less well equipped than I am. In fact, I have never been able to discover that there was anything disgraceful in being a colored man. But I have often found it inconvenient—in America.[17]

That Williams endured more than "inconvenience" is apparent from a letter he wrote to a friend shortly before his death. "I was thinking about the honors that are showered on me in the theater," he observed, "how everyone wishes to shake my hand or get an autograph, a real hero you'd naturally think. However, when I reach a hotel, I am refused permission to ride on the passenger elevator, I cannot enter the dining room for my meals, and am Jim Crowed generally. . . ."[18]

Biographer Ann Charters describes an experience, one of a number, that occurred when Williams spent some time in October 1918 in an effort to cope with poor circulation, especially in his feet, which swelled painfully after a night's performance. In the Indiana sanitorium where he went for a cure, he was required to ride a bicycle. Pedaling along a country road one afternoon, he was stopped by the local sheriff, who accused him of stealing the bike. Refusing to listen to Williams's explanation, he confiscated the new-looking bicycle, forcing Williams to return to the sanitorium on foot.

Comedian Eddie Cantor (1892–1964) told the story of Bert entering a St. Louis bar and ordering a gin. Obviously unwilling to serve a Negro, the bartender said: "I'll give you gin but it's $50 a glass!" Without hesitating, Bert opened his wallet, placed a $500 bill on the bar, and said, "Give me 10 of them."

Apart from the humiliating encounters with prejudice, the more stressful aspect of Williams's life was having continually to work in blackface, a role he found it impossible to abandon. He was a man "who hated the stigma of his color," Charters states, "but the only way he had found to success in the theater was by wearing the minstrel mask of burnt cork."[19]

Comedian W. C. Fields, with whom Williams worked in the *Follies* and with whom he talked freely, said: "I often wonder whether other people sensed what I do in him—that deep undercurrent of pathos. . . . It did seem a pity that any artist who contributed so much that was of the best to our theater, should be denied even the common comforts of living when on the road in cities like St. Louis and Cincinnati."[20]

Perhaps the pathos was the result of a situation in which, feeling humiliated and suffering prejudicial treatment, he nevertheless took no part in activities protesting, in biographer Charters's words, "mob law, segregation, 'Jim Crowism,' and many other indignities to which the race is unnecessarily subjected in the United States."[21] But he was a proud man, and quite conscious of his achievement.

"I am what I am," he concluded his *American Magazine* article, "not because of what I am, but in spite of it."[22]

Black Theater Composers

"Negroes were at last on Broadway and there to stay," Will Marion Cook wrote of the premiere of *Clorindy*. "Gone was the uffdah of the minstrel! Gone the Massa Linkum stuff! We were artists and we were going a long, long way . . . Nothing could stop us and nothing did for a decade!"[23]

The premiere of *Clorindy: or, the Origin of the Cakewalk,* its full title, occurred in July 1898, and the Broadway theater to which Cook referred was the Casino Roof Garden. Unable to interest producers in the one-hour musical, Cook had persuaded E. E. Rice, then producing a series of vaudeville *Summer Nights,* to include it as an extended afterpiece. When Cook raised his baton, there were only 50 people in the audience. But by the time the opening chorus had finished, the Roof Garden was packed—the audience drawn from the show downstairs in the Casino Theater, which had just let out, "by those heavenly Negro voices."

"When the last note was sounded," Cook rejoiced in his *Theater Arts* article, "the audience stood and cheered for at least ten minutes . . . I was so delirious that I drank a glass of water, thought it was wine and got glorious drunk."[24]

With comedian Ernest Hogan in the lead, *Clorindy* produced such Cook hits as "Who Dat Say Chicken in Dis Crowd?" "Darktown Is Out Tonight," "Hottest Coon in Dixie," and "That's How the Cakewalk's Done," the last-mentioned, a feature of the audience-rousing cakewalk finale. Characterized by the *Times* as "sensational," *Clorindy* was the first all-black musical to play a New York theater patronized exclusively by whites, although the theater was a roof garden. But Cook was also the composer of the first full-length black musical to be presented at a *major* Broadway house. It was *In Dahomey,* the Williams and Walker musical written and performed by blacks, which played the New York Theater in 1903. Another musical for which Cook served as composer, *The Southerners* (1904), employed an all-black chorus that appeared onstage in one scene together with the white actors. The historic departure and challenge that this represented was indicated in the review by the critic of *The New York Times,* who wrote: "When the chorus of real live coons walked in for the cake last night at the New York Theatre, mingling with the white members of the cast, there were those in the audience who trembled in their seats."[25]

Will Marion Cook was one of a group of black composers who gave a new cast to theater music in the first decade of the twentieth century and prepared the ground for the dazzling emergence of *Shuffle Along* in 1921. With Bob Cole and Rosamond Johnson, as well as Joe Jordan, Will Vodery, and of course, Eubie Blake, Cook helped bring the black musical out of the womb of the minstrel show and vaudeville.

The career of Cook, one of the best trained of the group, embraced music in the concert as well as theatrical field, and he was a successful conductor, choirmaster, and composer. Studying violin at Oberlin when he was 15, he continued his study abroad with the distinguished violinist Josef Joachim of Berlin, and later, on his return to the United States, attended the National Conservatory of Music, where his teachers included Anton Dvořák.

Duke Ellington (1899–1974) was among his contemporaries who acknowledged his influence and pedagogy. "We would ride around Central Park in a taxi," the Duke said, "and he'd give me lectures in music. . . . Some of the things he used to tell me I never got a chance to use until years later when I wrote the tone poem, *Black, Brown and Beige*."

It was the success of *Clorindy*, incorporated after a time in Williams and Walker's *Senegambian Carnival* as an afterpiece, that led to an association of Cook with the comedic duo. In an eight-year period, the most fruitful for Williams and Walker and for Cook in the theater, he functioned as composer-in-chief and musical director of *The Sons of Ham* (1900), *In Dahomey* (1903–1905), *Abyssinia* (1906), and *Bandana Land* (1908). Both before and after, he composed quite a number of musicals, which were produced but did not contribute to his reputation as a theater composer or to the popular repertoire of the time. But *The Southerners* of 1904, which featured white minstrel Eddie Leonard in blackface as a plantation slave, and which did not make it as a show, brought this comment from the *Times:* "The negro [sic] composer of the score, Mr. Will Marion Cook . . . succeeded in harmonizing the racial broth as skilfully as he harmonized the score."[26]

In the years that followed the Williams and Walker productions until his death in 1944, Cook pursued a productive career in the concert world as a conductor and the organizer/choirmaster of a number of impressive choral groups, including Afro-American Folk Singers, Negro Choral Society, and others. Probably the most exciting of these undertakings occurred in 1918–1919, when his New York Syncopated Orchestra toured the country and, while in England, gave a Command Performance before King George V. Duke Ellington, who conferred with Cook during his early days in Harlem, came away revering him as "the master of all the masters of our people."[27]

More successful in producing song hits than Cook and, perhaps, more crucial in the transformation of the minstrel show into musical comedy were Robert "Bob" Cole and J. Rosamond Johnson. Before he teamed with Rosamond, Bob Cole (1868–1911) was in partnership with another Johnson, Billy Johnson (1858–1916), with whom he produced and starred in *A Trip to Coontown.* Antedating *Clorindy* by more than a year—it opened in April 1897—it has been singled out by some as the "first black musical comedy"[28] and by others as "a landmark in that it was entirely written, performed and produced by blacks.[29] But it played in an off-Broadway house, the Third Avenue Theater.

Before he achieved this breakthrough, Cole was associated as a comic with Sam T. Jack's *Creole Show,* establishing a reputation as the youngest stage manager in the theater; as an actor with the All Star Stock Company at Worth's Museum in New York, the first American stock company organized by blacks; and with the Black Patti Troubadours, when he and Billy Johnson first joined forces and became the talk of the country. For the Troubadours, Cole wrote the hour-long farce *Jolly Coon-ey Island,* in which he introduced the tramp, Willie Wayside, who became a central figure in *A Trip to Coontown.* A controversy, resulting in litigation over the ownership of music he composed—other black songwriters faced the same problem with producers at the time—led to Cole's leaving the Troubadours and organizing his own company, which presented *A Trip to Coontown.*

The closing of *Coontown* led to the dissolution of the partnership between Cole and Billy Johnson, and the formation of a new team, Bob Cole and J. Rosamond Johnson. A schooled musician who had studied at the New England Conservatory of Music and with Samuel Coleridge-Taylor in London, Rosamond collaborated with Cole initially on songwriting and in a high-class vaudeville act, and, later, on a number of significant theatrical productions. In 1901 they worked on *Toloso,* a little-known musical that lampooned America's imperialistic activities. Although it was not produced—largely, it is said, because producers feared public reaction as a result of America's involvement in the Spanish–American War—two of its songs became very popular. "My Castle on the Nile" was interpolated by George Walker in both *Sons of Ham* and *In Dahomey.* "Under the Bambo Tree," whose melody is supposedly based on the Spiritual, "Nobody Knows the Trouble I've Seen," became a hit vehicle for Marie Cahill, a turn-of-the century musical comedy star, when she interpolated it in *Sally in Our Alley.*

James Weldon Johnson, who collaborated on the lyrics of "My Castle on the Nile," was the younger brother of J. Rosamond. A poet–writer, he worked on songs with the duo but never on stage with them, and is remembered for having helped to inaugurate the Harlem Renaissance with the publication of *Fifty Years and Other Poems* in 1917.

"The Johnson brothers were emphatically new Negro," music publisher Edward B. Marks wrote in his autobiography.

> Even men like Williams and Walker were outwardly resigned to all sorts of discrimination. They would sing "coon," they would joke about "niggers," they accepted their success with wide-mouthed grins as the gist of the gods. Rosamond Johnson, benevolent, mellow-voiced, industrious, and his brother, who was to become the national leader of his race, were of a different stamp. They wrote songs, sometimes romantic, sometimes whimsical, but they eschewed the squalor and the squabbles, the razors, wenches, and chickens of the first ragtime. The word "coon" they banished from their rhyming dictionary, despite its tempting affinity with moon. The coon song died. The coon shouter vanished from the scene during the years of their ascendency. "We wanted to clean up the caricature," says Rosamond Johnson.[30]

The brothers later wrote "Lift Every Voice and Sing" whose popularity with blacks gave it the subtitle, "The Negro National Anthem." Together, they also produced two significant collections: *The Book of American Negro Spirituals* (1925) and *The Second Book of Negro Spirituals* (1926). J. Rosamond Johnson, who provided the musical arrangements for these, himself edited *Shout Songs* (1936) and *Rolling Along in Song* (1937), a folk-song collection. Musical director of Hammerstein's Opera House in London, a staff member for several years at the Music School Settlement in New York City, and founder–director of the Rosamond Johnson Quintet, J. Rosamond composed a number of choral works, including *Walk Together, Children* for chorus and orchestra, demonstrating a rare ability to infuse European musical forms with the idioms and sound of Negro folk music.

In 1901, Cole and the Johnsons became the first black songwriters to sign a contract, providing for advance monthly payments against future royalties, with a Broadway music publishing company. The contacts with Joseph W. Stern and Co., later Edward B. Marks Music Corporation, led to the popularization of their songs by such white performers as Marie Cahill ("Congo Love Song"), Anna Held ("Maiden with the Dreamy Eyes"), Eddie Leonard ("Mandy, Won't you Let Me Be Your Beau?"), May Irwin ("Nancy Brown"), and Lillian Russell.

In 1906 James Weldon Johnson was appointed Consul to Venezuela, and, having written the lyrics, left Cole and his brother to produce *Shoo-Fly Regiment,* advertised as "The First Real American Negro Play with Original Music." The operetta that followed, *The Red Moon* (1908), was the last Cole–Johnson production: Cole appeared in the role of a show manager, and J. Rosamond, as a Ragtime pianist. As *The Red Moon* was completing a two-year run, Rosamond wrote the score for *Mr. Lode of Koal,* working with J. A. Shipp, Alex Rogers, and Bert Williams, who starred in the short-lived vehicle.

In 1910, Cole and Johnson returned to vaudeville, touring the Keith circuit at $750 a week. On the last night of their engagement at New York's Fifth Avenue Theater, Cole collapsed. Apparently suffering from a nervous breakdown, he spent much of 1911 in hospitals. Late in July, he left for a private sanitorium in the Catskills. Early in August 1911, he drowned in a lake, prompting those who knew him as an excellent swimmer to conjecture that he had taken his own life. In his autobiography, *Along This Way,* James Weldon Johnson characterizes Cole as "one of the most talented and versatile Negroes ever connected with the stage."[31]

The musical director of the Cole–Johnson shows *The Shoo-Fly Regiment* and *Mr. Lode of Koal* was James Reese Europe, who also served in the same capacity with the famous dancing Castles, Irene and Vernon, in 1913–1914. The first black bandleader to make recordings, Europe organized the first New York bands specializing in syncopated music, and is credited with introducing Jazz to Europe.

Born in Mobile, Alabama, Europe was raised in Washington, D.C., where he studied piano and violin. By 1904 he was in New York City, where, the following year, he performed at Proctor's Theater with the Nashville Students. After touring Europe with the Tennessee Students, he was associated with Cole and Johnson from 1906 to 1908 on the two shows mentioned earlier.

Starting in 1910, when a national dance craze began sweeping the country, he organized the Clef Club Orchestra and Tempo Club Orchestra, which played syncopated music and became society favorites. The first time that popular music and Jazz were heard in Carnegie Hall was at a concert he gave, perhaps as early as 1911, according to some sources, or as late as 1914, according to others.[32] Sometime in this period, when he was performing at Baron Wilkins's Harlem nightclub, reports have it that young George Gershwin, unable to gain entry, sat for hours on the curb, enchanted by the syncopated sounds emanating from the club. Europe's bands, composed of schooled musicians, were well trained.

According to Eubie Blake, although they could not enter through the front door of many of the places where they played, "that Europe gang were absolute reading sharks. They could read a moving snake and if a fly lit on that paper, he got played. We were only twelve men sounding like sixty. Jim would come in, bow, raise his baton, count, 'One, two,' hand me the stick and walk out."[33]

Europe met the Castles at a private society party. Thereafter they opted for his orchestra in all of their performances and enterprises. Vernon and Irene Castle—his surname was Blythe, but he appropriated his stage name from Windsor Castle—were at the height of their popularity from 1912 to 1917, with all society and dancing America trying to do the dances they created, such as the Castle Walk, Castle Lame Duck, Castle Maxixe, and so on. In a world that had gone dance-crazy, the Castle dances were markedly different from the two types of public dancing that had prevailed until then — the Two-Step (with the Bunny Hug and Turkey Trot as variants) and the Waltz. In this period, until Vernon was killed in a wartime Texas plane crash when he tried to save the life of another flier, the Castles had a teatime dancing school called Castle House, a Castles-in-the-Air on the roof of the 44th St. Theater, and even a Castles-by-the-Sea at Long Beach. With Ford Dabney (1883–1958), the pianist in his band, Jim Europe wrote and/or arranged the "Castle Walk," "Castle House Rag," and "Castle Valse Classique," among others. Publisher Edward B. Marks claimed they wrote so many dance numbers that on some title pages, they had their names spelled backward, "Eporue" and "Yenbad."

At the outbreak of World War I, Europe was commissioned a lieutenant and named bandmaster of the 369th Infantry Band, a Negro regiment. Playing for the Allied troops and others in France, he captivated audiences with performances of "Memphis Blues" and the sound of America's new syncopated music. At an Allied military concert at the Tuilleries in France, after the other orchestras had played the classics, he scored a sensation with "St. Louis Blues."

Returning after the war to national acclaim — thousands turned out to greet him and his Hell Fighters — he set forth on a nationwide tour with a concert at the Manhattan Opera House on March 17, 1919. During a concert in Boston on May 9, 1919, he was stabbed to death by snare drummer Pvt. Herbert Wright, ostensibly enraged by sarcastic remarks Europe made about his performance.

> "He was brought back to New York," according to Douglas Gilbert, and buried from St. Mark's Methodist Episcopal Church in West 53rd St. after a parade from a Harlem undertaker's parlor. Throngs witnessed it, and among the spectators were Col. William Hayward (commander of the 369th Regiment) and John Wanamaker, Jr. He was buried in Arlington, not in his uniform but in the famous dress clothes that he wore as a jazz-band leader, which included a white, pleated silk shirt and striped vest.[34]

At his death, Jim Europe was just 38 years old, and left a legacy not only of sterling musicianship but of having contributed immensely to the betterment of the black musicians' lot through the Clef Club, which he organized, and other social-minded activities.

Fanny Brice, the celebrated "funny girl" who became a star comedienne/singer of the *Ziegfeld Follies,* made her debut in the 1910 edition, the same year in which Bert Williams first appeared.

On opening night, Ms. Brice, who had until then been performing in obscure burlesque houses, stopped the show with her delivery of "Lovey Joe," a ragtime love song by Will Marion Cook and Joe Jordan.

Jordan began his career as a Ragtime composer, functioning at first in St. Louis and later in Chicago, where he was part of an active Ragtime coterie. His Rag output includes "Double Fudge—Ragtime Two Step (1902), "Nappy Lee—A Slow Drag" (1903, and "Pekin Rag, Intermezzo" (1904).

His first challenging assignment came in 1905 when actor/songwriter/producer Ernest Hogan, of "All Coons Look Alike to Me" notoriety, put together a group of versatile performers, named them the Memphis Students, though none was a student or came from Memphis, and retained as composers for the group James Reese Europe and Joe Jordan, who also served as musical director. So innovative were the concerts—involving instrumentalists who sang as they played; an orchestra using saxophones, mandolins, and banjos instead of the then-accepted instruments of dance bands; the hijinks of a "dancing conductor"; and the first public concert of syncopated music—so excited was audience reaction that the scheduled two-weeks at Hammerstein's Victoria Theater on Broadway stretched into a five-month engagement. In the fall of 1905, Will Marion Cook assumed direction of the group in a highly successful European tour, which took it into theaters in London, Paris, Berlin, and other cities.

By 1906 Jordan had become director of the new Pekin Theater Orchestra in Chicago and was working with leading men Flourney Miller and Aubrey Lyles on a musical *The Man from 'Bam,* the stock company's first production. That year, Jordan contributed material to *Rufus Rastus,* starring Ernest Hogan. Succeeding Pekin Theater musical productions for which Jordan wrote music included *The Husband* (1907) and *Captain Rufus* (1907), both of which also played Hurtig and Seamon's Music Hall.

A high point in Jordan's musical life came in October 1939, during ASCAP's Silver Jubilee Festival at Carnegie Hall. The second evening of a week of concerts, dedicated to Negro music, found Jordan directing an orchestra of 75 musicians and a chorus of 350 voices singing the unofficial Negro anthem by the Johnson brothers, "Lift Every Voice and Sing."

Will Henry Bennett Vodery (1885–1951) was another black theater composer/conductor who came to the fore in the first decade of our century. Establishing a reputation as one of the foremost arrangers of the 1920s and 1930s, he became the first black to invade the Hollywood film scene. Born in Philadelphia and later a scholarship student at the University of Pennsylvania, he became professionally involved in music through Bert Williams, who brought him to New York and helped him secure his first major assignment: composing the music for the Black Patti Troubadours' production *A Trip to Africa* (1904). In the succeeding eight years, he wrote music for a dozen shows, the most important of which were the Williams and Walker production of *Abyssinia* (1906), Ernest Hogan's *Oyster Man* (1907), and Miller and Lyle's *The Man from 'Bam,* for which he composed one of his best-known songs, "After the Ball Is Over."

In 1910 he served as musical director of Williams and Walker's *Bandana Land*—which he also arranged—as it traveled through the United States and Europe. One indication of his growing stature was his being selected that year to conduct the orchestra for the ceremony in Washington, D.C., celebrating the opening of Howard University. On his debut in the *Ziegfeld Follies of 1910,* Bert Williams commissioned Vodery to write his songs, an action that prompted Ziegfeld to engage Vodery as arranger of the *Follies* from 1913 into the late 1920s. It was Vodery who orchestrated George Gershwin's first attempt at writing a black opera, *Blue Monday,* composed by the future composer of *Porgy and Bess* for the George White *Scandals* of 1922 and played by the orchestra of Paul Whiteman in the pit.

During the 1920s and 1930s, Vodery was in constant demand as a theater arranger, whose numerous assignments involved some of the most significant black musicals of the day. These included *Shuffle Along* (1921), *Keep Shufflin'* (1928), Lew Leslie's *Blackbirds of 1928* and *Blackbirds of 1929,* and the legendary *Cotton Club Parade* of 1935. Vodery also served as arranger for the famous Jerome Kern–Oscar Hammerstein II path-breaking musical *Show Boat,* which was produced by Ziegfeld in 1927 and pioneered the subject of miscegenation. Then in 1929, Vodery moved to Hollywood, where he was retained by Fox Films until 1933 as an arranger and musical director, the first black to function in such a capacity.

Apart from his achievements as a conductor/composer/arranger, Vodery was revered as a man who was generous in opening doors for others. Among these was a young William Grant Still (1895–1978) whose first rewarding assignments as an arranger came through Vodery's intervention and whose works in the symphonic and operatic fields later earned him recognition as the "dean of Afro-American composers."

The Passing of the Minstrel Show

During the 1890s, a number of black musicals deviated from the minstrel-show pattern, introducing elements that led to the development of musical comedy and its flowering in *Shuffle Along* (1921).

The first of these was *The Creole Show*, produced in 1890 by a white burlesque theater owner and manager, Sam T. Jack. The idea for the show originated with Sam Lucas, later known as the "dean of black performers." Maintaining the framework of the minstrel show, including plantation sets and the olio, it departed from it by introducing a female chorus of 16 in what had once been an all-male form. In addition to the pretty girls, it shattered tradition by using, for the first time, a female interlocutor, who sat, as was the custom, in the center of an all-male semicircle. In successive editions, *The Creole Show* continued running until almost the end of the decade, playing all the top burlesque houses in the East and scoring a sensation in New York, where it drew crowds for five seasons at the old Standard Theater in Greeley Square.

In *Octoroons*, produced in 1895 and one of the most successful road shows for eight seasons, John William Isham, who had been an advance man for *The Creole Show*, moved further away from the minstrel-show format. Employing music from comic and grand opera and a cast of 17 women in addition to 16 men, Isham disregarded the traditional sequence of segments in the minstrel show. Part one of *Octoroons* consisted at times of an opening chorus plus a medley of songs by the principals; at other times of a travesty involving a group of comics. Part two, instead of the traditional olio, offered a burlesque sketch, with the specialities strung on a thin story thread. Part two emphasized spectacles, such as a cakewalk jubilee, a military drill, and a "charm march." Bob Cole not only wrote an opening skit but found his wife, Stella Wiley, in the cast.

With *Oriental America* of 1896, Isham continued his assault on the content and structure of the minstrel show, featuring a Japanese dance, a quartet of girls cycling in bloomers, and other exotic novelties. Believed to be the first black show of the 1890s to play on Broadway (at the old Palmer Theater), *Oriental America* emphasized music from the great operas—*Lucia di Lammermoor, Rigoletto,* and others. J. Rosamond Johnson sang the Armorer's song from *Robin Hood* in costume. Instead of the traditional walk-around, it presented a rousing medley of operatic selections, earning plaudits as one of the best singing shows in decades, both here and in England.

Building a musical around an opera star now appears in retrospect as an inevitable development, and that was what Voelckel and Nolan did in 1897 to compete with *Oriental America*. As their star they chose Sissieretta Jones, (1870–1933), dubbed the "Black Patti" by the influential New York *Clipper* for her magnificent operatic singing at the Grand Negro Jubilee at Madison Square, April 26–28, 1892. Even before then, her voice had given her such renown that she was invited to sing at the White House before President Harrison in February 1892. For the opening number of Black Patti Troubadours, as the company came to be called, Voelckel and Nolan retained Bob Cole, who produced the skit "At Jolly Coon-ey Island." Although the show at first followed the minstrel pattern, the finale, titled, "The Operatic Kaleidoscope," was devoted entirely to Black Patti, who sang operatic selections with the chorus. Touring the United States and Canada with changing personnel, the Troubadours continued to feature Black Patti as their draw during the many years of their existence (1897–1920). In time, to accord with its altered format, the billing of the Troubadours was changed to Black Patti Musical Comedy Company. Under this banner it presented *A Trip to Africa,* as produced in two acts by John Larkins, in the Bowery section of New York City in 1908, presumably the first time that an all-black show was performed before a white audience.

An operatic finale was also used in *Darkest Africa,* which opened shortly before the first production of the Black Patti troupe and boasted a narrative thread: "the delineation of Negro life, carrying the race through all its historical phases from the plantation into Reconstruction days, and, finally, painting our people as they are today, cultured and accomplished in the social graces."[34] Sam Lucas headed a cast of 50, and versatile Billy McLain, with a long career in minstrelsy dating back to Lew Johnson's Minstrels in 1883, served in the dual capacity of performer and manager. The closing scene, titled "The Operatic Ball," featured Cordelia McLain as prima donna, tenor Lawrence E. Chenault, baritone Edward Winn, Billy McLain, and a chorus, singing arias from several operas, including *Cavalleria Rusticana.*

The use of operatic material and the starring of a black competitor to famous soprano Adelina Patti (1843–1910) suggests that producers of black musicals were seeking to bring the musical culture of white society to blacks but also, perhaps, to broaden their audience. In the adventuring and experimentation of these black "variety" shows of the 1890s, most still retaining vestiges of the minstrel show but all departing in one way or another from its plantation setting, its subject matter, and format—and some making tentative steps in the direction of a story line—one detects the search for a new form. Unquestionably, here are the rudimentary beginnings of the revue and the black musical comedy of the 1920s.

Black Stock Companies

The death in 1911 of songwriter Bob Cole of Cole and Johnson and *A Trip to Coontown* fame occurred roughly at the same time as the deaths of comedian/songwriter/producer Ernest Hogan (1909) and of George Walker of Williams and Walker (1911). Although other members of the black theatrical world remained active—Jesse Shipp, Alex Rogers, Paul Laurence Dunbar, Will Vodery, Joe Jordan, and the Johnson brothers—*Mr. Lode of Koal* (1909), Bert Williams's last all-black show, was also the last show written and produced by blacks on Broadway until *Shuffle Along* shook up the American musical theater in 1921.

Despite the absence of black musicals on New York's main stem, the black theater, musical and dramatic, did not languish during the decade. In truth, road shows, stock companies, and new theaters in black neighborhoods afforded increasing outlets for black actors, dancers, singers, lyricists, composers, musicians, and producers. In Harlem in 1914, a new Lincoln Theater played host to the Anita Bush Stock Company, providing an outlet, among other performers, for Dooley Wilson, later of *Casablanca* film fame. At the nearby Lafayette Theater, known in Harlem as the House Beautiful, a new play opened every Monday from 1914 to 1921. In 1913 the Negro Players opened at the Lafayette Theater in a tabloid musical comedy titled *The Traitor;* Will Marion Cook assisted with the music. Companies of the Lafayette Players were organized and performed at the Howard Theater in Washington, D.C., Dunbar Theater in Philadelphia, and the Avenue Theater in Chicago.

The first successful stock company apparently was established in Chicago, when Robert Motts founded the Pekin Company at his Pekin Theater. Disbanded in 1911 when Motts died, it helped launch the careers of Miller and Lyles, later of *Shuffle Along* fame, and of composer/conductor Will Vodery, among others. In 1913, comic/impresario Sherman H. Dudley of the Original Smart Set Company organized the first black theater circuit. From 1915 until 1923, the Billy King Stock Company presented new and original musicals and tabloids every week at the Grand Theater in Chicago. By 1921 Harlem boasted the first theater owned and managed by blacks in the Renaissance at 133rd St. and Seventh Avenue.

Between 1910 and 1925 the most prolific producing, acting, and writing team was that of the brothers Salem Tutt Whitney and J. Homer Tutt. Associated in 1905 with the Original Smart Set Company, organized by Billy McLain, Ernest Hogan, and white producer Gus Hill, they later joined the Black Patti Troubadours. In 1909 they founded a second Smart Set company, which they merged with the original. They reportedly "produced, wrote and directed over 25 tabloids, two dramas, sixteen musical comedies, at least 150 vaudeville sketches, 300 poems and 50 songs."[36]

From this outpouring of Negro talent and creativity, the climate was created for the climactic emergence of *Shuffle Along*.

Shuffle Along

When it opened on May 23, 1921, in New York, *Shuffle Along* offered little promise of what it was to become. Underfinanced, it had played a series of one-night, out-of-town stands in New Jersey and Pennsylvania, tottering on the edge of bankruptcy. The settings and scenery were flimsy. The costumes were hand-me-downs, purchased from a folded Eddie Leonard vehicle, *Roly-Boly Eyes*. Postwar discrimination forced the production away from the center of Broadway's theatrical district into Daly's dilapidated music hall on 63rd St. Curiously, these limitations eventually worked to the show's benefit. Broadway critics who bridled at blacks seeking to emulate the opulent mountings of white productions were won over by the unadorned simplicity of *Shuffle Along,* not to mention such positive features as charismatic performers, hit songs, hilarious comedy sketches, and whirlwind dancing.

In addition to established comics Miller and Lyles, who wrote the book, the cast included such future theatrical greats as Josephine Baker (1906–1975), Hall Johnson, and Florence Mills (1895–1927), and the pit orchestra included not only Eubie Blake at the piano but William Grant Still on oboe. The songs were by Noble Sissle and Eubie Blake, and before the show closed, after a substantial run of 504 performances, six numbers were being sung and played around town and on their way to becoming standards. These included the title tune, "I'm Just Wild About Harry," "Love Will Find a Way," "I'm Cravin' for That Kind of Love," "Bandana Rag," and "Gypsy Blues." The exuberance of ensemble numbers and the precision and explosive energy of the dancing thereafter set the standard for black musicals as well as white.

Shuffle Along is best described as a revue with continuity rather than as a book show. The thin thread of a story involved a mayoralty race in a place called Jimtown, where sharp Steve Jenkins (Flourney Miller) and dull Sam Peck (Aubrey Lyles) jointly owned a grocery store, from which each was slyly taking money to finance his political ambitions. When Jenkins is elected Mayor with the help of a crooked manager, he appoints Peck the Chief of Police. A high point of the show was a fight between the two, a comedy routine developed by them during their vaudeville days. Eventually, the two are ousted by a reform candidate, Harry Walton, who inspires the memorable song, later used by Harry Truman in his campaign for the presidency, "I'm Just Wild About Harry."

The humor of Miller and Lyles relied on a well-known pattern—the sharpie versus the schlemiel—exploited by Williams and Walker, among other blackface duos. If *Shuffle Along* was following tradition in this respect, it represented a departure in several other ways. It was the first black musical in which the female chorus was scantily clad in the provocative style of such white revues as the *Ziegfeld Follies* and *George White's Scandals.* It was also the first musical in which a black man and woman, alone on stage, made an open display of romantic feelings, expressing them in the ballad "Love Will Find a Way." Finally, the show was not only fast-paced, but the high-stepping dancing was a display of such vitality, it left audiences breathless. Perhaps the most significant contribution of *Shuffle Along,* beyond its theatrical power, was to demonstrate that an all-black show could be a money-maker on Broadway. In all these ways, it not only motivated white and black entrepreneurs to produce black musicals, but it became the yardstick by which these were judged.

A measure of the popularity of the show was indicated by the opening of a new club in Harlem at 131st St. and Seventh Avenue, which called itself Shuffle Inn. Purchased by George and Connie Immerman, for whose delicatessen Fats Waller worked as a delivery boy, Shuffle Inn became the famous Connie's Inn in 1923.

Through the 1920s, Miller and Lyles made several attempts to repeat their success with *Shuffle Along.* Jimtown and the Steve Jenkins–Sam Peck duo figured in *Keep Shufflin'* (104 performances) in 1928 and *Sugar Hill* (11 performances) in 1931. The lively presence of Fats Waller at one of the pianos in the former contributed to its modest run, without helping it turn into a success.

Less than successful were such other black musical comedies of the 1920s as *Strut Miss Lizzie* (1922), by Henry Creamer and Turner Layton; *Liza* (1922), with a score by Maceo Pinkard; *Plantation Revue* (1922), whose cast included composer Shelton Brooks, Florence Mills, and Will Vodery; *How Come?* (1923); *Chocolate Dandies* (1924), and *Elsie* (1925), which not even scores by Sissle and Blake saved; *Lucky Sambo* (1925); and *Deep River* (1926).

Of all these, it was only *Runnin' Wild* (1923) that approached *Shuffle Along* in popularity. *Runnin' Wild,* once more concerned with the adventures of Steve Jenkins and Sam Peck in Jimtown, roles again played by Miller and Lyles, was produced and written by them. The attractive score was by Cecil Mack and James P. Johnson. For the finale of Act I, Elizabeth Welch and the chorus danced the Charleston, launching one of the biggest dance crazes of the Jazz Age, and one that became emblematic of the dizzy decade.

So popular was the dance that, in 1924, New York's Roseland Ballroom ran a Charleston Marathon that lasted 22.5 hours, with the winner awarded a one-week engagement at the Rivoli Theater on Broadway. During the three years of the craze, a flock of songs appeared, trading on the magic of the word: "Just Wait Till You See

My Baby Do the Charleston Dance," "I'm Gonna Charleston Back to Charleston," "Charleston Is the Best Dance After All," and others. In the film *Our Dancing Mothers* (1928), Joan Crawford charmed audiences by dancing the Charleston, as did Vivien Leigh in a 1963 Broadway musical *Tovarich*.

While people were still dancing the Charleston, another dance of black origin began to take hold. The Black Bottom, which involved the slapping of the backside, was introduced in *Dinah*, a Harlem musical written and produced by Irvin C. Miller, with songs by Tim Brymn (1881–1946), who had collaborated with Joe Jordan on the music for the Pekin Theatre/Miller and Lyles comedy *The Husband* (1907). The dance was performed by Ethel Ridley, who learned it from blues songwriter/publisher/manager Perry Bradford (1890–1970), a claim he made in a *McClure's* magazine article in 1927.[37] Other sources assign the dance's invention to songwriter/singer Alberta Hunter (1897–1984), one of the classic Blues singers, who is supposed to have copyrighted it.[38] In either event, the dance became a craze only after it was performed in *George White's Scandals* of 1926, with diminutive Ann Pennington dancing it to a song, "Black Bottom," by the hit songwriting team of De Sylva, Brown, and Henderson. At the peak of the craze, it was said that the Ned Wayburn dance studio in New York drew 1,000 students daily for instruction.

Five years elapsed before Broadway audiences saw another black musical hit after *Runnin' Wild* (1923). *Blackbirds of 1928*, which opened on May 9 at the Liberty Theater, has been described as "an all-white creation for an all-black cast." The producer was Lew Leslie, whose success with the 1928 edition led him to try other editions, unsuccessfully, late into the 1930s. Scant on production—drapes were used for scenery—*Blackbirds of 1928* was rich in "players and numbers," as *The New York Times* saw it. The players included Bill Robinson (1878–1949), who brought the house down nightly with his elegant tap-dancing to "Doin' the New Low Down"; Adelaide Hall, who scored in a jungle setting with "Diga Diga Do"; and Aida Ward, whose contribution to "I Can't Give You Anything But Love, Baby" helped make an evergreen of it. The infectiously melodic numbers were the work of lyricist Dorothy Fields (1905–1974) and composer Jimmy McHugh (1894–1969), who were newcomers to Broadway but whose score helped the revue run for a record 518 performances.

Blackbirds of 1933 folded after three weeks, despite Bill Robinson's eye- and ear-arresting tap dancing, including the famous up-and-down-the-stairs routine. *Blackbirds of 1939* closed after nine performances, despite beauteous newcomer Lena Horne and a formidable array of creative talents: songwriters Johnny Mercer

(1909–1976), Mitchell Parish, and Sammy Fain (b. 1902) Ferde Grofe's (1892–1972) orchestrations; and J. Rosamond Johnson's vocal arrangements.

Although they were not on Broadway, the Cotton Club and Connie's Inn presented such lavish floor shows that their openings drew the social and theatrical set who never missed a Broadway opening. Scores were generally written by top white songwriters, who vied for the opportunity. However, Connie's *Hot Chocolates* of 1929 boasted a score by the inspired team of Fats Waller and Andy Razaf, which contained the unforgettable "Ain't Misbehavin'." Revised for Broadway, *Hot Chocolates* opened at the Hudson Theater in June 1929 and ran for over six months, the last successful black musical of the decade.

Bamboola, which opened at Broadway's Royale Theater six days after *Hot Chocolates,* lasted a mere four weeks, lambasted by New York critics for its presumed effort to imitate white musicals in its scope. Although dancing was the main feature, as it was for most black musicals, a tribute to Bill Robinson involved 20 dancers imitating his celebrated routine of tapping his way up and down a staircase. Preconceived prejudices, shared with other reviewers, as to what a black musical should be were apparent in the comment: "The Negro is very funny when he's allowed to be funny in his own way."[39]

Successes or failures, these many black musicals introduced or featured some of the best Negro artists of the time, including among others, Josephine Baker, Louis "Satchmo" Armstrong, vocalist/trumpeter Jabbo Smith (b. 1908), Monette Moore (1902–1962), Lena Horne (b. 1917), Duke Ellington, Cab Calloway (b. 1907), Ivie Anderson (1904–1949), Buck and Bubbles, Nicholas Brothers, and Ethel Waters, who made her Broadway debut in an unprepossessing revue, *Africana* (1927).

Regardless of the failures, the black musicals brought a new tempo, sound, and elan into the American musical theater. No musical of the era or later could afford to disregard the challenge of the whirlwind dancing and the pacing of *Shuffle Along*. But the impact of the Sissle–Blake score went beyond these things; its primacy was in introducing the sound, rhythms, and spontaneity of Jazz into the theater.

The White Synthesis

The 1920s were the years of Prohibition, when the consumption of illicit booze brought bootleggers, speakeasies, hip flasks, rum runners, hijacking, mob violence, and padlocked nightclubs onto the

American scene. With average citizens flouting an unpopular law, it became a free-wheeling, anything-goes time—an up-tempo, libidinous era for which Jazz seemed the perfect accompaniment.

New York first heard Jazz in 1917, when the Original Dixieland Jazz Band came up from New Orleans, played at Reisenweber's restaurant and dance palace on 58th St. and Eighth Avenue, made the first recordings of the new dance music. Chicago began hearing Jazz about the same time when a group of jazzmen, including famed trumpeter King Oliver, also came up from New Orleans and began gigging around the Windy City. But it was not until 1922 that the famous Creole Jazz Band of King Oliver, with young Louis Armstrong on second trumpet, began making jazz history at the Lincoln Gardens. Sometime in the 1920s, legendary novelist F. Scott Fitzgerald (1896–1940) stamped the decade with the label that has stuck, the Jazz Age. And it was "the national rage for jazz," according to theater historian Gerald Bordman, "that polarized the musical stage."[40]

Shuffle Along made its appearance at just the right moment, imbued with and initially reflecting the unbuttoned, improvisatory spirit of the new music but also of the era.

White musicals reacted dynamically, manifesting a change in tempo, mood, and animation that became evident even in the titles: brief, sharp, staccato phrases such as *Hit the Deck, Follow Thru, Good News, Here's How, Great Day! Be Yourself, Sky High, Allez-Oop, Take the Air, Make It Snappy, Lady, Be Good!*

The two dances of black origin that dominated the era, the Charleston and the Black Bottom, soon attracted a flashy competitor in the form of the Varsity Drag, devised by the white team of De Sylva, Brown, and Henderson for their collegiate musical, *Good News* (1927). And *Lady, Be Good!* offered "Fascinating Rhythm," its syncopated accents deftly enunciated in the nimble footwork of Fred Astaire and his sister Adele.

Lady, Be Good!, the work of the Gershwins, was on Broadway in the year that Paul Whiteman (1890–1967) introduced George Gershwin's jazzy *Rhapsody in Blue* (1924). If ever a songwriter/composer drew inspiration from the well of Negro music, the Blues, Ragtime, and Jazz, it was Gershwin. As early as his first hit song, "Swanee," in 1919, there was evidence of the rhythmic inventiveness and danceable melodies that marked such hits as "Somebody Loves Me" *(George White's Scandals of 1924);* "Clap Yo' Hands" and "Do-Do-Do" *(Oh, Kay);* " 'S Wonderful" and "My One and Only" *(Funny Face);* and "I Got Rhythm" and "Embraceable You" *(Girl Crazy).*

In 1922 for the *Scandals* of that year, Gershwin and B. G. De Sylva wrote a 20-minute "jazz opera" called *Blue Monday;* performed by white cast members in blackface and concerned with Negro life, it foreshadowed the crowning achievement of Gershwin's brilliant career. In its own way, *Porgy and Bess* represented also a flowering of the seeds planted by *Shuffle Along* and the black musicals of the 1920s and 1930s. As a tale centering around a black ghetto in Charleston, South Carolina, the "American Folk Opera," as it was called, used street cries, work songs, spirituals, shouts, and blues-inflected arias. To create this operatic fusion of Negro folk sounds and Jazz, Gershwin spent time in Charleston's Cabbage Row slum and on Folly Beach, off the Carolina coast, absorbing firsthand the songs he heard in churches, on the streets, at black picnics, and among fishing crews. It took a bit of time for the initial quibbling about whether *Porgy and Bess* is an opera to come to rest. But this powerful drama of love and infidelity in a black setting stands today as the most celebrated, most recorded, and most performed of indigenous American operas.[42]

Walking closely behind Gershwin in his use of Blues and Jazz in theater and film music is Harold Arlen (b. 1905), whose endeavors have at times involved Jazz-oriented lyricist Johnny Mercer. Of Arlen, Alec Wilder has said in his probing musicological study *American Popular Music:* "Even in Arlen's later, more mature and more ambitious melodies, he never drew upon or was influenced by European music of any kind. He is wholly a product of American jazz, big band music and American popular song."[42] To which one should append Stanley Green's observation: "Arlen is best-known for his *blues* [emphasis added] and rhythm songs that have a strong affinity with the emotion of Negroes."[43]

Partnered with Ted Koehler (b. 1894), Arlen wrote the songs for five annual editions of the *Cotton Club Parade* from 1930 on. Out of these Harlem floor shows came such Blues/Jazz popular hits as "I've Got the World on a String," performed by Aida Ward (c.1900–1984); "Stormy Weather," introduced by and a perennial of Ethel Waters's (1897–1977); "As Long As I Live," a duet for Lena Horne and Avon Long (1910–1984); and many others. Betweentimes, Arlen wrote "I Gotta Right to Sing the Blues" for *Earl Carroll's Varieties* (1932), a song that became the theme of jazz trombonist Jack Teagarden (1905–1964), and "It's Only a Paper Moon" for a 1933 film, *Take a Chance,* which provided hit disks for the Mills Bros. and Nat "King" Cole (1917–1969).

Johnny Mercer lyrics for film collaborations yielded such Arlen evergreens as "Blues in the Night (My Momma Done Tol' Me)," first recorded by the great band of Jimmie Lunceford (1902–1947), and an Academy Award nominee in 1941; "That Old Black Magic," an Academy Award nominee in 1943 and an audience-grabber of all of

Billy Daniels's (b. circa 1920) appearances in nightclubs during the 1940s and 1950s; and "One for My Baby (And One More for the Road)," introduced by Fred Astaire in the film *The Sky's the Limit* (1943). Another evocative torch song from Arlen's piano was "The Man That Got Away," with lyrics by Ira Gershwin (1896–1983), and an Academy Award nominee for Judy Garland's (1922–1969), heart-rending performance in *A Star Is Born* (1954).

As for Broadway musicals, Arlen was involved mainly with all-black or predominantly black casts and themes—*St. Louis Woman* (1946), in which Pearl Bailey (b. 1918) made her Broadway debut; *House of Flowers* (1954), starring Pearl Bailey and Diahann Carroll (b. 1935); and *Jamaica* (1957), starring Lena Horne. *Bloomer Girl* (1944), with a Civil War setting, and *Saratoga* (1959), with a New Orleans setting, both involved questions of Negro rights.

Arlen seldom ventured outside the realm of theater, film, and popular song. But he did compose an instrumental work, *Americanegro Suite,* and a blues opera, *Free and Easy,* an expansion of the music in *St. Louis Woman.* It is little wonder that when Edward Jablonski came to write Arlen's biography, he called it *Happy with the Blues.*

CHAPTER FIVE

"SINGIN' THE BLUES"

In August 1920, a heavy-hipped black vaudevillian named Mamie Smith (1883–1946) entered the OKeh studios in New York City to record what became a runaway Blues best seller. Mamie was backed by a small combo of five black instrumentalists—clarinet, cornet, trombone, the typical front line of a New Orleans jazz band, plus violin and piano. The session was produced by Fred Hager, recording director of General Phonograph Corporation, who had been prodded into recording a black singer by a persistent, cigar-chomping vaudevillian/songwriter named Perry Bradford.

The story has sometimes been told that the session was supposed to have been done by Sophie Tucker, a popular white vaudevillian also on the OKeh label, and that Mamie Smith cut "Crazy Blues" when the Last of the Red Hot Mamas, as Ms. Tucker was known, suddenly canceled. The story has no validity. The particular session on which Mamie Smith cut "Crazy Blues," originally known as "Harlem Blues," was not her first, but her second, OKeh date. In February 1920, Hager had recorded "That Thing Called Love" and "You Can't Keep a Good Man Down" with Mamie, again at Bradford's urging. Despite fears that blacks did not have the money to buy disks and that whites would not buy a record by a black singer, Mamie's first disk sold so well that Hager assented to the August session.

Instead of using a white combo, as he had done on the first date, he used a black group. As described by Bradford in his autobiography, *Born with the Blues,*[1] the band employed "hum and head arrangements"; that is, its members did not play from a written score. But they did apparently rehearse for two days before they came to play their "head arrangement," in today's terminology.

"Crazy Blues" proved a surprise and a sensation, to which the song on the back, "It's Right Here for You (If You Don't Get It, 'Tain't No Fault Of Mine)," may have contributed. The record sold so well that OKeh experienced difficulty pressing records fast enough to keep up with the demand. In a backward glance, this is more readily understood than it was in 1920. During World War I, which ended in 1918, there had been a large migration of black people from the South into northern cities, where the war effort afforded blacks employment opportunities not accessible in the South; they were a made-to-order market. To whites, unfamiliar with the Blues, Mamie's disk must have had an appealing, exotic sound. Incidentally, her billing on the record was "contralto," a designation arising from the then-interest of the record industry only in black *concert* artists.[2]

Thinking back to that period, Alberta Hunter, co-writer of Bessie Smith's first hit, "Down Hearted Blues," said: "There was Sara Martins, Ida Cox, Chippie Hill, Victoria Spivey, Trixie Smith and Clara Smith, and Mamie Smith, who made it possible for all of us with her recording of *Crazy Blues,* the *first* blues record."[3]

Born in Cincinnati in 1890, or possibly as early as 1883, Mamie Smith was typical of the group of black female vocalists who became known as the Classic Blues Singers of the 1920s. She was a vaudevillian and a cabaret singer, not really a Blues singer, who at 15 was dancing and singing in the well-known *Smart Set* company of Salem Tutt Whitney. Settling in Harlem in the era when it was just beginning to boom as the entertainment center of New York and when Lenox Avenue was known as the International Boulevard, she performed at such Harlem night spots as Baron Wilkins's, Leroy's, and Edmund's, as well as at Harlem vaudeville theaters.

In 1917 she was in the cast of *Sergeant Ham of the 13th District,* a musical starring and produced by Jeanette and Perry Bradford. The association eventually led to Bradford's becoming Mamie's manager. The success of her OKeh records having made her a draw on the Theater Owners Booking Association (T.O.B.A.) circuit, she toured the country with her own revue, which included six dancing girls and her own band. The Jazz Hounds, as they were called, involved at various times such outstanding musicians as pianist Willie (The Lion) Smith (1897–1973), clarinetist Buster Bailey (1902–

1967) and tenor-saxist Coleman Hawkins (1907–1969). With the Jazz Hounds, she starred in a musical, *Struttin' Along* (1923), whose cast included Edward Anderson, then featured on the *Jack Benny Show* as Rochester. Other productions in which she starred included *Black Diamond Express* (1928), which she also produced, and *Sepia Vagabonds* (1930). She also appeared in a number of RCA film shorts, the most attractive of which was "Jail House Blues," with Porter Grainger and J. Homer Tutt. At the peak of her career, she owned two apartment houses, and performed in a $3,000 cape, decorated with ostrich plumes. Although she recorded close to 100 sides, she apparently died poor.

Perry Bradford, who was so instrumental in her career, was born on Valentine's Day in 1893 (not 1890) in Montgomery, Alabama (not Atlanta, as some believe), and died, after a long, productive life, on April 20, 1970. He was a capable entertainer, a resourceful manager, an astute judge of talent, a commercial songwriter, a successful publisher, and a pioneer in Jazz, Blues and the dance song. Even when he was attending Atlanta University, from the ages of 12 to 15, he toured with the New Orleans Minstrels, singing, dancing, and playing piano. From 1908 to 1919, he was part of the vaudeville team of Bradford and Jeanette, acquiring the nickname of "Mule," because of a piano/vocal specialty involving the command, "Whoa, mule!" The nickname fitted him: he was both stubborn and persistent in an era when a black songwriter/manager did not find too many doors open.

Even before "Ballin' the Jack" opened the market for songs describing a dance, he wrote "The Bullfrog Hop," "Messin' Around," and "The Baltimore Buzz," all dance songs. "The Bullfrog Hop" antedated the popularity of the Shimmy, featured later by Gilda Gray. Bradford persuaded Ethel Waters to use "Messin' Around" in her T.O.B.A. tour in 1912. Other Bradford dance songs included "Stewin' the Rice" (1904), "The Possum Trot" (1915), and "Scratchin' the Gravel" (1917), the last of which he sold to Charles K. Harris, a publisher whom he described as receptive to black talent. The most important of his dance songs was "The Original Black Bottom Dance," which he wrote and published in 1922, four years before it became a national craze.[4]

"Crazy Blues" shook up the record business of the day in a triple sense: It prompted the launching of a series of "race" records, as they came to be called, by the then active companies; it motivated the rise of new black-oriented labels; and it motivated a search for black singers who could compete with Mamie Smith. The first to introduce a race roster with its 8000 series in 1920, OKeh soon had competitors in Paramount's 12000 series (1921), Columbia's

14000D series (1922), Vocalion's 1000 series (1925), Perfect's 100 series (1925), Brunswick's 7000 series (1926), and Victor's V38500 series (1927).

To Mamie Smith, OKeh added a number of black artists: teenager Victoria Spivey (1906–1976), Sara Martin (1884–1955), and Sippie Wallace (b. 1898); and boasted in its advertising: "The World's Greatest Race Artists on the World's Greatest Race Records." Paramount's black roster included Alberta Hunter; Ida Cox (1889–1967), "Uncrowned Queen of the Blues," also called "The Sepia Mae West"; and Ma Rainey, "Mother of the Blues." To OKeh's claim that its 8000 series was "The Original Race Record," Paramount countered that it had "The Popular Race Record." With its 14000D series in motion, Columbia acquired Bessie Smith, later called the "Empress of the Blues," and Clara Smith (1894–1935), the "World's Champion Moaner." There were at least five Smiths among the Classic Blues singers, and none was related to another.

The growing popularity of the Blues was indicated not only by the scramble for black female singers among the record companies but by a Blues singing contest held in New York's Manhattan Casino as part of the fifteenth Infantry's First Band Concert and Dance. Four singers competed for the prize: Lucille Hegamin (1894–1970), Harlem's favorite, who sang "Arkansas Blues," Alice Leslie Carter, singing "Decatur Street Blues," Daisy Martin, with "If You Don't Believe I Love You," and the "Southern Nightingale," Trixie Smith (1895–1943), who won the silver loving cup for her own song, "Trixie Blues." Trixie was immediately signed by Harry Pace for his recently established Black Swan label.

In 1922, as in 1921, at least 50 Blues records were issued, without satisfying the demand. Between 1920 and 1942, "almost 5,500 blues and 1,250 gospel records, involving all told about 1,200 artists" were released.[5]

Bessie Smith

The year 1923 witnessed the rise of Bessie Smith, soon recognized as the biggest-selling blues artist of the era. Her recordings are still extant in a two-record set, titled *The World's Greatest Blues Singer,* and in a four-volume anthology, *The Bessie Smith Story.*[6]

"Of all the great vocal artists I've been lucky enough to produce," John Hammond has said, in an introductory note to the two-volume set, "including Billie Holiday, Mildred Bailey, Peggy Lee, Joe Turner, and Dinah Washington, Bessie Smith is the most powerful and the most original." Frank Walker, who produced her first sides, said: "I never heard anything like the torture and torment she put into the music of her people."[7]

These strong reactions have been shared in different ways by the musicians who worked with Bessie. "She dominated the stage," guitarist/banjoist Danny Barker (b. 1909) said. "You didn't turn your head when she went on." Drummer Zutty Singleton (1898–1975) said: "She always did pack the Lyric Theater in New Orleans, every show, with big lines always waiting. She was a *big* woman with that beautiful bronze color and stern features. Stately just like a queen. . . ." Reedman Buster Bailey (1902–1967) said: "She had a powerful pair of lungs. There was no microphone in those days. She could fill up Carnegie Hall, Madison Square Garden, or a cabaret. . . . Bessie was the Louis Armstrong of the blues singers." White reedman Mezz Mezzrow (1899–1972) recalled: "She was tall and brown-skinned, with great big dimples creasing her cheeks, dripping good looks—just this side of voluptuous, buxom and massive, but stately, too, shapely as a hourglass, with a high-voltage magnet for a personality. . . ."[8]

Novelist and patron of the arts Carl Van Vechten, at whose apartment she sang, had this to say about her: "It was the real thing—a woman cutting her heart open with a knife until it was exposed for us all to see, so that we suffered as she suffered, exposed with a rhythmic ferocity, indeed, which could hardly be borne."[9] Songwriter/Blues singer Alberta Hunter remembered:

> Bessie Smith was the greatest of them all. There never was one like her and there'll never be one like her again. Even though she was raucous and loud, she had a sort of tear—no, not a tear, but there was *misery* in what she did. It was as though there was something she had to get out, something she just had to bring to the fore. Nobody, least of all today, could ever match Bessie.[10]

It was Alberta's song, *Down Hearted Blues,* with music by bandleader Lovie Austin (1887–1972), that became the first side Bessie cut, on February 16, 1923. She was accompanied just by pianist/songwriter Clarence Williams (1898–1965), whom Frank Walker, Columbia's A and R Director, remembering her from an Alabama honky-tonk, had sent to find her in the South. The released record, on which she was curiously billed, "Comedienne," was the product of a second session, on February 17. Although the song was selling on several labels, on a piano roll, and on a Paramount record by Alberta Hunter herself, *Down Hearted Blues* became a hit for Bessie. "We thought it was exhausted," Alberta later said, "but it sold 780,000 copies!"[11]

Between 1923 and her last session, in December 1933, Bessie

cut 180 sides for Columbia; the masters of 20 have been lost. The good years were between 1923 and 1927, when Bessie produced such classics as "Baby, Won't You Please Come Home," "Keeps on A-Rainin' (Papa, He Can't Make No Time)," and " 'Tain't Nobody's Bizness If I Do," accompanied by Clarence Williams; the pseudo-Spiritual, "Moan You Moaners," accompanied by James P. Johnson and the Bessemer Singers; "St. Louis Blues," with Louis Armstrong on cornet; "Yellow Dog Blues," with a combo that included Coleman Hawkins (tenor sax), Buster Bailey (clarinet), and Fletcher Henderson (piano).

But even after she had passed her peak and various excesses began to take their toll, there were such memorable sides as the rent-party song, "Gimme a Pigfoot" (1933), with a combo that included Jack Teagarden (trombone), Frankie Newton (trumpet), Chu Berry (tenor sax), and Benny Goodman (clarinet); "Me and My Gin" (1928), with Joe Williams on trombone and Porter Grainger at the piano; and the immortal "Nobody Knows You When You're Down and Out" (1929), with Clarence Williams (piano), Ed Allen (cornet), and Cyrus St. Clair (tuba). By the time she recorded these last two songs, they had inescapable autobiographical overtones.

A heavy drinker from the years when she was performing in cheap tent-shows, carnivals, and honky-tonks, she became profligate in her consumption of food, liquor, and sex. Breaking with Frank Walker, who handled her affairs with scrupulous honesty and intelligence, she quickly misspent her earnings, mishandled her affairs (assisted by her husband, a Philadelphia policeman), and, with changes in public taste and her arrogance in choosing inferior material for recording, was soon "down and out." Where she had once toured in her own Pullman train and was recognized as the highest-paid entertainer on the Negro vaudeville circuit, by 1928 she had to accept work at any price to cover expenses and was taking engagements for which she had to sing bawdy, third-rate Blues or do mammy routines in costume.

By 1931 Frank Walker reluctantly conceded that Bessie was finished as a recording artist. Her last session, on November 24, 1933, was largely a sentimental gesture, engineered by John Hammond. It was the only one she made in the last six years of her life. Where she had once commanded $1000 a session, in 1933 the best she could get was a flat $50 a side—"and the sales at that time," according to Hammond, "did not justify that expense."[12]

On a Sunday afternoon in 1936, Bessie Smith made her one appearance on 52nd St., then in its heyday as the Mecca of Jazz. It was a jam session sponsored by the United Hot Clubs of America at the Famous Door. It was, perhaps, as a result of this brief appearance that Hammond began considering a comeback record session for Bessie. In the spring of 1937, Bessie, then on tour with Winsted's Minstrels in North Carolina, was unable to participate in a planned session. Then, on September 25, 1937, on the eve of Hammond's departure for Mississippi to bring her back to New York, Bessie was in a car crash just below Clarksdale.

> "Her arm was almost tore out of its socket," Mezz Mezzrow said. They brought her to the hospital but it seemed like there wasn't any room for her just then—the people around there didn't care for the color of her skin. The car turned around and drove away, with Bessie's blood dripping on the floor mat. She was finally admitted to another hospital where the officials must have been color-blind, but by that time, she had lost so much blood that they couldn't operate on her, and a little later she died . . . That was how the lonesome road ended up for the greatest folk singer this country ever had—with Jim Crow directing the traffic.[13]

Mezzrow's charge that racism contributed to Bessie's death had its beginnings in a 1937 *Down Beat* story by John Hammond, which bore the headline: "Did Bessie Smith Bleed to Death While Waiting for Medical Aid?" Hammond stated bluntly: "She was refused treatment because of her color and bled to death while waiting for attention"—but he did ask Mississippi citizens to confirm the story. Protests from Mississippi hospital authorities prompted *Down Beat* quickly to publish a second article, acknowledging that Bessie had been taken to a black hospital in Clarksdale, where she died from loss of blood. Despite the "retraction," the story about her racist treatment continued to be repeated,[14] so that as late as 1960, Edward Albee wrote his prize-winning play, *The Death of Bessie Smith,* further circulating the myth.

The account of the accident, now generally accepted, appears in John Chilton's *Who's Who of Jazz:*

> On Route 61, about 10 miles north of Clarksdale, Miss., the Packard in which Bessie was a passenger, hit the back of a stationary truck. The impact sliced off the roof of the car and turned the vehicle on its right side. Shortly afterwards, the driver of the relatively undamaged truck drove from the scene of the accident to call an ambulance. Dr. Hugh Smith, a noted surgeon from Memphis, who was driving to do some night fishing, came upon the scene of the accident. He found Bessie lying on the road in critical condition, having suffered some injuries to her chest, abdomen and right arm. Having rendered first aid to Bessie, Dr. Smith and his companion began clearing the back of his car to make room for the injured woman. Shortly afterwards they were forced to jump clear just before the back of his Chevrolet was rammed by another car—two passengers in the oncoming vehicle were both

injured in the collision. Two ambulances arrived, one drove Bessie to the Afro-American Hospital in Clarksdale. After being operated on for the amputation of her right arm, she died at 11:30 A.M. from a combination of shock and severe injuries. She was buried in the Mount Lawn Cemetery, near Darby, Pa.[15]

Shortly after her death, John Hammond wrote:

To my way of thinking, Bessie Smith was the greatest artist American jazz ever produced; in fact, I'm not sure that her art did not go beyond the limits of the term 'jazz.' She was one of those rare beings, a completely integrated artist capable of projecting her whole personality into music. She was blessed not only with great emotion but with a tremendous voice that could penetrate the inner recesses of the listener.[16]

Mahalia Jackson (1911–1972), the Queen of Gospel Music, said: "Bessie was my favorite but I never let people know I listened to her. Mamie Smith, the other famous blues singer, had a pretty voice, but Bessie's had more soul in it. She dug right down and kept it in you. Her music haunted you even when she stopped singing."[17]

Ma Rainey

While performing in Chattanooga, Tennessee, where she was born sometime between 1895 and 1900 on a date that cannot be verified, teenage Bessie Smith had the good fortune to be heard by Gertrude Melissa Nix Pridgett. Ma Rainey, as Gertrude Pridgett came to be known (Rainey was her married name), was traveling through Chattanooga with the Rabbit Foot Minstrels. She was so impressed by young Bessie that she arranged to take her on tour—a child singer in short skirts—and made Bessie her protégée. The two became major exponents of Classic Blues, southern style, a barrelhouse style that went with singing in tent, medicine, carnival, and circus shows.

Although Ma Rainey was 13 or more years older than Bessie, she did not make her own record debut until the year after Bessie scored with "Down Hearted Blues." But at 14 she made her local debut in Columbus, her native city, at the opera house, in a show titled, *A Bunch of Blackberries,* and by 1902 began singing the Blues. With her husband, William "Pa" Rainey, she worked for the Tolliver Circus for several years (1914–1916).

Her recording career, involving some 90-odd titles on the Paramount label, was sandwiched into four years, 1924–1928. She is best remembered for "See See Rider," one of the most famous and most recorded of all Blues songs. Hers was the first recording of that song, giving her a hold on the copyright, and one of the best of the more than 100 versions. The southern country tenor of much of her repertoire is suggested by recordings of such traditional Delta blues as "Bo Weevil Blues," "Lost Wandering Blues," "Levee Camp Moan," "Southern Blues," and "Moonshine Blues." The last title was frequently her opening number as she emerged onstage from the horn of a large, old-style Victrola.

Although she toured on the black vaudeville circuit, her style was in the raw, earthy spirit of down-home Blues. She made a number of recordings with Jazz artists, including Louis Armstrong, Kid Ory (trombone), Buster Bailey, Don Redman (saxes), Coleman Hawkins, Tommy Ladnier (trumpet), Fletcher Henderson and Claude Hopkins (piano), and Willie "The Lion" Smith, calling the groups the Wildcat Jazz Band or the Georgia Jazz Band. She also worked with two guitars, and with guitar and banjo. Toward the end of her career on Paramount, she recorded with Tampa Red (1900–1981) and Georgia Tom (b. 1899), cutting such songs as "Sleep Talking Blues," "Runaway Blues," and "Sweet Rough Man."

A short, round-faced, homely woman with a frankly expressed yen for young boys, she performed onstage wearing a necklace of 20-dollar gold pieces—and there was gold in the uneven teeth of her grin. She retired comfortably in 1935 after the death of her mother and sister, spending her time running two theaters she had bought in Columbus and Rome, Georgia, the Lyric and the Airdrome. Little known in the North, she had a tremendous following in the South, and influenced the styles of many down-home Blues artists, starting with Bessie Smith. In 1984, she was the central character in a play that opened on Broadway, titled *Ma Rainey's Black Bottom.*

Novelist Alice Walker, who won a Pulitzer Prize for her novel *The Color Purple,* indicated that when she started working on the book, "I was listening to a lot of Bessie Smith, Ma Rainey, the women on the Mean Mothers album. I loved the way they dealt with sexuality, with the relationships with men. They showed you had a whole self and you were not to succumb to being somebody else's—as they would say—'play toy.' "[18]

Black-Owned Record Labels

As OKeh, Paramount, and Columbia Records all moved to establish race series in the wake of the large sale of "Crazy Blues," the first black-owned record label came into existence. The enterprising entrepreneur was Harry pace (1884–1943), who had been part of Pace and Handy, the music publishing company established as a result of the collaboration of the two on several songs. Pace was a professor of Greek and Latin at Lincoln University in Missouri when he and W. C. Handy, then a teacher of music in Memphis, began working together. By 1918, the company had grown so large, due to Handy's Blues compositions and to recordings by Bert Williams, that it was moved from Memphis's Beale Street to New York City. Three years later, after Pace and Handy dissolved their partnership, Harry Pace established the Pace Record Company, and launched the Black Swan label. It was named in honor of Elizabeth Taylor Greenfield, the nation's first black opera singer, who was known as the Black Swan.

Pace started his operation conservatively in the basement of his home at 2289 Seventh Avenue, but was so successful that, within a year, he moved to a formal office at 257 West 138th Street. In his opening *Chicago Defender* announcement, he described his company thus: "Only bonafide Racial company making talking machine records. All stockholders are colored, all artists are colored, all employees are colored." He added: "Only company using Racial Artists in recording high class song records. This company made the only Grand Opera records ever made by Negroes."

Having appointed Fletcher Henderson (1898–1952) as recording director and William Grant Still (1895–1978) as arranger and later music director, he proceeded to release disks by Alberta Hunter, Ethel Waters, Trixie Smith, and Lucille Hegamin—three of them classic Blues singers. Ethel Waters's "Down Home Blues," together with Alberta Hunter's "How Long, Sweet Daddy, How Long," became Black Swan's first hit disks, garnering such sales that Pace sent Ethel Waters on the road with the Black Swan Troubadours, led by Fletcher Henderson, to promote the company's product.

Black Swan's product reached into several areas besides the Blues. Included were baritone and soprano solos, vaudeville duos, violin solos, vocal groups, dance orchestras, and jazz bands. Having purchased the Olympic Disc Record Company in April 1922, Pace even began issuing records by white singers from the Olympic catalogue, reneging on his promise to be exclusively black. It all came to a rapid, dismal end. Price-cutting by the established labels and, unquestionably, Black Swan's too-rapid expansion forced Pace to declare bankruptcy in December 1923. In March 1924 Black Swan was absorbed by Paramount.

Just three years later, a second attempt to establish a black-owned record label also failed. The ambitious executive was J. Mayo Williams, who had done an exceptional job in building the race roster of Paramount Records, including the acquisition of Ma Rainey. In May 1927, having left his Paramount post, Williams announced the formation of the Chicago Record Company and the first release on his Black Patti label. As Harry Pace had named his label after a black opera singer, Williams honored Sissieretta Jones, the concert singer known as Black Patti. Like black Swan, Black Patti was a conglomeration of choirs, Jazz bands, Blues singers, and even included two white crooners. Williams's venture did not last the year. By August 1927, Black Patti was out of business and Williams was functioning as talent scout for Vocalion Records' 1000 race series.

A number of other short-lived labels, not necessarily owned by blacks, came into existence as a result of the Blues explosion. In November 1920, in Orange, New Jersey, a small company named Arto began releasing disks by blues singer Lucille Hegamin, and even achieved a substantial seller with her version of "I'll Be Good but I'll Be Lonesome," b/w "Arkansas Blues." The company went bankrupt in 1923. Before this, Cameo Records signed Lucille Hegamin to an exclusive contract, and released a flock of her recordings before its demise. In Los Angeles, two black music-store proprietors launched an "all-colored" label, Sunshine Records, that lasted for three releases.

In March 1922 a black vaudeville team produced six records on its C & S label and vanished. Two labels that announced formative plans but apparently never released disks were Echo Records—OKeh spelled backward?—and an abortive attempt at a company that W. C. Handy advertised. Ajax Records, manufactured by the Compo Company of Quebec, lasted from October 1923 to August 1925, during which its releases included recordings by Mamie Smith and Monette Moore (1902–1962), a Texan who performed at Connie's Inn between 1927 and 1932 and later served as Ethel Waters's understudy in *As Thousands Cheer* and *At Home Abroad*. Meritt Records, produced by a singer/music-store owner of Kansas City, operated from late 1925 until about 1929, when the Winston Holmes Music Company, as it was called, after its black owner, went out of business.[19]

Considering the contribution of black artists to popular music, it is ironic that no black-owned label developed into a substantial enterprise until the 1960s, with the formation of the Motown complex. Before Motown, there was Vee Jay Records of Chicago, which was a thriving label for almost 10 years before it went bankrupt. Of this, and the success of Philadelphia International, founded in the 1970s, more later.

Delta and Country Blues

With the market for Blues records continuing to expand, the search for talent became critical. Once the available female vaudevillians —the classic Blues singers—had been signed and recorded, the companies had only one direction in which to go. They began to send field units into the South to the towns and cities in which the Blues had originated and been developed. Godrich and Dixon report that, between 1927 and 1930, "Atlanta was visited seventeen times by field units in search of race talent, Memphis eleven times, Dallas eight times, New Orleans seven times, and so on."[20]

In addition to field trips by traveling units with portable equipment, record companies employed scouts, many of them owners of music stores, to ferret out local talent. Among the best known of these was Henry C. Speir, who owned a music store on North Farrow Street in Jackson, Mississippi.[21] Midway on a line between Meridian to the east and Vicksburg to the west, Jackson is outside the Delta region, an area formed by the Mississippi River (to the west) and the Yazoo River (to the east), with Memphis as roughly the most northerly point and Vicksburg the most southerly. Looking like an elongated sweet potato on a map, the area is regarded as the most likely and, certainly, the most important, source of the Blues.

Speir scouted for Paramount Records of Grafton, Wisconsin. It was he who sent Charley Patton (1887–1934), generally recognized as the Father of Delta Blues, to Arthur Laibley, a Paramount producer. As a result, Patton made his first recording ("Pony Blues") at the Gennett Record Studios in Richmond, Indiana, on Friday, June 14, 1929. Later, in 1933, when the recording industry was suffering from the Great Depression, Speir made test recordings of Patton, Willie Lee Brown (1900–1952), and Son House (b. 1902), and sent them to W. R. Callaway and Art Satherly of American Record Company (ARC). Callaway came from New York to record what were Patton's last sides (on Vocalion), in January 1934. On this date, Patton also recorded duets with Bertha Lee, the young woman, many years his junior, who was Patton's common-law wife until his death later that year from a heart ailment.

Speir was also responsible for getting Nehemiah Skip James (1902–1969) and a score of other bluesmen on wax, making the Paramount catalogue the most important source of Delta Blues. James recorded 26 sides in February 1931. Through Charley Patton, Son House also made his first recordings for Paramount in the summer of 1930, producing some of his most compelling performances in "Dry Spell Blues," "My Black Mama," and, especially, "Preachin' the Blues."

Ralph Limbo, or Lumbo, who was located in Itta Bena, Mississippi, was another store owner—mainly of furniture, including phonographs—who served as a field scout. Through a deal he made with Ralph Peer, Victor's recording director, Bukka White (1906–1977) recorded 14 sides in May 1930, including the classic "Panama Limited" and "The New 'Frisco Train." Booker T. Washington White, as he was baptized, who wanted to be a "great man like Charley Patton" and was tough enough to be known as "Barrelhouse" in Parchman Penitentiary (where he spent two years), built on Patton's raw vocal style and hard rhythmic thrust.

Jesse Johnson, who was married to Blues singer Edith North Johnson (b. 1905) and operated the De Luxe Music Shop in St. Louis, served as talent scout for several labels, including OKeh and Paramount. (Edith, who recorded for QRS, Paramount, OKeh, Vocalion, and Brunswick in 1928–1929, was herself a talent scout.) Johnson was an aggressive promoter who used airplanes to publicize new record releases via circulars dropped on crowds at baseball games. In 1925 he sponsored a talent contest for Blues singers, which netted Lonnie Johnson (1889–1970) a seven-year contract with OKeh. Johnson's role was so widely known that when Victoria Spivey, who was born in Houston, wanted to make records at age 16, she traveled to St. Louis to see Jesse. Several days later she was in a recording studio, cutting tunes, for an OKeh field unit, that included her well-known "Black Snake Blues."

In 1923 Polk Brockman, who was OKeh's distributor in Atlanta as well as a talent scout, arranged for recording director Ralph Peer, himself the son of a Missouri storekeeper, to bring equipment to record a favorite hillbilly singer, Fiddlin' John Carson. But advance notice of Peer's arrival attracted a long line of local talent to the Nassau Street loft where he set up a makeshift studio. Peer's recording of two little-known local Blues singers, Lucille Bogan and Fannie Goosby, became the first race records made outside of New York and Chicago. It led to OKeh's boasting in ads that new race artists "have been discovered by special recording expeditions into the South."[22] OKeh might also have boasted that Peer's trip led to the birth of the hillbilly industry.

Sometimes a local record store served as an ad hoc recording studio. This was the case in July 1927, when Gennett Records went to Birmingham, Alabama, and proceeded to record local talent, a preacher, quartet, harmonica player, and Blues singers, all unfortunately undistinguished.

But on the many field trips, the companies recorded an enormous number of root groups and Blues singers, virtually all of them men and some of them soon forgotten: jug bands such as Cannon's

Jug Stompers, Memphis Jug Band, Whistler's Jug Band, King David's Jug Band, and Birmingham Jug Band; quartets including the Mt. Zion Baptist Quartet, Morris Brown Quartet, and southern college and university quartets; such gospel solo singers and groups as Rev. J. M. Gates and the Memphis Sanctified Singers, Birmingham Jubilee Singers, Seventh Day Adventists' Choir, and Heavenly Gospel Singers.

Out of this rash of recording activity, a number of major figures emerged in the years between 1926 and the onset of the Depression. It was during this time that the down-home, or Delta, sound of the Blues entered popular music. Because of the isolation of these bluesmen from white and Pop/Jazz influences, their style was more immediately derived from the field holler and the gang-work song than those of other bluesmen. Their vocal style, as Sam Charters has described it, was "hard and unrelenting, the voice unusually heavy, the tone produced in the back of the throat with rougher growling tones, and the falsetto voice used for contrast or emotional strength."

The Origin of the Blues: Delta Blues

A number of notable bluesmen came to the fore as a result of record-company treks into the South. Among those who helped document Delta Blues, there were Charley Patton, Bukka White, Son House, Robert Johnson, Willie Brown, John Hurt, and Sonny Boy Williamson.

Dating the beginnings of the Blues is largely an exercise in conjecture, since its origin is shrouded in the distant days before recordings might have provided documentation. Moreover, as a folk art transmitted orally, the Blues attracted musicologists later than the Spirituals, which began to be notated during the Civil War. Symptomatic is the contrast between *Slave Songs of the United States,* which was published in 1867, and the watershed collection, *Blues: An Anthology,* produced by W. C. Handy in 1926.

But let me hazard the idea that we can, with some measure of understanding and, perhaps, even accuracy, fix the likely beginnings of the Blues by considering the psychology and sociology of the form.[24] In this connection, the blues of the Delta bluesmen are particularly revealing.

In the 70 titles Patton recorded before his death, there are details of place, people, and incidents that give his work a distinctly local, if not autobiographical, character. In "Tom Rushen," whose title identifies a local sheriff, we meet a Mr. Holloway and a Tom

Day, the latter a sheriff of Bolivar County before Rushen, who arrested him for drunkenness. In "High Sheriff Blues," alcohol also accounts for Patton's difficulties, only the scene is Belzoni, in Humphreys County, where the sheriff was a Mr. Ware, and a plantation owner, Mr. Purvis, apparently tried to arrange his release through a Mr. Webb.

The floods of 1927 provoked Patton's longest blues, "High Water Everywhere," in which fear of the onrushing waters leads him to consider the various places to which he might flee — Greensville, Rosedale, Vicksburg, Sharkey County, Stover, Tallahatchie, Blytheville, and Joiner — all of which he enumerates. But the water keeps "risin'" ominously, with "families sinkin' down," "fifty men and children, come to sink and drown," — which leads to his final crushing line: "I couldn't see nobody home an' was no one to be found."

More significant than the localization marking Patton's blues is the personalization. "They run me from Will Dockery's," he sings in "Thirty-four Blues," naming a place where he farmed from childhood and from which he was dismissed. He goes on to interweave his own economic problems with those engendered by the Great Depression, with "women and children flaggin' freight trains for rides." In "High Sheriff" he explains that for him "thirty days seem like years in a jailhouse where there is no booze. . . . It takes boozey booze, Lord, to carry me through. . . ."

By contrast, when Bukka White is in jail, he does not miss booze, but his wife and children. In "Parchman Farm Blues," having indicated that he was given a life sentence, he laments: "I wouldn't hate it so bad, but I left my wife and my home." In "Sleepy Man Blues," where he describes himself as being "troubled in mind," he does not resort to alcohol, as Patton might have. What he wants instead is "to sleep all the time," for "he knows if he can sleep all the time/The trouble won't worry his mind."

Born Booker T. Washington White on November 12, 1906, Bukka White learned to sing in church and became acquainted with the guitar as a youngster, through his father, who was a musician and a fireman on the M & O railroad. Working on his uncle's farm or carrying water for a local construction gang, he dreamed of being as popular as Charley Patton, whom he saw at plantation shows. In the summer of 1937, according to reports, he shot a man. Set free on bond, he fled to Chicago, where, in the middle of a September recording session for ARC, arranged by producer/publisher Lester Melrose, he was apprehended by the Mississippi sheriff. The two sides that were released sold so well that Melrose worked at getting White out of jail, a procedure that took two years. But in that period of separation from his family and the deprivations endured at Parchman Farm, White wrote one of the most moving, introspective series of Blues about prison life ever produced. Although he recorded two Blues when Alan Lomax visited the prison for the Library of Congress in May 1939, he did the bulk of the Parchman Prison songs in March 1940, on the ARC labels OKeh and Vocalion, after his release.

Seldom has the dismal sense of being a prisoner been communicated with such deep feeling as in his simple song, "I wonder how long 'fore I can change my clothes." Prison garb was obviously not very protective in the rain and cold. But more consequential was the feeling of shame: "Walking down the road," he sings, "I could hardly walk with looking down on my clothes." And consider the poignance of his closing line: "Never will I forget that day when they taken my [civilian] clothes and throwed them away."

Suffering from a fever, he laments the absence of his wife to comfort him: "They don't allow my lover come and take my hand." But he also fantasizes: "They say it ain't the fever, just your lover has another man." And he concludes: "I want my lover come and drive my fever away/Repeat/Doctor says you do me more good than he would in all his days."

Looking at himself in the mirror one day, he decides he is "looking funny in my eyes," and adds, "I believe I'm fixin' to die." Acknowledging his awareness that he is born to die, what troubles him is the effect of his death on his children: "I hate to leave my children crying." He thinks back to his departure for prison and the tears shed for so many nights by his wife, "who treated me, children, like I was her baby child." And so, in his imagination, he pleads with hs wife: "Mother, take my children back/before they let me down/And don't leave them screaming and crying on the graveyard ground."

Delta Blues reached a high point of artistic beauty in the affecting simplicity of Bukka White's poetry, the result of the introspective character of his writing.

Eddie James House, Jr., known as Son House, was born on a farm outside of Lyon, Mississippi, in 1902, and did not start playing the guitar until he was 26 years old. The impetus came from a chance encounter with a bottleneck guitarist who drew such a crowd that Son was overwhelmed. He went and bought himself a $1.50 guitar, which Willie Wilson repaired for him and from whom he learned his first song. Two years later, he made his first recordings for Paramount. He received $40 for the session.

"Forty dollars!" he exclaimed to an interviewer. "Making it that easy and quick! It'd take me near about a whole year to make forty dollars in the cotton patch."[25]

Among the songs he recorded in the session was "Preachin' the Blues," a title that embodies an ambivalence from which Son suffered all through his life. He had been brought up in the church, and until he himself began playing guitar, became angry when he saw a man with a guitar singing the Blues. Although he enjoyed the benefits derived from being a bluesman, he was unable to resolve the conflict within himself between the spiritual rewards of the Christian life and the "sinfulness" of the Blues life. "I can't hold God in one hand," he would say, "and the Devil in the other."[26]

Another song he recorded in his first session, "Dry Spell Blues," documented the suffering of people during a drought that parched all the cotton and corn, forcing some to become moonshiners for a livelihood—all at a time when pork chops were "forty-five cents a pound and cotton is only ten." The churchgoer in House came out in the concluding stanza: "Oh, Lord, have mercy if you please/Make your rain come down and give our poor hearts ease. . . ."

Thirty years after he recorded "Preachin' the Blues," Son House was still talking about the Blues versus the church. Samuel Charters cites an unnamed observer who remembered seeing Son at a performance with Charley Patton when "House got drunk and climbed up on a table to give a sermon."[27] The persistent anxiety and inner turmoil contributed a heightened emotionalism to his work, characteristic of Delta Blues at its best.

The bluesman who brought that tradition to a peak of autobiographical richness and poetic expressiveness was Robert Johnson (c. 1912–1938), who studied guitar as a youngster by watching Son House at performances. Johnson recorded the fewest sides of the influential Delta bluesmen—just 29 in five brief sessions, three in San Antonio, in November 1936, and two in Dallas, in June 1937. When Vocalion sought him for another date, in 1938, he was dead.

Johnson's death is shrouded in mystery. "He was poisoned," according to Johnny Shines, who worked with him, "by one of those women who really didn't care for him at all. . . . That was down in Eudora, Mississippi. . . . And I heard that it was something to do with the black arts. . . ."[28] Son House heard three different accounts: In one, Johnson was stabbed to death by a jealous husband; in another, stabbed by a woman; and in a third, that he was poisoned.[29] The most recent research verifies murder by a jealous husband. Dying at 26, Johnson contributed to the romantic legend, described alliteratively by Peter Guralnick, of the artist, "doomed, haunted, dead at an early age, desperate, driven—a brief flickering of tormented genius."[30]

With his limited output and abbreviated life, Johnson has exercised a degree of influence that underlines the awe in which he was held by his contemporaries as well as his "teacher," Son House. "The first one [of his records] I heard," House told Julius Lester, "was *Terraplane Blues*. Jesus, it was good. We all admired it."[31] The first song learned by the great Muddy Waters (1915–1983) was Johnson's "Walking Blues." Elmore James (1918–1963) named his group the Broomdusters after Johnson's song, "I Believe I'll Dust My Broom," which was his theme. "Ramblin' on My Mind" was Johnny Shine's favorite song. Rock artist Johnny Winter is said to have learned to play the guitar by making an intensive study of Johnson's first album. Recovering from a nervous breakdown, the result of a broken love affair, British guitarist Eric Clapton adapted the melody of Johnson's "Love in Vain" to express his longing for Patti Harrison.

What accounts for this far-reaching impact is not only the power of Johnson's performances but also the immediacy of his poetry. His songs were introspectively autobiographical: The man in his blues is the weird, sexually driven, devil-hounded wanderer his contemporaries knew. A shy man who could not face a group of strange musicians he was asked to play for, he was completely uncontrolled in his aggressiveness toward women. "He'd go up to a girl he saw at one of the dances," Son House said, "and try to take her off, no matter who was around, her husband or boyfriend or anybody."[32] Whether their names are real or not, the number of different girls mentioned by name in his songs hints at the intensity of his sexuality.

Legend has it that Johnson met a giant black man (the Devil) at a crossroad and had his guitar tuned and handed back to him, invested with magical power.[33] But Johnson was not just aided by the Devil; he was terrorized by him, as he sang in "Hellhound on My Trail," and possessed by him, as he chanted in "Me and the Devil." Mistreating his "sweet little rider," he consoles her: "When I'm dead and gone/ You may bury my body down by the highway side/So my old evil spirit can get a Greyhound bus and ride. . . ."

"I have to ride the blinds," Johnson sings in "Walking Blues." Johnny Shines has said: "If anybody said to him, 'Let's go!' It didn't matter to him where it was they were going; he'd just take off and go. It didn't matter what time of day or night it was."[34]

The memory that Johnson's fellow bluesmen had of him was of the man mirrored in his Blues. He was in constant flight, driven by fears, imagined or real, unwilling or unable to elicit any response from women except sexual, paranoid in terms of seeing enemies around him, blocking his passway with stones (as he says in "Stones in My Passway"), always traveling a road "dark as night." It was a life of terror, but one that produced poetry with an emotional wallop and expressive intensity unapproached by any of his contemporaries.

In the Blues of all four Delta bluesmen, one finds a chronicle of personal experiences that allows each to emerge as an identifiable individual. This type of self-description, self-exploration, self-projection was largely impossible for Afro-Americans until after the Civil War.

During the slavery years, black folk were not only owned by the slaveholder, as horses and cattle were possessions, but they were part of a conclave in which they had no rights, no power, and, literally, no existence as individuals. The children of slaves frequently did not even bear the surname of their fathers, but of the slave owner. The average slave could not think of himself as "I," except, perhaps, on those occasions when out of reach and hearing of the white overseer, a cotton-picker could pretend to be singing but was actually "conversing" with a not-too-distant slave in a type of fragmented melody, later known as a *holler* or *arhoolie*. (And, of course, hollers are regarded as the most likely antecedents of the Blues.)

It was not until the slave became self-dependent, not until the family unit superseded the communal unit of slavery, not until "we" became "I," that the door to personalized expression was opened. This did not occur until some time after the issuance of the Emancipation Proclamation and, more specifically, the adoption of the Thirteenth and Fifteenth Amendments, between 1865 and 1870. These abolished slavery and guaranteed blacks the rights of citizenship and the right to vote. These constitutional amendments were adopted during the era of Reconstruction, sometimes also known as "the tragic era."

Now the slave was free—free to own land, free to move about, "free" to declare his preference as an individual at the ballot box, free to choose his employer and place of employment, and free to take care of dependents. Can one conceive of the psychological change that occurred in Afro-Americans as a result of this changed status? "Changed outlook" would be a more realistic description, since Southern whites—through the Ku Klux Klan; intimidation, violence, lynchings; and discriminatory legislation—sought to prevent blacks from exercising these rights.

As we know, blacks—they were then known as *freedmen*—had to struggle to gain these constitutional rights, not just during the Reconstruction era but for decades. Yet the potential existed. True, having never worked for wages and lacking finances, blacks might still be forced to become sharecroppers or tenant farmers, so that economics deprived them of some of their new freedoms. But now they had dependents, whereas once their dependents were not theirs, but possessions, as they were, housed, clothed, and fed, as they were. With dependents, they were now the heads of families, facing the challenges and the fears of being self-sufficient, of making lives for themselves, in short, of becoming *individuals*.

Was it not inevitable that in this difficult period of adjustment, Afro-Americans would begin ruminating about their new world, its promises and deprivations? Herein we have the beginnings of the expressiveness of the Blues. It remained a rural folk art during the latter decades of the nineteenth century, transmitted orally, until, after the turn of the century, it erupted in the incandescent, personalized poetry of the Delta bluesmen and others.

In his autobiography, *Father of the Blues*, W. C. Handy mentions the years between 1892 and 1903 as those in which he first heard and was moved by the sound of the Blues.[35] Big Bill Broonzy (1893–1958) likewise thinks of the 1890s as the period in which he heard his uncle, Jerry Belcher, play and sing "Joe Turner Blues," the first Blues he remembered.[36] This time slot accords with my thought that the sociological and economic atmosphere of the Reconstruction era, roughly 1865–1877, initiated psychological changes in the outlook of Afro-Americans that found expression first in folk Blues and ultimately in the creative subjectivity of twentieth-century bluesmen.

Although Mississippi was the source of the most important and the greatest number of bluesmen, other southern states contributed vital figures to down-home blues. From Texas came Blind Lemon Jefferson (1897–1929), who recorded mostly for Paramount; whose lead boys included T-Bone Walker (1910–1975), Leadbelly (1889–1949), and Josh White (1908–1969); and whose affective blues, "See That My Grave Is Kept Clean," was recorded by Bob Dylan (b. 1941) in his debut album. Texas also accounted for Henry Thomas (1874–?), who was known as Ragtime Texas; Texas Alexander (c. 1880–c. 1955), who recorded mostly on OKeh and worked frequently with his cousin, Lightnin' Hopkins; and Sam "Lightnin'" Hopkins (b. 1912). One of the most prolific writers of the Blues, Mack McCormick said of Hopkins: "His only understanding of music is that it be as personal as a hushed conversation."[37]

Tennessee bluesmen included Walter "Furry" Lewis (b. 1893) whose main locale was Memphis, where, between 1908 and 1916, he worked with W. C. Handy's Orchestra or as a single, entertaining in local taverns, dance halls, house parties, fish fries, or passing tent and medicine shows, and, in the late 1920s, made recordings, mostly on Vocalion. Another important Tennessee bluesman was John Adams "Sleepy" Estes (1899–1977), one of the most recorded of down-home blues singers, with disks on many labels; a man who became a legend in his own time, appearing in the 1960s at the Newport Folk Festival and in the 1970s at the Newport Jazz Festival in New York; and whose version of Kokomo Arnold's "Milk

Cow Blues" inspired one of Elvis Presley's first recordings while he was still on the Sun label of Memphis.[38]

From Louisiana, where the Blues intersected with Jazz, came two significant bluesmen, among others. Rufus Perryman (1892–1973), known as Speckled Red, because of his pink and speckled skin pigmentation—he was an albino black—recorded for Vocalion and Brunswick in the late 1920s and for Bluebird in the late 1930s, popularizing "Dirty Dozens," the well-known insult song; and established himself as an outstanding barrelhouse and boogie pianist. Lonnie Johnson, who worked solo in the red-light district of Storyville between 1910 and 1917, recorded with both Louis Armstrong and Duke Ellington in the late 1920s; and in a long career, managed to achieve a Pop hit record, "Tomorrow Night," when he was in his late fifties. Although his beginnings were in down-home Blues, he moved successfully in a Pop/Jazz direction in time.

The Form of the Blues

Unique in its simplicity and singularity is the form in which the Blues crystallized: three chords, three lines of lyric (A-A-B), in a 12-bar sequence. Here is how it appears on paper:

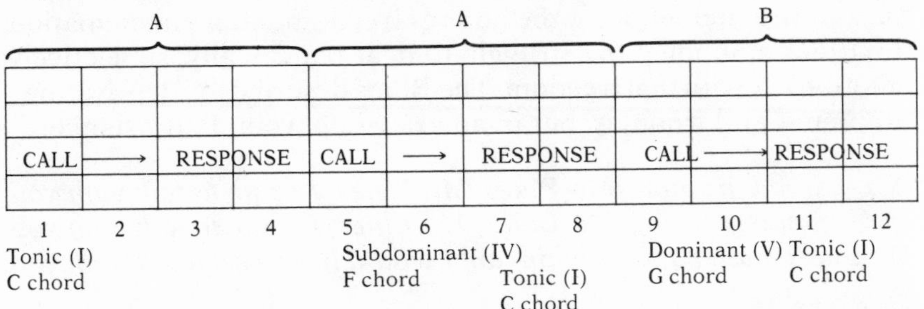

As a 12-bar form, the Blues departs from the 8-bar units of Pop (producing a 32-bar structure) and the 16-bar units of Gospel. The three-line arrangement in which the first line is repeated (A-A-B) has no counterpart in prosody. Within each 4 bars of the 12, a call-and-response pattern, deriving ultimately from African music, is maintained. In Delta, or Country, Blues, the response is made by guitar, or "harp." The scale used in the Blues is also unique, involving a flatted third and seventh, which puts it outside the major–minor diatonic system of Western music. "Bent" or "blue" notes—that is, notes that are partially flatted—give the Blues a sound of its own. Of the greatest significance is the use of these flatted or partially flatted notes over major chords.

Dictionaries today still employ the word *sad* in defining the

Blues. The mistaken characterization arises, perhaps, from the singing style of rural bluesmen, which may be described as moaning, crying, or high-pitched, nasal whining. Musically, however, the Blues does not have a sad sound, since its three chords are resolute major chords and the overall mood is not one of sadness. The clue to the character of the Blues is in the paradoxical or ambiguous relationship between the chords and the flatted melodies. What one senses is tension, and tension is as indigenous to the Blues as stress is and was to the lives of the freedmen and their descendants.

As we know, the Emancipation Proclamation and the constitutional amendments designed to make ex-slaves true citizens did not free them politically or socially. What they did was to separate them from the land and give them mobility. For the first time in over 200 years on American soil, blacks were free to go where their needs, desires, and abilities would take them. The obstacles to carving out their own destinies were tremendous. The freedom acquired by the former slave was the freedom to seek and not find, to look for work and not get it, to labor for food, shelter, and clothing and not secure them, to hunger for love and not find it. The life of the ex-slave became an exercise in deprivations and thwarted hopes.

The Blues is the music of hunger—hunger for the necessities and the pleasures of life in a free society. During slavery, the Spirituals were a metaphor for the hope of freedom. After emancipation, the Blues embodied the struggle to deal realistically, subjectively, emotionally with that freedom. The Blues describe the deprivations, problems, and troubles, but in an *existential* vein. For instance:

Good morning, Mr. Blues, Mr. Blues, I come to talk with you,
Good morning, Mr. Blues, Mr. Blues, I come to talk with you,
Mr. Blues, I ain't doin' nothin' an' I would like to get a job from you.

And there is laughter in the Blues, the laughter of looking reality in the eye:

High yeller, she'll kick you, that ain't all,
High yeller, she'll kick you, that ain't all,
When you step out at night 'nother mule in your stall.

Barbecue Bob (1902–1931)

Well, that old mule sat down when he heard what the police said.
(the police threatened to arrest him if he hit the mule)
Well, that old mule sat down when he heard what the police said.
That mule looked back at me and smiled, bucked his head and crossed his legs.

Florida Kid

"The most astonishing aspect of the Blues," Richard Wright has written, "is that though replete with a sense of defeat and downheartedness, they are not intrinsically pessimistic; their burden of woe and melancholy is dialectically redeemed through sheer force of sensuality into an almost exultant affirmation of life, of love, of sex, of movement, of hope."[39]

The Blues represent a fusion of opposites—melancholia but not without mirth, frustration but not without anticipation, despair but not without determination, suffering but not without endurance, defeat but not without hope. Out of these contrasting feelings come the emotional intensity and enduring appeal of the style.

Urban Blues

In 1933, a Blues contest was held in Chicago. The entrants included a little lady who had the face of a librarian but the musical muscle of a longshoreman. "She played guitar like a man," said Big Bill Broonzy, who was one of her competitors.[40]

The little lady came from Louisiana, born in a little town called Algiers, in either 1897 or 1900. By 15, she was singing for handouts on Memphis's Beale St., in its barbershops and saloons. Her name was Minnie Douglas. As the result of a brief marriage and collaboration with another Blues singer, Kansas City Joe McCoy (1905–1950), she became Minnie McCoy, but was best known as Memphis Minnie. A Columbia scout who happened to hear her on Beale Street trundled her up to Chicago, where she made her first of many recordings, in 1929, becoming in time associated with "Me and My Chauffeur," "Black Rat Swing," "Crazy Cryin Blues," "Picking the Blues," and "Bumble Bee," which became the basis of Muddy Waters's "Honey Bee."

In the Blues contest of 1933, Minnie performed "Lookin' the World Over" as well as "Me and My Chauffeur." According to Big Bill in his autobiography, she overwhelmed not only the audience but the judges as well.[41] Tampa Red, Sleepy John Estes, and Richard M. Jones (1892–1945), who were the judges, gave the prize to Minnie, of whom Big Bill wrote: "She can make a guitar cry, moan, talk and whistle the Blues."[42]

Memphis Minnie was part of a group of bluesmen, exiles from the South, who had begun as down-home singers, settled in Chicago in the 1920s and 1930s, and developed a style that became known as Urban Blues. Georgia Tom (Thomas A. Dorsey), born in 1899, came from Georgia at 19. Jazz Gillum (William McKinley Gillum; 1904–1966) came from Mississippi at 19. Washboard Sam (Robert Brown;

1910–1966) came from Arkansas at 22. Sonny Boy (John Lee) Williamson of Jackson, Tennessee (1914–1948), came to Chicago at the age of 23. Bumble Bee Slim (Amos Easton), born in 1905, came from Georgia at 25, and Tampa Red (Hudson Whittaker) migrated from Georgia at 25. Big Bill (1893–1958) arrived in Chicago in 1920 at the age of 27.

A photograph of the period shows a paunchy, white-haired man, surrounded by a group of bluesmen. To his right were Jazz Gillum and Big Bill with his guitar; seated below him, Washboard Sam; and to his left, Roosevelt Sykes (1906–1983) and St. Louis Jimmy (James Oden), 1903–1977. The gent around whom these bluesmen were clustered was Lester Melrose, who originally owned a music store in Chicago, and became after a time the most powerful figure in the Chicago blues scene—manager of many artists, record producer, talent scout, contractor, and music publisher.[43]

After the Depression, the Blues underwent changes that were the result not only of the migration of bluesmen, already mentioned, but of developments in the recording scene. During the Depression, virtually all of the race series launched by the main record companies were phased out, starting with Columbia's 14000D series in 1931. By 1937, when the ARC black dime-store labels were discontinued, Paramount's 12000 series, Vocalion's 1000, Victor's 23250, OKeh's 8000, and Perfect's 100 had all been withdrawn. However, in 1934 Decca established its all-important 7000 series, and in 1932 the Bluebird label began its noteworthy flight.

"Noteworthy" because, in the 1930s, the era when the Blues became urbanized, Chicago became the hub of Blues recording as a result of the Bluebird label. Two men were central to this development, Lester Melrose and Big Bill Broonzy. Melrose managed, among others, Bumble Bee Slim, Washboard Sam, Casey Bill (b. 1909), and Lil Johnson. He published Arthur "Big Boy" Crudup (1905–1974), whose recording career began when Melrose heard him on a Chicago street, who sued Melrose for nonpayment of royalties toward the end of his life,[44] and who was a major influence on Elvis Presley. Working with Bluebird, Vocalion, and the new Decca of Jack and David Kapp, Melrose was instrumental in securing recording dates for a large and varied number of Blues artists, including Tampa Red, Lonnie Johnson, Memphis Slim, Memphis Minnie, Victoria Spivey, Sonny Boy Williamson, Tommy McClennan (whom he went down to Mississippi to fetch at Big Bill's urging), Bukka White, whose release from Parchman Penitentiary he secured, and even Muddy Waters before he began recording for the Chess brothers. Bassist/songwriter Willie Dixon also recorded for Melrose before he became Loenard Chess's right-hand man.

In the period when Melrose was in charge of Bluebird Records, Victor's new race subsidiary, Big Bill Broonzy became the house guitarist and the contractor who selected musicians for record sessions. It was a powerful post that contributed to his becoming the central figure of Urban Blues. Of 1,200 bluesmen with record releases between 1920 and 1942, according to Dixon and Godrich, Big Bill and Tampa Red each had the greatest number, more than 100 disks. Broonzy was named by young Presley, together with Big Boy Crudup, as one of "the real low-down Mississippi singers" to whom he was forbidden to listen. The illustrious British guitarist Eric Clapton also singled out Big Bill as one of the early bluesmen he "dug."

William Lee Conley Broonzy, born in Scott, Mississippi, and raised in Arkansas, arrived in Chicago at the age of 27, in 1920. He originally played a cigar-box fiddle and banjo in country string bands, learning guitar only after 1920 from Papa Charlie Jackson (?–1938). Living in the booming city of Chicago in the years when Joe "King" Oliver, Louis Armstrong, and others were bringing the sound of hot Jazz into popular music, Broonzy slowly divested himself of his country origins. Like other exiles working in Chicago clubs, he began using a piano accompanist, Joshua Altheimer (1910–1946), succeeding Black Bob, and then added bass and/or drums. The piano superseded the guitar in Urban Blues, and the harmonica was superseded as a melody instrument by alto or tenor sax or clarinet. Urban Blues developed as the confluence of Blues and Jazz.

A photograph of Washboard Sam (Robert Brown) epitomizes the ambivalence of outlook in Urban Blues. There he stands, attired in a neat, double-breasted suit, wearing a tie, and with spats on his feet—but he holds an ordinary washboard, mounted with two cowbells, and there are thimbles on the fingers of his right hand. The man has become a city slicker, but his instrument is a down-home contraption. Here is a fusion of the rural and the urban, of country tradition and city sophistication. This ambivalence found expression in an early urban style known as *hokum*.

Big Bill was lead guitarist of the Famous Hokum Boys, one of a number of groups that went by such names as the Hokum Trio, Harum Scarum, and Hokum Jug Band. Their music and outlook represented a fusion of old and new, of acquired urbanity and the condescension of the converted Chicagoan, mixed with a bit of nostalgia for the life of rural simplicity they had left. Big Bill lived in a house in Chicago but maintained a farm in Arkansas, to which he returned periodically.

After a time, there was the Chicago Five, a group that played stomps and fast "jive" tunes, using clarinet or sax and boogie piano.

Tampa Red and Georgia Tom recorded with Ma Rainey and her Georgia Jazz Band, and managed an erotic hit of their own in "It's Tight Like That." Pianist Leroy Carr (1905–1935) worked with jazz guitarist Scrapper Blackwell, singing in a suave, melodious voice that made lasting hits of his moody "How Long, How Long Blues" and especially "In the Evening (When the Sun Goes Down)."

Presented in Chicago clubs after the Depression and the repeal of Prohibition in 1933, the Blues were for entertainment and dancing. Big Bill was in demand onstage as well as on disk. He delivered his songs in an easy, relaxed style, singing with little emotional tension and making memorable his "Key to the Highway," an unconventional blues of 16 bars and a nonclassic progression, later hits for Brook Benton and Joe Williams, of Count Basie fame. When the record companies began issuing Blues after the Petrillo recording ban of 1944, Big Bill, along with Memphis Minnie, who had beat him in 1933, was in circulation again on Columbia, which had bought Vocalion and the ARC dime-store catalogues. In the 1950s, Broonzy enlarged his following as a result of appearances in England, France, and Belgium.

In 1957, just a year before his death from cancer, Big Bill went into a recording studio in Chicago and played, sang, and talked for 10 hours. Bill Randle and Studs Terkel, two disk jockeys of the era, who produced the sessions, occasionally asking questions, edited the tapes down to five LPs. Together with Big Bill's autobiography, these constitute one of the most enlightening, firsthand discourses on the Blues ever put on record.[45]

Boogie-Woogie

In December 1938, Carnegie Hall was the scene of a unique concert, *From Spirituals to Swing,* "An Evening of American Negro Music." Conceived, produced and em-cee'd by the legendary John Hammond, it offered samples of black music by outstanding black artists: "Spirituals and Holy Roller Hymns," "Soft Swing," "Harmonic Playing," "Blues," "Boogie-Woogie Piano Playing," "Early New Orleans Jazz," and "Swing." The concert was dedicated to the memory of Bessie Smith, who had died a year earlier.[46]

Among the black artists who came from various parts of the country, there were two whom Hammond had difficulty finding. He located Meade Lux Lewis (1905–1964) washing cars in a Chicago South Side garage and Albert Ammons (1907–1949) driving a taxi, also in Chicago. Together with Pete Johnson (1904–1967), who had accompanied bartender Joe Turner (b. 1911) in Kansas City's famous Sunset Café, the two scored a hit playing Boogie-Woogie. "They were stirring to the audience individually and collectively," *New York Times* critic Howard Taubman wrote. "They could barely contain themselves when the music was under way. And what endurance!"[47] Touring the country afterward and making records as the Boogie Woogie Trio, they launched the craze that swept popular music for roughly three years.

As a sound, Boogie-Woogie is related to the Blues, whose chord sequence, whether in classic 12- or 8-bar patterns, it maintains. Its most inescapable feature is the presence of eight eighth notes or an alternating series of dotted eighths and sixteenths in each measure, performed repeatedly by the left hand of the piano player. The right hand plays freewheeling melody against the basic ostinato, melody that incorporates the flatted third and seventh of the Blues.

As in the case of the Blues, the origin of Boogie-Woogie is shrouded in the uncertainty of folk art. The general consensus is that the style developed in logging and turpentine camps of the South, because these usually had a beat-up upright piano on which itinerant keyboard players could entertain the work crew at night. That it was a Western and possibly a Texas development is suggested by the recollections of several jazz- and bluesmen. Leadbelly claimed to have first heard Boogie-Woogie in Caddo County, Texas, and Richard M. Jones, who wrote the immortal "Trouble in Mind," recalled hearing a pianist named Stavin Chain play it in Donaldville, Texas, during the building of the Texas–Pacific Railway in 1904. Trumpeter Bunk Johnson (1879–1949) said he heard the style performed in the lumber camps of western Louisiana. W. C. Handy remembered hearing three pianists—Sonny Butts, Seymour Abernathy, and Bennie French—play it in Memphis in about 1909. Apparently, the style was originally known as "Fast Western," a fact confirmed by Pete Johnson, who recalled pianists of his early days in Kansas City playing "the same sort of Western rolling blues."[48]

It is believed that the style reached Chicago during or after World War I, with the migration of Southern blacks seeking employment. By the time of the Great Depression, in 1929, when "rent parties" (known as "boogies") became a means of raising the monthly payment, Boogie-Woogie was an entertainment staple.

The first time that the descriptive term appeared on a record was apparently in 1928, when Vocalion released "Pine Top's Boogie Woogie," as played by Clarence "Pine Top" Smith (1904–1929), an Alabama pianist who worked with Ma Rainey in the late 1920s, was accidentally shot to death in a dance hall fracas on Chicago's Orleans Street, and achieved posthumous fame as an innovator.

But the sound was actually put on wax in the year preceding

Pine Top's disk, except that the descriptive identification was not used. In December 1927 Meade Lux Lewis recorded "Honky Tonk Train Blues," a boogie-styled piece, despite its title, which has suggested to some historians that the ostinato of Boogie-Woogie is an imitation of the rolling wheels of a train. The Paramount Record apparently made no great impression until John Hammond was moved by his worn-out copy to go looking for its performer, whom he discovered in a Chicago car wash. Lewis than rerecorded his "Honky Tonk Train Blues." The year was 1936, and Count Basie was inspired to record "Boogie Woogie (I May Be Wrong)," with a rousing vocal by Mr. Five-by-Five, Jimmy Rushing (1903–1972).

It was two to three years before Boogie-Woogie became a dominant trend in popular music, and it was the white artists who latched onto the sound and made it a mainstream phenomenon. In 1938 Meade Lux Lewis composed and recorded "Yancey's Special," a tribute to Jimmy Yancey (c. 1894–1951), whom the black Chicago pianists regarded as the "father of the style." Bob Crosby (b. 1923) recorded it with his orchestra and Bob Zurke (1910–1944) at the piano. Crosby followed it with an orchestral version of Lewis's "Honky Tonk Train." Tommy Dorsey (1905–1956), sensing a growing response to the sound, recorded and scored with "Boogie Woogie," based on "Pine Top's Boogie," in 1938.

Jimmy Yancey, who was born in Chicago and died there of diabetes, toured vaudevile as a dancer and singer, appearing also in Europe before World War I. After settling in Chicago, he became a favorite of "pitchin' the boogie" parties and as a performer at local clubs. But beginning in 1925 and continuing for about 25 years, he held a position as grounds keeper at Comiskey Park, home of the Chicago White Sox baseball team. During those years, his home at 35th St. and State became a hangout for Boogie-Woogie players, to whom he was a teacher and, in time, a father figure. These included Albert Ammons, Meade Lux Lewis, Pine Top Smith (the nickname based on his red hair), and Cripple Clarence Lofton (1896–1957). Despite his in-group importance, Yancey did no recording until 1939, when the Boogie-Woogie craze was in full swing; and then his sessions were on Solo Art, an offbeat label owned by a New York bartender, Dan Qualey, who was a Boogie-Woogie fanatic and recorded Ammons, Johnson, and other eight-to-the-bar performers. Later, Yancey left examples of his superlative artistry—he was not a flashy performer, but resembled Count Basie in the economy of his playing—on Vocalion, Sessions, and Atlantic, recording on the last-mentioned with his wife, Estella "Mama" Yancey (b. 1896).

With the Boogie Woogie Trio touring the country and playing to appreciative crowds, white performers latched onto the sound in growing numbers. In 1940 the big band of Will Bradley (b. 1912), with Freddie Slack (1910–1965) at the piano and vocals by drummer/coleader Ray McKinley (b. 1910), made best sellers of "Beat Me Daddy, Eight to the Bar"[49] and "Scrub Me, Mama, with a Boogie Beat," the latter based on the traditional "Irish Washerwoman" folk ballad. These songs were the work of two Tin Pan Alley songwriters, Don Raye (b. 1909) and Hughie Prince (1906–1960), who quickly capitalized on the trend with "Rhumboogie" and, in 1941, with "Boogie Woogie Bugle Boy" and "Bounce Me, Brother, with a Solid Four."

In 1940 "Rhumboogie" was recorded and sung in a film, *Argentine Nights,* by the Andrews Sisters, a brash-sounding trio, who had become known as a result of "Bei Mir Bist Du Schön (Means That You're Grand)," a hit in 1937, and "Hold Tight—Hold Tight" and "Beer Barrel Polka," hit records in 1939. In 1941 the Andrews Sisters made resounding best sellers of "Boogie Woogie Bugle Boy" (revived successfully in 1973 by Bette Midler) and "Bounce Me, Brother, with a Solid Four." Performed by the trio in *Buck Private,* "Bugle Boy" gained an Academy Award nomination in 1941. This was the year that Lewis, Ammons, and Johnson recorded "Boogie Woogie Prayer," and the Glenn Miller (1904–1944) band, with a vocal by Tex Beneke and the Modernaires, recorded "The Booglie Wooglie Piggy," a bit of nonsense also recorded by the Andrews Sisters.

One of the first disks released by newly formed Capitol Records and, actually, the Hollywood company's first bestseller in 1942, was "Cow Cow Boogie," as recorded by the big band of drummer Freddie Slack, with a vocal by Ella Mae Morse (b. 1924). "Cow Cow Boogie" was apparently based on "Cow Cow Blues," a number written and recorded by Charles Davenport (1894–1955), who used the stage name, Cow Cow Davenport, based on a childhood pet name stemming from the cow-catcher on railroad engines. An early Ragtime pianist, he was a pioneer of the Boogie-Woogie style, and recorded many blues for OKeh, Paramount, and Vocalion. After threatening legal action on the adaptation of his "Cow Cow Blues," which he recorded three times—once for Paramount, once for Vocalion, and once for Brunswick—he sold the rights to the number.

Two black woman pianists who came to the fore in the early forties, Hadda Brooks on Modern and Hazel Scott (1920–1981) on Decca, each started her career by recording Boogie versions of classics. Scott's variations on "Fantasie Impromptu," "Prelude in C Sharp Minor," "Minute Waltz," and others led to an improvisation of her own, "Hazel's Boogie," which was b/w "Blues in B Flat."

Like all explosive trends, Boogie-Woogie was largely passé by 1942–1943. But its metrics, particularly Shuffle rhythm, became a basic component of the Jump Blues that evolved in the 1940s and became known as Rhythm and Blues.

William Christopher Handy

If any single Blues is known throughout the world, it is unquestionably "St. Louis Blues." In a list of the 40 Most Recorded Songs, published in America between 1900 and 1950, "St. Louis Blues" stood at the top, above such other giant songs as "Tea for Two" and "Star Dust."

"That's a pretty tune," T-Bone Walker said of "St. Louis Blues," "and it has kind of a bluesy tone, but that's not the blues. You can't dress up the blues. The only blues is the kind that I sing and the kind that Jimmie Rushing sings and Basie plays. I'm not saying that *St. Louis Blues* isn't fine music, you understand. But it just isn't blues."

To understand what it is, one must become aware of William Christopher Handy's background. Born in Florence, Alabama, he studied solfège in the Florence District School for Negroes, learning to sing in all keys, measures and movements; became a bandmaster at the A & M College at Huntsville, Alabama; and became trumpet soloist and band director of Mahara's Minstrels (1896–1903). While he was serving as director of a "colored" Knights of Pythias band in Clarksdale, Mississippi, "life suddenly took me by the shoulder and wakened me with a start."[51]

Dozing in a railroad station at Tutwiler, waiting for a train that was nine hours late, he heard "a lean, loose-jointed Negro . . . plucking a guitar . . . [and singing] *goin' where the Southern cross the Dog,* a line which he repeated three times to "the weirdest music I had ever heard. . . ."[52] Handy had been studying traditional books on theory, Steiner's *First Lessons in Harmony,* Moore's *Encyclopoedia of Music,* thinking that everything worthwhile was to be found in books.

"But the blues did not come from books," he observes. "Suffering and hard luck were the midwives that birthed these songs. The blues were conceived in aching hearts."[53]

The Tutwiler experience was underscored by an encounter some time later in Cleveland, Mississippi. He was leading his orchestra at a dance when he agreed to let a local "colored" band play a few numbers. It was a three-piece band, consisting, he wrote in his autobiography, "of a battered guitar, a mandolin and a worn-out bass. . . . They struck up one of those over-and-over strains that seem to have no very clear beginning and certainly no ending. . . ." But it drove the dancers wild, who responded with a steady shower of coins. "There before the boys lay more money than my musicians were being paid for the entire engagement. Then I saw *the beauty of primitive music*" [emphasis added].[54] After returning to Clarksdale, Handy set to orchestrating a number of local tunes. Came the mayoralty campaign of 1909 in Memphis, and Handy wrote a song for Edward H. Crump, one of the candidates, which he later published in an instrumental version as "Memphis Blues" (1912).

It was his first Blues composition, and it adheres in part to the classic or ethnic form. It has three sections, with a total of 40 measures. The first and third sections are in the traditional 12-bar form, and use is made of the flatted third and seventh of the so-called Blues scale. But the middle section consists of 16 measures, and it departs entirely from the traditional chord sequence of the Blues. In 1913 came "The Jogo Blues," another instrumental, and then, in 1914, "The St. Louis Blues." This famous work is again a longer song, made up of four sections. Only the third breaks away from the 12-bar form, consisting once again of 16 bars. Here he employs the sophisticated rhythm of the tango or habanera, a dance rhythm with which Handy had made contact on a trip to Havana with Mahara's Minstrels. However, even in the 12-bar sequences, he does not adhere either to the chord pattern of the Blues or to the lyric A-A-B form.

Clearly, Handy's role was that of an adapter, a popularizer, and, later, a collector. Isaac Goldberg correctly described Handy's contribution when he wrote: "William Christopher Handy, the Father of the Blues, is not the inventor of the genre; he is its Moses, not its Jehovah. It was he who, first of musicians, codified the new spirit in African music and set it forth upon its conquest of the North."[55]

Handy's long list of publications includes, in addition to other types of music, two types of Blues. There are adaptations of such well-known folk blues as "Joe Turner Blues," "Yellow Dog Blues," which Bessie Smith recorded, "John Henry Blues," and others. Then there are the composed Blues, with lyrics by Langston Hughes ("Golden Brown Blues"), J. Tim Brymn ("Aunt Hagar's Children Blues"), Margaret Gregory ("Wall Street Blues"), and others. One of Handy's most significant contributions came in 1926, with the publication of *Blues: An Anthology*. It was a watershed collection that enriched the black man's search for identity during the Harlem Renaissance, and that helped make the white world cognizant of the riches in black folk music. Twelve years later, he amplified that awareness of black artistry with his anthology *Book of Negro Spirituals,* which Handy Brothers Music Co. published.

Late in his career, he took his "Memphis Blues," "Beale Street

Blues," "Harlem Blues," and "St. Louis Blues" and wove them into a symphony in four movements, *Blue Denim. Father of the Blues* helped establish his role as perhaps the greatest popularizer of the Blues. The word *father* should be understood to mean, not that he generated the form, but that he nurtured, protected, enhanced, and boosted it.

Anticipating and gaining momentum during the vogue of the classic Blues singers, his "St. Louis Blues"[56] early attracted prominent popular singers such as Sophie Tucker and Ethel Waters, who was the first woman to sing it, not to mention the great Bessie Smith, who recorded it in 1925 with Louis Armstrong. His "Memphis Blues" and "Beale St. Blues" drew performances by the jazz bands of the day. The popularity of his pieces contributed greatly to the flood of Blues that inundated Tin Pan Alley during the 1920s as an offshoot of the Harlem Renaissance. In this way, he was (though black) among the synthesizers who adapted, refined, polished, sweetened, and whitened the Blues for popular consumption.

The White Synthesis

The 1920s are variously described as the Dizzy Twenties, the Roaring Twenties, and, of course, the Jazz Age—all of these epithets connoting an era in which people were on a binge, consuming illicit booze in speakeasies from dusk to dawn; and flappers and collegians, in F. Scott Fitzgerald's memorable words, "danced in a champagne haze on the rooftops of the world."[57] Curiously, it was in this era of unbuttoned revelry and gaiety that the Blues enjoyed their greatest vogue.

A measure of the popularity of the Blues is given by a ridiculous parody of one of the era's biggest novelty hits, "Yes! We Have No Bananas." Interpreted by ebullient comic, Eddie Cantor, in a 1922 revue, *Make It Snappy,* the hit went on to become a runaway best-seller, with performances ad nauseam in vaudeville, on the radio, and in clubs. Before it was laid to rest, a parody appeared. It was titled, "I've Got the Yes! We Have No Bananas Blues."

Considered from the standpoint simply of numbers, the vogue of the style is inescapable—and this as a mainstream phenomenon with a large market among whites. A survey of the publications of Tin Pan Alley firms reveals that more than 200 Blues figured prominently in the decade's recorded songs. In the year of Bessie Smith's first best seller, "Down-Hearted Blues" (1923), no fewer than 46 different Blues appeared on record and in print,[58] and this statistic does not include such songs as "Nobody Knows You When You're Down and Out," which did not use the word *Blues* in the title.

The largest number of Blues was written and introduced by the classic Blues singers, including Alberta Hunter, Clara Smith, Ida Cox, Sara Martin, and Bessie Smith; and by such black Broadway songwriters as Perry Bradford, J. Tim Brymn, Maceo Pinkard, Porter Grainger, and prolific Clarence Williams. Blues were also created in this period by jazzmen such as King Oliver, Jelly Roll Morton, Fletcher Henderson, Fats Waller, and James P. Johnson, among others.

Among white songwriters, it was the theater composers who reacted early to the spell of the Blues. The impact of the style on George Gershwin and Harold Arlen has already been described in the discussion of black musicals. In 1920, show and film tunesmith Jerome Kern (1885–1945) composed "Left All Alone Blues" for *The Night Boat* and the following year created "Blue Danube Blues" for *Good Morning, Dearie*. For *Spice of 1922*, the Gershwins wrote "The Yankee Doodle Blues," and for *Lady Be Good* (1924), "Half of It Dearie Blues." From London, Noel Coward (1899–1973) came with "Russian Blues" in the revue *London Calling* (1923), which three years later was sung by Gertrude Lawrence in *Andre Charlot's Revue of 1926*. That year, Rodgers and Hart wrote "Atlantic Blues" for the London production of *Lido Lady* (1926), which became "Blue Ocean Blues" in *Present Arms* (1928). In the *Ziegfeld follies of 1927*, Ruth Etting was "Shaking the Blues Away," a song by Irving Berlin. Jimmy McHugh and his longtime partner, Dorothy Fields, wrote "Out Where the Blues Begin" for the show *Hello Daddy!* (1928); and back in 1922, McHugh, working with Jack Frost, penned "When You and I were Young Maggie Blues," introduced in vaudeville by the famous duo Van and Schenck, and a best-selling record years later for Bing and Gary Crosby (1951).

The theater song that epitomized the era's embrace of the Blues came in the 1926 *George White's Scandals*. Written by the high-flying team of De Sylva, Brown, and Henderson, "The Birth of the Blues" quickly caught on to become one of the standards of the Pop music repertoire. Delivered by dashing Harry Richman (1895–1972), "The Birth of the Blues" became the title of a film in 1941, when it was sung by Bing Crosby, and a featured song in the film *The Best Things in Life Are Free* (1956), when it was crooned by Gordon McRae (b. 1921). The *George White Scandals* that sent "The Birth of the Blues" into orbit was also the show that introduced one of the era's big dances, the Black Bottom.

Apart from Harold Arlen, whose mastery of the Blues produced some of the greatest songs of our time, the songwriter for whom Blues was the marrow of his craft was Hoagland Carmichael. Hoagy, a Hoosier who practiced law briefly and then became a star of films, radio, and TV, is the only major white songwriter with genuine roots in Ragtime and Jazz. "Ragtime on the piano were Hoagland's lullabies," said his mother, who played piano for silent films, pounded out Ragtime pieces at college proms, and performed Joplin's "Maple Leaf Rag" at his wedding reception in 1936.[59]

Booking bands as a college student at Bloomington, he became a "jazz maniac," in his words, leading a surface existence as an academic and "an almost underground one as a jazz revolutionary," mesmerized not by "the music of comfortable well-bred people" but by "the hungry notes of the disinherited, the enslaved and the ignorant."[60] By 1923 he was involved with the Wolverines of Chicago, the best white Jazz band of its day, with the legendary Bix Beiderbecke on cornet. "Bix loved the real old Blues," Hoagy wrote in *Sometimes I Wonder,* "and adored the phrasing of Bessie Smith and Ma Rainey."[61] On a visit to Chicago to see Bix, Hoagy spent many hours listening to King Oliver, Louis Armstrong, and other Jazz musicians.

A few months after King Oliver and his Creole Jazz Band recorded the historic "Dipper Mouth Blues" on Gennett Records in the spring of 1926, the Wolverines made their first recordings, and these included Hoagy's "Riverboat Shuffle." In the succeeding year, Curtis Hitch's Happy Harmonists recorded his "Washboard Blues," with Hoagy himself at the piano. The piece was subsequently cut by Red Nichols and his Five Pennies (Brunswick, 1920), by Paul Whiteman and his Orchestra (Victor, 1927) and by Mildred Bailey and her Orchestra (Vocalion, 1938), among others. It was the Whiteman recording that made Hoagy decide to forsake the law; Bing Crosby was standing by in case he bombed on the vocal, but he gave so creditable a performance that he felt ready to devote himself to music.

"Star Dust" was written in 1927, and Hoagy recorded it with Emil Seidel and his Orchestra, again on Gennett Records, keyboarding it as a Ragtime instrumental. Two years later, after Mitchell Parish added the evocative lyric, Isham Jones made the recording that launched the song as one of the all-time beautiful ballads. Later performances that contributed to the song's legendary rise in the Pop firmament include Mary Healy's singing of it in *Star Dust,* a film of 1940, the year in which Artie Shaw and his Orchestra made a best-selling disk.

In the early 1930s, Carmichael produced a succession of engaging song hits, including "Georgia on My Mind" (1930), "Rockin' Chair" (1930), "Lazy River" (1931), which he introduced on disk with his own orchestra, and "Lazy Bones" (1933), which was introduced by Mildred Bailey, as were "Georgia on My Mind" and "Rockin' Chair." All of these were marked by locutions, curves of feeling, and turns of melody that reflected Hoagy's deep immersion in the Blues. The many performances by Ray Charles (b. 1930) of "Georgia on My Mind" in the 1970s, which moved the state of Georgia to adopt it as its Official Song,[62] are indicative of the soulfulness of Hoagy's lyrics and music. The imprint of Jazz and the Blues is also to be found in such later hits as "Hong Kong Blues," which he sang and wrote for the Humphrey Bogart film *To Have and To Have Not* (1945); "Ole Buttermilk Sky," which he sang in the film *Canyon Passage* (1946), winning an Academy Award nomination; and "Watermelon Weather" (1952), which was recorded by both Perry Como and Eddie Fisher.

Hoagy did win an Academy Award for "In the Cool Cool Cool of Evening" as Best Song of 1951, a song for which Jazz-oriented Johnny Mercer wrote the lyric. Mention should also be made of "I Get Along Without You Very Well (Except Sometimes)," a song he wrote based on an unsigned lyric given to him while he was a student at Indiana University. After an extended search, the author was identified as a Mrs. James Brown Thompson. She died the night before the song was introduced by Dick Powell on a network radio show. It was a "torch" ballad, the type of song described as a white Blues. Carmichael later sang it himself with Jane Russell in a film, *The Las Vegas Story* (1952).

Mildren Rinker Bailey, who helped make hits of three of Hoagy's songs of the early thirties, became identified with one of them as the "Rockin' Chair Lady." Using the song as her theme, she occasionally employed a rocking chair as an onstage prop. Part Indian and a sister of Al Rinker, of Paul Whiteman's famous Rhythm Boys—young Bing Crosby was part of the trio—she sang with the Whiteman band (1929–1933), to become the first female to front a Jazz orchestra. On leaving Whiteman, she joined the band of her new husband, jazz xylophonist Red Norvo (b. 1908), the two performing and winning plaudits as Mr. and Mrs. Swing. It was in those years (1936–1939) that she established her reputation as a sterling Jazz artist, prompting Jazz critic Leonard Feather to observe: "Where earlier white singers with pretensions to a jazz identification had captured only the surface qualities of the Negro style, Mildred contrived to invest her thin, high-pitched voice with a vibrato, an easy sense of jazz phrasing that might almost have been Bessie Smith's overtones."[63] In those years, Bessie Smith and her husband visited the Norvos at their home in Forest Hills.

"Bessie was crazy about Mildred," Red Norvo later reported. "She and Mildred used to laugh at each other and do this routine. They were both big women, and when they saw each other, one of them would say: 'Look, I've got this brand-new dress, but it's too big for me, so why don't you take it?' "[64]

Other visitors to the Norvo home included Fats Waller, pianist

Jess Stacy (b. 1904), of the Benny Goodman band, singer Lee Wiley (1915–1975), trumpeter Bunny Berigan (1908–1942), and even the French Jazz historian Hugues Panassie. In short, Mildred and Red identified with the world of Jazz socially as well as musically. After she split with Red, Mildred worked with Benny Goodman, and was well received on the coast-to-coast Camel Caravan network radio show. Recording frequently, she was accompanied by some of the most illustrious jazzmen of the day, who held her in high repute. She was the forerunner of an impressive line of white female Jazz singers, including Peggy Lee, Anita O'Day, June Christy, and Chris Connor, among others.

If the warmth of the Blues was in Mildred's voice, the animation of hot Jazz was the mark of Sophie Tucker's style. But even though she was billed for a time as Queen of Jazz, she was not a jazz singer. More to the point were such characterizations as World-Reowned Coon-Shouter, The Mary Garden of Ragtime, and what became a lasting description, The Last of the Red Hot Mamas. Sophie's roots were in black music, and early appearances at Tony Pastor's turn-of-the-century Music Hall found her performing in blackface, billed as a Coon-Shouter. And that was what basically she remained through a long career, which stretched from the Ragtime and Vaudeville eras to a 1963 performance at the Prince of Wales Theatre in London—the Royal Family being present—with the Beatles.

Irrepressible, flamboyant, and raucous, Sophie was the first white female singer to perform W. C. Handy's classic "St. Louis Blues" in vaudeville. As a result of her performances, two songs by black songwriter/entertainer Shelton Brooks (1886–1975) became evergreen hits: "Some of These Days," with which she was permanently identified after 1910, and "Darktown Strutters' Ball," a Ragtime classic of 1915. Appearing at the Broadway shrine of vaudeville, the Palace Theater, during the Ragtime craze, she featured Irving Berlin's "International Rag." In 1920 when, black songwriter Perry Bradford was pressuring OKeh's recording director to record some of his blues, Fred Hager initially wanted Sophie Tucker to sing them; but since she was under contract to another company, he accepted Mamie Smith instead.

In the early thirties, when the film studios were embarking on a binge of musicals, Sophie was summoned to Hollywood to appear in a motion picture, appropriately titled for her, *Honky Tonk.* The robust shout tradition in which she styled her singing found later practitioners in Willie Mae "Big Mama" Thornton, the great black singer, who very likely had no acquaintance with Sophie Tucker, and in white Bette Midler, the blonde bombshell of the 1970s.

CHAPTER SIX

"SAY IT WHILE DANCING"

"I invented Jazz," Jelly Roll Morton boasted, naming 1902 as the year and the Tenderloin District, also known as Storyville, in New Orleans, as the site of his creation. Two years before his death in 1941, Ferdinand La Menthe Morton, as he was baptized, expanded on his achievement: "Everyone today is playing my stuff and I don't even get credit. Kansas City style, Chicago style, New Orleans style —hell, they're all Jelly Roll style."[1] That the man who played the piano artfully contributed to the evolution of the turn-of-the-century style is unquestioned. But many other musicians, known and unknown, also contributed—and, probably, horn players and reed men played a really crucial role in developing what was initially an instrumental style.

As a piano player in the bordellos of the Crescent City, Morton doubtless was intimate with the music of minstrelsy, the coon songs of the nineties, cakewalk tunes, and Ragtime. As we have noted earlier, he was quite familiar with Scott Joplin's pieces, an intimacy he did not admit when St. Louis musicians tested his reading ability. This fact would serve to emphasize the contribution of Ragtime piano to Jazz. But Ragtime itself followed a form derived from the March.

Now, marching bands were as numerous in New Orleans as there were firehouses, police stations, and fraternal organizations.

All had their complement of amateur musicians for picnics, fish fries, fairs, funerals, etc. Buying brass and woodwind instruments inexpensively was no problem. As the port of embarkation for troops in the Spanish-American War, New Orleans was flooded with marching-band instruments, left in pawn shops, when the war ended abruptly. Accordingly, the marching band became an incubator of Jazz, an inescapable fact, considering the front line of New Orleans Jazz combos—cornet, clarinet, trombone.

Jelly Roll established his creativity as a solo pianist with recordings he made in 1923 of his own compositions: "Milenburg Joys," "Wolverine Blues," "The Pearls," and "Kansas City Stomp," among others. All of these he later developed into band numbers with his Red Hot Peppers, who began recording in 1926 and produced about 50 historic sides between then and 1929. In such numbers as "Black Bottom Stomp," "Smoke House Blues," "Doctor Jazz," and "The Chant," to name a few, we can hear the transition from Ragtime to Jazz taking place in the playing of the seven-piece combo, some of whose cornet and clarinet parts were written out by Jelly Roll.

Of greater consequence, perhaps, to Jazz were the recordings made by Louis (Satchmo) Armstrong and His Hot Five, also his Hot Seven, between 1925 and 1928. Out of these sessions and more than 50 recorded numbers came such rip-roaring Jazz classics as "Muskrat Ramble," "Cornet Chop Suey," "Gully Low Blues," "Potato Head Blues," and a best seller of 1926, "Heebie Jeebies," generally cited as the source of "scattin'."[2] Perhaps, the contrast between the Morton sessions and the Armstrong dates, which took place in the same years, is the result of the inspired genius of one being a pianist and of the other, a cornetist.

The Creole Jazz Band of King Oliver, which Satchmo joined in Chicago in 1922, began making its mark on disk in 1923, the year that Jazz began to be extensively recorded. Landmark sides produced by the combo included "Dippermouth Blues," "Jazzin' Baby Blues," and "Canal Street," among others, sides that are among the best examples of classic New Orleans Jazz style in the rich polyphony of a group of instruments playing variants of a melody simultaneously.

In addition to Jelly Roll, Satchmo, and the King, the Jazz scene of Chicago had strong proponents of the music in such New Orleans exiles as cornetist Freddie Keppard (1889-1933), drummer Baby Warren Dodds (1898-1959), sterling soprano saxist Sidney Bechet (1897-1959), clarinetist Johnny Dodds (1892-1940), reed man Jimmy Noone (1895-1944), and the legendary multi-instrumentalist (trombone, cornet, string bass, alto sax) Kid Edward Ory (1886-1973).

The priority of giving the world outside of the Crescent City a taste of the new music cannot be credited to any of the foregoing. In June 1915, it was Tom Brown's Jass Band—Jazz was then spelled that way—that became the first band to travel north and play at Lamb's Café, in Chicago. The following year, the Dixie Land Jass Band, originally named after clarinetist Alcide "Yellow" Nunez (1884–1934) also went to Chicago to play at the Booster Club. Drummer Johnny Stein's hot combo, whose personnel became the Original Dixieland Jazz Band (ODJB), began playing Chicago's Schiller Café in March 1916. All of these were white bands, as was the ODJB, which opened late in 1916 at Reisenweber's, in New York City.

Consisting of cornetist Nick La Rocca (1889–1961), trombonist Eddie "Daddy" Edwards (1891–1963), clarinetist Larry Shields (1893–1953), pianist Henry Ragas (1890–1919), and drummer Tony Sbarbaro (1897–1969), the ODJB was the band that set off the jazz explosion. An overnight sensation, its fee rocketed to an unheard-of $1,000 a week. And on February 26, 1917, when it went into the Victor studios, it made the first jazz recordings in history. "Livery Stable Blues" and "Original Dixieland One Step" also exemplified New Orleans collective, polyphonic style, with virtually no solos. "Livery Stable Blues" was recorded with a whinnying cornet and a mooing trombone to emphasize the novel nature of the new music. Jazzmen of this era sometimes indulged in so-called audience-grabbing ploys, clowning, mugging, holding their instruments at odd angles, etc.

One of Jelly Roll's earliest recordings was made with the New Orleans Rhythm Kings (NORK), the most important white band after ODJB. They began performing in Chicago in about 1919–1920, after ODJB had left, working at the Friars' Inn, which was frequented by members of the infamous Al Capone gang. Led by trumpeter Paul Mares (1900–1949), who imported clarinetist Leon Rappolo (1902–1943) and trombonist Georg Brunies (1900–1974), NORK began recording in 1922, at the Richmond, Indiana, studio of Gennett Records, producing sides that inflamed the imagination of a group of young white Chicagoans.

"Boy, when we heard *Farewell Blues* by NORK," cornetist Jimmy McPartland later reported,

> I'll tell you, we went out of our minds. Everybody flipped. It was just wonderful. So we put the others on—*Tiger Rag, Discontented, Tin Roof Blues, Bugle Call,* and such titles. We stayed there from about three in the afternoon until eight at night, just listening to these records one after another over and over again. Right then and there we decided we would get a band and try to play like these guys . . . One way or

another we all got instruments, and that was the nucleus of the Austin band.[3]

The nucleus consisted of Bud Freeman on C melody sax, Frank Teschmacher on clarinet, Jim Lannigan on bass tuba, Richard McPartland on banjo, and Jimmy McPartland on cornet; they were later joined by Davey Tough on drums. How deep their emulation of NORK went is further explained by Jimmy:

> What we used to do was put a record on—play a few bars and then all get our notes. We'd have to tune our instruments up to the record machine, to the pitch, and go ahead with a few notes. Then stop! A few more bars of the record, each guy would pick out his notes and boom! we would go and play it. . . . In three or four weeks, we could finally play one tune all the way through—*Farewell Blues.*[4]

Because on records NORK was called the Friars Society Orchestra, after the Friars' Inn, the Austin High School gang (not all went to Austin High) called itself the Blue Friars. What we know as white Dixieland Jazz had its beginnings with this group. As used in relation to New Orleans music, the word *Dixieland* did not signify a particular style. But with the white imitation of New Orleans Jazz that developed in Chicago and other parts of the Midwest, Dixieland came to mean a white, up-tempo, peppy, accent-on-the-afterbeat or two-boat style.

When F. Scott Fitzgerald dubbed the 1920s the Jazz Age, he was thinking of the new social attitudes—the freewheeling approach to sex; females bobbing their hair, wearing above-the-knee skirts, smoking, drinking and petting in the back seats of automobiles; the anything-goes spirit of the time. But the music that came roaring out of New Orleans via Jelly Roll, King Oliver, and Satchmo was emblematic. However, the sound of the Jazz Age was more in the music of the white adapters, which had an exuberant recklessness, a happy, high-flying verve, and a bouncy drive that provided stimulating accompaniment for such up-tempo dances as the Charleston, Black Bottom, and Varsity Drag. James Lincoln Collier attributes the contrast between black and white to the fact that the whites were "rebelling against a highly ordered and emotionally reserved culture,"[5] a rebellion that in large measure was the essence of the Jazz Age.

The White Synthesis

At the birth and emergence of Jazz, a pattern was established in which the adaptation and synthesis by white musicians brought a style, originated by blacks, into the mainstream. As we have seen, this was largely, but not entirely, true of New Orleans Jazz. What should not be overlooked, however, is that Jazz "was made in the first instance by blacks, that the majority of superior players have been black, and that most of the significant advances have been worked out by blacks."[6] J. L. Collier cites Paul Mares, one of the early New Orleans trumpeters: "We did our best to copy the colored music we'd heard at home. We did the best we could, but naturally we couldn't play real colored style."[7] Collier adds: "Whites have played important roles in giving Jazz its shape."[8]

Among the white jazzmen of the 1920s whose imaginations were fired by New Orleans players, black and white, there were, in addition to the Austin High School crowd: cornetist Bix Beiderbecke, who came from Davenport, Iowa; clarinetist Charles Ellsworth "Pee Wee" Russell, from St. Louis; guitarist Albert Edwin (Eddie) Condon, from Indiana; trumpeter Rowland Bernart "Bunny" Berigan, from Wisconsin; drummer George Wettling, from Topeka, Kansas; trumpeter Phil Napoleon, of Boston, and pianist Frank Signorelli, of New York, both founding members of the Original Memphis Five; clarinetist Benjamin David (Benny) Goodman, of Chicago; trombonist Weldon Lee (Jack) Teagarden, of Texas; and cornetist Francis Joseph "Muggsy" Spanier, of Chicago. Spanier said: "I would go down to the South Side and listen hour after hour to those two great trumpeters, Joseph King Oliver and Louis. That's when they were at the old Lincoln Gardens. It got so that I knew every phrase and intonation they played, just from listening, so that, in spite of myself, I was doing the same things."[9]

Jack Teagarden (1905–1964), who worked around Texas, listening to "the colored orchestras" when he could,[10] came to New York City in 1927 with a little-known group, the Doc Ross Jazz Bandits, which quickly split up. Playing jam sessions as a result of his contact with Pee Wee Russell (1906–1969) and Wingy Manone (1904–1982), he rapidly became an in-demand trombonist on free-lance gigs. From 1928 to 1951, he worked steadily with three major bandleaders: Ben Pollack (1903–1971), a drummer who had been with NORK; Paul Whiteman; and, for five years (1946–1951), with an "all-star" band, led by Louis Armstrong.

"Teagarden was the first white player," Collier writes, "to understand thoroughly the essence of black jazz playing."[11] That understanding manifested itself in his artful use of the blue third and the blue seventh, the two tones that blacks introduced into our major scales, as well as in his "lazy" way of playing around the beat. To his accomplishments as an outstanding Jazz trombonist, Teagarden added the singular achievement of being the outstanding white male singer in Jazz, and virtually the only male. In a long-range recording career with many of the top jazzmen, his most memorable sides include: "Makin' Friends," with the Kentucky Grasshoppers; "Basin Street Blues," b/w "Beale Street Blues," with the Charleston Chasers, a Benny Goodman unit; and "I Gotta Right to Sing the Blues," his theme, with the Benny Goodman band. "The Yogi Berra of Jazz" was what Goodman called him. Saxist Gerry Mulligan said: "Jack has everything a good musician needs: a beautiful sound, a wonderful melodic sense, a deep feeling, a swinging beat, and the ability to make everything, even the most difficult things, sound relaxed and easy."[12]

The white Jazz musician who epitomized the Jazz Age, but in retrospect, was Leon Beiderbecke, known as Bix Beiderbecke. Recognized as a brilliant, creative musician by his peers, he was little known to the public until after his premature death at 28. A romantic novel, *Young Man with a Horn,* by Dorothy Baker (later a film), helped enhance a legend that was in the making when alcoholism, reckless living, and pneumonia killed him in 1931.

To many, as to James Lincoln Collier, Bix was the first great white Jazz musician. "He was superior to every jazz player of his day except Louis Armstrong," Collier states, "and has been matched since by very few . . . His influence on his contemporaries was both direct and pervasive . . . Nor was it only whites."[13] Creating unforgettable and much-imitated masterpieces in recordings of "Singin' the Blues" and "I'm Coming Virginia," on both of which he played with C-melody saxist Frankie Trumbauer (1901–1956), Bix gave historical importance to the Wolverines, with whom he worked in 1923–1924, and later, even to the Paul Whiteman band, with whom he blew intermittently from 1927 to 1931.

A burgeoning composer, he was much involved with the modern tonalities of the French impressionists Debussy and Ravel, and of several Americans, especially the piano pieces of Eastwood Lane and Edward MacDowell *(Woodland Sketches).* This interest led to his producing a series of piano compositions—"Candlelights," "Flashes," "In the Dark," and "In a Mist"—which emanated from late-at-night keyboard rambling. The influence of the whole-tone scale and harmonies of Ravel and Debussy is audible in his cornet improvisations as well as in these piano works. He himself recorded only "In a Mist," which he performed with Lennie Hayton (1908–1971) and Roy Bargy (1900–1974) in a three-piano version at Carnegie Hall in October 1928. Had he lived, Bix might have been a seminal force in the development of so-called Third Stream Jazz, a fusion of Jazz and European modernism attempted in the 1950s by John Lewis (b. 1920) of the Modern Jazz Quartet and others.

On the fourth anniversary of his death on August 6, 1931, reports have it that over a thousand people attended a graveside memorial service at Oakdale Cemetery in Davenport, Iowa. The young man with a horn is exemplary not only of the dialectic interplay of black and white but of black and European music, which has shaped our popular music.

In considering why Jazz entered the Pop mainstream through white rather than black players, one must be aware of two factors. More clubs and theaters were accessible to white bands than to black ones. Even in New York, few black performers made it to midtown Manhattan until the rise of Swing Street; Count Basie did not play a midtown venue until 1938, when his band was booked at the Famous Door. Differences in repertoire were also accountable. While the black Jazz bands played New Orleans standard numbers and Blues-oriented tunes, whites focused on the popular songs of the day and played for dancing.

The Jazz Singers

"I don't think I'm singing," Billie Holiday said. "I feel like I'm playing a horn. I try to improvise like Les Young, like Louis Armstrong, or someone else I admire. What comes out is what I feel. I hate straight singing. I have to change a tune to my own way of doing it."[14] Many disquisitions have been written on Jazz singing. Has anyone described it better than Lady Day (1915–1959)?

One of the most influential of Jazz singers, Billie Holiday was preceded in the territory by two luminaries. Ethel Waters is rejected by many as a Jazz singer. She was potent onstage, but her style was more dramatic and histrionic than Jazz-oriented. Nonetheless, she recorded with Duke Ellington (1932), Benny Goodman (1933), and a formidable array of jazzmen. Her emotive handling of certain commercial songs such as "Stormy Weather," "Taking a Chance on Love," and "Lady Be Good" put her on the rim of Jazz if not outside the realm of popular singing.

Although he is largely viewed as one of the great Jazz trumpeters of all time, Louis Armstrong scored as a swinging singer almost from the beginning of his exciting career. The hoarse, gravelly sound of his voice was not only unique but hardly a pop sound. "Scatting"—the substitution of nonsense syllables for words—was an instrumental use of the voice, allowing for horn-like improvisation, which he initiated on a recording of "Heebie Jeebies" in 1926. Because some of his vocal records, such as "Hello Dolly" and "Mack the Knife," have been best sellers, there is a tendency to dismiss them as not being Jazz. But in his singing, Satchmo employed the same techniques—changes in timbre, melodic and rhythmic variation, a swinging beat—that made him one of the great instrumentalists. "I don't need words," he has said. "It's all in the phrasing."[15]

Billie Holiday, whose vocal style acknowledged Armstrong's instrumental style as an influence, began recording in 1933 after ubiquitous John Hammond of Columbia Records heard her at Monette Moore's, a Harlem club. ("I decided that night," he later said, "that she was the best jazz singer I ever heard."[16]) She made her disk debut simply as a band vocalist with the recently formed Benny Goodman band. Her artistry as a soloist became more evident in the sides she cut with the band of pianist Teddy Wilson (b. 1912) between 1935 and 1942. Later she recorded for Decca (1944–1950) and for Clef/Verve (1952–1957); but since her death, dozens of albums have appeared from many sources, including off-the-air checks.

She sang with Count Basie for a year, beginning in March 1937, and for a shorter period with Artie Shaw. She became a star as a result of a summer appearance at Café Society Downtown, in New York. Thereafter, through the 1940s, she became the highest-paid and most in-demand performer on 52nd St., playing Kelly's Stable, Onyx, Downbeat, and Spotlite, among other clubs on Swing Street.

Unlike Sarah Vaughan (b. 1924) and Ella Fitzgerald (b. 1918), each of whom has a more than two-octave vocal range, Billie had a small voice and limited range. An unfriendly "admirer" said she sang as if her shoes were too tight. But that tight little voice, with its bittersweet sound, could and did express feeling with such depth and intensity that it overpowered audiences. Singing most frequently behind the beat, she was a highly expressive musician whose economical departures from the melody line and the beat were in the Satchmo lyrical tradition.

A singer who learned from listening to records—of Bessie Smith and others from her teenage days—she had an intuitive grasp of the songs that were for her. They had to do with hunger and love, as she herself indicated and demonstrated in two imperishable songs that she cowrote and recorded: "God Bless the Child" and the torch ballad "Fine and Mellow." Leading a sordid, tormented, and traumatic kind of life—rape at an early age, a jail sentence for prostitution, broken marriages involving men who were drug addicts, her own addiction and alcoholism—she found singing an outlet for the anguish of living. For her, singing was autobiography.

What has sometimes not been sufficiently recognized is that Billie was not only a superb Jazz singer but a consummate Pop singer as well. Her repertoire consisted largely of the popular hits and show songs of the day. She brought to them a depth of expressiveness and poignancy, which changed the nature and course of Pop singing. Before her, singing stars including Al Jolson, Bing Crosby (1904–1977), Ruth Etting, Connie Boswell (c. 1907–1976), and others sought to entertain and appeal. Billie sought to express and communicate. One of the men who sat her feet in the halcyon days of 52nd St. was Frank Sinatra (b. 1915), who said later: "It is Billie Holiday, whom I first heard in the 52nd St. clubs in the thirties who was and still remains the greatest single musical influence on me."[17] That influence has been evident in Sinatra's phrasing, emotive involvement with his songs, and the use of songs as a form of self-expression.

It was tenor saxist Lester Young (1909–1959), the father of Cool Jazz, who nicknamed Billie "Lady Day." An obvious play on her surname, it also embodied recognition of the fierce pride that was a counterpart of Billie's tragic lack of self-esteem. In the early Harlem years, when she and her mother were struggling to eke out a living and she worked as a waitress, Billie refused to accede to the owner's demoralizing and obscene demand that, like other waitresses, she pick up tips without the use of her hands.

In her earliest appearances on 52nd St., a segregated street in the 1930s and 1940s, she was not permitted to mingle with white patrons, and in a booking at the Famous Door, was compelled to sit upstairs outside the ladies room during her breaks. Working with Count Basie, she had to use makeup in theaters to darken her light complexion. Singing with Artie Shaw, she had to use makeup to whiten her face. On touring with the band, she wrote: "Eating was a mess, sleeping a problem, but the biggest drag of all was a simple thing like finding a place to go to the bathroom."[18] Singing with the Shaw band at a midtown hotel, she could not enter through the main lobby but was forced to use the service entrance when she came to work.

The hurt and scars found partial expression in Billie's mordant recording of "Strange Fruit." Although lynching had been the subject of "Supper Time" in the Irving Berlin show *As Thousands Cheer* (1933), where it was treated sentimentally—a mother brooding over how to tell her children that their father had been lynched—the stark realism of "Strange Fruit" was a challenge. It took courage to put it on wax in 1939. The Commodore Records sessions at which "Strange Fruit" was recorded, together with a flock of torch songs such as "I'll Be Seeing You" and "Lover Come Back to Me," represent a high watermark in the history of Jazz and Pop singing.

Imprisoned in 1947–1948 as the result of a drug bust, set up by one of her drug-addicted husbands to save his skin, she was refused a cabaret card and prevented from working in any New York club in the latter years of her life. Hospitalized in 1959, she was arrested for possession on what proved to be her deathbed, when a so-called friend slipped her some heroin. Dead at the age of 44, Billie left a legacy of recordings whose emotionalism reflect her distraught existence and establish her as a superlative Jazz singer. Ralph J. Gleason, Jazz critic of the *San Francisco Chronicle,* wrote: "When Billie was in her prime, she was the most magnetic and beautiful woman I have ever seen, as well as the most emotionally moving singer I have ever heard."[19]

Winning one of the Wednesday night amateur contests at the Apollo Theater in Harlem in 1942 with her singing of "Body and Soul," Sarah Lois Vaughan joined the band of Earl "Fatha" Hines as vocalist and second pianist. The following year, she performed with the first Bop band in history, newly formed by Billy Eckstine (b. 1914), with a personnel that included Bop pioneers Dizzy Gillespie (b. 1917) and Charlie "Bird" Parker (1920–1955). In 1945 she recorded with the small Bop combos formed by alto saxist Parker and trumpeter Gillespie; later, with an orchestra directed by pianist Tadd Dameron (1917–1965). Winner of the New Star award in *Esquire's* 1947 Jazz Poll, she rated top Female Vocalist honors in *Down Beat's* annual poll from 1947 through 1952.

In the 1950s, Sassy, as she came to be called—she was the Divine Sarah in Jazz—allowed herself to be moved into the Pop field by A & R chieftains Hugo and Luigi, at Mercury Records. Scoring a hit with the seductive "Make Yourself Comfortable," she produced a series of moderate sellers that peaked with the Jazz-flavored "Broken Hearted Melody," a top-ten disk in 1959.

With a voice whose suppleness allows her to drop easily from high soprano to low baritone notes and a sureness of pitch that makes her a tasteful improviser, she continues to astonish audiences with the operatic range of her voice. Approaching 60 years of age, Sarah sang to the accompaniment of the Los Angeles Philharmonic, conducted by Michael Tillson Thomas, in an album released as *Gershwin Live!* There was no diminution in the quality, scope, or excitement of her performances, which also involved a sellout tour of the United States. With Thomas at the piano in "The Man I Love," Sarah delivered a free-ranging, introspective variation of the song's melodic line that was a brilliant bravura performance, rare in Jazz. Sinatra has said: "Sassy sings so good I want to cut my wrists with a dull blade and let her sing me to death."[20]

The name of Ella Fitzgerald conjures up a vocal sound, mellifluous, fluid, and relaxed, unapproachable by others either in the Pop field or in Jazz. As the result of winning an amateur contest in 1934, she became associated with the great band of hunchback drummer Chick Webb (1902–1939), remaining with it until his premature death from pleurisy. She assumed leadership of the band for a short time, having scored a million-copy seller in 1938 with her swinging version of "A-Tisket, A-Tasket," based on the well-known nursery rhyme. She achieved a second million-copy disk in a 1944 collaboration with the famous Ink Spots on "Into Each Life Some Rain Must Fall."

"Of course, I goofed where Ella was concerned," John Hammond has admitted. "Fletcher Henderson and Benny Carter played for her [at Fletcher's house on One Hundred Thirty-fourth Street] and I thought she was nice. She had this lovely, smooth, silky voice, but for me, she didn't have any of the excitement and sex Billie Holiday had."[21]

The truth is that Ella does not "have" excitement or sex, except, perhaps, when she is "scattin'," the improvisatory vocal technique in which she vies with Satchmo. Like Sarah, she has remarkable range and perfect control of pitch. Unlike Billie, who improvised on the words of a song, Ella improvises on the music, achieving a rare liquid loveliness of sound. The magic of her voice, apart from its beauty, is in the warmth she communicates, the warmth of an aural cocoon out of which a butterfly of melody soars on delicate wings. This achievement is particularly evident in a series of sterling *Songbooks* she recorded for producer Norman Granz of Jazz at the Philharmonic—four- and five-album collections, in each of which she covers the major output of such top show composers as Gershwin, Cole Porter, and Richard Rodgers.

"I never knew," Ira Gershwin said, "how good our songs were until I heard Ella sing them." Richard Rodgers said: "Whatever Ella does to my songs, they sound better."[22]

Of the more recent followers in the vocal Jazz tradition of Lady Day, Sassy, and Ella, there are such artists as beauteous Nancy Wilson (b. 1937), who worked with Cannonball Adderly (1928–1975); Abbey Lincoln (b. 1930), who popularized husband Max Roach's *Freedom Suite* (1960); Ivie Anderson (b. 1905), who embellished Duke Ellington's music with her vocals from 1931 to 1942; and Helen Humes (1931–1981), who is remembered for the three years she served as Count Basie's vocalist, 1938–1941.

Perhaps the most significant of these latter-day jazz singers is Carmen McRae (b. 1922), whose admiration for Billie Holiday led to an album of songs associated with her. "She could do no wrong," Carmen said of her idol. "She sings the way she is. . . . Singing is the only place she can express herself the way she'd like to be. . . . Only way she's happy is through a song."[23] Sensitive in her perception of Billie, Carmen makes no attempt to imitate Lady Day's style or sound. Selecting 12 songs that are part of the Holiday mythos, including "Yesterdays," "My Man," "These-There Eyes," "Some Other Spring," and "Lover Man (Oh, Where Can You Be)," Carmen garbs them with clothes from her own tonal wardrobe. The contrast in approaches is illuminating. Where Billie's sound is tender and tart, Carmen's is full-blown. Billie's is an art of understatement, while Carmen tends toward embroidery. Billie is intent on wringing every bit of feeling from the words, while Carmen seems more concerned with rhythmic and harmonic exploration.

It was in the early sixties that McRae appeared on the music scene, and drew from Ralph J. Gleason the comment: "the most unusual and exciting jazz singer to emerge in a generation." Gleason added: "The melding of words and music and performance . . . happened with Bessie Smith and Ma Rainey, and it happened with Billie Holiday, and now is happening with Carmen McRae."[24]

Curiously, jazz singing has been more a female than a male domain, despite Louis Armstrong's priority in this area. Apparently, men with the improvisatory urge take up instruments. Jimmy Rushing (1903–1972), regarded as the father of the vocal Swing tradition, came out of Oklahoma, sang occasionally with Jelly Roll Morton, and then, successively, with Walter Page's Blue Devils, Bennie Moten's band, and Count Basie, as these bands metamorphosed, one into the other. All of the latter were part of the Kansas City Jazz scene and tradition in the late 1920s and early 1930s.

With Count Basie (1904–1984), Jimmy worked steadily from 1935 to 1948, serving not only as vocalist but as confidant and collaborator. Together the two wrote original Blues or reworked traditional Blues in such songs as "Sent for You Yesterday and Here You Come Today," "Goin' to Chicago," "Good Morning Blues," "Take Me Back, Baby," and "Boogie Woogie (I May Be Wrong)," the last, a contribution to the Boogie-Woogie craze of the late thirties. All of these may be heard on *The Essential Jimmy Rushing,* an album that includes Ma Rainey's "See See Rider" and Leroy Carr's "How Long, How Long Blues" and was produced by John Hammond. That Rushing was basically a Blues-shouter, high-pitched and exuberant, is quite clear. But since he sings around the beat, not on it, as folk Blues singers tend to do, his delivery has a swinging quality that gives it a Jazz feeling.

Not very tall, and extremely fat throughout his life, he inspired the song, "Mr. Five by Five," which he helped develop into a Pop hit in 1942. Novelist Ralph Ellison, who grew up in Oklahoma City when Rushing was singing with the Blue Devils, later wrote: "When you stood on the rise of the school grounds, two blocks to the East, you could hear Jimmy's voice jetting forth from the dance hall like a blue flame in the dark, now soaring high . . . above the shouting of the swing band."[25] He was the epitome of the theme used by Basie at the Reno Club in K.C.—"Swingin' the Blues."

There is a line that separates the Blues from the Jazz singer. It is a line that fades in and out, depending on the songs and the apropos treatment, when one considers an artist like Jimmy Witherspoon (b. 1923). His first employer was Kansas City jazzman Jay McShann (b. 1909). Influenced by Walter Brown ("Confessin' the Blues") and Joe Turner ("Piney Brown"), he accounted for the 1949 Rhythm and Blues hit "Ain't Nobody's Business." Then there's Ray Charles (b. 1932), whose recorded output runs the gamut from Jazz to Blues to Rhythm and Blues to Soul and to Country music; who started recording in 1949–1950 with a Jazz trio modeled on Nat "King" Cole's then-popular Jazz trio and who made Jazz recordings on solo sax, but whose greatest impact during the 1960s was as the "father of Soul," music followed by a series of staggering Country hits.

The achievement of Jack Teagarden as a Jazz trombonist is so formidable that limited attention is generally given to his prodigious talent as a Jazz/Blues singer. Teagarden made contact with black music as a boy and teenager in the small Texas town where he was born, fascinated by the Spirituals he heard and avidly seeking out black bands upon whom to model his playing. By the time he arrived in New York in 1927, his mastery of the trombone was such that he never lacked work during the rest of his life. As a vocalist, Teagarden delivered in a muddy, nasal baritone that at times echoed the smooth sound of his trombone. Among his most memorable vocals are those on "Basin Street Blues" (made with a Benny Goodman-led combo called the Charleston Chasers) and "Beale Street Blues" (made with an Eddie Lang–Joe Venuti combo). Additional favorites include "Up the Lazy River," "Rockin' Chair," and "I Gotta Right to Sing the Blues," which he used as a theme with the big band he led in about 1938. Terming him "the leading and virtually the only white male singer in Jazz" as well as "the first white player throughly to understand the essence of black jazz playing," James Lincoln Collier concludes: "Had he never played trombone, he would have earned a place in jazz history for his singing."[26]

Another elusive line is that separating Jazz singers from vocalists in the small combos and big bands of the Swing era, many of whom were really Jazz singers and all of whom were white.

The White Synthesis: Jazz Singing

Lee Wiley (1915–1975), who was, like Mildred Bailey, part Indian (Cherokee) and who also worked with Paul Whiteman (on his radio show), had the independence of mind so necessary to the Jazz singer: "I always sang the way I wanted. If I didn't like something, I just wouldn't do it."[27] But that independence may have accounted for a lack of direction in a career that ended 25 years before she died, except for occasional gigs and recordings. Hailing from Oklahoma, she was singing at 16 with the big band of Leo Reisman (1897–1961) at the elegant Central Park Casino in New York (1931–1933). She made recordings with the great Casa Loma Band. In 1943 she sang with a big band she formed with her new husband, Jazz pianist Jess Stacy (b. 1904), who worked with Benny Goodman for a number of years. Her enduring fame is based on a series of albums she cut in the early forties of the show songs of George Gershwin, Cole Porter, and Rodgers and Hart. Her accompaniment on these was by small Dixieland Jazz groups that included some of the day's outstanding jazzmen—Bunny Berigan (1908–1942), Bobby Hackett (1915–1976), Fats Waller, and Eddie Condon (1905–1973), among others. A striking-looking woman with olive skin she attributed to her Cherokee blood, she had a sexy, husky voice and sang in an easy, laid-back, sensuous style that made her a favorite of the top show composers and jazzmen of the day. ("She has a voice and style," wrote Boston columnist George Frazier, "that have long since made me extremely eager to go to bed with her.")[28] With composer Victor Young (1900–1956), on whose Kraft radio show she sang, she wrote a number of songs, including "Got the South in My Soul" (1932) and "Any Time, Any Day, Anywhere," which became a Pop hit in 1933.

In the Swing bands of Benny Goodman, Stan Kenton, Jimmy Dorsey, and Gene Krupa, other aspiring Jazz singers were nurtured. Stan Kenton (1912–1979) was fortunate with a succession of canaries, as they were sometimes called in those days. Anita O'Day, born Anita Colton in Chicago (1919)—Colton became O'Day, pig Latin for dough—grew up listening to Billie Holiday and Mildred Bailey, and at 19 was singing in one of Chicago's top Jazz clubs, the Three Deuces. Working with the band of Gene Krupa (1909–1973) and sharing vocals with Jazz trumpeter Roy Eldridge (b. 1911), Anita and Little Jazz, as Roy was called, produced one of 1941's hit singles in "Let Me Off Uptown." A stint with Woody Herman (b. 1913) led to a two-year association in 1944–1945 with Stan Kenton. Singing like a Jazz musician, she proved that she was "one of the boys" by becoming a narcotics addict, a problem she did not lick completely until 1967, after she nearly died from an overdose. Prior to that, a show-stealing performance in the 1958 Newport Jazz Festival film *Jazz on a Summer's Day,* led to her cutting a series of albums for Norman Granz's Jazz label. Anita had a husky voice, and as a soloist was fond of surprise shifts in tempo and key, and liked to scat.

When Anita left the Stan Kenton band in 1945, she recommended June Christy as her successor. Husky-voiced like Anita, Shirley Luster, as she was baptized in 1925, sang with Kenton for four years (1945–1949), scoring a hit with "Tampico" early in the association. The third in the succession of Kenton songbirds was Chris Connor, born in 1927 in Kansas City, Missouri. Singing briefly with a Bob Brookmeyer combo in the late 1940s, she worked with Claude Thornhill (1909–1965) and Jerry Wald (1919–1973) after settling in New York. A year with the Kenton band in 1952–1953 led to her emergence as a Jazz soloist. Her albums include *Chris Connor Sings Lullabies of Birdland,* a collaboration with modern Jazz trumpeter Maynard Ferguson (b. 1928), whom she met during the Kenton stint; and two albums devoted to the music of George Gershwin.

Blonde Helen O'Connell (b. 1920), who sang with a flock of bands, came to renown with the band of Jimmy Dorsey (1904–1957) in the years between 1939 and 1943. Paired with Sinatra competitor Bob Eberle (1916–1981), she can be heard on the Dorsey hits "Amapola," "Green Eyes," and "Tangerine." Helen was less a Jazz singer than a Swing, big-band vocalist.

By contrast, blonde, impassive-faced Peggy Lee sang Jazz from the start, although she vocalized with a number of bands, including that of suave Will Osborne (b. 1906). Born Norma Jean Egstrom in North Dakota in 1920, Peggy Lee achieved her maturity with the band of Benny Goodman in 1941–1943, and has actively pursued a distinguished career into the 1980s. With guitarist Dave Barbour (1912–1965), to whom she was briefly married, she wrote the hit "Mañana" (1948). In 1955 she was nominated for an Oscar for her singing and acting in the film *Pete Kelly's Blues.* In 1969 she received two Grammys for her record of "Is That All There Is."

Of all the white Jazz singers, she has been the most involved with black music. Her first big hit, "Why Don't You Do Right?" was based on a Blues she learned from Mississippi Blues singer Lil Green (1919–1954), which she persuaded Goodman to record late in 1942. Among later hits, "Alright, Okay, You Win" was based on the Joe Williams–Count Basie best seller; "Hallelujah, I Love Her So" was derived from the well-known Ray Charles song and recording; and her biggest single hit, "Fever," was a cover of the 1956 R & B disk by Little Willie John (d. 1968). An album of the songs in *Pete Kelly's Blues* involved a Peggy Lee–Ella Fitzgerald collaboration.

A survey of white female Jazz singers should not omit two ladies who began as Pop vocalists and turned to Jazz in their late careers. Rosemary Clooney (b. 1928), who sang with the band of Tony Pastor (1907–1969), became an overnight sensation in 1951 with her boisterous recording of the harpsichord-backed "Come on-a My House." There followed a series of Pop hit disks: "Tenderly," "This

Ole House," and "Hey There," among other best sellers of the fifties. When she returned to the music scene after an almost 20-year retirement, occasioned by marriage to actor José Ferrer and divorce, child-raising, and health problems, Rosemary paid tribute to the music of Duke Ellington in two albums, for one of which, *Blue Rose,* the Duke wrote and dedicated the title tune to her. The blues-infected songs of Harold Arlen and the sophisticated songs of Cole Porter accounted for two other albums. In 1983 she collaborated with Woody Herman and his Big Band on an album titled, *My Buddy.* Clooney takes limited liberties in her singing but works on the lyrics with a comcentration characteristic of Jazz singers.

Unlike Clooney, Teresa Brewer (b. 1931) did not serve her apprenticeship with a big band. She burst on the Pop record scene in 1950 with a hit novelty song, "Music! Music! Music! (Put Another Nickel In)," having spent six years or so, from the age of five, touring with a road unit of the Major Bowes Amateur Hour. Cute, perky novelty songs were her métier for several years after "Music! Music! Music!" Like Clooney, when she returned to active recording again in the seventies, she moved in a Jazz direction, and for her, too, the attraction was the songs of Duke Ellington. Two albums bear witness to her love of such great Ellington standards as "Solitude," "Mood Indigo," and "It Don't Mean a Thing If It Ain't Got That Swing," which was the subtitle of a 1973 collaboration with the Duke. It was the music of Duke that figured again in an album of *Teresa* with Shelly Manne, at which time Duke Ellington was quoted as saying: "She's completely true to herself at all times. She swings and that's what Jazz is all about."[29] There was also an album with jazz pianist Earl "Fatha" Hines, titled, *We Love You Fats.* The year 1983 brought two albums: *I Dig Big Band Singers* and *The Songs of Bessie Smith.* The latter was a collaboration with Count Basie, which included nine songs associated with the Empress of the Blues, starting with Bessie's first hit, "Down Hearted Blues" and presenting individualized Brewer interpretations of such standards as "St. Louis Blues," "Gulf Coast Blues," "I Ain't Gonna Play Second Fiddle," and the demanding "Gimme a Pigfoot." Contending that some years ago, the combination of Teresa Brewer singing Bessie Smith songs with the Count Basie Band would have seemed most unlikely, Jazz critic Nat Hentoff concluded: "Teresa has fulfilled [the unusually challenging assignment] so well that she has to be included now among the ranking jazz singers. Not jazz-influenced singers only. Teresa sings like a horn with jazz time. That's jazz singing."[30]

CHAPTER SEVEN

"IT DON'T MEAN A THING IF IT AIN'T GOT THAT SWING"

When we opened at the Palomar [in Los Angeles]," Benny Goodman recalled,

> we had a "what've we got to lose" attitude and decided to let loose and shoot the works with our best things like *Sugar Foot Stomp, Sometimes I'm Happy,* and the others. Actually though, we were almost scared to play. [They had just laid a big egg in Denver and were pretty low.]
>
> From the minute I kicked them off, the boys dug in with some of the best playing I'd heard since we left New York. I don't know what it was, but the crowd went wild and then—boom! That was the real beginning.[1]

The date was August 21, 1935, and it was the beginning of Swing as a mainstream development in popular music. As Jazz, later generally a cult music, was the Pop music of the twenties, the music played by the big bands was the popular music of the years from the mid-thirties until the end of World War II. Swing was the music to which people began dancing as the country climbed out of the economic morass of the Great Depression. It was the music of FDR and the NRA and all the alphabetical agencies spawned to assist recovery.[2] It was the music of the post-Prohibition era, when speakeasies became nightclubs and a concentration of clubs on 52nd St. made it Swing

Street.[3] It was a bouncy music of hope and togetherness before the onset of World War II.

The big bands became the medium through which songs became best sellers and popular singers learned the craft that made them stars after World War II. The Swing era was the era of Benny Goodman, of Artie Shaw, Glenn Miller, the Dorsey brothers, Charlie Barnet, Harry James, Woody Herman, Gene Krupa, and others.

But before the big bands of these white star instrumentalists arose to dominate the airwaves and to draw SRO crowds to the country's numerous ballrooms, there were the big black bands of Fletcher Henderson, Count Basie, and Duke Ellington; also of Jimmie Lunceford and Chick Webb. "Before the twenties were over," Marshall W. Stearns has observed,

> Negro bands led by Chick Webb, Earl Hines, Cecil Scott, William McKinney, Charlie Johnson, Luis Russell, and, of course, Duke Ellington were all playing in a style in which *the whole band swung together* [emphasis added]. And before 1935 when Goodman arrived, these bands were joined by Cab Calloway, Jimmie Lunceford, Teddy Hill, Les Hite, Andy Kirk, Don Redman, and especially, Bennie Moten. This music was swinging, relaxed, powerful but for the most part unheard.[4]

In short, while the Swing era gave prominence and large rewards to the big white bands, the style was originated and developed by black musicians during the 1920s.

The Black Pioneers of Swing

If any one man deserves credit for the origin of Swing, it is James Fletcher "Smack" Henderson (1898–1952), who launched his first band in the summer of 1923 at the Club Alabam in New York City. Henderson had come to the city from Georgia to study chemistry at Columbia University; become a song demonstrator for the music publishing firm of Pace and Handy; served as Music Director of Black Swan Records, organized by Harry Pace—the first black-owned record label—and toured as bandleader with Ethel Waters, Black Swan's outstanding artist. The band at the Club Alabam on West 44th St. consisted of nine pieces, three brass, three saxes, and three rhythm, plus Henderson at the piano, and it played dance music rather than Jazz.

From 1924 to 1929, Henderson led the band at the Roseland Ballroom, and it was here that the Swing style took shape, and his band became the ultimate in Negro bands. The group now consisted of 12 men, 5 brass, 3 saxes, and 4 rhythm, which, with an added sax, became the standard Swing instrumentation. Louis Armstrong, Joe Smith, Coleman Hawkins, or Rex Stewart were its star soloists, and Benny Carter and Don Redman, its arrangers. A child prodigy who played trumpet at three years of age and who, during his childhood, mastered every band instrument as well as harmony, theory, and composition, Don Redman (1900–1964) remained with Henderson until 1928, when he took over as music director of McKinney's Cotton Pickers. His pioneering work in Swing can be heard on such titles as "Sugarfoot Stomp," "Henderson Stomp," "Whiteman Stomp," and "Stampede"—all numbers written by Fats Waller and given to Henderson, according to legend, one number for each hamburger Fletcher bought a hungry and indigent Waller.

A stint at Connie's Inn in Harlem in the fall of 1930 was the beginning of the end for the Henderson Band, which ran into problems and bad luck, until it disbanded in the winter of 1934. But during the late twenties and early thirties, Henderson brought to a peak of perfection the style that had begun to take shape in the arrangements of Benny Carter (b. 1907) and Don Redman. By the time that Benny Goodman was playing a coast-to-coast radio show called *Let's Dance* in 1934, Fletcher was the chief architect of its style and had developed a formula that was soon imitated by other big bands and that made Goodman's the top Swing band of the era.

The Henderson arranging formula, which became the earmark of the time, involved a steady, chugging, four-to-the-bar rhythm, unison riffs behind improvising soloists, harmonized swinging section choruses, and call-and-response interchanges between the brass and reed sections. During the 1930s, there was a constant demand for Henderson arrangements, and he wrote for the Dorsey brothers, Isham Jones, and other bands. Among his best arrangements for the Goodman band, memorable titles include "Sometimes I'm Happy," "Blue Skies," "Down South Camp Meeting," "Sugarfoot Stomp," and "King Porter Stomp."

Reorganizing his band in about 1935, Henderson alternated between gigs at New York's Roseland Ballroom and the Grand Terrace in Chicago for several years. A number by Andy Razaf (words) and Leon Berry (music), "Christopher Columbus," arranged by his brother Horace Henderson (b. 1904) and later recorded by many bands, became his theme and a top recording for his band. In 1939 he joined Benny Goodman on piano and as staff arranger, creating an in-demand number in "Stealin' Apples," another Fats Waller tune. He was back again writing arrangements for Goodman in the mid-1940s. Late in that decade, health problems developed when he was touring with Ethel Waters as her pianist. In 1950, he made another attempt to come back, working with J. C. Johnson on *Jazz*

Train (a revue), leading his own band at Bop City (a new Broadway club), and playing with his own sextet at Café Society, which was his last job. A stroke incapacitated him in December 1950, resulting in his death in December 1952.

When Columbia Records issued a four-volume retrospective, *The Fletcher Henderson Story,* it was subtitled, "A Study in Frustration." The title was, unfortunately, apt. The originator of the Swing style and its creative arranging force, he remained the arranger, while Goodman and others became celebrated bandleaders. He had to endure the experience over and over of making fine recordings that garnered marginal sales, while others, using his arrangements on the same numbers, achieved best sellers. That color line had much to do with this situation is unquestioned. But there was also a problem of personality. Fletcher Henderson was apparently too easygoing and too lacking in leadership qualities to command a band. In the booklet accompanying the retrospective, John Hammond, one of his strongest supporters and admirers, tells of how, during a week when he booked the band in the pit of a stage show, there were "fifty instances of tardiness" by his sidemen.[5] Frank Driggs, who documented the booklet, concludes:

> Fletcher Henderson lived and worked far—perhaps too far—in advance of his time. He never profited from his own ideas. Yet he built a musicians' band, a swinging band years before the word came into general usage. It was the Henderson style and arrangements that precipitated the Swing Era. . . . Even with his subsequent bands, Goodman clung to the Henderson style. Basie's band, too, continued the Henderson tradition. . . . Fletcher Henderson's approach remains the foundation for big bands in jazz.[6]

Two other towering giants of popular music, starting in the big band era but continuing into other areas and times, were the Count and the Duke. Both had a command of their personnel and a charisma onstage lacking in Fletcher Henderson. But both suffered from the same discrimination that limited his visibility and popularity. Duke Ellington was nominated for a Pulitzer Prize but was rejected by the governing board, which usually approves nominees recommended by its specialists.

From his youth, Edward Kennedy "Duke" Ellington (1899–1974) manifested a strong sense of confidence, contrasting sharply with Fletcher Henderson's feeling of insecurity. An intuitive talent for leadership was enhanced by an elegance of manner, a nattiness of dress, and a way with words that found expression in a colorful speaking style. (He was the cowriter of a novelty number titled, "You're Just a Old Antidisestablishmentarianismist.") He led his first band, The Washingtonians, in 1924–1927 at the Hollywood (later the Kentucky Club) on Broadway, developing "East St. Louis Toodle-oo," written with trumpeter, James "Bubber" Miley (1903–1932), as the theme. The band did not become a Jazz band until it settled at the Cotton Club for a five-year run, by which time it was known as the Duke Ellington Band.

It was during this period (1927–1932) that Ellington emerged as the leading composer of Jazz, producing such songs and instrumentals of lasting appeal as "Black and Tan Fantasy," "Mood Indigo," "It Don't Mean a Thing (If It Ain't Got That Swing)," "Rockin' in Rhythm," and "Sophisticated Lady." The flow of attractive songs, involving fresh melodies and chords, deriving from Jazz and the Blues, continued unabated until 1953 with "Satin Doll." In a list of over 100 songs and instrumentals, there were such gems as "Solitude," "In a Sentimental Mood," "Caravan," "Prelude to a Kiss," the bluesy torch ballad "I Got It Bad (And That Ain't Good)," and "I'm Beginning to See the Light," one of 1944's big pop hits. Two best sellers were developed by lyricist Bob Russell (1914–1970) from instrumental melodies recorded previously by Ellington: "Don't Get Around Much Anymore," based on "Never No Lament," and "Do Nothin' Till You Hear from Me," based on "Concerto for Cootie." Although these made their mark in the mainstream of popular music, they were quite removed from typical Tin Pan Alley pap.

As early as 1931, when he composed the instrumental "Creole Rhapsody" for a Cotton Club production, and somewhat later, when he wrote "Reminiscing in Tempo," composed for his mother on her death in 1935, Ellington's interest in more extended forms of composition became evident. They anticipated the longer works, including *Black, Brown and Beige,* his first major suite; *The Deep South Suite,* premiered at Carnegie Hall in 1946; *The Liberian Suite,* commissioned for the centenary of the black republic and premiered at Carnegie Hall in 1947; and *Night Creature,* also premiered at Carnegie Hall by his band and Symphony of the Air. Ellington responded to criticisms that these extended works were not Jazz with the comment that he was a composer who *also* wrote Jazz. Starting in 1965, he gave a number of sacred concerts (Grace Cathedral, San Francisco; Coventry Cathedral, England; Cathedral Church of St. John the Divine, New York), at which he presented extended works in an ecumenical vein.

A description of his work as a composer would be incomplete without mention of *Jump for Joy,* a musical revue (1941); film scores he wrote for *Anatomy of a Murder, Paris Blues,* and *Assault on a Queen;* a musical suite he wrote for a Shakespeare Theater production at Stratford, Ontario, of *Timon of Athens;* and *My People,* a major show he wrote and produced in 1963 for the Century of Negro Progress Exposition in Chicago.

In 1956 Ellington made the cover of *Time* magazine after a "comeback" appearance at the Newport Jazz Festival. Two years later, he was presented to Queen Elizabeth and the Royal Family. Through the years, his stature was recognized in a flock of honorary degrees bestowed on him by major American universities; as well as by titles with which he was invested by the governments of various foreign countries. Formal American recognition came to him with the President's Gold Medal, given by Lyndon Johnson in 1966, shortly after the Pulitzer citation denial, and the Medal of Freedom, the highest civilian award, presented at the White House by President Nixon on the Duke's seventieth birthday.

From the beginning, a considerable part of Ellington's compositions was inspired by and written for specific members of his band. At first, there was trumpeter James "Bubber" Miley, whose growl effects and gut-bucket playing became basic to the "jungle" music of the Cotton Club years. Then there was Charles Melvin "Cootie" Williams (b. 1910), for whom he wrote "Concerto for Cootie." The delicate, silk artistry on alto sax of John Cornelius "Rabbit" Hodges (1906–1970) found melodic expression in such songs as "Sophisticated Lady" and "Satin Doll." The sound of clarinetist Leon Albany "Barney" Bigard led to "Mood Indigo," written by Ellington with him; and the horn of trombonist Juan Tizol (b. 1900) can be heard in "Caravan," composed by Ellington with him.

Ellington kept his band in operation throughout his career, supporting it himself when the band did not have bookings. The work of no other American songwriter/composer was as directly a product of his constant involvement with his instrumentalists. It has been said, and it is a truism, that while Ellington played the piano, initially as a Ragtime and Stride eighty-eighter, and frequently conducted from it, his real instrument was the big band.

In the pantheon of Swing bands, Count Basie's was close to Ellington's. Unlike Ellington, William "Count" Basie (1904–1984), of Red Bank, New Jersey, built his reputation largely on his style as a pianist and his stature as a bandleader, and only to a degree on his work as a Blues and Jazz composer. His launching pad was Kansas City, where he played with two outstanding Jazz bands: Walter Page's Blue Devils (1928–1929) and Bennie Moten's Band (1929–1935), eventually drawing members of the latter, after Moten's sudden death, into his own first big band. It was in K.C. that he acquired his cognomen: During a broadcast from the Reno Club in 1936, a radio announcer suggested that, since bandleaders included an Earl (Hines) and a Duke (Ellington), there should be a Count.

Kansas City also contributed the style that was the basis of the

Basie band throughout its long existence. Blues and Boogie-oriented, it involved an extensive riff technique in which phrases were varied as themes or were passed from section to section of the band. It was a style developed by the bands with which Bill Basie played originally, as well as by such other K.C. bands as those of Andy Kirk, Harlan Leonard (b. 1905), and Jay McShann (b. 1909). Jo Jones (b. 1911), who drummed with Basie from the Reno Club days into the late forties, adds: "Bennie Moten's band played a two-beat rhythm such as one-and-three. Walter Page's band played a two-and-four. It wasn't that they would stop to accent the beat, it was sort of like a bouncing ball, and when those rhythms met in the Basie band, there was an even flow—one,two,three,four—like a bouncing ball.[7]

The Reno Club opened the door to Basie's emergence on the national scene when John Hammond caught late-at-night broadcasts while he was in Chicago in 1936. Hammond was so impressed, he arranged for the band to appear at the Grand Terrace in Chicago and then at Roseland Ballroom in New York. Boasting such star jazzmen as Lester Young (1909–1959) and Herschel Evans (1909–1939) on tenor saxes, Earl Warren (b. 1914) on alto, Harry Edison (b. 1915) and Buck Clayton (b. 1911) on trumpets, Dickie Wells (b. 1909) and Benny Morton (b. 1907) on trombones, a rhythm section of Jo Jones, Freddie Green (b. 1911) on guitar, and Walter Page (1900–1957) on string bass, with Jimmy Rushing (1903–1972) handling vocals, the Basie band began recording for Decca in 1937. An engagement at the Savoy Ballroom in Harlem drew attention to the band that year. But it was radio broadcasts from the Famous Door on Fifty-second Street, a booking arranged by John Hammond, that brought national recognition in 1938–1939. (Hammond also arranged for the Door to get much-needed air conditioning during the summer, on the understanding that he could bring Negroes into the segregated club as his guests.) So that the band could play at full volume during broadcasts, patrons had to leave their tiny tables and nurse their drinks on the sidewalk outside the small club.

Like Duke Ellington, Count Basie led a band continuously, throughout his entire career. Through almost five decades, from 1938 on, there were few bands that could approach, let alone match, the drive and wallop of the Basie aggregations. "One O'Clock Jump," written by Basie and adopted in 1938, remained its theme; "Everyday I Have the Blues," a best-selling record in 1952 for Joe Williams (b. 1918) with the Count Basie band, remained one of its biggest request numbers; and "Swingin' the Blues," cowritten by Basie with arranger Eddie Durham (b. 1906), typified its style. More so than Ellington's, Basie's was truly a Blues band.

Among other black bands that were in the forefront of the Swing phenomenon, there were aggregations led by Chick Webb, Jimmie Lunceford, Cab Calloway, Andy Kirk, and a Benny Goodman alumnus, Lionel Hampton.

Before his name became synonymous with the Savoy Ballroom in the mid-1930s, diminutive Chick Webb (1909–1939), a hunchback as a result of tuberculosis of the spine, played at various New York clubs and theaters: at the Black Bottom Club with a 5-piece band in 1926; at the Paddock Club with an 8-piece combo; and, finally, with an 11-piece big band at Rose Danceland at the end of 1927. There were also gigs at the Cotton Club (1929), Roseland, a *Hot Chocolates* revue, and a theater tour with Louis Armstrong. Settling at the "track," as it was known, Chick became the acknowledged King of the Savoy and of Harlem's own favorite band.

Commenting on the famous "battles of the bands," a big audience draw at the Savoy, Duke Ellington said: "Webb was always battle-mad, and those eight guys used to take on every band that came up there to play. And most times, they did the cutting, regardless of the fact that half the time, the other bands were twice the size. The unforgettable and lovable Webb ate up any kind of fight, and everybody in the band played like mad at all times."[8] Calling him "the most luminous of all drum stars, the master, the little giant of the big noise," Gene Krupa (1909–1973), himself a behemoth of the hides, said of Webb: "Chick gassed me, but good, on one occasion at the Savoy, in a battle with Benny's band, and I repeat now what I said then: I was never cut by a better man."[9]

Although the bouncy "Let's Get Together" was the Webb band's theme, it might as well have been "Stompin' at the Savoy." Both were reportedly written by sax man Edgar Melvin "The Lamb" Sampson (1907–1973), responsible for many of the band's arrangements, although Chick is credited with the theme song, and several names appear on "Stompin' at the Savoy"—Andy Razaf (words), Benny Goodman (music), Chick Webb, and Edgar Sampson.[10] Chick recorded "Stompin'" before publication in 1934, but Benny Goodman produced a best-selling record in 1936.

When Chick died in 1939 in his native Baltimore, on an operating table, Ella Fitzgerald, whom he had brought into the band in 1935, took over as leader for a three-year period. In 1947, the city of Baltimore established a recreation center as a memorial to the hunchback, who had saved pennies as a newsboy to buy his first drum.

"Precision" is the word that comes to mind when one thinks of the big band of James Melvin Lunceford (1902–1947). A music graduate of Fisk University and a teacher of music in a Memphis high school, Jimmie elicited from his bandsmen a gemlike attention to detail. Concerned about accuracy in performance, he insisted that his men play in tune and observe note values scrupulously, matters that later figured in the mainstream impact of the white Swing bands. If this demand for precision suggests that the Lunceford band did not swing, that is a mistaken impression. Trombonist-arranger Fernando Arbello (1907-1970), who played with Lunceford from 1942 to 1946, said: "When you talk about bands that could swing, don't forget the Lunceford band! I was with them for three or four years, and I'm telling you that that was one swinging band! There were times when we played in some places and even the walls would shake."[11]

Playing with two-beat accents under a chugging four, the band enunciated its concern in its theme, "Rhythm Is Our Business." Trumpeter Sy Oliver (b. 1910) produced arrangements with wide-voiced sax parts and a distinctive high-register brass section. While Lunceford could play all the saxes, flute, guitar, and trombone—and occasionally filled in—he dedicated himself to leading the band. From 1929, when he organized his first full-time band in Memphis, until his sudden death from a heart attack in 1947, he succeeded in making his one of the most celebrated and admired black bands of the era.

Mention of Cab Calloway inevitably evokes an image of a comic scat singer who made "Hi De Ho" a national catch phrase in about 1934; it does not immediately suggest an involved bandleader. But the fact is that in the late 1930s and early 1940s, the Cab Calloway Band was among the 10 highest-earning bands in the country, and its personnel included some of the top jazzmen of the day: trumpeters Dizzy Gillespie (b. 1917) and Jonah Jones (b. 1908), tenor saxists Chu Berry (1910-1941) and Ben Webster (1909-1973), bassist Milt Hinton (b. 1910), and drummer Cozy Cole (b. 1909).

Although he went to law school in Chicago, Cabell Calloway quickly switched to music in 1929, and soon was fronting two bands, Alabamians and Missourians, playing in Connie's *Hot Chocolates* and at the Savoy Ballroom, before he made his initial impact at the Cotton Club in 1931-1932. The sensation he scored in the club turned into national renown as the result of radio broadcasts, leading to a flock of film appearances from 1932 to 1945. In 1958 he played in *St. Louis Blues,* the film bio of W. C. Handy. It is said that the role of Sportin' Life in the Gershwin opera *Porgy and Bess* was written with him in mind—and he did appear in a 1952-1954 revival of the opera. In the 1960s he played in an all-black version of *Hello Dolly*.

Calloway was himself involved in the writing of "Minnie the Moocher (The Ho De Ho Song)," which he introduced at the Cotton

Club in 1931, sang in the film *The Big Broadcast* in 1932, and which brought him fame. He also appears as co-writer of "The Scat Song (Scat 'n' Skeet 'n' Hi De Hi)," which he introduced in 1932. That year he also sang, in the *Cotton Club Parade,* "Minnie the Moocher's Wedding Day," by Ted Koehler (words) and Harold Arlen (music), who wrote the 1932 Cotton Club score. He appeared at the Cotton Club as late as 1939, when he demonstrated his skill at handling a ballad, "Don't Worry 'bout Me," with words (w) by Ted Koehler and music (m) by Rube Bloom.

A list of recordings by the Calloway Band includes such Ellington perennials as "Mood Indigo" and "Take the *A* Train," Blues-oriented numbers such as "Bye Bye Blues" and "Chattanooga Choo Choo," and classic Blues including "Down Hearted Blues" and "St. James Infirmary," popularized by him in 1930. Singer, actor, and songwriter, Cab tends to be remembered largely because of his great comic talents. But he led a "truly great outfit of the big band era," in George T. Simon's words,[12] and did not fully disband until 1948.

Andrew Dewey Kirk, better known as Andy Kirk (b. 1898), led the Twelve Clouds of Joy, one of the highly praised bands of the Swing era and one that initially carried on the Kansas City tradition of Jazz. Born in Kentucky, Kirk was raised in Denver, where he studied tuba and bass sax. In 1929 he began fronting a band in Dallas when Terrence Holder walked out on his Dark Clouds of Joy. Although he played both the Roseland and Savoy ballrooms in the early 1930s, Kirk made his reputation at the Pla-Mor Ballroom in Kansas City, where after a time he rivaled the famous Bennie Moten for having the best band in the roistering city. Like Moten, he played a Blues-oriented Boogie style, using the favored riff technique.

In 1936, when the band was at its peak in K.C., it had a national record hit in "Until the Real Thing Comes Along," its theme; with a vocal by falsetto singer Pha Terrell (1910–1945). A large measure of the band's success was traceable to Mary Lou Williams, who joined Kirk in 1929, soloed at the piano, composed outstanding Jazz originals for it, and wrote many of its arrangements. From the mid-1930s until 1942, when she left Kirk to become a noted free-lance Jazz and Swing arranger, Mary Lou was billed as the Lady Who Swings the Band, the title of one of her originals recorded by the band. During the 1930s she was an in-demand arranger, turning out charts for the big bands of Benny Goodman, Louis Armstrong, Earl Hines, Tommy Dorsey, and Glen Gray, among others. During the 1940s, when she created *The Zodiac Suite,* played by the New York Philharmonic Symphony Orchestra (1946) and soloed at Café Society and the Village Vanguard in New York, she traveled with the Duke as staff arranger, and again with Benny Goodman. It was quite an accomplishment for a woman in what was then exclusively a man's world, and Mary Lou Williams had not only the talent but the character.

Lionel Hampton (b. 1909), who began leading his own band in 1936 at the Paradise Café in Hollywood, brought the vibraphone into Swing and Jazz. His training in Chicago in the 1920s was as a drummer, and after settling in California, he played drums with the big band of Les Hite (1903 – 1962). His association with the vibraphone is supposed to have begun accidentally. In 1930, the story goes, when he was at a recording session with Louis Armstrong at OKeh Records in Los Angeles, Satchmo spotted a vibraphone in a corner and, out of curiosity, asked Hamp to play something on it. As a result, the Armstrong disk of "Memories of You" contains an eight-bar introduction on vibes, supposedly the first use of the instrument on a jazz record. Hamp's association with Benny Goodman also happened accidentally. Visiting Hollywood, Goodman and drummer Gene Krupa came to the Paradise Café, where Hamp's band was playing, and joined him in a spontaneous jam session. Both were so impressed, that Hamp was invited to join the Goodman Trio, making it a Quartet, with Hamp on vibes—and he did occasionally play drums with the big band. During his tenure with Goodman, from November 1936 to July 1940, Hampton also recorded with many small combos, producing some of the best small-band Swing of the time. By contrast with Red Norvo (b. 1908), who switched from xylophone to vibraphone, Hampton plays a hard-driving, riff-inflected style.

In 1940, after leaving Goodman, Hamp returned to the West Coast and organized his own big band, which made its debut in November of that year and continued in action into the 1970s. "Flying Home," a song on whose music he collaborated with Benny Goodman (who introduced it on disk), became the band's theme. Wailing in a hard Boogie style with a sledgehammer beat, the Hamp band specialized in jump tunes, and even took off in a Bop direction after Jazz turned modern with Gillespie and Parker. Hampton himself was a flashy performer, bouncing, grunting, grinning, and sweating in a manner that was an attention-getter for Gene Krupa. In recent years, Hampton's musicianship received recognition at the White House, where he performed both during the Carter administration (June 1978) and the Reagan years (September 1981).

Small Band Swing

Swing played by small combos was a not-insignificant phase of the era, a phenomenon that developed largely because of the minuscule size of many of the Manhattan clubs, especially those on 52nd St.

Although it became known as Swing Street—a fact now memorialized by signs on the lampposts on the corners of Fifth and Sixth avenues[13]—52nd St. was hospitable to small combos playing Dixieland Jazz (at clubs such as Jimmy Ryan's) and, in the 1940s, to Bop (at the Onyx, Kelly's Stable, and so on). But the heyday of the Street coincided with the era of Swing, and during any week, one could hear trios, quartets, and quintets swinging for listeners; few of the clubs had space for dancers. Ad hoc trios were built around such star performers as pianists Art Tatum (1910–1956), Erroll Garner (1921–1977), Fats Waller, saxist Coleman Hawkins (1904–1969), trumpet players Roy Eldridge (b. 1911) and Dizzy Gillespie (b. 1917). Also white artists, including pianist Johnny Guarnieri (b. 1917), pianist Marian McPartland (b. 1920), and clarinetist Tony Scott (b. 1921) could be heard. But there were also small bands with set personnel, such as Stuff Smith and his Onyx Club Boys, Louis Prima and his New Orleans Gang, and Slim and Slam.

The group that inaugurated the Swing era on 52nd St. in February 1934 was Leo Watson and his Five Spirits of Rhythm. The comic antics of their musical novelty act brought as much applause as their bouncy music. Their two big request numbers were "Dr. Jekyll and Mr. Hyde" and "My Old Man," the latter based on an original Jazz riff. Leo Watson (1898–1950) was the main draw, a fabulous scat singer and a man who could vocally produce a trombone sound that could not be distinguished from the instrument itself. But he was also a schooled musician who could play drums, trombone, and tipple, and who performed, after the 52nd St. years, with Artie Shaw and Gene Krupa, among other bands.

There have been few Jazz fiddlers in the history of the art form. Joe Venuti (1898–1978), who soloed with Paul Whiteman, was a remarkable improviser; Eddie South (1904–1962), who became known as the Dark Angel of the Violin, was another; and Stuff Smith, a third, was as accomplished as each and, doubtless, more into modern Jazz than either. Hezekiah Leroy Gordon Smith (1909–1967) came to the Onyx with a six-piece combo that developed its style in a residency at various Buffalo venues. With Jonah Jones on trumpet and Cozy Cole on Drums, the Stuff Smith gang drew overflow crowds and made record hits of his "I'se a Muggin'" and "Youse a Viper," the latter with a rare vocal chorus by trumpeter Jones. Employing an electric amplifier on his instrument, Stuff also foreshadowed later developments in Jazz with his use of flatted fifths and whole-tone scales. Although his music bounced, he played with a full-bodied, resonant tone and the technique of a virtuoso violinist—all qualities documented on such albums as *Have Violin, Will Swing* and *Swingin' Stuff*.

The Onyx successor to Stuff was the combo of John Kirby (1908–1952), who was raised in a Baltimore orphanage. He originally studied trombone, then worked as a Pullman-car porter to buy a tuba, which he took up after settling in New York in the late 1920s. From 1930 to 1936 he played with a number of big bands, including those of Fletcher Henderson, Lucky Millinder, and the Mills Blue Rhythm Band. When he was performing with Chick Webb in 1933–1935, he switched from tuba to string bass.

The popular combo Kirby led at the Onyx included Buster Bailey (1902–1967), clarinet; Billy Kyle (1914–1966), piano; Russell Procope (1908–1981), saxes; O'Neil Spencer (1909–1944), drums; and Charlie Shavers (1917–1971), trumpet. Later a Tommy Dorsey stalwart, Shavers not only wrote most of the arrangements but composed two of the group's most successful numbers, "Pastel Blue" and "Undecided." Performing in eye-catching white tails, the group gained overnight acceptance, enhanced in the fall of 1937, when it was joined by pretty Maxine Sullivan (b. 1911). Almost immediately, Maxine scored with a hit recording of "Loch Lomond" b/w "Annie Laurie," Scottish ballads arranged in Swing style by Claude Thornhill (1909–1965).

The popularity of "Loch Lomond" provoked a brouhaha about swinging the classics. The controversy erupted when singer Ella Logan charged that Sullivan had copied her, and asserted that she was the first to swing old songs. Even before Logan had raised the issue, a Detroit radio station cut Tommy Dorsey off the air during a Swing version of "Loch Lomond." Two days later, radio stations in Cleveland and Los Angeles announced a ban on Swing versions of any old-time songs. Stations in New York and Milwaukee announced that they would give the public what it wanted. But in the meantime, the Cleveland station published a list of songs that could not be swung. In addition to "Loch Lomond," "Annie Laurie," and "Comin' thru the Rye," it included "Love's Old Sweet Song," "I Love You Truly," "Darling Nellie Gray," "Last Rose of Summer," "Juanita," "Sweet Genevieve," "Drink to Me Only with Thine Eyes," and Brahms's "Lullaby." Nevertheless, John Kirby recordings included lilting versions of such classics as "Anitra's Dance" from *Peer Gynt Suite,* "Humoresque," "Sampson and De-Li-Lah," and "Drink to Me Only with Thine Eyes."

Married in 1938, Kirby and Maxine Sullivan carried over their brief period of domestic bliss—they were divorced in 1941—into a CBS show, *Flow Gently, Sweet Rhythm.* It took its style from the light Swing played at the Onyx, yielding an album of the same title. The Kirby sextet continued in action until 1942, playing clubs in Chicago and Los Angeles as well as on 52nd St. What Kirby introduced into small-band Jazz, which tended to be a freewheeling, slam-bang type of music, was an orchestral precision, finesse, and a light, swinging beat. The Biggest Little Band in the Land, as it was billed, thus added a new dimension to combo Jazz.

The White Synthesis

In 1937 the Benny Goodman Band engaged in a musical "battle of the bands" with the band of Chick Webb. It is said that 4,000 people packed the Savoy Ballroom, while another 5,000, unable to gain entrance, milled about on Lenox Avenue, listening to whatever sounds drifted into the street and waiting for news of the winner. The Goodman Band, then at a peak of its popularity, lost the competition. To many, it seemed poetic justice, in view of the origins of Swing as a musical style.

The big bands have been so extensively written up in histories, discographies, and personal memoirs that we shall concern ourselves with three matters: the debt to black music, the nature of the white synthesis, and the black–white equation of the Swing years.

Benny Goodman (b. 1909) was at the epicenter of all three. An all-time great clarinetist, a fine Jazz improviser as well as classical musician, and a masterful bandleader, Goodman formed his band in 1934. By then he possessed at least a dozen years of experience behind him, starting at the age of 13, when he played dance dates in Chicago, continuing on alto sax and clarinet with the bands of Arnold Johnson (1893–1975), Art Kassel (1896–1965), and Ben Pollack (1903–1971); pit band work in Broadway shows; studio band work with the radio orchestras of Don Voorhees, Andre Kostelanetz, Paul Whiteman, and others; and a band of his own, accompanying crooner Russ Columbo (1908–1934) in the summer of 1932.

By 1934 Goodman had recorded extensively with many small combos and even backed the great Billie Holiday on her record debut. That summer, the big band he organized played Billy Rose's Music Hall, from June 1 to October 17. That year he was chosen for the famous *Let's Dance* program on NBC, a three-hour show sponsored by the National Biscuit Company, in which three bands alternated, one playing Latin music (Xavier Cugat), another, sweet dance music (Kel Murray), and the third, Swing (Benny Goodman). Thus, the Goodman Band was heard every Saturday night coast-to-coast during prime time, from December 1934 to May 1935. It was with high hopes that it set forth on a cross-country tour, only to meet disappointments in city after city, with a four-week stand in Denver turning into a dismal fiasco. The repeated complaint was that the band was too loud.

Then came the surprise reception at the Palomar Ballroom in Hollywood in August 1935, when the fans, who had developed into a following as a result of the *Let's Dance* broadcasts, went wild. In the period between November 1935 and May 1936, when the band played at the Congress Hotel in Goodman's hometown (Chicago) and broadcast nightly, it established itself as the foremost Swing aggregation, and Goodman emerged with the title of King of Swing. It was a title that most historians properly believe belongs to black pioneers of the style, such as Fletcher Henderson, Count Basie, or Duke Ellington.

What is consequential is that the success of the Goodman Band was based largely on the arrangements of Fletcher Henderson. This is not intended to denigrate the contribution of such talented arrangers as Jimmy Mundy (b. 1907), Spud Murphy (b. 1908), Horace Henderson (b. 1904), Edgar Sampson (1907–1973), and Mary Lou Williams. In the year of the *Let's Dance* program, John Hammond arranged for Goodman to buy as many as 36 scores—the figure varies according to different sources[14]—from Henderson, who was having some financial problems. These were "arrangements of current pop tunes with a beat and an irreverence Fletcher had never dared to employ with his own band." Hammond concludes: "I firmly believe that it was this approach to ballads that gave the Goodman Band the style that made it conquer the nation the following year."[15]

Another significant black influence on Goodman was Count Basie, about whom Marshall W. Stearns writes: "Goodman adopted Basie numbers such as *One O'Clock Jump*—the first Goodman recording to sell over a million—and then began to use Basie and some of his musicians on recordings."[16]

Goodman actually began to make records with black musicians as early as 1933. "For this," Goodman has said, "the responsibility must be given almost entirely to John Hammond, who really put me in touch with the kind of music they could play."[17]

Of course, Henderson and his band were not alone in playing a swinging kind of music. In addition to the black bands already discussed, there were bands led by Earl Hines, Cecil Scott (1905–1964), William McKinney (1895–1969), Charlie Johnson (1891–1959), Luis Russell (1902–1963), and others, all of whom, in the words of Marshall Stearns, "were playing in a style in which the whole band swung together."[18] This was happening before the 1920s were over, and before 1935, when Goodman arrived, these bands were joined by Teddy Hill (b. 1909), Les Hite (1903–1962), Don Redman (1900–1964), and Bennie Moten (1894–1935), among others.

Of what did the white synthesis consist? Goodman and the other big white bands contributed precision, accuracy of pitch and polish, producing "a refined and swinging blend that the general public at that precise moment was ready to enjoy."[19] In Marshall Stearns's words, "It was Goodman's precise style of playing the Henderson arrangements that hit the great American public as something new and exciting."[20]

In considering the rewards enjoyed by Goodman, Glenn Miller, Artie Shaw, and other white bandleaders, one cannot disregard the segregation that was an inescapable aspect of the American scene. In 1936, when the Cradle of Swing, as 52nd St.'s Onyx Club was known, presented New York's first Swing music concert, of the 16 bands and groups that performed at the Imperial Theater, only two were black—Louis Armstrong and Stuff Smith. In 1940, when disk jockey Martin Block, of the celebrated *Make Believe Ballroom*, ran a big-band popularity poll involving 21 radio stations, there was not a single black band in the top 10 finalists. Glenn Miller led the voting, with 44,446 votes, followed by Tommy Dorsey, Benny Goodman, Sammy Kaye, Kay Kyser, Gene Krupa, Charlie Barnet, Jimmy Dorsey, Artie Shaw, and Jan Savitt.

One obvious explanation for the absence of black bands was, of course, the tremendous exposure given by radio to the white bands. Glenn Miller (1904–1944) was on the air for Chesterfield cigarettes over the entire network on Tuesdays, Wednesdays, and Thursdays. Old Gold presented Artie Shaw, while Benny Goodman rode the Camel caravan—and so it went.

Segregation also marked the personnel of bands, as it did locals of the American Federation of Musicians. There were some exceptions. It was John Hammond again who persuaded Benny Goodman to add Teddy Wilson (b. 1912) to his personnel. "Nobody had attempted obvious racial mixing in major locations," notes James Collier. "Goodman was worried, and so no doubt was Wilson; but Hammond was persuasive, and Goodman was willing to take the risk."[21] To mitigate against possible adverse reaction and sniping, Wilson at first did not play with the band but only with the Goodman Trio. At a later date, as we know, Goodman added Lionel Hampton, making the trio into a quartet evenly balanced between black and white.

There were a few other intrepid bandleaders. Artie Shaw featured both Hot Lips Page (1908–1954) and Roy Eldridge (b. 1911) as solo trumpeters, and in 1938 employed Billie Holiday as his female vocalist. Trumpeter "Peanuts" Holland (b. 1910) appeared as a star soloist with Charlie Barnet, as did Howard McGhee (b. 1918). Jimmy Dorsey featured singer June Richmond (1915–1962) for a time, and toward the end of the Swing era, Tommy Dorsey hired his first black musician in Charlie Shavers (1917–1971). Generally speaking, most white bandleaders made no effort to breach the color line.

In December 1946, eight big bands called it quits. These were Woody Herman, Benny Goodman, Harry James, Les Brown, Jack Teagarden, Benny Carter, Ina Ray Hutton, and Tommy Dorsey. To all intents, with these major groups gone, the Swing era was over. By then, something initially known as Be-Bop or Re-Bop, and finally as Bop, was being heard, mainly on 52nd St.

The Black Backlash

> In 1945, as World War II was nearing its end, several white jazzmen wandered into the Three Deuces where a combo led by Dizzy Gillespie (b. 1917) was holding forth. Al Haig (b. 1924) was at the piano, Curley Russell (b. 1920) on bass, Stan Levey (b. 1925) at the drums, and Charlie "Bird" Parker (1920–1955) on alto. The sounds emanating from the combo were strange to ears accustomed to the predictable diatonics and two-beat drive of Dixieland. So was the song and its chord line. And the tempo was a runaway race.
>
> The visitors mounted the small bandstand, intending to jam a bit. They figured that the first number was an original and therefore strange in its chord line and accelerated, offbeat rhythms. But the next tune proved just as much of a puzzle. (It was not a pop or jazz standard that was part of the common pool in which jazz musicians had been swimming for years.) The visitors were baffled, but having sensed something of the chord line, waited patiently for the traditional signal that one player gives to another to invite participation. The nod of the head or the motion of the horn never came. Instead, the Gillespie player who had been soloing just stopped. There was an awkward pause as several measures went by with nothing except rhythm sounding. Finally, one of the visitors came in and tried to fumble his way through a solo. All three of the visitors made an effort to join the ensemble chorus. There was no "ride-out" as the final chorus of a tune was known in the old days. The Three Deuces group simply quit in the middle of a measure the way a car makes a sudden stop. And then Dizzy and his men vanished from the bandstand, leaving three bewildered instrumentalists looking as if their flies had been found open. "They really scared the shit out of us," one of the visitors later admitted."[22]

And while that may have been partly what the black boppers wanted to do, their more basic concern, as several indicated, was to create something that "Charlie," meaning white musicians, could not steal—as Charlie had done with Swing. The new Jazz was unabashedly antiwhite, and that included audiences as well as musicians.

Dizzy and other boppers played with their backs to the paying customers, and Dizzy occasionally waved his rump rhythmically in their faces, as if he were conducting. Boppers did not wait for or acknowledge applause. As for the musicians, they consciously sought to make the music a tantalizing puzzle to the listeners. They searched out new chord structures involving ninths, elevenths, and thirteenths (instead of using the smaller triads and sevenths), explored new scales such as the whole-tone scale, and favored an interval generally avoided in traditional Jazz and even in classical music, the so-called flatted fifth. Instead of working within the framework of the traditional repertoire known to musicians from the twenties on, they turned to recent show tunes, with their more complex chord patterns—and even these, they did not identify. Using hit songs from Broadway shows, they concealed the chord sequences behind new titles and invented new melodies over them.

"What Is This Thing Called Love" became "Hot House." "How High the Moon" became "Ornithology," and "Lover" became "Diggin' for Diz." Drummer Kenny Clarke (b. 1914) told Leonard Feather: "We'd play *Epistrophy* or *I've Got My Love to Keep Me Warm* just to keep the other guys off the stand, because we knew they couldn't make those chord changes. We kept the riffraff out and built our clique on new chords."[23]

Louis Armstrong called Bop "the modern malice," and boppers returned the compliment by referring to proponents of New Orleans and Dixieland Jazz as "moldy figs." Eddie Condon (1905–1973), a leader of the Dixieland crowd, taunted the Bop crowd: "We don't flat our fifths. We drink them."

Bop polarized the world of Jazz, with black artists pointedly rejecting whites, as they had been rejected over the years. The motivation is not difficult to understand. Black musicians had gone through the Swing years watching their white brothers reap the glory and the rewards. They had fought in the war to end racism, anticipating and hearing promises of a new world to come. But once World War II was over, it was segregation, discrimination, and exploitation all over again. Except for occasional tokenism, studio orchestras and executive positions in the recording industry and broadcasting studios continued to be white. The pit bands of Broadway shows remained white. Opportunities for blacks in symphony orchestras and the concert world showed little signs of improving.

Christy's Melodies, Boston, 1844. Harvard Theatre Collection.

Thatcher, Primrose and West's Minstrels, n.p., n.d. [1800s], program. Harvard Theatre Collection.

"James Bland's 3 Great Songs," Boston, 1879. Harvard Theatre Collection.

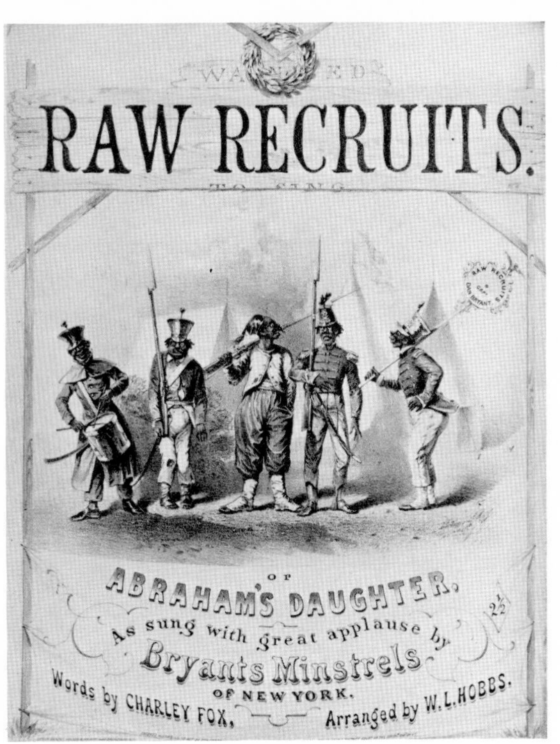

Bryant's Minstrels, "Raw Recruits," New York, 1862. Harvard Theatre Collection.

George Washington Dixon, "Zip Coon," New York, n.d. [1830s]. Harvard Theatre Collection.

Chuck Berry

Lena Horne

Otis Redding

Aretha Frankl

James Brown

Ray Charles

B.B. King

Little Richard

In social and psychological terms, Bop was an expression of anger, frustration, resentment—and challenge.

The birth of Bop had been quietly prepared in experimental sessions held beginning in the early forties at two Harlem venues—Clark Monroe's Uptown House and Henry Minton's Playhouse in the Hotel Cecil. Here trumpeter Dizzy Gillespie, saxist Charlie Parker, drummer Kenny "Klock" Clarke, pianist Thelonious Monk (1920–1982), and bassist Oscar Pettiford (1922–1960), among others, began working with new repertoire and seeking new modes of expression.

One of the major changes introduced into Jazz by Bop was with regard to tempo and the role of the drummer. From the 1920s on, Jazz had been dance music, whether the dancers were doing the Charleston, Black Bottom, Shag, Lindy Hop, or Truckin'. The boppers took the dance beat out of the music. Maintenance of rhythm was moved to the light chink-chink of the high-hat cymbals, while the bass drum was used for offbeat accents—"dropping bombs," in Kenny Clarke's lingo. Playing at breakneck tempi, the boppers also turned around the traditional triplet figure of classical music and Jazz. Instead of accenting the first note of three, as had been done for centuries, they threw the accent on the middle note. It became buh-DEE-dat or buh-RE-bop, whence the name of the music.

An up-tempo treatment of "How High the Moon" from a 1940 revue, *Two for the Show*, a song with an artfully modulating melody, became the early anthem of Bop. Original compositions were also written by Oscar Pettiford ("One Base Hit"), Thelonious Monk ("'Round About Midnight"), Budd Johnson ("Bu-Dee-Daht") and Dizzy Gillespie ("Salt Peanuts"). The last-mentioned embodied the upended triplet, with the second, accented syllable, Salt PEA-nuts, being voiced an octave above the first syllable.

Fragments or echoes of the new sounds were actually heard in several of the big bands. Among these were Earl Hines's Orchestra when Charlie Parker was a member, in 1943. Even earlier, in 1940, when Dizzy played with Cab Calloway's Band, adverse comments sometimes greeted his strange-sounding improvisations. In 1944, when both Dizzy and Bird played in Billy Eckstine's Band—as did trumpeter Benny Harris (1919–1975)—so much of the new Jazz was heard that the band is sometimes recognized as the first big Bebop band.

But it was 52nd St. that was the proving ground for Bop. In the 1944–1945 period, four clubs provided exposure for the new sounds—Spotlite, Three Deuces, Kelly's Stable, and the Onyx. The last-mentioned became the first to showcase a Bop combo. Advertised as the Gillespie–Pettiford Quintet, it consisted of Max Roach (1924–1984) on drums, George Wallington (b. 1924) at the piano, and Don Byas (1912–1972) on tenor sax, as well as the two leaders. The unintentional addition of Don Byas, who had been hired by the club as an alternate combo, led to the development of a unison trumpet–tenor-sax style, which became a mark of Bop. On a February 1944 record date for Apollo, Coleman Hawkins used four members of the group (sans Wallington) to record two Bop classics, Budd Johnson's "Bu-Dee-Daht" and Dizzy's "Woodyn You."

Despite the early controversy and, frequently, the animosity provoked by Bop, what started as a backlash to Swing became, as this author wrote in *52nd St.: The Street of Jazz,* "the herald of all modern jazz and developed at a time when the music was stagnating. Improvisation had become repetition and the music was no longer 'the sound of surprise.' Bop brought new resources into the field of Jazz, fresh melodic lines, startling rhythms, complex chords, and new repertoire."[24]

CHAPTER EIGHT

"MAMA'S GOT THE RHYTHM, PAPA'S GOT THE BLUES"

"With my little band," Louis Jordan (1908–1975) told me shortly before his death, "I did everything they did with a big band. I made the Blues jump."[1]

The little band to which he referred was the Tympany Five, which he organized in 1938 after playing saxes and singing for two years with the big band of Chick Webb, a resident band at the Savoy Ballroom in Harlem. The Tympany Five was a slimmed-down version of a big band, consisting of a rhythm group and two melody instruments, sax and trumpet. It played for fun and dancing in a joyful Shuffle–Boogie rhythm, pioneering the style that later became known as Rhythm and Blues and earning for Jordan the title, Father of R & B. Although the style had its beginnings in the dance rhythms of the big bands, with afterbeat accents imposed on an eight-to-the-bar meter, it did not fully mature until 1949, when the new black sound was formally christened Rhythm and Blues in *Billboard* magazine. It was not until World War II that the term *race records,* in use since the 1920s for records by black artists, began to be questioned for possible pejorative overtones. For a time, *Billboard* used *Harlem Hit Parade* on charts dealing with black disks, and in stories employed the word *sepia* instead of *Negro;* but in its issue of June 25, 1949, it led the music industry in adopting R & B as a descriptive term.

The Boogie strain in Jordan's work was not just a matter of meter but of songs as well. The early recordings of the Tympany Five included "Pinetop's Boogie" and "Caldonia Boogie" (recorded before Woody Herman's best-selling version). The most popular, perhaps the biggest, seller of his career, was "Choo Choo Ch'Boogie," which reportedly went over the million mark in 1946. By then, Jordan had demonstrated an ability to produce records that crossed over into the mainstream, even though the subject matter, the locution, and the point of view were black. In 1944 his "Is You Is or Is You Ain't My Baby," which he co-wrote, made the Top Ten on the Pop as well as the race charts, and commanded such a wide audience that Jordan was signed to sing it in the film *Follow the Boys.* (The Delta Rhythm Boys sang it the following year in the film *Easy to Look At.*) "Saturday Night Fish Fry," again with a black ethnic slant, proved a crossover in 1949.

Jordan's impact on other artists was far-reaching, embracing a performer/producer/songwriter like Johnny Otis (b. 1921) and the Song Laureate of Teenage Rock, Chuck Berry (b. 1926). The humor in many of Berry's songs, such as "Too Much Monkey Business" and "Brown-Eyed Handsome Man," owes a debt to Jordan. Chuck Berry has said: "If I had to listen through eternity to music, it would be Nat Cole, and if I had to work through eternity, it would be with Louis Jordan." Jordan's willingness to deal humorously with indigenous aspects of black life ("Ain't Nobody Here But Us Chickens," "Beans and Cornbread," etc.) was itself a testament of pride.

The Components of R & B

Rhythm and Blues may be described as an indigenous black music played by small combos in which the downbeat accents of popular music ($\overset{>}{1}$,2,$\overset{>}{3}$,4) are superseded by strongly accented upbeats or afterbeats (1,$\overset{>}{2}$,3,$\overset{>}{4}$), and in which singers abandoned the resonant vibrato of Pop singing for a raw, shouting style.

Two instruments became important in Rhythm and Blues. The electric guitar, whose use was pioneered by Charles Christian (1916–1942) in the Benny Goodman Band, grew in significance as a result of Aaron "T-Bone" Walker (1909–1975). Working in his early days with Blues pioneers Ida Cox and Ma Rainey, he developed an intimacy with the Blues that led to his introducing and popularizing "Stormy Monday," one of the most recorded of all Blues. In 1940 he joined the big West Coast band of Les Hite (1903–1962). As in Christian's case, his desire to solo led to his discarding the acoustic for the electric guitar. He developed such proficiency on it that few R & B guitarists have escaped his influence. Among those who idolized him, B. B. King (b. 1925) has said: "T-Bone and Elmore James and that Frenchman, Django Reinhardt. These three combined to one is the basis of my playing."[2]

The other instrument that became a vital component of R & B was the tenor sax, still the lead instrument of so-called society combos that play at confirmations, weddings, etc. In these combos, the tenor has a smooth, warm, euphonious sound, similar to what it had in the white "sweet" Swing bands. But early R & B tenormen favored the instrument for the raucous, snarling roar it could also produce. They used it to express the same feelings that were embodied in the rise of Bop—a sense of postwar disillusionment with the black's status.

The tenorman who was the precursor of the abrasive style known as honking was Battiste Illinois Jacquet (b. 1922) of Broussard, Louisiana, whose solo on Lionel Hampton's disk of "Flying Home" (1941) created a sensation among black musicians. Deriving from the Coleman Hawkins tradition of the big-voiced, vibrant tenor, Jacquet, who later worked with Count Basie, forged a reputation as an exhibitionist who could hype an audience to a frenzy, which he did in 1944 at a Jazz at the Philharmonic concert. His use of repetitive phrases and dissonant intervals became an earmark of a style that relied on the repeated sounding of a deep, low, resonant note followed by high, squeaking, freak notes.

Among the tenormen who made honking instrumental records, there were Hal Singer (b. 1919), who worked with Jay McShann, Lucky Millinder, and Duke Ellington, among other bands, until his "Cornbread" hit in 1948 made it possible for him to tour with his own small combo[3]; Wild Bill Moore (b. 1918), whose 1947 recording of "We're Gonna Rock, We're Gonna Roll" was one of the earliest pre-Rock uses of the words that came to identify the Presley revolution[4]; and Big Jay McNeely (b. 1928), whose recording of "Deacon's Hop" was a 1948 hit and whose steamy, erotic playing so excited a fan at the Shrine Auditorium in Hollywood that he fell out of the first balcony.

The biggest of the records made in the late-1940s time slot—all appearing on the Savoy label of Newark, New Jersey—was "The Hucklebuck" by Paul Williams, the No. 1 R & B disk of 1949, whose enormous popularity drew white competitive covers by Tommy Dorsey and Frank Sinatra. An even more popular R & B instrumental was the two-sided disk of "Honky Tonk" by pianist/organist Bill Doggett (b. 1916). Featuring an extended solo by tenorman Clifford

Scott, marked at points by honking, it went to No. 1 and remained a seven-month resident of best-seller charts into 1957.

William Ballard Doggett, who worked as an arranger for the Ink Spots and was associated at various times with Lionel Hampton and Ella Fitzgerald, mastered the electric organ when he played with Louis Jordan, who had previously been using Wild Bill Davis (b. 1906) on the instrument. Performed in a four-to-the-bar meter, "Honky Tonk" was a riff-styled, studio-developed arrangement in which the four musicians on the date participated — Doggett, tenorman Clifford Scott, drummer Berisford "Shep" Shepherd (b. 1917), and Billy Butler. It was a solid, medium-tempoed dance record, which, according to King Records, sold over 400,000 copies, making it the biggest instrumental R & B disk.

Virtually all R & B records were produced by small, independent labels. But Mercury Records, with its main office in Chicago, accounted for "Slow Walk," a hit R & B instrumental of 1956. It was by tenorman Sylvester "Sil" Austin (b. 1929), originally of Florida, who worked with trumpeter Roy "Little Jazz" Eldridge (b. 1911), Cootie Williams (b. 1908) and Tiny Bradshaw (1905–1958).

A tenorman whose talent was prized by many R & B artists but who never came into the limelight was (Thomas) Maxwell Davis (1916–1970), a West Coast arranger and saxist throughout the 1950s and 1960s. Working with Aladdin Records of Los Angeles, he recorded, among others, Lowell Fulson (b. 1921) and Clarence "Gatemouth" Brown (b. 1924). The latter was the bluesman with whom Don Robey of Houston launched his Peacock label. But Davis can also be heard on recordings by Red Prysock (b. 1929) and B. B. King.

Jack McVea (b. 1914), also a West Coast tenorman, worked as the leader of the studio band at Black & White Records, another R & B indie, and backed, among others, T-Bone Walker on his celebrated recording of "Stormy Monday." But before and after this association, he played with such bands as Lionel Hampton's, Count Basie's, and Benny Carter's, and on recordings with Slim Gaillard (b. 1916) of Slim & Slam fame. The peak of McVea's career came in 1946, when he recorded a novelty song that not only was a Pop crossover but became a national catchword with comics and in the media. The novelty, titled "Open the Door, Richard," was based on a funny skit, performed for years in black vaudeville by two comics, Dusty Fletcher and John Mason, who apparently originated the gag. A lawsuit was required to work out the writer credits, which ultimately included not only McVea, but Fletcher, Mason, and Dan Howell. The McVea disk on Black & White Records, employing a catchy musical riff, caught on so fast that it soon faced the competition of 14 other versions, 6 on major labels and 8 on small independents. Among the majors, there were disks by Count Basie (Victor), Louis Jordan (Decca), and the Pied Pipers (Capitol). The independent versions were by Dusty Fletcher himself (National), Hot Lips Page (Apollo), Big Sid Catlett (Manor), Hank Penny (King) and the well-known Merry Macs (Majestic). The commotion initiated by McVea resulted in "Open the Door, Richard" climbing to the No. 1 spot on *Billboard*'s Honor Roll of Hits on March 1, 1947.[5]

King Curtis (1934–1971), born Curtis Owsley in Forth Worth, Texas, also functioned as a studio musician. His association in a life that ended prematurely—he was stabbed to death by a drifter loitering in front of a Harlem brownstone he owned—was with Atlantic Records. The exciting tenor sax solos on disks by Aretha Franklin (b. 1942), Wilson Pickett (b. 1941), The Rascals, and other Atlantic artists of the 1960s, are invariably by Curtis. His precocious mastery of the instrument was such that he went directly from secondary school into the Lionel Hampton Band—and shortly thereafter, was the most sought-after tenorman for R & B record sessions. He scored his first hit with his own group (Noble Knights) on a small label (Enjoy) at the height of the Twist craze in 1962, with "Soul Twist." Although he placed a number of other disks on R & B charts with a combo called King Pins, his second biggest hit was "Memphis Soul Stew" on the Atco label, an Atlantic Records subsidiary, in 1967. In recordings of Bill Doggett's "Honky Tonk" and Big Jay McNeely's "Something on Your Mind," he acknowledged some of his predecessors in the evolution of the tenor-sax sound. To their raucous honking and screeching, he added a confident expressiveness that gave his playing an emotional kick.

The Giants of R & B

Just as the sound of the tenor sax changed in R & B, so the singing style underwent a drastic alteration. Pioneer Delta bluesmen moaned, sighed, and cried. Urban bluesmen added vibrato and Pop–Jazz influences. The most potent influence in R & B singing was Gospel music, whose exultation and excitement R & B singers sought to capture. With the head thrown back and the mouth open wide, they shouted. In the 1930s, Joe Turner (b. 1911), singing in a Kansas City bar as he mixed drinks, bellowed to attract customers off 12th Street. He was still a shouter when he surfaced on Atlantic Records in the 1950s with "Chains of Love," and followed it with a series of disks that climaxed in the 1954 hit, "Shake, Rattle and Roll." But his shouting in the 1950s was freighted with the postwar sense of disappointment and frustration felt by blacks. Turner had himself gone through years of rejection both professionally and, as he toured, as a black. When Ahmet Ertegun first approached him, he was hesitant about going back into the recording studio. The world of the 1950s still was segregated, excluding blacks from Broadway theaters, movie houses and nightclubs.

But as R & B developed, and in it, blacks were moving toward the feeling of pride and dignity that burst forth in the black nationalist movement of the 1960s and in the music known as Soul. R & B male shouters were not moaning the rural, nasal Blues of Blind Lemon Jefferson, the "hellhound on my trail" Blues of Robert Johnson, or the "fixin' to die" Blues of Bukka White—but the roaring "Shake, Rattle and Roll" Blues of the new, macho black male. *"Get outa that bed,"* Joe Turner sang, *"and make with those pots and pans!"*

The shouters were not just male. Ruth Brown (b. 1928) singing "5-10-15 Hours" and "Mama, He Treats Your Daughter Mean" was an assertive shouter, as was La Vern Baker on "Tweedle Dee" and "Jim Dandy." The towering figure of the female shouters was Willie Mae "Big Mama" Thornton (1912–1984), whose raucous yell at the opening of "(You're Nothin' But a) Hound Dog" was an announcement of the beginning of a new era in popular music—and an assertion of female independence. *"I ain't gonna feed you no more!"* But mainstream listeners were not paying attention then to the R & B charts and the disks coming out of the small record companies. They were unaware that "Hound Dog" was the No. 3 R & B song of 1953, and they were still unaware of Big Mama's rip-roaring record when Elvis Presley (1935–1977) made a confused, wrong-tempo version of the song three years later and became identified with it.[6] Although Big Mama recorded for a number of labels other than Peacock, on which she made "Hound Dog"—Arhoolie, Mercury, and Vanguard, among others—and though she made appearances at the Monterey and other jazz festivals, she never received the recognition due her talents—and she died alone in a run-down rooming house in Los Angeles. But her influence is to be heard in the soulful music of Aretha Franklin (b. 1942) and most impressively in Janis Joplin (1943–1970), who idolized, imitated, and learned from her and who made several overpowering recordings of her song "Ball and Chain."

Among the male giants of R & B, Fats Domino (b. 1929) and B. B. King (b. 1925) made their initial impact on the record scene in 1951–1952, Domino with "Goin' Home" and King with "Three O'Clock Blues." They come from contrasting environments, the former from the New Orleans Jazz scene and the latter from the Mississippi/Memphis Blues scene. Domino played a Boogie-styled,

Jazz inflected piano, while King mastered a vibrant, T-Bone Walker-styled electric guitar.

Although "Goin' Home" went to No. 1 in R & B, it was "Ain't It a Shame," followed by "Blueberry Hill" and "I'm Walkin'," that established a pattern of crossovers for Fats, who continued to make Gold Records into the pre-Beatles sixties. Early in his life, when he was working in a bedsprings factory, Fats's hands were mangled in an accident; but he outwitted doctors who said he would never be able to play again. Except for such standards as "Blueberry Hill," Fats wrote the songs he recorded in collaboration with Dave Bartholomew, a former Duke Ellington trumpet player who led a band at a New Orleans hotel. Bartholomew served as Domino's arranger, conductor, and record producer, the two cutting Fats's disks mostly in Cosimo Matassa's J & M Studio in New Orleans. In a long list of recordings, 19 of which reportedly sold over a million Imperial disks, the standout titles include "My Blue Heaven," a ballad of the 1920s; "I'm in Love Again," "I Want to Walk You Home," and "Blue Monday," which was introduced by Fats in the film *The Girl Can't Help It* (1957).

By comparison, B. B. King has had a limited number of best-selling records, doubtless the result of his deep Blues style. But he has never veered from his determination to become as celebrated as Sinatra, despite his immersion in the Blues. Born Riley B. King on a cotton plantation in the Mississippi Delta and a cousin to Bukka White, he became B. B. King as the result of a singing disk jockey program on Station WDIA in Memphis, where he was billed as the Blues Boy from Beale Street, shortened in time to B. B. Employing Pete Chatman's "Every Day I Have the Blues" as his theme, King sings in a high-pitched voice that rises easily to an intense falsetto, with Lucille, as he calls his guitar, serving as a responsorial voice. (Lucille got her name as the result of a dance-hall battle in which two men "killed" themselves over a girl called Lucille.) B. B. is not a shouter, and uses vibrato as well as modern harmony on his guitar. He identifies the antecedents of his high-pitched, single-string playing as T-Bone Walker and Jazz guitarist Django Reinhardt.

Although B. B. has placed as many records on R & B charts as Fats, he has not been able to move as consistently into top slots. After "Three O'Clock Blues," he scored a No. 1 hit with "You Know I Love You," and then had content himself with No. 2's in "Please Love Me," "You Upset Me Baby," "Sweet Sixteen," and "Don't Answer the Door." Perhaps the most popular of his recordings, "The Thrill Is Gone," did not chart until 1970, and only rose to No. 3. But B. B.'s following is white as well as black, achieved as the result of pursuing an unremitting and grueling program of country-wide personal appearances—more than 300 one-nighters, and as many as 342 in one year. In 1982 his artistry brought him three awards: a Grammy for the album *There Must Be a Better World Somewhere,* as the Best Ethnic or Traditional Recording of the Year; a Handy award on being named Blues Entertainer of the Year at the Second National Blues Awards, held annually in Memphis; and a Commendation for Excellence from BMI for his creativity in R & B.

A comparatively little known but most significant pioneer of R & B was country Bluesman Arthur Crudup, whom they started calling Big Boy because of his height, when he started recording in the early forties. Born in 1905 in around Forest, Mississippi, he traveled to Chicago with a Gospel group and became involved in singing and recording but remained a rural laborer throughout his life, returning to his farm and jobs in southern lumber and levee camps between record sessions. When he separated from the Harrington Four, Crudup sang for handouts on Chicago streets, "living" in a wooden crate beneath the stairs of the elevated station at 39th St. He made his first recordings on September 11, 1941, cutting "Black Pony Blues," "Death Valley Blues," "Kind Lover Blues," and "If I Bet Lucky" on the Bluebird label. He played his own acoustic guitar, accompanied by Joe McCoy (1905–1950) on an imitation string bass; that is the rural, homemade Brownie Bass, which was constructed of a washtub, a broom handle, and a clothesline.

On his second Bluebird date, in April 1942, he played an electric guitar and recorded one of his best-known originals, "Mean Old Frisco Blues." Thereafter, except for 1943 and 1948, Crudup did one or two sessions a year on Bluebird until 1952. After recording for several labels in Jackson, Mississippi, he returned to Victor, Bluebird's parent label, to do two sessions in 1953–1954, both for the Groove subsidiary, but now accompanied by a tenor sax combo. He quit recording after that because, as he said, "I was making everybody rich and I was poor." Apparently he was paid little or no royalties by his publisher, Lester Melrose of Melrose Music in Chicago, with whom he finally broke in 1947 because "he was gypping me," and later by Hill & Range, the firm that bought the Melrose catalogue. A lawsuit brought in his behalf against the latter company by AGAC/The Songwriters Guild was still unsettled at his death in 1974.[7] "I was born poor," he said at one point, "I live poor and I'm going to die poor," which he unfortunately did.

Bluesman Big Bill Broonzy said: "You hear Elvis Presley, you hearin' Big Boy Crudup."[8] By the time he died, Crudup had achieved some renown as the result of an album released by RCA with the title *The Father of Rock and Roll* (1971–1972). It was an appropriate title, accorded him because of his acknowledged influence on Presley, whose first record release, on Memphis's Sun label, and the second, on RCA (after it bought the Sun masters), was Crudup's song, "That's All Right Mama." Presley also recorded Crudup's "My Baby Left Me" and "So Glad You're Mine"; and shortly after his rise, he sent Crudup a plaque acknowledging his debt to "That's All Right." In 1959 Presley reportedly put up the money to finance an LP by Crudup, cut by Fireball Records of Nashville and leased to a small label, Fire Records.

Among other artists who have recorded Crudup songs, there are Creedence Clearwater Revival, Elton John, Rod Stewart, Johnny Little, Paul Butterfield, Buffy St. Marie, Tina Turner, Canned Heat, and B. B. King, whose recording of "Rock Me Mama" was a chart-maker. Although Crudup recorded with an R & B combo on his last session and though he early made use of an electric pickup on his guitar, he was basically a country Blues-man. Presley's imitation of his blue notes and high tessitura emphasizes that Rockabilly, the first stage of Rock 'n' Roll, derived vocally from Delta Blues rather than R & B.

The Chicago scene, which had been the locus of the evolution and dissemination of Urban Blues, was equally important to R & B. Just as Harlem and the Bedford-Stuyvesant areas of New York nurtured Doo-Wop vocal groups, at about the same time, the Maxwell Street market of Chicago became the spawing ground of Chicago Electric Blues. With Bluebird, Vocalion, Brunswick, and other race labels curtailing or eliminating their releases because of wartime restrictions, the door was open for a new independent to move in—and the Chess brothers did.

In the rise of Chicago Electric Blues, two Delta bluesmen were pivotal. Both men were born with elegant names, McKinley Morganfield and Chester Arthur Burnett, names that are little known, since their cognomens are so colorful that they are recognized respectively as Muddy Waters and Howlin' Wolf. A later member of the school followed their pattern, with Ellas McDaniel being known as Bo Diddley.

Of Muddy, generally regarded as the Father or King of Chicago Blues, it is sometimes said: He electrified the Blues. This is not quite accurate, since T-Bone Walker used and recorded with the instrument before Muddy. But Waters did form what is regarded as the first fully electrified band. This also is not quite true, for he always used harp players, frequently two of them, in his combos. But he did produce more chart-makers and standards than either T-Bone or his Chicago colleagues, and he did develop a larger following and more disciples than either.

The following, larger in Great Britain than here, was partly the result of an appearance by Waters in London. "When Muddy came to England in 1958," Mick Jagger of the Rolling Stones has said, "he shocked the English public by playing electric guitars and electric basses and electric harmonicas. Instead of one salty Negro man playing the blues . . . he came out with the band and made a deafening noise. And they all walked out and asked for their money back."[9] But Muddy's impact on British musicians was completely at variance with the audience reaction. Keith Richards (b. 1943) said: "When I heard him, I realized the connection between all the music. . . . He was like the code book. I was incredibly inspired by him as a musician."[10] The man most affected was guitarist Eric Clapton (b. 1945), who said: "I'd never heard electric Delta Blues before. I couldn't believe it. It changed everything . . . [His playing] was the subtlest of them all [including Elmore James and B. B. King]. It wasn't fancy or fast. It was just the deepest. . . . I felt so much love for him. I felt like he was my father and I was his adopted son."[11] (In 1972 Chess did release an album titled *Fathers and Sons,* in which Muddy Waters and his longtime pianist, Otis Spann (1930–1970) were heard performing with such "sons" as Michael Bloomfield, Paul Butterfield, Donald "Duck" Dunn, and Buddy Miles.) Muddy's appearance in London gave impetus to the British Blues movement of the sixties, which had already taken off from Skiffle.

His disk of "Rolling Stone," the second release of the newly formed Chess label, led to Brian Jones (1944–1969) naming the group he formed with Mick Jagger (b. 1944) and Keith Richard "the Rolling Stones." Himself a traditional jazzman, Jones decided to master slide guitar, the down-home technique Muddy had learned during his Delta days; involving the use of the broken head of a Coke bottle on the pinky finger to fret the instrument, it gives the acoustic guitar a ringing sound like that of the Hawaiian guitar and was not discarded by Muddy even after he adopted the electric guitar. Bob Dylan's "Like a Rolling Stone" was likewise a tribute to Muddy, as was the naming of the American Rock magazine *Rolling Stone.*

Born in Rolling Fork, Mississippi, in April 1915 and raised by a grandmother on Stovall Plantation, near Clarksdale, Mississippi, the youngster who loved to play in a muddy stream (hence Muddy Waters) sold a horse to buy his first guitar. Influenced by the blues of Son House (b. 1902) and Robert Johnson (c. 1912–1938), he achieved such renown as a Delta slide guitarist that when Alan Lomax came to Clarksdale for the Library of Congress in 1941–1942, he recorded Muddy for its archives. Arriving in the Windy City in 1943, Muddy later described his early Chicago days as "pretty ruggish." But through Big Bill Broonzy, then still a dominant figure on the Chicago record scene, he was able in 1947 to record some sides (never released) for Mayo Williams at Columbia. Later that year, through Sunnyland Slim (b. 1907), who played piano on some of the sides, he recorded for Aristocrat, the label launched by the Chess brothers before they founded Chess.

His first chart disk was "Louisiana Blues" (1951), hardly noteworthy in comparison with "Rolling Stone," which was his first recorded Chess side and, curiously, did not make the charts. Overall, his record sales never approached his power as an in-person performer or his influence and importance in the history of the Blues. When Martin Scorsese produced *The Last Waltz,* Muddy appeared in close-up shots, giving an enthralling performance of his "Mannish Boy."

Although Muddy was primarily responsible for the transformation of Delta, down-home Blues into electric, ensemble Blues, he retained the harmonica in his bands, providing a forum for such harp bluesmen as Little Walter (1930–1968), Walter "Shakey" Horton (b. 1917), and the redoubtable James Cotton (b. 1935). Frequently using two harmonicas, he developed a tight ensemble style, which became the trademark of postwar Chicago Blues.

Among American followers, one finds, in addition to those who appeared with him on the *Fathers and Sons* album, bluesmen Son Seals (b. 1942) and Luther Johnson (b. 1934), both of whom came to Chicago from the South because of him; such modern bluesmen as Otis Rush (b. 1934), Freddie King (1934–1976), Junior Wells (b. 1934), and Magic Sam (1937–1969); funky electrician Jimi Hendrix (1942–1970); and, among white disciples, Bonnie Raitt (b. 1949), Johnny Winter (b. 1944), and John Paul Hammond (b. 1942).

Among the numerous awards that Muddy has won are Grammy awards in 1971 for the album *They Call Me Muddy Waters,* in 1972 for *The London Muddy Waters Sessions,* and in 1975 for *Muddy Waters Woodstock.* Waters's original songs that have become a permanent part of the Blues repertoire and have been recorded by other artists include "Got My Mojo Working," "I'm Your Hootchie Coochie Man," "Just Make Love to Me," and "I'm Ready," all Top Ten R and B disks in 1954 and all an expression of the macho black male; "Long Distance Call," a Top Tenner in 1951; and "Mannish Boy," Top Ten in 1955. Although Muddy has a strong following in white audiences, his Blues are too pristine, too elemental—in short, too black—for his disks to cross over.

The extended five-page obituary that *Rolling Stone* ran on Muddy's death in 1983 at the age of 68 ended with Bonnie Raitt's encomium: "I think they should put up a statue like the one in Thailand of the Buddha. You know, the ones that are fifty feet high . . . I think they should do one of those of Muddy in Chicago."[12]

Howlin' Wolf was physically a big man, six feet tall and weighing 250 pounds, and when he crawled out onstage on all fours, baring his teeth in a snarl and casting his black, beady eyes around the audience, he shocked people with his wolf-like appearance. The voice that came crackling out of him rose to a deep-chested, animal-like howl. Originally, his desire had been to yodel in imitation of the "blue yodels" of Jimmie Rodgers (1897–1933), the Meridian, Mississippi, father of Country music. But his voice box was not built for the rapid, high-pitched switching from falsetto to normal voice that produces the yodel. "I couldn't do no yodelin'," he said frankly, "so I turned to growlin', then howlin'." In addition, to the Singing Brakeman, whom he idolized, he was an admiring follower of Blind Lemon Jefferson, the enigmatic Robert Johnson, with whom he worked for a spell, and, most of all, the raucous bluesman Charley Patton, regarded as the father of Delta Blues. As with his Chicago colleague, Muddy Waters, whose dominance he resented, much to Muddy's benign amusement, the Wolf's real power lay in personal appearances, not on disk.

Born in the eastern part of Mississippi in West Point, and living in Ruleville in the Delta as a teenager, he got his first guitar when he was 18 and was working with his father on Boosey's Plantation. Pursuing the pattern of Charley Patton, he played harmonica and guitar on the plantations of Mississippi and Arkansas between farm chores—and remained an active farmer through his life. It was not until after he served in World War II and had moved to West Memphis, in Arkansas, that he bought an electric guitar, formed his first band, with two excellent harp players, James Cotton (b. 1935) and Little Junior Parker (1932–1971), and began broadcasting over a local West Memphis station. He made his first recordings through Ike Turner (b. 1933), who was then producing records for both Modern of Los Angeles and Chess of Chicago. The success of "How Many More Tears" b/w "Moanin' at Midnight"—the former made the charts in 1951, even before he settled in Chicago—led to an extended association with Chess.

Muddy reportedly helped the Wolf secure his first club date, and before long he was appearing at the West and South Side clubs where Muddy performed and ensemble, electric Blues was being showcased. His Chess dates brought him into contact with bassist Willie Dixon (b. 1915), whom Leonard Chess called his "right hand" and whose songwriting brought "Little Red Rooster," "Back Door Man," and "Wang Dang Doodle," among other songs, to his repertoire. One of his favorite numbers was the sardonic "I'm Sitting on

Top of the World (Now She's Gone)," which he acquired from the Mississippi Sheiks. His best-known songs include "Killing Floor," "Evil Is Goin' On," and the powerful "Smokestack Lightning," recorded by the Yardbirds, one of the pioneer British rock groups of the 1960s.

The bellowing howl was still to be heard in 1973, after he had suffered several heart attacks and gone back into the studio to record *The Back Door Wolf*, an album produced by Ralph Bass, whose history as a record producer dates back to the early days of Savoy and Black & White Records. The 10 new 12-bar Blues recorded by the Wolf reveal no diminution in his declamatory power. The raucous, raspy hoarseness is there, and in "Trying to Forget You," one hears once again the eerie, wolf-like moaning that had marked "Smokestack Lightning" in 1956.[13]

The Sepia Sinatras

Late in 1944, a buck army private stationed in Los Angeles went into a garage and, singing and accompanying himself on piano, recorded a moody ballad he had co-written, titled, "I Wonder." The homemade recording equipment belonged to a former worker at a Los Angeles record-pressing plant, who was able to press his own disks in a unit he built behind his garage. By March 1945 Gilt Edge Records, as the upstart firm called itself, was apologizing in a trade-paper advertisement for its inability to keep up with the unprecedented nationwide demand for the Cecil Gant disk. Competitive versions on the National and Bluebird labels only served to energize the Gilt Edge disk into the runaway hit it had become. If any record, other than Louis Jordan's "Choo Choo Ch'Boogie," also a 45 hit, ignited the postwar Blues explosion, it would be Cecil Gant's "I Wonder"—he was billed as "Pvt." Cecil Gant, which contributed to the disk's appeal to wartime fervor. As a garage recording, "I Wonder" was highly instrumental in motivating the growth of small R & B labels on the West Coast. The Bihari brothers, who owned jukeboxes in black locations, later indicated that their inability to keep up with the demand for the disk led to their going into the record business and starting Modern/RPM Records.

The ballad style in R & B, exemplified by Gant's disk, is perhaps best described in the words of Charles Brown (b. 1922), a pioneer Blues balladeer, who said: "I would not call myself really a blues singer. I think I'm a blues ballad singer because I sing ballads my way and yet they sound bluesy."[14] The war years, with their agonies, sacrifices, separation from loved ones, and shortage of young men, were receptive to the romanticism and sentimentalism of balladry, as the hysterical bobby-soxers' embrace of Sinatra in the same time span as the Gant disk would indicate. University-trained and a high-school science teacher, Texas-born Charles Brown started as a cocktail pianist, playing the light classics and show tunes, but made his mark singing with Johnny Moore's Three Blazers. A recording of "Drifting Blues" won him the *Cash Box* award for the Best R & B Record of 1946.

The progenitor of the style, Leroy Carr (1905–1935), came from Nashville, grew up in Indianapolis (where he died prematurely of alcoholism), and exerted great influence on Chicago bluesmen of the 1930s. In the five-volume album, *The Bill Broonzy Story,* Big Bill tells of how a group of Chicago bluesmen drove all night from the Windy City to Indianapolis in order to hear Carr sing his song, "In the Evening When the Sun Goes Down." Carr wrote and recorded such moody Blues as "In the Evening When the Sun Goes Down" and "How Long, How Long," working with Jazz-oriented guitarist Scrapper Blackwell, and sang in a Pop-inflected style that foreshadowed the transformation of Delta Blues into the Urban Blues of the 1930s.

The movement gained impetus from the songs written and recorded by Ivory Joe Hunter (1911–1974), a piano-playing Texan who settled in the Bay area of California and whose ballad style involved the pop/jazz influences of Leroy Carr and Charles Brown. Baptized Ivory Joe, he was a towering figure as a record producer, singer, pianist, and songwriter among early modern bluesmen. One of the first blacks with a record label of his own—Ivory Records was a short-lived venture in Oakland, California, in 1945—and known for a time as the Baron of the Boogie for his piano records, he achieved crossover hits with his songs "I Need You So," "Since I Met You, Baby," and as early as 1950 with "I Almost Lost My Mind." All of these were chordally based on the classic 12-bar blues progression. Revived six years later, "I Almost Lost My Mind" became a No. 1 Pop hit and million-copy seller for young Pat Boone (b. 1934). Elvis Presley (1935–1977) recorded Ivory Joe's "My Wish Came True" and Jimmy Reed's "Ain't That Lovin' You, Baby."

In the late forties, on King Records, Ivory Joe recorded with members of Duke Ellington's Orchestra, achieving a chart disk with his "Guess Who," which featured a memorable alto solo by the celebrated Johnny Hodges (1906–1970). Shortly before he died of cancer, Ivory Joe, in a wheelchair, was given a tribute by the Grand Ole Opry, an appropriate gesture, since he anticipated Ray Charles as a black artist who recorded Country material (Hank Williams songs). Joining Atlantic Records in 1956, Ivory Joe recut his "I

Almost Lost My Mind" to compete with the Pat Boone cover—and asserted that the scope of his writing and performing had made the designation *Blues singer,* inapplicable to him. *He,* not just some of his songs, was a crossover.

What developed in the 1940s as a widespread Oklahoma/Texas musical migration to California involved Lowell Fulson (b. 1921); Percy Mayfield (b. 1920) and Roy Brown (b. 1925) both of whom hailed from Louisiana but came to the West Coast via Houston; and Texan Amos Milburn (b. 1927), among others.

Part Indian and born in Tulsa, Oklahoma, Lowell Fulson worked in the shipyards of Oakland, California, where he cut his first records for local producer Bob Geddins in 1946, including "Three O'Clock Blues" before it became a hit for B. B. King. Originally a down-home bluesman who played with the legendary Texas Alexander (c. 1880–c. 1955) for several years, he soon found his idols in T-Bone Walker and Jimmy Rushing, and moved into R & B. Between 1950 and 1954, recording with Texas pianist Lloyd Glenn (b. 1909) and with jump combos, he produced chart-makers in "Every Day I Have the Blues," later B. B. King's theme; Lloyd Glenn's "Blue Shadows" (No. 1 in R & B in 1950); and his own classic, "Reconsider Baby." (On tour, Ray Charles, who later recorded his "Sinner's Prayer," was his piano player.)

If anyone merited the term *sepia Sinatra,* which trade papers then used to characterize Blues balladeers, it was Percy Mayfield, who hailed from Shreveport, Louisiana. With his smooth, murmuring baritone, he made a million-copy, No. 1 disk of his song, "Please Send Me Someone to Love," on Los Angeles' Specialty label in 1950–1951—followed quickly by another Top Ten hit with "Lost Love."

Roy Brown (b. 1925), who was born in New Orleans, attended high school in Houston, and organized a Spiritual quartet in his teens, sang Bing Crosby hits to win first prize in a Los Angeles amateur contest and initially made his way as "a Negro who sounded white." Nevertheless, to the repertoire of Blues and Rock standards, he contributed the classic "Good Rocking Tonight," a hit for Wynonie Harris in 1949, who rejected the song at first; a tune that was eventually recorded by Arthur Prysock (b. 1929) and James Brown (b. 1928) as well as such Rock 'n' roll pacemakers as Elvis, Pat Boone, and Ricky Nelson (b. 1940). Brown himself scored a million-copy disk in 1950 with his song, "Hard Luck Blues," on the De Luxe label of New Jersey.

Although Amos Milburn of Houston, Texas, began recording for Aladdin Records of Los Angeles in 1946, it was not until 1949 that he made the charts. But then his acceptance was so great that *Bill-*

board's year-end survey of best-selling R & B disks listed his "Chicken Shack Boogie" as the No. 9 disk. In 1949, too, "Hold Me Baby," which he co-wrote, and "Rooming House Boogie," written by Jessie Mae Robinson, were best sellers. In 1950 "Bad Bad Whiskey," a song written by tenorman Maxwell Davis, went to No. 1, initiating a cycle of whiskey-song recordings that culminated in "Good, Good Whiskey" in 1953, the year in which Milburn stopped recording. More of a Boogie bluesman than some of his Texas colleagues, he anticipated Rock 'n' Roll in his fast jump versions of "Let's Rock Awhile" (1951) and "Rock, Rock, Rock" (1952).

The culmination of the Blues ballad trend came with artistry of two superlative singers, Nat "King" Cole and Dinah Washington (1924–1963). Born of an ordained minister in Montgomery, Alabama, raised in Chicago, and a West Coaster before he was 20, Nat Cole first attracted attention as a Jazz pianist, playing in an Earl Hines single-note style. The King Cole Trio, formed in 1957 with Oscar Moore (b. 1912) on guitar and Wesley Prince on string bass, produced hits in "Sweet Lorraine," a revival of the oldie associated with crooner Rudy Vallee (b. 1901), and "Straighten Up and Fly Right," introduced by the Trio in the film *Here Comes Elmer* (1943). The Trio became the first black Jazz combo to have a commercially sponsored radio series.

From 1944 to 1947, the Trio won the Small Combo award in *Down Beat's* annual poll, duplicating the record in *Metronome*'s polls from 1945 to 1948. As a Jazz pianist, Nat won *Esquire*'s Gold Award in 1946 and *Metronome*'s poll between 1947 and 1949. Later, in 1956–1957, Nat became the only black artist with his own series on network TV, but the series was without a commercial sponsor, for which Cole, in quitting the show, blamed the network.

Conficting stories have been circulated as to how Nat began singing, presumably without intending to become a singer. One tale places his first impromptu public performance in Hollywood circa 1945. In a tale he told me at length, Ralph Watkins, owner of Kelly's Stable on 52nd St., claimed that he had to force Nat to sing when he accidentally caught him rehearsing a song at the piano one afternoon.[15] However it happened, Nat rapidly became one of the superstar voices of the day, also the first Jazz-oriented singer since Louis Armstrong to achieve worldwide popularity.

The record that brought him international fame was "Nature Boy," a Capitol disk of 1948, with a Nelson Riddle arrangement. (It was a curious song, written by eden ahbez, a Brooklyn-born Yogi who believed that only divinities deserved to capitalize their names, and who walked the streets of Hollywood, in prehippie days, wearing long hair, sandals, and a blanket-cape.) That same year, the Trio scored with "Little Girl," a revival of a rhythm ballad of the 1930s, popularized by Guy Lombardo and His Royal Canadians. "Nature Boy" was followed in 1950 by "Mona Lisa," a Gold Record that brought an Academy Award to the songwriters (Ray Evans and Jay Livingston), who had written it for the film *Captain Carey, U.S.A.* Ahead of its time as a song dealing with the generation gap, "Too Young" became another Gold Record in 1951. As a result of Cole's disk, "Too Young" became the song that was No. 1 on *Your Hit Parade* for the greatest number of weeks in the history of the show.

To people in the music business of the 1950s, Cole was the singer to whom they turned with romantic songs whose lyrics mattered. For he articulated with a clarity and precision surpassed only by Sinatra, and he had a warm, supple, velvet baritone that captivated with the beauty of its sound.

Dinah Washington, born Ruth Jones also in Tuscaloosa, Alabama, in 1924,[16] started as a Gospel singer and pianist in her church, went on to work in a duo with her mother, performing in churches around Chicago, and finally as a member of the noted Sallie Martin Gospel Singers. The association with the Martin troupe came after Dinah, at 15, had won an amateur contest at the Regal Theater and worked some nightclubs without fiscal or emotional rewards. Nevertheless, by 1941–1942, she had left the Gospel field and was performing in various Chicago clubs, including the Garrick Stage Bar, where Billie Holiday was appearing in the main room, downstairs, and she was singing in the upstairs room. It was during her year at the Garrick that Ruth Jones became Dinah Washington, with several people claiming credit for the change.[17]

Among those who were impressed by her performance at the Garrick was Lionel Hampton, with whom she sang for almost two years but recorded only one side. Decca was then, like other record companies, interested only in band recordings. In 1943, while she was still singing with Hampton, Leonard Feather, Jazz critic and historian, recorded Dinah for a small label, singing a group of Blues he had written. Although Dinah cut an album of Gospel songs for Apollo, a small Harlem label, after she left Hampton, she spent the R & B years between 1943 and her death in 1963 recording a wide range of material that established her as the Queen of the Jukeboxes. Mercury Records used her marvelous versatility to record for black listeners any song that was breaking for a hit—Blues, Country, Jazz, Show, and Pop tunes.

In truth, Mercury resisted her moving into the mainstream, until she recorded "What a Diff'rence a Day Made" in 1959. Then, largely as a result of the initiative of the song's publisher, without the support of the record company, her disk climbed into the Top Ten on *Billboards's* pop Honor Roll of Hits.[18] It also finished in the Top Fifty of the year's pop hits at the same time that it won Dinah a Grammy for the Best R & B Record of the Year—it was hardly that. In the few years that remained before her accidental death, Dinah's disks, mostly revivals of Pop ballads of the 1930s and 1940s, were easy crossovers.

Dinah Washington's unique sound was compounded of Gospel, Jazz, and Blues elements, all fused into a tonality of liquid loveliness. She was an effortless singer, who could produce superb recordings in one or two takes, and she articulated with a bell-like clarity of diction. *Imperious* was the word for Dinah as a person, who had the *chutzpah* to announce to a British audience, with Queen Elizabeth sitting in a box: "There is but one Heaven, one Hell, and one Queen, and your Elizabeth is an impostor!" She was referring, of course, to her title as Queen of the Jukeboxes.

Among later artists, Dinah's influence is audible in a varied group of singers, including Etta James, Ruth Brown, Esther Phillips, Dionne Warwick, Nancy Wilson, and Diana Ross.

Doo Wop and Group R & B

In its initial stage, R & B singing tended to be a group rather than a solo phenomenon. As late as 1951–1952, when Johnny Otis offered Jackie Wilson to Ralph Bass at King Records, Bass passed in favor of the Dominoes. When Atlantic Records compiled its invaluable eight-volume anthology *History of Rhythm and Blues*, the first two tracks were by the Ravens ("Ol' Man River") and the Orioles ("It's Too Soon to Know").

The impetus for the formation of black singing groups doubtless came from the successful invasion of the Pop market by two earlier groups, both originating in the Midwest. The Mills Bros., who came from a small Ohio town, made their debut on Cincinnati's Station WLW in 1925, as did the Ink Spots, who came from Indianapolis not 10 years later. From the start, the Mills Bros. were swingers, which they remained over a 50-year period, while the Ink Spots were basically balladeers.

For the Mills Bros., their stint on WLW led to a three-year contract on CBS, the first of its kind for a black group. By 1930 they had their first million-copy disk in "Tiger Rag," credited to the Original Dixieland Jazz Band in 1917, backed with "Nobody's Sweetheart," the oldie Jazz standard of 1924. Their biggest hit came in 1942–1943 with "Paper Doll," a revival of a 1915 song written by Johnny Black (who, incidentally, was killed in a roadhouse brawl over 25 cents in

1936). It is said that Black persuaded a reluctant publisher, Edward B. Marks, to accept the song, by playing it over and over on a violin, with a trained canary perched on his shoulder, chirping along. As a revival, "Paper Doll" not only sold a million disks but, much to the publisher's amazement, over a million copies of sheet music.

In 1944 the Mills Bros. produced another million seller in "You Always Hurt the One You Love," followed in 1948 by "Lazy River," a million-copy disk whose melody was composed by Hoagy Carmichael in 1931 and revived in a 1946 film, *The Best Years of Our Lives*. Perhaps their strangest hit was "Glow Worm," a song originally published in Germany in 1902, for which Johnny Mercer, working on his own, wrote an updated lyric, electrifying the worm. Between 1925 and 1975, recording beautifully blended, swinging arrangements, which sometimes included dazzling horn imitations, and collaborating with such artists as Louis Armstrong, Boswell Sisters, Cab Calloway, Duke Ellington, or Count Basie, the Mills Bros. recorded almost 2,500 songs.

All through their 50 years, except for brief intervals when deaths reduced them to a trio, the Mills Bros. remained a family quartet. Of Harry Mills (b. 1913), who was the spokesman of the group, Dean Martin has said: "He had more influence on my singing style than anyone in show business. Few people know that Bing Crosby was also influenced by Harry, who set the pattern for me."[19]

The Ink Spots achieved their renown through a stylized presentation in which Bill Kenny (1923–1978) sang a chorus in a high-pitched, partly falsetto tenor and was followed by Orville "Hoppy" Jones (d. 1944) reciting the lyric, with some interpolations, in a slow, deep baritone voice, full of heartfelt concern. The group acquired its name, we are told, during a conference in their New York manager's office, when an overturned inkwell spattered a blotter with ink spots. The year was 1939, and "If I Didn't Care," the record that brought recognition. That year, the Ink Spots appeared at the New York Paramount with the Glenn Miller Orchestra as an "extra added attraction." There was so much demand for their services that they doubled at the Apollo Theater in Harlem, and after the last show at the Paramount, raced to 52nd St.'s Famous Door. To keep up with their heavy schedule, they used an ambulance to take them through Manhattan's traffic.

Nineteen forty-six was a banner year, with two-million-copy disks in "To Each His Own" and "The Gypsy," plus a best seller in "For Sentimental Reasons," a cover of a hit version of the song by Deek Watson, who had been part of the Ink Spots. An earlier recording with Ella Fitzgerald yielded the memorable disk of "Into Each Life Some Rain Must Fall." As has happened with a number of groups, success ignited the ambitions of individual members and led to squabbles. By 1952 there were two Ink Spots groups, one headed by Bill Kenny, and the other by guitarist/bassist Charles Fuqua—and neither was as successful as the original. But there was no gainsaying the inspiration of the Ink Spots and the Mills Bros. to young blacks seeking a way out of the black ghetto and second-class citizenship.

While the Ravens were basically a jazzy combo, singing and recording Mills Bros.' versions of such standards as "White Christmas" and "Ol' Man River"—both of which made race charts in 1947–1948—they had considerable impact on young R & B groups. Their success led groups of the late 1940s and early 1950s to adopt bird names, and soon there were the Penguins on Dootone Records, Flamingos (Chance), Robins (Savoy), Larks (Apollo), Meadowlarks (RPM), Swallows (King), Falcons (Unart), Cardinals (Atlantic), and Wrens (Rama), among others. The Ravens' treatment of "White Christmas" was imitated by the Drifters in their version of the Irving Berlin perennial. The Dominoes made "Sixty Minute Man" with the bass-voice lead of Bill Brown, following Jimmy Ricks's bass-voice lead on "Ol' Man River," Another young group, working in the Mills Bros.' swing tradition, was the Four Tunes, who delivered a rousing best seller in "Marie."

The Orioles, the first thoroughgoing R & B group, reacted to the superstition about bird names by substituting Orioles for Vibranaires, the name by which they were originally known in Baltimore. They were also one of the first Doo-Wop groups, as the street-corner singing groups came to be known. *Doo-Wop* was one of the nonsense syllables like *Sh-Boom, Sha Na Na, Eh-Toom-Ah-Ta, Dum-Bee-Oo-Bee,* etc., used by young singing groups in the absence of instrumental accompaniment, to give a rhythmic beat and for "fills" under sustained notes. The Doo-Wop groups emerged mostly in the country's black ghettos, coming together either in secondary schools or in churches, and rehearsing on street corners, in school yards, tenement hallways, and in New York's subways. Among R & B groups that started as Doo-Wop amateurs, there were the Harptones, Crows, Belmonts, Flamingos, Imperials, Dells, and Spaniels, as well as the Shirelles, a female group from Newark, New Jersey.

The Orioles, who coalesced in a Baltimore high school, made a practice of singing at the foot of the staircase leading down from the Baltimore station of the Pennsylvania Railroad. Here they were spotted by an aspiring songwriter, Deborah Chessler, who taught them one of her songs, bundled them after a time into her second-hand car, and drove up to New York City. An enterprising woman, she got them an audition with the owner of a small label, a record contract, and a booking at Harlem's Apollo Theater. Her song "It's Too Soon to Know" (1948), the first release of Jubilee Records, became a modest R & B hit for the Orioles, who continued to place disks on R & B charts into 1953, when they produced their biggest hit, singing by then with authority and polish, "Crying in the Chapel."

In 1950 Johnny Otis (b. 1921) placed three Savoy disks among the year's best-selling R & B records—"Double Crossing Blues," "Cupid's Boogie," and "Mistrustin' Blues"—all involving Little Esther, later called Esther Phillips (1935–1984), as a squeaky teenager and deep-voiced Mel Walker. The following year saw the emergence as best sellers of two key R & B groups. The Dominoes, organized by choirmaster Billy Ward (b. 1921) as a Gospel group, produced the year's No. 1 R & B disk in his erotic "Sixty Minute Man," and launched the careers of Clyde McPhatter (1933–1972) and Jackie Wilson (c. 1932–1984), who succeeded McPhatter in 1953 as the lead singer of the group.

The Clovers, earliest of three top groups on Atlantic Records, came together in a Washington, D.C., high school. Their first hit, "Don't You Know I Love You," was written by Atlantic Records's president, Ahmet Ertegun, under the pseudonym A. Nugetre—his last name spelled backward. Hits recorded by the Clovers throughout the 1950s included "Fool, Fool, Fool" (1951) and "Ting A Ling" (1952), both also written by Ertegun and both No. 1's, the former being covered by Kay Starr (b. 1922).

When high tenor Clyde McPhatter left the Dominoes, an excited Ahmet Ertegun tracked him down and persuaded him to organize a new group. This became the Drifters, who recorded chart-makers from "Money Honey" in 1953 until 1967, a period in which their lead singers and producers changed. One of the first Atlantic groups to record with strings and written arrangements, and to embody Latin influences, they delivered chart-makers in "There Goes My Baby" (1959), "Save the Last Dance for Me" (1960), "Up on the Roof" (1962), and "On Broadway" (1963), among others.

The best of the Atlantic groups was the Coasters, which emerged from binary fission of the Robins, West Coasters (hence the name), and that brought humor into R & B. Recorded by two of Rock's finest songwriters and earliest independent producers, Leiber and Stoller, they cut an evergreen group of "playlets," as L & S called their songs. The first, after two of the Robins flew East to become the nucleus of the new group, was "Down in Mexico" (1956), followed by such humorous story-songs as "Young Blood," "Charlie Brown," "Poison Ivy," and "Yakety Yak," the last-mentioned an incisive cameo of teenage–parent conflict. In the entertaining disks of the Coasters, R & B reached one of its peaks, demonstrating, incidentally, that the style could have substance as well as excitement, drive, and danceability.

The Five Royales, who came from North Carolina, began singing Gospel in 1948 and switched to R & B four years later, delivering two hits on Apollo, a Harlem label, with "Baby, Don't Do It" and "Help Me Somebody," both in 1953. Lead singer, group director Lowman Pauling, who wrote these hit songs, was also cowriter with record producer Ralph Bass of "Dedicated to the One I Love," a hit for the Royales on King Records in 1958, an even bigger hit for the Shirelles three years later on Scepter Records, and in 1967 for the Mamas and the Papas on Dunhill Records.

When King Records signed the Five Royales, a Detroit group named the Royals changed its name to the Midnighters (later Hank Ballard & the Midnighters), and shortly made the charts with "Work with Me, Annie" (1954), a song that stirred a storm over its erotic implications. These were denied by King/Federal producer Ralph Bass. But the follow-up by the Midnighters, innocently or arrogantly, was titled "Annie Had a Baby." Hank Ballard (b. 1936), who wrote the "Annie" songs, later was responsible for "Let's Go, Let's Go, Let's Go," No. 1 in 1960, and for "The Twist."

The dance craze of the early 1960s was not triggered by the Midnighters' original disk but by the recording made more than a year later by Chubby Checker (b. 1941), whose sensational dancing on Dick Clark's *American Bandstand* electrified the day's teenagers and launched the dance that swept the world beginning in 1961. Checker, whose baptismal name was Ernest Evans, chose his pseudonym because of its similarity to the name of the singer he idolized, Fats Domino.

The longest-lived of the groups to arise in the pre-Rock era was the Platters, a mixed group of four males and a female whose first of a long list of hits, "Only You," came in 1955. This was cowritten by their arranger/producer/manager, Buck Ram, who also wrote their succeeding million-copy disk, "The Great Pretender" (1956) and who has kept the group in action with a constantly changing personnel into the 1980s. The versatility and appeal of the original group, whose lead singer was Tony Williams—unsuccessful later as a solo artist—was demonstrated when they recorded revivals of a 1939 British oldie, "My Prayer," and the 1933 Jerome Kern show tune, "Smoke Gets in Your Eyes," each of which became a Gold Record.

The year of the Presley explosion, 1956, brought the Dells as well as the Coasters onto national best-seller charts. The initial hit of this five-man group, originally Gospel singers from Harvey, Illinois, was

"Oh, What a Night" on Vee Jay Records. It accomplished the unusual feat of becoming a million seller for a second time on Cadet Records, a subsidiary of Los Angeles' Modern label, 13 years later (1969). With only one change in personnel from 1954 to 1973, the Dells scored a Gold Record as late as 1973 with "Give Your Baby a Standing Ovation," also on the Cadet label.

One of the most interesting phenomena of the R & B era, by contrast with those just discussed, were the groups known inside music business as "one-hit wonders." These were instances in which groups scored a single best seller and then were unable to produce another, regardless of how many records they made. One might attribute this development to the fickleness of the public. Additional contributing factors were the amateurishness of groups that lacked the discrimination to select good songs as well as the professionalism to know how to arrange and present them; also, the small, new record companies were amateurs, generally lacking the insight in recording and the finances needed for promotion.

During the pre-Rock 1950s, the following groups and songs were among the one-hit wonders: *1950:* Ray-O-Vacs, "Besame Mucho" (Decca); *1954:* Penguins, "Earth Angel" (Dootone), Chords, "Sh-Boom" (Cat); *1955:* Cadillacs, "Speedoo" (Josie), El Dorados, "At My Front Door" (Vee Jay), Marigolds, "Rollin' Stone" (Excello), Turbans, "When You Dance" (Herald); *1956:* Teen Queens, "Eddie My Love" (RPM), Willows, "Church Bells May Ring" (Melba); *1957:* Rays, "Silhouettes" (Cameo); *1958:* Chantels, "Maybe" (End), Imperials, "Tears on My Pillow" (End); *1959:* Impalas, "Sorry (I Ran All the Way Home)" (Cub).

The R & B Chronicle

The excitement, drive, buoyancy, and danceability that Rhythm & Blues brought into black music and, after a time, into the mainstream, had their beginnings in the early forties and attained maturity in about 1949, the year that the style became identified as R & B.

Viewed in musical terms, there was no esthetic reason why a style derived from big band, Boogie-Woogie, Gospel music, and down-home Blues, and fusing the sounds of "shout" singing, the electric guitar, and the boisterous tenor sax, should have developed into a popular art form. But substantial sociological, technological, psychological, and economic factors came into play between the early 1940s and the world of post-World War II that created a fertile soil for the growth of what became known as R & B.

Sociological: Despite wartime promises, when the country returned to "business as usual," it was "discrimination as usual," with blacks still being excluded from the white areas of entertainment. Thus, they were compelled to turn for entertainment to their own ghettos, where, for working- and middle-class blacks, the jukebox, whose use expanded greatly during the wartime shortage of musicians for live entertainment, was the major instrument for listening and dancing.

Psychological: As Bop was an indigenous black development, arising from mixed feelings of rage, resentment, and pride in black musicians' own commercially undervalued artistry and creativity, so R & B stemmed from the same boil of emotions. The motivation was not articulated in R & B, whose direction was an escape into revelry and fun. A style developed out of blacks' own resources, untainted until later by white intervention.

Economic: Faced with shellac quotas and other stringencies during World War II, the major record companies stopped recording and releasing records by blacks, and devoted themselves to producing white mainstream merchandise. This occurred at a time when blacks, as a result of the war and new employment opportunities, possessed increased purchasing power and money to spend on leisure-time enjoyment.

Technological: The development of tape and its extensive use in communication during the war brought the development of comparatively inexpensive taping machines. In place of the costly and massive equipment required for cutting masters, it now became possible to record in a garage or living room. And with the rise of the disk jockey and the introduction of the transistor radio, the ears of the public could be reached by small labels lacking the staffs and finances to expose their product through network radio and TV.

To dancers and young people of the 1940s, the big bands had a dull and lifeless sound, while the pallid music of the crooners lacked a beat. The demand for recordings by black artists in their own indigenous style, growing at a time when the major companies were not supplying them, opened the door to the rise of the small, independent labels. During the 1940s, an estimated 400 small labels released disks, of which perhaps 100 were able to keep afloat into the early 1950s. Only a handful developed into substantial operations.

Among the earliest of the R & B labels, there was a group of New York-based outfits with almost forgotten names, some of which released Blues, Gospel, and big-band swing, as well as the new jump Blues: Varsity, founded in late 1930s with reissues of the Mississippi Sheiks; Beacon, which developed such artists as Una Mae Carlisle (1926–1964), Five Red Caps and Savannah Churchill (b. 1919), who also recorded for Manor Records of New Jersey; Apollo, an outgrowth of a Harlem record store that accounted for the Five Royales, the Larks (a Harlem Doo-Wop Group), and, especially, the great Gospel artist Mahalia Jackson (1911–1972); Keynote, a Jazz label on which Dinah Washington made her solo debut, singing Blues written by jazz journalist turned indie producer Leonard Feather; Jubilee, which introduced the Orioles, Della Reese (b. 1932), and, later, the Four Tunes and the Cadillacs; and National, whose A & R director was Herb Abramson, later a cofounder of Atlantic Records, and whose artists included the Ravens, Pete Johnson (1904–1967), Joe Turner (b. 1911), the big band of Billy Eckstine (b. 1914)—he made the erotic Blues hit "Jelly, Jelly" in 1946—and Charlie Barnet (b. 1913) whose band accounted for the classic "Cherokee" disk on Bluebird in 1939. The metropolitan scene would also include De Luxe, a New Jersey label with its own pressing plant that introduced Otis Williams and the Charms, and Roy Brown (b. 1925), who wrote and made the original version of the Wynonie Harris hit, "Good Rockin' Tonight."

The most important of all these New York–New Jersey indies, in terms both of its artists and longevity, was Savoy Records, founded in 1942 by the owner of a Newark record shop, Herman Lubinsky, who remained at the helm until his death in 1974. At that time, Fred Mendelsohn, one of his producers and formerly with De Luxe Records, took over and ran the company, mainly as a Gospel label, until the catalog was purchased by Arista Records. Among the artists who recorded for Savoy, there were Varetta Dillard; teenage Little Esther; Big Maybelle (1924–1972), whose career was wrecked by drug addiction, which also shortened Little Esther Phillips's life; and Nappy Brown, who came out of a Gospel group. These were recorded by a bunch of highly talented producers, retained by Lubinsky, who had a reputation for being a tightfisted businessman. They included Teddy Reig, who built the label with the Swing and Bop artists of 52nd St.; Lee Magid, who moved the label in an R & B direction; Fred Mendelsohn, who accounted for one of its outstanding best sellers, "The Hucklebuck," by Paul Williams; and Ralph Bass, who manned the West Coast operation and produced a series of best sellers in 1950–1951, and later built the King Records' roster, as he had earlier developed Black & White before moving to Savoy.

Pointing to Roy Milton, Joe Liggins, T-Bone Walker, Charles Brown, and himself, among artists who were located on the West Coast, Johnny Otis has said that "R & B started here in Los Angeles."[20] Despite the importance of these performers, credit for starting R & B would have to be given to the New York area. But Los Angeles was, perhaps, more involved in triggering the explosion, and became the center for an upstart group of R & B labels. The earliest apparently were the short-lived Gilt Edge label, on which Cecil Gant scored with the garage-produced disk of "I Wonder," and the longer-lived Specialty Records, originally Jukebox Records, whose roster included Roy Milton, Lloyd Price (an early crossover with "Lawdy Miss Clawdy" in 1952), Little Richard, and Sam Cooke, initially as part of the Soul Stirrers Gospel group.

The year 1945 witnessed the rise of three family-owned companies. Paul Reiner's Black & White company produced the classic version of "Stormy Monday" by T-Bone Walker and later, in 1946–1947, the runaway crossover hit "Open the Door, Richard." The Mesner family's Aladdin, initially a Jazz label with artists including Helen Humes, King Cole Trio, cool tenorman Lester Young and K.C. bandleader/pianist Jay McShann, became, after 1946, the home of Amos Milburn, Charles Brown, Lightnin' Hopkins, the Five Keys, and Shirley & Lee, a duo who recorded one of the classic teenage standards, "Let the Good Times Roll" (1956), which is not the same as the song with that title recorded by Louis Jordan 10 years earlier.

Like Savoy on the East Coast, Modern/RPM, the third of the family-owned Los Angeles enterprises, became the longest-lived of the West Coast labels, operated up to the present time by one of the Bihari brothers. Its roster of artists is one of the most impressive in R & B, including, as it does, John Lee Hooker (b. 1917), one of the most-recorded of bluesmen; Lowell Fulson (b. 1921); Elmore James; Jimmy Witherspoon (b. 1923), remembered for his classic 1949 version of "Ain't Nobody's Business"; Etta James, whose "Wallflower," an answer to "Work with Me Annie," led to Georgia Gibbs's million-copy cover, "Dance with Me Henry"; and seventeen years of B. B. King disks (1951–1968).

Los Angeles was also the locus of Imperial Records, begun in 1945 by Lewis Chudd, a former radio executive, who found and signed Fats Domino on a visit to New Orleans in 1949. Imperial's other major artist was young Ricky Nelson, who was signed by Chudd when Nelson made a cover record of Domino's hit "I'm Walkin'" in 1957. Imperial possessed two other artists who prevailed in the R & B market: Smiley Lewis (b. 1920) with "I Hear You Knockin' (But You Can't Come In)," which crossed over in 1955; and the Spiders, who produced a back-to-back hit in "I Didn't Want to Do It," backed with "You're the One."

Chicago was the headquarters for two top labels, both family-administered, at least at the start. Chess/Checker was launched by the Chess brothers, Leonard and Phil, two Polish immigrants who owned the Macomba nightclub and operated out of a Michigan Avenue storefront office and studio. With an artist roster that included Muddy Waters, Howlin' Wolf, Bo Diddley, and Chuck Berry, they made a mark not only on R & B but on Rock 'n' Roll as well. Theirs was one of the sturdy, long-lived enterprises of the era.

By contrast, Vee Jay Records of Chicago went out of business after a dozen sparkling years. Founded in 1952–1953 by Vivian Carter Bracken, a Gary, Indiana, disk jockey, her husband, James Bracken, and Vivian's brother, Calvin Carter, Vee Jay came into being as one of the few black-owned record companies in the history of the record business. Emerging in the transitional period when black R & B was rapidly evolving into white R 'n' R, Vee Jay successfully spanned the changeover. Its roster included such black groups as the Spaniels, El Dorados, Dells, and Impressions, downhome bluesmen including John Lee Hooker and Jimmy Reed, as well as Rock groups and singers such as Dee Clark (b. 1938), Gene Chandler (b. 1937), Four Seasons, and even the Beatles.

Although it is generally overlooked, Vee Jay was the first American record company to release a Beatles album. The year was 1963, and the album was titled *Introducing the Beatles*. Vee Jay was enabled to do this because Capitol Records of Hollywood, which had first refusal rights, rejected the group. In 1963 Vee Jay also released three singles, possibly four, by the Beatles: "Please Please Me," backed with "Ask Me Why," "From Me to You," backed with "Thank You Girl," and "Love Me Do," backed with "PS I Love You." When Capitol saw the light and began releasing Beatles disks, they had to call their first album *Meet the Beatles*. The curious fact is that the group that took the American record scene by storm in 1964, failed to excite very much interest in 1963, when Vee Jay was releasing their disks in this country.

Despite the sagacity that gave Vee Jay priority in the history of the Beatles in this country and its unusual success in producing chart records, it failed to become the first major black-owned record company, an achievement of Motown Records. But Vee Jay was still on the scene when Motown got started, declaring bankruptcy in 1966. Why and how it failed has never been fully explained. But the explanation seems to lie in a combination of factors: mismanagement, black–white tensions on the executive level, misappropriation of funds, and perhaps even outright larceny.[21]

King Records, launched in a defunct Cincinnati ice house in 1945 by Syd Nathan, former owner of a general store, was one of the few R & B companies that could produce a record from start to finish—from taping a master to putting a finished album on the market. Its catalog covered the gamut from instrumental hits such as Bill Doggett's "Honky Tonk" to such male vocalists as Lonnie Johnson (1889–1970), Ivory Joe Hunter, and Wynonie Harris, to groups including the Dominoes, Charms, and Midnighters, and to such superstars as James Brown (b. 1928). (Because it was located in Cincinnati, King also possessed a large Country catalog.)

In the R & B era, there was one other company beside Vee Jay that was black-owned. Peacock Records of Houston owed its beginnings, like Chess of Chicago, to a nightclub owned by Don Robey, who died in 1975. Starting with Gatemouth Brown (b. 1924), who was then appearing at his Bronze Peacock club, Robey developed a roster that included Big Mama Thornton; Bobby "Blue" Bland (b. 1930), whose soulful output on Duke, a sister label, has continued from 1957 into the 1980s; Little Junior Parker (b. 1935), who recorded for Duke for almost 10 years (1957 – 1967); and Johnny Ace (1929 – 1954), the first of the Rock 'n' Rollers to become a cult figure, when he accidentally killed himself playing Russian Roulette during a Christmas Eve performance in Houston.

The mushrooming of R & B labels from the early forties into the fifties represents one of the most remarkable chapters of small enterprise in the history of American business. However, out of the hundreds of independents that helped produce a resplendent storehouse of song, only a few attained a "lasting" status: Modern/RPM in Los Angeles; Chess in Chicago; King in Cincinnati; Peacock/Duke in Houston; and Savoy and Atlantic in New York and New Jersey. All of these except Modern are now owned by successors.[22]

The White Synthesis

The impact of Rhythm and Blues was so great that the white transformation of the style involved several stages, and it took place in Great Britain as well as in the United States. The American synthesis embraces four developments: (1) the "cover" syndrome; (2) Rockabilly; (3) Teenage Rock; and (4) Surfing music. In England, the white synthesis involved Skiffle and a number of key Rock groups, including the Rolling Stones, Animals, and Yardbirds.

The "Cover" Syndrome

During the early years of Rock 'n' Roll, a certain number of unfriendly members of the musical establishment and the older generation advanced the claim that this new, rambunctious style was foisted on the public by a conspiracy of small record labels, upstart publishers affiliated with Broadcast Music, Inc., disk jockeys "on the take," and new, teenage artists and their managers. The claim of a force-fed public accepting a music it did not want is made occasionally even today. What these claimants face is a curious phenomenon that has slowly come to light and that involved listeners, singers, and others, in different parts of the country in the early 1950s. The import of what I am about to describe arises precisely from the circumstance that the development occurred in *different* parts of the country, in areas as disparate as Cleveland, Philadelphia, Gallatin (Tennessee), Memphis, the upper Midwest, and Albert Lea (Minnesota).

Sometime in 1951, Alan Freed, a disk jockey on Station WJW in Cleveland, visited the record shop that sponsored his radio show. The owner had told Freed of a strange change in the buying pattern of teenagers frequenting the store from a nearby high school. What Freed saw was young people who were passing by bins containing records by top contemporary artists such as Como, Sinatra, Patti Page, and Kitty Kallen, and crowding around the bins that held records by the Dominoes, Johnny Ace, Ruth Brown, the Clovers, and other R & B groups. Freed was so impressed by what he witnessed that he returned to the station and persuaded the management to let him change the title of his program from *Record Rendezvous* to *The Moon Dog Rock 'n' Roll House Party.* Although he used the phrase "Rock 'n' Roll," it was then a subterfuge: he was not certain how his listeners would react to records by black artists, and chose a non-identifying term for Rhythm and Blues disks. Cleveland listeners were obviously positively impressed, because Freed was soon on the air 23 hours a week and was being heard on a number of stations outside of the Cleveland area. In 1952, when Freed and several promoters ran a "Moon Dog Coronation Ball" at the Cleveland Arena, 18,000 tickets were sold for a hall that could accommodate only 10,000. Every artist on the program was black, but at least half of the audience was white. (To leap ahead to 1955, still more than a year before Elvis had his first national hit, Alan Freed ran a "Rock 'n' Roll Party" at the St. Nicholas Arena in New York. This occurred after he had moved from Cleveland to station WINS. Over 15,000 paid admission, and thousands were turned away. Once again, every artist on the program was black—Buddy Johnson Orchestra, Joe Turner, The Clovers, Fats Domino, The Moonglows, The Harptones, The Drifters, Ella Johnson, Danny Overbea, Dakota Staton, Red Prysock, and Nolan Lewis. And once again, at least half of the audience consisted of white teenagers.)

In 1951 Bill Haley (1927–1981), born in a suburb of Detroit, and frontman of a Country & Western combo known as the Saddlemen, was recording for a small Philadelphia label, Essex Records. In 1951, owner Dave Miller persuaded Haley to "cover" Jackie Brenston's hit disk of "Rocket 88," which went to No. 1 on R & B charts.

Although Haley's platter was hardly world-shaking, it changed his orientation. The following year, he wrote and recorded "Rock a-Beatin' Boogie," employing words that he might have derived from the Dominoes' disk of "Sixty Minute Man": namely, "Rock . . . Rock . . . Rock, everybody/Roll . . . Roll . . . Roll, everybody."[23] (The Dominoes' bass lead had sung: "I'll rock 'em, roll 'em all night long . . .") In 1953 Haley wrote and recorded "Crazy, Man, Crazy," adapting a black teenage expression of the day. Haley's Essex disks opened the door to a Decca recording contract, and in 1954, for his first session, he recorded two epic-making disks: "Rock Around the Clock" and a cover of Joe Turner's "Shake, Rattle and Roll"—his record producer being the man who had served in that capacity for Louis Jordan.

It was "Shake, Rattle and Roll," specifically the Turner original, and not the Haley cover, that midwifed the birth of an R & B fan in the upper Midwest. As Barry Hansen, later a popular San Francisco disk jockey known as Dr. Demento, explained in a liner note to the Turner album: when the dance master of a class in the Lindy Hop put on the Turner disk—Hansen already had the Haley white cover at home—"I simultaneously forgot my unfortunate partner, the Lindy Hop and Bill Haley."[24]

In Memphis, Tennessee, another teenager was turning away from the country played by most local radio stations and secretly listening to records by Big Bill Broonzy, Arthur "Big Boy" Crudup, and other black artists. "They would scold me at home," Elvis Presley said, "for listening to them. *Sinful music,* the townsfolk in Memphis said it was. Which never bothered me, I guess."[25]

Not far from Memphis, in Gallatin, Tennessee, the owner of a mail-order record business, Randy Wood, was studying orders received from teenagers that seemed to indicate a developing trend. Young country listeners, responding to his commercials on WSM, the Grand Ole Opry radio station, appeared to be buying more and more R & B disks. When he established Dot Records, all of Pat Boone's early recordings were covers of black hits: the El Dorados' "At My Front Door," Charms' "Two Hearts," Fats Domino's "Ain't That a Shame," etc. Wood followed this pattern with his female artists as well: the Fontane Sisters covered the Charms' "Hearts of Stone," Gale Storm covered Smiley Lewis's "I Hear You Knockin' (But You Can't Come In)," and so on.

Eddie Cochran (1938–1960) was born in Albert Lea, Minnesota, grew up in Oklahoma City, Oklahoma, and settled in California at the age of 15. What he was listening to became clear in 1958, when he recorded his own "Summertime Blues," and later in his short career and abbreviated life, Ray Charles's "Hallelujah, I Love Her So" and Sleepy John Ester's version of Kokomo Arnold's "Milk Cow Blues," singing in a style that was distinctly black. An early interest in Country songs such as John Loudermilk's "Sittin' in the Balcony" soon yielded to the influence of R & B artists.

What must be inescapably clear from this survey is that the interest in R & B by white teenage listeners and singers was a *spontaneous* development, and one that was not limited to a single area of the country.

Now, the cover syndrome has been viewed in some quarters as an attempt by the major record companies to invade the popular market, which they had yielded by default to the small, new R & B labels during and after World War II.[26] The statistics do not support this contention: out of a list of 29 successful covers, the only major company extensively involved in the cover syndrome was Mercury Records of Chicago. RCA Victor managed one impressive cover with Perry Como of Gene & Eunice's "Kokomo," and Capitol gave Peggy Lee the biggest single of her distinguished career with her cover of Little Willie John's "Fever."

Most of the cover disks were made by new, young artists. The Crew Cuts, a white group out of Canada, covered the Penguins' "Earth Angel"; incidentally, without superseding the Dootone group's version. The McGuire Sisters, three women in their twenties out of Middletown, Ohio, covered the Spaniels' "Goodnight, Sweetheart, Goodnight," but really scored with their version of the Moonglows' "Sincerely." Young Pat Boone was the cover artist par excellence, with covers of recordings by the Charms, Fats Domino, Little Richard, Roy Brown, Ivory Joe Hunter, and the Flamingos. But established white artists, facing dwindling sales on the type of ballad that had brought them fame, also tried to maintain their position in the record world with covers.

The cover syndrome involved mostly two labels in addition to Mercury—Dot and Coral. The segregation of radio, with the 50,000-watt white stations refusing to play black records, opened the door to covers. Ahmet Ertegun, president of Atlantic Records, indicated how impossible it was to get plays of their records, while disk jockeys would play the same songs in white versions.

There was also an economic factor at play in the syndrome. The small labels that made R & B disks generally owned the publishing rights to the songs they recorded. This meant that what they lost in sales of their records was more than made up by the royalties they received on the white covers of their songs. As a result, the small-label "publisher" frequently sought white covers, since their sales generally far exceeded those of the original black recordings. Exposure by the white powerhouse stations and network radio accounted for the difference.

"Sh-Boom," regarded as the first Rock 'n' Roll hit, was the result of a cover. Recorded originally by the Chords, a Doo-Wop black group on Cat, an Atlantic Records subsidiary, it was quickly covered by Mercury Records' Crew Cuts. To get that cover, Atlantic gave up 50% of the publishing rights. It turned out to be quite unnecessary, for Mercury made the cover without the urging of the publisher, to whom Atlantic ceded half of its publishing royalties. Like the publishing house that paid a sizable advance for the 50% share, Mercury had discovered that the Chords' disk was selling like a hit in the Los Angeles market.[27]

White covers of black disks have been called rip-offs by this author and other historians—and they were that, in a sense. There was always the possibility, as in the case of Fats Domino, Bill Doggett ("Honky Tonk"), and Louis Jordan ("Choo Choo Ch'Boogie"), that the black record might cross over if a white cover did not monopolize airplay on the powerhouse white stations. That was La Vern Baker's contention when a cover of her "Tweedle Dee" yielded a million-copy seller to Georgia Gibbs, and left her record in the lurch. In fact, La Vern was so furious that she went to her congressman and sought to have a law introduced banning the copying of arrangements, something which is not possible under the copyright law. (Copyright protects the creator.) Nevertheless, there is one respect in which the white cover performs a positive function: by its widespread impact, it does publicize the original black artist and thereby enhances the earning capacity of such a group or artist in personal appearances.

From a historical standpoint, the cover syndrome was of great signifigance. It was operative in the early 1950s, reaching a peak during the two years before the emergence of Presley. It served as the bridge between Rhythm and Blues and Rock 'n' Roll. The mainstream of these years was still dominated by so-called good music, the ballads of the 1930s and 1940s, as well as by the baritones whose versions made these into hits. A statistical study of the top artists of the 1950s—the entire decade, that is—places Elvis Presley in the No. 1 position and includes Pat Boone (No. 2) and Fats Domino (No. 4). But the No. 3 and No. 5 spots are occupied by Perry Como and Nat King Cole, respectively.

Until 1956, when the Rock revolution was in full swing, black music (R & B) and Country music (C & W) were regional undercurrents. In the cover records—Hank Williams records were also covered in the early 1950s by Tony Bennett, Jo Stafford, and other mainstream singers—the undercurrents were developing into a swell that would soon overwhelm the mainstream. In the first stage of Rock 'n' Roll, the two regional streams came together.

Rockabilly

In 1955 Country guitarist Carl Perkins (b. 1930), son of a Tipton County, Tennessee, farmer, who was living in a government project in Jackson, Tennessee, got up at 3:00 A.M., went downstairs, and wrote out the words of a new song on a potato sack. "We didn't have reason to have writing paper around," he explained.[28] The song was "Blue Suede Shoes," an early anthem of the Rock generation, and the melody he wrote for his words used the chord progression and structure of classic 12-bar Blues. In describing Rockabilly music, as it became known, Perkins, who made the original record of his song, although people think of it in connection with Elvis Presley, later said: "Rockabilly is Blues with a country beat."[29]

The white transformation of R & B also found expression in Bill Haley, a precursor of Presley, whose pattern of development he anticipated. Haley's musical roots were in Country music. As a young man, he wanted to be a champion yodeler, a style of singing practiced by Jimmie Rodgers (1897–1933), the Father of Country Music. Winning an amateur contest in an outdoor C & W park near his home in Chester, Pennsylvania, he made contact and became friendly with Nashville singer Hank Williams (1923–1953). His first singing job, at 15 or 16, was on a Wilmington radio station, singing with a country group called Cousin Lee. His first network show, in Fort Wayne, Indiana, was again with a Country combo, called the Down Homers. Traveling, he worked with the WLS Barn Dance in Chicago, where he met Red Foley (1910–1968), another idol, as well as a well-known Country duo of the day, Lulu Belle and Scotty.

Betweentimes he visited New Orleans, presumably at Hank Williams's suggestion, where he heard the music of Louis Jordan. In an interview I had with him, he characterized Hank Williams as a "great Blues Singer" and credited him with stimulating "my interest in R & B music, race music, as it was then called."[30] The black influence crystallized when Haley became associated with a small station in Chester, where he worked as record librarian, sportscaster, and a performer with his own group. Before he went on the air each day, he was preceded by a show in which an hour of R & B was played. It prompted him to think: "Why shouldn't a country-and-western act sing Rhythm & Blues music. It was unheard of in those days (the early 50s). I didn't see anything wrong in mixing things up. I liked to sing R & B tunes and I sang them."[31] In short, when he was approached by Dave Miller of Essex Records in Philadelphia, who had been listening to his broadcasts, he began recording covers of R & B hits, such as Jackie Brenston's "Rocket 88," and such R & B originals as "Rock-a Beatin' Boogie," which he wrote.

The fusion of C & W and R & B, represented by both Perkins and Haley, came to a climactic explosion with Presley, who was doing on Sun Records what Haley was doing on Essex somewhat earlier. But there were other young Country singers in different parts of the country who were duplicating the pattern. Jerry Lee Lewis (b. 1933) came to Sun Records from Louisiana to record "Whole Lot-ta Shakin' Goin' On" and "Great Balls of Fire," the latter co-written with Otis Blackwell, a brilliant black songwriter who wrote two of Presley's biggest hits, "Don't Be Cruel" and "All Shook Up." Johnny Cash (b. 1932) came to Sun from Arkansas and recorded his own well-known song, "I Walk the Line."

Eddie Cochran (1939–1960), an Oklahoman who settled in Hollywood, first recorded "Sittin' in the Balcony" by a Nashville songwriter, John Loudermilk, but followed it with his own "Summertime Blues" and other songs, including Ray Charles's "Hallelujah, I Love Her So" and Kokomo Arnold's "Milk Cow Blues," in which he affected a black sound and style. Other young singers who became part of the Rockabilly development included, among others, Gene Vincent (1935–1971), of Norfolk, Virginia, with "Be-Bop-A-Lula"; Ricky Nelson (b. 1940), of New Jersey and Los Angeles, with "I'm Walkin'," a cover of the Fats Domino hit; Conway Twitty, (b. 1935) of Arkansas, with "It's Only Make Believe"; Johnny Burnette (1934–1964), of Memphis, with "You're Sixteen"; and Roy Orbison (b. 1936), of Texas, with "Only the Lonely."

Apart from Presley, the most important proponents of Rockabilly were the Everly Bros., Buddy Holly, Jerry Lee Lewis, Carl Perkins, and Bill Haley, and, coming from the other end of the spectrum, Chuck Berry.

The Everly Bros.—Donald Isaac (b. 1937) and Phil (b. 1939)—worked as part of a Kentucky/Tennessee family group, singing Country songs on local radio stations from the time they were six and eight years old. Shortly after they were out of high school, Wesley Rose, of the Nashville music publishing company Acuff-Rose, became their manager, and arranged for them to record for Cadence Records of New York. Their first hit, "Bye Bye, Love," (1957) as well as several succeeding hits ("Wake Up, Little Susie," "All I Have to Do Is Dream," etc.) were written by the Nashville husband-and-wife team Felice and Boudleaux Bryant.

That the brothers had listened to R & B as well as Country music is clear from a recording they made in 1958 of Ray Charles's "This Little Girl of Mine." Black influence is apparent in their driving style, which might be described as Country Rock if not Rockabilly. Their harmony was derived from southern Country singers, but the beat came from rock. In fact, in a 1959 recording of Don's song, " 'Til I Kissed You," cut with former members of the Crickets, they had Buddy Holly's drummer use a whole set of drums, a first in Country music. The popularity of the duo resulted in Gold Records for all of their early releases. And their impact reached across the sea, so that a British group in its formative stage not only modeled its singing style on the brothers, but actually considered calling itself the For Everlys. The British group eventually settled on the name the Beatles.

Buddy Holly (1936 – 1959) vaulted national record charts in the year after Presley mounted them, influenced by Elvis's high-spirited style. Hailing from Lubbock, Texas, and recording in Clovis, New Mexico, Holly's sound was described as Tex – Mex, a not-too-precise characterization but one that may have had something to do with the radiant, ringing sound of his guitar, produced by a technique known among Country pickers as "brush and broom." A chord is struck (the broom), and with the same movement, the fingers are flipped across the same or a related chord (the brush). While in high school Holly formed a group known as the Western and Bop Band, which included Bob Montgomery, later a prominent Nashville songwriter/publisher.

Although he recorded initially for Decca, the sides went unreleased. But when Holly cut some of the same songs with the Crickets at Norman Petty's studio in Clovis, "That'll Be the Day" became a No. 1 record, both in England and the U.S. Holly's first solo hit on Coral was "Peggy Sue," followed by "Rave On." As in the case of the Everlys, he listened to R & B, deriving buoyancy, rhythmic punch, and repertoire from it. His album *20 Golden Greats* contains versions of Ellas McDaniels's "Bo Diddley" and Chuck Berry's "Brown Eyed Handsome Man."

His untimely death in a plane crash on February 3, 1959, along with the Big Bopper ("Chantilly Lace") and Ritchie Valens ("Donna"), was a staggering blow to a large following he had developed in only two years of recording. Years later, in 1971, Don McLean (b. 1947) wrote the classic "American Pie," in which he recalled the devastating impact of Holly's death and used it as a symbol of the decline of popular music. "The day the music died" was the memorable phrase that McLean attached to Holly's demise. Buddy Holly was another influence on the Beatles, who displayed their feelings for his group, the Crickets, by their choice of a related insect for their name.

Although he is black, Chuck Berry (b. 1926) is part of the white synthesis of R & B, by virtue of his style and the subject matter of his original songs. That there were Country roots in his work is evident from the first song he recorded for Chess. "Maybelline" was, in its first audition for Leonard Chess, a Country song, "Ida Red." It was the Chess coowner who prompted Chuck to rework it and then added a rocking beat in the recording process to make it a pioneer Rock 'n' Roll hit in 1955.

Born in San Jose, California, Charles Edward Anderson Berry grew up in a Missouri town about 30 miles from St. Louis, where he sang in the choir of the Antioch Baptist Church. But he was obviously listening to Country music as well as Louis Jordan, whose flair for humor influenced such Berry songs as "Too Pooped to Pop," "Too Much Monkey Business," "Brown-Eyed Handsome Man," and the classic "Roll Over, Beethoven." The last-mentioned, in which Beethoven is asked to "tell Tchaikovsky the news" and "dig those rhythm and blues," used the traditional chord progression of the Blues to encapsulate the jukebox regimen of the young reel-and-rock-it generation.

Despite the fact that Berry was a 30-year old man in 1956, there is no songwriter-singer of the period whose songs provide such an in-depth picture of teenage life. In "School Day," "Rock and Roll Music," "Almost Grown," "Johnny B. Goode," "Maybelline," and other hits of the 1955–1959 period, he delineated the world of the teenager in remarkably vivid and entertaining terms—not to mention danceable disks. His records are now part of a historical collection of material buried in a capsule to be opened 100 years from now, and designed to give the world of 2078 a picture of the teenage world of 1956.

As Rockabilly hits, sung with an enunciation that is white, Berry's songs found an audience across the board, among Country, Pop, and R & B record-buyers, appealing to white as well as black listeners. In the early 1960s his song "Sweet Little Sixteen" was adapted by the Beach Boys for their surfing music. His Pop/Rock orientation reached a fitting climax in 1972, when his erotically humorous gang song, "My Ding-a-Ling" went to the top of the Pop charts and became a Gold Record. He remains a giant of the Rock scene, still active in 1984, meriting, as no one else does, the title, Song Laureate of the Teenage Generation.

Teenage Rock

Rockabilly was a spontaneous phenomenon. White teenagers in various parts of the United States, mostly the South, responding to the drive and bounce of R & B, drew from it qualities that infused their singing with a new excitement, electricity, and beat. By contrast, Teenage Rock, a stage rather than a distinct style, was *ersatz*, a manufactured sound produced by record makers anxious to invade an expanding market, one they had thought was just a passing phenomenon. The change in outlook was the result of the introduction by the American Broadcasting Company of *American Bandstand,* a show featuring and addressed to teenagers. Having allowed the small independents to dominate the R & B market, the major record companies and music publishers moved to capture the new audience.

Now skilled old-time arrangers like Don Costa, at the helm of ABC–Paramount Records, took the most prominent features of R & B and embroidered recordings with a pronounced afterbeat, raucous tenor sax interludes, Boogie and/or shuffle rhythm, high-register piano triplets, and a small combo sound dominated by the electric guitar. The search was for adolescent singers whose popularity was insured by a youthful sound, regardless of how amateurish or crude they seemed to be. The new stars included Paul Anka (b. 1941), Connie Francis (b. 1938), Ricky Nelson, Bobby Vee (b. 1943), Ritchie Valens (1941–1959), Leslie Gore (b. 1946), and George Hamilton IV (b. 1937), among others.

Suddenly, the word *teenage* became freighted with the emotional and sociological overtones of *citizen* in the French Revolution or *comrade* in the Russian Revolution. Songs exploited the sentiment on records, including "Teen-Age Love," by Frankie Lymon & the Teenagers; "Teen Age Crush," by Tommy Sands; "A Teenager's Romance," by Ricky Nelson; "A Teenager in Love," by Dion & the Belmonts; and "Ballad of a Teenage Queen," by Johnny Cash. A number of songs focused on the clothes worn by the young: "Short Shorts," by the Royal Teens; "Black Slacks," by the Sparkletones; "Rubber Sole Shoes," by Julius LaRosa; "Bobby sox to Stockings," by Frankie Avalon; and "A White Sport Coat and a Pink Carnation," by Marty Robbins.

There were songs about such teenage expressions as "All Shook Up" (Elvis Presley), "Raunchy" (Bill Justis), and "Rumble" (Link Wray); and songs about teenage life-styles such as "At the Hop," by Danny & the Juniors; "A Rose and a Baby Ruth," by George Hamilton IV; and "Queen of the Hop," by Bobby Darin. Unrequited love was a theme, but on an adolescent level, as in Paul Anka's "Diana," about the young boy in love with an older girl, and "Born Too Late," by the Poni Tails, in which the young girl is in love with an older man. The problem of children versus parents found expression in "Yakety Yak" (The Coasters), "Get a Job" (The Silhouettes), and "Why Don't They Understand" (George Hamilton IV). Loneliness and the loner figured in Dion's "Lonely Teenager," Paul Anka's "I'm a Lonely Boy," and The Coasters' "Charlie Brown."

From a sociological point of view, all of these songs, simplistic though they were, charted a generation in search of its identity. While conflict between parents and children may be traditional, the children of World War II early began to experience a group alienation from their elders. By the mid-1960s that alienation had found expression in the work of such songwriters as Bob Dylan (b. 1941), Paul Simon (b. 1942), Randy Newman (b. 1944) the Beatles, and other protest and satiric writers. The initial, if traditional, conflict in the 1950s about chores, hairstyle, dress, and speech was just a superficial indication of a more deep-seated conflict over values that became paramount in the generation gap of the 1960s.

The singer par excellence of the white transformation of R & B was Pat Boone (b. 1934). Born in Jacksonville, Florida and raised in Nashville, he went to North Texas State College in Denton, graduated from Columbia University, and married the daughter of Country star, Red Foley (1910-1968). Pat concentrated on covers of R & B records, providing polished white versions in a smooth baritone of disks by such black artists as Fats Domino, Little Richard, Ivory Joe Hunter, Roy Brown, the Charms, Flamingos, and El Dorados. And he and his handlers worked at creating an image of the All-American Boy, a good student, a loving husband, and a sweet father. The image of purity, wholesomeness, and righteousness was visually symbolized by the white buckskins he wore on his TV show. These served to make viewers aware that he was not part of that wild, rebellious, rough crowd in the blue suedes.

Dick Clark (b. 1929), the affable, clean-cut, handsome host of *American Bandstand,* also participated in the movement to give Rock 'n' Roll a respectable image. The youngsters who were seen dancing on his shows had to follow strict dress requirements: the girls had to wear skirts, not jeans or dungarees, and the boys all wore jackets. Tight-fitting sweaters and T-shirts were a no-no. Most of the artists who came to "lip-sync" their records were white. Clark himself avoided the frenzied announcing style of Alan Freed, his major competitor nationally, who did favor black artists. Instead, Clark was cool, friendly in a detached way, and a host who was like a big brother, parent, or teacher but clearly not one of the crowd dancing to the disks on his turntable.

With *Bandstand* being telecast daily over more than 100 TV stations, Clark and the City of Brotherly Love became a major pivot of the music business, with an interlocking circle of new, local record labels, music publishers, songwriters, artists, and promotion men all clustering around the program's genial host. During the payola investigation of 1959-1960, it was revealed that Clark's conflict-of-interest holdings included shares in six music publishing companies, three record labels (Chancellor, Cameo/Parkway, and

Swan), a record distributor, a local record-pressing plant, and an artist-management firm. (He was compelled to divest himself of all these—at a handsome profit—in order to retain his post on *American Bandstand.*)

With the exposure that records received under Clark's aegis, many new artists sprouted from the Philadelia music scene. Swan Records came up with winners in Freddy Cannon and Billie and Lillie. Bob Marcucci, recently the subject of a film, *The Idolmaker,* and his Chancellor label scored with Fabian (b. 1943) and Frankie Avalon (b. 1940). Cameo/Parkway, the most successful of the group, achieved best-selling disks with Charlie Gracie, the Rays, Bobby Rydell, and Chubby Checker, among others. Some of these exemplified a new criterion in popular music: they "looked like singers"; none proved to have very much staying power.

Chubby Checker, born Ernest Evans (1941), was the young man whose Parkway recording of "The Twist" ignited the dance craze that swept the world in 1961–1962. Checker's disk was a cover of a record by the Midnighters on the King label; the song, written by Hank Ballard, the lead singer and organizer of the Midnighters, was recorded a year before Checker cut his version. What spelled the difference, unquestionably, was Checker's appearances on *Bandstand* to demonstrate the dance. An excellent dancer, who could make any dance look attractive, Chubby Checker became the dance specialist of Rock, introducing and/or popularizing such dances as the Pony, Mess Around, Hitchhiker, and Limbo Rock, all of which he recorded but none of which approached the popularity of the Twist.

To the teenagers of the late 1950s and early 1960s who did their homework before their TV sets, *American Bandstand* was the arbiter of not only how they danced, but how they dressed, combed their hair, talked, and dealt with their parents and friends.

Skiffle and British Blues

In March of 1956, American record charts included a British (actually a Scottish) import, a record by Lonnie Donegan and his Skiffle group of a Leadbelly up-tempo song, "The Rock Island Line." The London recording remained on the charts for 11 weeks, climbing into the Top Ten. A little more than a year later, in June of 1957, "Freight Train," by the Charles McDevitt Skiffle Group, made its appearance on the charts. Although the word *Skiffle* is of American origin, these were the first instances of its visibility in over 30 years.

During the 1920s, a Country Blues singer, Charlie Spand, recorded "Hometown Skiffle." As a style, Skiffle may date back to the earliest days of the Blues, since it refers to music played on homemade or nonstandard instruments, constructed by people who could not afford or did not have access to standard instruments. Among skiffle instruments, one finds combs, jugs, washboards, guitars, and fiddles made out of cigar boxes and wire, and the Brownie Bass. For the last-mentioned, an overturned washtub was used as a sounding device, the fretboard was a broom handle, and the player plucked and fretted a clothesline stretching from a hole in the middle of the tub to the top of the broom handle.

The two recordings, imported from Great Britain in 1956 and 1957, were indicative of a Skiffle craze that swept British Pop music circles in the 1950s, when young musicians and just youngsters, imitating impoverished black American bluesmen, devised and played instruments of their own making. The craze was inaugurated by Scottish-born Lonnie Donegan (b. 1931), an avid Folk/Blues/Jazz musician whose given name was Anthony until he and his group performed with black bluesman Lonnie Johnson (1889–1970) at London's Royal Festival Hall—after which Anthony became Lonnie.

Before they became part of the Beatles, John Lennon (1940–1980), Paul McCartney (b. 1942), and George Harrison (b. 1943) all played with the Quarrymen, a Skiffle group formed by friends of John Lennon, who attended the Quarry Rank High School in Liverpool. The impetus for the group's formation, according to Hunter Davies, came from three records: Bill Haley's "Rock Around the Clock"; Lonnie Donegan's "Rock Island Line"; and Elvis's "Heartbreak Hotel." Suddenly, in 1956, British youngsters felt that "for the first time music wasn't the property of musicians. Any one could get up and have a go. It was like giving paint sets to monkeys . . . There was overnight about a hundred dances in Liverpool with skiffle groups queuing up to perform."[32] Davies adds: "Like John and the others, Paul was influenced by the skiffle phase and Bill Haley's early rock numbers, but like John again, not until Elvis Presley was he really bowled over."[33] (But Paul was also excited by Little Richard both before and after he took the Beatles with him to Hamburg's Reeperbahn.) George Harrison said: "Lonnie Donegan and Skiffle just seemed made for me."[34]

Even while the Skiffle craze was in vogue, Alexis Korner (1928–1984), an ardent Blues and Boogie-Woogie fan, joined forces with Cyril Davies (1932–1964), another Blues aficionado, who played banjo and harmonica, to open the London Blues and Barrelhouse Club in the upstairs of a Soho pub. Korner's love for the Blues came from recordings by Blind Willie Johnson (b. 1923), Jimmy Yancey (1898–1951), Leadbelly (1889–1949), and Scrapper Blackwell (1903–1962), a Jazz guitarist/songwriter, who worked with bluesman Leroy Carr (1905–1935). Cyril Davies, who played in several Jazz bands in the early 1950s and participated in the Skiffle craze, moved afterward toward the electric instruments of R & B and was particularly influenced by harpist Little Walter (1930–1968), who worked with Tampa Red, Big Bill Broonzy, and Memphis Slim but mostly with Muddy Waters. Together, gravel-voiced Korner and Davies ran and performed at the Blues and Barrelhouse Club from 1957 until 1961, laying the groundwork for England's Blues-derived rock explosion.

Ejected from their Soho location for using amplification, they formed Blues Incorporated in February 1962, a band that continued to perform, with shifts in personnel, through September 1966. On March 17, 1962, they opened London's first R & B club, in the basement of a café in Ealing, a suburb. Both the club and their band "acted as a magnet for the growing body of blues aficionados," according to Pete Frame, "who journeyed from all over Britain. Audience participation was encouraged; aspiring bluesers were able to test their wings on stage with the band."[35] Starting in May 1962, Blues Incorporated played a weekly stint at the Marquee, initially a Jazz stronghold and later an R & B and Rock venue. "By 1963, the R & B boom was in full swing in England," Frame has observed.[36]

Throughout the more than four years of the existence of Blues Incorporated and the seven major incarnations through which it went as a result of musicians who came and went, Alexis Korner remained as the pivot and inspiration. Among the future top British musicians who were part of Blues Incorporated for varying periods, there were bassist Jack Bruce (b. 1943) and drummer Ginger Baker (b. 1943), who formed Cream with Eric Clapton (b. 1945), of John Mayall's Bluesbreakers. Brian Jones (1944–1969), who fathered the embryo of the Rolling Stones in May 1962, was, with Mick Jagger (b. 1944), drummer Charlie Watts (b. 1941), and guitarist Keith Richard (b. 1943), part of Blues Incorporated. Inspired by Korner's enthusiasm, his disciples formed other Blues/Rock bands of their own, including Manfred Mann, Chris Farlowe's Thunderbirds, John Mayall's Bluesbreakers, the Animals, Zoot Money's Big Roll Band, and the Graham Bond Organization.

Korner's associate, Cyril Davies, launched his own R & B Stars in November 1962, which operated until his untimely death in 1964. This band was the incubator for Long John Baldry's Hoochie Coochie Men (with a bow to Muddy Waters) and Steam Packet, both of which included vocalist Rod Stewart (b. 1945). On Korner's death in January 1984, *Rolling Stone* gave recognition to his seminal role in the British R & B movement, which transformed British Pop music as it had done American Pop, by printing a genealogy of British Blues bands as a eulogy.[37]

The repertoire and recordings of these white British groups reveal a large debt to American rhythm-and-bluesmen. Bo Diddley's "I'm A Man" and Howlin' Wolf's "Smokestack Lightning," delivered in clipped British accents, are in a *Greatest Hits* album of the Yardbirds, a pioneer group that succeeded the Rolling Stones at the famous Crawdaddy Club. "You Got What It Takes," recorded by Marv Johnson (b. 1938) and cowritten by Berry Gordy, Jr., who founded the Motown complex, became the title song of an album by the Dave Clark 5, the first group to play the Ed Sullivan Show after the Beatles. The Tremoloes covered "Too Many Fish in the Sea" by the Marvelettes and Ashford and Simpson's "Running Out." Out of 10 selections in the *Best of the Cream,* there were "Spoonful," of Chess bassist Willie Dixon, "Crossroads," of influential bluesman Robert Johnson, and "Born Under a Bad Sign," of Stax Records' Booker T. and William Bell.

Ray Charles and Bo Diddley (b. 1928) were the special favorites of the British group that started as the Alan Price (b. 1942) Combo—all five were self-taught—and became famous as the Animals. Playing R & B from the start, they became the resident group at the Club a Gogo in Newcastle, where they developed a large local following, as the Beatles did in Liverpool. A demo disk became a local best seller, motivating the group to move to London, where they made their radio debut on the BBC's Saturday Club late in December 1963. By 1964 they were on American charts with "House of the Rising Sun," a bawdy Blues popularized by folk singer Josh White (1908–1969). It went to No. 1 and earned a Gold Record on the MGM label. That year, they made a tour with Chuck Berry of Great Britain and United States. Two years later, they produced a million-seller with a *Best* collection that included covers of John Lee Hooker's "Boom, Boom," "Dimples," and "I'm Mad Again," Jimmy Reed's "Bright Lights, Big City," and Ray Charles's "Talkin' 'Bout You."

Chuck Berry hits figured in albums by the Dave Clark 5 ("Reelin' and Rockin") and the Youngbloods ("Monkey Business"). But the group that was most partial to Chuck's songs was the Rolling Stones. Until the *Aftermath* album, when Mick Jagger and Keith Richard began writing all the Stones' songs, a Chuck Berry song was included in each of their albums of 1964 and 1965: "Carol," "Around and Around," "You Can't Catch Me," and "Talkin' About You." More involved than any British group in the white transformation of R & B, they recorded songs by Stax's Rufus Thomas; Atlantic's Wilson Pickett; Specialty's Sam Cooke; Chess's Bo Diddley, Willie

Dixon, and Muddy Waters; and, reaching back into 1941, "Confessin' the Blues," by Kansas City pianist/bandleader Jay McShann (b. 1909).

Surfing Music

They said, "We're white and we sing white," suggesting a backlash, but the Beach Boys took the melody of Chuck Berry's "Sweet Little Sixteen" (with accreditation) and adapted it for the type of song that became known as Surfing Music in 1963, a concept rather than a musical style.

The Beach Boys started as many such groups did in the Rock era, with three brothers. Hailing from Hawthorne, California, Brian, Dennis, and Carl Wilson (b. 1942, 1944, and 1946, respectively), a cousin, Mike Love (b. 1941), and a neighborhood friend, Al Jardine (b. 1942), played music just for fun, until they coalesced into a Rock group. Hawthorne, a suburb of Los Angeles, was only five miles from the Pacific coast, where surfing, imported from Hawaii, had developed into a teenage fad. Dennis, the middle brother, who drowned in 1984, was an avid surfer, and when the boys, anxious to distinguish their group from the myriad other such groups, were searching for fresh song ideas, he suggested surfing. After Brian and Mike wrote "Surfin'" to Chuck Berry's melody, they paid to make a demo record, arranged to have it released on a small local label, and created enough excitement in the area to attract a Capitol Records contract.

They adopted the name Beach Boys to accord with the song, and in personal appearances dressed accordingly: in slacks and candy-striped, short-sleeved sports shirts. Their first single on Capitol, "Surfin' Safari," which became the title of their debut album, was a sizable seller, with best-seller singles developing in the follow-up disks of 1963, "Surfin' U.S.A." and "Surfer Girl." Although Surfing Music attracted only another duo, Jan and Dean, who also wrote and recorded surfin' songs, it exercised a spell that made it a nationwide craze between 1963 and 1965.

The music had no real individuality. With the Chuck Berry tune as a base, it was a white version of a 12-bar Blues. A gentle afterbeat was sounded with hand claps: rest/clap-clap, rest/clap; rest/clap-clap, rest/clap. The identity of Surfing Music inhered in an image, romantic and thrilling. It was a matter of sunshine, sea, surf, and sand, lolling on a sun-drenched beach with an attractive girl, savoring the gentle ocean breezes, and, most of all, escaping from the boredom and tensions of everyday living. And, of course, it meant plunging into the ocean, paddling out on a surfboard, and riding the crest of an onrushing wave to shore, to the admiring eyes of envious onlookers. Implicit was the sense of exhilaration, freedom, swift movement, and challenging the elements. The necromancy of the concept was perhaps best indicated by reports that youngsters in the Midwest, thousands of miles from an ocean, drove around, as did their Pacific Coast cohorts, with surfboards strapped to the roofs of their cars.

CHAPTER NINE

"BLACK IS BEAUTIFUL"

In 1968 James Brown (b. 1928) wrote and recorded a two-sided single, "Say It Loud—I'm Black and I'm Proud," which became the evocative title of a best-selling album. It was an emotional declaration of black independence, in which Brown called upon a group of black youngsters to "say it loud" and they responded, again and again, "I'm black and I'm proud," while he asserted in his choked, high-pitched tenor that it was time for blacks to do things "for ourselves," independently of whites. Despite its patently didactic character—perhaps because of it—the single went to No. 1 on R & B charts, where it remained for 12 weeks.

"Say It Loud—I'm Black and I'm Proud" was a testament of the polarization that marked black song and singing during the 1960s and that had its origin in the growth of black nationalism and a black power movement. The 1960s were an era of bloodied driveways, bloodied kitchen pantries, bloodied stages, bloodied motel balconies, and bloodied automobiles, an era of persuasion by assassination—Medgar Evers, John Fitzgerald Kennedy, Robert Kennedy, Che Guevara, Malcolm X, and Martin Luther King, Jr.

James Brown shrieked and howled on his records; so did Aretha Franklin (b. 1942) and Jackie Wilson (1934–1984). If R & B singers were shouters, Soul singers were screamers. Gospel music was one of the sources from which R & B derived its excitement. But Gospel, with its unbuttoned emotionalism, was the essence of Soul.

It was in the 1920s, and especially during the Depression years, that Gospel music blossomed. In storefront Baptist churches, to the rhythm of handclapping, foot-stamping, rattling tambourines, and a thumping, tinny upright piano, black people sought to escape the deprivations of the lean years and find solace in the embrace of Jesus and the Lord, and to hope for a brighter future. Jesus was the rock, the healer, the teacher, the doctor, and as the Reverend James Cleveland (b. 1931) boomed, "I don't need nobody else!"

As a youngster in Chicago, Cleveland was Mahalia Jackson's paper boy, hopefully pressing his ear against her door to hear her sing. At eight, he made his first public appearance, boy soprano in the Pilgrim Baptist Church, where Thomas A. Dorsey (b. 1899) was leader of the Angelic Choir. Later Cleveland used so much voice to praise the Lord that he strained it; and "that's why it sounds like a foghorn," he says. "Lots of folks call me the Louis Armstrong of Gospel."[1]

Mahalia Jackson, the Queen of Gospel Song during her dedicated life, called Thomas A. Dorsey "our Irving Berlin." Starting as a writer of Blues and a top-notch Jazz pianist, who accompanied Ma Rainey but also played with the great Bessie Smith, Dorsey attained an early peak with an erotic Blues he wrote and recorded as Georgia Tom with Tampa Red. "It's Tight Like That" became a sizzling hit in 1928, which Dorsey sometimes tried to forget later in his career. Shortly after the success of the song, Dorsey turned to religious music, following in the footsteps of the Reverend C. Albert Tindley, the Methodist minister/author of "Stand By Me" and other tabernacle songs, used by the raucous Holiness sects (1890–1906), and the spiritual songwriter credited with originating Gospel-styled music.

From 1939 to 1941, Dorsey traveled as accompanist to Mahalia Jackson. In time, he became the celebrated writer of such gospel classics as "Peace in the Valley," "If You See My Saviour," and "Precious Lord," the song requested by Martin Luther King, Jr., the night of his assassination. Dorsey wrote neither hymns nor spirituals but religious songs with a popular orientation, for which he coined the designation *Gospel songs.* In 1932–1933, he and the famous Sallie Martin founded the National Convention of Gospel Choirs and Choruses, whose annual festivals he administered into the 1980s.

Of greater consequence to Soul music than the songs themselves was the rapturous style in which they were sung, especially in services conducted in the Holiness, Sanctified, Pentecostal, and other unorthodox Baptist churches. "I have never seen anything to equal the fire and excitement that sometimes without warning, fill a church, causing it to rock," wrote author James Baldwin, who was himself once a Harlem storefront preacher. "The cries of 'Amen!' and 'Hallelujah!' and 'Yes, Lord!' and 'Praise His Name!' 'Preach it, brother!' sustained and whipped on my solos until we became equal, wringing wet, singing and dancing in anguish and rejoicing at the foot of the altar."[2]

If R & B was the music of revelry, Soul was the music of ecstasy: It aimed at evoking an emotional response. Possessed, the singer sought to make the music possess the listener.

Richard Penniman, now the Reverend Richard Penniman and better known as Little Richard (b. 1935), is not generally classified as a Soul singer. But when he burst on the record scene in 1955 with the hysterical scat-howl, "Wop/Bop-a-lou/Bop-a-lop/Bim-bam-boom!" there was no mistaking the gospel fire in his voice. That the high-powered intensity of expression came from Gospel music should have been evident from his background in Augusta and Macon, Georgia; and later, in a backward glance, from his desertion of Rock 'n' Roll for the church in the 1950s, and ultimately from his full-time work as an evangelist preacher since 1975. But "Tutti Frutti," a rewrite of a risqué original, was so erotic, as were such succeeding sizzlers as "Rip It Up," "Long Tall Sally," "Keep A-Knockin'," and "Send Me Some Lovin'," that it was not easy to associate Little Richard's fire with spiritual fervor rather than impassionated sex. Moreover, the libidinous lyrics were underscored by fey mannerisms, which Little Richard now frankly characterizes as homosexual. Thus, the explosive energy of his delivery, antedating Elvis's emergence on record charts by almost six months, became an earmark of Rock 'n' Roll.

It was that, as was readily evident in Elvis's imitative recordings of such songs of the Macon firebrand as "Tutti Frutti," "Rip It Up," "Long Tall Sally," and "Ready Teddy." Elvis's debt was exceeded by Jerry Lee Lewis (b. 1935), who not only copied Little Richard's racing piano style and his wild, whooping song style, but imitated his eccentric stage mannerisms—playing his pumping piano standing up, bouncing on the keyboard with his rump, and banging the keys, as he sat, with the heel of an outstretched foot.

Pioneer of the Rock revolution, Little Richard exerted considerable influence on a number of consequential black artists. Foremost of these were two Macon residents, the late Otis Redding (1941–1967) and James Brown (b. 1936), whose albums bore such tear-it-up titles as *Mr. Dynamite, Cold Sweat,* and *Raw Soul.* As a teenager, Otis Redding grew up idolizing and listening to Little Richard, whose impact was also evident in such Soul artists of the sixties as Wilson Pickett (b. 1941) and Aretha Franklin.

Of Ray Charles, Urban bluesman Big Bill Broonzy, admittedly not a churchgoer, said: "Ray is mixin' the Blues with Spirituals. That's wrong. . . . He should be singin' in church."[3] Charles's intrepid fusion of the two genres first became evident in the same year as Little Richard's entry into the record scene—and Ray became, together with Penniman, a forerunner of the Soul movement of the 1960s, developing it simply as a musical style and not as a postural response to a time and to changes in the black condition and outlook. In Charles's transformation, "My Jesus Is All the World to Me" became, in 1955, "I've Got a Woman," and "This Little Light of Mine," a hymn to Jesus popularized by the Clara Ward (1924–1973) Singers, became "This Little Girl of Mine."

When Charles first proposed these secularizations of Gospel song for recording, executives of Atlantic Records were dismayed, if not horrified. They well knew with what antithetical feelings religious blacks would view a fusion of the music of the Lord (Gospel) with the music of the Devil (Blues). How could one justify turning a paean to Jesus into a rosuing love/sex song, as Charles did in "Hallelujah I Love Her So." But Ray was determined, and won a large, perhaps new, audience with the sensual emotionalism of recordings that reached a climax in the call-and-response excitement of "What'd I Say" (1959), the title song of his first million-copy album.

The intensification of the black struggle for equal rights in the 1960s and the rise of a black power movement created an atmosphere so charged with tension that few black singers, regardless of their political or social outlook, could avoid reacting to it. Singers became "witnesses," not just entertainers. Their disks became so suffused with feeling, regardless of subject matter, that they lapsed into shrieks, screams, yelps, groans, screeches, shrill and choked falsettos.

"It makes no difference what kind of song you sing," Sam Cooke (1935–1964) once said. "You have to stir up the emotion of the 'congregation' and literally lift them from their chairs. I learned this lesson at an early age in church."[4]

Cooke's involvement with spiritual music began in his boyhood, when he sang in his father's Chicago church, as part of a family quartet; continued in his high school days, when he was lead singer of the Highway QC's, a church-touring quintet; and culminated in his recording with the famous gospeleers the Soul Stirrers. When he wanted to record secular R & B ballads by himself, he encountered the same opposition that Ray Charles had experienced with secularized versions of Gospel song. The head of Specialty Records felt it would be injurious to the standing of the gospel group if its lead singer became involved with nonsacred material. Cooke left the label with one of its producers and cut independently "You-oo-oo-oo Send Me," the disk that launched him on his short-lived (1960–1964) and tragically terminated life as an R & B singer. (He was shot and clubbed to death by the black owners of a motel where he had registered with a white girl; the suspicious circumstances have never been fully explained, but his death was ruled a justifiable homicide.)

RCA Victor signed Cooke in 1960, after he had spent three years with chart-making releases on the independent Keen label. Then he scored a remarkable succession of Top Ten records. He was not a shouter, not a screamer, but sang ballads like "Nothing Can Change This Love" with a soulful tenderness, an emotional warmth, and mellow melisma derived from his Gospel years. But even in such up-tempo numbers as "Chain Gang," "Twistin' the Night Away" (No. 1 at the height of the Twist craze), Little Richard's "Send Me Some Lovin'," and Willie Dixon's "Little Red Rooster," he delivered with a depth of feeling that likewise was Gospel-derived. The two-sided hit single is comparatively rare. But Cooke succeeded in producing three singles on which both sides soared to the top of best-seller lists: "Bring It On Home to Me," b/w "Having a Party" (1962), "Somebody Have Mercy," b/w "Nothing Can Change This Love" (1962), and "Shake," b/w "A Change Is Gonna Come" (1965). The last-mentioned song, a posthumous hit, revealed Cooke's sensitivity to the dynamics of the black experience in the 1960s. One of the best instances of the soulful handling of a ballad is to be found in his "(I Love You) For Sentimental Reasons," an early Keen recording, in which the insistent repetition of "I Love You" and other words produces a brimming intensity of feeling, despite the caressing softness of his voice.

Few records are suffused with the kind of unrestrained feeling projected by James Brown (b. 1928) in his supplication for love in "Please, Please, Please" (1956), the disk that first brought him before the American public. It was harbinger of a style of explosive emotionalism suggested by such album titles as *Pure Dynamite, Cold Sweat,* and *Raw Soul.* Calling himself "America's No. 1 Soul Brother," Brown expressed himself in the most dynamic form of Soul, resorting to shrieks, screams, and screeches that make him sound at times like a feline in pain. His appeal to black audiences was such that, between 1956 and 1971, he placed 59 disks on R & B charts, of which 19 mounted to the No. 1 and No. 2 slots, a record equaled by no other black artist. His power to sway black people was displayed during riots in the sixties, when his appearances on TV in Boston and Washington, D.C., helped draw young blacks off the streets.

Among Brown's No. 1 hits, there were "Papa's Got a Brand New Bag," which won him a Grammy in 1965 for Best R & B Record, "It's a Man's Man's Man's World," "Mother Popcorn," and "Super Bad." That Brown could compete with other types of singers in the handling of a ballad is apparent in recordings he made of such songs as "Nature Boy," "I Love You, Porgy," and "Mona Lisa," the Academy Award song of 1950, originally recorded by Nat "King" Cole. In the 1970s, Brown became a leading exponent of Funk with numbers like "Funky Drummer" and "Make It Funky."

Like James Brown and Berry Gordy, Jr., who co-wrote his early hits, Jackie Wilson (1934–1984) was a prize fighter for a time, winning the Golden Gloves as a welterweight at the age of 16—he said he was 18. Like Brown, he was also an incredibly dynamic performer, who danced and sang with such furious energy that he stained leather outfits with his sweat. (It may have been a factor in the heart attack/stroke that he suffered onstage in 1975 and left him in a coma until his untimely death in 1984.) Unlike Brown, he possessed a voice of almost operatic range, which he displayed on "Night," a million-seller adaptation of an aria from the opera *Samson and Delilah.*

Wilson's first million seller was "Lonely Teardrops," written by Berry Gordy, Jr., Gwen Gordy, and his cousin Tyran Carlo, a trio that also wrote "I'll Be Satisfied" and "That's Why." "Lonely Teardrops" is replete with a choked falsetto that became a facet of his soulful style, which reached a peak of expressiveness and acceptance in "(Your Love Keeps Lifting Me) Higher and Higher" (1967), later a hit in a cover by Rita Coolidge. Coolidge's disk offers an instructive contrast in that the rhythmic background of her record has the drive and beat of Wilson's but her vocal is laidback country. Hailing from Detroit, Wilson sang lead with the Dominoes, succeeding Clyde McPhatter, during their years as a Gospel group, an experience that colored his style.

Nina Simone's creative journey is indicative of the challenge of the 1960s, especially to black artists. Born Eunice Kathleen Waymon (1933) in a small North Carolina town, she was valedictorian of her high-school class and endured the pain of a fracas about where her parents were to sit during the graduation ceremony. A piano prodigy, she won a scholarship to the prestigious Juilliard School of Music in New York, where she studied with noted piano pedagogues of the day. When the possibility of a concert career evaporated, as it did for most blacks in that era, Nina began playing in a nightclub and discovered that she had to sing as well as play piano if she wanted to be paid.

It was at this time that she adopted the name by which she is known, concerned about offending her religious parents, to whom a nightclub was anathema. Although her metier is jazz piano, she became known as the result of a soulful version of "I Love You, Porgy," a song from the Gershwin folk opera *Porgy and Bess*. Released on a small, independent label (Bethlehem) in 1959, it became her sole million seller, opening the door to a recording contract in Colpix, a subsidiary of Mercury, and, in the late 1960s, on RCA.

Events strongly affected Nina Simone, as they did other artists in the sixties. Two that particularly upset her were the Ku Klux Klan bombing of a church in Alabama in which four children were killed, and the wounding of James Meredith, the first black admitted to the University of Mississippi, during a protest march. Outraged and in a fury, Nina wrote and recorded a song seldom or never heard on the radio. Its title: "Mississippi God Damn"—"and I mean every word of it," she sang. In it, she aired many of the grievous situations blacks have had to endure, sneered at those who urged blacks to "go slow" in trying to right injustice, and voiced a demand for equality—"you don't have to live next to me." At about the same time, she also wrote and recorded "Four Women," a mordant satire of prejudices arising from skin color.

Otis Redding (1941–1967), who came from the area that produced Little Richard, James Brown, and Ray Charles, idolized Sam Cooke, but was a soulful stylist in the exuberantly energetic tradition of Brown and Little Richard. Nevertheless, he seldom gave a performance that did not include Cooke's "Shake," which he also recorded in 1967, with pronounced sexual overtones. One of the most important songs of his short career (1963–1967) was "Respect," which he wrote and recorded in (1965); it earned a Gold Record for Aretha Franklin in 1967. In Redding's version, the demand for respect from his spouse assumes inescapable sexual overtones.

A choir singer in his youth, Redding became nationally known as a result of his appearance at the Monterey Pop Festival in 1967. He was the last artist on a program that had been running for three days, and people were beginning to leave when he came onstage. But he was such a dynamic and charismatic performer that the audience not only remained but gave him a standing ovation. It was in the same year that Redding wrote and recorded his biggest hit, "(Sittin' On) The Dock of the Bay," which he never lived to enjoy. On tour in December 1967, his plane crashed into an icy lake near Madison, Wisconsin, just three days after he recorded "The Dock of the Bay"—cowritten with white guitarist Steve Cropper of the M.G.'s—carrying to their death with him four members of the Bar-Kays, his backup group. In the view of Jerry Wexler, an executive of Atlantic Records, distributors of Redding's Volt and Atco disks, Otis was "responsible for the fact that so much of the young white audience dug Soul the way the black does."[5]

Sex was always more than a subliminal aspect of Soul music. But the degree of eroticism varied, reaching high levels in Wilson Pickett (b. 1941) as well as Otis Redding. Born in Alabama and raised in Detroit, where he sang Gospel, Pickett joined the Falcons, an R & B group, for a four-year stint, after which (in 1963) he began recording alone for Lloyd Price's Double L label. The biggest disk of his career came in 1965, shortly after he moved to Atlantic. "In the Midnight Hour," his first of half a dozen million-copy sellers, was recorded in Memphis's Stax studio under Steve Cropper, who collaborated on the song, as he had on Redding's "Dock of the Bay." Its enticing sensuality led to Pickett's being known as "wicked" Wilson Pickett. In the succeeding six productive years, he scored million sellers with "Land of a Thousand Dances," "Mustang Sally," "Funky Broadway," "Don't Let the Green Grass Fool You," and "Don't Knock My Love." The last two titles, both Gold Records in the year 1971, were produced by Gamble and Huff, the founders of Philadelphia International, and were wild, soulful wailers.

The voice of Aretha Franklin, who became known as Lady Soul, had passion, not sex. In "I Never Loved a Man (The Way I Love You)," her first Soul hit, she expressed feelings of love with a breathless, mounting intensity never heard before on a record by a female. Accompanying herself on piano in a Gospel style, on which she had been coached as a youngster by the Reverend James Cleveland, she produced her first No. 1 hit. It was the beginning of a striking seven-year series of Top Ten chart songs and Grammy awards. Only Soul Brother No. 1 exceeded her achievement in terms of chart-makers and No. 1 best sellers—she scored 35 numbers on the charts, with 13 No. 1 and 2's—although he did not come close to collecting the number of Grammy awards given to Aretha. From 1967 to 1974 she was cited as the Best Female R & B Vocalist every year.

Before coming to Atlantic in 1967, Aretha had spent six years at Columbia, where she recorded many different types of songs in a fruitless attempt to find an expressive group for her. For her first Atlantic session, producer Jerry Wexler, instead of recording her in Harlem with local musicians, flew her down to a then little-known recording studio in Muscle Shoals, Alabama. "The liberal southern white is a hell of a lot closer to the Negro soul," he later explained, "than the Northern white liberal. And besides there was the Memphis Sound."[6] Out of that session also came the powerful declamatory version of Otis Redding's "Respect," which outsold "I Never Loved a Man," became a Gold Record, and brought Aretha her first two Grammys. It was a banner year, bringing million-copy sellers in

"Baby, I Love You," "A Natural Woman," and "Chain of Fools." All of these were delivered with an emotional thrust that tapped into Aretha's Gospel roots, something that Columbia had neglected to do.

The daughter of the Reverend C. L. Franklin, she began singing as a youngster in the choir of the New Bethel Baptist Church, her father's pastorate. During her girlhood, frequent visitors to the Franklin home included not only the Reverend James Cleveland, but Gospel singer Clara Ward, who mothered her when Aretha's own mother left the family, as well as the great Mahalia Jackson, whose protégé she became. At 14 Aretha joined her father's evangelistic tours, and spent the next four years singing in churches of the Midwest. In 1960 the door to an audition at Columbia was opened for her by bassist Major "Mule" Holly of pianist Teddy Wilson's band. Despite the nurturing of John Hammond, who signed her to Columbia, she spent the years until she moved to Atlantic, singing, as she said, "to the floor."

In succeeding years, Aretha demonstrated again and again her power to make hits of songs previously associated with other artists, so unique and forceful was her style. In 1968 she scored million sellers with "I Say a Little Prayer," originally a hit for Dionne Warwick (b. 1941) and "My Song," originally a hit for Johnny Ace (1932–1954). Two of Ben E. King's hits, "Don't Play That Song" in 1970 and "Spanish Harlem" in 1971, became best sellers for her. In 1971, too, Aretha took Paul Simon's giant hit of 1970, "Bridge Over Troubled Water," and made a Grammy Award winner of it. As late as 1981, she repeated the gambit, producing a best seller with Sam and Dave's "Hold On, I'm Coming." What one hears in many of her disks, perhaps the product of a troubled life—breakup of a stormy marriage, falling out with her father, bouts with alcohol—is a degree of anguish, the full baring of a heart in pain, rare in record literature.

If Aretha could not have happened without Big Mama Thornton, Janis Joplin (1943–1970) could not have happened without both, and young Jennifer Holiday was a natural in the succession of female anguish-singers with her Gospel-dramatic styled "(And I Am Telling You) I'm Not Going" in *Dreamgirls*.

The Memphis Sound

The history of Soul music involves two additional sounds—the Motown Sound, sometimes known as the Detroit Sound, and the Stax Sound, frequently designated the Memphis Sound. "If Motown is the northern ghetto expanding into the white world of sleek automobiles and plush clubs," this author wrote in *The World of Soul*, "Stax is the Mississippi River overflowing the banks of the 1960s. Inescapably, the Memphis Sound had more grit, gravel and mud in it than the Detroit Sound."[7] In fact, viewed in perspective, the Motown Sound represents a white transformation of Soul by blacks.

Launched in 1959 by Jim Stewart and his sister, Estelle Axton, who mortgaged her home to raise $2,500 for an Ampex recorder—Stax is a conjunction of the first two letters of their surnames—Stax developed its Soul sound as much through its studio band as through its vocalists. The M.G.'s (Memphis Group), as they called themselves, was an integrated combo, composed of two blacks—pianist/organist Booker T. Jones (b. 1944) and drummer Al Jackson, Jr. (1934–1975), and two whites—guitarist Steve Cropper (b. 1941) and bassist Donald "Duck" Dunn (b. 1941). Except for Missouri-born Cropper, who settled in Memphis before he was 10, the others were Memphis-born. Blues was their heritage as well as white Country and black church music—and the integration of styles as well as personnel seemed to account for the unique Memphis Sound.

Booker T described that sound as one that "started in the Negro church in the South. The music was really soul-searching. It was enough to make the listener cry at times. We've retained the basic elements of this church music in the Memphis Sound."[8]

Robert Palmer, now a *New York Times* critic but an aspiring R 'n' R saxophonist in 1965 who came to the Stax studio from Little Rock, Arkansas, describes the Memphis Sound as "a combination of white song form, black vocal treatment, simple arrangement, rhythmic restraint and pure understated elegance of expression."[9] One might add that the Sound had a relaxed, behind-the-beat rhythm in which C & W bass lines fused with gospel sounds in the piano, horns, and voices.

Settling in the defunct quarters of a former vaudeville–movie house on East McLemore Street, in the heart of Memphis's blacktown, Stax shortly erected on what was once the triangular marquee of the Capitol Theater, "Soulsville/USA," contrasting markedly with Motown's "Hitsville/USA" legend.

Three years after Stax and its allied company, Volt, produced its first release, Booker T. and the M.G.'s recorded "Green Onions," an instrumental that went to No. 1 on R & B charts, crossed into the Top Ten of Pop charts, and eventually became a Gold Record (1967). That year, the group superseded Herb Alpert and the Tijuana Brass as the Top Instrumental combo in *Billboard*'s year-end poll. "Green Onions" was the first of a best-selling series of soulful instrumentals that included "Hip Hug-Her" (1967), "Groovin'," "Soul Limbo," and "Time Is Tight." The last-mentioned was from the soundtrack of *Up Tight,* a black remake of *The Informer,* for which Booker T. wrote the score.

Before Stax, there was Satellite, named after Estelle Axton's record shop, which continued to operate in the shadow of the defunct theater's reconstituted marquee. Satellite acquired the momentum that led to the founding of Stax from a 1960 duet, " 'Cause I Love You," by Rufus Thomas (b. 1917), textile-mill janitor, vaudevillian, and Station WDIA disk jockey, with his daughter Carla (b. 1942). Thomas had previously, in 1953, produced a small hit in "Bear Cat," on the Sun label. In 1963 he scored with "Walking the Dog," replete with a dance routine he performed in personal appearances. Through the years, it led to a succession of chart-topping dance disks, including "Do the Funky Chicken" (1970), a two-sided "(Do the) Push and Pull" (No. 1 in 1970), "The Breakdown" (1971), and "Do the Funky Penguin" (1971).

Thomas's daughter Carla, who went on to acquire a master's degree in English literature from Howard University, launched her solo record career in 1961 with a song she wrote, "(Gee Whiz) Look at His Eyes." On Atlantic Records, she continued, singing in a robust Dinah Washington-derived style, until 1965, when a switch to Stax yielded "B-A-B-Y," a hit in 1966. That year she acquired the title, Queen of Memphis Soul, largely as the result of an album, *The King and the Queen,* with Otis Redding.

The year 1966 was a stellar one for Stax, with three new artists scaling the charts: William Bell, Johnny Taylor (b. 1940), and Sam and Dave, whose "Hold On! I'm Coming" was followed by "Soul Man," a Grammy winner in 1967. An accomplished songwriter, William Bell recorded *A Tribute to a King* following the untimely death of fellow Stax artist Otis Redding. Johnny Taylor, who succeeded Sam Cooke as lead singer of the Soul Stirrers, racked up a million-copy seller in "Who's Making Love" in 1968 and a Gold Record in "I Believe in You" in 1973.

The two most important artists in the Stax/Volt Soul stable were Otis Redding and Isaac Hayes (b. 1943). The intensity of Redding's singing found support in his substitution of a stomp beat for the afterbeat of R & B: accents on every beat of a four-note measure added wallop to his delivery, especially when a trumpet-led brass choir lifted the dynamic level.

Isaac Hayes, a multi-instrumentalist, began at Stax as a songwriter, collaborating with David Porter on hits for Johnny Taylor, Sam and Dave, and Carla Thomas. His debut album, *Presenting Isaac Hayes,* in 1967 (later retitled *Blue Hayes*), offered little to foreshadow the innovative character of *Hot Buttered Soul,* the album that brought him national renown in 1969. Spoken introductions, an 18-minute version of "By the Time I Get to Phoenix," and an almost symphonic use of a large, string-dominated orchestra, all bespoke a creativity that peaked in 1971 with two albums.

One was the soundtrack for the film *Shaft,* the first movie presenting blacks in heroic roles. Hayes's score, fusing driving R & B with soulful string arrangements, became the fastest-selling album in Stax's history. Released as a double album in August 1971, it went to No. 1 in both the Jazz and R & B charts, remained a best seller for more than a year, and brought Hayes a composer's Grammy for Best Original Score written for a Motion Picture. The "Theme from *Shaft,*" written and produced by Hayes and arranged by him and Johnny Allen, sold over a million as a single and won an Academy award.

In 1971 Hayes also produced a double album, titled *Black Moses,* on whose cover he appeared as a robed Messiah. On tour with a massive 40-piece orchestra, he fortified the cover image, appearing stripped to the waist and draped with heavy gold chains. He was a striking figure, with his clean-shaven head, heavy black beard, and dark shades. By then the Black Moses had established the Isaac Hayes Foundation to help poor and needy old people, regardless of race, and was reportedly pouring more than estimated savings of $1.5 million a year into community projects. It came as a shock when he declared bankruptcy in 1976, a dismal development that seemed also to mark his loss of creativity.

Although the Staple Singers became known as "the first family of Gospel," Mississippi-born Pop Staples (b. 1914), who founded the group, was inspired to study the guitar by Delta bluesmen Robert Johnson and Blind Blake (c. 1890–1895—c. 1933), and he took up the harmonica after hearing Howlin' Wolf. Singing in Chicago churches with his daughters, Cleo and Mavis, and son Pervis, and then on the radio, they began recording for United Records in about 1954. On Vee Jay, they produced their first modest hit, in 1956, with "Uncloudy Day," singing Gospel to a Rock 'n' Roll beat. It was on Stax, after a stint with Epic Records, that they became internationally known in the 1970s for a style described as "Soul Folk"—it was the title of their first album on Stax—and characterized as soft-textured and introspective, rather than exhibitionist.

The change from pure Gospel to sweet Soul was frankly dictated by a desire to reach a larger audience, which they succeeded in doing. With Mavis (b. 1940), whose contralto ranges from near-baritone to high soprano, succeeding Pop in the lead, and Yvonne (b. 1939) replacing Pervis, the Staple Singers achieved a million seller in "Heavy Makes You Happy (Sha Na Boom Boom)," followed in the same year by "Respect Yourself." Nineteen seventy-two yielded "I'll Take You There," with a Caribbean sound, and in 1973 they had "If You're Ready (Come Go with Me)," a Gold Record. By 1975 the group had moved to Curtis Mayfield's label, Curtom, where they added another Gold Record to their collection with "Let's Do It Again," written by Mayfield.

That Stax was well aware of the roots of its sound became clear when it signed Albert King (b. 1923) of Mississippi, the six-foot four-inch half-brother of B. B. King. What makes King so interesting is that he began as a Delta bootleneck bluesman and remained one, although he enjoyed many other types of music. By his own admission, he listened early to the Mills Bros. and the Golden Gate Quartet. He was not only crazy about the bands of Woody Herman (b. 1913) and the Dorsey Bros. but recalled numbers that he loved —Herman's "Uptown Blues" and the Dorsey Bros.' "Jumpin' at the Woodside." He also admired Bob Wills (1905–1975) and his Texas Playboys. Familiar with Fats Domino and Ray Charles, he taught himself guitar by listening to records of T-Bone Walker and Blind Lemon Jefferson, and learned the bottleneck technique of fretting from country bluesman Bukka White.

Albert King recorded for a number of labels before he came to Stax, starting with Parrot in 1953 and including Bobbin (1959–1962), King (1962), and Coun-tree (1965). "The old blues made sense in their day," he has said, "but the problems today are different."[10] And so he brought the traditions of old Blues into a 1960s setting, accompanying himself on electric guitar and updating the imagery of his songs—"Laundromat Blues" (1966) and "(I Love) Lucy" (1968). Although his style was contemporary and some even characterized it as modern, he lacked the appeal of B. B. King, and his records have remained in-group favorites without becoming best sellers.

Structured as an interracial company, in which Jim Stewart was white and his major assistant, Al Bell, of Little Rock, Arkansas, was black, Stax developed an interracial sound through its integrated studio band. It prided itself on functioning as a family (which Motown did too), whose motto was, during a period of vaulting racial tensions, "Look What We've Done Together." But by the time that Johnny Taylor and Isaac Hayes, propelled by the untimely death of Otis Redding, became the biggies of Stax and set the tone for the 1970s, black nationalism was moving the label in an all-black direction. Although later bands, such as the Bar-Kays and the Isaac Hayes Movement, based themselves on the sound of the M.G.'s, what came out was harder, tougher, and more abrasive.

The Stax Sound, early and late, is still audible on the record scene, remembered in reissues by San Francisco's Fantasy Records, which acquired the masters some time after the flourishing company went bankrupt. Unfortunately, like Vee Jay before it, the family and the multimillion-dollar organization came to a dismal end. Stewart filed for bankruptcy in 1975. Al Bell was indicted for fraud shortly before the company's publishing subsidiary was auctioned off to a local bank. In 1976, Isaac Hayes, who had ridden around Memphis in a gold-plated Cadillac and a Jaguar, filed a $6 million bankruptcy plea. In the preceding year, Al Jackson, Jr., the M.G.'s fine drummer, was shot to death during a burglary at his home.

When the company's prime movers gathered in the spring of 1984 for a Stax Family Reunion dinner at the Peabody Hotel and for a concert the next evening at the Mid-South Coliseum, elder statesman Rufus Thomas called Stax "a label to love." But a number of the lovers were absent, including Jim Stewart, Al Bell, Isaac Hayes (who had moved to Atlanta), and Booker T. Jones.

A word should be added about the sound of Memphis, which has a history antedating Stax Records. Although W. C. Handy's Blues are not generally associated with it, there is no reason why they should not be. After all, "Memphis Blues" (1912), "Beale Street Blues" (1917), and the world-famous "St. Louis Blues" (1914) were all written in the city whose name and celebrated street provided the titles for two of his popular blues. In W. C. Handy's metier, the sound of Memphis was that of the Blues, flavored with Jazz and Pop tonalities.

With the advent of Sam Phillips and Sun Records in the early 1950s, the city's sound underwent a significant change. It embodied elements of R & B, as in Jackie Brenston's "Rocket 88" and Howlin' Wolf, whose masters Phillips sold to such R & B labels as Chess; it also encompassed Rockabilly. While Elvis Presley became the most important exponent of the fusion of R & B and C & W with his recordings between 1953 and 1955, Sam's studio also, as we have seen, accounted for Jerry Lee Lewis, Johnny Cash (b. 1932), Carl Perkins, Roy Orbison, and Conway Twitty, all eminent proponents of Rockabilly.

Even during the period when Stax was developing its definition of Soul, there were a number of other Memphis labels contributing to its sound. Hi Records used the advertising slogan, "The Label that created the Memphis Sound," based largely on the combos of Rock-a-Boogie bassist Bill Black (1926–1965) and trumpeter Willie Mitchell (b. 1928) whose albums include *Soul Serenade* and *Solid Soul*. Jerry Wexler, then an Atlantic Records producer, who brought Aretha Franklin south for her first sensational session, included that studio in the sound of Memphis; as well as the Quin Ivy Recording

Studio at Sheffield, Alabama. Not to be overlooked, there was the American Recording Studio of Chips Moman, who played guitar and served as coproducer of Aretha's Muscle Shoals session. A producer at Stax in its formative days, Moman developed a reputation that drew artists to American Recording from different parts of the country, diffusing the identity of its sound. In 1969, shortly after Elvis cut a flock of sides with Moman, Dionne Warwick flew in from New York to record under Moman, who became coproducer of her album *Soulful.*

Recognizing that these producers and studios contributed to the sound of Memphis, one would have to acknowledge Stax's priority in its creation in the 1960s and early 1970s.

The White Synthesis

The white transformation or commercialization of Soul took several different forms, some purely a matter of fabricating a sound, as in the case of the Righteous Brothers or theBlues Brothers; others, a genuine expression of anguish, as with Janis Joplin. The white synthesis will be examined under three headings: the Motown Sound, whose crossover sound became blacker in time; Blue-Eyed Soul; and Heavy Metal, which is parallel to rather than derived from Soul.

The Motown Sound

When Berry Gordy, Jr. (b. 1929), decided to launch his own record label after he had successfully produced masters and placed them with other labels, he chose Tammy as its name. Unfortunately, the name was being used by another corporation, so that Gordy settled for Tamla as an alternative title. His initial choice is both significant and revealing. "Tammy" was the title of a hit song from the film, "*Tammy and the Bachelor*, popularized on records by Debbie Reynolds (b. 1932). The selection of a Pop song title for his record label suggests that Gordy had his eyes on the mainstream market. When he used strings on his records, he chose players from the Detroit Symphony Orchestra. As soon as any of his artists became established on disk, they were guided into cutting albums such as *The Supremes Sing Rodgers & Hart, The Four Tops on Broadway,* etc., and were booked into major white showrooms in Las Vegas, New York, Philadelphia, and Los Angeles. To insure that his artists moved comfortably in white, middle-class society, Gordy established a finishing school, whose function it was to tutor in such matters as table manners, etiquette generally, appropriate dress, and the niceties of small talk. As for the choice of material for recording, the emphasis was on romantic subjects, with an avoidance generally of controversial or topical themes—this at a time when the struggle for civil rights was mounting in intensity and making it difficult for concerned whites or blacks to avoid speaking out. In short, the Gordy design was to take black elements and use them to build a black audience base, but also to flavor them so that records would cross over into the white market. Whether the Motown Sound is characterized as Pop Soul or Pop Gospel, Gordy was so successful in achieving his goal that when Motown celebrated its twenty-fifth anniversary in 1983, it had become a far-flung conglomerate of record labels (Tamla, Gordy, Raw Earth, V.I.P., Soul, and others), music publishing companies, booking and managerial corporations, film and television production firms, with a combined income in 1982 of $104 million, prompting *Newsweek* to call it "the largest black-owned company in America."[11]

The white synthesis of Soul by black producers and artists—that synthesis is not a matter of skin color but style color—began in 1959 when Gordy settled in a rundown white clapboard house at 2648 West Grand Boulevard in Detroit. By then, he had been a prize fighter, owner of a record store, nightclub photographer, and Ford Motor Company worker. More to the point, he had co-written several of Jackie Wilson's early hits and produced masters with singer Marv Johnson (b. 1938), which he had leased to United Artists Record Co. and to Anna, a label owned by his sister. Johnson's first release, "Come to Me," was described as a "clean R & B record that sounded as white as it did black."[12] When he opened shop on West Grand Boulevard, it was said that Gordy slept in the upstairs of the clapboard house that soon carried the sign, "Hitsville, USA."

It was not until 1961 that Gordy produced best sellers on Tamla. "Shop Around," co-written by Gordy and lead singer Smokey Robinson (b. 1940), was a hit for the Miracles and later in a white cover by the Captain and Tenille. It went to No. 2. "Please Mr. Postman," by the Marvelettes, another Detroit group, made No. 1. While the Marvelettes, a female group, continued recording into the late 1960s, they never duplicated their success with "Please Mr. Postman." But the Miracles (four men and a woman at the beginning), led by high-pitched, falsetto-voiced Smokey Robinson, produced No. 1 chartmakers in "You've Really Got a Hold on Me" (1963), "I Second that Emotion" (1967), "The Tears of a Clown" (1970), and "Love Machine" (1976).

With Mary Wells (b. 1943), Gordy's first successful solo artist, Motown—a contraction of Motor Town—came into being as a label and umbrella for a steadily growing list of labels. Having worked for a time on the Ford assembly line, it is said that Gordy sought to pattern his operational setup on the efficient mechanization of the auto company; the word "factory" kept cropping up not only in casual conversations of Motown family members but in descriptions of its operation and expansion.

Mary Wells achieved her first chart-makers in 1962, in rapid succession, with "The One Who Really Loves You," "You Beat Me to the Punch," and "Two Lovers," followed by "My Guy" in 1964. Wells was the first of a fairly long line of female singers — Brenda Holloway, Kim Weston, Yvonne Fair, Barbara McNair, among others — with limited life in the Motown complex. An early departure from the Gordy menage, Wells never did as well on a series of labels for which she recorded.

Marvin Gaye (1939 – 1984), who was shot to death by his father during a family quarrel, sang as a boy in his father's Pentecostal church in Washington, D.C., and in his teens with several R & B groups, including the Rainbows, Marquees, and the Moonglows. An accomplished musician who played several instruments (organ, guitar, and drums, his favorite) and who developed into a composer, writing a film score in the 1980s, Gaye was one of the few Motown artists whose choice of material stemmed from situations in his life and changes in his outlook. Although he became associated with Gordy early, playing drums with the Miracles and singing backup on Marvelette records, his first solo chart-maker was "Stubborn Kind of Fellow" (with the Vandellas), in 1962. Major records after that included "How Sweet It Is To Be Loved By You" (1964), later a best seller for James Taylor; "I Heard It Through the Grapevine" (1968), originally a hit for Gladys Knight & the Pips; and "Let's Get It On" (1973), one of the biggest-selling singles, and one of the most erotic, in Motown's history, a No. 1 on both Pop and R & B charts.

Gaye's masculinity led to a series of duets with Motown females — with Mary Wells in 1964, Kim Weston in 1967, and, eventually, with Diana Ross, after she left the Supremes, in 1973 – 1974. His most successful partnership was with Tammi Terrell in 1967 – 1969, the duo producing Top Ten disks in "Your Precious Love," "If I Could Build My Whole World Around You," "Ain't Nothin' Like the Real Thing," and "You're All I Need to Get By." Her sudden death in March 1970, at the age of 23, was a devastating shock that took Gaye from the recording scene for a time and deepened his outlook on life and the world.

It led to an album concerned with social issues, a rarity in the Motown catalogue, titled *What's Goin On,* whose songs he wrote or co-wrote. The title number, sounding the keynote for a conceptual album, sold a million copies as a single, as did "Mercy, Mercy, Me

(The Ecology)," a caustic commentary on how people were destroying the environment, and "Inner City Blues (Makes Me Wanna Holler)," an angry look at the world from the black ghetto. So impressive were the songs that Gil-Scott Heron (b. 1949) recorded "Inner City Blues"; Diana Ross cut "Save the Children"; Aretha Franklin cut "Wholly Holy"; and Quincy Jones (b. 1934) and Roland Kirk (1936–1977) recorded the title tune, "What's Going On."

An album he produced in the late 1970s, *Here My Dear,* occasioned by a lack of finances to pay for a divorce, offered a frank, detailed scenario of the life and death of his marriage. It did not remove the pain of having discovered that his wife had had an affair with Teddy Pendergrass, whom he regarded as a close friend. Nor did it solve his difficulties with the IRS, a situation that caused him to flee to Hawaii, where he reportedly lived in a converted bread-delivery truck. A tour in England in the early 1980s drew comments about his being both unpredictable and unmanageable—he turned up too late to sing for a Command Performance before H.R.H. Princess Margaret, among other escapades.

But it was in this period that he began working on a new album, recorded in Belgium and Munich and released in 1982 on Columbia Records. *Midnight Love* included the slyly erotic song, "Sexual Healing," which won him a Grammy, his first after eight nominations. On the back of the cover, he wrote: "I still love Jesus, all praises to the Heavenly Father." He was living in Los Angeles with his parents when an argument led to the tragic fatal shooting in January of 1984. Posthumously, Gaye became "something of a soul saint," in the words of Jim Miller (*Newsweek,* July 1, 1985, p. 60). The Commodores produced a hit with his song "Nightshift," while Diana Ross gave one of the most emotional performances of her career on her recording of his "Missing You." The climax came with Gaye's own *Dream of a Lifetime,* a posthumous album of new material. The provocative songs provided a poignant insight into the decline that led to the fatal encounter with his father, a decline generated by drugs as well as a desperate, destructive struggle to resolve sacred yearnings with profane, erotic obsessions. Some of the song titles were themselves revealing: "Savage in the Sack," "It's Madness," "Masochistic Beauty," and "Sanctified Lady," which depicted the excitement of making love to a religiously-consecrated woman. None of these compared, except as self-relevation, with "I Heard It Through the Grapevine" (his great single of 1969) and his masterful album, *What's Going On* (1971).

The Contours, a Detroit sextet, were, together with the Supremes, Miracles, and Marvelettes, among the first groups in the Motown stable. Their 1962 hit, "Do You Love Me," written by Berry

Gordy, not only went to No. 1 on R & B charts but climbed to No. 3 in Pop. Although they continued to make records into 1967, the promise of the initial hit was never realized. Also on the Gordy label, Martha and the Vandellas began as a backup trio for Marvin Gaye and other artists. (Martha Reeves [b. 1941] was a secretary at Motown, part of whose job was to put lyrics on tape for artists to learn.) Between 1963 with "Heat Wave" and 1967, the group scored Top Ten records with "Quicksand," "Dancing in the Street" (their biggest), "Nowhere to Run," "I'm Ready for Love," and "Jimmy Mack" —and that was it.

"Heat Wave," like Marvin Gaye's "Can I Get a Witness" and the Miracles' "Mickey's Monkey," was the work of a trio of songwriters/producers, Eddie Holland (b. 1939), Lamont Dozier (b. 1941), and Brian Holland (b. 1941), soon widely known as H-D-H. Eddie Holland started as vocalist who made demos on songs that Berry Gordy had submitted for Jackie Wilson's consideration. In 1962, before he became part of the songwriting/producing trio, he achieved a moderate hit in "Jamie" on R & B charts. While a number of factors went into the making of the Motown or Detroit Sount—among them, the superlative studio band; 9 other producer/songwriters, including Norman Whitfield (b. 1943) and Barrett Strong (b. 1941), Nick Ashford and Valerie Simpson, and Mickey Stevenson, head of A & R from 1959 to 1967; and Berry Gordy's creative savvy—H-D-H were its major architects, and the Temptations and Supremes, its major exponents. Once H-D-H left Motown and other producers took over, the Sound took on a blacker hue.

During the period 1964–1965, the "Sound" reached its full flowering. As one hears it in "My Girl" of the Temptations and in "Where Did Our Love Go" and a flock of hits by the Supremes, the Motown Sound embodied a number of Gospel elements: rattling tambourines, handclapping, and call-and-response. The vocals were not the product of harmony: Diana Ross, Levi Stubbs, and David Ruffin sang lead, with responses, echoes, and interjections by other members of the Supremes, Four Tops, and Temptations, respectively. R & B's afterbeat was retained but was sounded on the tambourine and/or snare drum, supported by a booming bass line laid down by James Jamerson (d. 1983). To make the Sound attractive to Pop or Rock record-buyers, strings were added, with members of the Detroit Symphony playing the type of sustained harmonies audible on records of the Pop balladeers. This transformation of the Gospel/R & B base of the music made the Motown Sound so accessible that from October 23, 1963 to January 30, 1965, *Billboard* eliminated its R & B charts because the Pop and R & B charts, as a result of Motown hits, were duplicates of each other.

Holland-Dozier-Holland are also to be credited with a critical transformation of the traditional song form, avoiding the 12-bar blues, 16-bar Gospels and 32-bar Pop ballads. For these, they substituted a repetition of two or three 8-bar strains in which the cadences (the resolutions) of these other forms were elided. The music went round and round, with the "hook" (most memorable phrase) being repeated over and over. It was said that this cyclical handling of small phrases was particularly effective for listening on transistor radios, then part of an expanding market.

It was with H-D-H that the Supremes—Diana Ross (b. 1944), Mary Wilson (b. 1944), and Florence Ballard (b. 1943), from a black ghetto housing project—attained their majority and became the most important female group of the 1960s. They had been recording for almost two years when "Where Did Our Love Go," in 1964, initiated a record-breaking series of 11 No. 1 disks on Pop charts that carried them into 1969. The best sellers of 1964 included "Baby Love" and "Come See About Me." They were written and produced by H-D-H, as were the three giant hits of 1965: "Stop in the Name of Love," "Back in My Arms Again," and "I Hear a Symphony." The last-mentioned became the title of an album that contained songs from three Broadway shows: "With a Song in My Heart," from Rodgers and Hart's *Spring Is Here,* "Without a Song," from Vincent Youmans's *Great Day!* and "Strangers in Paradise," from *Kismet,* all done in an orchestral ballad style indistinguishable from a Pop treatment. The Pop/Gospel treatment was reserved for such H-D-H songs as "You Can't Hurry Love" and "You Keep Me Hangin' On," both No. 1 in 1966, and "Love Is Here and Now You're Gone" and "The Happening," both No. 1 in 1967. (Hollywood composer Frank DeVol wrote the music for the last-mentioned, which was also recorded by Herb Alpert and the Tijuana Brass.)

In 1967 Cindy Birdsong, of Patti LaBelle & the Bluebelles, succeeded Florence Ballard, whose short-lived solo career ended in 1976 in an untimely death at the age of 32; and the Supremes became known as Diana Ross and the Supremes. The change was well deserved, since it was the purring voice of Diana, with its engaging little erotic shriek, that gave the group its tremendous appeal. When they scored a No. 1 with "Someday We'll Be Together" in 1969, only the Beatles and Elvis Presley exceeded their tally of No. 1's and no female group could approach it.

By 1968 the Supremes had lost the services of the trio that shaped their style and accounted for their amazing track record. During a discussion of the renewal of their contract, H-D-H, according to reports, were summarily fired by Berry Gordy. No explanation was ever made, although there were reports that a demand by the trio for a financial accounting precipitated a heated discussion, which may have led to the breakup. By then the Motown Sound had passed its prime. When the Supremes appeared on the Ed Sullivan Show together with the Temptations and joined forces later that year (1968) for a TV special on NBC, both groups sang a varied program appropriate for a Las Vegas showroom, including the pseudo-operatic "Impossible Dream," from the Broadway show, *Man of La Mancha*. The goal patently was to reach the Pop "easy listening" crowd as well as the Rock generation.

Both Diana Ross and Motown underwent major changes in 1970. Diana left the Supremes and Berry Gordy moved his operation from Detroit to Hollywood, settling in a skyscraper at Hollywood and Vine. (The story of the Supremes later was the theme of the 1982 Broadway musical *Dreamgirls*.) With Jean Terrell replacing Diana in her old group, Ross embarked on a solo career, achieving her first No. 1 hit in "Ain't No Mountain High Enough," originally an Ashford-Simpson duet for Marvin Gaye and Tami Terrell in 1967. Two years later, Diana proved herself an accomplished actress in the starring film role of Jazz singer Billie Holiday. In *Lady Sings the Blues*, financed by Motown and based on Holiday's 1956 autobiography, Diana sang with sensitivity and power 17 songs associated with the career of Lady Day, producing a double soundtrack album that soared to No. 1. For her acting in the title role, Diana received an Academy Award nomination. Starring roles in two films followed: *Mahogany*, a Berry Gordy production in 1975; and *The Wiz*, a 1978 movie version of the Broadway/black version of the memorable Judy Garland film, *The Wizard of Oz*. Neither attracted the accolades of Diana's debut film, but the theme song of *Mahogany*, "Do You Know Where You're Going To?" became a million-copy disk for Diana, by then a superstar of the Las Vegas strip.

When the Supremes were still a Doo-Wop Detroit group, the Primettes, a nucleus of the Temptations was known as the Primes. Next to the Supremes, Motown's powerhouse group was the Temptations, a male quintet that approached the acceptance of the Supremes with 10 No. 1's in R & B between 1965 and 1971. Led by David Ruffin, formerly with the Dixie Nightingales Gospel group, whose robust tenor found a foil in Eddie Kendricks's high tenor, the Temptations scored their first No. 1 Pop hit with "My Girl," an outstanding sampler of the Motown Pop/Gospel sound.

As producers, Holland-Dozier-Holland and Smokey Robinson were largely responsible for the development of the Motown or Detroit Sound, with Smokey serving as the Temptations' producer from 1964 into 1967. After Norman Whitfield became the group's major producer around 1967, the Temptations veered away from romantic pop ballads to songs that dealt more and more with social issues and to a style that frequently was psychedelic.

Producers Barrett Strong and Norman Whitfield accounted in 1968 for "I Wish It Would Rain" and "Cloud Nine," a Grammy winner with a psychedelic theme; in 1969 for "I Can't Get Next to You," No. 1 on Pop charts, as was "Just My Imagination" in 1971; and in 1972 for the triple Grammy winner, "Papa Was a Rolling Stone." Despite Berry Gordy's tendency to steer clear of social issues, the Temptations touched on the color problem in "Beauty Is Only Skin Deep," a Top Tenner in 1966, and the tense racial situation of the time in "Ball of Confusion (That's What the World Is Today)," again a Top Tenner in 1970. Although David Ruffin left the group in 1968, Eddie Kendricks in 1971, and Paul Williams in 1973—he died at the age of 34—the group continued to produce best sellers through the 1970s.

Formed in 1954 as an R & B group with a Mills Bros. sound, the Four Tops, originally known as the Four Aims, have preserved the same lineup for 30 years. Led by Detroit-born Levi Stubbs, they recorded, not very successfully, for a number of labels, including Chess, Singular, Riverside, and Columbia, before they made it on Motown. Their most productive period was between 1965 and 1967, when their songs were written and produced by H-D-H. While "Baby I Need Your Loving" was a best seller in 1964, it was "I Can't Help Myself" (1965) that went to the top of Pop charts, as did "Reach Out, I'll Be There" (1966), later a Diana Ross favorite. Although they racked up best sellers in "Standing in the Shadows of Love" (1966) and "Bernadette" (1967), the departure of H-D-H from Motown foreshadowed their own several years later. Norman Whitfield, who succeeded Holland-Dozier-Holland, was interested in a funkier and tougher style than suited the Tops, whose disks included such Pop songs as "It's All in the Game" and Rock numbers such as "MacArthur Park." It was not until they departed Motown for ABC/Dunhill Records that they returned to the Top Ten with "Keeper of the Castle" (1972) and "Ain't No Woman (Like the One I've Got)" (1973). A versatile group, they traveled as part of the road shows of Billy Eckstine (b. 1914).

The career of Gladys Knight & the Pips, a family group out of Atlanta—brother Merald and cousins William Guest and Edward Patten—was launched by a homemade recording of Johnny Otis's ballad, "Every Beat of My Heart." Released locally, the disk attracted so much attention that two independent R & B labels—Vee Jay of Chicago and Fury of New York—became involved in a lawsuit over its ownership; it reportedly went on to sell a million for Vee Jay in competition with a remake on Fury, which won the group. Before making this disk, Gladys Knight (b. 1944) sang with two Gospel groups, Morris Brown Choir and Wings over Jordan Choir. At the age of eight, she won $2,000 for her rendition of "Too Young" on the Ted Mack Amateur Hour TV show. After the Fury association, the group recorded briefly for an offbeat label, Maxx, which gave them a small chart-maker in "Giving Up." Signed by Berry Gordy to his Soul label in 1967, the group quickly garnered a million-copy seller with Normal Whitfield and Barrett Strong's classic song, "I Heard It Through the Grapevine." The same songwriter/producing team gave them a follow-up hit in "The End of the Road" (1968). In 1970 they had a Top Ten disk in "If I Were Your Woman," but "Neither One of Us (Wants to Be the First to Say Goodbye)" went to No. 2 in 1973.

But that year, switching from Soul to Buddah Records, they had a No. 1 hit in "Midnight Train to Georgia," which also brought them their first Grammy. Now, in rapid succession, they had "I've Got to Use My Imagination," "Best Thing That Ever Happened to Me," and "On and On," all hits in 1973–1974. With *Imagination,* a Gold album, they won their second Grammy. "On and On," a song written and produced by Curtis Mayfield (b. 1942), was on the soundtrack of the film *Claudine.* Gladys Knight has a powerful set of pipes, and she delivers with the fire of a Gospel-trained singer, vocalizing generally against sustained harmonies by the male trio behind her.

The Jackson 5, second-generation artists in the Motown family, were also a family group. Attending a campaign benefit for the mayor of their hometown (Gary, Indiana), they gave a performance that so impressed Diana Ross that she brought them to the attention of Berry Gordy, who immediately put them under contract; their first album was titled, *Diana Ross Presents The Jackson 5.* Composed of five brothers, ranging in age from 10 to 18—Michael, 10; Marlon, 12; Jermaine, 14; Toriano, 15; and Sigmund, 18—the group caught on instantly, and between 1969 and 1971, produced a succession of four No. 1 disks and two No. 2 records. Incidentally, the first album included "Zip-a-Dee Doo Dah," a pop standard from the 1946 film *Song of the South,* suggesting that the traditional Berry Gordy interest in crossover still prevailed.

Like their first hit, "I Want You Back," their second million-copy single, "ABC," was written and produced by a group that signed itself simply "the Corporation"; it was a collaboration involving Freddie Perren, Fonso Mizell, Deke Richards, and Berry Gordy, Jr. *ABC* became the title song of the group's second million-selling album. In 1970 their *Third Album* became a million-seller, hanging on the charts, like the previous album, for just under a full year. Out of this album came "I'll Be There," reportedly enjoying a sale of 3.5

million, with a global estimated sale of 5 million — figures that made the teenage quintet one of the most formidable in Motown's history. In 1971 the group continued its overpowering assault on the record market, accounting for million sellers in "Mama's Pearl," again by the Corporation, and in "Never Can Say Goodbye." The latter, by Clifton Davis, is said to have sold 1,213,000 copies in the first five days of release, a pace of sales unparalleled since the heyday of the Beatles. Absent from the million-copy charts for several years, the Jackson 5 returned in 1974 with "Dancing Machine," a cut from their *Get It Together* album.

By 1971 young Michael Jackson (b. 1959) had his first solo disk on the market, scoring a best seller with "Got To Be There," and launching one of the most phenomenal careers in the history of music business. More about Michael in the final section of this book.

Unique as the Jackson 5 were, Stevie Wonder (b. 1950) was an even more remarkable artist; perhaps, the most original of all on the Motown roster. Blinded by an incubator accident—he was born prematurely—Steveland Judkins Morris, of Saginaw, Michigan, began "devouring" instruments before he was in school. By the time he was 13, he had his first Gold Record in "Fingertips, Part 2," playing a vibrant Blues on harmonica. The unique character of *Little Stevie Wonder; 12-Year-Old Genius,* as his first album was titled—it, too, went to No. 1 —was not just a matter of his mastery of an untold number of instruments, but in a virtuoso ability to absorb and transmute many different styles—Blues, R & B, Gospel, Reggae, Jazz, adult Pop. This prodigious scope is unquestionably at the bottom of a rare openness and readiness to cope with new material, sounds, and themes.

For the first eight years of his Tamla association, Stevie was part of the Motown "family." The songs he recorded were mostly by staff writers. The arrangements were by staff arrangers, who masterminded his sessions so that he frequently came into sing and play after the rhythm and structure were set. As with other Motown artists, they published whatever he wrote and booked his tours—and, since he was underage, held his money in trust. This was the period of such hits as "Uptight (Everything's Alright)" (1965); "I Was Made to Lover Her" (1967); "For Once in My Life" (a cover of a Tony Bennett hit in 1968); "My Cherie Amour," and "Yester-me, Yester-you Yesterday" (both in 1969). But even in this period, Stevie, who later showed a strong concern with social themes and universal love, tried to follow his own bent and remain outside the Motown assembly line, recording, among other numbers, the unofficial anthem of the civil rights movement, Bob Dylan's "Blowing in the Wind."

The recognition of Stevie's individuality began in 1971, when he reached maturity and gained access to his million-dollar trust fund. One of his first moves was to build a $250,000 recording studio in his own home, out-fitting it with all the latest synthesizers and electronic gadgetry. He began branching out in his recordings, using many different types of synthesizers and electronic instruments, all of which he quickly mastered and played himself. He had already produced in its entirety the album, *Signed, Sealed and Delivered,* which had been named the Best Soul album of 1970, a category whose quasi-racial overtone did not please him. Now his new interest in computerized and radical keyboard instruments found expression in an album, *Music on My Mind,* in which he used the Moog, and ARP synthesizers, etc. But it was in *Talking Book* (1973), an album that stayed on the charts for over two years, that his liberated spirit and approach first attained fruition. His first platinum album, *Talking Book* yielded two million-copy, No. 1 singles in "Superstition" and "You Are the Sunshine of My Life," the latter a Pop-styled original that remains his best-known song and that won a Grammy, one of five out of six for which he had been nominated.

In August 1973 Stevie was almost killed in a North Carolina auto accident when a log rolled off a truck, smashed through the front window of the car in which he was riding, and struck him in the forehead. He had begun work on a new album, which when it was released, bore the enigmatic title, *Fulfillingness' First Finale,* taken by some to refer to the possible "first" ending of his life, and by others, to the finale of the first stage of his career. The brooding album sold over a million copies, as did two singles, "You Haven't Done Nothin'" and "Boogie on Reggae Woman." Once again, as in the preceding year, Stevie walked off with five Grammy awards at the NARAS ceremony in March 1975. "Boogie on Reggae Woman," on which Stevie played his first instrument (harmonica) as well as synthesizers, was an adaptation of the Jamaica-styled sound with which a few American and British artists (Johnny Nash, Paul Simon, Eric Clapton) were beginning to experiment.

October 1976 brought *Songs in the Key of Life,* which raised Stevie's total of Grammy awards to 14, as he added to his previous collection, Best Album, Best Producer, Best Male Pop Performer, and Best R & B Performer. So many songs were involved in the album that the two-album format had to be extended to include a separate 7-inch, 33-rpm disk. The range of material was impressive, embracing a tribute to Duke Ellington in "Sir Duke" as well as disquisitions that some critics dismissed as heavy-handed preaching.

The most demanding and audacious undertaking of his career

was the writing and production of a double album, released in 1979 as *(Journey Through) The Life of Plants.* What made the project so incredible was that Stevie had accepted the assignment to write the music for a film, a difficult task even for a sighted composer because of the technical problem of synchronizing sight and sound to the split second. (Film composers use what is known as a "click track" which ticks off the seconds in order to achieve such synchronization.) How Stevie solved the problem was never explained, although there is a curious credit on the album cover "for your help in coordinating sound effects" to the Air Traffic Controllers, Dallas–Fort Worth, Texas, Airport. Apart from this problem, *The Secret Life of Plants,* a semi-documentary, required a wide variety of music and lyrics, including love ballads, insect effects, Japanese song, African music, and background instrumental music. Stevie not only wrote all the material but played all the instruments used on the soundtrack. It was a virtuoso performance that won critical acclaim if not commercial acceptance.

In *Hotter Than July,* released late in October 1980, Stevie once again made extensive use of the new musical resources, playing the Fender Rhodes, flute synthesizer, Vocoder, bass synthesizer, clavinet, ARP, bass Melodon, Fairlight Synthesizer, not to mention cabasa, celeste, harpsichord, harmonica, and drums. Besides writing the songs, he also accounted for the arrangements and production. His intimacy with contemporary musical and political developments was evident in at least three songs: the Top Ten single, "Master Blaster (Jammin')," a tribute to Reggae master, Bob Marley, which contained references to peace in Zimbabwe; "Happy Birthday," homage to slain civil rights leader Martin Luther King, Jr.; and "I Ain't Gonna Stand for It," whose very title suggests the indignation that Stevie feels about life for black people. Despite his total immersion in music, Stevie manages to be actively involved in the problems of Third World people and in the campaign to have King's birthday declared a national American holiday. A plea for support of the campaign appeared in the inner sleeve of *Hotter Than July,* together with a photograph of Martin Luther King and a personal devotional.

In 1982 Stevie sang a duet with ex-Beatle Paul McCartney on a McCartney song, "Ebony and Ivory," which dealt with the racial problem and went to No. 1 on the Pop chart, where it remained securely ensconced for seven weeks. Using the image of the black and white keys on a piano keyboard living "together in perfect harmony," it asked the question: "Oh, Lord, why don't we?"

Stevie Wonder has been included in this segment on the Motown Sound because he has remained with the Berry Gordy company from the beginning of his career up to the present, perhaps the only artist, with the exception of Smokey Robinson, who has maintained this long-range association. But almost from the beginning, Stevie possessed a kind of individuality that made him resist being squeezed into the Motown mold, and as soon as he became legally competent, he took complete control of his work. He is too complex and too unique an artist to be included in the white synthesis as developed by Berry Gordy, and he has recorded songs and become involved in projects that were limited in their appeal and possible sales. In an overall view, his work has breadth that places him outside black music as such, although there is a discernible black base both in his outlook and, frequently, sound.

A word must be said about the musicians who made up the Motown studio band, the "Unsung Session Men of Hitsville's Golden Era," as a writer termed them in *The Musician*. Noting that Motown's Twenty-fifth Anniversary was celebrated on May 16, 1983, on NBC, the writer observed that the two-hour TV special "neglected to even mention the quintessential members of what was once the best band in America." By contrast with the session men at Stax Records in Memphis, "Booker T & the M.G.'s became darlings of the music world . . . [while] . . . the men of Motown toiled in anonymity."[13]

The members of the band all came from southern cities, their families drawn, like Berry Gordy's, from Georgia, to Motor Town by the booming automobile industry of the 1920s, 1930s, and 1940s. Leader Earl Van Dyke's family came from Kentucky, keyboardist Johnny Griffith's from Mississippi, and bassist James Jamerson from South Carolina. The comparative affluence of the Detroit economy provided parents with enough income to afford music lessons. Jamerson, Griffith, and Van Dyke grew up in the Bop era of the 1950s, helping one another learn the new changes, but they early turned to R & B, which provided a livelihood.

Other members of the Motown house band were drummers Benny "Papa Zito" Benjamin and Uriel Jones, guitarist Robert Waite, and tenor saxist Dan Turner. Benjamin, who was idolized by young Stevie Wonder almost as a second father, died of a stroke in 1969, by which time the Motown Sound had begun to wane. Working together day and night—sessions sometimes started early in the morning, others late at night—the men played with a sharing of insight and feeling achieved only through such intimacy. "When we locked into a groove," Johnny Griffith said, "it was hellacious."[14]

Granting the rhythmic clout of Motown disks, the contribution of the session men has never been fully evaluated or recognized.

"There is sometimes a tear," Jamerson said, shortly before his death in August 1983, "because I see how I was treated and cheated." Except for string segments, played from charts by members of the Detroit Symphony, Motown recordings were "head" arrangements, devised, created, and developed in the studio. Producers like H-D-H, Norman Whitfield, and others came in with outlines of the songs, hints of fills and patterns, a few chord suggestions—and the session men did the rest. "We were doing more of the job than we thought," Jamerson said, "and we didn't get any songwriting credit. They didn't start giving any musician credits on records until the 70s."[15]

The presence of Motown contributed to a flourishing night life in Detroit, with such clubs as the Chit Chat Lounge and Twenty Grand, where session men gigged. After Motown moved to Hollywood, the Detroit music scene bogged down. The move had wider repercussions for black popular music, promoting a flow of R & B musicians from Chicago, Memphis, New Orleans, Atlanta, Philadelphia, and even New York to Tinseltown. The consequence was a loss of regionalism in black music. After a time, back in Detroit, the promise of a new sound was in the hands of George Clinton and the United Sound Studios, who tried to bring blackness back, the style that became known as Funk.

Blue-Eyed Soul

They called themselves the Righteous Brothers, an adaptation of the churchly accolade: "Man, that was really righteous, brother." One sang in a deep, roaring bass, reminiscent of Jimmy Ricks of the Ravens, and the other shrieked like James Brown. In 1964 they recorded "You've Lost That Lovin' Feelin'," a record that climbed to No. 1 on Pop charts and No. 3 on R & B charts in the period when the Temptations scored with "My Girl" and the Supremes with "Stop! In the Name of Love." But R & B disk jockeys were in for a shock when the Righteous Brothers came to call. Bass Bill Medley (b. 1940), who played piano and guitar, and shrieker Bobby Hatfield (b. 1940) were white Anglo-Saxons. They sang black, so that the term "Blue-Eyed Soul" was applied to and originated with them—and that before they recorded for Phil Spector's Philles label in 1964.

First known as the Paramours when they began recording for Moonglow Records, their black sound on "Little Latin Lupe Lu" (1963), a song written by Bill Medley, invited the name change to Righteous Brothers. By 1964 they were associated with Spector, for whom they delivered four Top Ten chart-makers, and were featured on ABC-TV's popular *Shindig* show. In addition to "Lovin' Feelin'," their Philles hits included "Just Once in My Life," "Unchained Melody" (a mid-1950s hit for Al Hibbler) and "Ebb Tide." On Verve in 1966, they again sent a disk to No. 1, "(You're My) Soul and Inspiration," a Gold best seller, but did not fare as well with "He," another Al Hibbler hit. While all the other titles found a welcome on R & B stations, "He" did not. Apparently, as word spread that the duo was white, their appeal to black listeners—despite their sound—seemed to disappear. Their sound was rejected as a gimmick rather than a genuine expression.

Another group that modeled itself on the Soul singers of the 1960s was the Young Rascals, or the Rascals, as they were later called. Three of the quartet's members—Felix Cavaliere (b. 1944), Eddie Brigati (b. 1946), and Gene Cornish (b. 1945)—were originally associated with Joey Dee's Starlighters, the combo that hit with "Peppermint Twist" and became known during the Twist craze as the house band at the Peppermint Lounge. Felix played keyboards, Gene played guitar, and Eddie handled percussion and sang. When they left the Starlighters in 1965, they joined with Dino Danelli (b. 1945), a Jersey City drummer who had worked with Lionel Hampton and several R & B road shows. Playing and singing on the Barge, a floating Long Island nightclub off the waters of Southampton, during the summer of 1965, they attracted the interest of Sid Bernstein, a canny New York agent who had promoted the Beatles' first American tour. Bernstein's skilful "hyping" of the group stirred several New York record labels to bid for their services, with Atlantic coming out the victor.

"Good Lovin'," in a heated, soulful style reminiscent of Otis Redding, became a Gold Record in 1966, as did "Groovin'" in 1967. By the following year, the group had dropped "Young" from its title and was modulating its soulful thrust in favor of meaningful lyrics. "A Beautiful Morning" and "People Got to Be Free," both written by Cavaliere and Brigati, were million sellers in 1968. By 1971 they had left Atlantic and were recording—briefly—for Columbia, where they continued their experimentation, moving in a Jazz direction and concerning themselves with Yoga in *Peaceful World*.

During the 1970s and into the 1980s, at least three artists came forth to continue the white fascination with the black sound and the Blues. These were Delaney and Bonnie, Joe Cocker, and Hall and Oates.

Bonnie Bramlett (b. 1944), a white Blues-shouter, originally from Granite City, Illinois, met Delaney Bramlett (b. 1939), a white Country Gospel singer of Pontotoc, Mississippi, in Los Angeles in 1967; they were married seven days later. Organizing the fluctuating group that became known as Delaney and Bonnie and Friends—which at one point included no lesser figures than ex-Beatle George

Harrison, superstar guitarist Eric Clapton (of whom Delaney said, "Eric plays guitar like a black man"),[16] and Rock guitarist Dave Mason (b. 1946)—they became known as the outstanding purveyors of Gospel Rock, along with Leon Russell (born Hank Wilson, 1941) and the Shelter People.

Before he joined forces domestically and musically, Delaney mastered the Country-styled Gospel music that was indigenous to rural Mississippi, where he grew up and began playing guitar at eight years of age, on a Playtime guitar his mother bought him for Christmas. After a stint in the Navy, he developed a musical reputation around the Chicago area, where he had been stationed, even playing a date with the Everly Brothers in 1959. Settling in Los Angeles after his discharge, he played his Gospel-Rock style with Country and Western bands, performing in the Palomino, the best-known country club in the area.

Bonnie, whose singing career began in her mid-teens, left small-town Illinois for Memphis, where her raucous Blues style got her work with Stax/Volt Soul and Rock groups. Later, she toured the country as the only white Ikette with the Ike & Tina Turner Revue.

After their marriage, Delaney and Bonnie became one of the first white acts signed by the Stax label. On their debut album, *Down Home,* the members of the mixed band, Booker T & the MGs, served as their backup. Later, an Elektra album, *Accept No Substitutions—The Original Delaney and Bonnie,* was acclaimed for its forceful fusion of Soul, Gospel, Country, and Rock. The praise by critics and respect from fellow musicians such as Harrison and Clapton continued when they switched to Atco Records and produced their *Original Delaney and Bonnie* album. In 1971 they finally made the Top 20 with "Never Ending Song of Love" and "Only You Know and I Know." In 1972, after they moved to Columbia Records, they broke up.

Joe Cocker (b. John Cocker, 1940) is English, and representative of the tremendous impact and hold of American Blues on the singers/musicians of the Beatles generation. A "Blue-Eyed Soul" singer, he toured the United States extensively, collaborated with American artists, and was on American best-seller charts mainly from 1970 to 1975. A working stiff out of Sheffield, he graduated from a trade school, and in his apprentice years in music, earned a living by installing and repairing gas lines during the day. Lonnie Donegan (b. 1931) and Skiffle stirred him at the age of 13 to buy a cheap drum kit and to begin messing around with kids who bought guitars.

At about the time that Skiffle began to fade, he was attracted to Little Richard and Gene Vincent (1935–1971). "But I was especially attracted to the Blues," he said, "which seemed to have a great honesty compared to all the bullshit English pop."[17] Muddy Waters was the next influence. By the late 1950s, working with a group called the Cavaliers, Cocker manifested the impact of Buddy Holly and Chuck Berry. But the major influence at this time was Ray Charles, whose disk of "What'd I Say" (1959) inflamed him and led, some years later, when he worked with Vance Arnold & the Avengers, to his recording a cover of Ray's "Georgia on My Mind." The 1960s were lean years, despite tours with the Rolling Stones, Manfred Mann, and the Hollies. Playing Blues-Rock, he later toured American bases in France, scoring with blacks and alienating white listeners. Still later, he organized Joe Cocker's Big Blues Band and made moderately successful disks for British record companies and on the American A & M label.

A tour of the United States in the summer of 1969, including an appearance at the legendary Woodstock Festival, won critical applause for his boisterous vocals and weird dancing—in which he outdid Elvis—and an appearance on the Ed Sullivan Show. At an A & M session in Los Angeles, or it may have been at Woodstock, he met Leon Russell, the white American bluesman, who returned to England with him and helped produce his first single chart-maker, "She Came through the Bathroom Window," written for him by Paul McCartney. Touring the States in 1970 with a 40-piece group, billed as Mad Dogs and Englishmen, assembled by Leon Russell, he achieved a Top Ten single with "The Letter," recorded with Russell and the Shelter People. The tour was filmed and was a box-office success in American theaters in 1971.

That year, he hit American charts with "High Time We Went," followed in 1972 by "Feeling Alright" (reentry of a 1969 disk) and "Midnight Riders," recorded with the band of Chris Stainton, who was part of Cocker's backup group on "She Came through the Bathroom Window." His last appearance on American charts for the rest of the 1970s was with "You Are So Beautiful," which climbed to No. 5 in 1975. But in 1982, he returned to best-seller lists, racking up his first No. 1 (for three weeks) with an Island disk of "Up Where We Belong," the love theme from the hit film *An Officer and a Gentleman,* on whose soundtrack he appeared with Jennifer Warner. By then he was infusing his Blue-Eyed Soul with elements of Rock and balladry, as evidenced in the LP *Sheffield Steel.*

Recognized as the most successful singing duo of the 1980s, Oates and Hall, sometimes known as the Blue-Eyed Soul Brothers, met in 1967. If the story, as told in *Dangerous Dances,* an authorized biography, is to be accepted, it happened at a record hop in West Philadelphia at which they were the only two white faces in a crowd of soul brothers. Their mastery of the black sound of Rhythm and

Blues was such that they had been invited by Station WDAS to appear at the Adelphia Ballroom with their respective bands, the Temptones and the Masters, along with the best black bands of Philadelphia. At the dance, they realized an added kinship: they were both students at Temple University, in Philadelphia. Two years later, in 1969, they began a lasting partnership, eventually developing into what many regard as the best Blue-Eyed Soul duo ever.

Between 1980 and 1984, adapting soulful sounds emanating from Philadelphia International recordings, they managed 12 consecutive Top Ten singles, 5 of which went to No. 1, as well as 5 albums, each of which sold over a million. Among their hit singles, there were "Kiss on My List," "Private Eyes," "I Can't Go for That," "Maneater," and "You've Lost That Lovin' Feeling," the 1964 hit of the pioneers of Blue-Eyed Soul, the Righteous Brothers.

Daryl Hall, born Daryl Franklin Hohl—and named after film producer Daryl Zanuck—is the tall, blond keyboardist/guitarist of the duo, while John Oates, short, dark, with a black moustache, sticks to the guitar. Their earliest successes came in the mid-1970s, when, together with the Bee Gees and Boz Scaggs (b. 1944), they hung their music on the dance beat of black music, refining the hard, harsh sound for the Pop market. "Sara Smile" and "Rich Girl" were hit singles from the landmark album of mid-1970s Blue-Eyed Soul, *Abandoned Luncheonette.* While the Bee Gees took the Disco route, producing the monster seller *Saturday Night Fever,* Hall and Oates tried unsuccessfully to make it as a duo in a market brimming with the hustle of big-band instrumentation.

Voices, their twelfth album, the first produced by them, went multi-platinum in 1980 and marked the turnaround. To Motown/Philadelphia Soul, they added the bounce of Rock and the densities and textures of Techno-Pop. In 1984 *Bim Bam Boom,* title suggesting exuberance, became a Top 5 album, with the single "Out of Touch" scaling No. 1. It offered substantial evidence of their ability to react to changes in the market—critics have taken them to task for their flexibility—in material that bore the marks of the new black sounds of Hip-Hop.

The white artist who raised the sound and style of Soul to a seething boil was Janis Joplin (1943–1970), the ugly duckling out of Port Arthur, Texas, for whom the liberated female was as stylistically crucial as self-pride and black power were to the ethnic Soul artist. "She was the only woman," wrote Ellen Willis, "to achieve the kind of stature in what was basically a male club, the only Sixties culture hero to make visible and public woman's experience of the quest for individual liberation. . . . Janis' favorite metaphors [were] singing as fucking (a first principle of rock and roll) and fucking as liberation (a first principle of the cultural revolution) . . ."[17]

The unbuttoned expression of passion by a female was first assayed with considerable impact by Aretha Franklin at just about the time that Janis was making the San Francisco scene. As we have seen, it became the mark of Aretha's emergence as a Gospel-rooted shouter in songs such as "I Never Loved a Man (The Way I Love You)" and in Otis Redding's blazing demand for "Respect" in 1967. The succession was rather direct from Aretha to Janis, and both owed a debt to the pioneer of women's independence in song—Big Mama Thornton and her walloping "Hound Dog" disk.[18] Janis's debt to Big Mama was more direct and immediate than Aretha's.

Big Mama's song "Ball and Chain" became Janis's own resounding masterpiece. It exists in several versions, dating back to the debut album of Big Brother and the Holding Company, the San Francisco group with whom Janis made her record debut and was briefly associated. Although Big Brother's debut album made little impact, the follow-up, *Cheap Thrills,* in 1968, went to No. 1. On this album, Janis's version of the song is considerably longer than that in her own soundtrack album, *Janis* (1975). But in both and in her stage presentations, her singing involves the most violent contrasts of dynamics, from hoarse yells and heart-torn, melismatic screams to virtually inaudible moans.

In comparison with Big Mama's classic rendition of "Ball and Chain," one hears a contrast of two approaches. Big Mama is singing a Blues, balancing toughness and tenderness, rebelliousness and acquiescence, challenge and resignation, and seeking to transcend her hurt by confronting it with grace. Curiously, Janis's is the Soul version, blacker than Big Mama's; she is the Soul singer protesting, pleading, despairing, but in an extreme state of frenzy: "All I ever wanted to do was to love you. . . . The pain is killing me, dragging me down . . . maybe you can help me—c'mon help me!" At moments she is drowning in her tears—as in the song that Ray Charles introduced in 1957—and again, bleeding with love, a duality one heard also in "Piece of My Heart."

Whether she could ever have resolved this dichotomy, we will never know, since Janis, having recorded *Pearl* during the summer of 1970, was dead of an overdose on October 4, 1970, in a Hollywood motel room. She had once said: "Onstage I make love to 25,000 people, then I go home alone." In the three brief years of her burgeoning career, it was to the abysmal loneliness of a motel room like the one in which she died that she frequently went after a performance.

After Janis Joplin came Jennifer Holiday, the southern Gospel singer who became an overnight sensation with the heartbreak rendition of "And I Am Telling You I'm Not Going," a song that, in its outcry, combined the dual elements of anger and pleading so basic to Janis's style.

The circle was complete, from Big Mama (thesis) to the white transformation by Janis (antithesis), and, dialectically, to the synthesis by Holiday.

Heavy Metal

American or British, Heavy Metal bands are mostly made up of white instrumentalists. As a sound phenomenon, Heavy Metal marks the triumph of amplifiers, synthesizers, and electrical distortion in the 1970s. As a musical style, it emanates from emotions similar to those that were given expression in black Soul. It is angry music, aggressive music, music that is an expression of inner disturbance; perhaps, most of all, of frustration. It is on the instrumental level as extreme a form of expression as Soul was on the vocal level. Since its greatest appeal is to young listeners whose ears can withstand the high-decibel thunder, it is not an exaggeration to say, as Lester Bangs has written: "There is, perhaps, no music which more accurately conveys the screaming nerves of pubescent frustration than Heavy Metal."[19]

Iron Butterfly, a California band, is generally recognized as America's first Heavy Metal rock band. It made the Top 40 in 1968 with a single titled, "In-a-Gadda-Da-Vida," their way of saying, "In the Garden of Eden," or "Life." Among British groups, the Yardbirds and the Who vie for honors as the pioneers of the style. But Jimi Hendrix is really the original heavy metallurgist. After one tour, his engineer announced: "I think I've gone deaf . . . I am going home to Scotland for two weeks to see if my hearing comes back to normal."[20]

At the Monterey Pop Festival in June 1967, where the Jimi Hendrix Experience first became known to American audiences, Jimi came onstage shortly after the Who had overwhelmed the crowd with their slambang destruction of their instruments. In a matter of minutes, playing his guitar at a level they had not heard in the five concerts of the Festival, Hendrix stunned the crowd with his virtuosity, a staggering display of instrumental mastery in which he played complex patterns, holding the instrument behind his back, over his head, between his legs, and plucking the strings with his teeth. Then, in a mind-boggling bit of shoddy showmanship, before he left the stage, he poured lighter-fluid over his expensive instrument, touched a flame to it, and watched it burn to a crisp, hovering over it like a priest over a sacrificial lamb.

The promise of his performance was more than realized in the brief three years and three months that remained of his career and life. There was virtually no guitarist of the time, including such British giants as Eric Clapton, Peter Townshend (b. 1945), and Jeff Beck (b. 1944), and American virtuosos including Mike Bloomfield (1942–1981), who was not intimidated by him. After he heard Jimi in person, Bloomfield, who was an outstanding instrumentalist, told *Guitar Player* magazine: "I didn't even want to pick up a guitar for the next year."[21]

Apart from what he played (his music was deeply rooted in the Blues) and his technical virtuosity, it was his ingenious use of distortion and amplification that fellow guitarists could not unravel. "He plays both amplifiers full up," his engineer said.

> Most people just touch the wah-wah pedal with their foot. Jimi jumps on it with his full weight. . . . He ruins a lot of tremolo bars, too. He bends the strings with the bars, and they get bent way past the distortion level. That starts the feedback. . . . He also burns up a lot of tubes because of the great volume. . . . One night he burned out four amplifiers. You see, his amplifiers are turned up full and pushing what they're supposed to, but then all the speakers are pushing plus fuzz and the wah-wah, so there's more power than the amplifiers can take."[22]

"Maybe if we play loudly enough," he said, "we can shut out the world."[23]

But he could not—and the world made a troubled being out of him. It started in Seattle, where he listened to white Rockabilly singer Eddie Cochran (1935–1960), and where, it is reported, he was disciplined in high school for holding hands with a white girl. By 1963 he was playing guitar in backup bands for the Isley Brothers, Wilson Pickett, Jackie Wilson, King Curtis, and Little Richard. It was the "Tutti Frutti" man who cut him to pieces after a performance because, wearing a flashy shirt, he was accused of drawing attention away from the star of the show, Little Richard.

He was playing Blues in New York's Greenwich Village—and edgy about singing because of his poor voice until he heard Bob Dylan—with a group he called Jimmy James and the Blue Flames when the ex-bassist of the British Animals persuaded him to move to England. (His departure from the Blue Flames was not without travail.) Working with two British musicians, bassist Noel Redding (b. 1945) and drummer Mitch Mitchell (b. 1946), as the Jimi Hendrix Experience, he developed a following on the Continent as well as in Great Britain.

The year of his American debut in Monterey saw his first album, *Are You Experienced?* climb to No. 5 on the charts. It was followed in 1968 by *Axis Bold as Love* (No. 3) and *Electric Ladyland* (No. 1), the last-mentioned serving as the name of the recording studio he built in New York City. A reprise album, *Smash Hits,* made No. 6 in 1969. But by then, Hendrix was struggling to cope with a number of pressures, some external, some internal. He could not reconcile his own desire for instrumental perfection with audience and managerial demands for best sellers. Anxious to press forward artistically, he formed an experimental group he called his "electric sky church," whose direction is suggested by the "weird" version of the "Star Spangled Banner" he played at the Woodstock Festival in 1969.

At a time when many black artists were declaring themselves politically, Jimi resisted pressures by black militants to become involved. However, in an apparent move to satisfy criticism, he dissolved the Experience and formed the Band of Gypsies, in which he substituted two black musicians (bassist Billy Cox and drummer Buddy Miles) for the white Englishmen with whom he had made his original triumph. Still reacting to criticism, he played joints in Harlem with the Gypsies, whose performance, recorded live at New York's Fillmore East on New Year's Eve 1970, may be heard on *Hendrix Band of Gypsies,* a No. 5 chart-maker.

That these pressures were taking their toll was evident early in 1970 when, at a peace benefit in New York's Madison Square Garden, he suddenly stopped playing in the middle of a set and, in what appeared to many like a dazed state, he wandered off the stage. It was not too many months before he went to bed in the London flat of a girlfriend after a night of heavy drinking and took some sleeping pills. The coroner could not determine whether his fatal inhalation of vomit during barbiturate intoxication was an accidental death or suicide. The date was September 18, 1970, and Jimi was not yet 28 years old.

Hendrix's entry into the record scene in 1967 came just before the Heavy Metal explosion of 1968, when Iron Butterfly *(Heavy),* Velvet Underground *(White Light-White Heat),* Blue Cheer *(Vincebus Eruptus),* and the British Deep Purple *(Shades of Deep Purple)* all turned up the volume of their playing to ear-shattering levels.

Although they performed organist Jon Lord's *Concerto for Group and Orchestra* with both the London Philharmonic and the Los Angeles Philharmonic Orchestra, Britain's Deep Purple, of which Lord is a member, holds the title, "World's Loudest Rock Band," according to the *Guiness Book of World Records.* Debuting in 1968, the group produced a Gold album *(Machine Head)* in 1972, a platinum album *(Made in Japan)* in 1973, with other albums bearing titles such as *Fireball* 1971), *Burn* (1974), *Stormbringer* (1974), and *Powerhouse* (1977).

The Led Zeppelin took off in 1968, when guitarist Jimmy Page of the legendary Yardbirds formed the group to complete scheduled dates in northern Europe. Known for their "rave-ups," as they called the extended free-form instrumental breaks in which they indulged —comparable to the Iron Butterfly's 17-minute extemporization, "In-a-Gadda-Da-Vida"—the Yardbirds pioneered the artistic use of feedback. Led Zeppelin exploited all the available resources of distortion but derived its impact from the bluesy, hard-Rock guitar of Jimmy Page (b. 1945), the roaring vocals of Robert Plant (b. 1947), and the booming drums of John Bonham (1947–1980). Their R & B roots were audible in such selections as Willie Dixon's "You Shook Me" and"I Can't Quit You Baby," both of which appeared in their double debut album of 1969. Their classic "Stairway to Heaven" came from *Led Zeppelin IV*, one of four Gold and platinum eponymous albums they made into 1980. When they dissolved in 1980, as a result of John Bonham's drinking himself to death, they were still playing with the drive and power of their early work.

Steppenwolf, which took its name from the famous novel by Herman Hesse, took its thunder from political events of the time. The grinding terror of Russian tanks in the streets of Czechoslovakia was echoed, it is said, in "Born to Be Wild," a hit single of 1968 whose puissant qualities peaked in *Minster* (1969). "Born to Be Wild" was heard as the motorbike theme of the film *Easy Rider*. Five Steppenwolf albums appeared between 1968 and 1971, pinning listeners to their seats, a reviewer wrote, "by their eardrums."

The critical outcry against Grand Funk Railroad was almost as loud as their head-banging music. But it did not prevent the group, formed in 1968 and folded in 1976, from achieving No. 1 singles in "We're an American Band" (1973) and "Locomotion" (1974). At the height of its popularity—Capitol released four albums, one after the other, in 1970—the group advertised itself with 60-foot portraits on the largest billboard in the world, one that stretched across two Broadway blocks in New York City's Times Square. The magnitude of the advertisement was, perhaps, chosen to reflect visually the volume of its sound.

Black Sabbath, a British band, did not fare any better at the hands of the critics. Starting as a Blues band in Birmingham, it changed its name from Earth to Black Sabbath in 1969 and proceeded to cultivate a quasi-"evil" image, accompanying it with a hammer-driving sound that made it a pioneer Heavy Metal band. In a review of a 1972 performance in Los Angeles, a reviewer described their songs as consisting of "anguished screeching about war pigs, rat salads, iron men and gloomy topics set to an endlessly repeated two-chord riff."[24] Nevertheless, and despite changes in personnel, Black Sabbath has commanded a sizable following from its eponymous debut album of 1970 to the present.

Blue Oyster Cult, one of the prime American exponents of Heavy Metal, was formed in Long Island, New York, and secured a contract from Columbia Records in 1971 as the result of critical applause in *Crawdaddy* magazine. *Secret Treaties,* their breakthrough album of 1974, included "Career of Evil" by poetess, later Punk songstress, Patti Smith (b. 1946), who also contributed songs to their *Agents of Fortune* LP in 1976, the year that gave them a Top Twenty single in "(Don't Fear) The Reaper." (Chart singles are infrequent among the Heavy metallurgists.) *Cultosaurus Erectus* (1980), out of which came another chart single ("Burnin' for You"), offers a striking example of the type of mythic concept and cover cultivated by some of the ear-exploding combos. On the front cover: the horrible-looking, magnified head of the fictitious dinosaur in an artist's rendering; on the back cover: photographs of the unfertilized eggs and skeletal head of the monster, the latter "courtesy of the Underbelly Institute" plus an artist's conception, based on skeletal remains of the dinosaur, "thought to be a distant relative of the Horn-Swooped Bango-Pony." The entire put-on was similar to mythic "philosophies" and images presented by Devo, Black Sabbath, and other Heavy Metal groups.

During the 1970s, interest in sledge-hammer rock music assumed international proportions. While the largest component of head-bangers came from England and the United States, the Scorpions was a trio founded by the Schenker brothers in Germany; Triumph, inspired by a fellow-riveter group (Rush), came from Canada; and AC/DC, organized by the Young brothers, emigrated from Australia.

Among adherents of the sonic assault formed in England, there were UFO, which started as a hard-Rock group; Queen, which moved in a Rockabilly direction in the 1980s; Judas Priest, out of Birmingham, which scored a platinum album with *Screaming for Vengeance;* Iron Maiden, the first group to appear live on BBC TV's "Top of the Pops" program after the Who in 1973, four years earlier; and the Blizzard of Oz, formed by Ozzy Osbourne of Birmingham after he left Black Sabbath and with whom he engaged in competitive dueling, recording some of the numbers he had recorded with that group.

The American representatives of Heavy Metal, included, among others, ZZ Top, who drew on Country and Delta Blues for their brand of high-energy music in the Gold album *Rio Grande Mud* and the platinum LP *Fandango;* Kiss, who hid their faces behind circus makeup and dressed in comic-book costumes; Van Halen, whose organizers (the Van Halen brothers) were born in the Netherlands but raised in Pasadena, California, where they studied to be concert pianists before turning to Rock, and who substituted skin-tight silk for the black leather of most Heavy Metal groups; Alice Cooper, stage name of Vincent Furnier (b. 1948), who grew up in Phoenix, Arizona; and Devo, a group that started at Kent State University and built its reputation with a furious multi-media campaign in which they projected an image and "philosophy" of devolution.

While almost all Rock groups donned bizarre attire and indulged in zany antics to draw media attention, the Heavy Metal brigade tended to extravagances that opened the door to the scandalous behavior and monstrous hair and dress styles of the Punks of the late 1970s. In this respect, Kiss, sometimes described as "America's masters of outrage and arrogance," used heavy makeup so that one musician looked like a vampire or demon; another, like a catman; a third, like a starman; and the fourth, a spaceman—with all attired in appropriately grotesque costumes and boots. Live shows employed explosives and drum kits rising 40 feet high, while bassist Gene Simmons spit fire and fake blood as he rolled out a foot-long tongue.

The cannonball music inevitably was accompanied by pugnacious postures and bellicose themes. Album covers depicted a garish red baby with green slits for eyes, and fangs and claws (Black Sabbath); a bloodied, disheveled figure of a man with torn pants and bloodied thighs, glowering like a madman *(Diary of a Madman);* or, simply, a large reproduction of a cannon (AC/DC). Song titles abounded in intimations of violence: "Killer Queen" (Queen); *Killing Machine* (Judas Priest); *Killers* (title of an album by Iron Maiden as well as Kiss); *Dressed to Kill* (Kiss); "Whip It" (Devo), "Force It" (UFO); "Night of the Long Knives" (AC/DC); "This Planet's on Fire" (Sammy Hagar); "Inject the Venom" (AC/DC). In *The Game* (1980) and a hit single, "Another One Bites the Dust," Queen, with two members possessing degrees in physics, manipulated studio resources to simulate war effects.

When the Sex Pistols appeared on the British scene, their hair dyed in garish colors, safety pins stuck through their cheeks, and using four-letter cuss words in their TV appearances (including "F—— the Queen"), the Heavy Metal groups faced a real challenge. But the provocations and outrages of neither the Punk nor New Wave groups caused any lessening in the audience appeal of Heavy Metal. The 1980s brought the rise of new high-energy, high-decibel exponents in Motley Crue, Ratt, Quiet Riot, Def Leppard, and Twisted Sister, among others.

Heavy Metal has been condemned as appealing to an infantile

and immature love for loud sounds and loud noise. But proponents point to the Jimi Hendrix goal of drowning out the world through loud sound; the argument is that the ear-shattering decibels provide a sense of escape, if temporary, from the boredom, the monotony, and the futility of everyday living and work. Like Rock audiences generally, only more so, Heavy Metal listeners respond to the music vocally as well as physically. At high points in a show, proponents assert, the streams of sound flowing from the audience and the performers merge in an explosion of ecstasy. When that happens, the show approaches a religious rite, the type that James Brown and other Soul performers sometimes achieved. All together and alike are "possessed," enveloped by the roar of sound and elevated by it to a more intense level of existence.

CHAPTER TEN

THE DISCO CRAZE

In 1975, at a party in his Beverly Hills home, the late Neil Bogart (1943–1982), owner of Casablanca Records, fun-tested a new record he had just received from Giorgio Moroder, arranger/composer/producer of a German diskery, Oasis. "Love to Love You Baby" was recorded by a black American singer from Boston, Donna Summer (b. 1950), who also wrote the erotic number, which had her gasping, groaning, and moaning on the tape in an expression of ecstatic passion. People were so amused and the party was so enlivened by the song that the record had to be played again and again. The following morning, Bogart phoned Moroder in Germany and, on the basis of how his guests had been affected, requested that the 4-minute disk be extended to 20 minutes. The record that Moroder ultimately produced with Miss Summer was just 16 minutes and 50 seconds long; but it was described as one in which Miss Summer not only repeated the title "Love to Love You Baby" 28 times but simulated the sounds of female orgasm 23 times.[1]

From a musical standpoint, the disk represented a sharp turnaway from the sounds that had dominated American and British airwaves since the mid-1950s. Instead of electric guitars, one heard strings, woodwinds, and brass. Instead of a small four- or five-piece combo, which had become traditional with Rock, there was a large orchestra, one that was very much like the Swing bands of the big-band era, only larger, and with electronic textures and synthesized clusters of sound. But the most pronounced and novel sound was the thumpa-thumpa bass-drum beat, four to the bar, as in the Swing era, not only continuous but way out in front of the singer and the orchestra.

Curiously—and, perhaps, the source of this configuration—a record with a very similar sound was issued in the United States just about six months before the Summer disk. An instrumental disk by Van McCoy and the Soul City Orchestra, "The Hustle," composed by McCoy (1940-1979), not only became the biggest-selling dance disk of the 1970s but the basic dance of Disco. The main infectious strain of three was performed by an instrument seldom heard in Rock—the flute—with a vocal group, a sustained string section, and a brass choir handling the other strains as out-front counter-melodies. At moments, the vocal group interjected a staccato, "Do it!" or "Do the Hustle!" The thumping drum beat was as pronounced as on the Summer disk, and, like it, a steady four-to-the-bar.

It was almost two years before Disco erupted into the music-and-dance craze that swept the world of the 1970s as the Twist had done in the 1960s and Break Dancing was to do in the 1980s. The conflagration was ignited by a 1977 film, *Saturday Night Fever,* with a hit Disco score by the Bee Gees and a story that centered on the desperate struggle of a poor white kid, played by John Travolta, to win the Saturday-night competition and become the king of the local discotheque. The soundtrack album became one of the biggest-selling LP's in record history,[2] with the Bee Gee's disk of "Stayin' Alive" and "Jive Talkin'," and the Trammps record of "Disco Inferno," breaking as hit singles.

By 1978 it was estimated that more than 200 radio stations around the country had adopted wall-to-wall Disco formats, some, like Station WKTU of Queens, in New York, jumping from a no-show rating to the top audience draw of the area. Reports had it that there were more than 20,000 discotheques around the country—some, such as Phazes, in Atlanta, built at a cost of $1.5 million—and that more than 36 million people flocked to their dance floors. In New York City, Studio 54 became the center of the Disco scene, as the Peppermint Lounge once had been of the Twist scene, with luminaries of stage, screen, high society, television, politics, and Madison Avenue crowding its dance sessions.

Although the Hustle came out of the black ghetto, the Disco craze was, at its height, a white, middle-class, youth-to-middle age phenomenon. However, its popularity reached down to lower age groups, with discotheques holding afternoon soda-pop sessions for the Pepsi Generation, and roller-skating rinks sponsoring Roller Disco sessions for the country's 28 million roller skaters.

It should, doubtless, be noted that discotheques antedated the Disco craze by two decades or more. A word of French origin, the *discothèque* came into being after World War II, when Parisian cafe owners began dispensing with costly live bands and entertainment, and substituted instead an in-house disk jockey playing records for dancers. At some point in the 1960s, discotheques began to be opened in the United States, but operated as private clubs, frequented exclusively by the gay set. Some of these continued to function as private luncheon clubs in the daytime even after they opened their doors to the public at night. But by the 1970s, discotheques had become part of the black and Latin subcultures as well.

When it pyramided into a global social phenomenon after 1977, Disco attracted exhibitionists of all ages and sexes, for whom the discotheque floor, regardless of how crowded it was, became a private arena for personal display and ego gratification. Disco also gave prominence to the record producer and the disk jockey, the former for his skill in manipulating the new, sophisticated recording technology, and the latter for his ability to use changes in tempo, volume, and mood to manipulate dancers on the floor. The craze brought best sellers to a number of new labels—Casablanca, TK, Salsoul, Philadelphia International, among others—as the majors sat it out. Peaking at 112 beats to the minute, Disco dances were extended, endurance bouts that led to the introduction of 12-inch singles with only one or two selections on each side.

It was not until April 1979 that *Newsweek* gave recognition to the craze, blazoning the development of its front cover with a headline, "Disco Takes Over," spread across a large head shot of Donna Summer. But by October of 1979, the *Wall Street Journal* made its own evaluation of the trend in a long article headed "Disco-Music Craze/Seems to Be Fading/Record Makers Glad." Noting that the clubs still thrive, the *Journal* observed that radio stations were dropping the wall-to-wall Disco format. It was not surprising that the craze seemed so short-lived, a huge backlash having developed because of the monotonous, up-front thumpa-thumpa rhythm of Disco records, the resort to repetitious, meaningless lyrics, and the resentment of Rock artists at being pushed off the charts.

The backlash assumed its most violent form in Chicago, at Comiskey Park, on July 12, 1979. Spearheading an anti-Disco campaign, a Rock disk jockey who had lost his job when his station went all-out on Disco arranged to have fans admitted to the stadium for $.98 if they presented a Disco record at the gate. Between games of the White Sox/Tigers doubleheader, the 10,000 Disco records, collected at the gate, were blown up. It prompted 7,000 youngsters to spill onto the playing field, smashing records, burning banners, and ripping up the sod, so that the second game had to be canceled.

Nevertheless, at the Grammy awards in 1979, Disco artists and songs were in the forefront. The Bee Gees carried off three awards: two for *Saturday Night Fever* (Album of the Year and Best Group Vocal Performance) and Best Arrangement for Voice on "Stayin' Alive." The Disco song "Last Dance" won a Grammy for Paul Jabara (Best R & B Song) and for Donna Summer (Best Female R & B Performance). A Taste of Honey, a Disco band, was voted Best New Artist of the Year, and Barry Manilow won a Grammy for Best Male Performance of his Disco song, "Copacabana (At the Copa)." At the Oscar ceremony in Hollywood, "Last Dance" won out over four other film songs as the Best Original Song of the Year.

With the exception of the Village People, an integrated group, the major purveyors of Disco were black. The preeminent figure was the girl from Boston, Donna Summer, who idolized singer Mahalia Jackson and developed her career largely in Germany, where her first professional job was a role in *Hair* and where, as part of the Vienna Folk Opera Company, she played in *Porgy and Bess* and *Show Boat,* appearing later in German productions of *Godspell* and *The Me That Nobody Knows*. Working as a backup singer in Munich, she attracted the attention of Giorgio Moroder and Pete Bellotte of Oasis Records, which led to "Love to Love You Baby," her million-copy American debut disk.

Two years elapsed before she garnered another Gold Record ("I Feel Love"). But as the Disco development moved into high gear, her career likewise took off. "Last Dance," from the film *Thank God It's Friday,* became a Gold Record in 1978, followed quickly by a Gold version of "MacArthur Park." The peak year in Disco, 1979, was a climactic one for Summer, with a succession of Gold and platinum disks: "Heaven Knows" (Gold); "Hot Stuff" and "Bad Girls," both platinum sellers; and "Dim the Lights" (Gold). The flow of best-selling disks continued into 1980 with "On the Radio" and "The Wanderer," both Gold. But in 1980, the woman who had cultivated the image of a sex goddess suddenly did an about-face and, reacting to memories of her early upbringing, became a Born-Again Christian, with an attendant change in her choice of material.

The year 1979 produced an unusual pairing when the newly crowned Queen of Disco made a recording with the long-established Queen of Pop music, Barbra Streisand (b. 1942). Having demonstrated her power as a sensuous singer, an eye-catching stage personality, and talented songwriter—8 of the 15 songs in *Bad Girls* were written or cowritten by her—Donna proved that she could more than hold her own in a dramatic vocal performance with Streisand. "No More Tears (Enough is Enough)" went to No. 1 and became a platinum seller. A fusion of Pop and Disco, and a superb blend of two expressive voices, it was thematically a declaration of female independence—the woman was bored to tears and throwing the man over.

Another female singer had already struck a similar note in a late 1978 recording. In the soaring "I Will Survive," Gloria Gaynor (b. 1949) made an impassioned declaration that swept aside the traditional posture of the woman as an inescapable victim of unrequited love. To influences absorbed from studying the records of Sarah Vaughan, Nat "King" Cole, and Marvin Gaye (while she worked as an accountant), Gaynor added the commanding voice that could soar dramatically over a large orchestra. In the Gaynor opus as well as the Summer–Streisand song, but also in terms of the behavior and dress (and undress) of females on Disco dance floors, Disco reflected the impact of the day's Women's Liberation movement.

A number of black bands contributed to the Disco explosion. A Taste of Honey, the group named Best New Band of 1979 in the Grammy competition, featured two female lead vocalists playing guitar and bass, with a backup of males on piano and drums. "Boogie Oogie Oogie," a platinum disk in 1978, was one of just two disks that made the charts between then and the 1980s. Like a number of other groups that erupted during the Disco explosion, A Taste of Honey seemed unable to develop its potential.

This limitation applied to the Trammps, a large group that included three keyboard players, two Conga drummers, and two tambourine-shakers, in addition to three guitars, bass, and drum. "Disco Inferno," performed in *Saturday Night Fever,* was the culmination of a three-record climb on the charts. The selection emphasized Latin American sounds, an ingredient used by other producers to add spice to the Disco brew.

A third group that participated in the Disco trend was Kool and the Gang, a Jersey City group led by Robert "Kool" Bell (b. 1950), which made the charts initially in 1973 with "Funky Stuff," moved into the Top Ten the following year with "Jungle Boogie" and "Hollywood Swinging" (both Gold Records), and came back to the charts, after a hiatus of four years, in the Disco period. Performing "Open Sesame" in *Saturday Night Fever,* they achieved Top Ten singles in 1979–1980 with "Ladies of Twilight," "Too Hot," and, the most memorable, "Celebration."

Chic was a studio-developed band, as were other Disco aggregations, the creation of bassist Bernard Edwards (b. 1952), a Rock-and-Roller, and guitarist Nile Rodgers (b. 1952), who was classically trained and a jazzman. The two New Yorkers met in 1972 in a group appropriately called, the Big Apple. In 1977 they cut some demos, which, on being played at New York's Night Owl discotheque, led to an Atlantic Records contract. "Dance, Dance, Dance," one of the demos and their first single, became a Gold disco favorite in 1977–1978. Their debut album, *C'est Chic,* yielded two major Disco disks: "Le Freak," which climbed to No. 1, where it remained for five record-breaking weeks and eventually passed the platinum 2-million mark in sales; and "I Want Your Love," a Gold record. In 1979, too, Chic placed "Good Times" in the No. 1 spot on the charts and added another Gold Record to its collection.

If Chic was a creature largely of the oceanic Disco wave, Sister Sledge, a longer-lived vocal group, came to fruition through it and the fertile songwriting/producing talents of Edwards and Rodgers of Chic. Long, long before they broke through with the evocative "We Are Family"—in fact, when the four sisters were not yet in grade school—they performed with their grandmother, a former opera singer, at banquets, parties, and social events in their native Philadelphia. As teenagers, they became involved in session work, serving as backup singers in records made by Gamble and Huff, the Philadelphia International entrepreneurs and songwriter/producers. The girls managed to squeeze in college at Temple University before they were signed by Atlantic Records. A number of undistinguished albums climaxed in a meeting with Chic's Edwards and Rodgers, who wrote, arranged, produced, and performed in "We Are Family." Shortly after garnering a Gold No. 2 hit with this suggestively autobiographical song, sister Joni, in a family way, left the group to slim the quartet to a trio.

Peaches and Herb was a duo that made the charts in 1967–1968, with a memorable hit in "Close Your Eyes," and then disappeared from the charts for a decade. Reconstituted in 1979 with a new Peaches, although the duo kept its original billing, they clambered aboard the fast-moving Disco train of 1979 with two dance hits—"Shake Your Groove Thing," a Gold Record, and "Reunited"—which they were, in a manner of speaking—a platinum seller that sped to a four-week stay at No. 1.

In a sense, the epitome of the Disco development was the group that called itself the Village People and remained active into the 1980s. A racially mixed sextet (four blacks and two whites), they dress in uniforms that identify them as a policeman, cowboy, construction worker, Indian, leather man, and G.I. Curiously, the group came into being when its songwriter/producer, Jacques Morali, saw

Felipe Rose dancing at a New York City discotheque in a loincloth and feathered headdress. Later identified as the Indian, Rose became the inspiration for an all-male singing group, each member dressed as an identifiable Villager and singing ironic macho songs. For the eponymous debut album of 1977, Morali hired studio musicians to perform, and models posed for the cover photo. The success of the album compelled a search for performers who could sing and dance as well as model. To the three who were part of the original group—Indian chief, G.I./sailor and commander/policeman—Morali added an out-of-work chorus boy (construction worker), an Agnes De Mille dancer (cowboy), and a toll collector in the Brooklyn Battery tunnel with no singing or dancing experience (biker).

The cover of the Village People's *Cruisin'* album depicts them seated on motor bikes, a Jeep, horses, and a construction rig, against a rugged western background. On their *Macho Man* album cover, they stand looking hard at you, their hands challengingly on their hips. But they have made no secret of their homosexual proclivities, a subject that occupies them in "Y.M.C.A.," a platinum No. 2 single in 1978–1979. It was one of three enormous sellers in the Disco market, with "Macho Man" and "In the Navy" both going Gold.

The White Synthesis

At the height of the Disco explosion, John Rockwell told, in *The New York Times,* of receiving a fervent plea from a Rock fan, urging him to become a standard-bearer in the fight against Disco. Observing that white Rock loyalists rejected the dance craze as "a black and homosexual phenomenon," Rockwell expressed concern that the animosity might be racial in origin, if it was not a product of snobbery or of feeling threatened.

"Sitting in the Palladium [on 14th St. in New York City]," he wrote, "listening to a hallful of white rock fans chanting their anti-disco slogans over and over, is just a bit too reminiscent for comfort of *lumpen-proletariat* proto-Fascism."[3]

This attitude did not seem to carry over to artists of Pop and Rock music. In addition to the Bee Gees, Barry Manilow, and Streisand, such stalwarts of Rock as Rod Stewart (b. 1945) and even the Rolling Stones did not hesitate to work in the style. In "Do Ya Think I'm Sexy?" a disco disk of 1978–1979, hoarse-voiced Stewart, whose career had begun with the Jeff Beck group 10 years earlier and involved Faces (1969–1975), realized his biggest single record (No. 1 for four weeks), and one that became a certified R.I.A.A. (Record Industry Association of America) platinum seller. In roughly the same period, the Rolling Stones produced a No. 1 Gold Record in "Miss You," which was released in a short Rock version and an extended Disco treatment.

Other white artists who produced Disco disks were Cher ("Take Me Home"); Paul McCartney's Wings ("Goodnight Tonight," a Gold Record); California's Doobie Brothers ("What a Fool Believes," No. 1 and a Gold Record in 1979); Blondie ("Heart of Glass," their first No. 1 and a Gold Record); and Herb Alpert, sans the Tijuana Brass ("Rise," an instrumental Gold Record that went to No. 1). It is no wonder that in the first eight months of 1979, 11 of the 16 No. 1 singles were Disco records.

Inevitably, the craze attracted some strange participants. Frank Zappa (b. 1940) produced "Dancin' Fool," a take-off in the typical satirical style of the Mothers of Invention. A Disco album by Arthur Fiedler and the Boston Pops Orchestra parodied the title of Bee Gees award-winning album in its title, *Saturday Night Fiedler*. Perhaps the most unusual entrant in the Disco sweepstakes was Ethel Merman, who had made her debut in the Gershwin show *Girl Crazy* in 1931 and who, at the age of 80—after not recording for 10 years—made an album of Disco-styled show tunes, including "There's No Business Like Show Business," a song she had introduced in *Annie Get Your Gun* in 1946.

None of these white interpreters made any pretense of becoming deeply involved in the dance style. Nor was there any carry-over, as did occur with other white adaptations of a black style, notably in the case of Rhythm and Blues. It was just a matter of exploiting an immediately accessible market.

CHAPTER ELEVEN

THE CONTEMPORARY SCENE

"One Nation under a Groove" (Funk)

Although the Funk slogan, "One Nation under a Groove," and the Funk "U" sign (formed by clenching a fist and sticking up the pinky and index finger) did not come into being until the late 1970s, the word *funk* goes back into the murky recesses of black ghetto slang. In that context, it referred to unmentionable, earthy sights, sounds, and smells, but especially to a body odor produced during sexual excitement or intercourse. As a music term, *funky* became prominent in the 1950s, when pianist/composer Horace Silver (b. 1928), drummer Art Blakey (b. 1919), and other jazzmen sought to develop a style counter to the coldness, complexity, and intellectualism introduced into the music by Bop, Cool, West Coast, and Third Stream Jazz. Playing "funky" meant to return to the evocative feeling and expressiveness of traditional Blues, to play hard and on the beat, with the use of Blues shadings and sonorities. One of Silver's earliest recorded pieces (1953) bore, in fact, the title, "Opus de Funk."

In the period between 1967 and 1971, the term came back into prominence among black artists, with no fewer than 19 songs employing the word in their titles. "Funky Broadway," recorded early in 1967 by a little-known group, Dyke and the Blazers, was covered by Wilson Pickett, then at the height of his "wicked" record career, who sent it to No. 1 on R & B charts and into the Top Ten on Pop charts. In the following year, there were six songs that bore "funky" titles: "Funky Boo-Ga-Loo," "Funky Judge," "Funky Walk," "Funky Way," with Clarence Carter (b. 1936) and Arthur Conley (b. 1946), both on Atlantic Records, accounting for "Funky Fever" and "Funky Street," respectively. In 1971 six songs once again carried the word *funky* in their titles: "Funky L. A.," "Funky Nassau," "Funky Rubber Band"; James Brown recorded "Make It Funky"; and while the Chambers Brothers called their disk just "Funky," Edwin Starr of the Motown complex, sang "Funky Music Sho Nuff Turns Me On."

Clearly, funky music was turning on many artists and listeners between 1967 and 1971, as the accumulation of titles suggests. Developing as a trend in the same years that Disco swept the country and the world, Funk was antithetical to Disco, eschewing its mellifluous big band sound and harking back, instead, to the bark and bite of Rhythm and Blues. Not unlike Punk in the Rock area, Funk opposed the extensive reliance on the recording studio and the new, sophisticated technology, an animus that disappeared after a time. Developments within black popular music also accounted for Funk, especially an antagonism to the slick, Pop-Gospel sound on which Motown had built an empire.

In truth, shortly after founder Berry Gordy of Motown dismissed the producing team of Holland-Dozier-Holland, who were largely responsible for the sound of Motown's premier group, The Supremes—perhaps believing that it was time for a change—another producer, Norman Whitfield came to the studio one day and told the members of the house band: "I wanna do something different. I wanna do something fresh."[1] Out of this desire came a series of records by the Temptations—"Cloud Nine," "Psychedelic Shack," and "Ball of Confusion"—all of which did not bear the well-worn Motown imprint, and which attained a funky climax in "Papa Was a Rolling Stone," a No. 1 Pop-charter in 1972.

The key figure in the rise of Funk was James Brown, but early proponents included Sly Stone, George Clinton, Wilson Pickett, Clarence Carter, and Arthur Conley, among others. In "Sweet Soul Music" (No. 2, R & B, 1967), Conley (b. 1947) sang, "He's the king of them all y'all." The reference was to James Brown, who began as a major figure in Soul music. But with "Papa's Got a New Bag" (1965), Brown began developing an instrumental sound that involved the band riffing hypnotically on a single chord, staccato punctuation by the horns, and shrill, choked chording by the guitar—all coalescing into a powered expression of rhythmic thrust, raw and sensual. By the time he recorded "Cold Sweat," a No. 1 R & B-charter in 1967,

Funk had crystallized into an earthy, roaring extension of pristine Rhythm and Blues, but grittier and sexier. Brown did not have to ask "Ain't It Funky" in 1969, a question he answered fully in "Funky Drummer" (1970) and "Make It Funky," No. 1 on R & B charts in 1971. Cited frequently as the artist who invented Funk single-handedly, he is regarded as the source of such Funk bands as Blackbyrds; Earth, Wind and Fire; Maceo & the King's Men; Ohio Players; Sly & the Family Stone; and George Clinton's many aggregations. In 1984, after almost 30 years and 56 Top 40 hits, he was honored by the Black Music Association at a reception in Washington, D.C. He had then just completed a duet album with New York Hip-hop Guru Afrika Bambaataa.

Dallas-born Sylvester Stewart, or Sylvester Stone (b. 1944), has been called the Godfather of Psychedelic Funk. Stone goes by the stage name of Sly. It is quite appropriate, considering that he named one of the groups he recorded with in his teens, the Vejtables, and called one of his big hits, "Thank You Falettinme Be Mice Elf Again." He was a musical prodigy, displaying talent at the age of four, when he discovered rhythm: "That's all I had to play with," he has said, "no toys." From a family Gospel group, he went, in his senior year of high school, with the Viscanes, a Pop vocal quintet that enjoyed a modest hit. At Vallejo Junior College, in California, he studied theory and composition, being turned on by Walter Piston's academic text, *Harmony*.

After graduation, he settled in the Bay Area, where he became the talk of the town for his unconventional and eclectic style of programming as an R & B disk jockey on two black stations, KSOL (San Francisco) and KDIA (Oakland). In 1964 he became producer and songwriter at Autumn Records, a small indie label on which he recorded Bobby Freeman (b. 1946), who had already had a hit on Josie Records with his own song, "Do You Want to Dance" (1958); the Mojo Men; and a white group called the Beau Brummels.

In 1966 Sly brought together a seven-piece group that included his brother on guitar, his sister on electric piano, and four multi-instrumentalists whose main instruments were trumpet, saxophone, bass, and drums. After rehearsing in Sly's basement — he wrote and arranged their material as well as playing organ — they began making appearances at local Bay Area clubs, at the famous Fillmore Auditorium at the height of the psychedelic craze, and, in time, at clubs in major cities. Signed by Epic Records, a Columbia subsidiary, they had their first release in 1968, making Top Ten in England as well as the United States with "Dance to the Music," a powerhouse Funk disk. Their second release, "Everyday People," which rose to No. 1 and went Gold, sounded a utopian theme of integration, a carry-over of Sly's programming as a disk jockey. In the three succeeding years, the group produced Top Ten disks in "Hot Fun in the Summertime" (1969), "Thank You Falettinme Be Mice Elf Again" (No. 1 and Gold in 1970), backed with "Everybody Is a Star," and "Family Affair" (No. 1 in 1971).

"Family Affair" was one of three hits ("You Caught Me Smilin'" and "Runnin' Away" were the other two) that came from a Top Ten album titled *There's A Riot Goin' On*. It represented a change in Sly's position from a utopian concern with integration to a challenging black-nationalist stand. "Blood's thicker than mud," they sang in "Family Affair"—the "mud" referring to the three-day festival of love and peace at Woodstock.[2] Reprising the song, "Thank you Falettinme . . ." at the close of the album, Sly changed the lyrics to "Thank You for talkin' to me, Africa . . ."

The *Greatest Hits* album, released in 1970, not only became a platinum album with a sale of over a million, but is credited with playing a major role in moving the sound of black music in a funky direction. By 1971 Sly & the Family Stone had demonstrated so much record power and acceptance that Epic thereafter advanced more than half a million dollars for each album. But the group's popularity now took a steady downward dip, due in part, perhaps, to Sly's black-power position but also to the group's irregularity in personal appearance, Sly's high living style, apparent changes in his personality, once highly affectionate and charismatic, and fluctuations in the Family's personnel. At the peak of the group's popularity (1968–1971), Sly described it as a dance-and-concert combination and their sound as the first fusion of psychedelia and R & B. Sly's reemergence after the downdraft of the 1970s came in 1982, in a partnership with George Clinton, whose funky style he greatly influenced.

Hailing from a small town in Ohio, George Clinton (b. 1940) developed Funk as a philosophy as well as a musical style, with Funkadelic, a collective he formed when he lost the rights to the Parliaments, his original group. "(I Wanna) Testify," the initial hit of the Parliaments—and in a psychedelic vein—came in 1967, shortly before Atlantic Records bought the Revilot catalog and the Parliaments. Undaunted, Clinton converted his back-up band into the Funkadelics, and embraced Funk as "the elixir of life and the answer to the world's problems." This outlook he projected in flagrant displays of zaniness, colorful and unconventional costuming, and sexually magnetic dance music. Fusing the raucousness of Soul with the aggressiveness of Rock, the band operated largely as an underground group, with such albums as *Free Your Mind . . . And Your Ass Will Follow* and *Maggot Brain*.

Later, William Bootsy Collins, a Cincinnati, Ohio, associate of Clinton's, formed the Pacemakers, a quartet that functioned as the back-up band at Cincinnati's King Records for such artists as Arthur Prysock and Hank Ballard (b. 1936). When James Brown, also a King artist, fired his own band, the Pacemakers took over as Brown's Famous Flames from 1969 to 1971. On leaving Brown, they functioned as the House Guests and collaborated with Clinton's Funkadelics during 1972–1973 on *America Eats Its Young, Cosmic Slop,* and *Standing on the Verge of Getting It On.*

Operating under the umbrella of P-Funk, and appearing generally in space-age costumes, Clinton and Collins spawned a spate of groups, including the Brides of Funkenstein, Horny Horn, Bootsy's Rubber Band, and Parliament/Funkadelic; and a series of strange characters, including Sir Nosi D'Voidoffunk (a baddie), Bootzilla (an aggressive cat), and Casper (a peace-loving fellow, modeled on the cartoon character).

It was not until 1978 that Funkadelic surfaced with *One Nation Under a Groove,* the title also of a Gold single. This was followed in 1979 by the Funkadelic album *Uncle Jam Wants You,* plastered with the slogan, "Rescue Dance Music from the Blahs" and spattered with cartoons and minuscule messages, with a dancing Uncle Jam and the Funk hand-sign featured on the back cover.

Parliament/Funkadelic enjoyed the distinction of presenting the last live show at the famous Apollo Theater in Harlem, which closed in March 1980 after serving the Harlem community and the world of entertainment for almost half a century. "George Clinton bypassed Madison Square Garden," Ted Fox wrote, "to help keep the Apollo going. Clinton and P-Funk were here in the ghettos of America, the leading proprietors of the wild style and loose philosophy known as Funk. Their shows were spectacles of abandon perfectly in keeping with the theater's great tradition."[3] By way of closing his history of Apollo's existence from 1934 into 1980, Fox uses the Funk slogan, "One Nation, United, under Groove" as his concluding theme.

"As the band launched into its anthem, "One Nation, United, under Groove," Fox writes, "the audience stood. Everyone sang along and stomped their feet. Hands folded into the funk sign punctured the air. The band stopped singing, but the audience continued: 'One Nation, United, under Groove!' Suddenly, two smudge pots on stage exploded in a flash. Pow! Pow!"[4]

The rise in 1978 of Rick James (b. 1952) was greeted by some historians as the second coming of Funk, with his dance music being described as New Wave Punk-Funk. Wearing his hair in Masai-warrior style, Rick affected an aggressiveness and a degree of eccentricity, outrage, and eroticism that opened the door to the later excesses of P-Funk and other late funksters such as Grandmaster Flash & the Furious Five, and the spectacular Prince.

After a boyhood in Buffalo that involved strange antics and having gone AWOL from the Navy Reserves—for which he later served a year in detention—James Johnson settled in Canada. Sharing an apartment with Neil Young, he formed an R & B oriented band, the Mynah Birds, which included in addition to Young, Bruno Palmer (later with Young of the legendary Buffalo Springfield) and Goldie McJohn (later of Steppenwolf). After a nonproductive songwriter stint with Motown, whose executives persuaded him to accept detention for his Navy outing, and a tour of London, the formation of a Blues band, Main Line, brought him back to his native Buffalo and the Motown fold.

It was at this point that the popularity of George Clinton prompted him to assay a funkier approach than Funkadelic/Parliament. The result was 1978's hit single, "You and I," from the album *Come Get It!* a powerhouse, flamboyant brand of Punk-Funk that led to Rick's being named Top New Male R & B Singer of 1979 by two trade papers, *Cash Box* and *Record World*. His second best-selling album, *Bustin' Out of L Seven*, was followed by a provocative, capacity-crowd tour involving his Stone City Band and the Punk Funk Chorus.

Having scored with *Fire It Up*, in 1979 he produced the debut album *(Wild and Peaceful)* of Teena Marie, a petite blonde California singer with whom he continues to be associated; and the following year he produced the debut album *(In 'n' Out)* of his Stone City Band. Rick's own fifth album, *Street Songs* (1981), a Funk classic that sold over 3 million to go double-platinum, yielded two hit singles, the erotic "Give It to Me Baby" and "Super Freak." Not long afterward, Rick James confessed to *Rolling Stone* that keeping up with his flamboyant, erotic, funky image was destroying him. By then he was crossing swords in the press with MTV for its racist exclusion of video cassettes by black artists and with Prince, whose mounting funky popularity had become a challenge.

In the 1980s Funk underwent a change as a result of the new recording and sound-generating technology increasingly used by artists such as Prince, Marvin Gaye, Sweet Pea Atkinson, Chaka Khan, and by groups trying to ride Prince's resplendent coattails, including Instant Funk, Shalamar, and Midnight Star. Computerized electronic drums, polyphonic synthesizers, and sophisticated sequencers heightened the rhythmic drive and thunder of Funk.

As Teena Marie's record career was energized by Rick James, Chaka Khan's musicianship developed with Rufus from 1972, when she became lead singer at the age of 18, until she stepped forth on her own in 1978. During her association with the group that began as American Breed, three albums, *Rags to Rufus* (an R & B Grammy winner in 1974), *Rufusized,* and *Rufus featuring Chaka Khan,* were expressive of a brand of Funk that added Jazz overtones to the frothy fusion of R & B and Rock. All three albums became certified Gold albums, with the last mentioned, which contained "Jive Talking," going Platinum. (Christened Yvette Marie Stevens, Chaka Khan grew up in Chicago treasuring records by Dizzy Gillespie, Charlie Parker, and Sarah Vaughan.)

By 1984 when Chaka Khan reached a peak in her solo career with the Top Three single, "I Feel for You," written and originally recorded by Prince, her inventiveness led to her being typed the Thomas Edison of Funk. At this time, Ray Parker, Jr. (b. 1954), who was concerned with women as political victims of the sexual revolution in *Women Out of Control* and who was a "hook"-conscious craftsman of Funk Rock, was dubbed the Phil Donahue of Funk.[5] As part of Raydio, Parker had touched the theme initially in the platinum single of 1981, "A Woman Needs Love (Just Like You and I)."

No survey of Funk would be complete without consideration of the Isley Brothers, a family group out of Cincinnati, Ohio, who scored their first hit in 1962—their "Twist and Shout" was covered by the Beatles in an early album—and whose productivity has continued through associations with different labels and changes in the music scene up into the 1980s. When producer/songwriters Holland, Dozier, and Holland—with whom they worked in the mid-1960s—left the Motown complex, the brothers, Ronald (b. 1941), Rudolph (b. 1939), and O'Kelly (b. 1937), backed by three other family members—Ernest arranges, Marvin plays bass and Chris piano—founded their own T-Neck label. It happened shortly after James Brown electrified black popular music with his "Cold Sweat" brand of Funk—and the brothers took fire from it, scoring a Gold Record with "It's Your Thing" in 1969. "It's Your Thing" also brought a Grammy award for the Best R & B Vocal by a Group. During the 1970s, pursuing a funky route, the brothers earned two more Gold Records: for "That Lady" from the album *3 × 3* in 1973 and for "The Heat Is On" from *Fight the Power* in 1975, which eventually sold Platinum.

The title of the last-mentioned album suggests that the Isley Brothers, not unlike James Brown, Nina Simone, Temptations, and other black artists, reacted to the rising tide of black nationalism in their songs. They also began using synthesizers and the new technological equipment, employing the electronics to enhance their Funk.

In the 1980s and not long before he was tragically shot to death by his father, Marvin Gaye created the album *Midnight Love,* achieving a Top Ten/Gold Record in the erotic single, "Sexual Healing." The only musicians on the funky disk were Gaye and guitarist Gordon Banks. The vocal harmonies were produced by a procedure of recording layer on layer, as were the keyboard, synthesizer, and percussion sounds.

A similar process was involved in the synth-funk recordings made by Prince (b. 1962), of Minneapolis, who was widely hailed as the *wunderkind* of Funk for his *1999* album. Prince not only sang all the vocal parts but himself layered guitars, keyboards, bass, and drum on the disk. Using abrasive guitar riffs reminiscent of Jimi Hendrix (whose erotic manipulation of the instrument he imitated and advanced) and dancing orgiastically as James Brown once did, Prince was an overpowering sexual personality as a performer. In the lyrics of his songs ("Little Red Corvette," "Delirious," and the *Dirty Mind* album of 1980, among others), and in concert appearances (employing a brass bed and performing in bikini underwear and women's stockings), he projected a degree of explicit sex that was outrageous Funk.

In 1984, when Michael Jackson took the music scene by storm, drawing media coverage approximating that given the Beatles and Elvis, Prince was close behind the young new King of Rock in the ascension to the throne. As an album, *Purple Rain,* on which Prince recorded for the first time with a band (Revolution), went to the top of the charts for an extended stay, delivering a No. 1 hit single in the semiautobiographical "When Doves Cry." As a film that likewise involved autobiographical material—it was based on Prince's outline—*Purple Rain* was termed the *Citizen Kane* of Rock movies and applauded as better than Presley's *Jailhouse Rock* of the 1950s and the Beatles' *A Hard Day's Night* of the 1960s.[6] *The New Yorker*'s Pauline Kael called it "a landmark . . . the black crossover movie that many of us expected a decade ago when Diana Ross appeared in *Lady Sings the Blues* and showed the kind of talent that made her seem a natural to attract both black and white audiences. . . ."[7] Heading his article with a play on words, "The New Prince of Hollywood," *Newsweek*'s film critic concluded: "Prince is one of a handful of performers who've restored the urgency and danger—and the beat—to the rock scene. And *Purple Rain* gets that excitement on the screen."[8]

Prince and Michael Jackson, and Chaka Khan on the female side, were to Funk what Presley had once been to Rockabilly—the flowering, the acme of the style. Although other solo singers participated in the Funk movement—notably Wilson Pickett, Arthur Conley, Rick James—Funk is basically an instrumental dance style. What Heavy Metal is to Rock, Funk is to R & B—a dance music compounded of hypnotically repeated rhythm riffs, grinding guitars, thunderous drumming, and roaring bass lines, all designed to achieve a high degree of sensuality and danceability. Operating on that base, the solo singers produced a raw, heated, propulsive, sexually energetic music.

"Stir It Up" (Reggae)

In 1982, on a visit to the South Rim of the Grand Canyon, I took a burro ride down to the bottom of the Canyon. When the guide learned that I wrote books on contemporary popular music, he took me into the town café of Supai, where 400 Havasupai Indians dwell. There on the wall of the rural café, next to a Bible calendar and frayed pictures of tribesmen in loincloths, was a photograph of a "dreadlocked" Rastafarian. It bore the inscription, "I love Supai Rastafarians," and it was signed by Tyrone Downie, a Jamaican musician who had been a member of the band of Bob Marley (1945–1981), the legendary Father of Reggae music. I learned that early in 1982, Downie and the mother of Marley, Cedella Booker, had flown by helicopter into Supai and given a concert, and that when Marley died of cancer at the age of 36, in May 1981, his death had been mourned in Supai over a two-week period. The concert there had been arranged by Chris Blackwell of Island Records, a major Reggae recording label, who had discovered the Supai interest in Marley's music when he was in a Las Vegas record shop and spotted Havasupai Indians buying Bob Marley disks.

It was a startling and intriguing idea—Indians living on the floor of the Grand Canyon venerating the Jamaican proponent of Reggae music. It was a fact given further confirmation when, on a later visit to Phoenix, where Havasupai high-school youngsters attend the Phoenix Indian School, I found an issue of *The Arizona Republic* containing a long article with large pictures and headlined: "Spirit of Reggae Thrives at Bottom of Grand Canyon."[9] It indicated that Reggae records were played extensively not only in Supai huts but by Indians in the neighboring Grand Canyon village of Peach Springs, and that picture posters of Marley were to be found in the huts of many of the Indians and in the rooms of young Indians living in the dormitory of the Phoenix Indian School.

Unquestionably, the initial appeal of Reggae to the Havasupai was its sound and beat. But the Indians also found parallels between their oppressive and deprived lives and those of the black Jamaicans among whom Rastafarianism developed as a socio-political religion. The religion had its roots in the black-nationalist ideas of Marcus Garvey (1887–1940), the Jamaican who attracted a huge following among American blacks in the 1920s with his Universal Negro Improvement Association and back-to-Africa movement. Garvey had prophesied that a great black leader would come out of Africa to free Jamaicans from white domination. When an Ethiopian baron, Ras Tafari, was crowned Emperor Haile Selassie in 1930, black Jamaicans believed Garvey's prophecy had been fulfilled. They began to venerate Ras Tafari as a God and their Redeemer. Babylon became a symbol of the white man's world of exploitation and discrimination, while Africa loomed as their "Father's home."[10] The Rastafarians did not believe in combing or cutting their hair, their dreadlocks ostensibly serving as antennae to the spiritual world, which could be approached through smoking spliffs, or ganja, as marijuana is known in Jamaica. They rejected anything that was not "I-tal"—in Rasta, "pure" or "natural"—including alcohol, tobacco, meat, and salt. Extensive unemployment, depressed states of mind, and resentment of whites—all had their parallels in the lives of the Havasupai, who were ready to embrace Jah, the Rastafari God of Love, as theirs. These tenets are presented by Marley in such albums as *Burnin'* (1973) and *Exodus* (1977).

The origin of the word *Reggae,* like that of the word Jazz, is shrouded in mystery. Hux Brown, the Jamaican guitarist who devised the one-string-quiver trill that opens Paul Simon's Reggae-inflected disk "Mother and Child Reunion," has said: "It's a description of the beat itself," and adds inconclusively: "It's just a fun, joke kinda word that means the ragged rhythm and the body feeling."[11] Another explanation is that it is a bastardization of a Kingston street word for prostitute, *streggae.* A more remote and, probably, unlikely source is Regga, the name of a Bantu-speaking Tanganyikan tribe.

The first appearance of the word *Regga* on a record occurred in 1968, on the Mytals' disk of "Do the Reggay." The following year, Desmond Dekker's "Israelites" and his "It Mek"—"That's why" in West Indian parlance—made their appearance on American record charts. By then Reggae had evolved as a musical style from two earlier related sounds, Ska and Rock Steady. The word *ska* is said to come from *skat,* an onomatopoetic simulation of the scratching guitar sound made on Ska disks. Ska was presumably developed by Jamaican musicians as a result of listening to and trying to play Rhythm and Blues, which they heard on records broadcast by radio stations in Miami and New Orleans. The Ska sound, as it developed during the middle and late 1950s, at just about the time that Rock 'n'

Roll was emerging from R & B in the United States, used mainly horns, adapted Jazz riffs, and was played in a chug-a-lug tempo.

In England, with its West Indian exiles, Ska was performed by one of Britain's noted R & B artists, Georgie Fame (b. 1943), and his Blue Flames at the well-known Flamingo Club in London in the early 1960s. By 1964 American charts listed "My Boy Lollipop," a Ska novelty, as a hit for Millie Small, on whose recording hoarse-voiced Rod Stewart played harmonica.

Ska was superseded in Jamaica by the style identified as Rock Steady or Rub-a-Dub, which was rooted in American Soul music, as Ska was derived from American R & B. Under the influence of James Brown, Ska's chug-a-lug tempo became upbeat, and the sound of electric instruments and guitars superseded the horns of Ska. By 1966, Alton Ellis had set the pattern with a recording, which he called "Rock Steady."

Robert Nesta Marley, who became the reigning king of Reggae as well as a mythic figure during his abbreviated lifetime, recorded his first disk, a solo version of his song "Judge Not (Unless You Judge Yourself)," in 1961. A poor country boy, the son of a British army captain and a young Jamaican girl, who ran a grocery store and wrote and sang Spirituals, he had grown up in Trench Town, dreaming of hearing his voice on a jukebox. In 1963 he formed the Wailers with two boyhood friends, Neville O'Riley Livingston, who called himself Bunny Wailer and played bongos and conga, and Winston Hubert McIntosh, who played piano, organ, and guitar, and who became known as Peter Tosh — each of whom went his own way in 1974 and 1975 respectively.

In 1964 as "Judge Not" was released in England, the Wailers enjoyed their first modest hit in "Simmer Down," a romantic admonition to the rude boys (teenage hoodlums), who were terrorizing Jamaica in the mid-1960s in a parallel to America's Hell's Angels biker gangs. In charting the development of the Wailers, Timothy White describes 1964–1966 as their Ska period, with producer Clement Dodd; 1966–1967 as their Rock Steady years, with Leslie Kong as producer on the Beverly label; and 1967–1970 as the years under Lee Perry, when the group came into its own. In 1972 Marley became associated with the Island label of Chris Blackwell, a white Jamaican related to the Blackwell cannery family, who produced his first internationally distributed LP in *Catch a Fire* (1973).

By then, Marley, angered by the exploitative practices of Jamaican record companies and alienated by the materialistic values of the United States, where he spent some time in the late sixties, working on a Chrysler assembly line, had returned to Jamaica and become a Rastafarian. Included in the first Wailers' recordings for Blackwell's labels were tendentious songs of rage and fury, such as "Burnin' and Lootin'." The titles of later albums, including *Exodus* (1977), *Uprising* (1980), and *Confrontation* (1983), and such singles as "Get Up Stand Up" (in *Burnin'*) and "People Get Ready," suggest Marley's constant concern with the plight of the poor people of Jamaica. The songs of social protest were sometimes cited to explain Marley's limited exposure on American radio—even though he averred: "We're not talking about burning and looting for material things. We only want to burn capitalistic *illusions.*"

Thus, it was not through Marley but largely through a film, *The Harder They Come,* that Reggae received its first important exposure in the United States and in many other parts of the world. Jimmy Cliff, star of the film, played a black Jamaican rebel/singer at odds with the police, who hunt him down in a terminal chase through the black ghetto of Kingston. For a time, it appeared that Cliff might achieve the legendary recognition conferred upon Marley. *I Am the Living,* involving the production skills of Luther Dixon, largely responsible for the Shirelles and other American black artists, was released by MCA Records in 1980, and *Jimmy Cliff Special* was a CBS release in 1982. But Cliff's disks, except for a 1969 single ("Wonderful World, Beautiful People"), did not make the charts; neither did Marley's or Peter Tosh's records. It was disks by adapters, American and British, white and black, through whom Reggae reached American ears.

In 1975, when Marley performed at the Roxy, in Los Angeles, with his dreadlocks swirling around him, his in-person appeal and the impact of the trancelike music were apparent. Recognized by critics as a giant, despite limited sales, he was saluted as an innovator whose influence exceeded his impact. His artistry gained mythic status late in 1976 when seven gunmen stormed into his Kingston compound with automatic rifles and spattered his home with bullets, wounding his wife, his manager, a reporter, and Marley himself. Nevertheless, after treatment at a hospital, Marley performed at the *Smile Jamaica* concert, for which he had been rehearsing when the assassination attempt was made.

Perhaps the high point of Marley's reign as Reggae King came in 1978, when he made a triumphal appearance at New York's Madison Square Garden. It occurred at about the same time that he received a citation at the United Nations in behalf of the Third World nations. In *Playboy* magazine's annual readers' poll of 1980, he was acclaimed as Best Composer, just behind Stevie Wonder and Smokey Robinson. In the Best Group category, he placed fourth, behind the Blues Brothers, Earth, Wind & Fire, and the Commodores. Those attending the ceremony when Rhodesia became the independent nation, Zimbabwe, heard Bob Marley's name cited immediately after the British flag was lowered.

Black radio stations in the United States have been as little receptive to authentic Reggae as the Rock stations. Many reasons have been adduced for this rejection: Reggae's not easily understood patois; the social and political protest that underlies Marley's work and characterizes him as a revolutionary; his denunciation of colonialism, which has, in fact, made him so attractive to the Third World nations.

For his funeral in Kingston, 12,000 people filled the National Arena and heard a eulogy by the prime minister, who announced that a park would be set aside for Marley and other national heroes. Attendees included the governor-general of Jamaica, the former prime minister, a daughter of the president of Gabon, and American rock singer Roberta Flack.

Since his death in 1981, no one has emerged to fill Marley's position of Reggae leadership. The two major Jamaican contenders are Jimmy Cliff and Peter Tosh. The latter, who was a cofounder of the Wailers but left to pursue a solo career in 1975, belongs to the more radical wing of the Rastafarians. Disagreeing musically and politically with Marley, he has said: "I am a musical messenger . . . and I want to educate people through music."[12] Shortly after he left the Wailers, Tosh achieved a top-selling single in Jamaica with "Legalize It," a paean to the healing powers of ganja. In 1978 at the Kingston One Love Concert, he attacked both the prime minister and his leading opponent for unfulfilled campaign promises to correct the evils of the "shitstem." Some months later, he was brutally mishandled by the Jamaican police. Although Tosh has been befriended by Mick Jagger and Keith Richard of the famous Rolling Stones and signed to their record label, his disks have remained in-group favorites.

The White Synthesis

The musical world outside of Jamaica first became involved with Reggae in the early 1970s. Apart from Johnny Nash of Texas and Eric Clapton of Great Britain, who recorded Bob Marley songs, other adapters bypassed Reggae's Rastafarian ideology and worked with the style as an engaging sound. It was through these American and British artists, not really through Marley or his Jamaican associates, that Reggae became known and attractive to non-Jamaican record-buyers.

The first Reggae-inflected song and record to make American charts was Paul Simon's "Mother and Child Reunion," in February 1972. It was rhythmically closer to the authentic Reggae sound than many of the white adaptations that followed, perhaps because Simon used a Jamaican rhythm group on his disk. The charts of 1972 also included the Reggae-influenced "I'll Take You There" of the Staple Singers and, toward the end of the year, Johnny Nash's "I Can See Clearly Now," both of which became No. 1 singles.

If any one record must be chosen as the wellspring of Reggae in England and the United States, it would be "I Can See Clearly Now." It passed the million mark in sales, became the title of a best-selling album, established Johnny Nash nationally, and brought a polished version of the Jamaican sound to the ears of a wide audience. For Nash, his renown in 1972 was in the nature of a revival. Born in Houston, Texas, in 1940, and a singer of Baptist Gospel songs in his youth, he had been a regular on the celebrated radio and TV shows of Arthur Godfrey for seven years, from the age of 16. Although he enjoyed album releases during the 1960s and was active with his own record label (Joda), his new prominence on the national music scene was the result of "I Can See Clearly Now."

The song was the first of a group of Reggae songs that he recorded between 1972 and 1975—and appropriately so, since his parents came from Jamaica, where he made contact with both the music and Bob Marley on visits. In 1973 his version of Marley's "Stir It Up" made singles charts, though not as successfully as the "Clearly" number. (As an expression, "stir it up" appears to have been the Jamaican equivalent of Presley's "all shook up" and Sam Cooke's "you send me"). Other Marley songs recorded by Nash, with only a hint of patois pronunciation and a more musical sound, included "Guava Jelly" in 1972 and "Mellow Mood," "Rock It Baby," and "Reggae on Broadway," all in 1975.

Among artists who came to know Reggae through Nash, Paul McCartney, who heard the performer in New York's Bitter End in the 1970s, told a reporter that the sound might start a new trend, and added: "Reggae's the whole R & B beat turned around. That's what Reggae's all about. They've turned the R & B beat on its back."[13] McCartney experimented with the sound in *Wild Life,* an album by Wings, his post-Beatles group.

In 1974 another Bob Marley song, "I Shot the Sheriff," became No. 1 on American charts, this in a catchy version by British guitarist Eric Clapton, formerly of the Yardbirds, a pioneer Rock 'n' Roll group, and Cream. That year, Stevie Wonder produced "Boogie on Reggae Woman," employing synthesizers so extensively that the delicate West Indian flavor of the music was lost. Six years later, in

1980, Stevie paid tribute to Tuff Gong of the Kingston recording studio with his "Master Blaster (Jammin')," a free, Top Five adaptation of Bob Marley's "Jamming" in the *Exodus* album of 1977. In 1981 Wonder appeared at Jamaica's annual Reggae Sunsplash festival, performing with Third World, a Jamaican Reggae group for whom he co-wrote "Try Jah Love."

Among million-copy singles that trade on the Reggae sound, there are "Why Can't We Be Friends?" (1975), by War; "Hotel California" (1977), by the Eagles; and "The Tide Is High" (1980), whose sound and rhythm are clearly modeled on Marley's and Nash's "Stir It Up," by Blondie. Other recorded adaptations of Reggae include "Watching the Detectives," by Elvis Costello; "Movin' On," by Taj Mahal; "Protection," by Graham Parker; "Police and Thieves," by Clash; "Dreadlock Holiday," by 10cc; as well as selections in Led Zeppelin's *Houses of the Holy,* Johnny Rivers's *L.A. Reggae,* and Grace Jones's *Warm Leatherette* and *Nightclubbing.*

Reggae figured extensively in the rise of the blond, British, male trio known as the Police. Their first two albums, *Outlandos d'Amour* and *Reggatta de Blanc* were described as offering "leadsinger Sting's patois-laden words of demi-isolation set atop their own brand of New Wave reggae: dubby bass, phased guitar and explosive percussion."[14] *Zenyatta Mondatta* (1981), their first platinum album in the United States and the record that gave them international status, included "Don't Stand So Close to Me," a superlative use of Reggae that sent the single into the Top Ten. However, by the time they produced their fifth album, *Synchronicity,* in 1983, they "got rid of all that reggae stuff," according to drummer Stewart Copeland, "that middle America couldn't handle."[15]

In the 1983 *Rolling Stones* Music Awards, the Police walked off with four first-place awards: Band of the Year; Album of the Year, *Synchronicity;* Single of the Year, "Every Breath You Take"; and Songwriter of the Year, Sting. The awards included as a separate category, Reggae Artist, indicative of the continued presence of the trend. The winner was Eddy Grant, and the runner-ups UB40 and Bunny Wailer. But none had as yet produced a chart disk, suggesting that Reggae was still, after a dozen years, an in-group phenomenon.

The Oreo Singers (Black Pop)

The term *Oreo singer* has a pejorative overtone. To be black on the outside and white on the inside, like the tasty cookie, connotes a "conflict of interests," a sense of reneging on one's true color. By this time in our cultural history, we have really moved beyond this simplistic concept. Although the great Ray Charles was criticized by purists when he began singing and recording white Country songs, it was clear that he was as expressive and heartfelt an interpreter of a Country ballad like "I Can't Stop Loving You" as he was of such Soul songs as "What'd I Say" or "Hallujah, I Love Her So." Unquestionably he was addressing himself to a different audience than the one who bought his Gospel/R & B ballad, "This Little Girl of Mine." Other black singers have been condemned for directing their creativity toward white audiences and for singing and recording white repertoire.

Lou Rawls called the dingy clubs, noisy bars, and ill-paying lounges with out-of-tune pianos that a black artist had to play at the start of a career, the "chitlin' circuit." Is there any reason why a black artist should be chided for preferring the Copa or a major showroom on the Las Vegas strip? Or preferring to make a disk that crosses over and becomes a Gold or Platinum Record? The crux of the problem is not just a matter of audience, repertoire, or sales, but of honesty, being true to one's artistic instincts, making a given song a genuine expression of one's self—and that self, we have learned, can have a number of sides.

The sound of popular music in America until the advent of Rock 'n' Roll was forged by three black singers—Ethel Waters, Louis Armstrong, and Billie Holiday. All three are regarded as Jazz and Blues singers, but all three sang the Pop songs of their day.

It was Billie Holiday who said of Armstrong: "Pops Toms from the heart," a reference to his acceptance as a popular entertainer. But Billie cut to the heart of the problem. Armstrong genuinely felt what he sang. When he scored a hit with "Mack the Knife" from *Threepenny Opera* in 1956, and knocked the Beatles out of the No. 1 spot on pop charts with his version of "Hello Dolly" in 1964, his renditions were not concessions to the market but his interpretation of the songs.

To some listeners, Armstrong's achievement as a Pop singer may have come as a surprise, considering his acknowledged stature as the first great Jazz improviser on trumpet. But the fact is that in the years when he was making himself immortal with the Chicago recordings of his Hot Five and Hot Seven, he was also singing and recording such Pop songs and standards as "Star Dust," "Ain't Misbehavin'," "I've Got the World on a String," "The Music Goes 'Round and Around," and "Blueberry Hill"—singing in his unique gravel-voiced baritone with an expressiveness that prompted a recent biographer to call him "without question the finest jazz singer who ever existed."[16] But he also sang with a melodious clarity and perceptive phrasing that gave him access to the mainstream Pop market, favoring songwriters such as Hoagy Carmichael, Harold Arlen, and other contemporaries.

Ethel Waters, born illegitimately to a 12-year-old girl, began recording at about the same time as Armstrong, in the 1920s. Although she early assayed the Blues on Black Swan, the first black-owned record label in the United States, appearances in vaudeville and Broadway musicals, black at first and then mainstream (like Irving Berlin's *As Thousands Cheer*), moved her in a Pop direction. This was set even before she starred in the Berlin Broadway show when she made a hit of "Dinah" in 1925—later the theme of the *Dinah Shore TV Show*—in her first major nightclub appearance at the Paradise Club on Broadway. At the Cotton Club in 1933, she launched "Stormy Weather" as a standard. Her command of the Pop idiom embraced recordings of sophisticated songs, including Cole Porter's "Miss Otis Regrets." Historian/critic Henry Pleasants assesses her influence in the following terms: "In just about every popular singer who came after her, one hears a bit of Ethel Waters."[17]

With Billie Holiday, who did her best singing in the 1930s and early 1940s, Pop singing became an art, and through her influence, especially on Frank Sinatra, she exercised the ultimate power in shaping popular music. Because of her individual handling of songs, she also rates, like Armstrong, as one of the all-time great Jazz vocalists. She called her autobiography, *Lady Sings the Blues;* but the title had more to do with her unhappy, sordid, and tragic life than with the songs she sang. Her repertoire consisted almost entirely of Pop material, Tin Pan Alley ballads, and show tunes. But she sang them with a depth of feeling and personalized them to such a degree that she forever altered the tenor of popular singing. Quite naturally, she was the master of "torch songs," ballads of unrequited love like "Body and Soul," "I Can't Get Started," "Lover Man," and "Some Other Spring." With a thin voice of limited range but one that was a most affecting combination of sweetness and bitterness, she gave a bluesy cast to everything she sang, imparting to Tin Pan Alley songs an emotional depth they seldom had possessed on the printed page. "With few exceptions," Frank Sinatra said, "every major pop singer in the United States during her generation has been touched in some way by her genius."[18]

In his heyday, Billy Daniels (b. circa 1916) was as much a media sensation as any of the more sexy singers of the 1970s and 1980s. It was body language as well as a horny, high-pitched voice that spoke to a generation of girls and ladies in the nightclubs of the late 1930s and the 1940s. Born in Jacksonville, Florida, Billy went to school in

Harlem, where he lived with his grandmother. A star-struck youngster, he admittedly spent much time hanging around Harlem theaters and clubs in the hope of meeting the big black entertainers of the day — Bill Robinson, Ethel Waters, Eubie Blake, Fletcher Henderson, Duke Ellington, and others. Although he wrote his father that he was attending high school, he quit to work as a waiter at Dickie Wells, then the Hotcha club, and, finally, Ubangi, where, as a dancer and production singer, he really got his start as an entertainer. A stint as band vocalist with Erskine Hawkins (b. 1914) led to a singing job, first at the Black Cat, and then at Ernie's in Greenwich Village.

The year was 1936, memorable to him because that was the year that 52nd St. suddenly came alive, with everybody talking about the Onyx, Famous Door, Hickory House, and other clubs. It was on that street that recognition came to Daniels, as it did to a host of black singers and jazzmen — Billie Holiday, pianist Art Tatum, saxist Coleman Hawkins, pianist Errol Garner, pianist/comic/songwriter Fats Waller, fiddlers Stuff Smith and Eddie South, and the Count Basie Band, among others.

A brief sojourn at the Club 18 led to Kelly's Stable, then still on 51st St., and to Mammy's Chicken Koop, the two clubs that became Daniels's 52nd St. venues, although he also played the Yacht Club, Spotlite, Tondelayo's, and Three Deuces. However, it was at the Ebony, on Broadway between 53rd and 54th Sts., later renowned as Birdland, that Daniels first performed the song with which he became irrevocably associated, Johnny Mercer and Harold Arlen's "That Old Black Magic," a song that he recorded at least twice on the Mercury label. A visit by Walter Winchell, famed columnist of the day, led to a write-up in which Daniels was described as "the sexiest singer of the day."[19]

Other songs that became part of Daniels's métier included "Symphony," a French ballad, which he introduced at the Three Deuces, and "Intermezzo," originally a violin solo, which he sang with Stuff Smith (1909–1967) at the Stable and, later, with famed Eddie South (1904–1962), the Dark Angel of the Violin, at the Riviera, on the banks of the Hudson, high up on the Palisades.

Daniels began recording before his longtime association with Mercury, when Leonard Joy of Victor-Bluebird came into the Stable, and persuaded him to record "Diane" and "Penthouse Serenade," two other songs in his repertoire. The 1930s and 1940s were a period in popular music when club performances were to an artist's rise what charts became after the 1960s and when records frequently were made as a result of talked-about club performances. That was how tenor-saxist Coleman Hawkins came to record his famous Jazz version of "Body and Soul," the torch ballad that he generally played in the wee hours of the morning at the Stable. Leonard Joy was once again the record-man who heard about it, came to the club, and persuaded the Hawk to cut it in 1939.

"Things started moving for me," Daniels later said,

> after I played the Savannah Club down in the Village. The excitement sent me to the Park Avenue at 52nd St. & Park Avenue, one of the best clubs in the city, with a decor by Joseph Urban. From the Park Avenue to Cafe Society Downtown, to the Riviera, the Copa, back to the Riviera, the Copa again—and boom! I was off like a rocket. Played all over the world, made five pictures for Columbia, and Old Black Magic for Universal.[20]

Apart from appearances on TV and on the Las Vegas strip in the 1970s, Daniels's last major engagement was in the Broadway musical *Golden Boy*, starring Sammy Davis, Jr.

The first black male singers to ascend to the topmost rungs of popular music were Billy Eckstine and Nat "King" Cole. Like the three seminal figures—Satchmo, Mama Stringbean, and Lady Day—Cole began his career in Jazz. In fact, his achievement as a Jazz pianist was so notable that Jazz critics lamented his defection to Popular music when, after establishing the Nat "King" Cole Trio on radio, in clubs, and in films, and producing such song hits as his own "Straighten Up and Fly Right," he began making Pop records. "Nature Boy" launched an impressive career in 1948 that involved a succession of million-copy hits: "Mona Lisa," the Academy Award song of 1950; "Answer Me, My Love" (1954); "A Blossom Fell" (1955); and "Ramblin' Rose" (1962). The last-mentioned became the title of an album, which remained on best-seller charts for a record-breaking 162 weeks. Possessed of a baritone of heady loveliness, Cole phrased and articulated with a graphic clarity that made him sought after by songwriters whose lyrics approached poetry.

Handsome William Clarence Eckstine (b. 1914) began his professional career as a vocalist with the band of Earl Hines, singing and recording with the famed Jazz pianist's combo from 1939 to 1943. When he turned solo Pop singer in 1947, it was cause for lamentation among Jazz aficionados, for in 1944 he formed (with the aide of saxist Budd Johnson [1910–1984]) and fronted a big band that included an incredibly large array of outstanding jazzmen—altoist Charlie "Bird" Parker, drummer Art Blakey, and trumpeters Fats Navarro, Howard McGhee, Miles Davis, and Dizzy Gillespie, among others, with Sarah Vaughan as vocalist. It was the first big Bop band, and it left a permanent mark on Jazz history.

But after three years of one-nighters, changes in personnel, and financial stringencies, the band folded. That year (1947), Eckstine, who had sung and played trombone in the band, produced his first Pop hit as a solo singer of "Everything I Have Is Yours." His echoing baritone, enhanced by a sometimes too-pronounced vibrato, accounted for a series of million-copy hits: Rodgers & Hart's "Blue Moon" (1948); Duke Ellington and Juan Tizol's "Caravan" (1949); Victor Young's "My Foolish Heart," from the film of the same name (1950); and "I Apologize" (1951), a revival of the 1931 Bing Crosby hit. Eckstine's popularity was so great that he became recognized as "Mr. B" in a period when superstar Perry Como was known simply as "Mr. C."

Although neither Sarah Vaughan nor Ella Fitzgerald has ever lost her standing among this century's great Jazz singers, both have at times worked with Pop material and Pop arrangements. Ella's foray in Pop was of the briefest. In 1938, while she was still singing with the Chick Webb Band, which she joined in 1934 and whose leadership she assumed on Webb's death in 1939, she recorded an adaptation of the old nursery rhyme, "A-Tisket, A-Tasket." It took off in the Pop market and sold steadily into and after 1944, when Ella scored her second million-copy hit. "Into Each Life Some Rain Must Fall" was a collaboration with the Ink Spots, for whom it became their first Gold Record. By then she was widely recognized as the First Lady of Song.

One of the most rewarding periods of his distinguished career came in the 1950s, when her association with Jazz at the Philharmonic led to her making for its producer, Norman Granz, a series of *Songbooks,* as they were called. These were in the nature of comprehensive anthologies, sometimes involving as many as five LPs, of the songs of Cole Porter, Rodgers & Hart, Gershwin, and Harold Arlen. They were basically the work of a Jazz singer—not a Pop singer—for Ella's concern with the music was so great that the sense of the brilliant show lyrics was frequently sacrificed to melodic Jazz improvisations.

Sarah Vaughan's involvement with the Pop market came in the period (1954–1959) when she was recording for Mercury under A & R chieftains Hugo & Luigi. Songs were written or selected for her that exploited a certain little-girl coyness in her voice. The titles are indicative: "Make Yourself Comfortable" (1954); "Whatever Lola Wants (Lola Gets)" from the Broadway show *Damn Yankees* (1955); "Experience Unnecessary" (1955); "C'est La Vie" (1955). Suggestive and sophisticated without being sexy, all of these went into the Top Twenty on Pop charts, climaxed by "Broken-Hearted Melody," which made the Top Ten. The last-mentioned was backed with Errol Garner's classic "Misty." None of these was without embellishments, timbral changes, rhythmic alterations, and showy melodic leaps that were and are part of the Vaughan metier qua Jazz singer. But Sassy—a nickname more appropriate for these than the Divine Sarah, her other nickname—tempered her improvisation, and the records were promoted and handled as Pop items. That they were not and are not her favorites is suggested, perhaps, by her failure, once they had run their course, to keep them in her repertoire.

Unlike a vast number of black singers whose vocal beginnings are in the church, Sammy Davis, Jr. (b. 1925), began as a vaudeville and nightclub entertainer—this at the age of two. By the time he was eight, he was an integral part of the Will Mastin Trio, a family group that included his uncle, Will Mastin, and his father, Sammy Davis, Sr. Before he became a singer, Sammy was a great mimic and impressionist, a fabulous dancer, and a virtuoso instrumentalist who played piano, bass, drums, vibraphone, and trumpet. The decision to devote himself to singing, urged upon him by Frank Sinatra, may have been the result of a car crash in which he lost an eye, in 1954.

The following year (1955) saw three Davis recordings on Pop charts: "Something's Gotta Give" from the film *Daddy Long Legs;* "Love Me or Leave Me," a revival of the Ruth Etting/*Whoopee* hit of 1928; and "That Old Black Magic," the Johnny Mercer/Harold Arlen perennial. But the song that established him as a top-notch singer was "What Kind of Fool Am I," from the Leslie Bricusse/Anthony Newley Broadway hit musical of 1962, *Stop the World—I Want to Get Off,* a show in which he later starred. He himself had already played a starring role in *Mr. Wonderful* (1956), the title song of which yielded chart recordings that year, not for him, but naturally for three ladies: Sarah Vaughan, Teddi King, and Peggy Lee. The biggest recording for Davis came in 1972 with "The Candy Man," a song by the writers of "What Kind of Fool Am I," which they wrote for the film *Willy Wonka and the Chocolate Factory.* Davis's singing style involved no concessions on his part to the tastes of white listeners. It was theatrical and declamatory, clearly a natural product of his early years as a vaudeville and nightclub entertainer.

Like Sammy Davis, Johnny Mathis's roots were in vaudeville, not as a result of his own early experiences, but through his father, a former vaudevillian, who began teaching him songs from the age of 10. But his early interest was in sports. He was an all-round athlete in high school, an outstanding high-jumper at San Francisco State College, and planned to teach physical education. Helen Noga, the wife of a local jukebox operator, changed his plans when she heard him singing in San Francisco's Black Hawk club, became his manager, and quickly secured a contract with Columbia Records for him. His first release, "Wonderful, Wonderful," in 1956, became his first giant record, together with two other million-copy disks in 1957: "Chances Are" and "It's Not for Me to Say."

Although he made his record debut at the height of the Presley–Jerry Lee Lewis–Buddy Holly frenzy and during the days when Rock 'n' Roll records were beginning to dominate Pop charts, Mathis sang old-style romantic ballads—all three of his debut songs were written by established Tin Pan Alley songwriters—[21] in a rangy, trained baritone that made a sparkling use of contrasting timbres. It was a course that he continued to pursue with notable success. Issued in 1958, *Johnny's Greatest Hits,* composed of romantic ballads—new, old, and his chart-makers—not only sold over two million copies but remained on album charts continually for a record-breaking period of 490 weeks, or nearly 10 years. Two albums, issued in 1959, *Merry Christmas* and *Heavenly,* the latter composed of film and show tunes, became Gold Records. *Heavenly* also contained a lyric version of Errol Garner's "Misty," which became a Gold single. Mathis's popularity continued through the 1960s, during which he attracted listeners to "Gina" (No. 6 in 1962) and "What Will Mary Say" (No. 9 in 1967). However, almost 15 years intervened before a Mathis single approached his earlier sales. But in 1978, more than two decades after his first hit, "Too Much, Too Little, Too Late," a duet with Deniece Williams, not only became a Gold Record, but climbed to No. 1 on Pop charts, where it remained for five solid weeks.

Unlike Sammy Davis and Johnny Mathis, Sam Cooke (1937–1964) was deeply involved in Gospel music from his early years until he scored his first Pop ballad hit, in 1957. The son of a Chicago Baptist minister, he sang with a touring church group, Highway Q C's, as a high-school student. By the early fifties, he was lead singer of a major Gospel group, Soul Stirrers, which recorded for Specialty Records of Los Angeles. His desire to turn to secular material led to his leaving the label with one of its producers and recording what became his first Pop hit, "You Send Me." Written by his brother, the ballad went to the top of Pop singles charts in the year (1957) that saw another million-copy seller in "I'll Come Running Back." The latter was released by his old label, which had allowed him to record it, together with several other R & B songs, but had then refused to release it, fearing injury to the standing of the Soul Stirrers among religious blacks.

That Specialty's fears were well grounded was demonstrated some years later. The Soul Stirrers, spotting Cooke in the audience at an anniversary concert in Chicago, invited him onstage to sing with them. As soon as the religious crowd realized who he was, they began hissing and booing, and stalled the program until he left the stage, thereby reinforcing the well-established posture among religious blacks against the mixing of spiritual and secular music. Of course, once Cooke had left the group, Specialty had no compunction about releasing an R & B ballad in its vaults to cash in on the popularity of "You Send Me."

Cooke's impact as a Pop balladeer anticipated the later acceptance of Al Green and Lionel Richie, two baritones whose voices were also tender, sensuous, and romantic. Between 1957 and 1965 —the year after he was shot and clubbed to death in a bizarre, still unexplained motel incident—Cooke racked up an extraordinary list of 29 chart-makers, 17 of which were in the Top Twenty. The most impressive of these was "Chain Gang," in 1960; "Twistin' the Night Away," which he wrote and cut at the height of the Twist craze; and "Shake," a posthumous hit that became a favorite of Otis Redding. Cooke never erased the Gospel influence of his early years from his singing, as one can hear even in a ballad such as "(I Love You) For Sentimental Reasons," where the insistent repetition of words and phrases imparts a quasi-religious intensity to the song.

Brook Benton (b. 1931) came to New York City from a South Carolina Gospel group. Baptized Benjamin Franklin Peay, he wrote songs and played small clubs, while he drove a truck or trundled a hand truck through the city's garment district. Clyde Otis, the first black A & R Director of a major label, produced his first two hits in 1959. "It's Just a Matter of Time," co-written by Otis, Benton, and arranger Belford Hendricks, was backed by "So Many Ways," and each side became a million-copy single. Benton's rich baritone, attractive in its low register, also produced a giant best seller in "The Boll Weevil Song," a rewrite by Otis and Benton of an old folk ballad. The following year (1962), Benton climbed to No. 3 on Pop charts with "Hotel Happiness." His biggest seller came in 1970, with "Rainy Night in Georgia," a moody ballad by singer/songwriter Tony Joe White. Shortly after his record debut in 1959, Benton cut two sides with Dinah Washington whose playful artlessness on disk provided an engaging foil for Benton's macho baritone. Two Top Ten hits came from the pairing: "Baby (You've Got What It Takes)" and "A Rockin' Good Way (To Mess Around and Fall in Love)."

Ray Charles, blinded by illness at 6 and orphaned at 15, is an artist of such scope that Pop is only a small phase of his capacious talent. Master of the alto sax, clarinet, organ, and piano, he first made his mark in Jazz, modeling a trio on the popular Nat Cole Trio, and securing the first sponsored TV show by a black group in Seattle. His initial recordings on Atlantic, also in a Jazz idiom, earned him the title of the Genius. The turn to Rhythm and Blues in the mid-fifties led to his pioneer work as the Father of Soul music.

Having made a controversial fusion of Blues and Gospel song with "This Little Girl [originally This Little Light] of Mine" and other Soul records, he then went on to startle the world by applying his artistry to white Country and Pop material.

In 1960, having moved from black-oriented Atlantic Records to ABC-Paramount, he recorded Hoagy Carmichael's great standard, "Georgia on My Mind." This paean to a southern state hardly sat well with many blacks. Nevertheless, his disk won two Grammy awards: Best Male Recording 1960 and Best Pop Single Performance. Returning briefly to the R & B field, he received the NARAS award for Best Rhythm and Blues Recording 1961 for Percy Mayfield's "Hit the Road, Jack." That year, he also recorded "One Mint Julep," a revival of a Rudy Toombs hit for the Clovers.

In 1962, however, he made a full-fledged foray into Country music, becoming one of the few blacks, and probably the first, to score in this area of white southern song. *Modern Sounds in Country Music,* embracing songs popularized by such country notables as Eddy Arnold, Floyd Tillman, the Everly Brothers, Don Gibson, and the legendary Hank Williams, ascended to No. 1 where it remained for 14 amazing weeks, was named a Gold Record by the RIAA, and yielded two hit singles: "You Don't Know Me," a lovely 1955 ballad by Cindy Walker and Eddy Arnold, and Don Gibson's 1957 hit, "I Can't Stop Loving You." The last-mentioned, a million-copy seller, remained at the top of Pop charts for five weeks and garnered a Grammy as Best R & B Recording 1962. "Busted," a song introduced by Johnny Cash, was named Best R & B Recording 1963 in the NARAS awards.

Through the 1960s and into the 1980s, Charles's choice of material for recording/performing ranged from a Frankie Laine hit, "That Lucky Old Sun," to a Pop waltz ballad, Guy Mitchell/Mitch Miller's "My Heart Cries for You," to such Beatles songs as "Yesterday" and the acerbic "Eleanor Rigby," to show tunes, including Rodgers & Hammerstein's "Some Enchanted Evening." Charles used his chesty, churchy voice and its mellifluous sound to create appealing versions in a style that was his natural fusion of Jazz, Country, and Gospel music.

Charley Pride, born in Sledge, Mississippi, in March 1938, became the first black singer to appear on Nashville's *Grand Ole Opry.* The year was 1967, and by then, Pride, who has no trace of the Blues in his voice, had had two singles. "I Know One" and "Just Between You and Me" in the Top Ten Country charts. Baseball, not singing, was his early interest, and he was good enough at it to pitch for the minor-league Memphis Red Sox for several seasons. A visit to Nashville and an audition before RCA producer-executive Chet Atkins

(b. 1924) brought a recording contract. Since then, apart from Ray Charles's Country recordings, he has remained the only black artist performing and recording in an authentic Country style.

In 1968 he placed two more singles and two albums on Country charts. His 1969 album, *The Best of Charley Pride,* produced by Chet Atkins and containing songs by such top contemporary country songwriters as Jack Clement, Mel Tillis, and Dallas Frazier, plus a revival of the Fred Rose/Hank Williams classic "Kaw-Liga," was declared a Gold Disk in 1970. That year he also won *Billboard* plaques for Best Male Country Vocalist and Best Country Album. His 1971 recording of "Kiss an Angel Good Mornin'" crossed the million-copy line in March 1972, bringing him a Gold Disk and songwriter Ben Peters a Grammy for Best Country Song (Songwriter Award) 1972. It has been estimated that between 1969 and 1982, Charley has had 27 No. 1 hits in the Country field. Despite his black origin in Mississippi, Country music and style seem quite natural to him.

For Lou Rawls (b. 1936), of the Windy City, as for fellow Chicagoan Sam Cooke, Gospel music was the beginning. From the age of seven, he sang in the choir of the Mount Olive Baptist Church. Later, from 1955 to 1959, he was part of the Pilgrim Travellers, a Gospel group that included Sam Cooke. A stint in the Army may have proved the turning point, for on his return to civilian life, he began singing in black clubs, first in the Midwest and then in Los Angeles, working before such difficult audiences and for so little pay that he never forgot these travails. However, it was during this harsh apprenticeship that he developed a style of soliloquizing his way into a song, which proved a unique departure on his disks. (In clubs, he found that he could use the rapidly spoken monologues to quiet noisy audiences, after which he could go into his songs.)

He did not begin recording until 1966. His first disk came out of a session in which he assembled a group of friends to react to his "chitlin'-circuit" monologue song style. The resultant album, *Lou Rawls Live,* was followed by *Soulin',* his term for the speak/singing technique, exemplified impressively in the song, "Dead End Street." His biggest single came in 1976 with "You'll Never Find Another Love Like Mine," a million-seller on Philadelphia International Records. Through the years, the United Negro College Fund has benefited tremendously from his singing and his activity on its behalf. His singing sound is close to the crackling, metallic voice in which he speaks.

Al Green (b. 1946), who grew up on an Arkansas dirt farm and then in the black ghetto of Grand Rapids, Michigan, and lived and recorded in Memphis in his peak years, has been called the last of the great Soul singers. Singing lead in a family Gospel quartet, the Green Brothers, he was dismissed from the group and ejected from the house when his father caught him listening to Jackie Wilson (1935–1984). Green later said: "Sam Cooke, Jackie Wilson — I didn't make distinctions between spiritual and secular music to any great extent back then. If they sang with feeling, from their hearts, I loved the music."[22]

By 1969 he was recording for Willie Mitchell, an ex-trumpet player who was his producer at Hi Records of Memphis, and working with a studio band that included drummer Al Jackson, formerly of the M.G.'s at Stax/Volt. Together, Green and Mitchell sought to forge a style that combined the Pop–Soul of Detroit's Motown with the down-home Soul of Memphis's Stax, aiming for a black–white synthesis that blended black Soul and white Pop. Nevertheless, there was in Green a constant tug of war between the sacred and the profane, between the Gospel roots of his early life and the Pop–sex drive of his musical persona, a problem that Ray Charles apparently did not encounter.

Green tried to resolve the dualism and to quiet an inner voice by occasional excursions into religious recordings. In 1978 he cut *Truth N' Time,* a Motown album that included such standard Gospel songs as the Statons' "Blow Me Down" and "King of All," as well as Pop religiosos such as Bacharach and David's "Say a Little Prayer," his "Happy Days," and the film theme, "To Sir, with Love." Again in 1983, on Hi Records, he recorded an album containing original religious songs, written by himself, Willie Mitchell, and others. Titled *Sings the Gospel,* its cover depicted a church steeple. By the end of the 1970s, Green had, in fact, become an ordained minister, serving the Full Gospel Tabernacle of Memphis, Tennessee.

But Green became a music-world notable by walking in the flashy accoutrements of singing sex studs such as wicked Wilson Pickett, cooing Sam Cooke, stomping Otis Redding, and aggressive Teddy Pendergrass (b. 1950). Stylistically, Green alternated between the warm soulfulness of Cooke and the hard-hitting Soul of Otis Redding. In 1971, he won RIAA Gold Records for sales of over a million on "Tired of Being Alone," which he wrote, and "Let's Stay Together," cowritten with Willie Mitchell and drummer Al Jackson.

The next year brought a flock of million-sellers, including singles "Look What You Done for Me," "I'm Still in Love with You," and "You Ought to Be with Me," and two albums, *Let's Stay Together* and *I'm Still in Love with You.* The flow of million-copy sellers continued into 1973 with "Call Me" and "Here I Am (Come and Take Me)"; in 1974, "Sha La La (Makes Me Happy)"; and in 1975, "Love." The titles suggest songs that are traditional romantic fare whose impact came from Green's sensuous style and his seductive charisma as a performer.

Again, with five albums for the Christian label Myrrh Records, Green played on Broadway in 1982 in the Gospel-oriented show, *Your Arms Too Short to Box with God.* His performance was described as "electrifying." But he did not fare as well in a Manhattan night-long Gospel extravaganza in which he appeared as the closing performer in 1984. "The Reverend Green seemed somewhat lost," reviewer Christopher Connelly wrote, "as he tried to be both a pop-soul vocalist and a gospel singer."[23] In short, there is little indication that his immense success as a popular entertainer has brought the serenity he seeks in his colloquies with God.

Teddy Pendergrass had the makings of what Lionel Richie became in the 1980s until a car crash paralyzed him from the waist down. A most handsome, statuesque man, Pendergrass operated in the tradition of black singers like Billy Eckstine and Harry Belafonte, whose attractiveness added a zinger to their singing and made them "matinee idols," as they were once called. By contrast, Pendergrass, who became *the* black male singer/sex symbol of the late 1970s, exuded a kind of animal sexuality, almost savage in character. Reviews of his concerts at the Hollywood Greek Theater told of hysterical young women who fainted, as in the days of young Sinatra. A female talent scout of Geffen Records said: "When Teddy sang, there was something savage about him. He's so handsome. You have it in your mind that he could ravage you and you wish he would. . . . When Teddy sang *Close the Door,* you could hear the door click shut with you locked in with him, and you loved it!"[24]

Originally lead singer of Harold Melvin & the Blue Notes, tall, bearded Pendergrass made a million-copy seller of his solo version of "Close the Door" in 1978, and in 1981 scored a chart single with "Two Hearts," a duet with Stephanie Mills, star of the Broadway show *The Wiz.* Although he recovered from the paralyzing auto accident of 1982 sufficiently to work from a wheelchair and to record a new album, *This One's For You,* the macho sex image was inevitably gone. Without it, the gruff-voiced sex singer had lost the sine qua non of his power to overwhelm the ladies.

Tall, stately Joe Williams, born Joseph Goreed (1918) in Cordele, Georgia, but raised in Chicago, attained his greatest renown during the years that he sang with the Count Basie Band (1954–1961) when his swinging delivery of "Every Day I Have the Blues" and "All Right, Okay, You Win" became his continuing flag-wavers. Before the Basie years, he worked with various Jazz bands, including those of Jimmie Noone, Coleman Hawkins, Lionel Hampton, Andy Kirk (b. 1898), and others. Possessed of a crackling, booming baritone, equipped with its own echo chamber, he is able to infuse whatever he sings with a jaunty kind of sincerity.

Through the 1960s and 1970s, and into the present, he made occasional appearances with the Basie band but gigged mostly on his own in concert, in Vegas showrooms, and at Jazz festivals, most frequently with the Newport Jazz Festival, held in New York. His solo albums bear titles such as *Have a Good Time* and *A Swinging Night at Birdland,* and include LPs with trumpeter Harry "Sweets" Edison (b. 1915), pianist George Shearing (b. 1919), and the Thad Jones–Mel Lewis Orchestra. Clearly, the emphasis is on Jazz. But Williams has, since the 1960s, been turning more and more to popular singing and a repertoire of ballads such as "Imagination" (a 1940 hit), "What a Difference a Day Makes" (popularized by Dinah Washington), and Billy Joel's "Just the Way You Are," without bypassing the Memphis Slim Blues, "Every Day I Have the Blues," or Leroy Carr's classic "In the Evening." He has played a dramatic role in the folk musical, *Big Man: The Legend of John Henry,* by Nat and Cannonball Adderley. "I'm not a Blues singer," he has said, "but a singer who sings the Blues."

Until Diana Ross left the Supremes in 1970 to develop into the superstar she became, Dionne Warwick (b. 1941) was the most potent female singer in black Pop music. Hailing from East Orange, New Jersey, Marie Dionne Warwick was singing in New Hope Baptist Church at six, and in time played organ and sang with the Drinkard Singers, a Gospel group headed by her father. While studying on a scholarship at the Hartt College of Music in Hartford, Connecticut, she formed the Gospelaires, a family trio that included her sister and a cousin; it flourished from 1954 to 1961. Sometime in 1961, songwriter Burt Bacharach (b. 1928) heard her singing backgrounds with the Gospelaires for a Drifters record session. Demos that she made of songs written by Bacharach and lyricist Hal David (b. 1921) brought a recording contract from Scepter Records, an independent R & B label, and a production deal for the two songwriters.

"Don't Make Me Over" was the first of a remarkable series of hits produced by the three from 1963 into 1970. Except for a period when Bing Crosby worked with Burke and Van Heusen, and later Frank Sinatra's "personal" songwriters were Cahn and Styne, followed by Cahn and Van Heusen, no singer was so completely identified with one team of songwriters—and with Dionne, the identification was closest, since the songwriters were also her producers, which was not the case with either Crosby or Sinatra.

Out of an impressive group of 22 chart songs, the three achieved Top Ten records with "Anyone Who Had a Heart" and "Walk on By" in 1964, "Message to Michael" in 1966, "I Say a Little Prayer" in 1967, "(Theme from) Valley of the Dolls" and "Do You Know the Way to San Jose" in 1968, "This Girl's in Love with You" in 1969, and "I'll Never Fall in Love Again," from the Broadway show *Promises Promises,* for which Bacharach and David wrote the score.

In the early 1970s, after writing the score for a musical film version of *Lost Horizon*—the film and the score "bombed"—Bacharach and David came to a parting of the ways. With Dionne, they had left Scepter Records, eventually suing the company for underpayment of royalties, and made a deal with Warner Bros. Records for three albums. Only one had been completed when the pair broke up, preventing Dionne from fulfilling her commitment. Alleging breach of contract, she sued B and D, about whom she had once said: "These men and their songs have been the best friends I ever had." An out-of-court settlement was reached. In the meantime, all three, whose collaboration had been so magical, found themselves floundering as they tried to work out their creative destinies alone or with other collaborators.

It was not until 1975 that Dionne returned to the charts—and this as the result of a recording with a group called the Spinners. "Then Came You" went to No. 1 and sold over a million. Again, four difficult years of experimenting with different producers and different studios intervened. Signing with the Arista label of Clive Davis, former Columbia Records executive, gave a lift to Dionne's career. Working with Barry Manilow as her producer brought her a million-copy hit in "I'll Never Love This Way Again" in 1979, and that year, she received a Grammy award for "Deja Vu."

No one was surprised by Diana Ross's rise as a superstar after her departure from the Supremes. Her purring vocals and catlike hauteur as lead singer had more than indicated her potential power as an entertainer and singer. Before 1970 was torn from the calendar, Diana had two tremendous chart-makers, with the Ashford/Simpson dramatic ballad, "Ain't No Mountain High Enough" making No. 1 for a three-week run. In the decade of her career as a soloist, she added 14 best sellers, among which four became No. 1 disks: "Touch Me in the Morning" (1973); "Theme from *Mahogany* (Do You Know Where You're Going To?)" (1975); "Love Hangover" (1976); and the most puissant of all, "Upside Down" (No. 1 for four weeks in 1980, during which its sale soared over the million mark).

During this period, Ross starred in three motion pictures: *Lady Sings the Blues* (1972); *Mahogany* (1975); and *The Wiz.* The most successful of these was *Lady Sings the Blues,* based on the autobiography of Jazz singer Billie Holiday. So striking was Diana's portrayal of the tormented and tragic life of Lady Day that she was nominated for an Academy Award. A double soundtrack album, composed of 17 songs sung by and associated with the legendary Holiday, sold over a million globally. Diana made no effort to imitate the immortal singer but managed to plumb the depth of hurt and longing, and the bittersweetness with which Holiday artlessly imbued her songs.

In 1980–1981 Diana left Motown, despite the many years of association and Berry Gordy's role in producing/financing two of her films, and joined RCA. Apart from financial considerations, it was, perhaps, a move designed to emphasize a broadening of outlook, a move away from the Supremes/Motown image to a Pop singer/entertainer/actress image. The expanded Pop image had already been initiated in a double album recorded live in Hollywood's Ahmanson Theater in September 1976, with Berry Gordy as executive producer. It was a bravura performance in which Diana sang, in addition to the songs of the Supremes years, show tunes by Rodgers and Hart ("The Lady Is a Tramp"), Stephen Sondheim ("Send in the Clowns"), and Marvin Hamlisch ("Dance: Ten; Looks: Three" from *A Chorus Line*), as well as songs associated with such giant predecessors as Josephine Baker, Ethel Waters, Billie Holiday, and Bessie Smith, a set richly spanning the gamut from Blues to Jazz to Pop.

Yet her first hit on RCA was a revival of the Frankie Lymon/Teenagers Rock 'n' Roll hit of 1956, "Why Do Fools Fall in Love" (1981). It made the Top Ten, as did "Mirror Mirror" and "Muscles" (1982), the latter written and produced by Michael Jackson, once her protégé along with his brothers in the Jackson 5. However, in 1981, "Endless," a Pop-inflected ballad duet with Lionel Richie, not only made No. 1 for nine shattering weeks but went on to become a platinum seller.

The move to RCA signaled not only Diana's expanded scope as a singer, but that she was taking full command of her career. Her 1982 album, *Silk Electric,* which included the hit single, "Muscles," and for which she chose famed artist Andy Warhol to design the cover, listed her as producer of the album for Diana Ross Productions. (She also collaborated on a number of the songs.) Diana also produced one of the songs in her 1983 album, *Ross,* which included the hit single, "Pieces of Ice," produced by songwriter/producer Gary Katz. Cover photos of Diana on these albums depict a sultry-looking lady, with a head of flowing hair and bare shoulders—an image in accord with the lady who superstars in the Circus Maximus of Vegas's Caesars Palace and who dueted on disk in 1984 with Julio Iglesias, the new Latin American Sinatra.

Looking like the wholesome girl next door receiving a bouquet of tulips on the cover of *Let's Hear It for the Boy* (1984), Deniece Williams (b. 1949) came up with an album that sold triple platinum (more than 5 million). It happened after years of "paying dues," as performers term it. At three, in Gary, Indiana, she was singing in a church choir. Fourteen years of Gospel singing later, she managed to make a record (with the help of the owner of a record shop in which she worked). It attracted so little attention that she registered in college to become a nurse. In 1969, sick of bedpans, she joined Stevie Wonder's back-up group; and for the next five years she toured with him, recorded on all his albums, and even relocated in Los Angeles when he moved his operation there. Work with Wonderlove permitted her to record with Minnie Riperton and Roberta Flack, to write songs, to launch a publishing company, and to make demos for songwriters and publishers. It was a demo that attracted the notice of Maurice White of Earth, Wind & Fire, and it was he who arranged for her debut album, *This is Niecey,* in 1976.

What gave her career a major lift was the duet disk she cut with Johnny Mathis, "Too Much, Too Little, Too Late," on which she received costar billing and which went to No. 1 in 1978. However, it took another six years, during which she slowly became her own producer and business administrator, before her career went into orbit with *Let's Hear It for the Boy.* Having come out of a deeply religious background, she has confessed that singing R & B/Pop music has "caused me a lot of grief and guilt—and a lot of the elder members of my family were very, very upset with me for doing it. . . . I still wonder on occasion, 'Am I doing the right thing?' But I think it would have been wrong not to indulge my talent . . . My creativity comes undoubtedly from God."[25]

That talent and creativity involve a voice which, like Sarah Vaughan's—she sometimes sounds like her in the low register—spans four and a half octaves, although she sings basically in only three and a half. (The average voice seldom can manage more than two octaves.) One can hear echoes of several different singers in different songs—Roberta Flack, the shrill high register of Diana Ross, the gloss of Minnie Riperton—but Deniece Williams's sound is really her own.

Just about the time that Teddy Pendergrass splintered a brilliant career in a paralyzing car crash, Lionel Richie (b. 1950), lead singer of the Commodores, decided to embark on a solo career. During his tenure as lead and songwriter, the soft-voiced group, singing medium- to slow-tempoed ballads, achieved Top Ten chart-makers in "Sweet Love" and "Just to Be Close to You" (both 1976), and "Easy" and "Brick House" in 1977. Its most popular numbers were "Three Times a Lady" (1978) and "Still" (1979), both of which made No. 1 and were written by Richie.

Formed in 1969 after all six members had graduated from Tuskeegee Institute, in Alabama, the Commodores were signed by Motown in 1972. Insisting on their own choice of material, they made their album debut with *Machine Gun* in 1973. The style was Heavy-Metal Funk, putting them in a competitive position with Sly & the Family Stone and Earth, Wind & Fire. By late 1980, having switched from Funk to Richie balladry, they had produced three Gold, three Platinum, and three multi-Platinum albums, grossing a worldwide record sales of over 25 million. In 1981, they continued their run of chart-makers with "Lady (You Bring Me Up)" and "Oh No." At just about the time when Richie was taking off, they scored with a Richie Gospel song, "Jesus Is Love," from their album, *Heroes*. It won a Grammy for Best Inspirational Performance 1981.

Richie's eponymous debut album yielded a monster ballad hit, "Truly" in 1982, which he frankly said he sang in Sinatra style. His succeeding album, *Can't Slow Down*, which reportedly sold over 10 million copies, included four hit singles: "All Night Long," "Running with the Night," "Stuck on You," and "Hello." As Pop music headed for the mid-1980s, Lionel Richie stood at its pinnacle. In the year in which Michael Jackson and Prince smashed box-office records, racked up record-breaking sales, and were inundated with media coverage, Lionel Richie outstripped both in terms of the charts. In the *Rolling Stone* review of *Can't Slow Down*, there was, perhaps, an explanation. "If he were white," the reviewer wrote, "and couldn't sing, he'd almost be Barry Manilow."[26] Underlying the facetious comment was the reviewer's observation that Richie's style and songs had only the most "tenuous connection" with black music.

During the summer of 1984, Lionel Richie's opening act was Tina Turner, once part of Ike and Tina Turner, who succeeded in invading the Pop market after a seven-year struggle, but on her own Gospel-rooted terms, "an ageless soul survivor." "What I like to sing," she told *Newsweek*, "are ass-kickers. I want to get crazy. That's who I am."[27]

Onstage, Tina (b. 1939) is, in a sense, the apotheosis of Funk—raucous, strenuous, voluptuous, sweating, rasping, purring, belting. But on disk, her style is an ambivalent combination of Soul, Pop, R & B, and Rock, defying easy characterization. Moreover, her first No. 1 Pop single ever, "What's Love Got to Do with It," and the Platinum 1984 album from which it came, *Private Dancer*, contain elements of Reggae and New Wave synth-pop—all of which adds up to a black style that is her own and that is sometimes jocularly characterized as "raunch and roll."

Born Anna Mae Bullock in Nutbush, Tennessee, of a sharecropper father and a half-Cherokee mother, she met Izear Luster Turner

(b. 1931) of Clarksdale, Mississippi, in St. Louis in 1956. By then Ike Turner had, as a scout for Modern Records of Los Angeles, recorded such pioneers of R & B as B. B. King, Sonny Boy Williamson (1899–1965), and Robert Nighthawk (1909–1967), and had produced Jackie Brenston's sensational hit of 1951, "Rockert 88," issued by Chess Records of Chicago. With his Kings of Rhythm, formed originally when he was still in high school, Ike was performing at three St. Louis night spots, Club Imperial, Club De Lisa, and the R & B Club Manhattan, where Anna Mae managed to gain an audition. After he worked her into his stage show, she had a son by another member of the band and he had two sons by a common-law wife. But eventually they drifted together, married against her better judgment, and had a son.

Written by Ike, their first record release, "A Fool in Love," was a Top Ten R & B hit, as were the follow-ups of 1960 and 1961—"I Idolize You," "It's Gonna Work Out Fine," "Poor Fool," and "Tra La La La La," all on the minor Sue label. During the remainder of the sixties, they recorded constantly—Turner was an enterprising promoter—moving from label to label without producing any real hits. Even an attempt by the noted producer Phil Spector to create a classic, wall-of-sound disk in "River Deep—Mountain High" proved such a classic failure that Spector sidelined himself as a record-maker for several years. It was not until 1971, when they covered a number of rock hits, the Rolling Stones' "Honky-Tonk Women" and the Beatles' "Together," that they made the Top Ten again with a version of Creedence Clearwater Revival's "Proud Mary."

But all through these years, the marriage was a disastrous misadventure, in which, as reported by *Rolling Stone,* Tina "was battered and brutalized."[28] It was in Dallas, when she was beaten mercilessly by Ike that she finally mustered the courage to walk out. The year was 1976—she had endured more than 15 years of being, in her words, "a little slave girl"[29]—and she left with $.36 in her purse, requested nothing in the divorce proceedings, and ended deeply in debt over engagements she had broken by her walkout.

Although she had already demonstrated marked dramatic ability as the Acid Queen in the film version of the rock opera *Tommy,* and though she managed to keep working in Vegas and Reno showrooms, as a sort of "Rock-and-Roll Ann Margret," it was not until 1984 that the lean years came to an end. Things began to change when she recorded Al Green's classic "Let's Stay Together" with members of the British group Heaven 17, and it became a hit in England, subsequently catching on in New York dance clubs. With Capitol Records offering $150,000 for a quick follow-up album, Tina rush-recorded *Private Dancer,* her first solo album in years, using several British producers and songwriters. It shot up to No. 1 on the black album chart and moved into the Top Ten on Pop album charts.

In the discerning view of Stephen Holden, *Private Dancer* "is a landmark not only in the career of the 45-year-old singer but in the evolution of pop-soul music itself . . . an innovative fusion of old-fashioned soul singing with New Wave synth-pop."[30] In it, one hears the soulful sound of southern Gospel music. But the Baptist is now a Buddhist, and there is a new depth not only in her outlook but in her singing. Tina may still be sex in motion, with her svelte figure, long, lithe legs and sensual mouth, but in her singing there is by turns cool composure, defiance, cynicism, passion, and vulnerability.

"We've become more pop-oriented," said Anita Pointer of the dayglo Pointer Sisters, reflecting recent movements of various black artists. "We cut back on the nostalgia and the Jazz in the late 70s," she told the *Las Vegas Review-Journal* on March 29, 1985.

The four daughters of two West Oakland, California, Church of God ministers, the girls were forbidden as they grew up to sing popular, R & B, or film songs. Thus, they gravitated to scat singing, and without being able to read music, mastered the jazzy Lambert, Hendricks, and Ross hit "Cloudburst." Through a San Francisco producer, Dave Rubinson, they became busy backup singers in the 1970s—even while they were working at various clerical jobs—lending their background voices to such artists as Grace Slick, Sly Stone's band, Esther Phillips, Dave Mason, Boz Scaggs, Elvin Bishop, and Tower of Power, among others.

Their first self-titled album, on ABC's Blue Thumb label, came in 1973 after they had been briefly managed by impresario Bill Graham (1971) and recorded unsuccessfully on Atlantic (1972). Allen Toussaint's song, "Yes We Can Can" made the charts (No. 11 Pop, No. 12 R & B), opening the door for them to bookings on top TV shows. On these, they attracted widespread comment because of their 1940s antique getup, involving high heels, below-the-knees dresses, and wide, floppy hats. But it was their hyperactive delivery, close harmony, and exotic fusion of gospel, be-bop, and R & B that won acclaim.

In 1974, "Fairytale," written by Anita and Bonnie Pointer for *That's A-Plenty,* their second album, won them a Grammy as Best Country Single of the Year, which led to their being the first black women to perform on Nashville's *Grand Ole Opry.* Elvis covered "Fairytale" as their first two LP's went Gold.

Between 1975 and 1977, problems beset the group: a lawsuit for back royalties against Blue Thumb Records; the mental breakdown of sister June, the youngest; and by 1978, the departure of Bonnie, who went solo and not too successfully on Motown Records.

Regrouping as a trio, Ruth (b. 1946), Anita (b. 1948), and June (b. 1954) signed with a new producer, Richard Perry, on whose Planet label they not only entered the mainstream but scored enormous hits with "Fire" (1978), a Bruce Springsteen song; "He's So Shy" (1980); and "Slow Hand" (1981)—all of them R.I.A.A. certified million sellers.

At the 1985 Grammy Award ceremony, they collected emblems for "Jump" (Best Pop Vocal by a Duo) and "Automatic" (Best Vocal Arrangement). Their most recent album, *Breakout,* included not only these songs but "I'm So Excited" and "Neutron Dance," and the highly danceable album went platinum, with a sale of over 2 million. By then, the Pointer Sisters had joined the small coterie of black superstars appearing in the main showrooms of the Vegas strip.

If 1940s nostalgic costuming contributed to the rise of the Pointer Sisters, it was lame space-cadet suits, introduced at a headline Bottom Line show in New York City, that brought notoriety to Labelle in 1973. The following year they became the first black group to appear at New York's Metropolitan Opera House where they introduced their resounding hit, "Lady Marmalade." A song about a Creole hooker, it went to No. 1 in 1975, became a million seller, and was the highlight of *Nightbirds,* the album produced by New Orleans' Allen Toussaint, co-writer of their hit song.

Formed as Patti LaBelle (b. Patricia Louise Holt, 1944) and the Blue Belles in Philadelphia in 1961, the group was a quartet until Cindy Birdsong (b. 1939) left in 1967 to replace Florence Ballard in the Supremes. In those years, the group was a typical black sixties girl group with the sequined gowns and bouffant hairdos. Their hits, such as "I Sold My Heart to the Junkman" (1962), were moderate noisemakers.

Recognition did not come until the mid-1970s when their management was assumed by British Vicki Wickham, who knew them from appearances on the mid-1960s British show *Ready Steady Go* and who steered them in a rock direction. But even then, theirs was a limited acceptance for they were voicing ideas, political and sexual, that seemed outrageous at the time and that women were then not ready to accept.

Although "Lady Marmalade" established the group, then known as Labelle, it broke up two years later, in 1977, over musical differences. It was then that an uneasy but peppery Patti LaBelle found an audience for her solo fusion of provocative social commentary and raw rock power. In the 1980s her star was in the ascendancy as she scored in several media besides records. Onstage, she appeared successfully with Al Green in the Broadway revival of *Your Arms Too Short to Box with God;* and on film, she performed with Oscar power as the blues-belting bistro owner in *A Soldier's Story*. On disk, she charted songhits from Eddie Murphy's blockbuster film, *Beverly Hills Cop*. The onstage firebrand continues to live quietly in Philadelphia with her high-school-principal husband and their three children.

"Rapper's Delight" (Hip Hop)

Sometime in 1974, in an apartment in the Bronx, Joseph Saddler, who was to become known as Grandmaster Flash, plugged two turntables, set on orange crates, into the same speaker. Placing a different record on each turntable, he switched from one to the other, capturing a 10-second drum explosion from one, a 15-second bass line from the other, a harmonic fragment from the first—until he had an exciting "mix" of sound. He later claimed that the impulse came from an early dissatisfaction with complete tracks of a piece. But he could have been influenced by the Dub development in Jamaica in the early 1970s, when producer/engineers dropped out the instruments on a commercial recording, except for bass guitar and drums, and faded the voices in and out.[31]

For fun, Saddler began playing his new mixes in a nearby park. Thus the group known as the Furious Five was born, made up of brothers Melvin and Danny Glover (known in the group as Melle Mel and Kid Creole respectively), Eddie Morris (Mr. Ness), Guy Williams (Rahiem), and Keith Wiggins (Cowboy). These would talk over the soundtracks created by Saddler, providing rhymed street-level narratives over the funky rhythm tracks. So many people were attracted to the group's performances that a local club owner persuaded Saddler to do the show inside for an admission charge of one dollar. Soon rival "Rap" groups, as they came to be called, sprang up. When the dee jays/producers of these groups came to Saddler's club to learn what records he was using in his "mix," he would allow them to look, without letting them know that he had switched labels.

Suggestions that he and his Furious Five make a commercial recording were rejected—who would buy a record with people jabbering street talk over a rudimentary rhythm track instead of singing? Then, in 1979, a disk called "Rapper's Delight" was released by Sugar Hill Records of New Jersey, a company formed by Sylvia Robinson, who had been half of the Mickey & Sylvia duo with a 1957 hit titled, "Love Is Strange." When "Rapper's Delight" began climbing the black charts and became a hit—No. 36 in a two-week rise on Pop charts—Grandmaster Flash and his Furious Five approached and made a tie-up with Sugar Hill Records.

By 1981 they had a moderate Rap hit in "Wheels of Steel." But in 1982, after sitting for a year on a song-poem about ghetto life written by Ed Fletcher, a member of the Sugar Hill house band, they finally recorded "The Message." It was released in the summer on a 12-inch single, over their uneasy protestations. In rapped lyrics, "The Message" projected images of inner-city decay, punctuated by a sinister cackle. It dealt with junkies, hustlers, derelicts, bag ladies, a numbers runner, and a suicide. In its brutish realism, Jim Miller of *Newsweek* found it "strident, histrionic and a record that made everything else on the radio seem cowardly by comparison."[32] Curiously, considering its impact, "The Message" did not make the Pop charts. But it was voted the best single of 1982 by the nation's Rock critics, and it quickly became recognized as the landmark disk that helped legitimize the Rap development.

"It changed not only the image of the group," rock critic Robert Hilburn wrote, "but also the status of rap music itself. Most hard-rock stations ignored the record because they rarely play records by black artists. Still, it picked up enough support in dance clubs, on black-oriented radio stations and adventurous rock fans to become a certified Gold Record ($1 million in sales)."[33]

In Grandmaster Flash's view: "Until then, Rap had a limited audience—something that was either a novelty for kids or dance music just for the black audience. We had always felt that we could reach all people, regardless of age or color. That's what The Message did for us."[34]

"The Message" came just a year before a *Newsweek* cover headline read: "BREAKING OUT! Dancing the summer away," superimposed upon a young black kid, Robert Taylor of the film *Beat Street,* spinning on his head. *Beat Street,* featuring New York City break-dancers and street musicians, had opened in June, a month after *Breakin',* about a trio of West Coast break-dancers. Born, like rapping, in the Bronx, break-dancing was described as an acrobatic style in which the dancer spins on the head, the back, and/or the hands. It had apparently caught on by then to such a degree that a how-to book, *Breakdancing,* was then at the top of *The New York Times* list of paperback best sellers.

Another type of street dancing had surfaced from the black ghettos. Known as Pop-locking (called the Electric Boogie in New York), it had apparently originated in Los Angeles with a group called the Lockers. In this type of break-dancing, the dancer looked as if an electric current were passing through his body, "locking" his joints for a moment and followed by his "popping" one joint out of line and back again. The robot-like, stiff-jointed style, performed standing up, was popularized by superstar Michael Jackson in his videos where he performed The Moonwalk, also called the Back Float. It involved shifting the weight from one leg to the other and sliding backward, movements that made the dancer look as if he were walking forward on air.

The two types of break-dancing plus rapping conjoined with graffiti to form the black/Hispanic subculture identified as Hip-Hop, a term that came from a rap song by high priest Afrika Bambaataa. Founder of the so-called Zulu Nation, a loose confederation of Bronx breakers (dancers), rappers (singers), scratchers (record spinners), and burners (graffiti artists), Bambaataa was featured in *Beat Street,* together with such Hip-Hop personalities as legendary dee jay Kool Herc, rapper Grandmaster Melle Mel & the Furious Five, Rock Steady Crew, New York City Breakers, and Robert Taylor, the 16-year-old spectacular break-dancer who had been discovered on a South Bronx playground and was making his film debut.

In 1983 Bambaataa & the Soul Sonic Force, working with keyboardist/producer Arthur Blake, had recorded "Looking for the Perfect Beat" and "Planet Rock." Both were ostensibly among the first instances of the electronic transformation of the Rap style evolved by Kurtis Blow, Grandmaster Flash, and the Sugarhill Gang. "Planet Rock," a hit on dance charts, reportedly sold over half a million records. Kurtis Blow, who had functioned for a period as a Disco disk jockey, himself made the charts in 1980 with a fast-talking disk titled, "The Breaks." The early 1980s saw a proliferation of rapper disks by such groups as The Funky Four Plus One *(That's the Joint),* Count Coolout *(Rhythm Rap Rock),* The Treacherous Three ("Body Rock"), and the erotic family trio Sequencer ("The Monster Jam"). All of these involved rapid-fire street talk, generally rhymed, spoken to a minimal musical accompaniment of a percussive ostinato, punctuated by an occasional guitar or bass chord. Bambaataa's disks added the clatter of electronic percussion and electronically altered vocals, as well as synthesized textures heard in *Beat Street.*

Folk singer/actor Harry Belafonte, King of Calypso in the mid-1950s and now the co-producer of *Beat Street,* said of the film:

> The real story about break-dancing isn't the wonderful feat of these kids being able to spin. . . . The more important story in this film is that Presidents Carter and Reagan have gone into this community, the South Bronx, have raped it with television cameras and with promises to this most most underprivileged group, and then, when they got into office, nothing at all was done to change the plight of these wretched people.
>
> Yet with all the dopetaking and gang wars suddenly out comes this social voice, this protest, this break-dancing, this rap singing, this graf-

> fiti art with some of them now making $15,000 to $25,000 a canvas. And all of this is saying from the Bronx: 'You're not going to be able to forget us. You'll see it on the sides of your subways. You'll see it on the walls of your city. You'll see it in our dancing on every corner . . . Our film is a look at the cultural phoenix that has risen out of the ashes of the South Bronx to replace the hopelessness, the drugs and the violence.[35]

Newsweek quoted the director of a Denver juvenile-delinquency program: "Break-dancing is a way to be No. 1 without blowing somebody away." And a San Francisco 16-year-old, identified by the street name of Jay Rock, said: "If you told me a few years ago that I'd be dancing, I'd laugh. It's like a thing: guys getting ready to fight, but instead we dance."[36]

Breakin', the film that antedated *Beat Street* by a month in its concern with the same black/Hispanic subculture, produced a soundtrack that sold Platinum as well as a hit single, "There's No Stopping Us," by Ollie and Jerry. It featured two West Coast break-dancers: Michael (Boogaloo Shrimp) Chambers and Adolfo (Shabba-Doo) Quinones.

Steve Allen was at pains to advise readers of the *Los Angeles Times* that break-dancing had developed some years before it was seen, in a 1980 film called *Wild Style:* "In 1973," Allen wrote,

> I performed a two-week comedy-and-music concert engagement at the Starlight in Kansas City. A Los Angeles street-dance group called The Lockers was featured. One of the group's members was Shabba-Doo, whom I subsequently booked on the premiere telecast of NBC's *The Big Show* in 1980. Shabba-Doo became a part of the standard opening sequence of the 11-Specials of the series. Bette Midler, at about the same time, was using Shabba-Doo in her concert act.[37]

Shabba-Doo himself claimed that he was doing the Robot as far back as 1968—and then on street corners of Chicago, where he was arrested for performing Pop-locking. Originally scheduled to serve as a choreographer, Shabba-Doo so impressed the producers of the low-budget *Breakin'* that he was co-opted as a featured player.

As a semidocumentary on the Hip-Hop subculture of South Bronx, *Wild Life* apparently enjoyed a limited audience. *Flashdance* of 1983 was doubtless more significant in making the general public aware of the revolutionary dance style. In the closing sequence, the heroine used break-dancing as a startling means to gain entry into a ballet school. By 1984, interest in the street-dance style had burgeoned so that the San Francisco Ballet opened its season with a gala featuring 46 break-dancers, while a troupe of 100 helped close the Los Angeles Olympics. As at the height of the Disco craze, clubs had by then sprung up all over the country where the Hip-Hop subculture met the white middle class. It was hoped that break-dancing had also superseded the rumble among street gangs as the hip way to settle scores.

The White Synthesis

In September 1984, an article in the Sunday *New York Times* bore the heading: "Pop Records Turn to Hip-Hop." It was a semaphore of how quickly elements of the black subculture were being adapted by white artists. Cited in the article by Stephen Holden were Daryl Hall and John Oates, and Barry Gibb of the Bee Gees.

In making their new album, *Bim Bam Boom,* Hall and Oates had consulted with Arthur Baker, the Hip-Hop producer–guru responsible for Afrika Bambaataa's electronic extension of Rap. The staccato sounds of Hip-Hop became a textural element, imposed on the recognized Hall and Oates's Rock and Pop-Soul sounds, its aural street acerbity adding bite to Hall and Oates's bark. Clipped melodic phrases superseded the extended Soul melodies generally created by Hall, with lyrics that reflected the slanginess of Hip-Hop. "All-American Girl," in fact, included a rapped segment, as did "Fine Line" in Barry Gibb's *New Voyager* LP, where a verse was rapped. Earlier instances of white adaptations were to be found in Lakeside's "Fantastic Voyage" and Blondie's "Rapture."

Black singers on a different wave-length also began to reveal the impact of the new subculture. In funky Chaka Khan's album, *I Feel for You,* Grandmaster Melle Mel appeared on the title track to introduce the exuberant singer in a rapped sequence. One of the songs, "My Love Is Alive," was co-produced by keyboardist John Robie, partner of Hip-Hop producer Arthur Baker. Using a large complement of electronic sound effects, Robie added the clatter of synthesized percussion and the wail of altered vocals to Khan's Pop Funk.

Holden found that Chaka Khan was successful in tying together three different aspects of American black music—Prince, who wrote the title song; Stevie Wonder, who played harmonica on the title track; and Grandmaster Melle Mel, who rapped on it. Holden concluded that "Hip-Hop, like the Funk and Soul styles that preceded it, will be exerting an influence on Pop for a long time to come."[38]

Ma Rainey's Black Bottom (Black Musicals of the 1970s and 1980s)

In 1982 an NBC-TV Special was on the beam when it spoke of the "Big Black Boom on Broadway." Not since the opulent decade of the twenties, which saw the birth of the legendary Blake and Sissle show, *Shuffle Along,* were there so many black musicals to be seen in the theaters of the main stem. The 20 and more shows—the first four years of the eighties added at least 10 more—offered an impressive variety of vehicles.

To begin with, there were four one-man (-woman) shows. *An Evening with Josephine Baker,* opening New Year's Eve 1974, held forth briefly at the Palace; while *Sammy,* a showcase for Sammy Davis, Jr., ran for two weeks in April 1974 at the cavernous Uris Theatre. In January 1985, an actress with the odd name of Whoopi Goldberg, a face as quizzical and a style as comic-dramatic as a rag doll's, was holding forth at the Lyceum, her six original monologues charming appreciative audiences.

The one-woman show that became an extraordinary event in the theater was *Lena Horne: The Lady and Her Music.* An autobiographical account of her career and life, told in stories that were as incredible as they were funny—with songs interspersed—it was hailed as "a shared journey of self-discovery about the human cost (to the audience as well as the singer) of being a symbol—a symbol of black gentility and sexiness in the 40s and 50s."[39] One of the most revealing moments in the evening's proceedings came when Lena allowed the audience to hear her at two different stages of her career. She first sang "Stormy Weather" as she did it in the period when Hollywood developed a special makeup to whiten her already light complexion and when her sequences were shot so that southern distributors could drop them out without affecting the continuity. Resentful of the treatment and feeling humiliated, Lena put a wall between herself and white audiences. It was as if she were saying, "You can have the singer but you can't have me." But even the singer held back. Having presented the inhibited "Stormy Weather," toward the end of the evening Lena offered a version of the song in the era of Martin Luther King, Jr., when it became a declaration of black identity and she let loose like Aretha Franklin or Big Mama Thornton. The contrast was stunning.

Playing to SRO crowds from the day of its opening in May 1981 into the following year, *Lena Horne* went on to wow audiences in Los Angeles, to garner a Special Grammy award in 1982, and, finally, to be captured on a live two-record set. "In the depth and range of its emotion," Stephen Holden wrote, "Lena Horne's singing hits peaks of ferocity, tenderness, playfulness and sheer delight that would have seemed unthinkable in her glamour-girl days, while, technically, her voice has lost little of its satin timbre and flexibility . . . all this from a woman who's a beautiful sixty-four."[40]

Revivals were a marked feature of the seventies, which witnessed, in September 1976, the first presentation of the complete score of *Porgy and Bess,* bowdlerized on its introduction in 1935 and during earlier revivals. The Gershwin opera was a production of the Houston Grand Opera Company, also responsible for the first full showing of Scott Joplin's Ragtime opera, *Treemonisha.*

Treemonisha was the first of three black productions on Broadway during the 1975–1976 season. The evening after it opened, *Me and Bessie* opened in the Ambassador Theater. The theater proved too large for such an intimate show, which soon found a rewarding house at the off-Broadway Edison Theater, in the Times Square area. Essentially a one-woman show, *Me and Bessie* presented Gospel/Blues singer Linda Hopkins narrating the tragic tale of the Empress of the Blues and singing the enduring Blues that she popularized during her stormy career.

The third black company that arrived on Broadway—in November 1975—offered an all-black revival of *Hello, Dolly!* with irresistible Pearl Bailey in the lead and veteran singer Billy Daniels in the main supporting role. The following July, an all-black version of *Guys and Dolls* was presented, with James Randolph (Sky), Ernestine Jackson (Sarah), Robert Guillaume (Nathan Detroit), and Norma Donaldson (the allergic-to-long-engagements Adelaide).

The most successful of the revivals was *The Wiz.* Not really a revival of *The Wizard of Oz* story, which was irrevocably associated with the Judy Garland film, it was an original black adaptation. The transformation had a book by William P. Brown and a score by Charlie Smalls. Starring Stephanie Mills as Dorothy, *The Wiz* held forth from January 1975 for a profitable three-year run that led to a film version in 1978. On screen, *The Wiz* boasted a stellar cast, including Diana Ross as Dorothy, Michael Jackson as the Scarecrow, Nipsey Russell as the Tinman, Lena Horne as Glinda the witch, and Richard Pryor as the Wiz. The problem was that Diana Ross, despite her vivacity, looked too old to be Dorothy, a charge that was also leveled at Stephanie Mills, who had matured from 18 to 26, when *The Wiz* was revived on Broadway in 1983. A two-record soundtrack of the film version, produced by the indefatigable Quincy Jones, included the show's hit single, "Ease on Down the Road."

Nostalgia figured through the decade in at least five black productions. *Bubbling Brown Sugar,* opening in March 1976 at the ANTA, where it played for two seasons, included some new songs but fared best in its recapitulation of the Savoy Ballroom melodies of Fats Waller, Duke Ellington, Shelton Brooks, Maceo Pinkard, and Eubie Blake. In addition, Bill Robinson's elegant style of tap-dancing was mimicked, and Bert Williams's rendition of "Nobody" was recalled by Avon Long.

Other nostalgic productions included *One Mo' Time,* at the Village Gate, a remembrance of the good old days of black vaudeville in New Orleans; *Shades of Harlem,* also a Village Gate offering, described as a Cotton Club cabaret musical, which followed in the footsteps of *Bubbling Brown Sugar,* trading on the songs of Ellington, Eubie Blake, Billie Holiday, and Kerry Mills, but including originals by Frank Owens, its gifted musical director; and *Haarlem Nocturne,* starring and conceived by Andre De Shields, whose ambisexuality adorned both *The Wiz* and *Ain't Misbehavin'*. Described as flashy, *Haarlem* brought the famous and capacious Latin Quarter back into operation.

Frank Owens was also the conductor of the 19-piece band at *Black Broadway,* a 1980 musical regarded by many as "the most authentic old-time revue."[41] Staged originally at the Newport Jazz Festival of 1979, *Black Broadway* was a vaudeville-style song-and-dance salute not only to the old music but to some of the artists who had performed it. Onstage was John Bubbles, of Buck & Bubbles, and the original Sportin' Life in *Porgy and Bess,* who appeared despite being partially paralyzed but sat in a chair as he reprised "It Ain't Necessarily So." Adelaide Hall, who starred in *Blackbirds of 1928;* Elizabeth Welch, celebrated as the popularizer of Cole Porter's "controversial" ballad, "Love for Sale"; and Edith Wilson, who starred in *Hot Chocolates* in 1930 with Fats Waller and Louis Armstrong, also appeared.

On viewing *Black Broadway,* the critic of *Newsweek* was moved to observe that "the most exciting shows to emerge from Broadway's mania for revivals have not been the blockbusters of the 50s and 60s . . . but the brash, bluesy recreations of an almost forgotten era: the exuberant Black Broadway of the 1920s whose rhythm and ragtime changed the pulse of American music forever." Annalyn Swan concluded: "As *Black Broadway* proves so delightfully, Broadway may be known as the Great White Way—but its heart belongs, at least in part, to Harlem."[42]

Inevitably, these reminders of the greatness of the music of Ellington, Blake, and Waller led to full-scale productions. First there was *Ain't Misbehavin'* in 1978, with the music of Fats Waller. Next came *Eubie!* a tribute to the songs of Eubie Blake. Then, in 1981, there was *Sophisticated Ladies,* celebrating the melodic genius of Duke Ellington.

All three were resounding hits, with *Ain't Misbehavin'* enjoying the longest run on Broadway. Originally produced in the intimate cabaret space of the Manhattan Theater Club, it drew such strong audience response that the move to a Broadway theater seemed and proved justified. The small cast of five operated in the self-mocking, comic style of Waller the buffoon, as well as presenting about 30 songs he had recorded or written. Among these were two songs, "I Can't Give You Anything But Love, Baby" and "Sunny Side of the Street," generally credited to Jimmy McHugh, but which the producers of the show identified as melodies written by Fats and sold to McHugh. Ken Page, who played Fats, never appeared onstage without the derby that Waller always wore atilt in his nightclub appearances. *The New Yorker*'s capsule comment: "Ain't Misbehavin' is a rip-roaring musical tribute by a superb small company whose energy would suffice to light Manhattan."[43]

While the Waller show made its tribute 35 years after his death in 1943 at the unripe age of 39, *Eubie!* celebrated Blake when he was a vital 95, and he came onstage opening night. Audiences knew fewer of his songs than those of Waller, although "I'm Just Wild About Harry," "Memories of You" (Blake's great favorite), and others were quite familiar. Jack Kroll of *Newsweek* found a historical dimension in *Eubie!* "Humor, sweetness, sex and jive," he wrote, "re-create the thermonuclear fusion of Vaudeville, operetta and musical comedy that Blake and Sissle brought to Broadway"[44] with their revolutionary *Shuffle Along* of 1921.

Gregory Hines, who tap-danced with his brother, Maurice, in *Eubie!* and again with him in the film *Cotton Club,* was the solo star of *Sophisticated Ladies,* in which an onstage band, conducted by Mercer Ellington, played some 35 numbers written by the Duke, alone or with collaborators. "Gregory Hines dances with a grace that ravishes the eye," Brendan Gill wrote, "and with a velocity that must alarm every cardiologist in the audience." But he was just one of a talented and high-energy cast that sang and danced to create an "exceptionally elegant" show, a "stunning potpourri of Duke Ellington numbers.[46]

Familiar melodies were also the basis of *Don't Bother Me, I Can't Cope,* a Spiritual/Blues/Gospel-oriented show that opened at the Playhouse in April 1972. Conceived and directed by Vinnette Carroll, it was developed as a workshop production at her loft on 20th St. where, with out-of-town try-outs, it slowly evolved into a musical entertainment by Micki Grant. Starring Ms. Grant and featuring the noted Gospel singer Alex Bradford (remembered for *Black Nativity*), it won the 1972 Outer Circle Critics Award and a 1972 Obie Award. "All heaven breaks loose on the stage," *Time* magazine observed. "This cast is so agile that it defies the laws of gravity, and the singers have such richly resonant voices that they could bring down the walls of Jericho. This is the kind of show at which you want to blow kisses."[47]

The three major figures of *Don't Bother Me, I Can't Cope*—

Vinnette Carroll, Micki Grant, and Alex Bradford—also created *Your Arms Too Short to Box with God,* which played at the Lyceum Theater in 1976. An adaptation of the Gospel according to St. Matthew, the show was originally mounted for the Spoleto Festival. In the starring role was an unknown Gospel singer from Houston, Jennifer Holliday, who toured with the national company for a year and a half, made her Broadway debut with the production in July 1980, and went on to stardom with *Dreamgirls* late in 1981. With its fervor, *Your Arms Too Short to Box with God* nightly set feet stomping and hand clapping as at a revival meeting. For a time, the male lead was played by Al Green, then at the height of his career in Pop music but soon to be known as Rev. Al Green.

In the early 1970s, two successful black plays appeared in musical versions. Aided by producer Philip Rose and Peter Udell, actor Ossie Davis turned his 1961 comedy *Purlie Victorious* into a libretto, for which Gary Geld composed music, much of it in a revival Gospel vein. *Purlie,* as it was called, starred Cleavon Little and Melba Moore, who helped keep it on Broadway for 686 performances and a successful road tour. Three years later, in 1973, *A Raisin in the Sun,* Lorraine Hansberry's insightful hit of 1959, became *Raisin.* It was produced by Robert Nemiroff, who had been married to Hansberry before her untimely death from cancer; he also collaborated on the libretto. With lyrics by Robert Brittan and music by Judd Woldin, it was recommended by *The New Yorker* as "worth seeing for its appealing and gifted cast, though the book is as old-fashioned as *Uncle Tom's Cabin.*"[48]

Out of this veritable flood of black musicals came three major new works. Opening on December 20, 1981, *Dreamgirls,* with book and lyrics by Tom Eyen and music by Henry Krieger, was directed and choreographed by Michael Bennett, who had done the same for the long-running hit *A Chorus Line.* No show in recent memory, except perhaps *Chorus Line,* was greeted with such thunderous rave reviews. *The Village Voice, The New York Times,* Associated Press, *Wall Street Journal, Time, New York* magazine—all sent their critical hats sailing in the wind. Representative of their applause are the following: *Newsweek:* "*Dreamgirls* is an entertainment unlike any other, a permanent contribution to our musical theater." *Hollywood Reporter:* "*Dreamgirls* is a dream musical. It's a miracle of stagecraft, has a well-nigh perfect cast, and is one of the most innovative productions in years." *London Times:* "*Dreamgirls* goes beyond any musical I have seen, including Mr. Bennett's own *A Chorus Line.* It actually thrusts the American musical into a new age."[49]

Out of the show, 21-year-old Jennifer Holliday emerged as an overnight star. Audiences and critics alike could not contain themselves over her performance, especially *And I Am Telling You I'm Not Going,* which she sang at the end of Act One. In *The New York Times,* Frank Rich wrote:

> When Broadway history is being made, you can feel it. What you feel is a seismic emotional jolt that sends the audience as one right out of its wits. While such moments are rare these days, Broadway history was made at the end of the first act of Michael Bennett's beautiful and heartbreaking musical, *Dreamgirls* . . . If the curtain didn't fall, the audience would probably cheer Jennifer Holliday until dawn.[50]

Jennifer won well-deserved Tony and Drama Desk awards as Best Actress in a Musical as well as the *Theatre World* award.

With a trio of black girl singers pursuing the American dream of making it big between the years 1962 and 1972—roughly the years of the Supremes—*Dreamgirls* was purportedly based on the careers of the famous trio. Composer Krieger specified Etta James as the musical model for Effie White, the portly singer played by Jennifer Holliday. The musical also involved the story of a Soul-type singer like James Brown. Its power derived from the skillful interweaving of the personal fortunes of the main characters with the manipulations and avarice involved in show business. The sociology of black–white relationships was explored most effectively in a song titled, "Cadillac Car," part of whose lyrics went: "If the big white men can make us think we need his Cadillac to make us feel as good as him, we can make him think he needs our music to make him feel as good as us."

Spare in dialogue, *Dreamgirls* relied greatly on recitative without going operatic. Composer Henry Krieger displayed a marvelous ability to fuse recitative and song, and to use the rhythms and tonalities of R & B in theater music. Revolutionary in the fluidity of its staging, so that scenes dissolved into one another as in a film, *Dreamgirls* was termed by many critics "the musical of the 1980s."[51]

Krieger, whose score contributed mightily to the emotional wallop of *Dreamgirls,* also wrote the score for *The Tap Dance Kid,* which opened at the Minskoff Theater on November 7, 1983. The world of show business, central to *Dreamgirls,* was peripheral to the *Kid,* which concerned itself with an ethnic problem: the black drive for middle-class respectability. Based on the novel *Nobody's Family Is Going to Change,* by Louise Fitzhugh, the central conflict in the musical was between a 10-year-old and his father, the youngster desiring to become a star hoofer, and the father—a self-made lawyer, who fought his way out of the black ghetto—demanding that his son *do* something instead of dancing.

There were other ethnic touches, as *Newsweek*'s Jack Kroll

noted in his perceptive review: Willie's overweight 13-year-old sister, "another icon of black culture, the fat woman who's both loser and winner, earth mother and blues lamenter, Hattie McDaniell or Bessie Smith."[52] With his understanding of the work's black roots, Kroll wrote a sympathetic critique, conceding its "over-earnest" character, unlike *The New Yorker*'s Brendan Gill, whose disregard of the black motivation led him to characterize the father and mother as simply "overachievers."[53]

To *The Tap Dance Kid* Krieger contributed at least one quasi-operatic aria in the vein of Jennifer Holliday's show-stopper. It came when Willie's father, depicted until then as a stubborn tyrant, poured out an anguished account of his frustrations and dreams. Alfonso Ribiero, the 12-year-old New York schoolboy who played Willie, danced like an "urban whirlwind," while Hinton Battle, playing the uncle sympathetic to Willie's dream, danced with "the balletic athleticism of a Gene Kelly and the rhythmic suavity of Charles 'Honi' Coles."[54] Small wonder that *The Tap Dance Kid* won a 1984 Tony and the 1984 Astaire Award for Best Choreography.

Ma Rainey's Black Bottom, which opened in October 1984, is not a musical but a drama or melodrama with music, concerned with the exploitation of black Jazz musicians in the 1920s and, in a larger sense, with racism as it affects both blacks and whites. *The New Yorker* called it "a genuine work of art," startling "in the same fashion that *The Glass Menagerie* startled us when it first came to Broadway."[55] Calling it "the first smash hit of the season," Judith Crist characterized it as "a stunner!"[56] And Frank Rich wrote in *The New York Times: "Ma Rainey* floats on the same authentic artistry as the blues music it celebrates. It's explosive, funny, salty, carnal and lyrical."[59]

The debut play of a Minnesota poet, August Wilson, *Ma Rainey's Black Bottom* was originally presented in the spring of the year at the Yale Repertory Theatre, whose artistic director, Lloyd Richards, made his Broadway debut with Lorraine Hansberry's *A Raisin in the Sun.* The setting of the play is a rundown Chicago race recording studio in 1927, where four black musicians and two white marginal entrepreneurs are awaiting the arrival of Blues singer Ma Rainey. Expert at needling her exploiters and a combination of fine artist and show-biz bitch, Ma Rainey personifies the "kiss my black bottom, whitey" attitude of a successful singer, fully aware that the $200 she is receiving is a pittance, compared to what the white entrepreneurs will earn from her records. Her contempt is the counterpart of the attitude of the white studio owner and Ma's manager — they have respect neither for the blacks they are exploiting nor for the work in which they are engaged.

Most of the play focuses on the conversation of the four studio musicians, underpaid and patronized, as they rehearse and await the star's arrival. Sharp, brilliant characterization distinguishes the fatalistic, patient trombonist (played by Joe Seneca, a songwriter in real life); the bassist, good-humored but cognizant of his humiliation; the pianist, the most politically alert; and, finally, the trumpeter, full of fun at the start, lusting after Ma's girlfriend, but so full of rage that he triggers the shocking and violent climax of the play. From the banter of the four, the funny and harsh insults, it becomes clear that each has been badly hurt by his blackness, each has survived at a great cost, and each is filled with self-hatred, knowing how they all have participated in their misuse.

In the course of the play, Theresa Merritt, a big woman in the great tradition of the Big Mamas of the Blues, does get to sing (and record) "Black Bottom Blues," based not on the De Sylva–Brown–Henderson "Black Bottom" of 1926, as some critics indicated, but on a Ma Rainey disk with the same title as the play and probably derived from a Jazz instrumental with that title, recorded by Eddie Heywood in 1923. Also heard during the play were "Doctor Jazz," written by the legendary Joe "King" Oliver and recorded by Jelly Roll Morton's Red Hot Peppers in 1927, and "Hear Me Talkin' to Ya," written by Gertrude "Ma" Rainey and recorded by her but remembered mainly for Louis Armstrong's recording, also made in 1928.

Appearing at a time when radio has, unfortunately, once again become segregated—Rock stations generally refused to play Funk, Soul, and R & B records (but not Pop black singers like Lionel Richie) and MTV avoiding the use of videos by black artists—*Ma Rainey's Black Bottom* seems a fitting note on which to close this history of black popular music. Apart from its artistic merit and probing insights into black–white relationships, the play recalls for us "the anger, pain and defiance that ride on the exultant notes of the Blues,"[58] the bone, tissue, and sinew of American popular music.

POSTSCRIPT

The musical divisiveness of the 1980s, not untainted by racial overtones in the discrimination against black videos and artists, was seemingly countered by two consequential developments in the spring of 1985.

In February, at the conclusion of the annual Grammy Awards ceremony, 46 white and black artists gathered at the A & M recording studios in Hollywood and, under the baton of award-winning conductor Quincy Jones, recorded a new song written by Michael Jackson and Lionel Richie. Although rock artists of the 1960s involved themselves in many social and humanitarian causes, nothing approached the collaborative effort, the display of feeling, and the degree of involvement evinced by the super-group that recorded "We Are the World." The song had been written specifically to aid victims of the African famine as part of a project conceived by singer Harry Belafonte. Cutting across record company labels, managers, and lawyers, the session exceeded in scope anything one could imagine, with artists of every conceivable style and color blending their voices in a selfless gesture of love.

Among the 46 artists who participated there were Tina Turner, Diana Ross, Ray Charles, Stevie Wonder, Lionel Richie, Michael Jackson, as well as Bruce Springsteen, Paul Simon, Billy Joel, Kim Carnes, Bob Dylan, Kenny Rogers, Cyndi Lauper, Johnny Oates, and many, many others. It was an array of talent whose fee for a commercial venture could not be estimated.

By early April, "We Are the World" was the No. 1 single in America, its sales pacing the newly released album of the same name to which various artists—Prince, Huey Lewis, Pointer Sisters, Kenny Rogers, Tina Turner, among others—had contributed singles royalty-free. The album also included "Do They Know It's Christmas" by the British Collective Band-Aid, whose effort in behalf of the starving Ethiopians had anticipated the American charity single and album. It also included the Canadian mercy tune, "Tears Are Not Enough," which involved a collaboration of Gordon Lightfoot, Anne Murray, Joni Mitchell, and Neil Young, among other Canadians.

Having raised a reported $60 million with the single and album, an idea emerged to augment the astronomical figure with a live concert. This event occurred on Saturday, July 13, 1985. It was a monster trans-Atlantic extravaganza, organized by Irish rocker Bob Geldof, in which a 10-hour concert at Wembley Stadium in London and a 14-hour concert at John F. Kennedy Stadium in Philadelphia were fused into a 16-hour program in which 50 artists, black and white, were broadcast and televised in part or completely to at least 100 stations. More than 160,000 fans of rock and black music jammed into the two stadiums for concerts, which were seen by 1.4 billion people around the world, and which drew donations estimated at $70 million.

The other event that found black and white artists joining in a common effort occurred in May. On Sunday, May 19th, in prime time from 8:00 to 11:00 P.M., NBC presented a special program titled *Motown Returns to the Apollo*. It was not just that Motown artists were returning to the Palace Theater of black vaudeville 23 years after their initial foray, but that the theater itself was returning to life on what would have been its 50th anniversary. From 1935 to the mid-1970s, the Apollo was both the home of all black performers and the Taj Mahal of the famous. It was the springboard to fame for a long line of illustrious black singers from Billie Holiday to Sarah Vaughan, Ella Fitzgerald, Dinah Washington, and Aretha Franklin, not to mention the great black comics and bands.

By the 1970s, the theater had fallen on dark days, with performers demanding outsized fees or resisting the grind of five shows a day, and the white–black tensions of the time reducing audiences that had always included whites. In 1976 the Schiffman family, which had developed the venue into the diadem of black live entertainment, sold it, and it appeared for a time that the great landmark might vanish in the mist of real estate renovation. A rising wave of citizen protest moved the city to declare the theater a historical landmark—and now, rebuilt and refurbished, it was being reborn as a showplace and TV production facility. Once again, the opening theme of all Apollo shows, "I May Be Wrong (But I Think You're Wonderful)" would be heard again.

Taped early in May at the new Apollo, with a black-tie audience for the benefit of the African/Ethiopian Relief Fund, the show drew all of Motown's artists and alumni to help celebrate the theater's rebirth. Included were Stevie Wonder, Smokey Robinson, Mary Wells, the Commodores, the Temptations, Diana Ross, and a host of others. There were many others, white and black, such as Rod Stewart, Billy Eckstine, James Brown, Drifters, Jennifer Holliday (star of *Dreamgirls*), and young Sam Harris, the sensational blue-eyed soul winner of TV's *Star Search.*

What gave the Special its significance in a period when radio was being racially divisive was the pairing of black and white singers in duets—Stevie Wonder and Boy George doing "Part-Time Lover" and "Love Is in Need of Love Today"; Luther Vandross and Boy George dueting "What Becomes of a Broken Heart"; George Michael of Wham and Smokey Robinson blending voices on "Never Gonna Dance Again"; and fiery Patti LaBelle and hoarse-voiced Joe Cocker winning a standing ovation with their emotion-drenched delivery of "You Are So Beautiful."

These duets served to affirm once again that the black–white fusion remains the ineluctable source of the appeal and impact of our popular music.

NOTES

Introduction

1. Paul Henry Lang, Ed. *One Hundred Years of Music in America* (New York: G. Schirmer, Inc., 1961), 141.
2. Alec Wilder, *American Popular Song* (New York: Oxford University Press, 1972), 162. Also 7, 28.
3. Henry Pleasants, *The Great American Popular Singers* (New York: Simon and Schuster, 1974), 15.

Chapter One. "That Great Gettin'-Up Morning"

1. In a photograph that has become part of the Fisk University seal, the original 9 Jubilee Singers were (seated left to right) Ms. Minnie Tate (contralto), Mr. Greene Evans (bass), Ms. Jennie Jackson (soprano), Ms. Ella Sheppard (soprano and pianist), Mr. Benjamin Holmes (tenor), Ms. Eliza Walker (contralto); and (standing left to right) Mr. Isaac P. Dickerson (bass), Ms. Maggie Porter (soprano), Mr. Thomas Rutling (tenor). The personnel of the group changed, increasing to 10 when it went on its European tour, and numbering 11 at one point.
2. W. E. Burghardt Du Bois, *The Souls of Black Folks* (Greenwich, Conn.: Fawcett Publications, 1961), 182–83.
3. John Lovell, Jr., *Black Song: The Forge and the Flame* (New York: The Macmillan Company, 1972), 403.
4. *Illustrated Christian Weekly* (May 4, 1872). Quoted by Lovell, *Black Song,* 404.
5. Lovell, *Black Song,* 404.

6. J. B. T. Marsh, *The Story of the Jubilee Singers; With Their Songs* (London: Hodder and Stoughton, 1877, 1903), 175.
7. Eileen Southern, *The Music of Black Americans,* Second Edition (New York and London: W. W. Norton & Co., 1983), 226–27.
8. Lovell, *Black Song,* 498–99.
9. The day that the Jubilee Singers set out on their first fund-raising tour is a day of special remembrance at Fisk, with a convocation at which honorary degrees are sometimes conferred on distinguished blacks. Shortly before his death, in 1983, ragtime composer Eubie Blake was so honored, along with Stevie Wonder.
10. Du Bois, *Black Folks,* 181–182.
11. Lovell, *Black Song,* 408.
12. Ibid., 409.
13. As Frederick J. Work and then his son, John W. Work, directed the singers at Fisk, collecting, arranging, and editing spirituals—the latter edited *American Negro Songs and Spirituals* in 1940—so the choir at Hampton was directed by two leading composer/conductors, R. Nathaniel Dett (1882–1943) and Clarence Cameron White (1880–1960).
14. James Weldon Johnson and J. Rosamund Johnson, *The Book of American Negro Spirituals* (New York: The Viking Press, 1925 and 1940), xxxviii. Howard Thurman, *Deep River* (Port Washington, N.Y.: Kennikat Press, 1945), 39. Henry Edward Krehbiel, *Afro-American Folksongs* (New York: G. Schirmer, 1914), 154.
15. Lovell, *Black Song,* 331–32, 386.
16. This epoch-making work contained 137 songs. William Francis Allen (1830–1899) worked with ex-slaves in contraband camps on Sea Islands, off the coast of Georgia. Lucy McKim Garrison (1842–1877) was a pianist who accompanied her father to the contraband camps on the Port Royal Islands, off the coast of South Carolina. Charles Pickard Ware (1840–1921), a cousin of William Allen's, collected slave songs at Coffin's Point, St. Helena Island.
17. See Howard Odum and Guy B. Johnson, *Negro Workaday Songs* (Chapel Hill: University of North Carolina Press, 1926). Also Dena J. Epstein, *Sinful Tunes and Spirituals* (Urbana, Chicago, and London: University of Illinois Press, 1977), Chapter 9.
18. Harold Courlander, *Negro Folk Music, U.S.A.* (New York and London: Columbia University Press, 1963), 81.
19. Southern, *Music of Black Americans,* 27–29, 187–88.
20. Three of Gottschalk's best-known compositions employed black folk tunes of his native city, New Orleans: *Bamboula, La Savane (Ballad Creole),* and *Le Bananier (Chanson Negre).* Gottschalk became the first American concert artist/composer to attain international renown.
21. Eileen Southern, ed., *Readings in Black American Music* (New York: W. W. Norton & Co., 1983), 27–28.
22. Dena J. Epstein, *Sinful Tunes and Spirituals* (Urbana, Chicago, and London: University of Illinois Press, 1977), 111.
23. William H. Tallmadge, "The Black in Jackson's White Spirituals", *The Black Perspective in Music* (Fall 1981), 139.

24. Eileen Southern, "An Origin for the Negro Spiritual", *The Black Scholar* (Summer 1972), 11.
25. See Tallmadge, "Jackson's White Spirituals," 156–58.
26. Henry Edward Krehbiel, *Afro-American Folksongs* (New York: G. Schirmer, 1914).
27. Tallmadge, "Jackson's White Spirituals," 156.
28. Ibid., 157.
29. Ibid., 158.
30. Dena J. Epstein, "A White Origin for the Black Spiritual? An Invalid Theory and How It Grew," *American Music* (Summer 1983), 56.
31. John A. Lomax and Alan Lomax, *Folk Song U.S.A.* (New York: Duell, Sloan and Pearce, 1947), 334.
32. Ibid., 335.
33. A much earlier description of the ring-shout, and quite similar in its major features, appeared in Thomas Wentworth Higginson's *Army Life in a Black Regiment* (Boston: 1870). Cited by Eileen Southern in *Readings in Black American Music* (New York, London: W. W. Norton & Co., 1983), 176.
34. Krehbiel, *Folksongs,* 30, 75.
35. See Lovell, *Black Song,* 637–56.
36. Du Bois, *Black Folks,* 181.
37. In the liner note to their album of *American Negro Slave Songs,* which includes "Hush, Somebody's Calling My Name" and "Follow the Drinking Gourd," Alex Foster and Michael Larue write: "Cult songs served the slaves a two-fold purpose: 1. To have the master think they were seeking salvation in the sky, and 2. To give codes and messages for escape and secret meetings through using religious themes."
38. See Lovell, *Black Song,* 284–85.
39. Hall Johnson, "Notes on the Negro Spiritual" (1965), cited in Southern, *Readings,* 279.
40. Frederick Douglass, *My Bondage and My Freedom* (Boston: 1855), cited in Southern, *Readings,* 87.
41. Cited in Southern, *Readings,* 198.
42. Ibid., 199.
43. Melville J. Herskovits, *The Myth of the Negro Past* (New York: Harper & Brothers, 1941), 97.
44. Transcriptions for piano, published in 1905 by Oliver Ditson Co. of Boston, the melodies were from Africa (7), West Indies (1), and the rest (16) from Spirituals. Coleridge-Taylor, born in England of an African father and British mother, had already made use of a Spiritual, "Nobody Knows the Trouble I See," in his celebrated *Song of Hiawatha* (1899), based on the work of the American poet Henry Wadsworth Longfellow, whose *Songs of Slavery* he also set to music.
45. In 1940 Edward B. Marks Music Corporation published *Album of Negro Spirituals*—there were 26—newly adapted and arranged by J. Rosamond Johnson. But the publication of H(enry) T(hacker) Burleigh's individual arrangements was by G. Ricordi & Co., the Italian publishers of opera composer Puccini. Beginning in 1917, Ricordi published Burleigh's arrangements of "Deep River," "Go Down, Moses," "Nobody Knows De

Trouble I've Seen," and "Swing Low, Sweet Chariot." They followed in 1918 with "Oh Peter Go Ring Dem Bells," "Sometimes I Feel Like a Motherless Child," and " 'Tis Me, O Lord—Standin' in the Need of Pray'r." In 1921 came the publication of three other Negro Spirituals, including "Little David, Play on Your Harp."

46. Cited in Southern, *Readings,* 277.
47. Ibid., 279.
48. John Rublowsky, *Music in America* (New York: Crowell-Collier Press, 1967), 112.
49. Edward MacDowell, who crossed words with Dvořák, went to Europe at the age of 15 and remained a music student in Germany until he was 27.
50. Quoted in Rublowsky, *Music in America,* 113–14.
51. Ibid., 117.
52. Ibid., 118.
53. Ibid., 118.
54. New York *Herald* (May 21, 1894), 28. Cited by Alan Howard Levy, "The Search for Identity in American Music, 1890–1921," *American Music* (Summer 1984), 75.
55. The development of an indigenous body of American music by American composers was hindered by a provision in the copyright law, which denied protection to the work of foreign composers. Relieved of the necessity of paying royalties to such composers, American publishers promoted and sold all the foreign music they could import and print. According to Russell Sanjek, who is at work on a definitive history of popular-music publishing in this country, "Only one-tenth of all music printed in the United States was by Americans. Even as late as the early 1900s, 70 percent of all piano rolls and recordings were of foreign music." See Russell Sanjek, *From Print to Plastic: Publishing and Promoting America's Popular Music (1900–1980)* (Brooklyn: Institute for Studies in American Music, 1984).

Bibliography

In addition to the books and articles cited in the footnotes, the following are of interest.

Ames, Russell. *The Story of American Folk Song.* New York: Grosset & Dunlap, 1955.

Chirgwin, A. M. "The Vogue of the Negro Spiritual," *The Edinburgh Review* (January 1928).

Conley, Dorothy L. "Origin of the Negro Spirituals," *The Negro History Bulletin* (May 1962).

Davis, Lenwood G., comp. *A Paul Robeson Research Guide, A Selected, Annotated Bibliography* (Westport, Conn.: Greenwood Press, 1983).

Graham, Shirley. *Paul Robeson, Citizen of the World.* Foreword by Carl Van Doren. (Westport, Conn.: Greenwood Press), reprint, 1946.

Sister Mary Hilarion, "The Negro Spiritual," *The Catholic World* (April 1, 1936).

Jackson, George Pullen. *White and Negro Spirituals* (New York: J. J. Augustin, 1943).

Jackson-Brown, Irene V. "Afro-American Sacred Song in the Nineteenth Century," *The Black Perspective in Music* (Spring 1976).

Johnson, James Weldon. *The Autobiography of an Ex-Colored Man* (New York: Alfred A. Knopf, Inc., 1927).

Lorenz, Ellen Jane. *Glory, Hallelujah: The Story of the Camp Meeting Spiritual* (Nashville: Abingdon, 1980).

Maultsby, Portia K. *Afro-American Religious Music: A Study in Musical Diversity* (Springfield, Ohio: The Hymn Society of America, 1981).

———. "Black Spirituals: An Analysis of Textual Forms and Structures," *The Black Perspective in Music* (Spring 1976).

Phillips, Waldo B. "Negro Spirituals in Retrospect," *The Negro History Bulletin* (December 1958).

Riis, Thomas. "The Cultivated White Tradition and Black Music in Nineteenth-Century America: A Discussion of Some Articles in J. S. Dwight's Journal of Music," *The Black Perspective in Music* (July 1976).

Southall, Geneva. "Black Composers and Religious Music," *The Black Perspective in Music* (Spring 1974).

Washington, Booker T. *Up from Slavery* (New York: Doubleday & Co., 1901).

Discography

Afro-American Spirituals, Work Songs and Ballads. Archives of Folk Song, Library of Congress, L 3.

American Negro Slave Songs, Alex Foster and Michael Larue. Tradition TR 2108.

Harry Belafonte. *Belafonte.* RCA Victor LPM 1150.

Paul Robeson in Live Performance. Columbia M 30424.

The Historic Paul Robeson. Everest FS 345.

The Gospel Ship. New World NW 294.

Georgia Sea Island Songs. New World NW 278.

White Spirituals from The Sacred Harp. New World NW 205.

Chapter Two. "Gentlemen, Be Seated!"

1. Edward B. Marks, *They All Sang, From Tony Pastor to Rudy Vallee* (New York: The Viking Press, 1935).
2. Gerald Bordman, *American Musical Theatre, A Chronicle* (New York: Oxford University Press, 1978), 251.
3. The National Broadcasting Company (NBC) was inaugurated on November 15, 1926. The Columbia Broadcasting System (CBS) was inaugurated on September 18, 1927.
4. With his brother, J. Rosamond Johnson, who wrote the music, James Weldon Johnson wrote "Lift Every Voice and Sing," known as the Negro national anthem.
5. Hans Nathan, *Dan Emmett and the Rise of Early Negro Minstrelsy* (Norman: University of Oklahoma Press, 1962), 118.

6. Eileen Southern, *The Music of Black Americans* (New York: W. W. Norton & Co., 1983), 89. See Nathan, *Negro Minstrelsy,* pp. 50–59.
7. Marshall W. Stearns, *The Story of Jazz* (New York: Oxford University Press, 1956), 112.
8. Nathan, *Negro Minstrelsy,* 110.
9. Ibid., 113.
10. Ibid., 114.
11. Ibid., 115.
12. National Theatre, Boston (June 15, 1840).
13. Nathan, *Negro Minstrelsy,* 115.
14. Ibid., 119.
15. Robert C. Toll, *Blacking Up: The Minstrel Show in Nineteenth Century America* (New York: Oxford University Press, 1974), 46.
16. Toll, *Blacking Up,* 38.
17. Nathan, *Negro Minstrelsy,* 230–31. "The walk-around was the invariable finale," according to Douglas Gilbert, "to the first part of the early-day minstrels. It was presented like this: At a chord from the orchestra, the company rose to their feet. As the orchestra began a lively tune in 2/4 time, one of the company would step down stage from the semicircle, walk around for sixteen bars of music and do one step of a reel, finish with a break, then resume his place in the semicircle as another stepped out and repeated the performance, varying, though, with a different step. This would continue until six or more dancers had appeared. Then all the dancers came down stage and danced together while the rest of the company patted time and shuffled. Curtain" (Douglas Gilbert, *Lost Chords: The Diverting Story of American Popular Song* [New York: Doubleday, Doran and Co., 1942], 13–14).
18. Nathan, *Negro Minstrelsy,* 263–66.
19. Ibid., 269.
20. Ibid., 275.
21. Ibid., 266–68.
22. Ibid., 269.
23. Charles Hamm, *Yesterdays, Popular Song in America* (New York: W. W. Norton, 1979), 227.
24. William W. Austin, *"Susanna," "Jeanie," and "The Old Folks at Home," The Songs of Stephen C. Foster from His Time to Ours* (New York: Macmillan Publishing Co., 1975), 203.
25. Hamm, *Yesterdays,* 206. Austin, *Stephen Foster,* xx–xxi.
26. Hamm, *Yesterdays,* 215.
27. Austin, *Stephen Foster,* xxiii.
28. John Tasker Howard, *Stephen Foster, America's Troubadour* (New York: Tudor Publishing Company, 1940), 385.
29. In 1940 a disagreement about new royalty rates prompted the country's radio stations to boycott songs licensed by ASCAP and to establish their own publishing/performing rights company. Among the earliest songs promoted by Broadcast Music, Inc. (BMI) was "Beautiful Dreamer," which was performed so extensively on the radio that it became a hit.
30. W. C. Handy, *Father of the Blues, An Autobiography* (London: Sidgwick and Jackson, 1957), 39.

31. Ibid., 43.
32. Toll, *Blacking Up,* 221.
33. Ibid., 219.
34. Ibid., 201.
35. Ibid., 215.
36. Ibid., 199.
37. Ibid., 211.
38. Ibid., 223.
39. Handy, *Father of the Blues,* 33.
40. Toll, *Blacking Up,* 227.
41. "In Retrospect: Gussie Lord Davis (1863–1899)," *The Black Perspective in Music* (Fall 1978), 189.
42. *The Black Perspective in Music* (Fall 1978), 191.
43. Maxwell F. Marcuse, *Tin Pan Alley in Gaslight* (New York: Century House, 1959), 151, 179. Quoted in *The Black Perspective in Music* (Fall 1978), 189.
44. David Ewen, *All the Years of American Popular Music* (Englewood Cliffs, N.J.: Prentice-Hall, Inc., 1977), 49.
45. Southern, *Music of Black Americans,* 234.
46. A number of historians have reported that Bland was graduated from Howard, and have given his birth year as 1854. A letter from the Assistant Registrar, dated November 4, 1983, states: "Our records do not reflect that James A. Bland graduated from Howard University. He was, however, admitted in 1870 at the age of 14 and continued his studies in Arithmetic, Geography and Reading through December, 1872." If he was 14 in 1870, his birth year would be 1856.
47. Toll, *Blacking Up,* 225.
48. John F. Perry & Co., music publisher of Boston.
49. Toll, *Blacking Up,* 251.
50. Handy, *Father of the Blues,* 17.
51. Ibid., 32–33.
52. Ibid., 34.
53. Ibid., 69.
54. Marks, *They All Sang;* 64, 69, 183.
55. Toll, *Blacking Up,* 154–55.
56. Appearing in 1909 in blackface with the Dockstader Minstrels at the Fifth Avenue Theatre in New York City, Jolson sang his first "mammy song" and received such acclaim that *Variety* commented: "Haven't seen a demonstration for a single act, or any act for that matter, as was given Al Jolson." Cited by Ewen, *American Popular Music,* 200.
57. Douglas Gilbert, *Lost Chords* (New York: Doubleday, Doran & Co., 1942), 144.
58. Toll, *Blacking Up,* 153.
59. Ibid., 152.
60. Ibid., 152.
61. Ibid., 145.
62. Ibid., 147.
63. Ibid., 205.
64. Ibid., 202.
65. Ibid., 202.

66. The blackface tradition did not die with the demise of minstrelsy. It persisted into the 1920s not only in the person of the great Bert Williams, by then of Ziegfeld Follies fame, but in the performances of singers and comedians like Al Jolson and Eddie Cantor. In fact, in the *Ziegfeld Follies of 1919,* Williams and Cantor, both in blackface, sang "I Want to See a Minstrel Show," written by Irving Berlin. The plot line of *Roly-Boly Eyes* (1919), starring the popular blackface minstrel Eddie Leonard, had him running away to join a minstrel show. At the same time, in a theatre farther downtown, the once very popular blackface team of McIntyre and Heath performed minstrel numbers in a show titled *Hello, Alexander.* The *Ziegfeld Follies of 1920* included the comedy team of Moran and Mack, known as the "Two Black Crows," clowning in blackface. And even the sophisticated *Greenwich Village Follies,* playing uptown at the Shubert Theatre in 1921, incorporated a singer in blackface. All of these nostalgic echoes of minstrel days suggest that the appeal of the form had not been entirely dissipated even after World War I.

Bibliography

In addition to the books and articles cited in the footnotes, the following are of interest:

Day, Charles H. *Fun in Black; or, Sketches of Minstrel Life, with the Origin of Minstrelsy* by Brown, Colonel T. Allston. New York: Robert M. DeWitt, 1874. Both the Day and Brown pieces are reprinted in *The Black Perspective in Music* (Spring 1975), pp. 77–83.

Dennison, Sam. *Scandalize My Name.* New York: Garland Publishing Co., 1982.

Fletcher, Tom. *100 Years of the Negro in Show Business: The Tom Fletcher Story.* New York: Da Capo Press, 1954.

Hillebrand, Fred. *Burnt Cork and Melody, A New Minstrel Folio.* New York: Edward B. Marks Music Corporation, 1953.

Mercier, Denis. "Collecting 'Black Americana' Song Sheets: The Music Never Stops," *The Sheet Music Exchange,* SMX (October 1983, Vol. 1, no. 7).

Minstrel Songs, Old and New. Boston: Oliver Ditson, 1882.

Mulligan, Harold V. *Stephen Foster, A Biography.* New York: G. Schirmer, 1920.

Paskman, Dailey. *Blackface and Music, A New Minstrel Folio.* New York: Edward B. Marks Music Corporation, 1932.

Rice, Edward LeRoy, comp. *Monarchs of Minstrelsy, from "Daddy" Rice to Date.* New York: Kenny Publishing, 1911.

Root, Deanne L. *American Popular Stage Music: 1860–1880:* Ann Arbor: UMI Research Press, 1981.

Wittke, Carl. *Tambo and Bones.* Durham, N.C.: Duke University Press, 1930.

Discography

Benny Fields and his Minstrel Men. Colpix CP 501.

Stephen Foster Favorites. The Gentlemen Songsters. Treasure Productions TLP 838.

The Parker Brothers. *Barber Shop Quartet Sing.* Pickwick K 146.

Gentlemen, Be Seated! (A Complete Minstrel Show) Epic LN 3238.
Minstrel Show. Somerset P 1600.

Chapter Three. "My Ragtime Baby"

1. Ann Charters, *Nobody, The Story of Bert Williams* (New York: Macmillan, 1970), 49–50. See also Isidore Witmark and Isaac Goldberg, *From Ragtime to Swingtime* (New York: Lee Furman, Inc., 1939), 195–96. "It is not generally known," Witmark and Goldberg write, "that the verse part of 'All Coons Look Alike to Me,' as now known, was the work of Isidore Witmark. Hogan's original melody did not fit in well with the refrain; Isidore thereupon wrote a new melody, together with some of the words for the second verse."
2. Sigmund Spaeth, *A History of Popular Music* (New York: Random House, 1948), 288.
3. Edward B. Marks, *They All Sang, from Tony Pastor to Rudy Vallee,* as told to Abbott J. Liebling (New York: Viking Press, 1935), 91.
4. Spaeth, *Popular Music,* 242.
5. "During the thirty year period between 1885 and World War I," Alec Wilder writes in *American Popular Song,* "our popular music underwent many fundamental changes. When these changes—rhythmic, harmonic, melodic—were consolidated, a unique kind of song emerged: American song." Wilder thereupon proceeds to discuss the songs that display "evolution and innovation," having already considered Stephen Foster as the creator of the "first truly native songs." He begins with Benjamin Robertson Harney and his song "You've Been a Good Old Wagon, But You Done Broke Down" and Kerry Mills's "At a Georgia Camp Meeting," observing that "the impact of Negro syncopation is the major force in the Americanization of our popular music." The songs that Wilder favors in the Americanization process are: "Hello! Ma Baby" (1899) in "ragtime genre"; "Under the Bamboo Tree" (1902); "Bill Bailey, Won't You Please Come Home?" (1902); Shelton Brooks's "Some of These Days," "a landmark in popular music, perhaps, *the* landmark of the transition era"; Lewis F. Muir's "Play That Barbershop Chord" (1910) and his "Waiting for the Robert E. Lee" (1911); Ernest Burnett's "My Melancholy Baby," the first *torch* song; "Alexander's Ragtime Band" (1911); W. C. Handy's historic "Memphis Blues" (1912) and his "Yellow Dog Blues" and "St. Louis Blues" (1914); Chris Smith's "Ballin' the Jack" (1913); Spencer Williams's "I Ain't Got Nobody" (1915); "Pretty Baby" and "Poor Butterfly" of 1916; "The Darktown Strutters Ball" of Shelton Brooks, "For Me and My Gal" and "Rose Room," of 1917; "Ja Da" and "After You've Gone" of 1918; "Baby Won't You Please Come Home" and "There'll Be Some Changes Made" of 1921 and 1922 respectively (pp. 3–28).

   Wilder regards the period preceding this transition era (1885–World War I)—the years between the Civil War and 1885—as a fallow period, marked by "a dreary melange" of published songs. Wilder attributes the situation to "the traumatic disruptions to Negro life" produced by the new status. What Wilder apparently disregards is the body of *oral* song that was being developed by black people in trying to deal with and adjust to the new world. This was the period when the Blues was born, the sound and form that did not become known until after 1910, with the publications of W. C. Handy and the recordings of the Delta bluesmen. See Chapter Five of this study, "Singin' the Blues."

6. Wilder, *American Popular Song*, 9.
7. Paul Henry Lang, Editor, *One Hundred Years of Music in America* (New York: G. Schirmer, Inc., 1961), 147.
8. William J. Schafer and Johannes Riedel, *The Art of Ragtime* (New York: Da Capo Press, 1973), 31.
9. Syncopation was to be found in some of the earliest tunes of the minstrel shows, including "Ole Dan Tucker" and "Zip Coon." Some writers on Ragtime have tried to distinguish between Ragtime and earlier forms of syncopated piano music with the contention that in Ragtime, the basic rhythmic figure (♪ ♩ ♪) is handled so that the last note is tied across the barline to the first note in the next measure (♪ ♩ ♪|♪ ♩ ♪). An examination of 100 rags in Max Morath's *100 Ragtime Classics* (Denver, Colo.: The Dunn Printing Company, 1963), reveals that the tying of the first note in a measure is as rare as the omission of that note. However, in Ben Harney's *Rag Time Instructor,* all the examples of how one rags a piece involve an elision of the first note of the measure.
10. Cincinnati *Commercial,* "Levee Life" (1876). Quoted at length in Gilbert Chase, *America's Music from the Pilgrims to the Present* (New York: McGraw-Hill, 1966), 431–33.
11. Addison Reed, "Scott Joplin, Pioneer," *The Black Perspective in Music* (Fall 1975), 271.
12. Arnold Shaw, "The Scott Joplin Renaissance: The Missing Link in Pop and Jazz," *High Fidelity* (October 1972), 81–83.
13. The concert on the evening of October 22, 1971, was recorded by The New York Public Library NYPL SJ. The liner note is by Vera Brodsky Lawrence, who had edited the facsimile edition for the library.
14. See the discography for this chapter.
15. David Ewen, *All the Years of American Popular Music* (Englewood Cliffs, N.J.: Prentice-Hall, 1977), 172.
16. In his collection *One Hundred Ragtime Classics,* Max Morath includes pieces by 17 other composers, including Louis Chauvin, George M. Cohan, James Reese Europe, Charles H. Hunter, J. Bodewalt Lampe (1896–1929), C. Luckeyeth Roberts, and Percy Wenrich.
17. William Krell's "Mississippi Rag" was copyright January 25, 1897.
18. Eileen Southern, *The Music of Black Americans, A History* (New York: W. W. Norton, 1983), 343.
19. Alan Lomax, *Mister Jelly Roll, The Fortunes of Jelly Roll Morton, New Orleans Creole and "Inventor of Jazz"* (New York: Duell, Sloan & Pearce, 1950), 68 et seq.
20. Gilbert Chase, *America's Music* (New York: McGraw-Hill Book Company, 1955), 478.

21. James Lincoln Collier, *The Making of Jazz* (Boston: Houghton Mifflin Company), 45.
22. Chase, *America's Music*, 477.
23. Eileen Southern, "Conversation with Eubie Blake, A Legend in his Own Lifetime," *The Black Perspective in Music* (Spring 1973) 59.
24. The cognomen "Tin Pan Alley" emerged later (in about 1911), when the Alley had moved uptown to Twenty-eighth Street. See Marks, *They All Sang*, about the Union Square era.
25. "Bill Bailey, Won't You Please Come Home?" and "Hello Ma Baby" are among a group of songs singled out by Alec Wilder in discussing how American popular music achieved a native idiom between 1890 and World War I. See Wilder, *American Popular Song*, 9–28.
26. Other white musicians who usurped royal titles were, of course, Paul Whiteman (King of Jazz) and Benny Goodman (King of Swing).
27. Hoagy Carmichael with Stephen Longstreet, *Sometimes I Wonder* (New York: Farrar, Straus, Giroux, 1965), 3.
28. Stanley Green, *The World of Musical Comedy* (New York: Ziff-Davis Publishing Company, 1960), 110.
29. Duke Ellington, *Music Is My Mistress* (New York: Da Capo Press, 1976), 34.
30. Among the songs written by others and popularized by Waller, there were Nat Cole's "That Ain't Right" (1933), "I'm Gonna Sit Right Down and Write Myself a Letter" (1935), "It's A Sin to Tell a Lie" (1936), Hoagy Carmichael's "Two Sleepy People" (1938), and "I Can't Give You Anything But Love" (1928). The last mentioned, generally credited to Jimmy McHugh, was described by the producers of the show as a song written by Waller and sold by him to McHugh.
31. Cited in Collier, *Making of Jazz*, 382.

Bibliography

In addition to the books ad articles cited in the footnotes, the following are of interest.

Berlin, Edward A. *Ragtime: A Musical and Cultural History*. Berkeley: University of California Press, 1980.

Blesh, Rudi, and Harriet Janis. *They All Played Ragtime: The True Story of an American Music*. New York: Alfred A. Knopf, Inc., 1950.

Burnett, James. *Bix Beiderbecke, King of Jazz*. New York: A. S. Barnes, 1961.

Charters, Ann. *The Ragtime Songbook*. New York: Oak Publications, 1965.

Confrey, Zez. *Modern Course in Novelty Piano Playing*. New York: Mills Music Company, 1923.

Gammond, Peter. *Scott Joplin and the Ragtime Era*. New York: St. Martin's Press, 1975.

Jay, Dave. *The Irving Berlin Songography, 1907–1966*. New Rochelle, N.Y.: Arlington House, 1969.

Kimball, Robert, and William Bolcom. *Reminiscing with Sissle and Blake*. New York: The Viking Press, 1973.

Kirkeby, Ed. with Duncan P. Scheidt and Sinclair Traill. *Ain't Misbehavin': The Story of Fats Waller*. New York: Dodd, Mead & Co., 1966.

Waldo, Terry. *This Is Ragtime*. New York: Hawthorn Books, 1976.

Waller, Maurice, and Anthony Calabrese. *Fats Waller.* New York: Schirmer Books, 1977.

Wareing, Charles H. and George Garlick. *Bugles for Beiderbecke.* London: Sidgwick and Jackson, 1958.

Discography

Ain't Misbehavin'. The New Fats Waller Musical Show. RCA CBL 2-2965.

E. Power Biggs Plays Scott Joplin. Columbia M 32495.

William Bolcom. *Heliotrope Bouquet Piano Rags.* Nonesuch H 71257.

In Hoagland. Georgie Fame, Annie Ross, Hoagy Carmichael. DRG SL 5197.

Dick Hyman. *Kitten on the Keys. The Music of Zez Confrey.* RCA XRL 1-4746.

The Entertainer: Scott Joplin. London Festival Ballet Orchestra. Columbia M 33185.

Marvin Hamlisch. *The Entertainer.* MCA 2115.

James P. Johnson 1921–1926. Olympic 89422X.

Al Jolson. *The Early Years.* Olympic 7114.

Scott Joplin. *The Magnetic Rag.* The Southland Singers. Angel S 36078.

Milton Kaye. *The Classic Rags of Joseph Lamb.* Golden Crest CRS 4127.

Max Morath. *Oh, Play That Thing! The Ragtime Era.* Epic LN 24106.

———. *The Best of Scott Joplin.* Vanguard VSD 39/40.

———. *Irving Berlin. The Ragtime Years.* Vanguard VSD 79346.

———. *The Ragtime Women.* Vanguard VSD 79402.

———. *The World of Scott Joplin.* Everyman SRV 310SD.

Itzak Perlman and André Previn. *The Easy Winners and Other Rag-Time Music of Scott Joplin.* Angel S 37113.

Roger Shields. *The Age of Ragtime.* Turnabout TV-S 34579.

The Golden Age of Ragtime. Transcribed from piano rolls. Riverside RLP 12–110.

Joshua Rifkin. *Piano Rags by Scott Joplin.* Nonesuch H 71248.

———. *Piano Rags by Scott Joplin.* Vol. II. Nonesuch H 71264.

Willie "The Lion" Smith. *Pork and Beans.* Black Lion BL 156.

———. *The Legend of.* Grand Award G.A. 33-368.

Sissle and Blake. Eubie Blake Music EBM 4.

Leo Smit. *The Masters Write Jazz.* Dot DLP 3111.

The Sting. Featuring the Music of Scott Joplin. MCA 2040.

The Essential Art Tatum. Verve V6-8433.

Art Tatum. *Works of Art.* Jazz 101.

Richard Zimmerman. Excerpts from *Treemonisha.* Olympic 8139.

Fats Waller plays Fats Waller. Everest FS 319.

Fats Waller and His Rhythm. *Handful of Keys.* RCA Victor LPM 1502.

Fats Waller in London. DRG Swing Disques.

Chapter Four. "Shuffle Along"

1. Dailey Paskman, *Blackface and Music* (New York: Edward B. Marks Music Corporation, 1936), 22. Also see Ann Charters, *Nobody, The Story of Bert Williams* (New York: The Macmillan Company, 1970), 135.

2. Charters, *Bert Williams,* 132.
3. Henry T. Sampson, *Blacks in Blackface: A Source Book on Early Black Musical Shows* (Metuchen, N.J.: Scarecrow Press, 1978), 329.
4. Ibid., 328.
5. Charters, *Bert Williams,* 40.
6. Quoted in ibid., 71.
7. Ibid., 71.
8. Ibid., 76. See Jeffrey P. Green, "*In Dahomey* in London in 1903," *The Black Perspective in Music* (Spring 1983), 22–40. The contrast between their social acceptance in Great Britain and their rejection in the U.S.A. was marked. "We were treated royally," Walker later said. "We had champagne from the Royal cellar and strawberries and cream from the Royal garden. The Queen was perfectly lovely and the King was as jolly as he could be . . ." (Quoted in Sampson, *Blacks in Blackface,* 80). In the U.S.A., "the highest honor paid to their company," Ann Charters writes, "was an invitation for 'the sixteen refined young Afro-Americans,' making up the Williams and Walker Glee Club to sing at a garden party given by Booker T. Washington at his summer home in South Weymouth" (Charters, *Bert Williams,* 77).
9. Ibid., 105.
10. Ibid., 107.
11. The pantomime poker game is preserved in a 1916 film short, *Natural Born Gambler* (Sampson, *Blacks in Blackface,* 81).
12. Quoted in Sampson, *Blacks in Blackface,* 82.
13. Bert Williams, "Comic Side of Trouble," *American Magazine* (January 1918).
14. Quoted in Sampson, *Blacks in Blackface,* 83.
15. Ibid., 85.
16. Ibid., 86.
17. Ibid., 90.
18. Quoted in Charters, *Bert Williams,* 138.
19. Charters, *Bert Williams,* 138.
20. Quoted in ibid., 132.
21. Charters, *Bert Williams,* 134.
22. Quoted in Sampson, *Blacks in Blackface,* 91.
23. Will Marion Cook, "Clorindy, the Origin of the Cakewalk," *Theater Arts* (September 1947), 61–65. Reprinted in Ed., Eileen Southern, *Readings in Black American Music* (New York: W. W. Norton, 1983), 233.
24. Ibid., 233.
25. Quoted in Gerald Bordman, *American Musical Theatre, A Chronicle* (New York: Oxford University Press, 1978), 201.
26. Quoted in Bordman, *Musical Theatre,* 201.
27. Quoted in Eileen Southern, *The Music of Black Americans, A History* New York: W. W. Norton, 1983), 380–81.
28. Sampson, *Blacks in Blackface,* 70.
29. Bordman, *Musical Theatre,* 158.
30. Edward B. Marks, as told to Abbott J. Liebling, *They All Sang, from Tony Pastor to Rudy Vallee* (New York: Viking Press, 1935), 96.
31. Quoted in Sampson, *Blacks in Blackface,* 73.

32. Eileen Southern, "In Retrospect: Black Music Concerts in Carnegie Hall 1912–15," *The Black Perspective in Music* (Spring 1978), 71.
33. Quoted in Charles E. Claghorn, *Biographical Dictionary of Jazz* (Englewood Cliffs, N.J.: Prentice-Hall, 1982), 102.
34. Douglas Gilbert, *Lost Chords, The Diverting Story of American Popular Songs* (New York: Doubleday, Doran & Co., 1942), 350.
35. Quoted in Sampson, *Blacks in Blackface*,.
36. Sampson, *Blacks in Blackface*, 96.
37. April 1927. See also Sampson, *Blacks in Blackface*, 341–43.
38. David Ewen, *American Popular Songs: From the Revolutionary War to the Present* (New York: Random House, 1966), 43.
39. Quoted in Bordman, *Musical Theatre*, 452.
40. Bordman, *Musical Theatre*, 388.
41. On February 6, 1985, the Metropolitan Opera presented its first performance of *Porgy and Bess*, an event heralded in *The New York Times* (Feb. 3, 1985) with a long article headed, "After 50 Years, 'Porgy' Comes to the Met as a Certified Classic" (Section 2, page 1).
42. Alec Wilder, *American Popular Song, The Great Innovators, 1900–1950* (New York: Oxford University Press, 1972), 389–90.
43. Stanley Green, *The World of Musical Comedy* (New York: Ziff-Davis Publishing Co., 1960), 211.

Bibliography

In addition to the books and articles cited in the footnotes, the following are of interest:

Carter, Lawrence T. *Eubie Blake: Keys of Memory*. Balamp Publications, 1979.

Emery, Lynn Fauley. *Black Dance in the United States from 1619–1970*. Palo Alto: National Press Books, 1972.

Ewen, David. *George Gershwin: His Journey to Greatness*. Englewood Cliffs, N.J.: Prentice Hall, 1970.

———. *New Complete Book of the American Musical Theater*. New York: Holt, Rinehart & Winston, 1970.

Gottfried, Martin. *Broadway Musicals*. New York: Harry N. Abrams, Inc., 1979.

Haskins, Jim. *The Cotton Club*. New York: New American Library, 1984.

Jablonski, Edward. *Harold Arlen: Happy with the Blues*. New York: Doubleday, 1961.

Kreuger, Miles. *Show Boat: The Story of a Classic American Musical*. New York: Oxford University Press, 1977.

Oberfirst, Robert. *Al Jolson: You Ain't Heard Nothin' Yet*. San Diego: A. S. Barnes, 1980.

Rose, Al. *Eubie Blake*. New York: Schirmer Books, 1983.

Shaw, Arnold. "Gershwin, Arlen and the Blues," *Billboard: The World of Soul*, June 24, 1967.

Woll, Allen. *Dictionary of the Black Theatre: Broadway, Off-Broadway and Selected Harlem Theatre*. Westport, Conn.: Greenwood Press, 1984.

Discography

Ain't Misbehavin'. The New Fats Waller Musical Show. (OCR) RCA CBL2-2965.

Blackbirds of 1928, Lew Leslie's. Columbia OL 6770.

Cotton Club Stars. Cab Calloway and the Cotton Club Orchestra and Others. Stash ST 124.

Billy Daniels. *The Masculine Touch.* Verve MGV 2085.

Eubie! (OCA) Warner Bros. HS 3267.

Hot Chocolates, Souvenir of Connie's. Smithsonian Collection R 012: P 14587.

Ella Fitzgerald *Sings the George and Ira Gershwin Songbook.* Verve MG V-4026.

———. *Sings the George and Ira Gershwin Songbooks.* Verve V-29-5.

———. *The Harold Arlen Songbook.* Verve 817 526-1.

Ella Fitzgerald and André Previn. *Do Gershwin.* "Nice Work If You Can Get It." Pablo Today D 2312140 Digital.

Funny Face. (OSTR-Paramount) Verve MGV 15001.

George Gershwin Plays Gershwin and Kern. Klavia KS 122.

The Music of George Gershwin. MGM 3El.

Harlem Comes to London. The Plantation Orchestra and others. DRG SW 8444.

Harold Sings Arlen. Columbia AOS 2920.

Hot Chocolates, Souvenir of Connie's. Smithsonian Collection R 012: P 14587.

Oh, Kay! Columbia ACL 1050.

Porgy and Bess. (OCA) Decca DE 79024.

———. (OSTR-Goldwyn) Columbia OS 2016.

———. (Complete) Odyssey 32 36 0018 (3-record set).

Shuffle Along. New World NW 260.

Sissle and Blake. (Early Rare Recordings, Vol. I) Eubie Blake Music EBM 4.

Maxine Sullivan. *The Great Songs from the Cotton Club.* Stash ST 244.

Michael Tilson Thomas and the Buffalo Philharmonic. *Gershwin on Broadway Overtures.* Columbia 34542.

Michael Tilson Thomas/Sarah Vaughan and the Los Angeles Philharmonic. *Gershwin Live!* CBS 37277.

Bert Williams. "Brother Low Down." Columbia 27664.

———. "It's Nobody's Business But My Own." Columbia 27663.

———. "Nobody." Columbia 33011, 3423.

———. "Play That Barbershop Chord." Columbia A929.

———. "Unlucky Blues." Columbia 27661.

———. "Woodman Spare That Tree." Columbia A1321.

———. "You Can't Trust Nobody." Columbia 27662.

Chapter Five. "Singin' the Blues"

1. Perry Bradford, *Born with the Blues* (New York: Oak Publications, 1965).
2. Robert Dixon and John Godrich, *Recording the Blues* (New York: Stein & Day, 1970), 9.
3. Nat Shapiro & Nat Hentoff, *Hear Me Talkin' to Ya* (New York: Rinehart & Co., 1955), 247.

4. See the discussion in the preceding chapter.
5. Dixon and Godrich, *Recording the Blues,* 19, 99.
6. Columbia CL 855.
7. Chris Albertson, "Empress of the Blues" booklet in Columbia GP 33, page 2.
8. Quoted in Shapiro and Hentoff, *Hear Me,* 245.
9. Ibid., 247.
10. Ibid.
11. Ibid.
12. *Bessie Smith: The World's Greatest Blues Singer,* liner note, 2.
13. Quoted in Shapiro and Hentoff, *Hear Me,* 246.
14. Chris Albertson, *Bessie* (New York: Stein and Day, 1972), 225.
15. John Chilton, *Who's Who of Jazz, Storyville to Swing Street* (New York: Time-Life Records Special Edition, 1978), 302–303.
16. Cited by George Avakian in his liner note on *The Bessie Smith Story,* Vol. 4, Columbia CL 858.
17. Cited in Chris Albertson, *Bessie,* on dust jacket.
18. Quoted in *The New York Times,* October 14, 1984, Section C, 7.
19. See Dixon and Godrich, *Recording the Blues,* 32ff.
20. Ibid., 41.
21. The role of music stores and their proprietors in finding talent and arranging for recordings still remains to be fully documented. One small indication of how little has been done is the number of variant spellings one encounters of Speir's name: Spier, Spiers, Spears, and Speir.
22. Quoted in Dixon and Godrich, *Recording the Blues,* 27.
23. Samuel Charters, *The Bluesmen: The Story and the Music of the Men Who Made the Blues* (New York: Oak Publications, 1967), 32.
24. The material and point of view presented in this section are based on a paper written by me and read in Liège, Belgium, at a Conference, "The Mississippi Blues Tradition," held at Liège State University in September 1984.
25. Quoted in Charters, *Bluesmen,* 62.
26. Ibid., 65.
27. Ibid., 57.
28. *Robert Johnson, King of the Delta Blues Singers*. Columbia C 30034. See Pete Welding's liner note.
29. Charters, *Bluesmen,* 99.
30. Peter Guralnick, *The Listener's Guide to the Blues* (New York: Facts on File, Inc., 1982), 34.
31. Quoted in Charters, *Bluesmen,* 89.
32. Charters, *Bluesmen,* 99.
33. Guralnick, *Listener's Guide,* 34.
34. Quoted in Charters, *Bluesmen,* 92.
35. W. C. Handy, *Father of the Blues, An Autobiography* (London: Sidgwick and Jackson, 1957), 72.
36. *The Bill Broonzy Story*. Verve MG V 3000-5. Vols. 1, 5.
37. Sheldon Harris, *Blues Who's Who* (New Rochelle, N.Y.: Arlington House, 1979), 244.
38. Although bluesman Kokomo Arnold (1901–1968) made the original re-

cording of "Milk Cow Blues" in February 1935 on Decca and is associated with the song, it was a boogie version by Sleepy John Estes that apparently inspired Presley's cover. RCA's *Elvis: The Sun Sessions* credits authorship of "Milkcow Blues Boogie" to Arnold, but the liner note by British critic Roy Carr makes reference to the Estes version.

39. Paul Oliver, *The Meaning of the Blues.* With a Foreword by Richard Wright. (New York: Collier Books, 1963), 9.
40. Quoted in Guralnick, *Listener's Guide,* 53.
41. *Broonzy Story,* Vol. 3.
42. Quoted in Bruce Cook, *Listen to the Blues* (New York: Charles Scribner's Sons, 1973), 122.
43. Paul Oliver, *The Story of the Blues* (Philadelphia: Chilton Book Company, 1969), 114. See the photo in which Lester Melrose is surrounded by a group of noteworthy bluesmen: William "Jazz" Gillum, Big Bill Broonzy, Roosevelt Sykes, James Oden (St. Louis Jimmy), and Washboard Sam (Robert Brown).
44. Arnold Shaw, *Honkers and Shouters* (New York: Macmillan Publishing Co., 1978), 34–35.
45. See *Broonzy Story.*
46. See *The Black Perspective in Music* (Fall 1974), 190–208, "In Retrospect: An Early Black Music Concert," in which an approximation of the original program is printed, together with program notes about each of the participants.
47. Howard Taubman, "Negro Music Given at Carnegie Hall," *The New York Times* (December 24, 1938). The review is reprinted in *The Black Perspective in Music* (Fall 1974), 207–208.
48. Max Harrison, "Boogie-Woogie," *Jazz.* Edited by Nat Hentoff and Albert J. McCarty (New York: Rinehart & Co., 1959), 108.
49. James Lincoln Collier, *The Making of Jazz* (Boston: Houghton Mifflin Co., 1978), 134–35. Collier claims that this song was inspired by a legendary pianist, John Dickson "Peck" Kelley, who refused to record or leave the Houston–Galveston–San Antonio area and with whom the legendary trombonist Jack Teagarden worked for about a year. Collier points to the song's opening line: "In a little honky-tonk village in Texas/There's a guy who plays the best piano by far. . . ."
50. Quoted in Shapiro and Hentoff, *Hear Me,* 250.
51. Handy, *Father of the Blues,* 74.
52. Ibid.
53. Ibid., 76.
54. Ibid., 77.
55. Isaac Goldberg, *Tin Pan Alley* (New York: John Day Co., 1930), 241. Cited by Alec Wilder, *American Popular Song: The Great Innovators 1900–1950* (New York: Oxford University Press, 1972), 18.
56. The song became the title of a Hollywood film biography featuring Nat "King" Cole as Handy. It premiered shortly after Handy's death in 1958.
57. Quoted in Nat Shapiro, ed., *Popular Music,* Vol. 5., 1920–1929, (New York: Adrian Press, 1969), 15.
58. Blues titles in 1920 numbered 4. In 1921, 14; 1922, 11; 1923, 46; 1924, 34; 1925, 19; 1926, 20; 1927, 20; 1928, 33; 1929, 18.

59. Quoted in Hoagy Carmichael with Stephen Longstreet, *Sometimes I Wonder* (New York: Farrar, Straus, Giroux, 1965), 14.
60. Carmichael, *I Wonder,* 58.
61. Ibid., 111.
62. Charles was an honored guest of the Georgia legislature on the occasion.
63. Leonard Feather, *The Book of Jazz* (New York: Horizon Press, 1957), 153.
64. Henry Pleasants, *The Great American Popular Singers* (New York: Simon & Schuster, 1974), 149. Quoted from a *New Yorker* profile in which Red Norvo reminisced with Whitney Balliett.

Bibliography

In addition to the books and articles cited in the footnotes, the following are of interest:

Blues Unlimited, 8 Brondrom Road, Lewishorn, London SE 13 5EA, England.

Broonzy, William. *Big Bill's Blues.* New York: Oak Publications, 1964.

Charters, Samuel. *The Legacy of the Blues.* New York: Da Capo Press, 1977.

———. *The Country Blues.* New York: Rinehart and Co., 1959.

———. *Sweet as the Showers of Rain: The Bluesmen,* Vol. 2. New York: Oak Publications, 1977.

Cone, James H. *The Spirituals and the Blues: An Interpretation.* New York: Seabury Press, 1972.

De Korte, Juliann. *Ethel Waters: Finally Home.* Old Tappan, N.J.: 1978.

Evans, David. *Big Road Blues: Tradition and Creativity in the Folk Blues.* Berkeley: University of California Press, 1982.

Fahey, John. *Charley Patton.* London: Studio Vista, 1970.

Ferris, William, Jr. *Blues from the Delta.* London: Studio Vista, 1970; New York: Da Capo Press, 1978.

Garon, Paul. *The Devil's Son-in-Law: The Story of Peetie Wheatstraw and His Songs.* London: Studio Vista, 1971.

zur Heide, Karl Gert. *Deep South Piano: The Story of Little Brother Montgomery.* London: Studio Vista, 1970.

Godrich, J. and R. M. W. Dixon. *Blues and Gospel Records 1902–1942.* London: Storyville Publications and Co., 1969.

Greenberg, Alan. *Love in Vain: The Life and Legend of Robert Johnson.* New York: Doubleday, 1983.

Guralnick, Peter. *Feel Like Going Home.* New York: Outerbridge & Dienstfrey, 1971.

Keil, Charles. *Urban Blues.* Chicago: The University of Chicago Press, 1966.

Knaack, Twila. *Ethel Waters: I Touched a Sparrow.* Waco, Tex.: Word Books, 1978.

Leadbitter, Mike, ed. *Nothing But the Blues: An Illustrated Documentary.* London: Hanover Books, 1971.

———. and Neil Slaven, *Blues Records 1943–1966.* London: Hanover Books, 1968.

———. *Delta County Blues.* Bexhill-on-Sea, England: Blues Unlimited, 1968.

Living Blues: The Journal of the American Blues Tradition. Center for the Study of Southern Culture, University of Mississippi, University, Miss.

Murray, Albert. *Stomping the Blues.* New York: McGraw-Hill Book Company, 1976.
Oliver, Paul. *Aspects of the Blues Tradition.* New York: Oak Publications, 1970.
———. *Bessie Smith.* Kings of Jazz Series. New York: A. S. Barnes, 1961.
———. *The Story of the Blues.* Philadelphia: Chilton Book Co., 1969.
———. *Conversation with the Blues.* New York: Horizon, 1965.
———. *Screening the Blues.* London: Cassell, 1968.
Olsson, Bengt. *Memphis Blues and Jug Bands.* London: Studio Vista, 1970.
Oster, Harry. *Living Country Blues.* New York: Minerva Press, 1975.
Palmer, Robert. *Deep Blues.* New York: Viking Press, 1981.
Pleasants, Henry. *The Great American Popular Singers.* New York: Simon and Schuster, 1974.
Mother of the Blues: A Study of Ma Rainey. Boston: University of Massachusetts Press, 1983.
Ramsey, Frederic, Jr., *Been Here and Gone.* New Brunswick, N.J.: Rutgers University Press, 1960.
Sackheim, Eric, comp. *The Blues Line: A Collection of Blues Lyrics.* New York: Grossman Publishers, 1969.
Shirley, Kay, Ed. *The Book of the Blues.* New York: Crown Publishers, Inc., 1963.
Stewart-Baxter, Derrick. *Ma Rainey and the Classic Blues Singers.* New York: Stein and Day, 1970.
Titon, Jeff Todd. *Early Downhome Blues, A Musical and Cultural Analysis.* Urbana: University of Illinois Press, 1977.

Discography

Mildred Bailey
Mildred Bailey with the Delta Rhythm Boys. Decca 3691/3755/3953.
Her Greatest Performances. 3 Vols. Columbia 3CL 22.
Me and the Blues. Regal 6032.
Rockin' Chair Lady. Decca DL 5387.
Rockin' Chair Lady. Realm RM 196.
The Uncollected, CBS Radio Shows (1944). Hindsight HSR 133.
The Perry Bradford Story, Pioneer of the Blues: As told to Noble Sissle by Perry Bradford. With 12 reissues from 1920 to 1924. Folkways FJ 2863.
Big Bill Broonzy
Big Bill's Blues. Columbia LP WL 111 o.p.
Big Bill's Blues. Epic EE 22017 o.p.
The Blues. Scepter S 529 o.p.
Portraits in Blues, Vol. 1. Storyville 154.
Sings Country Blues. Disc. D 112 o.p.
Sings Country Blues. Folkways 2326.
Sings Country Blues. Folkways 31005.
John Lee Hooker
The Blues. Crown CLP 5157 o.p./Kent 559.
Boogie Chillon. Fantasy 29706.
The Country Blues of John Lee Hooker. Riverside 12-838 o.p.

Folk Blues. Crown 5295 o.p./United 7729.
House of the Blues. Chess LP 1438 o.p.
Original Folk Blues. Kent 525.
Sings the Blues. Crown 5232 o.p.

Lightnin' Hopkins
Early Recordings. Arhoolie (A) R 2007.
Lightnin' and the Blues. Herald (A) LP 1012.
The Roots of Lightnin' Hopkins. Verve/Folkways (E) VLP 5003.

Son House
Blind Lemon Jefferson/Son House. Biograph BLP 12040.
Blues from the Mississippi Delta: Son House and J. D. Short. Verve FV 9035 o.p.
Mississippi Delta. Folkways 2467.
The Real Delta Blues. Blue Goose 2016.
Son House and Robert Pete Williams Live. Roots 501.

Alberta Hunter
Look for the Silver Lining. Columbia FC 38970.
Remember My Name. Columbia JS 35553. (OSR).
Young Alberta Hunter. The Twenties. Original Blues and Jazz Vocals. Stash ST 123.

Mississippi John Hurt
The Best of Mississippi John Hurt. Vanguard VSD 19/20.
His First Recordings. Biograph BLP C4.
The Original 1928 Recordings. Spokane SPL 1001 o.p.
Worried Blues. Piedmont 13161.

Elmore James
The Best of Elmore James. Sue ILP 918 o.p.
The Legend of Elmore James. Kent KST 9001/United 7778.
Original Folk Blues. Kent KLP 522.

Skip James
Greatest of the Delta Blues Singers. Melodeon 7321.
King of the Delta Blues Singers. Biograph 12029.

Robert Johnson
Robert Johnson. Kokomo 1000 o.p.
King of the Delta Blues Singers. Columbia CL 1654.
King of the Delta Blues Singers, Vol. II. Columbia C 3003/CBS (UK) 64102.
Delta Blues (Includes Charles Patton, Son House, Elmore James). Roots 339.

Furry Lewis
The Early Years, 1927–29. Spokane 1009 o.p.
Furry Lewis. Folkways FS 3823/XTRA (UK) 1116.
In His Prime, 1927–29. Yazoo 1050.

Memphis Minnie
Memphis Minnie. Blues Classics (A) BC I.
Memphis Minnie with Joe McCoy. Blues Classics (A) BC 13.

Charley Patton
The Immortal Charley Patton. Origin Jazz 1.
The Immortal Charley Patton. Origin Jazz 2.
Charley Patton: Founder of the Delta Blues. Yazoo L 1020.

Jimmy Reed
The Best of the Blues. VJ 1072 o.p.
Blues Is My Business. VJ 7303.
The Bossman of the Blues. VJ 1080 o.p.
Greatest Hits. Kent 553.
Jimmy Reed. Archives of Folk 234.
Roots of the Blues. Kent 537.
Gertrude "Ma" Rainey
The Immortal Ma Rainey. Milestone (A) MLP 2001.
Ma Rainey. Riverside (E) RLP 8807.
Ma Rainey, Vol. 3. London (E) AL 3558.
Sunnyland Slim
Chicago Blues Sessions (with Little Brother Montgomery). "77" LA 12/21.
Portrait in Blues. Storyville SLP 169.
Sunnyland Slim. Sonet 671.
Bessie Smith
Bessie's Blues: Bessie Smith 1923–24. Philips (E) BBL 7513.
The Bessie Smith Story, in 4 volumes. Columbia CL 855.
The World's Greatest Blues Singer. Columbia GP 33.
Sophie Tucker
Sophie Tucker and Ted Lewis. Soted 1200.
Bukka White
Country Blues. Sparrkussp. (German) 1.
Mississippi Blues. Takoma B 1101/Sonet 609.
"Sky Songs." Arhoolie F 1019, 1020.
Bukka White. CBS 52629 o.p.

Anthologies

Apollo Theater, Stars of (includes Bessie Smith, Mamie Smith, Ida Cox, Big Maybelle, Sarah Vaughan, Ella Fitzgerald). Columbia KG 30788
The Blues Tradition (includes Big Bill Broonzy and William Brown). Milestone 2016.
Jackson Blues 1928–1938. Yazoo L 1007.
Lonesome Road Blues: Fifteen Years in the Mississippi Delta 1926–1941. Yazoo L 1038.
Mississippi Blues 1927–1941. Yazoo L 1001.
Mississippi Blues. Vol. 1 (1927–1942), Vol. 2 (1927–1940), Vol. 3 (1928–1942). Roots RL 302, 303, 314.
The Mississippi Blues. 3 Vols. From the 1920s and 1930s. Origin OJL 5, 11, 17.
Mississippi Bottom Blues 1926–1935. Mamlish S 3802.
Mississippi Moaners 1927–1942. Yazoo L 1009.
Really Chicago Blues (includes Johnny Shines and Walter Horton). Adelphi 1005.
Sic 'Em Dogs on Me (includes Bukka White, Charley Patton, Furry Lewis, John Hurt, Ishman Bracey). Herwin 201.
They Sang the Blues (includes Skip James, Furry Lewis, and Robert Wilkins). Historical Records 22.

The Sound of Harlem, Vol III (includes "Crazy Blues" by Mamie Smith and Her Jazz Hounds, Bessie Smith, Alberta Hunter, Clara Smith, Victoria Spivey, Monette Moore, Gertrude Saunders, Edith Wilson, Lena Wilson, Ethel Waters, and Billie Holiday). Columbia C3L 33.

Chapter Six. "Say It While Dancing"

1. Quoted in Alan Lomax, *Mister Jelly Roll, The Fortunes of Jelly Roll Morton, New Orleans Creole and "Inventor of Jazz"* (New York: Duell, Sloan and Pearce, 1950), 62. Joachim Berendt, *The Jazz Book, from New Orleans to Rock and Free Jazz* (Westport, Conn.: Lawrence Hill & Co., 1975), 248.
2. James Lincoln Collier, *Louis Armstrong, An American Genius* (New York: Oxford University Press, 1983), 172–73.
3. Quoted in Nat Shapiro and Nat Hentoff, *Hear Me Talkin' to Ya* (New York: Holt, Rinehart & Winston, 1955), 119.
4. Ibid., 120.
5. James Lincoln Collier, *The Making of Jazz* (Boston: Houghton Mifflin Company, 1978), 129.
6. Ibid., 123.
7. Ibid., 124.
8. Ibid., 122.
9. Quoted in Shapiro and Hentoff, *Hear Me,* 116.
10. Collier, *Jazz,* 134.
11. Ibid., 136.
12. Quoted in George T. Simon and Friends, *The Best of the Music Makers* (New York: Doubleday & Company, 1979), 566.
13. Collier, *Jazz,* 172.
14. Quoted in Shapiro and Hentoff, *Hear Me, 201.*
15. Quoted in Simon, *Music Makers,* 18.
16. *Billie, Lena, Ella, Sarah.* Liner note.
17. Arnold Shaw, *52nd St.: The Street of Jazz* (New York: Da Capo Press, 1977), xiv.
18. Billie Holiday with William Dufty, *Lady Sings the Blues* (New York: Doubleday & Company, 1956), 90, 88.
19. *Billie, Lena, Ella, Sarah.* Liner note.
20. Quoted in Simon, *Music Makers,* 585.
21. *Billie, Lena, Ella, Sarah.* Liner note.
22. Quoted in Simon, *Music Makers,* 211.
23. Quoted in Shapiro and Hentoff, *Hear Me,* 199.
24. *Carmen, Billie.* Carmen McRae sings "Lover Man" and other Billie Holiday Classics. Columbia PC 37002. Liner note.
25. Quoted in Simon, *Music Makers,* 508.
26. Collier, *Jazz,* 139.
27. Quoted in Simon, *Music Makers,* 613.
28. Ibid., 612.
29. Liner note.
30. Teresa Brewer/Count Basie. *The Songs of Bessie Smith.* Doctor Jazz FW 38836. Liner note.

Bibliography

In addition to the books and articles cited in the footnotes, the following are of interest:

Allen, Walter C., and Brian Rust. *King Joe Oliver.* Belleville, N.J.: Walter C. Allen, 1955.

Armstrong, Louis. *Satchmo: My Life in New Orleans.* New York: Prentice-Hall, 1954.

Bechet, Sidney. *Treat It Gentle.* 1960. Reprint. New York: Da Capo Press, 1975.

Berendt, Joachim-Ernst. *The Jazz Book. From New Orleans to Rock and Free Jazz.* Westport, Conn.: Lawrence Hill and Company, 1975.

Berton, Ralph. *Remembering Bix: A Memoir of the Jazz Age.* New York: Harper & Row, 1974.

Brunn, H. O. *The Story of the Original Dixieland Jazz Band.* Baton Rouge: Louisiana State University Press, 1960.

Chilton, John. *Who's Who of Jazz: Storyville to Swing Street.* Philadelphia: Chilton Books, 1972.

Dahl, Linda. *Stormy Weather: The Music and Lives of a Century of Jazz Women.* New York: Pantheon, 1984.

Dexter, Dave. *The Jazz Story: From the 90s to the 60s.* Englewood Cliffs, N.J.: Prentice-Hall, 1964.

Down Beat, Chicago, 1934—.

Feather, Leonard. *The Book of Jazz from Then till Now.* New York: Horizon Press, 1957.

———. *The Encyclopedia of Jazz.* New York: Horizon Press, 1955.

———. *From Satchmo to Miles.* New York: Stein & Day, 1972.

Finkelstein, Sidney. *Jazz: A People's Music.* (1948). Reprint. New York: Da Capo Press, 1975.

Fox, Ted. *Showtime at the Apollo.* New York: Holt, Rinehart and Winston, 1983).

Goffin, Robert. *Horn of Plenty: The Story of Louis Armstrong.* 1947. Reprint. New York: Da Capo Press, 1977.

Hadlock, Richard. *Jazz Masters of the Twenties.* New York: Macmillan, 1965.

Hodeir, Andre. *Toward Jazz.* 1962. Reprint. New York: Da Capo Press, 1976.

James, Burnett. *Bix Beiderbecke.* Kings of Jazz Series. New York: A. S. Barnes, 1961.

Jones, LeRoi. *Blues People: Negro Music in White America.* New York: William Morrow, 1967.

Jones, Max, and John Chilton. *Louis: The Louis Armstrong Story, 1900–1971.* Boston: Little Brown, 1971.

Jones, Morley. *Jazz.* Ed. Alan Rich New York: Simon & Schuster, 1980.

Journal of Jazz Studies, Incorporating Studies in Jazz Discography. New Brunswick, N.J., 1973.

Keepnews, Orrin, and Bill Grauer, Jr. *A Pictorial History of Jazz: People and Places from New Orleans to Modern Jazz.* New York: Crown Publishers, 1955.

Lang, Iain. *Jazz in Perspective: The Background of the Blues.* 1947. Reprint. New York: Da Capo Press, 1976.

Leonard, Neil. *Jazz and the White Americans: The Acceptance of a New Art Form.* Chicago: University of Chicago Press, 1962.

Longstreet, Stephen. *Sportin' House: A History of the New Orleans Sinners and the Birth of Jazz.* Los Angeles: Sherbourne Press, 1965.

Littleton, Humphrey. *Best of Jazz: Basin Street to Harlem.* New York: Crescendo/Taplinger, 1978.

Marquis, Donald M. *In Search of Buddy Bolden: First Man of Jazz.* Baton Rouge: Louisiana State University Press, 1978.

Panassie, Hugues. *The Real Jazz. 1960.* Reprint. Westport, Conn.: Greenwood Press, 1973.

Ramsey, Frederic, Jr., and Charles Edward Smith, Eds., *Jazzmen.* New York: Harcourt Brace, 1930.

Rose, Al, and Edmond Souchon. *New Orleans Jazz: A Family Album.* Rev. ed. Baton Rouge: Louisiana State University Press, 1978.

Schafer, William J., and Richard B. Allen. *Brass Bands and New Orleans Jazz.* Baton Rouge: Louisiana State University Press, 1977.

Schiffman, Jack. *Harlem Heyday: A Pictorial History of Modern Black Show Business and the Apollo Theatre.* Buffalo, N.Y.: Prometheus Books, 1984.

Schuller, Gunther. *Early Jazz: Its Roots and Musical Development.* New York: Oxford University Press, 1968.

Smith, Jay D., and Len Guttridge. *Jack Teagarden: The Story of a Jazz Maverick.* 1960 Reprint. New York: Da Capo Press, 1976.

Smith, Willie, with George Hoefer. *Music on My Mind: The Memoirs of an American Pianist.* 1964. Reprint. New York: Da Capo Press, 1975.

Sonnier, Austin M., Jr. *Willie Geary "Bunk" Johnson: The New Iberia Years.* New York: Crescendo Publishing, 1977.

Stearns, Marshall W. *The Story of Jazz.* 1956. Reprint. New York: Oxford University Press, 1970.

Stoddard, Tom, ed. *Pops Foster — The Autobiography of a New Orleans Jazzman.* Berkeley: University of California Press, 1971.

Sudhalter, Richard M., and Philip R. Evans, with W. Dean-Myatt. *Bix: Man and Legend.* New Rochelle, N.Y.: Arlington House, 1974.

Tirro, Frank. *Jazz: A History.* New York: W. W. Norton, 1977.

Turner, Frederick. *Remembering Song: Encounters with the New Orleans Jazz Tradition.* New York: Viking Press, 1982.

Ulanov, Barry. *History of Jazz in America.* 1952. Reprint. New York: Da Capo Press, 1972.

Wareing, Charles H., and George Garlick. *Bugles for Beiderbecke.* London: Sidgwick and Jackson, 1958.

Williams, Martin T. *Jazz Masters of New Orleans.* 1967. Reprint. New York: Da Capo Press, 1979.

———. *Jelly Roll Morton.* Kings of Jazz series. New York: A. S. Barnes, 1963.

Discography

Delaunay, Charles. *New Hot Discography: The Standard Directory of Recorded Jazz.* Ed. by Walter E. Schaap and George Avakian. New York: Criterion, 1948.

Jazz Report. The Record Collector's Magazine. Ventura, Cal. 1958.

Jepsen, Jorgen Grunnet. *Jazz Records, 1942–1965.* A Discography. 8 Vols. Holte, Denmark: Karl Emil Knudsen, 1964–1965.

McCoy, Meredith, and Barbara Parker, comps. *Catalog of the John D. Reid Collection of Early American Jazz.* Little Rock: Arkansas Arts Center, 1975.

Ramsey, Frederic, Jr. *A Guide to Longplay Jazz Records.* New York: Long Player Publications, 1954.

Rust, Brian. *Jazz Records 1897–1942.* 4th and enlarged ed. 2 Vols. New Rochelle, N.Y.: Arlington House, 1978.

Schleman, Hilton R. *Rhythm on Record: A Complete Survey and Register of All the Principal Recorded Dance Music, 1906–1936, and a Who's Who of the Artists Concerned in the Making.* 1936. Reprint. Westport, Conn.: Greenwood Press, 1978.

Smith, Charles Edward, with Frederic Ramsey, Jr., Charles Payne Rogers, and William Russell, *The Jazz Record Book.* 1942. Reprint. Westport, Conn.: Greenwood Press, 1978.

Townley, Eric. *Tell Your Story: A Dictionary of Jazz and Blues Recordings, 1917–1950.* Chigwell, Essex, England: Storyville Publications, 1976.

Wilson, John S. *The Collector's Jazz: Traditional and Swing.* Philadelphia: J. B. Lippincott, 1958.

Louis Armstrong
- *Louis Armstrong Jazz Classics.* Brunswick 58004.
- *The Louis Armstrong Story:*
  - Vol. 1. *Louis Armstrong and His Hot Five.* Columbia ML 54383.
  - Vol. 2. *Louis Armstrong and His Hot Seven.* Columbia ML 54384.
  - Vol. 3. *Louis Armstrong and Earl Hines.* Columbia ML 54386.
  - Vol. 4. *Louis Armstrong Favorites.* Columbia ML 54386.
- *Louis Armstrong Classics: New Orleans to New York.* Decca DL 5225.
- *Chicago Days with Louis Armstrong,* Vol. 1. Jazz Panorama 1201.
- *Louis Armstrong Plays the Blues.* Riverside 1001.

Sidney Bechet
- *Sidney Bechet Solos.* Atlantic 118.
- *Jazz Classics,* Vol. 1. Blue Note 7002.
- *Jazz Classics,* Vol. 2. Blue Note 7003.
- *Days Beyond Recall* (with Bunk Johnson). Blue Note 7008.
- *Sidney Bechet,* Vol. 1. Jazz Panorama 1801.
- *Sidney Bechet,* Vol. 2. Jazz Panorama 1809.

Bix Beiderbecke
- *The Bix Beiderbecke Story:*
  - Vol. 1. *Bix and His Gang.* Columbia ML 4811, CL 844.
  - Vol. 2. *Bix and Tram.* Columbia ML 4812, CL 845.
  - Vol. 3. *Whiteman Days.* Columbia ML 4813, CL 846.

Teresa Brewer
- *It Don't Mean a Thing If It Ain't Got That Swing.* Columbia PC 37340
- *Songs of Bessie Smith.* Doctor Jazz FW 38836.
- *Sophisticated Lady.* Columbia PC 37363.

June Christy
- *June's Got Rhythm.* Capitol T 1076.
- *Something Cool.* Capitol T 516.
- *This Is June Christy.* Capitol 1006.

Rosemary Clooney
Rosemary Clooney Sings the Music of Cole Porter. Concord Jazz CJ 185.
A Tribute to Duke. Concord Jazz CJ 50.
Chris Connor
Stan Kenton: *Fabulous Alumni.* Creative World 1028.
——— *Some Women I Have Known.* Creative World 1029.
——— *Double Exposure.* (Jazzlore No. 21). Atlantic 90143-1.
Johnny Dodds
King Oliver and His Creole Jazz Band. Riverside RLP 1029.
Johnny Dodds Washboard Band. "X" LX 3006.
Johnny Dodds and His Orchestra. Decca ED 2352.
Warren "Baby" Dodds
Mr. Jelly Lord (Jelly Roll Morton). RCA Victor LPV 546.
The Blue Bechet (Sidney Bechet). RCA Victor LPV 535.
Ella Fitzgerald
Duke Ellington Songbook. Verve 4010-4.
Ella and Her Fellas, *A Tisket A Tasket.* Decca 8477.
Lullabies of Birdland. Decca 8149.
Ella Fitzgerald and Billie Holiday at Newport. Verve 8234.
Ella and Louis. Verve 4003.
Ella And Louis Again. Verve 4006-2.
Billie Holiday
Billie Holiday. Commodore Jazz Classics. Mainstream 56000.
Billie Holiday: The Original Recordings. Columbia 32060.
Lady Day. Columbia CL 637.
Lady Sings the Blues. Verve 8099.
Lover Man. Decca DL 5345.
The Golden Years, Vol. 1. Columbia C3L 21.
The Golden Years, Vol. 2. Columbia C3L 40.
Helen Humes
Black California. Savoy 2215.
From Spirituals to Swing. Vanguard VSD 47–48.
Lady Sings the Blues, Vol. 2. Savoy 2256.
Singin' the Blues. MCA 2-4064.
Freddie Keppard
New Orleans Horns (Anthology). Riverside RLP 1005.
Peggy Lee
All-Time Greatest Hits—Benny Goodman. Columbia PG 31547.
Best of Peggy Lee. MCA 2-4049.
Fever. Capitol 6014.
Is That All There Is. Capitol SM 368.
Carmen McRae
Greatest Of Carmen McRae. MCA 2-4111.
Carmen McRae Sings Lover Man and Other Billie Holiday Classics. Columbia PC 37002.
Take Five. Columbia Special Products JCS 9116.
Two for the Road. Concord Jazz 128.

Jelly Roll Morton
The Incomparable Jelly Roll Morton. Milestone MLP 2003.
King of New Orleans Jazz, Vol. 1. RCA Victor LPM 1649.
Jelly Roll Morton Piano Solos/New Orleans Memories. Commodore 30000.
The Saga of Mr. Jelly Lord. 12 vols. Circle L 14001-14012.

New Orleans Rhythm Kings
N.O.R.K. Riverside 12-102.

Jimmy Noone
Jimmie Noone Apex Club. Brunswick BL 58006.
Jimmie Noone and Earl Hines at the Apex Club, Vol. 1. Decca DL 9235.

Helen O'Connell
This Is Helen O'Connell. Victor VPM 6076.

Anita O'Day
At Mister Kelly's. Verve VMV 2550.
Stan Kenton: Fabulous Alumni. Creative World 1028.
Stan Kenton: Some Women I've Known. Creative World 1029.
Hi Ho Trailus Boot Whip. Doctor Jazz FW 39418.

King Oliver
King Oliver, Vol. 1. Brunswick BL 58020.
Lincoln Gardens. Jazz Panorama 1205.
King Oliver Plays the Blues. Riverside 1007.

Original Dixieland Jazz Band
Original Dixieland Jazz Band. Commodore 20003.

Kid Ory.
Kid Ory. Columbia CL 6145.
Kid Ory's Creole Jazz Band 1944/45. 2 Vols. Good Time Jazz 10, 11.

Jimmy Rushing
Jimmy: Jimmy Rushing—Mr. Five By Five. Columbia C2 36419.
The Essential Jimmy Rushing. Vanguard VSD 65/66.
Everyday I Have the Blues. Bluesway 6005.
The Odyssey of James Rushing, Esq. Columbia CL 963.
Sings the Blues. Vanguard VRS 8518.

Jack Teagarden
Big. T. Commodore 20015.
King of the Blues Trombone. 3 Vols. Epic SN 6044.
Jack Teagarden. RCA Victor LPV 528.

Sarah Vaughan
Gershwin Live! Sarah Vaughan/Michael Tilson Thomas. CBS 37277
Golden Hits!!! Mercury MG 20645.
Images. Emarcy MG 36109.
Sarah Vaughan. Emarcy MG 36004.
Sassy. Mercury MG 20441.

Lee Wiley
Night in Manhattan. Columbia Special Products JCL 656.
Singin' the Blues. MCA 2-4064.

Nancy Wilson
Best of Nancy Wilson. MCA 2-4049.

Jazz Origin. Pausa 9021.
Two Of Us. Columbia FC 39326/ 38-05424.
Nancy Wilson/Cannonball Adderley. Capitol SN 16210.

Of the songs discussed in this chapter, the author was himself involved in the development and popularization of "Broken Hearted Melody."

Chapter Seven. "It Don't Mean a Thing If It Ain't Got That Swing"

1. Nat Shapiro and Nat Hentoff, *Hear Me Talkin' to Ya* (New York: Rinehart & Co., 1955,) 314.
2. There were the CWA (Civil Works Administration), CCC (Civil Conservation Corps), FERA (Federal Emergency Relief Administration), AAA (Agricultural Act), WPA (Works Progress Administration), among others.
3. At various times between the thirties and the fifties, the block between fifth and sixth avenues housed a dozen or more clubs. Additional clubs, such as Hickory House, Kelly's Stable, Yacht Club, and others, were situated in the block between sixth and seventh avenues. See Arnold Shaw, *52nd St.: The Street of Jazz* (New York: Da Capo Press, 1977).
4. Marshall W. Stearns, *The Story of Jazz* (New York: Oxford University Press, 1956), 202.
5. Booklet accompanying *The Fletcher Henderson Story: A Study in Frustration*. Columbia/C4L 19.
6. Ibid.
7. Quoted in Nat Shapiro and Nat Hentoff, *Hear Me Talkin' to Ya* (New York: Holt, Rinehart & Winston, 1955), 298.
8. Ibid., 194.
9. Shapiro and Hentoff, *Hear Me*, 195.
10. In this period, it was not uncommon for bandleaders to receive writer credit (be "cut in") on songs they recorded.
11. Shapiro and Hentoff, *Hear Me*, 325.
12. George T. Simon, *The Big Bands* (New York: The Macmillan Company, 1967), 110.
13. The historic recognition came in 1979, when the Jazzwalk was launched on the Street. See *Dictionary of American Pop/Rock* by Arnold Shaw (New York: Schirmer Books, 1982), 194.
14. James Lincoln Collier, *The Making of Jazz* (Boston: Houghton Mifflin, 1978), 261; Stearns, *Story of Jazz*, 200.
15. Collier, 261.
16. Stearns, *Story of Jazz*, 213. See Benny Goodman, *The Kingdom of Swing* (Harrisburg, Penn.: Stackpole Sons, 1939), 129.
17. Stearns, *Story of Jazz*, 208.
18. Ibid., 202.
19. Ibid., 203.
20. Ibid., 209.
21. Collier, *Making of Jazz*, 213–14.
22. Shaw, *52nd St.*, 265.
23. Ibid., 267.
24. Ibid., 265.

Bibliography

In addition to the books cited in the footnotes, the following are of interest:

Allen, Walter C. *Hendersonia: The Music of Fletcher Henderson and His Musicians*. Highland Park, N.J.: Walter C. Allen, 1973.

Benny: King of Swing. A Pictorial Biography based on Benny Goodman's Personal Archives, with 212 illustrations. New York: William Morrow, 1979.

Calloway, Cab, and Bryant Rollins. *Of Minnie the Moocher and Me*. New York: Thomas Y. Crowell, 1976.

Condon, Eddie, and Hank O'Neal. *The Eddie Condon Scrapbook of Jazz*. New York: St. Martin's Press, 1973.

Condon, Eddie, and Thomas Sugrue, *We Called It Music: A Generation of Jazz*. New York: Henry Holt, 1947.

Connor, D. Russell. *BG—Off the Record: A Bio-Discography of Benny Goodman*. Fairless Hill, Pa.: Gaildonna Publishing Co., 1958.

Connor, D. Russell, and Warren W. Hicks, *B. G. on the Record: A Bio-Discography of Benny Goodman*. New Rochelle, N.Y.: Arlington House, 1969.

Dance, Stanley. *The World of Count Basie*. New York: Charles Scribner's Sons, 1980.

———. *The World of Duke Ellington*. New York: Charles Scribner's Sons, 1970.

———. *The World of Swing*, Vol. 1. New York: Charles Scribner's Sons, 1974.

———. *The World of Earl Hines*, Vol. 2: The World of Swing. New York: Charles Scribner's Sons, 1977.

Dance, Vince. *Bunny: A Bio-Discography of Jazz Trumpeter Bunny Berigan*. Rockford, Ill.: Vince Danca, 1978.

Down Beat, Chicago, 1934.

Easton, Carol. *Straight Ahead: The Story of Stan Kenton*. New York: William Morrow, 1973.

Ellington, Duke. *Music Is My Mistress*. New York: Doubleday, 1971; Da Capo Press, 1973.

Ellington, Mercer, with Stanley Dance, *Duke Ellington in Person*. Boston: Houghton Mifflin, 1978.

Esquire's World of Jazz. New York: Grosset & Dunlap, 1962; Thomas Y. Crowell, 1978.

Feather, Leonard. *Inside Bebop*. New York: J. J. Robbins and Sons, 1949.

———. *The New Edition of the Encyclopedia of Jazz*. Completely Revised, Enlarged, and Brought Up to Date. New York: Horizon Press, 1960.

Fernett, Gene. *Swing Out: Great Negro Dance Bands*. Midland, Mich.: Pendell, 1970.

Fernett, Gene. *A Thousand Golden Horns . . . The Exciting Age of America's Greatest Dance Bands*. Midland, Mich.: Pendell, 1966.

Flower, John. *Moonlight Serenade: A Bio-Discography of the Glenn Miller Civilian Band*. New Rochelle, N.Y.: Arlington House, 1972.

Gammond, Peter, ed. *Duke Ellington: His Life and Music*. 1958. Reprint. New York: Da Capo Press, 1977.

Gillespie, Dizzy, with Al Fraser. *To Be, or Not . . . to Bop: Memoirs*. New York: Doubleday, 1979.

Gitler, Ira. *Jazz Masters of the Forties*. New York: Collier/Macmillan, 1966.

Gleason, Ralph J. *Celebrating the Duke; and Louis, Bessie, Billie, Bird, Carmen,*

Miles, Dizzy, and Other Heroes. Boston: Atlantic Monthly Press Book/Little Brown, 1975.

Goodman, Benny, and Irving Kolodin. *The Kingdom of Swing*. New York: Stackpole Sons, 1939.

Gottlieb, William P. *The Golden Age of Jazz: On-Location Portraits, in Words and Pictures, of More Than 200 Outstanding Musicians from the Late Thirties through the Forties*. New York: Simon and Schuster, 1979.

Graham, Albert Powell. *Strike Up the Band! Bandleaders of Today*. New York: Thomas Nelson and Sons, 1949.

Harrison, Max. *Charlie Parker*. Kings of Jazz series. New York: A. S. Barnes, 1961.

Hobson, Wilder. *American Jazz Music*. 1939. Reprint. New York: Da Capo Press, 1976.

Horricks, Raymond. *Count Basie and His Orchestra: Its Music and Its Musicians*. 1957. Reprint. Westport, Conn.: Negro Universities Press, 1971.

Jewell, Derek. *Duke: A Portrait of Duke Ellington*. New York: W. W. Norton, 1977.

Kaminsky, Max, with V. E. Hughes. *My Life in Jazz*. London: Jazz Book Club, 1965.

Lee, Dr. William F. *Stan Kenton: Artistry in Rhythm*. Audree Coke, ed. Los Angeles: Creative Press of Los Angeles, 1980.

McCarthy, Albert. *Big Band Jazz*. New York: G. P. Putnam's Sons, 1974.

———. *The Dance Band Era: The Dancing Decades from Ragtime to Swing, 1910–1950*. New York: Da Capo Press, 1972.

Mezzrow, Milton, and Bernard Wolfe, *Really the Blues*. New York: Random House, 1946.

Miller, Paul Eduard, ed. *Down Beat's Yearbook of Swing*. 1939. Reprint. Westport, Conn.: Greenwood Press, 1978.

———. *Esquire's Jazz Book*. Chicago: Books, 1943–44.

———. *Esquire's 1946 Jazz Book*. New York: Smith and Durrell, 1946.

Mingus, Charles. *Beneath the Underdog*. Nel King, ed. 1971. Reprint. New York: Penguin, 1975.

Panassie, Hugues. *Hot Jazz: The Guide to Swing Music*. Trans.: Lyle and Eleanor Dowling. 1936. Reprint. Westport, Conn.: Negro Universities Press/ Greenwood Press, 1970.

Reisner, Robert George, ed. *Bird: The Legend of Charlie Parker*. 1962. Reprint. New York: Da Capo Press, 1975.

Russell, Ross. *Bird Lives! The High Life and Hard Times of Charlie (Yardbird) Parker*. New York: Charterhouse, 1973.

———. *Jazz Style in Kansas City and the Southwest*. Berkeley: University of California Press, 1971.

Rust, Brian. *The American Dance Band Discography 1917–1942*. 2 Vols. New Rochelle, N.Y.: Arlington House, 1975.

———. *The Dance Bands*. New Rochelle, N.Y.: Arlington House, 1974.

———. *Jazz Records 1897–1942*. 4th rev. and enlarged ed. 2 Vols. New Rochelle, N.Y.: Arlington House, 1978.

Sanford, Herb. *Tommy and Jimmy: The Dorsey Years*. 1972. Reprint. New York: Da Capo Press, 1980.

Shapiro, Nat, and Nat Hentoff. *The Jazz Makers*. 1957. Reprint. Westport, Conn.: Greenwood Press, 1975.

Shaw, Arnold. *The Street That Never Slept: New York's Fabled 52nd St.* New York: Coward, McCann and Geoghegan, 1971; Da Capo Press, 1977, reprinted as *52nd St.: The Street of Jazz.*

Simon, George T. *The Big Bands*. Rev. ed. New York: Macmillan, 1974.

———. *Glenn Miller and His Orchestra*. New York: Thomas Y. Crowell, 1974.

———. *Simon Says: The Sights and Sounds of the Swing Era, 1935–1955*. New Rochelle, N.Y.: Arlington House, 1971.

Spellman, A. B. *Four Lives in the Bebop Business*. New York: Pantheon Books, 1966.

Ulanov, Barry. *Duke Ellington*. 1946. Reprint. New York: Da Capo Press, 1972.

Walker, Leo. *The Big Band Almanac*. Pasadena, Calif.: Ward Ritchie Press, n.d.

———. *The Wonderful Era of the Great Dance Bands*. Berkeley, Calif.: Howell-North Books, 1964.

Wells, Dicky, as told to Stanley Dance. *The Night People: Reminiscences of a Jazzman*. Boston: Crescendo Publishing, 1971.

Discography

Mildred Bailey

Her Greatest Performances, Vols. 1, 2, 3. Columbia 3CL 22.

Rockin' Chair Lady. Decca DL 5387.

Count Basie

Blues by Basie. Columbia CL 901.

The Count. Camden CAL 395.

Count Basie. Victor LPM 1112.

Count Basie and His Orchestra. Decca 8049.

Count Basie Classics. Columbia CL 754.

Jumpin' at the Woodside. Brunswick BL 54012.

Lester Leaps In. Epic LG 3107.

Let's Go to Prez. Epic LN 3168.

One O'Clock Jump. Columbia CL 997.

Will Bradley

Boogie-Woogie. Epic 3115.

Cab Calloway

Cab Calloway. Epic 3265.

Cab Calloway and His Orchestra. Brunswick 58010.

Eddie Condon

Chicago Style Jazz. Columbia CL 632.

Dixieland. Columbia CL 319.

George Gershwin Jazz Concert. Decca DL 5137.

Jazz a La Carte. Commodore 20017, 30010.

Jazz Concert at Eddie Condon's. Decca DL 5218.

We Called It Music. Decca DL 5246.

Jimmy Dorsey

Fabulous Dorseys Play Dixieland Jazz 1934–35. Decca DL 8631.

Tommy Dorsey
Hawaiian War Chant. Victor LPM 1234.
He Really Digs Jazz. Decca 8314.
That Sentimental Gentleman. Victor LPT 6003.
Stringing the Blues, Vol. 2 (Joe Venuti and Eddie Lang). Columbia 2CL-24.
Tribute to Dorsey, Vol. 1. Victor LPM 1432.
Yes, Indeed! Victor LPM 1229.
Duke Ellington
The Duke and His Men. Victor LPM 1092.
The Duke Plays Ellington (piano solos). Capitol T 477.
Duke Ellington at the Cotton Club. Camden CAL 459.
The Ellington Era, 1927–1940. Vols. 1 and 2. Columbia C3L 27, 39.
Duke Ellington's Greatest Hits. Reprise R 6234.
Early Ellington. Brunswick 54007.
In A Mellotone. Victor LPM 1364.
Masterpieces by Ellington. Columbia CL 825.
The Music of Duke Ellington. Columbia CL 558.
Dizzy Gillespie
Dizzy Gillespie. RCA LPV 530.
Dizzy Gillespie. Savoy MG 12020.
Dizzy Gillespie Story, Vols. 1 and 2. Savoy MG 12110, 12047.
The Greatest. RCA LPM 2398.
At Home and Abroad. Atlantic 1257.
Benny Goodman
Carnegie Hall Jazz Concert 1938. 2 LP sets. Columbia OSL 160.
The Golden Age of Benny Goodman. RCA Victor LPM 1099.
The Golden Age of Swing. (5 vols.). RCA Victor LPT 6703.
This Is Benny Goodman. RCA Victor LPM 1239.
Benny Goodman Presents Fletcher Henderson Arrangements. Columbia CL 524.
Benny Goodman Trio-Quartet-Quintet. RCA Victor LPM 1226.
The King of Swing. (Air-shots). Vols. 1–3. Columbia CL 817, 818, 819.
Glen Gray
Casa Loma Caravan. Capitol 856.
Casa Loma in Hi-Fi. Capitol 747.
The Great Recordings of Glen Gray. Harmony 7045.
Lionel Hampton
The Genius of Lionel Hampton. Verve 8215.
Hamp! Verve MGV 8019.
Hamp's Boogie Woogie. Decca DL 5230.
Lionel Hampton and His Giants. Verve MGV 8170.
Jivin' the Vibes. Camden CAL 402.
Coleman Hawkins
Classic Tenors. Contact LP 3.
The Hawk Flies High. Riverside RLP 12-233.
Coleman Hawkins. RCA LPV 501.
Coleman Hawkins: A Documentary. Riverside 12-117/118.
Fletcher Henderson

The Big Reunion (Fletcher Henderson All-Stars). Jazztone J 1285.
Fletcher Henderson 1934. Swings the Thing. Decca DL 9228.
Fletcher Henderson Orchestra. Allegro 4028.
A Study in Frustration, Vols. 1–4. Columbia 4CL 19.

Woody Herman
Golden Favorites. Decca DL 8133.
The Swinging Herman Herd. Brunswick 54024.
The Thundering Herds. 3 LPs. Columbia C3L 25.
They Heard the Herd. Verve MGV 8216.
Woodchoppers' Ball. Decca 8133.

Earl Hines
Fatha Plays Fats. Fantasy 3217.
Grand Terrace Band. RCA LPV 512.
Earl "Fatha" Hines. Epic LN 3501.
Earl "Fatha" Hines Solos. Fantasy 3238.
Oh, Father! Epic 3223.

Harry James
All-Time Favorites. Columbia CL 655.
At the Hollywood Palladium. Columbia CL 567.
More Harry James in Hi-Fi. Capitol W 712.

Stan Kenton
Adventures in Blues. Capitol T 1985.
Contemporary Concepts. Capitol T 666.
Cuban Fire. Capitol T 731.
The Kenton Era. 4 LPs. Capitol W 569.

Andy Kirk
Instrumentally Speaking (1936–1942). Decca DL 9232.
A Mellow Bit of Rhythm. Victor LPM 1302.

Gene Krupa
Drum Crazy—The Gene Krupa Story. Verve MGV 6105.
Drummin' Man. Columbia C 2L 29.
Gene Krupa. Columbia 753.
Krupa-Hampton-Wilson. Verve MGV 8066.
Gene Krupa's Sidekicks. Columbia CL 641.
Swingin' with Krupa. Camden 340.

Jimmie Lunceford
For Dancers Only. Decca DL 5393.
Jimmie Lunceford and His Orchestra. Decca 8050.
Lunceford Special. Columbia CL 634 and 2715.

"Wingy" Manone
Sound of New Orleans (1917–1947) (anthology). Columbia C3L 30.
Swing Street, Vol. 1 (anthology). Epic SN 6042.
Trumpet on the Wing. Decca 8473.

Jay McShann
History of Jazz, Vols. 3 and 4. Capitol H 240 and H 242.
Kansas City Memories. Decca DL 9236.

Glenn Miller
Glenn Miller—A Memorial (1944–1969). RCA Victor VPM 6019.

The Best of Glenn Miller, Vols. 1, 2, 3. RCA Victor LSP 3377, LSP 3564, LSP 4125.
Glenn Miller on the Air, Vols. 1, 2, 3. RCA Victor LSP 2767, LSP 2768, LSP 2769.
This Is Glenn Miller and the Army Air Force Band. RCA VPM 6080.
The Original Recordings by Glenn Miller and His Orchestra. RCA Camden CAS 829.
The Unforgettable Glenn Miller. Reader's Digest RD 4-64.

Bennie Moten
Toby on Jazz. Vol. 10, Folkways FP 73.

Red Nichols
Meet the Five Pennies. Capitol T 1228.
Red Nichols and the Charleston Chasers. Thesaurus of Classic Jazz, Vol. 3. Columbia C4L 18.
Red Nichols and His Five Pennies: For Collectors Only. Brunswick BL 54008.

Red Norvo
Red Norvo and His All-Stars. Epic EE 22009.
Red Norvo Trio, Vols 1, 2. Discovery 3012, 3018.
Red Norvo Trio. Fantasy LP 3-12.
Red Plays the Blues. RCA Victor LPM 1729.

Charlie "Bird" Parker
Now's the Time. Verve 8005.
The Genius of Charlie Parker. Savoy 12014.
The Immortal Charlie Parker, Savoy 12001.
Charlie Parker. 4 Vols. Dial 201, 202, 203, 207.
Charlie Parker Memorial, Vol. 1. Savoy 12000.
Charlie Parker Memorial, Vol. 2. Savoy 12009.
The Charlie Parker Story. Savoy 12079.
The Charlie Parker Story. Vols. 1, 2, 3. Verve 8000, 8001, 8002.
Swedish Schnapps. Verve 8010.

Louis Prima
Chicago Jazz, Vol. 3 (Bud Freeman. Louis Prima). Jazz Panorama 1819.

Don Redman
Harlem Jazz, 1930 (Ellington, Redman, Henderson, Russell). Brunswick BL 58024.
The Fletcher Henderson Story, Vols. 1 and 2. Columbia C4L 19.
Master of the Big Band. RCA Victor LPV 520.
Park Avenue Patter. Golden Crest 3017.

Artie Shaw
The Great Artie Shaw. Camden CAL 465.
Artie Shaw and his Gramercy Five. RCA Victor LPM 1241.
Artie Shaw Swings Show Tunes. Camden CAL 515.
Artie Shaw withStrings. Epic 3112.
Reissued by Request. RCA Victor LPM 1648.

Stuff Smith
Dizzy Gillespie and Stuff Smith. Verve MGV 8214.
Have Violin, Will Swing. Verve MGV 8282.
Stuff Smith. Verve 8206.

Swingin' Stuff. Emarcy 26008.

Eddie South

Modern American Musicians: Norvo, Eddie South, Slam Stewart. Remington 1033.

Maxine Sullivan

The Great Songs from the Cotton Club. Stash ST 244.

"Loch Lomond/I'm Coming Virginia." Okeh 3654.

"Loch Lomond/Just Like a Gypsy." Decca 3954.

Chick Webb

Five Feet of Swing: Bob Crosby; Dorsey Brothers' Orchestra; Chick Webb plus Ella Fitzgerald; Jimmy Dorsey; Casa Loma Orchestra. Decca DL 8045.

Stompin' at the Savoy. Columbia CL 2639.

Chick Webb, Vols. 1 and 2. Decca 9222, 9223.

Teddy Wilson

Piano Moods. Columbia CL 6153.

Teddy Wilson and His Orchestra, featuring Billie Holiday. Columbia CL 6040.

Teddy Wilson and His Piano. Columbia CL 6098.

Teddy Wilson Trio. Mercury MG 25172.

Lester Young

Jumpin' at the Woodside: Count Basie. Brunswick BL 54012.

Lester Swings Again: The President. Verve MGV 8181.

Pres. Verve MGV 8162.

Pres Is Blue. Charlie Parker PLP 405.

Lester Young and His Tenor Sax. Aladdin 706.

Lester Young Memorial, Vols. 1 and 2. Savoy MG 12068, 12071.

Of the songs discussed in this chapter, the author was himself involved in the development and popularization of "Come On-A My House."

Chapter Eight. "Mama's got the *Rhythm,* Papa's got the *Blues.*"

1. Arnold Shaw, *Honkers and Shouters: The Golden Years of Rhythm and Blues* (New York: Macmillan, 1978), 74.
2. Charles Keil, *Urban Blues* (Chicago: University of Chicago Press, 1966), 107–108.
3. The advent of Rock 'n' Roll, rooted in R & B, elevated the electric guitar to the position occupied by the tenor sax in R & B. At the suggestion of Memphis Slim, Hal Singer went to Paris, where he met and married a French woman, had two daughters, and remained as part of an expatriate colony of jazzmen that included Dexter Gordon, Slide Hampton, Johnny Griffin, Art Farmer, Benny Bailey, and Thad Jones, who became director of the Copenhagen Radio Orchestra in 1980. But that year, Singer began thinking of returning home, feeling, as Michael Zwerin reported, "you've got to keep making hits or you go down." He also found that, while European musicians were generally friendly, the French were not, and worked to undercut American Jazz artists. See *International Herald-Tribune.* May 6, 1980.

4. Like other words—Jazz, Swing, Boogie—that came to identify popular-music styles, "rock" and "roll" had sexual connotations in black jargon, and are to be found in Blues recordings of the 1930s.
5. My first published article on popular music, appearing in *The New York Times Magazine* of May 18, 1947, was concerned with the phenomenon of "Open the Door, Richard."
6. "Confused" because the song was a put-down of a man who had been misusing a woman, and had to be sung by a woman, castigating the man as a lowdown hound dog. Although some changes were made in the lyric, it still made no sense when it was sung by a man.
7. See Shaw, *Honkers and Shouters,* for details, 31–35.
8. *The Bill Broonzy Story.* 5 Vols. Verve MGV 3000-5.
9. Quoted in *Rolling Stone,* June 23, 1983, p. 42.
10. Ibid.
11. Ibid., 40.
12. Ibid., 42.
13. Howlin' Wolf was among a group of black artists who have claimed under-payment and nonpayment of royalties by record companies and publishers. Among those who have aired their grievances publicly, either through lawsuits or statements to the media, are B. B. King, Big Mama Thornton, and John Lee Hooker, as well as Big Boy Crudup and the Wolf. For details of two lawsuits he brought, see Shaw, *Honkers and Shouters,* 305–306.
14. Shaw, *Honkers and Shouters,* 95.
15. Arnold Shaw, *52nd St.: The Street of Jazz* (New York: Da Capo Press, 1977), 214.
16. Different dates appear in different sources as Dinah Washington's birthday. None can be verified and she herself may not have known the exact date. When I was working on an article for the *Dictionary of American Biography.* I made a concentrated effort to ascertain the precise date. Correspondence with various government agencies in Alabama and the city of Tuscaloosa yielded the simple fact that in those years the births of blacks were frequently not recorded.
17. Joe Sherman, owner of the Garrick Stage Bar in Chicago, where her singing career really began, is generally credited with the change. But manager Joe Glaser, who brought her to Lionel Hampton's attention, and Hampton, with whom she sang for two years, have both claimed the responsibility. See the liner note on, *Dinah Washington: A Slick Chick on the Mellow Side,* Emarcy Jazz Series 814 184-1.
18. I happily accept responsibility for helping Dinah reach the wide audience she long deserved. As I wrote in the liner note to her recent album, I was long an admirer of her artistry. When Mercury Records appointed Clyde Otis as its A and R chieftain in 1959—he was the first black in such a key position at a major label—I approached him about reviving "What a Diff'rence a Day Made," originally a hit in 1934. Dinah's version, cut, as I recall, in two takes, was so potent that I went on a nine-week promotion tour, even though the Edward B. Marks Music Corporation, of which I was Vice-President, employed regional promotion men. A major reason for my activity was Mercury's game plan of promoting her disk only in black

markets. I directed my efforts at the country's pop disk jockeys, who reacted positively once they heard her record. See Arnold Shaw, *The Rockin' 50s: The Decade That Transformed the Pop Music Scene* (New York: Hawthorn Books, 1974), 258–59.
19. Ibid.
20. Shaw, *Honkers and Shouters,* 177.
21. Ibid., 337–340.
22. In 1985, Modern was in the process of being sold.
23. It was on the basis of this song that Bill Haley claimed credit for naming the music *Rock 'n' Roll.* But the junction of these two words and its popularization was performed by disk jockey Alan Freed, who deserves credit for giving the music its name.
24. See Barry Hansen ("Dr. Demento") liner note to *Joe Turner: His Greatest Recordings.* Atco SD 33-376.
25. Quoted in Shaw, *Honkers and Shouters,* xxiii.
26. Tom McCourt, "Bright Lights, Big City: A Brief History of Rhythm and Blues, 1945–1957," *Popular Music and Society,* Vol. IX, No. 2, 1983, 15.
27. Hill and Range paid $6,000 to Atlantic's publishing subsidiary for a 50% share of "Sh-Boom" 's earnings. Atlantic was willing to sell half the copyright because of a limited cash reserve and its desire to avail itself of H and R's publishing know-how. I was then Vice-President and General Professional Manager of H and R, and I negotiated the deal, having accidentally discovered that the Chords' disk was outselling all the major pop disks in the Los Angeles area. If H and R was to recoup and exceed the $6,000 advance, a white cover was a necessity—and this Mercury provided without any intervention by me. The Crew Cuts cover went to the top of Pop charts in the summer of 1954. In this instance, the Chords profited greatly from the cover, since they wrote "Sh-Boom" and received royalties on sales of the Crew Cuts' disk. See Shaw, *The Rockin' 50s,* 73–77, for details.
28. Quoted in Shaw, *The Rockin' 50s,* 164.
29. Quoted in Arnold Shaw, *Dictionary of American Pop/Rock* (New York: Schirmer Books, 1982). 317.
30. Quoted in Shaw, *The Rockin' 50s,* 139.
31. Ibid., 140.
32. Hunter Davies, *The Beatles* (New York: McGraw-Hill Book Co., 1968, 1978), 20.
33. Ibid., 30.
34. Ibid., 42.
35. Pete Frame, "Genealogy of British Blues Bands," *Rolling Stone,* March 15, 1984, 60.
36. Ibid.
37. Ibid.

Bibliography

In addition to the books and articles cited in the footnotes, the following are of interest:

Bane, Michael. *White Boy Singin' the Blues: The Black Roots of White Rock.* New York: Penguin, 1982.

Benjaminson, Peter. *The Story of Motown.* New York: Grove Press, 1979.

Bim Bam Boom: The Magazine Devoted to the History of Rhythm and Blues. Bronx, New York, 1972.

Bogle, Donald. *Brown Sugar: Eighty Years of America's Black Female Superstars.* New York: Harmony Books, 1980.

Broven, John. *Walking to New Orleans: The Story of New Orleans Rhythm and Blues.* Bexhill-on-Sea, Sussex, England: Blues Unlimited, 1974.

Escott, Colin, and Martin Hawkins. Sun Records: The Brief History of the Legendary Record Label. New York: Music Sales, 1980.

Ferlingere, Robert D., comp. *A Discography of Rhythm & Blues and Rock 'n' Roll Vocal Groups, 1945–1965.* Pittsburg, Calif.: Robert D. Ferlinger, 1976.

Fleese, Krista. *Chuck Berry: Mr. Rock 'N' Roll.* New York: Proteus Publications, 1983.

Gillett, Charlie. *Making Tracks, Atlantic Records and the Growth of a Multi-Billion-Dollar Industry.* New York: E. P. Dutton, 1975.

———. *The Sound of the City: The Rise of Rock and Roll.* New York: Outerbridge & Dienstfrey, 1970.

Given, Dave. *The Dave Given Rock 'n' Roll Stars Handbook: Rhythm and Blues Artists and Groups.* Smithtown, N.Y.: Exposition Press, 1980.

Gonzalez, Fernando L., comp. *Disco-File: The Discographical Catalog of American Rock & Roll and Rhythm & Blues, Vocal Harmony Groups,* 2d ed. 1902–1976: *Race, Rhythm & Blues, Rock & Roll, Soul.* Flushing, N.Y.: Fernando L. Gonzalez, 1977.

Groia, Philip. *They All Sang on the Corner: New York City's Rhythm & Blues Vocal Groups of the 1950s.* Branchport, N.Y.: Edmond Publishing, 1973.

Guralnick, Peter. *Feel Like Going Home: Portraits in Blues and Rock 'n' Roll.* New York: Sunrise Books/E. P. Dutton, 1971.

———. *Lost Highway.* New York: Random House, 1979. (See Part Four: "The Blues Roll On").

Haralambos, Michael. *Right On: From Blues to Soul in Black America.* New York: Drake Publishers, 1975.

Heilbut, Tony. *The Gospel Sound: Good News and Bad Times.* New York: Simon & Schuster, 1971.

Jones, Hettie. *Big Star Fallin', Mama: Five Women in Black Music.* New York: Viking Press, 1974.

Lewis, Myra, and Murray Silver. *Great Balls of Fire: The Uncensored Story of Jerry Lee Lewis.* New York: Morrow, 1982.

Leichter, Albert. *A Discography of Rhythm & Blues and Rock & Roll, circa 1946–1964: A Reference Manual.* Staunton, Va.: Albert Leichter, 1975.

Lydon, Michael. *Boogie Lightning.* New York: The Dial Press, 1974.

McCutcheon, Lynn Ellis. *Rhythm and Blues: An Experience and Adventure in Its Origin and Development.* Arlington, Va.: Beatty, 1971.

Millar, Bill. *The Drifters, The Rise and Fall of the Black Vocal Group.* New York: The Macmillan Company, 1971.

Morse, David. *Motown and the Arrival of Black Music.* New York: Macmillan, 1971.

Perkins, Carl. *Disciple in Blue Suede Shoes.* Nashville: Zondervan, 1978.

Propes, Steve. *Those Oldies But Goodies, A Guide to 50s Record Collecting.* New York: Collier Books, 1973.

Redd, Lawrence. *Rock Is Rhythm and Blues (The Impact of Mass Media)*. Lansing: Michigan State University Press, 1974.

Sawyer, Charles. *The Arrival of B. B. King: The Authorized Biography*. New York: Doubleday, 1980.

Tobler, John. *The Buddy Holly Story*. New York: Beaufort Books, 1983.

Tosches, Nick. *Unsung Heroes of Rock 'N' Roll: The Birth of Rock 'N' Roll in the Dark and Wild Years Before Elvis*. New York: Scribner's Sons, 1984.

Whitburn, Joel. *Top Rhythm & Blues Records 1949–1971: Facts About 4,000 Recordings Listed in Billboard's "Best Selling Rhythm and Blues (Soul) Singles" Charts, Grouped under the names of the 1,200 Recording Artists*. Menomonee Falls, Wisc.: Record Research, 1973.

White, Charles. *The Life and Times of Little Richard: The Quasar of Rock*. New York: Crown Publishers, 1984.

Williams, Richard. *Out of His Head: The Sound of Phil Spector*. New York: Outerbridge & Lazard, 1972.

Discography

This discography contains two sections. The first consists of collections (C), anthologies of more than one artist, arranged alphabetically according to the title of the collection. The second section lists albums of individual artists, arranged alphabetically under artists' surnames, except for artists who are better known under nicknames. The latter are arranged according to the first word in the nickname; for instance, *B*ig Mama Thornton, *L*ittle Anthony, etc. Where no albums are available, rather than omit the artist, I have listed single records, some of which are, unfortunately, collectors' items. The titles of single records appear between quotation marks; album titles are italicized. In a very few instances, I have included albums of foreign origin.

Collections

1C. *After Hours Blues*. Biograph 12010.
2C. *All Star Revue*. King 513.
3C. *Angry Tenors*. Savoy 14009.
4C. *Anthology of the Blues*, Vol. 12. Kent KST 9012.
5C. *Anthology of Rhythm and Blues*, Vol. 1. Columbia CS 9802.
6C. *The Birth of Soul*. Decca DL 79245.
7C. *The Blues: A Real Summit Meeting*. Buddah 2BDS 5144.
8C. *Blues Piano—Chicago Plus*. Atlantic SD 7227.
9C. *Blues Piano Orgy*. Delmark 626.
10C. *Original Boogie Woogie Piano Giants*. Columbia KC 32708.
11C. *Boogie Woogie Rarities, 1927–43*. Milestone 2009.
12C. *Bostic, Bradshaw, Dominoes*. King 536.
13C. *Classic Blues*, Vols. 1 and 2. Bluesway BLS 6061/2.
14C. *Coffee House Blues*. Vee Jay VJS 1138.
15C. *Collector's Record of the '50s and '60s*. Laurie SLP 2051.
16C. *Contry Blues Classics*, Vols. 1, 2, and 3. Blues Classics 3BC 5–7.
17C. *18 King Size Rhythm & Blues Hits*. Columbia CS 9467.

18C. *14 Golden Recordings from the Historical Vaults of Vee Jay Records,* ABC, ABCX 785.
19C. *Golden Goodies,* Vols. 1–19. Roulette R 25207; 25209–19; 25238–42; 24247/48.
20C. *Graffiti Gold,* Vols. 1 and 2. Vee Jay GG 9000A.
21C. *The Great Bluesmen,* Vols. 1 and 2. Vanguard VSD 25/6.
22C. *Great Groups.* Buddah BDS 7509.
23C. *History of Rhythm & Blues,* Vols. 1–4. Atlantic SD 8161–64.
24C. *The Jug, Jook and Washboard Bands.* Blues Classics BC 2.
25C. *Legend of Leadbelly.* Tradition TRD 2093.
26C. *Let the Good Times Roll.* Bell 9002.
27C. *Memphis Blues.* Kent KST 9002.
28C. *Milburn, Hopkins, Gene & Eunice.* Aladdin 710.
29C. *Negro Church Music.* Atlantic 1351.
30C. *Negro Religious Music: The Sanctified Singers,* Vols. 1 and 2. Blues Classics 2BC LP 17/18.
31C. *1950's Rock & Roll Revival.* Kama Sutra KSBS 2015.
32C. *Oldies But Goodies,* Vols. 1–10. Original Sound SR 8850–60.
33C. *The Old Time Song Service, Dr. C. J. Johnson.* Savoy MG 14126.
34C. *Orioles, Dominoes, Four Tunes.* Jubilee 1014.
35C. *Rhythm & Blues: Best Vocal Groups.* Dootone 204.
36C. *Rhythm & Blues, The End of an Era,* Vols. 1 and 2. Imperial LP 94003/5.
37C. *Original Rhythm & Blues Hits.* RCA Camden CAL 740.
38C. *Rock and Roll Festival.* Kent KST 544.
39C. *Rock 'n' Roll Solid Gold,* Vols. 1 and 2. Mercury SR 61371/2.
40C. *Rock 'n' Roll Survival.* Decca DL 75181.
41C. *Rock 'n' Soul,* Vols. 1–9. ABC 9ABCX 1955–63.
42C. *The Roots of Rock 'n' Roll.* Savoy 2221.
43C. *Stars of the Apollo Theatre.* Columbia 2KC 30788.
44C. *Story of the Blues.* Columbia G 20008.
45C. *Teenage Party.* Gee 702.
46C. *Texas Blues.* Kent KST 9005.
47C. *Texas Guitar.* Atlantic SD 7226.
48C. *This Is How It All Began.* Specialty SPS 2117.
49C. *Twenty Original Winners.* Roulette R 25249.
50C. *Underground Blues.* Kent KST 535.
51C. *Versus Rhythm & Blues.* Dootone 223.
52C. *Women of the Blues.* RCA Victor LPV 534.
53C. *Your Old Favorites.* Old Town OT LP 101.

Individual Artists

Johnny Ace: Memorial Album, Duke DLP 71. *See* 32C, Vol. 10; 41C, Vol. 1.
Faye Adams, *Softly He Speaks,* Savoy 14398. *Original Golden Blues Greats, Vol. 5,* Liberty 7525. *See also* 19C, Vols. 8 and 12; 32C, Vol. 2; 41C, Vol. 1.
Ray Agee. *See* 47C.
Arthur Alexander, Warner Bros. BS 2592.
John Marshall Alexander, Jr. *See* Johnny Ace.
Lee Allen. *See* 19C, Vol. 9.

Albert Ammons. *See* 10C.
Gene Ammons, *Soulful Saxophone,* Chess 1440. *Early Visions,* Cadet 2CA 60038.
Gary Anderson. *See* Gary "U.S." Bonds.
Lee Andrews & the Hearts. "Maybe You'll Be There," Rainbow 252. "Long Lonely Nights," Chess 1665. *See also* 19C, Vol. 3.
Sil Austin, *Everything's Shakin',* Mercury 20320; *Slow Walk Rock,* Mercury 20237.
"Baby" Cortez. *See* 19C, Vol. 13.
La Vern Baker, *Her Greatest Recordings,* Atco SD 33–372; Blues Ballads, Atlantic 8030. *See also* 5C; 23C, Vols. 2–4.
Hank Ballard. *See* 5C, 17C.
Jesse Belvin. "Goodnight My Love," Kent 45 MX 17. *See also* 19C, Vol. 8; 32C; 38C.
Chuck Berry's Golden Decade, Vol. 2, Chess 2CH 60023; Vol. 3, Chess 2CH 60028. *See also* 19C, Vols. 8 and 9; 32C, Vol. 10.
Big Bill Broonzy Story, Verve MG 5V 3000–5; *The Young Bill Broonzy,* Yazoo L 1011; *Big Bill Broonzy,* Columbia 30–153; Vocalion 04706; Vanguard VRS 8523–4.
Big Boy Crudup, *The Father of Rock and Roll,* Victor 20–3261. *See also* 7C, 37C.
Big Jay McNeely, *Big Jay in 3-D,* King 530. "Deacon's Hop/Blues in G Minor," Kent 45 MX 32. *See* 42C.
Big Joe Williams, 2 Arhoolie 1002/1053; *Blues Bash with Lightnin' Hopkins,* Olympia 7115.
Big Maceo Merriweather. *See* 37C.
Big Mama Thornton: She's Back, Backbeat BLP 68; *Sassy Mama,* Vanguard VSD 79354.
Big Maybelle: The Last of, Paramount 2PAS 1011. *Big Maybelle Sings,* Savoy 14005. *See* 42C.
Billie & Lillie, *See* 41C, Vol. 4.
Otis Blackwell Singin' the Blues, Davis JD 109.
Billy Bland. *See* 19C, Vol. 12; 49C; 53C.
Bobby Bland: Introspective of the Early Years, ABC/Duke 2BLPD 92. *See also* 27C; 32C, Vol. 9; 41C, Vols. 3, 7, 8, and 9.
Blind Boy Fuller, Blues Classics 11.
Blind Lemon Jefferson, The Classic Folk Blues of, Riverside 2RLP 12–125; 12–136M.
Blind Willie McTell: *Atlanta Twelve String,* Atlantic SD 7224.
Bo Diddley: *16 All Time Greatest Hits,* Checker 2989. *See also* 19C, Vol. 8; 25C; 32C, Vol. 10.
Bob & Earl. *See* 41C, Vol. 9.
Earl Bostic: Harlem Nocturne, King S1048. *See also* 19C, Vol. 8; 25C; 32C, Vol. 10.
Alex Bradford. *See* 48C.
Hadda Brooks, "Polonaise Boogie," Modern Music 123.
Louis Brooks & His Hi-toppers, "It's Love Baby," Excello 2056.
Buster Brown. *See* 19C, Vol. 17; 20C; 41C, Vol. 6.
Charles Brown: Great R & B Oldies, Blues Spectrum BS 102. *See also* 5C; 13C, Vol. 1.

Clarence Brown. *See* Gatemouth Brown.
James Brown: *The Unbeatable 16 Hits,* King 919. *See also* 5C, 17C.
Maxine Brown. *See* 19C, Vols. 8 and 9.
Mel Brown. *See* 13C, Vol. 1.
Nappy Brown, Savoy 14002. *See* 42C.
Robert Brown. *See* Washboard Sam.
Roy Brown: *Hard Times,* Bluesway BLS 6056. *See also* 13C, Vol. 1; 23C, Vols. 1 and 2.
Ruth Brown, Atlantic 8004.
Bull Moose Jackson. *See* 5C, 17C.
Bumble Bee Slim, "Ida Red" and "Lonesome Old Feeling," Fidelity 3004.
Carl Burnett. *See* Little Caesar.
Chester Burnett, *See* Howlin' Wolf.
Sam Butera, *The Big Horn,* Capitol T 1098.
Jerry Butler Sings Assorted Songs, Mercury SR 61320. *The Sagittarius Movement,* Mercury SR 61347. *The Best of Jerry Butler,* Vee Jay VJS 1048. *Jerry Butler Gold,* Vee Jay VJS 2–1003. *Just Beautiful,* Kent KST 536.
Robert Byrd. *See* Bobby Day.
The Cadets, "Stranded in the Jungle," Kent 45s MX 26, *See also* 19C, Vols. 10 and 17; 32C, Vol. 1; 38C.
The Cadillacs, *The Fabulous Cadillacs,* Jubilee 1045. *See also* 19C, Vol. 3; 41C, Vol. 1; 49C.
Cab Calloway: *St James Infirmary,* Epic LN 3265. *See also* 43C.
The Capris, *See* 31C.
The Cardinals. "Wheel of Fortune," Atlantic 958. "The Door Is Still Open," Atlantic 1054. *See also* 23C, Vol. 1.
Una Mae Carlisle, "Throw It Out Your Mind" and "That's My Man," Savoy 616.
Leroy Carr: Blues Before Sunrise, Columbia C 30496.
Champion Jack Dupree, Atlantic LP 8255; *Cabbage Greens,* OKeh OKM 12103. *See* 5C, 10C.
Gene Chandler, The Best Of, Vee Jay VJS 1199. *The Two Sides of Gene Chandler,* Brunswick BL 754149. *See also* 18C; 19C, Vol. 18; 20C, Vol. 7; 32C, Vol. 6; 41C, Vols. 8 and 9.
The Channels. *See* 19C, Vol. 11; 32C, Vol. 5; 41C, Vol. 2.
The Chantels. *See* 19C, Vols. 2, 3, 6, 10, and 11; 32C, Vol. 4; 41C, Vol. 4; 49C.
Jimmy Charles & the Revillettes. *See* 41C, Vol. 6.
Ray Charles: The Greatest Hits of, Atlantic 7101; *Hallelujah I Love Her So,* Atlantic 8006; *What'd I Say,* Atlantic 8029. *See also* 13C, Vol. 1.
The Charms. *See* Otis Williams & the Charms.
The Charts. *See* 32C. Vol. 2; 41C, Vol. 3.
Peter Chatman. *See* Memphis Slim.
The Checkers, "House with No Windows," King 4710. "White Cliffs of Dover," King 4675.
Clifton Chenier: Louisiana Blues & Zydeco, Arhoolie F 1024.
The Chords, "Sh-Boom," Cat 104. *See also* 23C, Vol. 2.
Chubby Checker, Twist, Cameo P. 7001. *See also* 26C, 48C.
Savannah Churchill, "Daddy Daddy," Manor 1004.
Jimmy Clanton. *See* 20C, Vol. 2; 41C, Vol. 4.

Dee Clark. *See* 18C; 19C, Vol. 9; 20C, Vol. 2; 32C, Vol. 6; 41C, Vols. 5 and 7.
The Cleftones. *See* 19C, Vols. 2, 7, and 19; 20C, Vol. 1; 41C, Vol. 7; 49C.
James Cleveland & the Cleveland Singers: He Leadeth Me, Savoy MG 14131. *James Cleveland & the Angelic Choir,* Vol. 7, Savoy 14171.
The Clovers, Atlantic 8009 and 1248. *Their Greatest Recordings: The Early Years,* Atco SD 33–374. *See also* 23C, Vols. 1, 2, and 3; 32C, Vol. 2.
The Coasters: Their Greatest Recordings: The Early Years, Atco SD 33–371. *Their Greatest Hits,* Atco 33–111. *See also* 19C, Vol. 2; 20C, Vols. 3 and 4; 26C.
Nat "King" Cole: Original Sounds, Up Front UP 151.
Sam Cooke: The Golden Sounds of, Trip 2TLP 8030. *Songs by Sam Cooke,* Keen 2001. *Encore,* Keen 2003.
Eddie Cooley & the Dimples. *See* 41C, Vol. 2; 49C.
Les Cooper & the Soul Rockers. *See* 41C, Vol. 8.
David Cortes Clowney. *See* Baby Cortez.
James Cotton Band, 100% Cotton, Buddah BDS 5620. *The James Cotton Band, High Energy,* Buddah BDS 5650. *See* 21C.
Ida Cox. *See* 21C, 42C.
The Crescendos, "Oh Julie," Nasco 6005.
The Crows, *Oldies But Goodies,* Vol. 2, Original Sound OSR 8652. *See also* 19C, Vols. 2 and 19; 32C, Vol. 2; 49C.
Arthur Crudup. *See* Big Boy Crudup.
The Crystals. *See* 19C, Vol. 16; 36C, Vol. 2.
The Cuff Links. *See* 19C, Vol. 15.
The Danleers. *See* 39C, Vol. 1.
Eddie "Lockjaw" Davis: The Cookbook of, Prestige P 24039.
Rev. Gary Davis. *See* 21C.
Maxwell Davis & His Tenor Sax, Aladdin 804.
Bobby Day. *See* 32C, Vols. 5 and 9.
The Dells: Greatest Hits, Vol. 2, Cadet CA 60036. *The Dells in Concert,* Vee Jay VJS 7305. *See also* 18C; 19C, Vols. 5 and 6; 32C, Vol. 3; 41C, Vol. 2.
The Delta Rhythm Boys. *See* 23C, Vol. 1.
The Del-Vikings: They Sing—They Swing, Mercury 20314; *Record Date,* Mercury 20353. *See also* 32C, Vol. 3; 39C, Vols. 1 and 2.
The Diablos, "The Wind," Fortune 511.
The Diamonds. *See* 23C, Vol. 1.
Varetta Dillard, "Easy, Easy Baby," Savoy 847. "Mercy Mr. Percy," Savoy 897. *See* 42C.
Dixie Hummingbirds: The Best Of, Peacock PLP 138.
Floyd Dixon, "Call Operator 210," Aladdin 3135. "Telephone Blues," Aladdin 3075.
Willie Dixon: Catalyst, Ovation OVQD 1433. *Memphis Slim & Willie Dixon: Blues Every Which Way,* Verve V 3007.
Bill Doggett, King 585. *See also* 5C, 17C, 32C, Vol. 6.
The Dominoes, King 536. *See* Billy Ward.
The Dootones, "Teller of Fortunes," Dootone 366.
Lee Dorsey. *See* 19C, Vol. 17; 20C, Vol. 1; 41C, Vol. 7; 49C.
Thomas A. Dorsey. *See* Georgia Tom.

K. C. Douglas, Cook LP 5002. "Mercury Boogie," Down Town 2004.
Minnie Douglas. *See* Memphis Minnie.
The Dreamlovers. *See* 19C, Vol. 11.
The Drifters: Their Greatest Recordings: Early Years, Atco SD 33–375; *Golden Hits,* Atlantic SD 8153. *See also* Vols. 3 and 19; 20C, Vols. 2, 3, and 4; 49C.
The Dubs. *See* 19C, Vols. 2 and 10; 20C, Vol. 1; 32C, Vol. 4; 41C, Vol. 3.
Amos Easton. *See* Bumble Bee Slim.
Billy Eckstine: Golden Hits, Mercury 60796.
The Edsels. *See* 19C, Vol. 10.
Tommy Edwards. *See* 32C, Vol. 7.
The El Dorados: Crazy Little Mama. Vee Jay 1001. *See also* 19C, Vols. 3 and 11; 20C, Vol. 2.
The Elegants. *See* 32C, Vol. 5; 41C, Vol. 4.
The Essex. *See* 19C, Vol. 18.
Ernest Evans. *See* Chubby Checker.
Bette Everett. *See* 18C; 20C, Vol. 2; 41C, Vol. 9.
The Falcons, "You're So Fine," Flick 001/Unart 2013.
Fats Domino: Sings Million Record Hits, Imperial 2103. *Rock & Rollin' with Fats Domino,* Imperial 9004. *This Is Fats Domino,* Imperial 9028. *Very Best of Fats Domino,* United Artists UA LA 233G. *See also* 26C; 32C, Vol. 10.
The Fiestas. *See* 19C, Vol. 19; 53C.
Five Blind Boys of Mississippi: The Best Of, Peacock PLP 139.
The Five Discs. *See* 15C.
The Five Keys: The Best Of, Aladdin 806; *On Stage!* Capitol T 828. *The Conoisseur Collection of,* Harlem Hitparade HHP 5004. *See also* 36C, Vol. 1.
The Five Red Caps, Davis DA 1. "Atlanta, Ga.," Davis 2102. "You Thrill Me," Joe Davis 7135.
The Five Royales, "Dedicated to You," King 580. *See also* 5C, 17C.
The Five Satins Sing, Ember 100. *See also* 19C, Vols. 6 and 11; 26C; 31C; 32C, Vols. 1 and 4.
The Five Willows, "My Dearest Darling," Allen 1000. "Lay Your Head on My Shoulder," Herald 433. "Church Bells May Ring," Melba 102.
The Flairs, "I Had a Love," Hollywood 185/Flair 1012.
The Flamingos. *See* 16C; 19C, Vols. 2, 3, 6, and 19; 20C, Vol. 1; 32C, Vol. 3; 40C; 41C, Vol. 5.
Frankie Ford. *See* 41C, Vol. 5.
The Four Clefs. *See* 37C.
The Four Fellows, "Soldier Boy," Glory 234.
The Four Flames. *See* 47C.
The Four Tunes, "Marie," Jubilee 5128.
Inez Fox. *See* 32C, Vol. 8.
Alan Freed: Go, Go, Go, Coral 57177; *Rock Around the Clock,* Coral 57213; *Rock 'n Roll,* Coral 57063; *Rock 'n Roll Dance Party,* Vol. 2, Coral 57115; *Rock 'n Roll Show,* Brunswick 54043.
Bobby Freeman. *See* 19C, Vol. 4; 20C, Vol. 1; 41C, Vol. 4.
Ernie Freeman. *See* 32C, Vol. 8.
Jesse Fuller. *See* 21C.
Johnny Fuller: California Blues, Kent KST 9003.

Rocky Fuller. *See* Louisianna Red.

Lowell Fulson: I've Got the Blues, Jewel LPS 5009; *In a Heavy Bag,* Jewel LPS 5003; *Tramp,* Kent KST 520; *Let's Get Started,* Kent KST 558; *The Ol' Blues Singer,* Granite GS 1006.

Furry Lewis: Slide 'Em on Down, Fantasy F 24703.

The G-Clefs. *See* 19C, Vols. 14 and 15.

Cecil Gant, Gilt Edge 501; *Rock Little Baby* (English), Flyright 4710.

Don Gardner & Dee Dee Ford. *See* 41C, Vol. 8.

Gary "U.S." Bonds. *See* 31C; 32C, Vol. 7; 41C, Vols. 6, 7, and 8.

Gatemouth Brown. *See* 7C.

Rev. Gatemouth Moore: After 21 Years, Bluesway BLS 6074.

Bob Geddins, "Irma Jean," Trilon 1058. "Thinkin' and Thinkin'," Cavatone 5/Modern 20-685.

Gene & Eunice. *See* 28C; 32C, Vol. 3.

Barbara George. *See* 32C, Vol. 7.

The Gladiolas, "Little Darlin'," Excello 2101. "Shoop Shoop," Excello 2136.

Lloyd Glenn: Chica-Boo, Aladdin 808. *See also* 7C.

Roscoe Gordon, "No More Diggin'," Kent 45s MX 31.

Lil Green: Romance in the Night, Vintage RCA Victor. *See also* 37C.

Guitar Slim. *See* 46C.

Arthur Gunter, "Workin' for My Baby," Excello 2204.

Shirley Gunter & the Queens, "Oop Shoop"/"That's the Way I Like It," Kent 45s MX 27. *See also* 38C.

Lionel Hampton, All American Award Concert, Decca 8088; *Golden Favorites,* Decca (7) 4296; *Lionel Hampton,* Glad-Hamp 3050. *See also* 6C.

The Harptones. Harlem Hitparade HHP 5006. *See* 19C, Vols 1, 7, and 17; 53C.

Eddie Harris: In Sound, Atlantic 1448.*See also* 18C.

Peppermint Harris, "I Got Loaded," Aladdin 3097.

Thurston Harris, "Little Bitty Pretty One," Aladdin 3398.

Wynonie Harris. *See* 5C, 17C.

Wilbert Harrison. *See* 19C, Vol. 17; 20C, Vol. 2; 41C, Vol. 5; 49C.

Dolores Hawkins: *Dolores,* Epic LN 3250.

Erskine Hawkins, "Tuxedo Junction," RCA Victor. "I've Got a Right to Cry," RCA Victor 20–1902.

Jalacy Hawkins. *See* Screamin' Jay Hawkins.

Ronnie Hawkins. *See* 19C, Vol. 8.

Roy Hawkins. *See* 4C.

Arthur Lee Hays & the Crowns, "Truly," RPM 424. "A Fool's Prayer," Dig 133.

The Heartbeats. *See* 19C, Vols. 1, 2, and 5; 20C, Vol. 1; 32C.

The Hearts, "Lonely Nights," Baton 208.

Joe Henderson. *See* 19C, Vol. 12; 41C, Vol. 8.

The Hollywood Flames, "Tabarin," Unique 005. "Wheel of Fortune," Specialty 429. "Buzz, Buzz, Buzz," Ebb 119.

John Lee Hooker: The Greatest Hits, Kent KST 559. *Detroit Special,* Atlantic SD 7228. *Boogie Chillun,* Fantasy 24706. *The Best of John Lee Hooker,* Vee Jay VJS 1049. *John Lee Hooker Gold,* Vee Jay VJS 2-1004. *See also* 13C, Vol. 1; 18C; 21C; 41C, Vol. 8; 48C; 50C.

Sam Hopkins. *See* Lightnin' Hopkins.

Walter Horton. *See* Little Walter.

Camille Howard, "Money Blues," Specialty 401. *See also* 47C.

Howlin' Wolf: The Back Door Wolf, Chess CH 50045. *Chester Burnett AKA Howlin' Wolf,* Chess 2CH 60016. *Moaning in the Moonlight.* Chess 1434. "Riding in the Moonlight," Kent 45s MX 12. *Howlin' Wolf,* Chess 2A CMB 201. *See also* 27C, 50C.

Helen Humes: Talk of the Town. Columbia PC 33488.

Ivory Joe Hunter, Atlantic 8008; Everest FS 289. *16 of His Greatest Hits,* King 605. *Ivory Joe Sings the Old & the New,* Atlantic 8015. *I Got That Lonesome Feeling,* MGM 3488. *See also* 17C; 23C, Vol. 3.

J. B. Hutto & His Hawks, *Hawk Squat,* Delmark DS 617. *Slidewinder,* Delmark DS 636. *See also* 21C.

The Impalas. "Fool, Fool, Fool," Polydor MVG 521. "Sorry (I Ran All the Way Home)," Polydor MVG 521.

The Impressions: Best of, ABC S 654. *Three the Hard Way,* Curtom CRS 8602. *See also* 41C, Vols. 7 and 9.

The Ink Spots, Best Of, MCA 2-4005; *18 Greatest Hits,* King 5001; *Greatest Hits,* Everest 4116.

Isley Bros.: Soul on the Rocks, Tamla 275; *Greatest Hits,* T Neck 3011. *See also* 32C, Vol. 10.

The Jacks, "Why Don't You Write Me," Kent 45s MX 18. *See also* 19C, Vol. 10; 38C.

Benjamin Jackson. *See* Bull Moose Jackson.

Mahalia Jackson: The World's Greatest Gospel Singer, Columbia CL 644.

Walter Jacobs. *See* Little Walter.

Illinois Jacquet, Epic BA 17033; *Message,* King S 1048; *How High the Moon,* Prestige P 24057.

Elmore James, The Legend of, Kent KST 9001; *Blues After Hours,* Crown 5168. "Dust My Blues," Kent 45s MX 15. "Standing at the Crossroads," Kent 45s MX 55. *See also* 38C, 50C.

Etta James, Chess CH 50042; Cadet S 4013. *Come A Little Closer,* Chess 60029. *Twist with Etta James,* Crown CLP 5250. "Roll with Me Henry/Good Rockin' Daddy," Kent 45s MX 17. *See also* 19C, Vol. 4; 32C, Vol. 1; 39C.

The Jarmels. *See* 15C.

Cathy Jean & the Romantics. *See* 32C, Vol. 9.

The Jesters. *See* 19C, Vol. 17.

The Jewels. *See* 32C, Vol. 5; 36C, Vols. 1 and 2.

Buddy Johnson: Walkin', Mercury 20322. *Rock & Roll with Buddy Johnson,* Mercury 20209.

Lonnie Johnson, Bluebird B 8779; OKeh 8775. *See also* 17C.

Pete Johnson. *See* 10C. *See* Joe Turner.

Robert Johnson: King of the Delta Blues Singers, Vol. 1, Columbia CC 1654; Vol. 2, C 30034.

Eddie Jones. *See* Guitar Slim.

Jimmy Jones. *See* 32C, Vol. 7.

Joe Jones. *See* 19C, Vol. 12; 20C, Vol. 1; 41C, Vol. 6.

Louis Jordan, Blues Spectrum BS 101; Decca 8593, 8627, 8638, 23631, 29018. *Let the Good Times Roll,* Decca 8551. *Greatest Hits,* Vol. 2, MCA 1337. *See also* 6C.

Don Julian. *See* Don Julian & the Meadowlarks.

Junior Parker, *I Tell Sad Stories and True,* United Artists UAS 6823.

Junior Walker. *Shotgun,* Soul 701. *Soul Session,* Soul 702. *See also* 4C.

Junior Wells, *South Side Blues Jam with Guy & Spann,* Delmark 628. *See also* 21C.

King Curtis: Everybody's Talkin', Atco SD 33–385. *The Best of King Curtis,* Atco SD 33–266; Prestige S 7709. *See also* 19C, Vol. 13; 42C.

B. B. King, Modern RLP 498. *Blues in My Heart,* Crown 5309. *Live at the Regal,* ABC S 509. "Please Love Me," Kent 45s MX 1. "Sweet Sixteen," Kent 45s MX 5. "Every Day I Have the Blues," Kent 45s MX 7. "3 O'Clock Blues," Kent 45s MX 9. *See also* 13C, Vol. 2; 38C; 50C.

Ben E. King: Greatest Hits, Atco SD 33–165. *See also* 19C, Vols. 12 and 18; 23C, Vol. 3.

Freddy King, Best Of, MCA 610. *17 Original Great Hits,* King 5012.

Gladys Knight & the Pips: Queen of Tears, Vee Jay VJS 1197. *See also* 18C; 32C, Vol. 6; 41C, Vol. 7.

Marie Knight: Songs of the Gospel, Mercury MG 20196. *See also* 6C.

Sonny Knight. *See* 32C, Vol. 1; 41C, Vol. 2.

The Larks: Super Oldies, Capitol T2562.

Annie Laurie. *See* 5C.

Leadbelly Soundtrack, ABC ABDP 939. *Huddie "Leadbelly" Ledbetter Memorial,* Stinson 17/19/48/51. *Huddie Ledbetter,* Fantasy F 24715. *Good Night Irene,* Allegro LEG 9025. *See also* 23C, Vol. 1.

Bobby Lewis. *See* 19C, Vol. 12; 49C.

Meade Lux Lewis, Tops 1533; Atlantic 133; Decca 3387. *See also* 8C, 10C.

Jimmy Liggins. *See* 48C.

Joe Liggins, Blues Spectrum BS 106. *See also* 47C.

Lightnin' Hopkins: And the Blues, Imperial 12211. *The Blues Giant,* Olympic 7110. *Early Recordings,* Arhoolie 2007/2010. *Fast Life Woman,* Verve V 8543. *Double Blues,* Fantasy 24702.

Lightnin' Slim, "Mean Old Lonesome Train," Excello 2106.

Mance Lipscomb: Texas Sharecropper & Songster, Arhoolie 1001. *See also* 21C.

Little Anthony & the Imperials, The Very Best Of, United Artists UA-LA 382. *See also* 19C, Vols. 2, 7, and 10; 20C, Vols. 1 and 2; 32C, Vol. 3.

Little Brother Montgomery: Tasty Blues, Bluesville BLP 1012. *Roosevelt Sykes/ Little Brother Montgomery,* Fantasy F 24717. *Blues Piano — Chicago, Plus,* Atlantic SP 7227. *See also* 1C, 8C.

Little Caesar & the Romans. *See* 32C, Vol. 6; 41C, Vol. 7.

Little Esther. *See* 32C, Vol. 9. *See* Esther Phillips.

Little Eva. *See* 19C, Vol. 4; 42C.

Little Junior Parker, Duke 72. *You Don't Have to Be Black to Love the Blues,* Groove 52.

Little Milton: Grits Ain't Groceries, Checker LPS 3011. *Greatest Hits,* Chess 50013. *Little Milton,* Chess 2A CMB 204.

Little Richard: Greatest Hits, OKeh 14121; Vee Jay VJS 1124; Specialty 2103. *Here's Little Richard,* Specialty 2100. *Little Richard Gold,* Vee Jay VJS 2–1002. *Talkin' 'Bout Soul,* Dynasty DYS 7304. *Little Richard's Back,* Vee Jay VJS 1107. *Greatest 17 Original Hits,* Specialty 5082–2113 M. "Tutti Frutti,"

Kent 45s MX 39. "Slippin' and Slidin'," Kent 45s MX 42. "Long Tall Sally," Kent 45s MX 40. *See also* 20C, Vol. 2; 26C; 32C, Vol. 3; 38C.

Little Son Jackson. *See* 46C.

Little Walter: The Best Of, Chess 1428. *Hate to See You Go*, Chess 1535. *Little Walter*, Chess 2A CMB 202. *See also* 27C.

Little Willie John: Fever, King 564; *Talk to Me*, King 596. *See also* 5C, 17C.

Lonesome Sundown, "My Home Is A Prison," Excello 2102.

Louisiana Red Sings the Blues, Atco SD 33–389.

Lucky Millinder, Tod 1037. *See also* 6C.

Frankie Lymon & the Teenagers. Gee 701. *Rock 'n' Roll*, Roulette 25036. *See* 19C, Vols. 1, 2, 9, and 19; 20C, Vol. 1; 41C, Vol. 2.

Jimmy McCracklin, "Just Got to Know," Art-Tone 825. "Think," Imperial 66129. "The Walk," Checker 885.

Ellas McDaniel. *See* Bo Diddley.

Gene McDaniels: The Facts of Life, Sunset SUS 5122.

Fred McDowell, Mississippi, Just Sunshine JSS 4. *Amazing Grace*, Testament 2219. *See also* 21C.

Ruth McFadden. *See* 52C.

Edna McGriff. *See* 19C, Vol. 12; 23C, Vol. 1.

Cecil J. McNeely. *See* Big Jay McNeely.

Clyde McPhatter: Welcome Home, Decca DL 75231. *See also* 23C, Vols. 2, 3, and 4. *See* The Drifters.

Jay McShann. *See* 6C, 7C.

Jack McVea, "Open the Door, Richard," Black & White 792.

Willie Mabon, "I Don't Know." Chess 1531. "I'm Mad," Chess 1538.

Magic Sam. *Genius: The Final Session*, Intermedia 5041. *Magic Blues Genius*, Intermedia 5025.

The Magnificents. *See* 19C, Vol. 6.

The Majors, "A Wonderful Dream," Imperial 5855.

Gloria Mann. *See* 19C, Vol. 16.

Bobby Marchan. *See* 41C, Vol. 6.

The Marigolds, "Rollin' Stone," Excello 2057.

Roberta Martin Singers, Savoy MG 14008.

Sallie Martin: The Living Legend, Savoy MG 14242.

Marvin & Johnny. *See* 38C.

Curtis Mayfield, Curtom 8005. *Roots*, Curtom 8009.

Percy Mayfield, Tangerine S 1505. *See also* 48C.

The Meadowlarks. *See* 19C, Vol. 14; 32C, Vol. 1.

The Medallions. *See* 19C, Vol. 15; 32C, Vol. 1.

The Mello Kings. *See* 31C; 32C, Vol. 1.

Memphis Slim, U.S.A., Candid 8024. *The Real Boogie Woogie, Piano Solos*, Folkways FA 3524. *Favorite Blues Singers*, Folkways FA 2387. *With Roosevelt Sykes: Memphis Blues*, Olympic 7136. *And Willie Dixon: The Blues Every Which Way*, Verve V 3007. *Raining the Blues*, Fantasy F 24705. *Honky Tonk Sound*, Folkways 3535. *Blue Memphis*, Warner Bros. 1899.

Mercy Dee Walton. *See* 4C, 48C.

Mickey & Sylvia: New Sounds, Vik LX 1102. *See also* 32C, Vol. 4; 37C.

The Midnighters: Greatest Jukebox Hits, King 41; Vol. 2, King 581.

Amos Milburn. *Rhythm & Blues Christmas,* United Artists UN 654. *See also* 28C.
William Rice Miller (Sonny Boy Williamson 2d). *"The Original" Sonny Boy Williamson,* Blues Classics BC 9. *One Way Out,* Chess CHV 417.
Lucius Millinder. *See* Lucky Millinder.
The Mills Bros., Best, 2 Decca DXS 7193E.
Roy Milton, Roots of Rock, Vol. 1, Kent KST 554. *Rhythm & Blues, Dooto 223. See also* 48C.
The Miracles, "Bad Girl," Chess 1734.
Mississippi John Hurt, Piedmont DLP 13157. *See also* 21C.
Mississippi Sheiks, "A Wonderful Thing," Riverside RLP 403.
The Monotones. *See* 19C, Vols. 5 and 19.
Eurreal Wilford Montgomery. *See* Little Brother Montgomery.
The Moonglows, Look, It's, Chess 1430. *Rock, Rock, Rock,* Chess 1425. *See also* 19C, Vols. 3, 6, 7, 10, 11, and 19; 49C.
The Moonlighters, "Shoo Doo Be Doo," Checker 806.
James Moore. *See* Slim Harpo.
Joe Morris. *See* 23C, Vol. 1.
Muddy Waters, The Best Of, Chess 1427. *AKA,* 2 Chess 60006. *Can't Get No Grindin',* Chess CH 50023. *Down on Stovall's Plantation,* Testament 2210. *Muddy Waters,* Chess 2A CMB 203. *See also* 7C, 21C.
Johnny Nash. *See* 41C, Vol. 3.
Jimmy Nelson, "T-99," Kent 45s MX 29. *See also* 4C.
The Nutmegs. *See* 19C, Vol. 6; 32C, Vol. 2.
Andrew "Voice" Odom: Further On Down the Road, Bluesway BLS 6055. *See also* 13C, Vol. 1.
The Olympics. *See* 20C, Vols. 1 and 2; 32C, Vol. 10; 41C, Vols. 4, 6, and 9.
The Orioles. *See* Sonny Til & the Orioles.
Johnny Otis, Blues Spectrum BS 103. *Cold Shot,* Kent 534. See 42C.
The Paradons. *See* 32C, Vol. 5.
The Paragons. *See* 19C, Vols. 14 and 15; 41C, Vol. 3.
Herman Parker. *See* Little Junior Parker.
The Pastels. *See* 19C, Vol. 11.
Pee Wee Crayton, Blues Spectrum BS 105. "Blues After Hours," Kent 45s MX 10. "Texas Hop," Kent 45s MX 22. *See also* 4C.
The Penguins: Decade of Golden Groups, Mercury S 2–602. *See also* 19C, Vols. 14, 15, and 19; 31C; 32C, Vol. 1; 49C.
Richard Penniman. *See* Little Richard.
Rufus Perryman. *See* Speckled Red.
Esther Phillips, Atlantic S 8102. *Black-Eyed Blues,* Kudu KU 14. *From a Whisper to a Scream,* Kudu 005.
Phil Phillips. *See* 39C, Vol. 2.
Piano Red, "Rockin' with Red/Red's Boogie," RCA Victor 0099.
The Pilgrim Travelers: Everytime I Feel the Spirit, Vee Jay VJS 18010.
Pine Top Smith. Vocalion 1245/1256; Brunswick 80008/BL 54014.
The Platters, King 549. *Encore of Golden Hits,* Mercury 60243. *See also* 2C; 17C; 39C, Vol. 2.
Lloyd Price: Greatest Hits, ABC S 324. *Mr. Personality,* ABC S 297. *See also* 19C, Vol. 14; 41C, Vols. 3, 4, and 5.

Arthur Prysock, Art & Soul, Verve V6 5009.
The Ravens: Write Me A Letter, Regent 6062. *The Ravens,* Harlem Hitparade 5007. *See also* 23C, Vol. 1; 41C, Vol. 1.
The Ray-O-Vacs. *See* 6C.
The Rays. *See* 19C, Vol. 16; 32C, Vol. 4.
Jimmy Reed, The Best Of, Vee Jay VJS 1039. *The Greatest Hits,* Vols. 1 and 2, Kent KST 553 and 562. *Root of the Blues,* Kent 2KST 537. *Blues Is My Business,* Vee Jay VJS 7303. *See also* 13C, Vol. 2; 18C; 41C, Vols. 1, 6, and 7; 50C.
Della Reese: Amen! Jubilee 1083. *Classic Della,* RCA LSF 2419. *See also* 41C, Vol. 3.
The Rivileers, "A Thousand Stars," Baton 200.
Robert & Johnny. *See* 19C, Vol. 6; 53C.
The Robins, Rock 'n' Roll, Whippet 703. *See also* 23C, Vol. 3; 36C, Vol. 2.
The Ronettes. Philles S 4006.
Rosie & the Originals. *See* 32C, Vol. 5; 41C, Vol. 6.
Diana Ross. *12 No. 1 Hits from the 70s,* Motown 5275. *An Evening with Diana Ross,* Motown M7-877R2. *Why Do Fools Fall in Love,* Victor AYL1 5162.
The Royaltones. *See* 52C.
Otis Rush, Blues Live! (Japanese) Trio PA 3086. *See also* 21C.
Jimmy Rushing, Essential, Vanguard 2VSD 65/66. *Listen to the Blues,* Vanguard Everyman SRV 73007. *Everyday I Have the Blues,* Bluesville BLS 6055. *You and Me,* RCA LSP 4566. *Sent for You Yesterday,* Bluesville BLS 6057. *See also* 13C, Vol. 2; 21C.
St. Louis Jimmy, Chicago Blues, Spivey 1003. *See also* 1C.
Screamin' Jay Hawkins, At Home With, Epic LN 3448. *See also* 43C.
Dee Dee Sharp, Biggest Hits, Cameo 1062. *See also* 32C, Vol. 6.
Shep & the Limelites. *See* 31C; 32C. Vol. 5; 41C, Vol. 7.
The Shields. *See* 32C, Vol. 3.
Johnny Shines. *See* 21C.
The Shirelles: Remember When, Scepter 2 SPS 599. *Greatest Hits,* Scepter S 507. *See also* 26C; 32C, Vol. 10; 40C.
Shirley & Lee, Let the Good Times Roll, Aladdin 807. *See also* 19C, Vol. 17; 32C, Vol. 1; 41C, Vol. 2.
The Silhouettes. *See* 19C, Vol. 7; 41C. Vol. 4.
Frankie Lee Sims. *See* 48C.
Hal Singer, *Honkers and Screamers.* Savoy 2234. *Roots of Rock 'n' Roll,* Savoy 2221. *See* 42C.
Sister Rosetta Tharpe: Precious Lord, Savoy 14214 (8-track cartridge). *Gospel Train,* Decca DL 8782; Mercury 20201. *See also* 6C.
The Six Teens. *See* 32C, Vol. 4.
Slim Harpo. *See* 41C, Vol. 7.
Smiley Lewis, "I Hear You Knocking," Imperial 5356.
Huey "Piano" Smith. *See* 41C, Vols. 3 and 4.
The Solitaires. *See* 53C.
Sonny Boy Williamson, John (No. 1), Blues Classics BC 3; Bluebird B 8580. *See also* 37C.

Sonny Boy Williamson, (No. 2). *See* William Rice Miller.
Sonny Til & the Orioles. *See* 19C, Vol. 2; 20C, Vol. 1; 23C, Vol. 1; 34C; 41C, Vol. 1.
The Soul Stirrers: Tribute to Sam Cooke, Checker LPS 10063. *Best,* Checker S 10015. *Gospel Music,* Vol. 1, Imperial 94007. *Original with Sam Cooke,* Specialty S 2137 E. *See also* 48C.
The Spaniels, "Goodnite, It's Time to Go," Vee Jay 1002. *See also* 19C, Vols. 5, 6, 10, and 11; 20C, Vols. 1 and 2; 21C.
Otis Spann Is the Blues, Barnaby 230246. *Heart Loaded with Trouble,* Bluesway BLS 6063. *See also* 13C, Vol. 2; 21C.
The Sparkletones. *See* 19C, Vol. 16.
Speckled Red: The Dirty Dozens, Delmark DL 601; Brunswick BL 58018/7116/7151. *See also* 9C.
Spiders. *See* 36C, Vol. 1.
Dakota Staton with Strings, United Artists UAL 3355. *Dynamic!* Capitol T 1054.
Arbee Stidham. *See* 37C.
Stick McGee. *See* 23C, Vol. 1.
Barrett Strong. *See* 32C, Vol. 4.
The Swallows, "It Ain't the Meat," King 4501. "Besides You," King 4525. "Tell Me Why," King 4515.
Swan Silvertones: Love Lifted Me, Specialty S 2122E. *My Book,* Specialty 2148. *See also* 48C.
Roosevelt Sykes Sings the Blues, Crown CLP 5237. *R.S.,* Bluebird 34–0721. *Hard Drivin' Blues, Delmark DS 607. Blues,* Folkways 3827. *And Little Brother Montgomery,* Fantasy F 24717. *Honeydripper,* Prestige 7722.
T-Bone Walker Blues, Atlantic 8020. *Stormy Monday Blues,* Bluesville S 6008. *Dirty Mistreater,* Bluesway BLS 6058. *Want a Little Girl,* Delmark DS 633. *See also* 13C, Vol. 1; 47C.
Tampa Red, The Guitar Wizard 1935–53, Blues Classics BC 25; Bluebird B 34–0711; Bluebird B 9024; Bluesville 1030. *See also* 37C.
The Tams. *See* 41C, Vol. 9.
Laurie Tate. *See* 23C, Vol. 1.
The Teenagers, featuring Frankie Lymon, Gee 701.
The Teen-Queens, "Eddie My Love," Kent 45s MX 14. *See also* 20C, Vol. 2; 32C, Vol. 1; 38C.
Joe Tex. *See* 17C.
Carla Thomas. *See* 23C, Vol. 4; 32C, Vol. 8.
Lafayette Thomas, "Cockroach Run," Jumping 5000. "Please Come Back to Me," Savoy 1574.
Tiny Bradshaw, King 536. *Tiny Plays,* King 501.
The Tune Weavers. *See* 19C, Vols. 10 and 19; 32C, Vol. 10.
The Turbans. *See* 32C, Vol. 2; 41C, Vol. 1.
Ike & Tina Turner: Greatest Hits, United Artists U 8512 (8-track Cartridge). *Please, Please, Please,* Kent 550. *River Deep, Mountain High,* A & M 4178. *From the Beginning,* Kent 2KST 533. "Good Bye, So Long," Kent 45s MX 44. *See also* 38C.
Joe Turner: His Greatest Recordings, Atlantic SD 33–376; *The Best Of,* Atlantic

SD 8144; *Sings K. C. Jazz,* Atlantic 1234. *Big Joe Rides Again,* Atlantic 1332. *And Jimmy Nelson,* Crown CST 383. *See also* 13C, Vol. 2; 21C; 23C, Vols. 1, 2, and 3; 32C, Vol. 2.

The Valentines. *See* 19C, Vols. 1 and 11; 52C.

The Vibrations. *See* 19C, Vol. 4.

Eddie "Cleanhead" Vinson, Riverside 3502. *See also* 7C; 13C, Vol. 2; 43C.

The Vocaleers, "Is It a Dream," Red Robin 114.

Mel Walker (with Johnny Otis Congregation), "Rockin' Blues," Savoy 766. "Gee Baby," Savoy 777. "Mistrustin' Blues," Savoy 735.

Billy Ward & the Dominoes, King 536; Decca 8621; Federal 548. *Yours Forever,* Liberty 3083. *See also* 5C; 12C; 17C; 32C, Vol. 5; 34C.

Clara Ward: Gospel's Greatest Hits, 2 Paramount 1028. *Lord Touch Me,* Savoy 14006. *Memorial Album,* Savoy 14308.

Dionne Warwick's Greatest Hits, Circle CS 581. *The 50 Greatest Hits of Dionne Warwick,* The Longines Symphonette Society.

Dinah Washington, What a Diff'rence, Mercury 60158. *Sings the Blues,* Grand Award 318. *The Beat of Bessie's Blues,* Emarcy 36130. *The Best in Blues,* Mercury 20247.

Hudson Whittaker. *See* Tampa Red.

Wild Bill Davis, OKeh Jazz; Epic EG 37315.

Wild Bill Moore: *Roots of Rock 'n' Roll,* Savoy 2221.

Larry Williams, Original Golden Blues Giants, Liberty 7572. *See also* 19C, Vol. 14.

Maurice Williams & the Zodiacs. *See* 19C, Vol. 12; 32C, Vol. 5.

Otis Williams & the Charms, King 570. *See also* 2C, 5C, 17C.

Paul Williams, "The Hucklebuck," Savoy 683. *See* 42C.

Robert Pete Williams. *See* 21C.

John Lee Williamson (No. 1). *See* Sonny Boy Williamson.

Chuck Willis: His Greatest Recordings, Atco SD 33–373. *King of the Stroll.* Atlantic 8018. *Wails the Blues,* Epic LN 3425. *See also* 23C, Vol. 3.

The Willows. *See* 19C, Vol. 11; 41C, Vol. 2.

Jackie Wilson: Greatest Hits, Brunswick BL 754185; Brunswick 754140. *Higher and Higher,* Brunswick BL 54130. *Nostalgia.* Brunswick BL 754199.

Jimmy Wilson, "Tin Pan Alley," Big Town 101.

Jimmy Witherspoon, The Best Of, Bluesway BLS 6051. *A Spoonful of Spoon,* Verve V6–5050. "Ain't Nobody's Business," Kent 45s MX 8. "No Rollin' Blues/Big Fine Girl," Kent 45s MX 23. *See also* 13C, Vol. 1.

Jimmy Yancey, Atlantic 525; Bluebird B 8630. *Jimmy & Mama Yancey,* Atlantic SD 7229. *See* 10C.

Johnny Young. *See* 21C.

Rockabilly

Big Bopper. *Chantilly Lace,* Mercury MG 20402.

Johnny Burnette: Hits & Other Favorites, Liberty LN 10144. *Johnny Burnette Trio,* Vol. 2, MCA 1561. *Listen to Johnny Burnette,* MCA 1513.

Johnny Cash: Original Golden Hits, 3 Vols., Sun 100, 101, 127. *Don't You Step On My Blue Suede Shoes,* Charly 30119. *Get Rhythm,* Sun 105.

Eddie Cochran, The Very Best Of, United Artists UA-LA428 E. 2 United Artists UAS 9959.

Everly Brothers: Golden Hits Of, Warner Bros. 1471. *24 Original Classics*, Arista AL 9-8207. *Wake Up Little Susie*, Harmony 11304.

Bill Haley: Golden Hits, MCA 2-4010. *Bill Haley Scrapbook*, Kama Sutra KSBS 2014. "Rock Around the Clock." Decca 29214.

Buddy Holly. *20 Golden Greats, Buddy Holly Lives*, MCA 3040. *Rock & Roll Collection*, MCA 2-4009. *Best*, 2 Coral 7CX. *Story*, Coral 757279.

Jerry Lee Lewis, Best Of, Sun Rockabilly VI, Charly 30123. *Golden Rock & Roll*, Sun 1000. *Original Golden Hits*, Vol. 1, Sun 102; Vol. 2, Sun 103; Vol. 3, Sun 128. *Rockin' Rhythm & Blues*, Sun 107.

Ricky Nelson. *Teenage Idol*, Liberty LN 10253. *Million Sellers*, Imperial S 12232.

Carl Perkins, Best Of, Sun Rockabilly VI, Charly 30123; Vol. 2, Charly 30124. *Blue Suede Shoes*, Sun 112. *Rockabilly Fever*, Sun CFM 510. *Original Golden Hits*, Sun 111E, 112.

Elvis Presley. *The Sun Sessions*, RCA APMI-1675.

Conway Twitty. *Memphis Country*, Sun 120. *Classic Conway*, MCA 5424.

Ritchie Valens. *American Graffiti*, Vol. 3, MCA 2-8008. *Best Of*, Rhino 200. *Oldies But Goodies*, Vol. 7, Original Sound Recording OSR 8857; Vol. 8, OSR 8518.

Gene Vincent. *Bop That Just Won't Stop (1956)*, Capitol N 16209. *Vincent's Greatest Hits*, Capitol 16208.

Teenage Rock

Paul Anka: His Best, United Artists LN 10000. *Anka's 21 Golden Hits*, Victor AYL1-3808. ABC-Paramount S 371.

Frankie Avalon: Greatest Hits, Everest 4117. *Grease*, RSO Records 2-4002. *Muscle Beach Party*, Liberty Ln 10193. *Oldies But Goodies*, Vol. 10, OSR 8860. Chancellor 5001.

Freddy Cannon. *14 Booming Hits*, Rhino 210.

Danny & the Juniors. *Original Rock 'n' Roll Hits of the 50s*, Vol. 1, Roulette 59001; Vol. 4, Roulette 59004. "At the Hop," MCA 2411; Roulette GG 121.

Bobby Darin. *This Is Darin*, Atco S 115. *Bobby Darin Story*, Atco 131. *Oldies But Goodies*, Vol. 6, Original Sound OSR 8858. "Queen of the Hop," Atco 13055. "Splish Splash," Atco 13055. "Mack the Knife," Atco 45-6147.

Dion & the Belmonts, Best Of, Laurie VI, LAU 4003. *Oldies But Goodies*, Vol. 6, "Teenager in Love," Laurie 102. *Great American Rock & Roll Revival*, Vol. 3, Laurie 4032. *Dion Do-Wop/Gold*, Vol. 3, Laurie 4025.

Fabian's Greatest Hits, Everest 4118. *American Pop*, MCA 1542.

Connie Francis, Very Best Of, MGM 4167. "Stupid Cupid," Polydoe MVG 511. *Greatest Hits*, MGM MGB 1-5410. *Rock 'n' Roll Million Sellers*, MGM S 3974.

Leslie Gore: Greatest Hits, Mercury 60124. "It's My Party," Mercury 30124. *I'll Cry If I Want To*, Mercury ML 8016.

Charlie Gracie. *Amazing Gracie*, Charly 30211. "Butterfly," Abkco 4012. *Rock-O-Rama*, Vols. 1, 2, Abkco 4222-23.

George Hamilton, IV. "A Rose and a Baby Ruth," Roulette GG-143. *Forever Young*, MCA 705. *At the Hop*, MCA AA-1111.

Bill Justis. *Raunchy,* Sun 109. *Original Memphis Rock & Roll,* Sun 116.

The Poni-Tails. "Born Too Late," MCA 2404, Roulette GG 127.

Marty Robbins. "White Sport Coat," Columbia 13-33013.

Royal Teens. "Short Shorts," MCA 2402, Roulette GG 126. *Original Rock 'n' Roll Hits of the 50s,* Vol. 2, Roulette 59002. *The Original 50s,* Pickwick SPC 3520.

Bobby Rydell. *Biggest Hits,* Vol. 1, 2, Cameo 1009, 1028. *Rock-O-Rama,* Vol. 1, 2, Abkco 4222, 4223.

Tommy Sands. *Steady Date,* Capitol T 848.

Neil Sedaka: Sings His Greatest Hits, RCA Victor LSP 2627, APLI 0928.

The Sparkletones. "Black Slacks," MCA 1553. "Boys Do Cry," Roulette GG 3. *The Original 50s,* Pickwick SPC 3520.

Bobby Vee's Golden Greats, United Artists LM 1008. *I Remember Buddy Holly,* Liberty LN 10223. "Run to Him," United Artists UA-XW023-A. "Take Good Care of My Baby," United Artists UA-XW022-A.

Link Wray. *Rock 'n' Roll Rumble,* Charly 30171.

British Blues/Skiffle

History of British Blues, including tracks by Fleetwood Mac, Savoy Brown, Aynsley Dunbar Retailiation, Chicken Shack, Climax Blues Band, John Lees Groundhogs, Jellybread, Downliners Sect, Key Largo plus others, Vol. I. Sire SAS 3701.

The Animals, Best Of, Abkco 4226. *Greatest Hits of Burdon* (Animals), MGM 4602. *Animals & Sonny Boy Williamson,* Charly 30199. *The Best of Eric Burdon and the Animals,* Vol. II, MGM E-4454.

Graham Bond Organization. *Beginning of Jazz-Rock,* Charly 30198.

Cyril Davies Rhythm & Blues All Stars, *History of British Blues,* Vol. I, Sire SAS 3701.

Lonnie Donegan, "Does Your Chewing Gum Lose Its Flavor," MCA 2780. Dot 15911. "Rock Island Line," London 1650.

Chris Farlowes Thunderbirds, Charly 30021.

Alexis Korner Blues, Inc. *History of British Blues,* Vol. I, Sire SAS 3701.

Charles McDevitt Skiffle Group, "Freight Train," Chic 1008.

Manfred Mann, Best Of, Capitol N 16073. "Rebel," Arista 9203. "Do Wah Diddy Diddy," United Artists UA XN048A. "Sha La La," United Artists UA XN048A.

John Mayall's Bluesbreakers, Best Of, Polydor 2-3006. *Last of the British Blues,* MCA 716. *Blues Breakers,* London PS 492 (CD) 80086-2.

Alan Price Combo. *House of the Rising Sun,* Townhouse SN 7126. *It's Priceless,* Accord SN 7143.

Yardbirds. "I'm a Man," Epic 15-2247. *Yardbirds,* Epic FE 38455, HE 48455. *Shape of Things* (Collection of Classic Yardbirds Recordings 1964–1966), Charly CDX. *Yardbirds* (featuring Jeff Beck), Charly 30195; (featuring Eric Clapton), Charly 30194.

Cover Records

This syndrome began to take shape in the early 1950s, with Bill Haley, and marked the early recordings of the Rockabilly artists and some Pop artists such as Perry Como, Peggy Lee, The Crew Cuts, Pat Boone, and others. Cover records flourished between 1954 and 1956. A comprehensive list will be found in Arnold Shaw, *Dictionary of American Pop/Rock* (New York: Schirmer Books, 1982), 96–98.

Chapter Nine. "Black Is Beautiful"

1. Tony Heilbut, *The Gospel Sound: Good News and Bad Times* (New York: Simon and Schuster, 1971), 233.
2. James Baldwin, *The Fire Next Time* (New York: Dial Press, 1963).
3. Quoted in Arnold Shaw, *The World of Soul: Black America's Contribution to the Pop Music Scene* (New York: Cowles Book Co., 1970), 284.
4. Ibid., 86.
5. Joseph Murrells, comp., *The Book of Golden Discs* (London: Barrie & Jenkins, 1974, 1978), 246.
6. Quoted in Arnold Shaw, *Honkers and Shouters: The Golden Years of Rhythm and Blues* (New York: Macmillan Publishing Co., 1978), 413.
7. Shaw, *The World of Soul,* 181.
8. Quoted in ibid.

8a. *The Rolling Stone Illustrated History of Rock & Roll* (New York: Rolling Stone Press/ Random House, 1976), 204.

9. Ibid., 197.
10. *Newsweek,* May 23, 1983, p. 75.
11. *The Rolling Stone Illustrated History of Rock & Roll,* op. cit., 222.
12. Nelson George, "The Motown Session Men," *The Musician,* October 1983, p. 62.
13. Quoted in ibid., 65.
14. Ibid., 66.
15. Quoted in Irwin Stambler, *Encyclopoedia of Pop, Rock and Soul* (New York: St. Martin's Press, 1974), 149.
16. Ibid., 117.
17. Ellen Willis, "Janis Joplin," in *The Rolling Stone Illustrated History,* 258.
18. Willie Mae "Big Mama" Thornton, *She's Back,* Backbeat BLP 68.
19. Lester Bangs, "Heavy Metal," *Rolling Stone Illustrated History,* 304.
20. Quoted in Arnold Shaw, *Dictionary of American Pop/Rock* (New York: Schirmer Books, 1982), 169.
21. Quoted in John Morthland, "Jimi Hendrix," in *Rolling Stone Illustrated History,* 276.
22. Quoted in Shaw, *Dictionary,* 169.
23. Quoted in Shaw, *World of Soul,* 267.
24. John Mendelsohn, "Black Sabbath," *Los Angeles Times,* March 15, 1972.

Bibliography

In addition to the books and articles cited in the footnotes, the following are of interest:

Charles, Ray, and David Ritz. *Brother Ray.* New York: Warner Books, 1979.

Clifford, Mike, consultant. *The Illustrated Encyclopoedia of Black Music*. New York: Harmony Books, 1982.

Ellison, Ralph. *Shadow and Act*. New York: New American Library, 1966.

Friedman, Myra. *Buried Alive, The Biography of Janis Joplin*. New York: William Morrow and Co., 1973.

Garland, Phyl. *The Sound of Soul*. Chicago: Henry Regnery Company, 1969.

Hirshey, Gerri. *Nowhere to Run: The Story of Soul Music*. New York: Times Books, 1984.

Hopkins, Jerry. *Hit and Run: The Jimi Hendrix Story*. New York: Putnam, 1983.

Jackson, Mahalia, with Evan McLeod Wylie. *Movin' On Up*. New York: Avon Books, 1966.

Kofsky, Frank. *Black Nationalism and the Revolution in Music*. New York: Pathfinder Press, 1970.

Larkin, Rochelle. *Soul Music!* New York: Lancer Books, 1970.

Lee, George W. *Beale Street, Where the Blues Began*. New York: Robert O. Ballou, 1934.

McKee, Margaret, and Fred Chirenhall. *Beale, Black and Blues: Life and Music of Black America's Main Street*. New Orleans: Louisiana State University Press, 1981.

Morse, David. *Motown and the Arrival of Black Music*. New York: The Macmillan Co., 1971.

Discography

The Memphis, Detroit, and Philadelphia Sounds (Soul and the White Synthesis).

Archie Bell and the Drells: *I Never Had It So Good*, Beckett 013.

William Bell. "I Forgot to Be Your Lover," Stax 0015. *15 Original Big Hits*, Vols 1–3, Stax 8501, 8502, 8516.

Bill Black's Combo: "Smokie," Part 2, Hi 2018. "White Silver Sands," Hi 2021. *Award Winners*, Hi 6005. *Cookin'*, Fontana Q 16243. *Memphis, TN*, Hi 8004.

Bobby "Blues" Bland, Best Of, MCA 27013; Vol. 2, MCA X-86. *Foolin' with the Blues*, Charly 1049. *Introspective of the Early Years*, MCA 2-4172. *Soul of the Man*, MCA X-79. *Tell Mr. Bland*, MCA 5425.

Booker T. and the MG's. "Green Onions," Stax 127. *The Best of Booker T. and the MG's*, Atlantic SD 8202.

James Brown. *Federal Years*, Parts. 1, 2, Solid Smoke 8023-24. *Best Of*, Polydor 1-6340. *Story: Ain't That A Groove* (1966–69), Polydor 422-821231-1 Y-1; *Doing It to Death* (1970–73), Polydor 422-821232-1 Y-1. *Say It Loud, I'm Black and I'm Proud*, King 5-1047.

Ray Charles. *A Life in Music*, Atlantic Deluxe AD 5-3700. *What'd I Say*, Atlantic 8029. *Rock & Roll*, Atlantic 8006.

Contours, Motown N 5-188. *Top 10 with a Bullet*, Motown Male Groups, Motown 5327.

Sam Cooke, This Is, Victor VPS 6027. *How It All Began*, Vol. 2, Victor SPE 2118. *The Gospel Sound Of*, Victor SPE 2116; Vol. 2, Victor SPE 2128.

Delfonics. *Oldies But Goodies*, Vol. 12, Original Sound 8862. "La-La Means I Love You." Philly Groove 150.

Marvin Gaye, Motown 5311 ML. *Midnight Love*, Columbia FC 38197. Marvin

Gaye and Tammi Terrell, *Greatest Hits,* Motown M5-225. Marvin Gaye and Kim Weston, *Anthology,* Motown M 9791. *Dream of a Lifetime,* Columbia FC 39916.

Four Tops. Motown 5314 ML.

Aretha Franklin. *Aretha's Gold,* Atlantic 8277. *Lady Soul,* Atlantic A 8176. *I Never Loved A Man the Way I Love You,* Atlantic A 8139. *Greatest Hits,* Atlantic SD 8295.

Isaac Hayes, The Best Of, Wattstax, Stax 8053. *Black Moses,* Stax 8509. *Greatest Hit Singles,* Stax 8515.

Jennifer Holiday, *Feel My Soul,* Geffen GHS 4014.

Intruders: Super Hits, Philadelphia PZ 32131.

Jackson Five. Motown 5312 ML.

Mahalia Jackson, Best Of, Kenwood 500. The Great MJ, Columbia CG 31379. *Sings the Best-Loved Hymns of Martin Luther King,* Columbia PC 9686.

Michael Jackson. *Off the Wall,* Epic FE 35745. *Thriller,* Epic QE 38112.

Albert King. *Blues for Elvis,* Stax 8504. *I'll Play the Blues for You,* Stax 8513. *San Francisco '83,* Fantasy 9627.

Gladys Knight and the Pips. *Every Beat of My Heart,* Accord SN 7103. *Greatest Hits,* Buddah BL 5-8083. *Letter Full of Tears,* Accord SN 7105.

Little Richard's Greatest Hits, Everest 4114. *Cast a Long Shadow,* Epic EG 30428.

Marvelettes. *Greatest Hits* Motown M 5-180. *Please Mr. Postman,* Tamla 54046, *Top 10 with a Bullet—Motown's Girl Groups,* Motown 5325.

Harold Melvin and the Blue Notes. *Collector's Item,* Philadelphia PZ 34232. *OKeh Chicago Blues,* Epic EG 37318. *Talk It Up (Tell Everybody),* Philly World 90187-1.

Miracles, Smokey Robinson and the, Motown 5316 ML.

Willie Mitchell, Best Of, Motown 5289. *Willie Mitchell Live,* Hi 8002.

O'Jays Collector Items, Philadelphia PZG 35024. *Greatest Hits,* Philadelphia FZ 39251.

MFSB: "TSOP (The Sound of Philadelphia)," Philadelphia International 3540.

Wilson Pickett: Greatest Hits, Atlantic 2-501. *In the Midnight Hour,* Atlantic 13024.

Otis Redding, History Of, Volt 418. *The Best Of,* Atco SD 2-801. *Otis Redding/The Jimi Hendrix Experience: Historic Performances Recorded at the Monterey International Pop Festival, June 16, 17, 18, 1967,* Reprise 2029. *Otis Redding Recorded Live, Previously Unreleased Performances (1966),* Atlantic SD 19346. *The Dock of the Bay,* Volt 419.

Smokey Robinson: Being with You, Tamla T8-375 M1. *Deep In My Soul,* Tamla T6-350 S1. *Blame It On Love and All the Great Hits,* Tamla 6064 TL.

Sam and Dave, Best Of, Atlantic 8218. *Soul Study,* Vols. 1–2, Fontana, 16257, 16258.

Nina Simone, The Best Of, Philips PHS 600-298. *I Put a Spell on You,* Philips PHM 200-172.

Staple Singers. *Great Golden Gospel Hits,* Vol. 1, Savoy 14069. *Our Best to You,* Stax 44001. *Turning Point,* Private I F 239460.

Spinners, Best Of, Atlantic 19179, Motown M 5-199. *Cross Fire,* Atlantic 80150-1. *Grand Slam,* Atlantic 80020-1. *Original Spinners,* Motown M 5-132. *Soul Years,* Atlantic 2-504. *Spinners,* Atlantic SD 7256.

Stylistics. *Philly Ballads,* Vol. 1, Philadelphia P 2-39255.

Supremes: Greatest Hits, Motown 2-663. *I Hear A Symphony,* Motown 643. *Where Did Our Love Go,* Motown 621. *Sing Rodgers and Hart,* Motown 659.

Johnnie Taylor. *Chronicle,* Stax 88001. *Super Hits,* Stax 8520.

Temptations. *Anthology,* Motown M 782 A3.

Tammi Terrell. *Irresistible Tammi,* Motown M5-231.

Carla Thomas. *Chronicle,* Stax 4124. *Echoes of a Rock Era, Later Years,* Roulette RE 113.

Rufus Thomas, Gusto 0064. *I Ain't Gettin' Older, I'm Gettin' Better,* AVI 6046.

Mary Wells, Greatest Hits Of, Powerpak 313, Motown M 5-233. *Old, The New and the Best Of Mary Wells,* Allegiance 444.

Jackie Wilson's Greatest Hits, Brunswick BL 754185. *Higher and Higher,* Brunswick BL 54130. *Spotlight on Jackie Wilson,* Brunswick BL 54119.

Stevie Wonder. *Little Stevie Wonder, the 12 Year Old Genius,* Tamla 240. *Fulfillingness' First Finale,* Tamla 332. *Hotter Than July,* Tamla T8-373 M1. *Innervisions,* Tamla 326. *Looking Back,* Motown M 804 LP 3. *The Original Musiquarium I,* Tamla 6002 TL2. *Signed, Sealed, Delivered,* Motown M5-176V1. *The Woman in Red,* Motown 6108 ML.

The Artists and the Songs that Inspired the Motown 25th Anniversary TV Show: The Incredible Medleys, Motown 5321 ML.

Philadelphia Classics, P. I. FZG 34940.

Philly Ballads, Vol. 1, Philadelphia International PZ 39255; Vol. 2, P. I. PZ 39308.

Philly International Dance Classics, Vol. 1, P. I. PZ 39254.

Top 10 with a Bullet—Motown's Girl Groups, Motown 5325.

Top 10 with a Bullet—Motown's Male Groups, Motown 5327.

20/20 (Twenty Hits in Twenty Years), Motown M9-937A2.

Blue-Eyed Soul

Joe Cocker: Greatest Hits, A & M 4670, 3257. *Mad Dogs and Englishmen,* A & M 6002. *An Officer and a Gentleman,* Island 90017-1.

Delaney and Bonnie. *Genesis,* Crescendo 2054. *On Tour,* Atco 326.

Hall and Oates. *Bigbamboom,* Victor AJL1-5309. *H_2O,* Victor AFL1-4383. *Nucleus,* Allegiance 5014. *Rock and Soul,* Part 1, Victor AYL1-4858.

Janis Joplin. *Cheap Thrills,* Big Brother and the Holding Company, Columbia KCS 9700. *Janis,* Columbia PG 33345.

Righteous Brothers: Greatest Hits; Vol. 1, Verve 6-5020. *Memories of the Cow Palace,* Philles 105. *Real Thing,* Verve 78027-IP.

Young Rascals: Greatest Hits (Time Peace), Atlantic 8190. *Super Hits,* Atlantic 2-501. *Big Chill,* Motown 6062.

Heavy Metal

AC/DC: *Dirty Deeds Done Cheap,* Atlantic 16033. *Highway to Hell,* Atlantic 19244. *If You Want Blood, You've Got It,* Atlantic 19212. *For Those About to Rock, We Salute You,* Atlantic SD 11111.

Black Sabbath, Warner Brothers 1871. *Master of Reality,* Warner Brothers 2562. *Paranoid,* Warner Brothers 1882. *Born Again,* WB 1-23978.

Blue Oyster Cult, Columbia 31063. *Cultosaurus Erectus,* Columbia JC 36550.

Alice Cooper. *Billion Dollar Babies,* Warner Brothers 2685. *Love It to Death,* WB 1883. *School's Out,* WB 2623.

Deep Purple. *Shades of Deep Purple,* Tetragrammaton 102. *Fireball,* WB 2564.

Def Leppard. *High 'n' Dry,* Mercury 422-818836-1MI. *On Through the Night,* Polygram SRM 1-3828. *Pyromania,* Mercury 422-810308-1 MI.

Devo. *Doctor Detroit,* Backstreet 6120. *Heavy Metal,* Asylum 90004. *Q: Are We Not Men,* WB 3239.

Grand Funk Railroad. *Closer to Home,* Capitol 471. *E. Pluribus Funk,* Capitol 853. *Grand Funk,* Capitol 406. *Love Album,* Capitol 633. *Survival,* Capitol 764. *We're an American Band,* Capitol 11207.

Jimi Hendrix. *Are You Experienced,* Reprise 6261. *Axis: Bold As Love,* Reprise 6281. *Electric Ladyland,* Reprise 6307. *Kiss the Sky,* Reprise 1-25119. *Smash Hits,* Reprise 2025. *Hendrix Band of Gypsies,* Capitol 472. *The Essential J. H.,* Reprise 2RS 2245.

Iron Butterfly. *In-a-Gadda-Da-Vida,* Atco 250. *Metamorphosis,* Atco SD 33-339.

Iron Maiden, Capitol ST 12094. *Killers,* Capitol ST 12141. *Powerslave,* Capitol SJ 12321.

Judas Priest, Best Of, Victor AYL1-4933. *Defenders of the Faith,* Columbia FC 39219. *Screaming for Vengeance,* Columbia FC 38160.

Kiss, Casablanca 7001. *The Originals,* Casablanca 7032. *Hotter Than Hell,* Casablanca 7006. *Lick It Up,* Mercury 422-814297-1-MI. *Dressed to Kill,* Casablanca 7016. *Love Gun,* Casablanca NBLP 7057.

Led Zeppelin, II, Atlantic 8236. *Led Zeppelin III,* Atlantic 7201. *Houses of the Holy,* Atlantic 7255. *Physical Graffiti (Swan Song),* Atlantic 2-200. *Coda,* Swan Song 90051-1.

Motley Crue. *Too Fast for Love,* Elektra El-60174. *Shout at the Devil,* Elektra 60289-1.

Ozzy Osbourne. *Diary of a Madman,* Jet F237492.

Queen, Elektra 75064. *A Night at the Opera,* Elektra 1053. *Sheer Heart Attack,* Electra 1026.

Quiet Riot. *Condition Critical,* Pasha OZ 39516. *Frankenstein and Other Monsters,* CBS FZ 39257. *Metal Health,* Pasha FZ 38443.

Ratt. *Out of the Cellar,* Atlantic 80143-1.

Scorpions, Best Of, Victor AFL1-3516; Vol. 2, AFL1-5085. *Animal Magnetism,* Mercury SRM-1-3825. *Love at First Sting,* Mercury 422-814981-1-M1.

Sex Pistols. *Never Mind the Bullocks,* WB K-3147.

Steppenwolf, MCA 37045. *16 Greatest Hits,* MCA 37049. *Wolftracks,* Allegiance 434.

Triumph. *Allied Force,* Victor AFL1-3902. *Progressions of Power.* Victor AYL 1-4561. *Thunder Seven,* MCA 5537.

Twisted Sister. *Stay Hungry,* Atlantic 80156-1. *You Can't Stop Rock 'N' Roll,* Atlantic 80074-1.

UFO. *Force It,* Chrysalis PV 41074. *Phenomenon,* Chrysalis PV 41059. *The Wild, the Willing, and the Innocent,* Chrysalis PV 41307.

Van Halen 1984, WB 1-23985. *Van Halen,* WB 1-3075; Vol. 2, WB HS 3312.

ZZ Top: *Tres Hombres,* London 631. *Fandango,* London 656.

Chapter Ten. The Disco Craze

1. "Disco Takes Over," *Newsweek,* April 2, 1979, p. 60.
2. At a ceremony in Lincoln Center in New York on December 5, 1984, the Record Industry Association of America honored the top winners in the Multi-Platinum category of sellers (albums that have sold more than a million copies). *Saturday Night Fever* came in third, with a sale of 11 million, behind Michael Jackson's *Thriller* (20 million) and Fleetwood Mac's *Rumors* (12 million).
3. *The New York Times,* Arts and Leisure section, Sunday, January 21, 1979, p. 22.

Bibliography

In addition to the articles cited in the footnotes, the following are of interest:

Peter Brown, "Ethel Merman: Making Debut as Diva of Disco," *Los Angeles Times,* "Calendar," Sunday, July 29, 1979, 5.

"Disco-Music Craze/Seems to Be Fading;/Record Makers Glad," *Wall St. Journal* (October 22, 1979).

Discothekin' Magazine (1976–1979).

Hanson, Kitty. *Disco Fever.* New York: New American Library, 1978.

Kornbluth, Jesse. "Merchandizing Disco for the Masses," *The New York Times Magazine* (February 18, 1979).

Pollock, Bruce. "Disco Sweeps the Nation," *Family Weekly* (May 20, 1979).

Discography

The Bee Gees, "Stayin' Alive," *Saturday Night Fever,* RSO RS 2-4001.

Jean-Marc Cerrone, "Love in 'C' Minor" (Part 1), Cotillion 44215.

Chic, C'est, Atlantic SD 19209. "Le Freak," Atlantic 3519.

Yvonne Elliman, "If I Can't Have You," RSO 884. *Saturday Night Fever,* RSO RS 2-4001.

Gloria Gaynor, "I Will Survive," Polydor 14508. *I've Got You,* Polydor PD 1-6063.

Andre Kostelanetz, "The Hustle" and "Salsoul Hustle" in *Dance with Me,* Columbia 34352.

Raymond Lefevre, "The Hustle" in *Rock and Rhythm in Hi-Fi,* Barclay 80-629.

Van McCoy, "The Hustle," Avco 4653.

Rolling Stones. "Miss You," Rolling Stones 19307.

Saturday Night Fever (OST), includes Bee Gees' "Jive Talkin'," Tavares' "More Than a Woman," K. C. and the Sunshine Band's "Boogie Shoes," Kool and the Gang's "Open Sesame," and others, RSO RS 2-4001.

Rod Stewart. "Do Ya Think I'm Sexy?" Warner 8724.

Donna Summer. *Greatest Hits On the Radio,* Volumes I and II, includes "Love to Love You Baby" and "No More Tears (Enough Is Enough)," duet with Barbra Streisand. Casablanca NBLP 2-7191. *Bad Girls,* Casablanca NBLP 2-7150.

Sylvester: Stars, Fantasy F-9579.

The Trammps: Disco Inferno, Atlantic SD 18211.
Village People: Cruisin', Casablanca NBLP 7118. "In the Navy," Casablanca 973. "Y.M.C.A.," Casablanca 945.

Chapter Eleven. The Contemporary Scene

1. Nelson George, "Standing in the Shadow of Motown," *The Musician* (October 1983), 64.
2. Held in August 1969 under extremely trying conditions—it rained steadily for the three days—the Festival was a triumph of the human condition, leading to the legendary designation of young people as the Woodstock Nation. Joni Mitchell celebrated the remarkable demonstration of kinship, amity, and love in "Woodstock," recorded by Crosby, Stills, Nash and Young. The high hopes that the spirit of Woodstock would spread were shattered by the violence that attended the Rolling Stones/Grateful Dead festival at Altamont, California, four months later.
3. Ted Fox, *Showtime at the Apollo* (New York: Holt, Rinehart & Winston, 1983), 307.
4. Ibid.
5. *Rolling Stone* (November 20, 1983), 72.
6. Robert Hilburn, *Las Vegas Review-Journal* (September 10, 1984), 3C.
7. *The New Yorker* (August 20, 1984), 87.
8. David Ansen, *Newsweek* (July 23, 1984). 65.
9. Judy Hille, *The Arizona Republic,* (Sunday, October 31, 1982), D1, D7.
10. Bob Marley, "Exodus" (1977), Island Records. Included in *Legend: The Best of Bob Marley,* Island Records.
11. Quoted in *Rolling Stone* (April 16, 1981), 85.
12. Quoted in Arnold Shaw, *Dictionary of American Pop/Rock* (New York: Schirmer Books, 1982), 308.
13. Quoted in Irwin Stambler, *Encyclopoedia of Pop, Rock and Soul* (New York: St. Martin's Press, 1974), 366.
14. *Rolling Stone* (March 1, 1984), 20.
15. Ibid.
16. James Lincoln Collier, *Louis Armstrong: An American Genius* (New York: Oxford University Press, 1983), 351.
17. Henry Pleasants, *The Great American Popular Singers* (New York: Simon & Schuster, 1974), 85.
18. Quoted in ibid., 166–67.
19. Arnold Shaw, *52nd St.: The Street of Jazz* (New York: Da Capo Press, 1977), 197.
20. Ibid., 198–99.
21. "Wonderful, Wonderful" was written by Ben Raleigh (words) and Sherman Edwards (music), the latter, later the composer/lyricist of the Broadway musical hit *1776*. "Chances Are" and "It's Not For Me To Say" were both written by Al Stillman (words) and Robert Allen (music).
22. Quoted in Ken Tucker, *Las Vegas Review-Journal* (August 5, 1984).
23. *Rolling Stone* (September 13, 1984), 44.

24. *Los Angeles Times,* Calendar section, (August 15, 1982), 3.
25. Quoted in *Grammy Pulse* (December 1984, Vol. 2, No. 6), 11.
26. *Rolling Stone* (December 20, 1984), 112.
27. Quoted in *Newsweek* (September 10, 1984), 76.
28. *Rolling Stone* (October 11, 1984), 19.
29. Ibid., 58.
30. *The New York Times,* Arts and Leisure section, (August 26, 1984).
31. Shaw, *Dictionary,* 113–14.
32. *Newsweek,* (August 30, 1982), 69.
33. *Los Angeles Times,* Calendar section, (March 27, 1983), 70.
34. Ibid.
35. Quoted in *Las Vegas Review–Journal* (June 17, 1984), 14C.
36. Quoted in *Newsweek* (July 2, 1984), 48.
37. *Los Angeles Times,* Calendar section, (January 8, 1984), 91.
38. *The New York Times,* Arts and Leisure section, (September 23, 1984).
39. Stephen Holden, "Horne aplenty," *Rolling Stone* (November 26, 1981), 70.
40. Ibid.
41. *Newsweek* (May 26, 1980), 84.
42. Ibid.
43. *The New Yorker,* April 27, 1981, 4.
44. *Newsweek,* October 2, 1978, 89.
45. *The New Yorker* (March 16, 1981), 61.
46. Ibid. (April 27, 1981), 4.
47. Ed Padula, Liner Note, Original Cast Album, Polydor PD 6013.
48. *The New Yorker* (November 4, 1974), 4.
49. Quoted in *The New York Times,* Arts and Leisure section (January 17, 1982), 2–3.
50. Ibid., 2.
51. Ibid.
52. *Newsweek* (January 9, 1984), 96.
53. *The New Yorker* (January 2, 1984), 81.
54. *Newsweek,* op. cit.
55. *The New Yorker* (October 22, 1984), 152.
56. Station WOR-TV.
57. *The New York Times* (October 13, 1984).
58. Jack Kroll, *Newsweek* (October 22, 1984), 106.

Bibliography

In addition to the books and articles cited in the footnotes, the following are of interest:

Bogle, Donald. *Brown Sugar: Eighty Years of America's Black Female Superstars.* New York: Harmony Books, 1980.

Brown, Geoff. *Diana Ross.* (New York: St. Martin's Press, 1981).

Clarke, Sebastian. *Jah Music, The Evolution of the Popular Jamaican Song.* London: Heinemann Educational Books.

Clifford, Mike, consultant. *The Illustrated Encyclopoedia of Black Music.* New York: Harmony Books, 1984.

Cole, Maria, with Louis Robinson. *Nat King Cole: An Intimate Biography*. New York: Morrow, 1971.

Davis, Stephen, *Bob Marley* (New York: Doubleday, 1985).

Davis, Stephen, and Peter Simon. *Reggae Bloodlines*. New York: Doubleday, 1977; Anchor, 1982.

———. *Reggae International*. New York: Knopf, 1983.

Johnson, Howard, and Jim Pines. *Reggae: Deep Roots Music*. New York: Proteus Publishing, 1984.

Horne, Lena, and Richard Schickel. *Lena*. New York: Doubleday, 1965.

Rolling Stone magazine, 1968—.

Shaw, Arnold. "The Music Scene" in *The New Book of Knowledge Annual*. Danbury, Conn.: Grolier, Inc., 1970–1984.

Spitz, Robert Stephen. *Barefoot in Babylon: The Creation of the Woodstock Music Festival, 1969*. New York: The Viking Press, 1979.

Whitburn, Joel. *The Billboard Book of Top 40 Hits, 1955 to Present*. New York: Billboard Publications, 1983.

———. *Music Yearbook—1983*. Menonomonee Falls, Wisc.: Record Research.

White, Timothy. *Catch on Fire: The Life of Bob Marley*. (New York: Harper and Row, 1983).

Young, Jean, and Michael Lang. *Woodstock Festival Remembered*. New York: Ballantine Books, 1979.

Zalkind, Ronald. *Contemporary Music Almanac 1980/81*. New York: Schirmer Books, 1980.

Discography

Bar-Kays As One, Mercury SRM 1-3844.

George Clinton. *Computer Games*, Capitol ST 12246. *You Shouldn't-Nuf Bit Fish*, Capitol ST 12308.

William Bootsy Collins. *One Giveth, The Count Taketh Away*. WB BSK 3667.

Con Funk Shun. *Touch*, Mercury SRM 1-4002.

Funkadelic: (Westbound) *Free Your Mind and Your Ass Will Follow, America Eats Its Young. One Nation under a Groove*, WB *Uncle Jam Wants You*, WB BSK 3371.

Isley Brothers, Greatest Hits, VI, T-Neck F239240. *Doin' Their Thing*, Motown M 5-143. *Go for Your Guns*, T-Neck PZ 34432.

Rick James/Stone City Band. *Reflections*, Gordy 6095. *Street Songs*, Gordy GB 1002. *Come Get It*, Motown 5263.

Chaka Khan, WB 1-23729. *Echoes of an Era*. Elektra E 1-60021. *I Feel for You*, WB 1-25162.

Ray Parker, Jr. *Chartbusters*, Arista AL 8-8266. *Ghostbusters*, Arista AL 8-8246. *Greatest Hits*, Arista AL 8-8027.

Parliament. *Clones of Dr. Funkenstein*, Casablanca. *Funkentelechy Vs. the Placebo Syndrome*, Casablanca. *Gloryhallastoopid—or Pin the Tale on the Funky*.

Kinky. *Instant Funk*, Salsoul SA 8564.

Rufus, ABC. *Rags to Rufus. Rufus and Chaka Khan, Live, (Stompin' at the Savoy)* WB 1-23679. *Masterjam*, MCA.

Horace Silver. *Jazz Messengers,* Blue Note LT 81508. *Silver's Blue.*

Sly Stone. Fresh, Epic 32134. *Greatest Hits,* Epic 30325. *Stand!* Epic 26456. *There's a Riot Goin' On,* Epic 30986.

Teena Marie. *Iron in the Fire,* Gordy G8-997. *Robbery,* Epic FE 38882. *Wild and Peaceful,* Motown 5271.

"Stir it Up" (Reggae)

Blondie, The Best Of, (includes "The Tide Is High") Chrysalis CHR 1337.

Eric Clapton. "I Shot the Sheriff," RSO 409.

Jimmy Cliff. *The Power and the Glory,* Columbia FC 38986. *I Am the Living,* MCA 5153.

Bob Marley and the Wailers. *The Birth of a Legend,* Calla 2-CAS 1240. *The Best Of,* Island 90169-1. *Bob Marley and the Wailers,* Magnum SSS 35.

Johnny Nash. *Stir It Up,* Hallmark SHM 3053.

Police. *Synchronicity,* A and M 3735. *Zanyatta Mondatta,* A & M 3720. *Reggatta de Blanc.* A & M 4792.

Reggae Sunsplash '81, A Tribute to Bob Marley, Elektra E1-60035.

Paul Simon. "Mother and Child Reunion," Columbia 45547.

Peter Tosh, Captured Live, EMI ST 17126.

Stevie Wonder. "Boogie on Reggae Woman," Tamla 54254.

The Oreo Singers (Black Pop)

Louis Armstrong. *Hello, Dolly!* Kapp KS 3364. *Disney Songs the Satchmo Way,* Vista 4044.

Brook Benton. *It's Just a Matter of Time: His Greatest Hits.* Mercury 822 321-1M1.

Jerry Butler. *Only the Strong Survive: The Legendary Philadelphia Hits,* Mercury 822 212 1M1.

Ray Charles. *Modern Sounds in Country and Western Music,* ABC 410; Vol. 2, ABC 435. *Ray Charles Invites You to Listen,* ABC 595.

Nat "King" Cole Story, 3 Vols., Capitol SN 16033–35. *Best Of,* Vols. 1, 2, Capitol N 16260–61. *A Blossom Fell,* Capitol DN 16165.

Commodores. *Natural High,* Motown M7-902R1. *Midnight Magic.* Motown 5348. *Heroes,* Motown 5353.

Sam Cooke, This Is, Victor VPS 6027 (e) 2. *The Unforgettable Sam Cooke,* Victor LPM 3517. *Sam Cooke at the Copa,* RCA ANL1-2658. *The Golden Sound of Sam Çooke,* Trip TLP 8030 (2).

Billy Daniels at the Crescendo, Crescendo 16.

Sammy Davis, Jr. *Hey There,* MCA 2-4109. *Stop the World, I Want to Get Off,* WB HS 3214.

Billy Eckstine: *Everything I Have Is Yours,* Metro MS 537. *25 Years of Recorded Sound,* DRG 2-2100.

Fifth Dimension. "Up-Up and Away," Soul City 753. "Aquarius/Let the Sunshine In," Soul City 772.

Ella Fitzgerald (with the Chick Webb Band). "A-Tisket, A-Tasket," Decca 1840. *The Harold Arlen Songbook* 817 526-1. *Cole Porter Songbook,* Verve 2-2511.

Rodgers and Hart Songbook, Verve 2-2519. *George and Ira Gershwin Songbook,* Verve 2-2525. *Duke Ellington Songbook,* Verve 2-2535, Vol. 2, Verve 2-2540.

Al Green. *Let's Stay Together,* Hi 32070. *Greatest Hits,* Hi 32089.

Billie Holiday, The Original Recordings, Columbia C 32060. *the billie holiday songbook,* Verve 823248-1.

Ink Spots. *Lost in a Dream,* Vocalion VL 73725.

Johnny Mathis's Greatest Hits, Columbia CL 1133, 34667.

Harold Melvin and the Bluenotes, *Talk It Up (Tell Everybody).* Philly World Records 90187-1.

Mills Brothers, Golden Favorites, Vols. 1, 2, Decca DL 75173, 75174. *Great Hits,* Dot DLP 25, 157.

Teddy Pendergrass. *Philly Ballads,* Vols. 1, 2, Philadelphia International P2 39255, 39308.

Charley Pride, Best Of, Victor AYL1-5148; Vol. 2, AYL1 4832. *Best of the 80s So Far,* Victor AHL1-5058. *Solid Country Gold,* Victor CPL1-4841.

Lou Rawls. *Too Much!* Capitol ST 2713. *The Best Of,* Capitol SM 2948.

Lionel Richie, Motown 6007 ML. *Can't Slow Down,* Motown 6059 ML.

Diana Ross, An Evening with, Motown M7-877R2. *To Love Again,* Motown M8-951 M1.

Maxine Sullivan. "Loch Lomond," OKeh 3654, Decca 3954.

Sarah Vaughan's Golden Hits, Mercury MG 20645. *Broken Hearted Melody,* Soul Parade HHP 8003.

Dionne Warwick's Greatest Hits, Circa 581. *The 50 Greatest Hits Of Dionne Warwick,* Longines Symphonette Society SYS 6074-77.

Dinah Washington. *What a Diff'rence a Day Makes!* Mercury MG 20479. *A Slick Chick on the Mellow Side,* EmArcy 814 184-1.

Ethel Waters Greatest Years, Columbia KG 31571. *Miss Ethel Waters, Performing in Person. Highlights from Her Illustrious Career,* Monmouth Evergreen MES/6812.

Deniece Williams. *Let's Hear It for the Boy,* Columbia FC 39366. *Footloose,* Columbia JS 39242.

Joe Williams: The Song Is You, Victor LPM 3343. *Count Basie Swings, Joe Williams Sings,* Verve 6-8488. *Everyday I Have the Blues,* Savoy 1140.

"Rapper's Delight" (Hip-Hop)

Afrika Bambaataa. *Beat Street,* Atlantic 80154-1. *Unity,* Tommy Boy 847.

Beat Street, (OMPST), Atlantic 80154-1.

Blasters. *Hard Line,* WB 25093-1. *Blasters,* Slash/War 23818.

Breakin' 2—Electric Boogaloo, Polydor 8236961.

Grandmaster Flash and the Furious Five. *They Said It Couldn't Be Done,* Elektra 60389-1.

Sugarhill Gang. *Rapper's Delight,* Sugarhill 542. *Greatest Rap Hits,* Vol. 2, Sugarhill 262. *Kick It Live From 9 to 5,* Sugarhill 454. *Livin' in the Fast Lane,* Sugarhill 32021.

Treacherous Three, *Beat Street,* Vol. 2, Atlantic 80158-1.

Ma Rainey's Black Bottom

(Black Musicals of the 1970s and 1980s)

Ain't Misbehavin': The New Fats Waller Musical Show. RCA CBL2-2965.
Don't Bother Me, I Can't Cope. Polydor PO 6013.
Dreamgirls. Geffen GHSP 2007.
Eubie. WB HS 3267.
Hello, Dolly! (Black version). RCA ANL1-2849.
Lena Horne: The Lady and Her Music. Qwest 2QW 3597.
One Mo' Time. WB HS 3454.
Sophisticated Ladies. 2RCA CBL2-4053.
Stop the World, I Want to Get Off (Black version). WB HS 3214.
Tap Dance Kid. Polydor 802101.
Whoopi Goldberg. Geffen GHS 24065.
The Wiz. Atlantic 18137. (OMPST) MCA 2-6010.

Of the songs discussed in this chapter, the author was himself involved in the development and popularization of "Wonderful, Wonderful" and "Hotel Happiness."

INDEX